Readings for Composition: EN 1103 and EN 1113

Mississippi State University Custom Edition

OXFORD
UNIVERSITY PRESS

Contents

culture

Other titles in this series include:

Globalization: A Reader for Writers
Maria Jerskey
(ISBN: 9780199947522)

Language: A Reader for Writers
Gita DasBender
(ISBN: 9780199947485)

Sustainability: A Reader for Writers
Carl Herndl
(ISBN: 9780199947508)

Identity: A Reader for Writers
John Scenters-Zapico
(ISBN: 9780199947461)

culture

A READER *for* WRITERS

John Mauk

Miami University of Ohio

New York Oxford

Oxford University Press

Oxford University Press publishes works that further Oxford University's objective of excellence in research, scholarship, and education.

Oxford New York
Auckland Cape Town Dar es Salaam Hong Kong Karachi
Kuala Lumpur Madrid Melbourne Mexico City Nairobi
New Delhi Shanghai Taipei Toronto

With offices in
Argentina Austria Brazil Chile Czech Republic France Greece
Guatemala Hungary Italy Japan Poland Portugal Singapore
South Korea Switzerland Thailand Turkey Ukraine Vietnam

Published by Oxford University Press.
198 Madison Avenue, New York, New York 10016
http://www.oup.com

Library of Congress Cataloging-in-Publication Data

Mauk, John.
Culture : a reader for writers / John Mauk, Northwestern Michigan College.
pages cm
Includes bibliographical references and index.
ISBN 978-0-19-994722-5 (pbk.)
1. College readers. 2. English language--Rhetoric--Handbooks, manuals, etc. 3. English language--Grammar--Handbooks, manuals, etc. 4. Report writing--Handbooks, manuals, etc. 5. Culture in literature. I. Title.
PE1417.M45655 2014
808'.0427--dc23

2013037247

Printing number: 9 8 7 6 5 4 3 2 1
Printed in the United States of America
on acid-free paper

Chapter 1

Work: What We Do

There are countless songs, television shows, novels, poems, and films dedicated to work—or more specifically to how much people hate their jobs. If there's one prevailing statement about Americans and work, it's that we desperately need more and that we hate it when it finally comes along. In short, Americans have a tangled relationship with work. The typical professional, across many fields, has among the world's smallest allotted vacation time, the least amount of sick leave, and the longest work week. We yearn to get free for a weekend and then take the overtime if it's available. But we also resist some of the worst jobs—those that have been shipped to countries with fewer labor, safety, and exploitation laws. We're gluttons for hard work, but for a particular kind.

Despite the conditions, there is another prevailing truth: The nature of work is changing. In his article "Of Apprentices and Interns," Ross Perlin says that work is "a shifting, uneven landscape, fought over and redefined in every culture and in every age." Whatever we mean by "a good job" will likely change as new tools replace old ones, as another generation moves into full-time employment, and as the economy accommodates global interconnectivity. When the markets shift, when a company gets downsized, when consumption in Europe or Asia slows even slightly, millions of jobs are affected. They get temporarily frozen, redefined, or obliterated. In this sense, work actually represents culture. It shows the perpetual state of movement—the collisions created by competing values, economic tremors, and personal hopes.

The readings in this chapter all focus on work: how to get a job, how to succeed in a particular work environment, how to make sense of employment trends, and even how to manage the hollow weirdness of white-collar professionalism. Amy Reiter and Julie Hanus deal with the complex politics of office life. Elizabeth Dwoskin and Mike Rose explore the issue of socioeconomic class that is often eclipsed by other, more visible, issues. Patricia Ann McNair dramatizes a unique class of workers—those fortunate enough to carry their jobs in their minds and through the streets of foreign cities. Finally, Christian Williams and Jason Storms connect work to broader economic worries.

Amy Reiter

Why Being a Jerk at Work Pays

Amy Reiter writes about pop culture and women's issues for such publications as *The Daily Beast*, *Glamour*, the *Huffington Post*, the *Los Angeles Times*, the *New York Times*, *Salon*, and the *Washington Post*. In the following *Daily Beast* article, Reiter considers the payoff of certain workplace behaviors.

For years, I tried to be a very nice person at work—a dream colleague, a team player, the sort of woman who gave women a good name in the workplace. I thanked people. I apologized. I expressed concern. I took responsibility for making things right, even when I wasn't the one who had made them go wrong.

Then one day I looked up from my under-challenging, midlevel job and noticed that my boss, who was generally regarded as kind of a jerk, but a smart and talented one, never, ever thanked people. He never apologized. And he didn't appear to give a rip about what was going on in the lives of anyone around him. He never took responsibility when things went wrong, preferring instead to label someone else the culprit and chew them out.

It suddenly occurred to me: he had gained responsibility, power and a big, cushy salary not despite the fact that he was a jerk, but because of it. Maybe no one liked him, but everyone respected him. Whereas I, arguably no less competent, but assuredly a whole lot more pleasant and agreeable, was drifting along in a rudderless career—pal to all, boss to none.

I'm not alone in my thinking: A recent study examining the relationship between agreeableness, income, and gender, published in *Journal of Personality and Social Psychology,* found that the workplace does tend to reward disagreeable behavior. Disagreeable men tend to earn more than agreeable men, and disagreeable women, though they earn less than both nice and not-nice guys, earn more than agreeable women, researchers found.

The study, entitled "Do Nice Guys—and Gals—Really Finish Last?" 5
(conducted by Timothy A. Judge of the University of Notre Dame's Mendoza College of Business, Beth A. Livingston of Cornell University's School of Industrial and Labor Relations, and Charlice Hurst of University of Western Ontario's Richard Ivey School of Business), provided an analysis of the data from three separate surveys conducted over the past two decades including responses from thousands of workers of various ages, salary levels, and professions. The authors also conducted a survey of their own, asking 460 business students to weigh in on hypothetical personnel decisions.

"'Niceness'—in the form of the trait of agreeableness—does not appear to pay," the authors concluded.

Although I could never pull off my boss's level of rudeness (nor would I have wanted to), I nevertheless decided to shed just a bit of my workaday warmth by making two seemingly small changes: to stop saying "thank you" or "I'm sorry." Straightaway. Cold turkey. Just to see what would happen.

I started with e-mail, where I had often signed off with a chipper "thanks!" or apologized for inconveniencing someone with a request or for taking a while to reply. I was no longer sorry it took so long to get back to anyone. Neither did I feel either regretful about asking them to do something or grateful to them in advance for doing it.

I painstakingly reread every message to make sure neither polite phrase had sneaked through. And after I'd carefully excised each self-effacing slip, I hit send with a new set to my jaw, a hard glimmer in my eyes.

10 The effect was immediate: Colleagues began to treat me with more respect. Celebrity publicists—a notably power-aware lot whom I often contacted in my job—were more responsive. Even interns (those pecking-order experts) seemed to regard me with a new sort of awe.

> "The effect was immediate: Colleagues began to treat me with more respect."

Emboldened, I sought to eliminate "sorry" and "thank you" from my spoken workplace interactions as well, sometimes literally covering my mouth (passing it off as a "thoughtful" pose) during meetings to keep from uttering them. I found myself smiling less and bargaining harder.

My new confidence gave me the inner wherewithal to launch a freelance business (I'm now my own boss). My career—and my income—lurched upward.

At first, my new sense of power and its rewards felt thrilling. I learned to bargain firmly and unapologetically and was paid fairly—and it seemed to me that, when people paid more for my work, they tended to value it (and me) more highly, further increasing my own sense of worth. But there were also times I pushed too hard and lost assignments. And I began to worry about my reputation. Had my new self-assurance made me overly demanding? Were people starting to think of me as a diva?

My concerns may have been valid. The recent study also found that the rewards of disagreeableness for women are limited—far more so than for men. What's more, if women push their disagreeable behavior in the workplace too far, they risk a major backlash.

15 "People attribute disagreeable—i.e., self-interested, tough, argumentative—behavior in men and women differently," study coauthor Judge told me. "If a man is disagreeable, he is thought to be tough and leader-like. If a woman is disagreeable, the 'b-word' is applied to her."

I had found myself bumping against these very boundaries: placing a higher value on respect and remuneration than likeability, I had advanced, but I feared I was becoming unlikable. Had I become, as Judge politely put it, a "b-word"?

This past summer, I had a breakthrough. It happened when I wrote an essay that was included in a collection of works by "mommy bloggers." An e-mail group was formed so that those of us who were involved could introduce ourselves to each other. Every single person, in their initial e-mails, included a sort of apology ("I've never been included in something like this before!") and an expression of thanks ("I'm so honored").

Reading through the e-mail chain, I saw these expressions not as displays of powerlessness, but of kindness, openheartedness and candor, a desire for connection and support. We were thankful. We were sorry. We were also in it together. I added my own expressions of modesty and gratitude to the highly agreeable chain, and felt the camaraderie surround me like a warm blanket.

In the intervening months, I've sought to find a middle ground. I will now allow the occasional "thank you" to pass, and I will apologize if I feel it is justified, though I still try not to do either reflexively.

That's the sort of balanced approach Judge, the study coauthor, recom- 20
mends. "I tell women there is a difference between disagreeing and being disagreeable," he says. "Be firm, logical, assertive, and persistent—but do not ever show hostility, anger, or other negative emotions."

We women are held to different standards of agreeability than men, Judge cautions, adding, "This of course is not fair—but fair does not always describe the world in which we live."

Sorry to break the news. And thanks!

Analyze

1. What is the difference between self-assured and demanding behavior? Why is the distinction important to Reiter's argument?
2. Given Reiter's descriptions of coworkers, how might she define a jerk? What behaviors make someone a jerk?
3. In your own words, describe Reiter's middle ground in communication—and how that constitutes a "breakthrough."
4. When describing a coworker, Reiter explains, "It suddenly occurred to me: he had gained responsibility, power and a big, cushy salary not despite the fact that he was a jerk, but because of it." Why is this statement especially important to her argument about work behavior and success?
5. What does Reiter's argument say about American culture?

Explore

1. In your experience, do nice people finish last? Why or why not?
2. Why do you think niceness might garner less respect than assertiveness?
3. Do you value likability over respect—or vice versa? What specific daily behaviors get you liked? What behaviors garner respect?
4. In your experience, are women "held to different standards of agreeability than men"? Give specific examples to support your answer.
5. Explain how Reiter's thinking about women might relate to Elizabeth Dwoskin's thoughts on "dirty" jobs.

Elizabeth Dwoskin
Why Americans Won't Do Dirty Jobs

A staff writer for *Bloomberg Businessweek*, Elizabeth Dwoskin writes on a range of issues related to politics, immigration, education, and health care. In the following article, Dwoskin examines the problems inherent in the immigrant labor subculture of the United States.

Skinning, gutting, and cutting up catfish is not easy or pleasant work. No one knows this better than Randy Rhodes, president of Harvest Select, which has a processing plant in impoverished Uniontown, Ala. For years, Rhodes has had trouble finding Americans willing to grab a knife and stand 10 or more hours a day in a cold, wet room for minimum wage and skimpy benefits.

Most of his employees are Guatemalan. Or they were, until Alabama enacted an immigration law in September that requires police to question people they suspect might be in the U.S. illegally and punish businesses that hire them. The law, known as HB56, is intended to scare off undocumented workers, and in that regard it's been a success. It's also driven away legal immigrants who feared being harassed.

Rhodes arrived at work on Sept. 29, the day the law went into effect, to discover many of his employees missing. Panicked, he drove an hour and a half north to Tuscaloosa, where many of the immigrants who worked for him lived. Rhodes, who doesn't speak Spanish, struggled to get across how much he needed them. He urged his workers to come back. Only a handful did. "We couldn't explain to them that some of the things they were scared of weren't going to happen," Rhodes says. "I wanted them to see that I was their friend, and that we were trying to do the right thing."

His ex-employees joined an exodus of thousands of immigrant field hands, hotel housekeepers, dishwashers, chicken plant employees, and construction workers who have fled Alabama for other states. Like Rhodes, many employers who lost workers followed federal requirements—some even used the E-Verify system—and only found out their workers were illegal when they disappeared.

In their wake are thousands of vacant positions and hundreds of angry 5
business owners staring at unpicked tomatoes, uncleaned fish, and unmade beds. "Somebody has to figure this out. The immigrants aren't coming back to Alabama—they're gone," Rhodes says. "I have 158 jobs, and I need to give them to somebody."

There's no shortage of people he could give those jobs to. In Alabama, some 211,000 people are out of work. In rural Perry County, where Harvest Select is located, the unemployment rate is 18.2 percent, twice the national average. One of the big selling points of the immigration law was that it would free up jobs that Republican Governor Robert Bentley said immigrants had stolen from recession-battered Americans. Yet native Alabamians have not come running to fill these newly liberated positions. Many employers think the law is ludicrous and fought to stop it. Immigrants aren't stealing anything from anyone, they say. Businesses turned to foreign labor only because they couldn't find enough Americans to take the work they were offering.

At a moment when the country is relentlessly focused on unemployment, there are still jobs that often go unfilled. These are difficult, dirty, exhausting jobs that, for previous generations, were the first rickety step on the ladder to prosperity. They still are—just not for Americans.

For decades many of Alabama's industries have benefited from a compliant foreign workforce and a state government that largely looked the other way on wages, working conditions, and immigration status. With so many foreign workers now effectively banished from the work pool and jobs sitting empty, businesses must contend with American workers who have higher expectations for themselves and their employers—even in a terrible economy where work is hard to find. "I don't consider this a labor shortage," says Tom Surtees, Alabama's director of industrial relations, himself the possessor of a job few would want: calming business owners who have seen their employees vanish. "We're transitioning from a business model. Whether an employer in agriculture used migrant workers, or whether it's another industry that used illegal immigrants, they had a business model and that business model is going to have to change."

On a sunny October afternoon, Juan Castro leans over the back of a pickup truck parked in the middle of a field at Ellen Jenkins's farm in northern Alabama. He sorts tomatoes rapidly into buckets by color and ripeness. Behind him his crew—his father, his cousin, and some friends—move expertly through the rows of plants that stretch out for acres in all directions, barely looking up as they pull the last tomatoes of the season off the tangled vines and place them in baskets. Since heading into the fields at 7 a.m., they haven't stopped for more than the few seconds it takes to swig some water. They'll work until 6 p.m., earning $2 for each 25-pound basket they fill. The men figure they'll take home around $60 apiece.

10 Castro, 34, says he crossed the border on foot illegally 19 years ago and has three American-born children. He describes the mood in the fields since the law passed as tense and fearful. Gesturing around him, Castro says that not long ago the fields were filled with Hispanic laborers. Now he and his crew are the only ones left. "Many of our friends left us or got deported," he says. "The only reason that we can stand it is for our children."

He wipes sweat from beneath his fluorescent orange baseball cap, given to him by a timber company in Mississippi, where he works part of the year cutting pine. Castro says picking tomatoes in the Alabama heat isn't easy, but he counts himself lucky. He has never passed out on the job, as many others have, though he does have a chronic pinched nerve in his neck from bending over for hours on end. The experiment taking place in Alabama makes no sense to him. Why try to make Americans do this work when they clearly don't want it? "They come one day, and don't show up the next," Castro says.

It's a common complaint in this part of Alabama. A few miles down the road, Chad Smith and a few other farmers sit on chairs outside J&J Farms, venting about their changed fortunes. Smith, 22, says his 85 acres of tomatoes are only partly picked because 30 of the 35 migrant workers who had been with him for years left when the law went into effect. The state's efforts to help him and other farmers attract Americans are a joke, as far as he is concerned. “Oh, I tried to hire them,” Smith says. “I put a radio ad out—out of Birmingham. About 15 to 20 people showed up, and most of them quit. They couldn’t work fast enough to make the money they thought they could make, so they just quit.”

Joey Bearden, who owns a 30-acre farm nearby, waits for his turn to speak. “The governor stepped in and started this bill because he wants to put people back to work—they’re not coming!” says Bearden. “I’ve been farming 25 years, and I can count on my hand the number of Americans that stuck.”

It’s a hard-to-resist syllogism: Dirty jobs are available; Americans won’t fill them; thus, Americans are too soft for dirty jobs. Why else would so many unemployed people turn down the opportunity to work during a recession? Of course, there’s an equally compelling obverse. Why should farmers and plant owners expect people to take a back-breaking seasonal job with low pay and no benefits just because they happen to be offering it? If no one wants an available job—especially in extreme times—maybe the fault doesn’t rest entirely with the people turning it down. Maybe the market is inefficient.

Tom Surtees is tired of hearing employers grouse about their lazy coun- 15
trymen. “Don’t tell me an Alabamian can’t work out in the field picking produce because it’s hot and labor intensive,” he says. “Go into a steel mill. Go into a foundry. Go into numerous other occupations and tell them Alabamians don’t like this work because it’s hot and it requires manual labor.” The difference being, jobs in Alabama’s foundries and steel mills pay better wages—with benefits. “If you’re trying to justify paying someone below whatever an appropriate wage level is so you can bring your product, I don’t think that’s a valid argument,” Surtees says.

In the weeks since the immigration law took hold, several hundred Americans have answered farmers’ ads for tomato pickers. A field over from where Juan Castro and his friends muse about the sorry state of the U.S. workforce, 34-year-old Jesse Durr stands among the vines. An aspiring rapper from inner-city Birmingham, he wears big jeans and a do-rag to shield his head from the sun. He had lost his job prepping food at Applebee’s, and after spending a few months looking for work a friend told him about a Facebook posting for farm labor.

The money isn’t good—$2 per basket, plus $600 to clear the three acres when the vines were picked clean—but he figures it’s better than sitting around. Plus, the transportation is free, provided by Jerry Spencer, who runs a community-supported agriculture program in Birmingham. That helps, because the farm is an hour north of Birmingham and the gas money adds up.

Durr thinks of himself as fit—he's all chiseled muscle—but he is surprised at how hard the work is. "Not everyone is used to this. I ain't used to it," he says while taking a break in front of his truck. "But I'm getting used to it."

Yet after three weeks in the fields, he is frustrated. His crew of seven has dropped down to two. "A lot of people look at this as slave work. I say, you do what you have to do," Durr says. "My mission is to finish these acres. As long as I'm here, I'm striving for something." In a neighboring field, Cedric Rayford is working a row. The 28-year-old came up with two friends from Gadsden, Ala., after hearing on the radio that farmers were hiring. The work is halfway complete when one member of their crew decides to quit. Rayford and crewmate Marvin Turner try to persuade their friend to stay and finish the job. Otherwise, no one will get paid. Turner even offers $20 out of his own pocket as a sweetener to no effect. "When a man's mind is made up, there's about nothing you can do," he says.

The men lean against the car, smoking cigarettes and trying to figure out how to finish the job before day's end. "They gotta come up with a better pay system," says Rayford. "This ain't no easy work. If you need somebody to do this type of work, you gotta be payin.' If they was paying by the hour, motherf—s would work overtime, so you'd know what you're working for." He starts to pace around the car. "I could just work at McDonald's (MCD)," he says.

Turner, who usually works as a landscaper, agrees the pay is too low. At $75 in gas for the three days, he figures he won't even break even. The men finish their cigarettes. Turner glances up the hill at Castro's work crew. "Look," he says. "You got immigrants doing more than what blacks or whites will. Look at them, they just work and work all day. They don't look at it like it's a hard job. They don't take breaks!"

The notion of jobs in fields and food plants as "immigrant work" is relatively new. As late as the 1940s, most farm labor in Alabama and elsewhere was done by Americans. During World War II the U.S. signed an agreement with Mexico to import temporary workers to ease labor shortages. Four and a half million Mexican guest workers crossed the border. At first most went to farms and orchards in California; by the program's completion in 1964 they were working in almost every state. Many *braceros*—the term translates to "strong-arm," as in someone who works with his arms—were granted green cards, became permanent residents, and continued to work in agriculture. Native-born Americans never returned to the fields. "Agricultural labor is basically 100 percent an immigrant job category," says Princeton University sociologist Doug Massey, who studies population migration. "Once an occupational category becomes dominated by immigrants, it becomes very difficult to erase the stigma."

Massey says Americans didn't turn away from the work merely because it was hard or because of the pay but because they had come to think of it as beneath them. "It doesn't have anything to do with the job itself," he says. In other countries, citizens refuse to take jobs that Americans compete for. In Europe, Massey says, "auto manufacturing is an immigrant job category. Whereas in the States, it's a native category."

In Alabama, the transition to immigrant labor happened slowly. Although migrant workers have picked fruit and processed food in Alabama for four decades, in 1990 only 1.1 percent of the state's total population was foreign-born. That year the U.S. Census put the combined Latin American and North American foreign-born population at 8,072 people. By 2000 there were 75,830 Hispanics recorded on the Census; by 2010 that number had more than doubled, and Hispanics are now nearly 4 percent of the population.

That first rush of Hispanic immigrants was initiated by the state's 25
$2.4 billion poultry and egg industry. Alabama's largest agricultural export commodity went through a major expansion in the mid-'90s, thanks in part to new markets in the former Soviet Union. Companies such as Tyson Foods (TSN) found the state's climate, plentiful water supply, light regulation, and anti-union policies to be ideal. At the time, better-educated American workers in cities such as Decatur and Athens were either moving into the state's burgeoning aerospace and service industries or following the trend of leaving Alabama and heading north or west, where they found office jobs or work in manufacturing with set hours, higher pay, and safer conditions—things most Americans take for granted. In just over a decade, school districts in once-white towns such as Albertville, in the northeastern corner of the state, became 34 percent Hispanic. By the 2000s, Hispanic immigrants had moved across the state, following the construction boom in the cities, in the growing plant nurseries in the south, and on the catfish farms west of Montgomery. It wasn't until anti-immigration sentiment spread across the country, as the recession took hold and didn't

let go, that the Republican legislators who run Alabama began to regard the immigrants they once courted as the enemy.

A large white banner hangs on the chain-link fence outside the Harvest Select plant: "Now Hiring: Filleters/Trimmers. Stop Here To Apply." Randy Rhodes unfurled it the day after the law took effect. "We're getting applications, but you have to weed through those three and four times," says Amy Hart, the company's human resources manager. A job fair she held attracted 50 people, and Hart offered positions to 13 of them. Two failed the drug test. One applicant asked her out on a date during the interview. "People reapply who have been terminated for stealing, for fighting, for drugs," she says. "Nope, not that desperate yet!"

Rhodes says he understands why Americans aren't jumping at the chance to slice up catfish for minimum wage. He just doesn't know what he can do about it. "I'm sorry, but I can't pay those kids $13 an hour," he says. Although the Uniontown plant, which processes about 850,000 pounds of fish a week, is the largest in Alabama and sells to big supermarket chains including Food Lion, Harris Teeter, and Sam's Club (WMT), Rhodes says overseas competitors, which pay employees even lower wages, are squeezing the industry.

When the immigration law passed in late September, John McMillan's phone lines were deluged. People wanted McMillan, the state's agriculture commissioner, to tell them whether they'd be in business next year. "Like, what are we going to do? Do we need to be ordering strawberry plants for next season? Do we need to be ordering fertilizer?" McMillan recalls. "And of course, we don't have the answers, either."

His buddy Tom Surtees, the industrial relations director, faces the same problem on a larger scale. Where McMillan only has to worry about agriculture, other industries, from construction to hospitality, are reporting worker shortages. His ultimate responsibility is to generate the results that Governor Bentley has claimed the legislation will produce—lots of jobs for Alabamians. That means he cannot allow for the possibility that the law will fail.

30 "If those Alabamians on unemployment continue to not apply for jobs in construction and poultry, then [Republican politicians] are going to have to help us continue to find immigrant workers," says Jay Reed, who heads the Alabama Associated Builders & Contractors. "And those immigrant workers are gone."

Business owners are furious not only that they have lost so many workers but that everyone in the state seemed to see it coming except Bentley, who failed to heed warnings from leaders in neighboring Georgia who said they had experienced a similar flight of immigrants after passing their own immigration law. Bentley declined to be interviewed for this story.

McMillan and Surtees spend their days playing matchmaker with anxious employers, urging them to post job openings on the state's employment website so they can hook up with unemployed Alabamians. McMillan is asking Baptist ministers to tell their flocks that jobs are available. He wants businesses to rethink the way they run their operations to make them more attractive. On a road trip through the state, he met an apple farmer who told him he had started paying workers by the hour instead of by how much they picked. The apples get bruised and damaged when people are picking for speed. "Our farmers are very innovative and are used to dealing with challenges," McMillan says. "You know, they can come up with all kinds of things. Something I've thought about is, maybe we should go to four-hour shifts instead of eight-hour shifts. Or maybe two six-hour shifts."

McMillan acknowledges that even if some of these efforts are successful, they are unlikely to fill the labor void left by the immigrants' disappearance. Some growers, he says, might have to go back to traditional mechanized row crops such as corn and soybeans. The smaller farmers might have to decrease volumes to the point where they are no longer commercially viable. "I don't know," says McMillan. "I just don't know, but we've got to try to think of everything we possibly can."

Since late September, McMillan's staff has been attending meetings with farmers throughout the state. They are supposed to be Q&A sessions about how to comply with the new law. Some have devolved into shouting matches about how much they hate the statute. A few weeks ago, Smith, the tomato farmer whose workers fled Alabama, confronted state Senator Scott Beason, the Republican who introduced the immigration law. Beason had come out to talk to farmers, and Smith shoved an empty tomato bucket into his chest. "You pick!" he told him. "He didn't even put his hands on the bucket," Smith recalls. "He didn't even try." Says Beason: "My picking tomatoes would not change or prove anything."

While the politicians and business owners argue, others see opportunity. Michael Maldonado, 19, wakes up at 4:30 each morning in a trailer in Tuscaloosa, about an hour from Harvest Select, where he works as a fish processor. Maldonado, who grew up in an earthen-floor shack in Guatemala, says he likes working at the plant. "One hundred dollars here is

700 quetzals," he says. "The managers say I am a good worker." After three years, though, the long hours and scant pay are starting to wear on him. With the business in desperate need of every available hand, it's not a bad time to test just how much the bosses value his labor. Next week he plans to ask his supervisor for a raise. "I will say to them, 'If you pay me a little more—just a little more—I will stay working here,'" he says. "Otherwise, I will leave. I will go to work in another state."

Analyze

1. Select one of Dwoskin's sentences that best captures the complexity of the immigrant/labor problem.
2. Beneath the obvious tension between the law and the need for labor, what does this article suggest about American workers and consumers?
3. Consider the historical information in paragraph 22. How does it change or affect Dwoskin's portrayal of the current problem?
4. Where do you think Dwoskin comes down on this issue? Is she for or against the immigration law in Alabama? Point to specific statements that support your understanding.
5. Consider the way Dwoskin uses quotations from laborers and employers. How do the specific quotations help to characterize the situation? How they portray both groups: workers and laborers?

Explore

1. Have you ever worked as a farm laborer or in a food processing plant? How does your answer (*yes* or *no*) influence your thinking on the immigrant labor issue?
2. Should U.S. law allow for migrant workers to enter the country? Why or why not?
3. If undocumented workers had to leave the United States suddenly and by the tens of thousands, what do you imagine would happen? What would be the most immediate result? What would be the long-term results?
4. What does Dwoskin's article suggest about a global economy?
5. What would you do if your company suddenly lost its workforce? What if you couldn't attract enough workers to process your stock?

Julie Hanus

White Collared: When Did Our Jobs Turn into a Joke?

Julie Hanus writes and blogs for *Utne Reader*, which describes itself as an enclave "of independent ideas and alternative culture." In her work, Hanus explores a range of topics such as the politics of food, digital culture, spirituality, the environment, and the arts. In the following article, Hanus analyzes the culture of white-collar work.

Remember *Laverne & Shirley?* Archie Bunker? Louie De Palma on *Taxi?* Norm and Cliff on *Cheers?* As these working-class characters live on in late-night reruns, a very different sort of everyperson is dominating the airwaves: the charmingly disengaged, sometimes bungling, always put-upon white-collar worker.

It's a logical trend. Since 1984, the number of U.S. workers has increased by more than 30 million, and 90 percent of that growth has been in the white-collar and service sectors. More citizens work at non-manual labor than ever before, and as technology, outsourcing, and offshoring continue to eliminate blue-collar jobs, pop culture has turned its attention to the office dweller.

The most popular and pointed TV treatment of this phenomenon is a biting satire more or less hijacked from Britain. In *The Office,* the interactions between big boss Michael Scott, played by comedian Steve Carell, and his underlings at Dunder Mifflin are governed by a rubric under which each character is reduced to his or her fundamental office identity. Dwight, assistant (to the) regional manager, is the guy guzzling the Kool-Aid. Sales rep Jim is smart, but often slacking. Pam, meekly poised behind the front desk, hopes to become an illustrator someday, because "no little girl ever dreams about becoming a receptionist."

The show's lead characters cleave into two groups: those who "get it" and those who don't. The latter class is represented by the clownish, not-so-lovable nerd Dwight who gullibly fawns over his foolish manager and mercilessly pursues advancement. He and his kind are the show's jesters. The better half, employees in the know, are its heroes.

5 They immediately spot the stupidity in empty managerial parables, sigh as they play along (for now, of course), and fend off lunacy by playing mostly harmless tricks on their naive officemates. They also demonstrate their superior grasp of the situation by casting incredulous glances at the camera, pained conspiratorial gazes that say: *Can you even believe this? You see that this is all B.S., right?*

For NBC, the formula has proven to be comedic gold. Lurking just below the public's laughter, though, is a grim reminder of what it means to be a modern-day worker bee.

The white-collar workspace hasn't always conjured up visions of monkey-like morons shuffling papers and wasting time on the Internet. When the United States began shifting to a postindustrial society in the aftermath of World War II, writes Nikil Saval in the Winter 2008 issue of the culture journal *n + 1,* corporations like General Electric and IBM offered a new breed of white-collar workers highly secure, salaried work, along with decent benefits and abundant vacation time. What's more, working *meant* something.

By the 1980s, however, economic instability had prompted companies to spread resources thin—to cut pay, slash benefits, and eliminate good jobs in favor of low-pay positions—in order to beef up profit margins. Swaths of Generation X watched their boomer parents get dropkicked in return for decades of good, hard work. Perhaps most notably, those who were affected responded by doing very little to protest—and white-collar workers have been rolling over ever since.

"Young technical and professional workers are as bewildered by the 'new economy' as manufacturing workers have been for a generation," labor activist Jim Grossfeld writes in the January 2007 issue of the online political journal the *Democratic Strategist.* However, in "White Collar Perspectives on Workplace Issues," Grossfeld's study for the Center for American Progress, an important difference between the two groups is revealed. Whereas blue-collar laborers organized to protest workplace issues such as unsatisfactory wages and benefits, white-collar workers have gone on the defensive with a disillusioned attitude. Believing instability and declining workplace conditions are "unavoidable in today's economy," and that corporations are too formidable, they've concluded that nothing can be done but to lower expectations and dodge disappointment. Reject loyalty and avoid betrayal.

10 The standards slid, unchecked. These days, U.S. workers put in longer hours than workers in any other developed country and take the least vacation. If they're actually insured, the benefits are often astronomically

expensive. There's no stability, either; white-collar workers hold an average of nine jobs before the age of 35. Instead of getting angry, they turn a scorned cheek to their employers, defiantly laughing along with *The Office* heroes at the absurdity of it all.

Assistant (to the) regional manager Dwight isn't mocked because he's an insufferable suck-up; he's ridiculed because he fails to recognize that it's all a waste of energy.

When the cartoon strip *Dilbert* first appeared in 1989, it depicted employees who knew better than their buzzword-slinging managers. In that two-dimensional universe, the people making things inefficient were the ones who were portrayed as fools; the evolving workplace was problematic, but the work had potential for value. Now the work itself is what's mocked, which, given the fact that most people spend a bulk of their lives at work, can't help but threaten the collective psyche and further damage the domestic workplace.

White-collar workers already report more occupational stress than their blue-collar counterparts and suffer twice as much from severe depression. Job satisfaction is falling, dropping from 60 percent in the mid-'90s to about 50 percent in 2005, according to a report from the Conference Board, a business-research organization. Forty percent of workers feel disconnected from their employers, and a quarter admit to showing up just to collect a check. In other words, some 35 million workers are either content to not care or have bought into the idea that there's no reason to. (Managers know it, too. Why else would they grit their teeth and bring in "fun" consultants who promise to boost sagging employee morale?)

This culturally sanctioned slacking that results from job insecurity is a self-fulfilling prophecy. Over the past few years, technology has made it possible for work once done in U.S. offices to be performed just as easily anywhere in the world. National Public Radio's *Morning Edition* recently likened the current threat to white-collar jobs to steelworkers' complaints of a generation past. "Fewer and fewer jobs are safe," said Ethan Kapstein, a guest expert in international economic relations. "It means that all of us, people like myself as well, have to continually upscale, we have to continually invest in our skills to maintain our productivity levels."

"What [white-collar workers] need is a new model of unionism that focuses on assuring their employability, mobility, and earning power rather than protecting specific jobs or compensation packages," Will Marshall, president of the Progressive Policy Institute, writes in the January 2007 issue of the *Democratic Strategist.* He echoes Kapstein, arguing that if U.S. white-collar workers want to keep their jobs, they'll have to focus on company productivity as much as on their own needs: "Modern labor associations . . . could operate, in short, like a back-to-the-future update on the old craft unions, which were defenders of quality workmanship as well as workers' interests."

To avert crisis, Kapstein and Marshall both call on the redeeming power of doing *good* work, of investing in skills and focusing on craftsmanship—which would require believing in the value of labor and the value of the laborer. Such a shift in mind-set could protect white-collar jobs, even transform domestic white-collar work. After all, the same technology that produced an outsourcing threat could just as easily make widespread telecommuting a reality. As Matt Bai writes in a November 2007 issue of the *New York Times,* "Why shouldn't more middle-class workers whose jobs can now be done remotely have the option to structure their own hours and still enjoy the security of a safety net? Why shouldn't . . . anyone who spends his day staring at a terminal in some sterile environment straight out of *Office Space* be able to work in shorts and spend more time around the kids?"

It's a lovely vision, shedding all those vestiges of cliché office work (the inflexible hours, the fluorescent-lit cubicles, the impossible work-home balance), but it can't happen if this generation of workers continues to find validation in checking out, backhandedly assuring themselves that they're better than their disappointing jobs and, in the process, proving to their employers that they're utterly replaceable and entirely outsourceable.

If white-collar workers seized this moment to check in, to believe in the value of their work and in themselves as workers, they might do more than save their jobs or even kick open the door for a reinvention of the workspace. They might remember what it feels like to care about what they do—or find out for the first time.

Analyze

1. How does *Office Space* function in Hanus's argument? What point does it help her to make?
2. Hanus explains that young professional workers are learning to "[r]eject loyalty and avoid betrayal." In your own words, explain the relationship between loyalty and betrayal. Why does it figure into jobs?
3. According to Hanus's article, what does it mean to be a "modern-day worker bee?"

Patricia Ann McNair
I Go On Running

A fiction writing professor at Columbia College Chicago, Patricia Ann McNair is an essayist, short story writer, and travel writer. She has published fiction and creative nonfiction in numerous magazines and journals as well as the 2011 story collection *The Temple of Air.* In the following essay, McNair examines the relationship between creativity and work.

I run along the banks of the River Avon on a path shared with walkers, bicyclists, other runners. I'm an American in Bath, in England, where I've been invited to teach creative writing for four months at a local university. Can I say I live here? How long must one stay in one place to be able to call it home? Jane Austen lived here. In fact, my flat (a simple, one bedroom gut rehab in a Georgian-era shell of buttery stone with tall windows) is on a street around the corner from one of the places Miss Austen resided. We are neighbors from different centuries. I've heard it said that Jane Austen didn't like Bath, or at least a number of her fictional characters didn't: "Do you know I get so immoderately sick of Bath . . ." Isabella Thorpe says in *Northanger Abbey*.

"Though I have built the best house I can build for you to stop at last and rest in, you go on running."
—From "My Brother Running" by Wesley McNair

I, however, love everything about this place, starting with my morning run by the river. The path goes alongside walls built decades ago, some built centuries ago. It skirts a crescent of terraced homes curving around a wide, green lawn. It dips under low-slung bridges and passes gently bobbing houseboats. The machines of a paper factory chug noisily nearby while workers gather at a picnic table to smoke and drink coffee from paper cups. If I run this way, I reach a housing estate of lookalike buildings, dog walkers, and kids in school uniforms waiting under a shelter for their bus. If I go that way, in the other direction, I will run in the shadows of Pulteney Bridge, first built in the 1700s. I listen for the sound of wings, the heavy "whomp whomp" that I know means the swans are close by, swooping toward the river's surface. Nearly every morning as I run, I pass this pair of elegant and awesome birds, or they pass me.

I carry with me my keys, my identification, and my stories.

When I am home in Chicago, I run through the city streets that are lined with *Pho* cafés, restaurants that serve noodles morning, noon, and night. There is a large population of Asian immigrants here, and the bright sound of chatter surrounds me, whole conversations I do not understand called across the sidewalks, from the doorway of the train station and the bakery, spilling out from the Asian grocery store. I am heading for the lakefront where the running path goes for miles past high rises and restored prairie lands and beaches. I know this place; I've lived here for close to all of my life. When I first started kissing boys in cars, this was one of the parking lots where I did it, here at the foot of this beach where my run on the lakefront starts.

The stories I am writing take my attention as I run, I move my lips 5 around the dialogue I hear a character say, I try out opening sentences in my head. Unlike Bath where I run full of the wonder that comes with a brand new place, my Chicago run is like something on autopilot. I must remind myself to look up from my story-making and out over the vast and shimmering water toward Wisconsin, toward Michigan.

In Interlochen, Michigan, I run through woods and by wetlands, along the curve of Green Lake (Wahbekenetta, it was once called, "Water Lingers Again"). The dirt road I come to passes through a cottage community of summer people mostly, folks who come to this place during warm months to float and to fish, to swim and to make meals on grills to eat on decks. I'm here to write and to teach, and it is the writing I mull over on my run, while I look out toward the still, blue lake, while I feel the warmth of the sunlight and cool of the tree shadow on my face, on my shoulders. I wind through the woods and the marshes and watch for deer, for their horizontal movement amidst this vertical landscape. I can feel their presence even when I can't see them, these deer. They are like an idea in the making: There. Close. There.

Some say that writers need to be away from the place they want to write about in order to make sense of that place. Sherwood Andersen wrote *Winesburg, Ohio* while he lived in Chicago. James Joyce wrote *Dubliners* while he resided in a number of European cities, none of them Dublin. While living in Paris, Ernest Hemingway wrote stories of Northern Michigan. In Bath I wrote about the Midwest; when I was in Interlochen, I wrote about Cuba, where I'd stayed in January 2000, where I ran along the sea. It wasn't until I was away from Interlochen that I could write about that place, about the first morning of my classes there when two planes flew into buildings in New York, when another crashed in DC, and another went down in a field in the middle of our country. Some weeks after the tragedy I flew home aboard a small plane; from the window I could see below me Interlochen and the cabin I lived in, I could trace the path I ran. We see best, perhaps, from some distance.

"The runner who's a writer is running through the land and cityscapes of her fiction, like a ghost in a real setting," wrote Joyce Carol Oates in an essay for *The New York Times*. In Prague I am not a ghost, judging from the looks I get from the people I pass. Perhaps more like an apparition, a surprising thing that doesn't exactly make sense. Every day on my run near the pension I share with my students, far away from the tourist section of the city, a place with few strangers, I pass an old man who walks a fluffy white dog on a leash. The man stops and stares at me while I run by. I nod, smile. *Dobry den.* Good day, I say. But it isn't until I've lived in this place for three weeks and made this run every day that he finally tips his head to me, that he answers me. *Dobry den.* This happens on the same day I figure out my story, recognizing as I wait to get through a crowd of locals at a bus stop—moving in place—that I have tried too hard with the tale set in a small Midwestern town; I have told too much. I finish the last leg of my run—down a long hill and along a blacktopped road that leads to the door of my home-away-from home and sit down at my desk and try again.

In Johnson, Vermont, my run takes me under/over a covered bridge and for a short while on a quiet highway. I pass a small, clapboard house close to the road where I pass another old man. He has gray hair and a garden of tiger lilies that grow orange against the home's white siding. Sometimes the man sits on a metal chair, watching the world (and me) go by. We always say good morning. And then I am running on a dirt road past an old mill, a dilapidated barn, cows. There are birds and butterflies in the weeds. A loud and arrogant jay calls at me most days. I call back. I can only see so far on this run because I've left my glasses behind on my writing desk in the house I share with other writers and artists. It isn't until I wear my glasses on a walk with a friend along this same path that I see the reindeer high on a ridge. They look down at us as we go by, and I know they have watched me before; they have seen me moving my hands over the shape of a story I have almost finished, building the structure in the air, paragraph by paragraph, section by section. When I hear the final sentence in my head one day on this run, I whoop and punch my fists toward the sky.

10 I am lucky to have work I can carry with me, work that takes me to new places. I am lucky to have new roads to run. It is when I am in my room at my desk (wherever that might be) that I get the words on the page, but I need this other time, too, on the running path. In each new place I'm like a cat: circling and circling and circling until I can settle down. The rhythm of the steps on the road, the sound of my breath, the things I see on the way—these help me get to the story, that creative place I want to be. I run the streets I don't yet know and those that become familiar, sniffing the air, taking the long way.

I'll get there sooner or later, that place I need to be in the story. But until then, I mustn't stop, I can't give up. I will go on running.

Analyze

1. What is McNair's main idea about her work?
2. What does McNair suggest about the nature of work—what it is, what it can be?
3. Would you say that work is, for McNair, tied to the particular locations in her life or somehow placeless? Refer to specific passages to support your answer.
4. Explain how the references to Anderson, Joyce, and Oates function in McNair's essay. What idea do they support?
5. Consider the animals in McNair's essay (the cows, butterflies, birds, even the kindly old men). What idea do they help to show?

Explore

1. McNair focuses on the way she gets creative, which is crucial for her work. What other jobs depend entirely on creativity?
2. Even if you are not a writer (or don't know any personally), try to imagine the difficult parts of the job. What kinds of politics or entanglements might they encounter?
3. How do you think writers make a living? How many books do you think someone has to sell to make an average annual salary? Explain your arithmetic in your answer.
4. Do you think you could maintain an intensive work life if you were your own boss? If you didn't have an immediate supervisor or time clock, could you keep working? What intellectual or psychological habits would help or hurt your work?
5. Many economists and cultural theorists imagine that the next century will see far fewer people going to an office or factory. Instead, people will move around the world and carry their work with them. Do you think this is possible in your chosen field? Why or why not?

Jason Storms
In the Valley of the Shadow of Debt

The founding editor of *Echo Cognitio: A Journal of Research and Creative Writing,* Jason Storms is completing a BA in English and psychology. In the following essay, he dissects the cultural conversation about college debt. Part rhetorical analysis, part research project, and part argument, his essay reveals the complexity—and the dangerously flawed thinking—related to debt.

College graduation is one of the great achievements in life. The pageantry of the graduation ceremonies is truly a spectacle: for roughly one month, every day presents stadiums and arenas filled to capacity as the country's most prominent leaders, thinkers, creators and innovators tell thousands of freshly-minted graduates essentially the same thing: *Life is a long journey with obstacles along the way. But you are college graduates, and with your college education, you can do anything you want.*

Yes, having a bachelor's degree doubles earning potential (United States Census Bureau). It enables social mobility. It is becoming the new standard for obtaining employment. Yet, as a soon-to-be undergraduate, I'm tempted to call shenanigans on the whole thing. The line into the adult world of jobs and money is bottlenecked, and I'm scared as hell to graduate. Debt almost rivals death as my fundamental, existential fear. And I've accrued enough debt to make a down payment on a house, and will soon enter a bleak job market with this debt-child to feed and a wife in grad school to support.

On one hand, this fear of debt and the need to eat and pay bills and maintain sanity is rational, but I question how much of this fear is driven by recent political discourse that characterizes spending and debt as the Great Satan. Whether the government spends money on college funding, health care or social services, current political rhetoric names any spending whatsoever as an existential threat to the American lifestyle.

Some level of debt *is* necessary. For example, almost no one buys a house by merely opening their wallet and taking the appropriate amount of cash. Certain necessities *do require debt.* Debt is necessary for social mobility and basic qualities of life for a majority of our country's citizens. President Obama, an African American raised by a single mother, made his way through Columbia and Harvard Universities by taking on college debt, and could pay off his student loan debt a mere four years before his election as president. His story highlights the balances and payoffs of a college education—you pay more in the short term, but reap more in the long term.

None of this is to say that college funding doesn't have its flaws; the inner workings of various for-profit schools have aptly demonstrated this. One need only look at how much money the U.S. government doles out to for-profit institutions (e.g., University of Phoenix, ITT Tech., et al.) and those institutions' abysmal graduations rates compared with how much money public institutions receive—and keep for profit—and those institutions' graduation rates (Randazzo). Naturally, this information has found its way into college debt discourse. Republican politicians vying for the 2012 GOP presidential nomination offered numerous proposals for fixing higher education. Ron Paul proposed eliminating financial aid altogether, and requiring college students to pay out of pocket. But this would further stratify the social classes, with the result being the rich remaining rich and the poor remaining poor. Education is the key to social mobility. Blocking access to this key would be like eliminating food stamps and insisting that every man, woman, and child pay for their own food. This borders on a false comparison, but I'll offer it nonetheless: a college education is as important to financial and social health as food is to physical health.

Conversely, a slightly less destructive idea has worked its way into the debt discourse: erasing college debt altogether. The recently-created Consumers Financial Protection Bureau has pressed Congress to reverse a 1977 law prohibiting bankruptcy from forgiving student loans (Pianin). Currently, student loan debts are one of the few loans on which you *cannot default*—and with good reason. Meanwhile, the Forgive Student Loan Act would forgive a portion of student loan debt altogether, after students have paid ten percent of their discretionary income for ten years. This idea seems to work well enough on paper.

Yet, these ideas still seem unsatisfying to me. I have had the privilege to receive a higher education because a financial institution, with promises from the U.S. government, agreed to loan me—a financially risky twenty-something—thousands of dollars. Others in my situation before me received this gesture and paid their loans, which kept the institution in business and stable enough to fund my education. It's only fair that I do the same for those who come after me; doing otherwise would be selfish. And it seems better to address crushing student loan burdens rather than to erase the debt altogether. Student loan bills must be paid so that those who attend college after this generation have the same access to education this generation has had.

The rub of this debt conversation comes when graduates can't get jobs or make their loan payments. It seems that the real specter is not debt but unemployment. My fear may not be debt, which has been a manageable constant in personal finance for decades. Rather, it's the intellectual arms race in which my cohorts and I find ourselves. As more people obtain college degrees, the competition for jobs increases, and I can't help but wonder if eventually the master's degree will become the new bachelor's degree, which seems on track to become the new high school diploma.

The conversation about college debt and funding really involves patterns of exclusivity, of finding ways we can preclude or include others in the ever-present quest to learn more and earn more. Right now, higher education, unlike primary and secondary education, costs money, and things like cost can act as a wall that financially or academically challenged individuals, and potentially their successive generations, have trouble breaking down. If we remove financial aid and college loans, we exclude a group—the financially needy—from having the option of attending college, and the subsequent opportunities a college education offers. If we make all funding based on academic merit, particularly academic merit in high school (as many college scholarships do), we keep a huge range of students who struggle through secondary education from having a second chance at social mobility.

10 One can't help but wonder if the hypothetical end of our country's technocratizing trajectory will result in graduates with too much knowledge but no flexibility or dynamism in their marketable job skills. My declared major is a good case in point here. With a bachelor's in English, I have numerous job options, such as writing, editing, teaching (market and geography depending, of course). These jobs may not pay me the same salary as, say, someone with a business or engineering degree, but a job still presents reliable income. Then comes grad school for English, and eventually, once a PhD is taken, there is really only one job available—teaching English in a college or university, and English PhDs only have a fifty-three percent chance of landing that coveted gig (Nared and Cerny, 2000). It seems that this could apply to almost any number of majors, particularly liberal arts majors that may not produce as much product as they do thought.

In the end, I view my college debt as a formidable adversary rather than the Grim Reaper. My wife has zero college debt. She actually had so much funding via scholarships and college trusts that she *made* money her senior year—and my debt is nothing that can't be wiped out quickly with modest living and aggressive repayment. It would have been a mistake *not* to attend college out of my fear of debt—a regret I've often seen in my mother, who turned down a basketball scholarship so she could live on my grandparents' farm for a few extra years and help with the chores. The only one of her siblings who went to college didn't graduate, and all of them churn up the rhetoric of debt each time they see me. But I am not afraid. Roughly a year from now, I will be everything a commencement keynote speaker will say I will be—a college graduate, capable of doing whatever I want in spite of life's obstacles. I just hope the commencement speech isn't too long and clichéd.

Works Cited

n.p. Educational Attainment. United States Census Bureau. Web. 22 August 2012.

Nared, Maresi & Cerny, Joseph. *From Rumors to Facts: Career Outcomes of English PhDs.* Modern Language Association, 2000. Web. 22 August 2012.

Pianin, Eric. "CFPB Pushes Bankruptcy Protection for Student Loans." *The Fiscal Times.* The Fiscal Times, 25 July 2012. Web. 22 August 2012.

Randazzo, Ryan. "For-Profit Colleges Bilking Public, Senator Says." *USA Today.* Gannett, 31 July 2012. Web. 22 August 2012.

Analyze

1. According to Storms, what is the core problem for graduating college students?
2. Of the possible solutions, which does Storms advocate?
3. Explain how personal testimony works for Storms. How does he use his own situation to provide insight on the complexity of the problem?
4. Explain how the sources operate in Storms's argument. What particular points do they support? How important are they in substantiating the claims?
5. Storms's essay might be seen as a two-layered argument. On one layer, he argues about college debt; on another, he argues about the way people argue. What is his concern about that second layer—or what he calls "the rhetoric of debt"?

Explore

1. To what degree are you concerned about college debt? On a scale of 1 to 10, are you mildly concerned (1) or terribly concerned (10)? Give reasons for your answer.
2. In the coming five years, how do you think college debt will figure into the economy at large?
3. Explain how student loans affected your college decisions: where you would attend, where you would live, what you would study, and so on.
4. Storms argues that college is the primary key to social mobility. Do you agree? And do you see the role of college education changing in the near future?
5. Storms explains that "the Forgive Student Loan Act would forgive a portion of student loan debt altogether, after students have paid ten percent of their discretionary income for ten years." What is your opinion of the Act? Why is it a good or bad idea?

Ross Perlin
Of Apprentices and Interns

Ross Perlin is a linguist and researcher for the Himalayan Languages Project in southwest China, where he studies the fading language Trung. He is the author of many articles on language and the 2011 book *Intern Nation: How to Earn Nothing and Learn Little in the Brave New Economy.* In the following magazine article, Perlin examines the historical and cultural value of internships.

After all the talk about amputating ears and public whippings, the Code of Hammurabi pauses to consider the plight of the intern. Well, not exactly—but that ancient litany of 282 laws, inscribed on diorite some 3700 years ago, did enjoin the master craftsmen of Babylon to pass on their trade and treat their apprentices fairly. Four millennia later, these are the basic rights that interns are still fighting for.

Interns, not apprentices, that is. Today, the contrast is stark, with the two groups seeming to inhabit completely different universes. The former are our favorite white-collar peons, often unpaid or paid a pittance, loaded with little indignities and unprotected in the workplace. Apprenticeships, on the other hand, represent a humane, professional model for training and beginning a career—the justified successor to the European tradition of craft apprenticeship, minus the cruelty, coercion, and familial arrangements, sensibly updated for the twentieth and now twenty-first centuries. If no longer ubiquitous, apprenticeships have nonetheless weathered the centuries. At this moment, there are nearly half a million active apprentices across the U.S. in fields as disparate as aerospace manufacturing, seafaring, cosmetology, and green energy.

Still, our archetypal apprentice is a cheerful, mildly rambunctious minion, probably straight out of medieval Europe (Goethe's "The Sorcerer's Apprentice," pre-Mickey Mouse), Colonial America (Ben Franklin), or Victorian England (a Dickens novel). Indeed, the institution has long since become a central model and metaphor for education more broadly. The Western apprenticeship tradition grew out of the medieval guilds, widely known in Latin as *universitates*. Some scholars assert that the first universities—early gatherings of scholars at Bologna, Paris, Oxford, and elsewhere—fancied themselves guilds of scholars, and that everything from set terms of student enrollment (inspired by indentures) to the concept of the dissertation (the "masterpiece" of a scholarly apprenticeship) drew on the model of guild apprenticeships.

In the English-speaking world, a typical term of "indenture" lasted seven years; the (mostly male) apprentices usually took up their indentures, with a nudge or a shove from their family, when they were around fourteen years old, the common-law "age of discretion." These indentures spelled out mutual obligations, more or less formally—the apprentice would work for such and such a period, at tasks relevant to the craft. (There were sometimes specific prohibitions against an apprentice performing grunt work considered the preserve of servants.) In return the master was obligated to teach the apprentice his trade, while also providing housing, meals, clothing, and so on. Numerous other kinds of stipulations also commonly bound both parties—that the apprentice should not marry during his term, for instance, or that the master should provide bedding or clothing of a certain quality.

In Britain, the Elizabethan-era Statute of Artificers enshrined this basic 5
setup until 1814. In the U.S., it began to come apart during the American Revolution, ironically enough since almost all of the Founding Fathers had

started out as apprentices. Apparently, the revolutionary spirit broadened the discourse of freedom in a way that threw indentures into a bad light, and runaway apprentices became an intractable problem. "Go West, young man," the Industrial Revolution, and the spread of mandatory schooling put further nails in the coffin of apprenticeship until the early twentieth century, when a coalition of enlightened employers, unions, and progressives managed to carve out the current, impressive niche.

So what about interns? In the late nineteenth century, the medical profession, eagerly standardizing, started pushing aspiring doctors to endure a year or two of purgatory between medical school and professional practice, "interning" them within the four walls of a hospital. Only after World War II did the model spread decisively to Washington, D.C., and corporate America. Yet the real internship boom is only three decades old—a sprawling, unstudied, unregulated mess gone global, allowing companies in every industry to save on costs and cut corners while millions of college students (and their families) scramble and sacrifice.

Every society has its gift economies—you probably don't pay a relative for babysitting, for instance—but young people working for free en masse is something new and frightening. What's amazing is how quickly we've become inured to it, how naturally we've accepted the idea of "investing in ourselves," bartering for connections and resume line-items. It's a useful reminder that the notion of work is hardly an eternal verity—more like a shifting, uneven landscape, fought over and redefined in every culture and in every age, in spite of hallowed old chiselings in stone.

Analyze

1. How does Perlin's reference to the Code of Hammurabi work? What idea or feeling does it help to establish for the article?
2. In your own words, describe a "gift economy." What part does the idea play in Perlin's thoughts about internships?
3. Why is it important, at least to this article, that apprenticeship may have begun with medieval universities?
4. How does the concept of "indenture" function in Perlin's article? How does it help to characterize or explain the value or peril of internships?
5. Is Perlin for or against modern internships? Or does he have some qualified stance? Refer to specific passages to substantiate your response.

Explore

1. Would you consider an unpaid internship in your chosen career field? Why or why not?
2. What is the most valuable aspect, from the perspective of a college student, of an unpaid internship?
3. Do you think the old-school method of training for a specific career is fundamentally better than getting a four-year university degree? Why or why not?
4. How young should someone start training for a career? Is there is a limit or should children begin as early as possible?
5. Consider the old-school method of adopting the family profession or craft. How do you think that would impact families? How would your family, for instance, be different if the children all supported or adopted the parents' profession?

Christian Williams

This, That, and the American Dream

Editor in chief for *Utne Reader*, Christian Williams writes on issues related to food, the environment, and politics. In his work, he strives to uphold *Utne*'s mission in "capturing emerging culture." In the following blog post, Williams examines the validity of American cultural ideals.

Remember how it felt when you graduated college?

Perhaps you're like me, and you grew up learning that a college degree was the key to a successful future. You knew you didn't want to spend the rest of your life flipping burgers like you did every summer. So you did it: you graduated college, and you proudly walked across the auditorium stage with a big grin. As you shook the dean's hand, all that was left to do was ask, "What's next?"

Back then, a loaded question like that was easy to answer: entry level job in a chosen career, graduate school—the options were endless. It was a question that was exciting to answer because no matter what route you chose, the degree all but guaranteed you'd start higher on the ladder than you would have if you'd only finished high school like your older relatives. You could see and feel what had been promised if you applied yourself and got a degree: the American Dream was real, and you were ready to stake your claim.

It felt good to look back on the previous four years of balancing school and work, knowing now that it was all worth it. Soon, you'd be settling into your career, making a comfortable living, buying a house, and starting a family. Sure, there'd be bills to pay, but you'd rest easy at night knowing that you'd continue to work your way up to better paying jobs in your field, and that you'd comfortably pay back your student loans and meet your mortgage payments.

5 Eventually, the loans would become a distant memory, and you'd be saving your money for your kids' future. They would share their goals of having a career and starting a family, and you'd be happy to do what you could to help them realize their version of the American Dream. You'd even pay off your house one day and still have enough money left to set aside for your retirement, ensuring you wouldn't have to work the rest of your life.

In *that* life, "fair" was getting out what you put in, so you worked hard and were compensated appropriately. And you knew that if you ever found yourself being taken advantage of, your college degree was always in your pocket and able to open another door if need be. In *that* life, there were safeguards put in place to make sure that the greediest among us weren't able to keep you under their thumbs. In *that* life, we celebrated on graduation day because it represented a gateway to opportunity for everyone who earned the right to walk through it.

But in *this* life, the concept of "fair vs. unfair" has disintegrated into an accusation of laziness by the advantaged toward the disadvantaged. In *this* life, greed has infiltrated every nook and cranny of our society to the point where we don't know whom to trust anymore. And in *this* life, insurmountable student debt and the lack of real opportunities to reach our potential have drained graduation day of its optimism and replaced it with the burden of concern. Soon, the event might be more appropriately symbolized by handcuffs than a handshake.

Perhaps there is no alternate reality to *this* life; an existence where everyone truly has the opportunity to realize their full potential, be successful, and find happiness. Perhaps the American Dream has always been an unattainable illusion created by the powers that be.

But if it is an illusion, the false hope it's meant to sustain is quickly fading. While people will recognize the illusion for what it is, they'll remember something important: it sure sounded pretty nice. And maybe then, with nothing left to lose, we'll all stand together, ask "what's next?" and do what it takes to make *that* life a reality.

Analyze

1. Within the framework of this article, what is the American Dream? Point to specific passages that suggest a definition.
2. In your own words, explain the essential difference between that life and this life—the one that Williams remembers and the one he currently describes.
3. As a magazine editor, Williams is writing to a specific audience—to the people familiar with the *Utne Reader*. Given the nature of his argument, what can you infer about that audience? What kinds of political views do they have? What social class might they inhabit?
4. This article was published in 2012—as the United States was climbing out of the deepest recession in modern history and as a presidential election approached. How do you think those factors figure into Williams's tone?
5. Sometimes, writers fall prey to the golden age fallacy—a belief that the past was inherently better for everyone: more innocent, more ethical, more supportive, and so on. Do you think Williams is guilty of the golden age fallacy? Or does he manage to dodge it somehow? Explain specific passages to support your point.

Explore

1. Do you buy the American Dream? Do your friends and family?
2. What decisions have you made—or been invited to make—in support of the American Dream?
3. Williams says, "In *this* life, greed has infiltrated every nook and cranny of our society to the point where we don't know whom to trust anymore." To what extent is this accurate? In your experience, does this statement ring true?
4. Williams says, "Perhaps the American Dream has always been an unattainable illusion created by the powers that be." In this respect, what

are the powers that be? As specifically as you can, explain the forces, institutions, people, even ideas that comprise the powers.

5. What do you expect to do after you graduate from college? Will you pursue the American Dream or will you venture in some other, more or less defined, direction?

Mike Rose
Blue-Collar Brilliance

A research professor at UCLA's Graduate School of Education and Information Studies, Mike Rose is an expert on educational psychology, language, and teaching. He is the author of numerous magazine, newspaper, and journal articles as well as books dealing with issues related to education and work. In the following magazine article, Rose considers the relationship between intelligence and social class.

My mother, Rose Meraglio Rose (Rosie), shaped her adult identity as a waitress in coffee shops and family restaurants. When I was growing up in Los Angeles during the 1950s, my father and I would occasionally hang out at the restaurant until her shift ended, and then we'd ride the bus home with her. Sometimes she worked the register and the counter, and we sat there; when she waited booths and tables, we found a booth in the back where the waitresses took their breaks.

There wasn't much for a child to do at the restaurants, and so as the hours stretched out, I watched the cooks and waitresses and listened to what they said. At mealtimes, the pace of the kitchen staff and the din from customers picked up. Weaving in and out around the room, waitresses warned *behind you* in impassive but urgent voices. Standing at the service window facing the kitchen, they called out abbreviated orders. *Fry four on two,* my mother would say as she clipped a check onto the metal wheel. Her tables were *deuces, four-tops,* or *six-tops* according to their size; seating areas also were nicknamed. The *racetrack,* for instance, was the fast-turnover front section. Lingo conferred authority and signaled know-how.

Rosie took customers' orders, pencil poised over pad, while fielding questions about the food. She walked full tilt through the room with plates stretching up her left arm and two cups of coffee somehow cradled in her right hand. She stood at a table or booth and removed a plate for this person, another for that person, then another, remembering who had the hamburger, who had the fried shrimp, almost always getting it right. She would haggle with the cook about a returned order and rush by us, saying, *He gave me lip, but I got him.* She'd take a minute to flop down in the booth next to my father. *I'm all in,* she'd say, and whisper something about a customer. Gripping the outer edge of the table with one hand, she'd watch the room and note, in the flow of our conversation, who needed a refill, whose order was taking longer to prepare than it should, who was finishing up.

I couldn't have put it in words when I was growing up, but what I observed in my mother's restaurant defined the world of adults, a place where competence was synonymous with physical work. I've since studied the working habits of blue-collar workers and have come to understand how much my mother's kind of work demands of both body and brain. A waitress acquires knowledge and intuition about the ways and the rhythms of the restaurant business. Waiting on seven to nine tables, each with two to six customers, Rosie devised memory strategies so that she could remember who ordered what. And because she knew the average time it took to prepare different dishes, she could monitor an order that was taking too long at the service station.

Like anyone who is effective at physical work, my mother learned 5
to work smart, as she put it, *to make every move count.* She'd sequence and group tasks: What could she do first, then second, then third as she circled through her station? What tasks could be clustered? She did everything on the fly, and when problems arose—technical or human—she solved them within the flow of work, while taking into account the emotional state of her co-workers. Was the manager in a good mood? Did the cook wake up on the wrong side of the bed? If so, how could she make an extra request or effectively return an order?

And then, of course, there were the customers who entered the restaurant with all sorts of needs, from physiological ones, including the emotions that accompany hunger, to a sometimes complicated desire for human contact. Her tip depended on how well she responded to these needs, and so she became adept at reading social cues and managing feelings, both the customers' and her own. No wonder, then, that Rosie was intrigued by psychology. The restaurant became the place where she studied human behavior, puzzling over the problems of her regular customers and refining her ability to deal with people in a difficult world. She took pride in *being among the public,* she'd say. *There isn't a day that goes by in the restaurant that you don't learn something.*

My mother quit school in the seventh grade to help raise her brothers and sisters. Some of those siblings made it through high school, and some dropped out to find work in railroad yards, factories, or restaurants. My father finished a grade or two in primary school in Italy and never darkened the schoolhouse door again. I didn't do well in school either. By high school I had accumulated a spotty academic record and many hours of hazy disaffection. I spent a few years on the vocational track, but in my senior year I was inspired by my English teacher and managed to squeak into a small college on probation.

My freshman year was academically bumpy, but gradually I began to see formal education as a means of fulfillment and as a road toward making a living. I studied the humanities and later the social and psychological sciences and taught for 10 years in a range of situations—elementary school, adult education courses, tutoring centers, a program for Vietnam veterans who wanted to go to college. Those students had socioeconomic and educational backgrounds similar to mine. Then I went back to graduate school to study education and cognitive psychology and eventually became a faculty member in a school of education.

Intelligence is closely associated with formal education—the type of schooling a person has, how much and how long—and most people seem to move comfortably from that notion to a belief that work requiring less schooling requires less intelligence. These assumptions run through our cultural history, from the post–Revolutionary War period, when mechanics were characterized by political rivals as illiterate and therefore incapable of participating in government, until today. More than once I've heard a manager label his workers as "a bunch of dummies." Generalizations about intelligence, work, and social class deeply affect our assumptions about ourselves and each other, guiding the ways we use our minds to learn, build knowledge, solve problems, and make our way through the world.

10 Although writers and scholars have often looked at the working class, they have generally focused on the values such workers exhibit rather than on the thought their work requires—a subtle but pervasive omission. Our cultural iconography promotes the muscled arm, sleeve rolled tight

against biceps, but no brightness behind the eye, no image that links hand and brain.

One of my mother's brothers, Joe Meraglio, left school in the ninth grade to work for the Pennsylvania Railroad. From there he joined the Navy, returned to the railroad, which was already in decline, and eventually joined his older brother at General Motors where, over a 33-year career, he moved from working on the assembly line to supervising the paint-and-body department. When I was a young man, Joe took me on a tour of the factory. The floor was loud—in some places deafening—and when I turned a corner or opened a door, the smell of chemicals knocked my head back. The work was repetitive and taxing, and the pace was inhumane.

Still, for Joe the shop floor provided what school did not; it was *like schooling,* he said, a place where *you're constantly learning.* Joe learned the most efficient way to use his body by acquiring a set of routines that were quick and preserved energy. Otherwise he would never have survived on the line.

As a foreman, Joe constantly faced new problems and became a consummate multitasker, evaluating a flurry of demands quickly, parceling out physical and mental resources, keeping a number of ongoing events in his mind, returning to whatever task had been interrupted, and maintaining a cool head under the pressure of grueling production schedules. In the midst of all this, Joe learned more and more about the auto industry, the technological and social dynamics of the shop floor, the machinery and production processes, and the basics of paint chemistry and of plating and baking. With further promotions, he not only solved problems but also began to find problems to solve: Joe initiated the redesign of the nozzle on a paint sprayer, thereby eliminating costly and unhealthy overspray. And he found a way to reduce energy costs on the baking ovens without affecting the quality of the paint. He lacked formal knowledge of how the machines under his supervision worked, but he had direct experience with them, hands-on knowledge, and was savvy about their quirks and operational capabilities. He could experiment with them.

In addition, Joe learned about budgets and management. Coming off the line as he did, he had a perspective of workers' needs and management's demands, and this led him to think of ways to improve efficiency on the line while relieving some of the stress on the assemblers. He had each worker in a unit learn his or her coworkers' jobs so they could rotate across stations to relieve some of the monotony. He believed that rotation would allow assemblers to get longer and more frequent breaks. It was an easy sell to the people on the line. The union, however, had to approve any modification in job duties, and the managers were wary of the change. Joe had to argue his case on a number of fronts, providing him a kind of rhetorical education.

Eight years ago I began a study of the thought processes involved in work like that of my mother and uncle. I catalogued the cognitive demands of a range of blue-collar and service jobs, from waitressing and hair styling to plumbing and welding. To gain a sense of how knowledge and skill develop, I observed experts as well as novices. From the details of this close examination, I tried to fashion what I called "cognitive biographies" of blue-collar workers. Biographical accounts of the lives of scientists, lawyers, entrepreneurs, and other professionals are rich with detail about the intellectual dimension of their work. But the life stories of working-class people are few and are typically accounts of hardship and courage or the achievements wrought by hard work.

Our culture—in Cartesian fashion—separates the body from the mind, so that, for example, we assume that the use of a tool does not involve abstraction. We reinforce this notion by defining intelligence solely on grades in school and numbers on IQ tests. And we employ social biases pertaining to a person's place on the occupational ladder. The distinctions among blue, pink, and white collars carry with them attributions of character, motivation, and intelligence. Although we rightly acknowledge and amply compensate the play of mind in white-collar and professional work, we diminish or erase it in considerations about other endeavors—physical and service work particularly. We also often ignore the experience of everyday work in administrative deliberations and policymaking.

But here's what we find when we get in close. The plumber seeking leverage in order to work in tight quarters and the hair stylist adroitly handling scissors and comb manage their bodies strategically. Though work-related actions become routine with experience, they were learned at some point through observation, trial and error, and, often, physical or verbal assistance from a coworker or trainer. I've frequently observed novices talking to themselves as they take on a task, or shaking their head or hand as if to erase an attempt before trying again. In fact, our traditional notions of routine performance could keep us from appreciating the many instances within routine where quick decisions and adjustments are made. I'm struck by the thinking-in-motion that some work requires, by all the mental activity that can be involved in simply getting from one place to another: the waitress rushing back through her station to the kitchen or the foreman walking the line.

The use of tools requires the studied refinement of stance, grip, balance, and fine-motor skills. But manipulating tools is intimately tied to knowledge of what a particular instrument can do in a particular situation and do better than other similar tools. A worker must also know the characteristics of the material one is engaging—how it reacts to various cutting or compressing devices, to degrees of heat, or to lines of force. Some of these things demand judgment, the weighing of options, the consideration of multiple variables, and, occasionally, the creative use of a tool in an unexpected way.

In manipulating material, the worker becomes attuned to aspects of the environment, a training or disciplining of perception that both enhances knowledge and informs perception. Carpenters have an eye for length, line, and angle; mechanics troubleshoot by listening; hair stylists are attuned to shape, texture, and motion. Sensory data merge with concept, as when an auto mechanic relies on sound, vibration, and even smell to understand what cannot be observed.

Planning and problem solving have been studied since the earliest days of modern cognitive psychology and are considered core elements in Western definitions of intelligence. To work is to solve problems. The big difference between the psychologist's laboratory and the workplace is that in the former the problems are isolated and in the latter they are embedded in the real-time flow of work with all its messiness and social complexity.

Much of physical work is social and interactive. Movers determining how to get an electric range down a flight of stairs require coordination, negotiation, planning, and the establishing of incremental goals. Words, gestures, and sometimes a quick pencil sketch are involved, if only to get the rhythm right. How important it is, then, to consider the social and communicative dimension of physical work, for it provides the medium for so much of work's intelligence.

Given the ridicule heaped on blue-collar speech, it might seem odd to value its cognitive content. Yet, the flow of talk at work provides the channel for organizing and distributing tasks, for troubleshooting and problem solving, for learning new information and revising old. A significant amount of teaching, often informal and indirect, takes place at work. Joe Meraglio saw that much of his job as a supervisor involved instruction. In some service occupations, language and communication are central: observing and interpreting behavior and expression, inferring mood and motive, taking on the perspective of others, responding appropriately to social cues, and knowing when you're understood. A good hair stylist, for instance, has the ability to convert vague requests (*I want something light and summery*) into an appropriate cut through questions, pictures, and hand gestures.

Verbal and mathematical skills drive measures of intelligence in the Western Hemisphere, and many of the kinds of work I studied are thought to require relatively little proficiency in either. Compared to certain kinds of white-collar occupations, that's true. But written symbols flow through physical work.

Numbers are rife in most workplaces: on tools and gauges, as measurements, as indicators of pressure or concentration or temperature, as guides to sequence, on ingredient labels, on lists and spreadsheets, as markers of quantity and price. Certain jobs require workers to make, check, and verify calculations, and to collect and interpret data. Basic math can be involved, and some workers develop a good sense of numbers and patterns. Consider, as well, what might be called material mathematics: mathematical functions embodied in materials and actions, as when a carpenter builds a cabinet or a flight of stairs. A simple mathematical act can extend quickly beyond itself. Measuring, for example, can involve more than recording the dimensions of an object. As I watched a cabinetmaker measure a long strip of wood, he read a number off the tape out loud, looked back over his shoulder to the kitchen wall, turned back to his task, took another measurement, and paused for a moment in thought. He was solving a problem involving the molding, and the measurement was important to his deliberation about structure and appearance.

In the blue-collar workplace, directions, plans, and reference books rely on illustrations, some representational and others, like blueprints, that require training to interpret. Esoteric symbols—visual jargon—depict switches and receptacles, pipe fittings, or types of welds. Workers themselves often make sketches on the job. I frequently observed them grab a pencil to sketch something on a scrap of paper or on a piece of the material they were installing.

Though many kinds of physical work don't require a high literacy level, more reading occurs in the blue-collar workplace than is generally thought, from manuals and catalogues to work orders and invoices, to lists, labels, and forms. With routine tasks, for example, reading is integral to understanding production quotas, learning how to use an instrument, or applying a product. Written notes can initiate action, as in restaurant orders or reports of machine malfunction, or they can serve as memory aids.

True, many uses of writing are abbreviated, routine, and repetitive, and they infrequently require interpretation or analysis. But analytic moments can be part of routine activities, and seemingly basic reading and writing can be cognitively rich. Because workplace language is used in the flow of other activities, we can overlook the remarkable coordination of words, numbers, and drawings required to initiate and direct action.

If we believe everyday work to be mindless, then that will affect the work we create in the future. When we devalue the full range of everyday cognition, we offer limited educational opportunities and fail to make fresh and meaningful instructional connections among disparate kinds of skill and knowledge. If we think that whole categories of people—identified by class or occupation—are not that bright, then we reinforce social separations and cripple our ability to talk across cultural divides.

Affirmation of diverse intelligence is not a retreat to a softhearted definition of the mind. To acknowledge a broader range of intellectual capacity is to take seriously the concept of cognitive variability, to appreciate in all the Rosies and Joes the thought that drives their accomplishments and defines who they are. This is a model of the mind that is worthy of a democratic society.

Analyze

1. Explain the role of Rose's mother in this article. What does she help to show or represent?
2. Cognitive variability is central to Rose's argument. He says, "In manipulating material, the worker becomes attuned to aspects of the environment, a training or disciplining of perception that both enhances knowledge and informs perception." Explain this concept in your own words.
3. Rose explains that "Verbal and mathematical skills drive measures of intelligence in the Western Hemisphere, and many of the kinds of work I studied are thought to require relatively little proficiency in either." How does this point fit into his main idea about work?
4. In your own words, explain the position or attitude that Rose seems to be pushing against. What assumptions is he trying to correct?

5. What is the strongest part of Rose's article? What passage strikes you as the most powerful and effective in getting you to celebrate the complexities of blue-collar work?

Explore

1. Are you from a blue-collar or white-collar family? How do you think your upbringing influenced your understanding of work?
2. How did your upbringing influence your understanding of intelligence? Be as specific as possible in your explanation. What kinds of intellectual skills did you learn to value or ignore?
3. Rose argues that "we rightly acknowledge and amply compensate the play of mind in white-collar and professional work, [but] we diminish or erase it in considerations about other endeavors—physical and service work particularly." Do you agree or disagree? What experiences support your position?
4. Rose argues, "Our culture—in Cartesian fashion—separates the body from the mind, so that, for example, we assume that the use of a tool does not involve abstraction." Consider a tool that you're familiar with—something you use often. Explain how that tool involves abstraction.
5. Rose explains that his mother studied human behavior in her job. How much do you, as a worker or college student, have to study and attend to the complexities of human behavior? In short, how are you a psychologist? How might you be better at your job if you knew more psychology?

Forging Connections

1. How much does work depend on social media? Consider a specific job—one that you have or may have someday. In an essay, explain how specific social media sites and services support or undermine the success of the work. Borrow insights from the following writers in Chapter 4: Lucy P. Marcus ("What It Means Today To Be 'Connected'"), Cynthia Jones ("Lying, Cheating, and Virtual Relationships"), Michael Erard ("What I Didn't Write About When I Wrote About Quitting Facebook"), or Steven D. Krause ("Living Within Social Networks").

2. Analyze the language of work. If you have a job, examine the particular phrases, words, and language habits of your associates. What specific words or phrases have unique meaning among you and your associates? What codes do you use? How do you conceal meaning from customers or bosses? In an essay, describe that language as thoroughly as possible. Consider the workplace as its own culture—or what is sometimes called a *microculture*. Describe specific situations and exchanges to help characterize the nature of the communication. Borrow insights and strategies from writers in Chapter 3, "Language: What We Mean," specifically Blake Gopnik ("Revolution in a Can"), Richard Chin ("The Science of Sarcasm? Yeah, Right"), and Autumn Whitefield-Madrano ("Thoughts on a Word: Fine").

Looking Further

1. Research the average salary in your chosen career field—or one that you're interested in. Does the salary depend on geography or advanced degrees? Or does it depend entirely on experience? Make a case that workers in your field should, on average, be paid more than professional athletes, movie stars, or even rock stars. Explain the particular value your field adds to the civilization. Take on and correct misunderstanding or inaccurate portrayals of people in your field. If necessary, point to mischaracterizations in popular culture. Integrate images, charts, or graphs to thoroughly present the sophistication and value of your field.
2. Look further into college loan debt. What might it mean for you and your generation? How will it impact the culture of college and broader trends in American culture? Think big. Make connections between financial struggles in your generation and broader academic practices. How might the cost of college and the shrinking government contributions to higher education impact students? How will that, in turn, impact the shared values and beliefs beyond college life?

Chapter 2

Consumerism: How We Spend

It's impossible to deny: If you attend college, work, drive, eat, use a computer, wear clothes, or talk on the phone, you're a consumer—not just a person who acquires things but an economic and cultural force. The average American citizen impacts the world simply by purchasing goods and services. Our needs and desires ripple outward. We influence labor trends, currency, production, and even political policy around the globe. In short, how we shop impacts how millions of others live.

Of course, we don't usually see ourselves in this light. We tend to see our purchasing decisions as personal—simple extensions of our own yearnings and needs. But while we select our next pair of pants, cell phone plan, caffeinated beverage, or house, we are being studied and tracked. Like at no other time in history, shoppers are being watched. Our next consumer move has been predicted, imagined, and charted out by those who want to shape our desires and then capitalize on them. In an unprecedented international spy game, we have been labeled according to our geography, age, race, gender, and fashion sense. In other words, as consumers, we are both agents and objects—targets of study and engines of commerce. We have immense power; yet, we are always nudged into decisions by trends and forces beyond us. And whether we admit it or not, American consumers are largely predictable and profoundly obedient to the marketing messages that surround us.

The readings in this chapter focus on the tensions of consumerism—on the forces behind and the effects of our consumption. Sara Davis, Dan Heath and Chip Heath, and Sharon Begley and Jean Chatzky all examine the power of products to lure us in and even dictate our tastes. Drew Harwell shows how appetites work in a particular social setting. David E. Procter and Charles Kenny show the holes in our otherwise powerful system of production and consumption. Fredrik deBoer and Sharon Angel reveal the historical complexity of our own desires. Finally, Damien Walter calls for a new culture entirely—one that supports creativity rather than consumption.

Sara Davis
Freshly Minted

A PhD candidate in literature, Sara Davis is the advertising and direct mail manager at University of Pennsylvania Press and a freelance puzzle editor for Kappa Publishing Group. She writes and blogs on the intersection of food and culture. Her columns appear in the online magazines *Table Matters* and *The Smart Set.* In the following *Smart Set* article, Davis examines a common ingredient in an everyday product.

Once, and only once, I saw a stranger behaving curiously in the toothpaste aisle. He was standing with his arms crossed and brow furrowed; his eyes seemed to scan everything from the top shelf to bottom, then back to the top again. I waited some time for him to move before I realized that he was doing the same thing I had come to do: Read the labels and frown. Cool Mint, Strong Mint, Radiant Mint, Fresh Mint, Clean Mint, Vanilla Mint, Spearmint, Cinnamint, Now With Intense Mint Flavor: There were no options without mint.

I can't speak for the stranger, but my disappointment with this stunning variety was dermatological. In my early 20s I was diagnosed with a skin condition that was aggravated by among other things, mint oil. At the time, I was a serious mint user: I always had a pack of gum in my bag and thought Altoids were a required final course after every meal. I replaced the breath mints with xylitol-based fruit gums and the old-fashioned remedy of fresh fruit after a meal, but mintless toothpaste is a specialty item, difficult to find: for most toothpastes, mint is an essential feature, not an optional flavor.

But in the history of dental hygiene, the ubiquity of mint is a relatively recent phenomenon. Humankind has devised itself breath fresheners and dental abrasives throughout recorded time, but these varied greatly among cultures, depending mostly on what materials were available. Crushed shells, chalk or brick dust, and even powdered bone could serve to scrub teeth and clean the gums until the invention of toothpaste in the late 19th century. To sweeten the breath, medieval Europeans could crush herbs into their tooth scrub or vinegar mouthwash; mint was sometimes used for this purpose, but so were rosemary, parsley, and sage. Other cultures chewed aromatic seeds—fennel seeds, cardamom, star anise—to abrade and sweeten the mouth; some of these fragrant seeds still appear in the bowls of colorful mukhwas you see at Indian restaurants.

The twentieth century brought several changes to this homemade, all-natural dental care: improved science led to a better understanding of hygiene and new technology led to the industrialization of materials that had previously been made in the home, as well as brand new products. One of these products, Listerine, made good use of another twentieth-century device—advertising.

5 The Listerine company didn't invent halitosis—neither the word nor the condition—but they did invent an extremely effective marketing campaign for an extremely foul-tasting liquid. Originally a surgical antiseptic, Listerine destroys the primary cause of malodorous breath, bacteria that live in the mouth. But science aside, the acrid antiseptic won its way into the mouths of the American public by way of social insecurities. No one wants

bad breath, and if everyone else is gargling with Listerine, then those who don't will become social pariahs.

A campaign like that, which exaggerates a social ailment and normalizes the cure, can rewrite cultural history. Suddenly, daily mouth care was considered the new normal, a recognizable routine that other products could capitalize on. By 1932, Lifesavers advertisements could not only borrow a character from Listerine's campaign, reanimating the halitosis-suffering social and romantic outcast, but could also build on the normalized practice of mouthwash. It's not enough to rinse the mouth, these ads claimed; you should be ready to pop a breath-sweetening candy throughout the day.

"A campaign like that, which exaggerates a social ailment and normalizes the cure, can rewrite cultural history."

There's not a single ingredient in a Lifesaver that combats halitosis or cleans the mouth, but each of the candies offered in that period features a flavor agent that has historically been used as a breath freshener: Pep-O-mint, Wint-O-green, Cl-O-ve, Lic-O-rice, Cinn-O-mon, and Vi-O-let. Violet and licorice seem like old-fashioned flavors to us now, but both have sweet and slightly astringent tastes that made them good crossover candies for a breath-saving sweet. Clove and cinnamon still appear in toothpastes today, particularly European and Middle Eastern brands, thanks to their strong and fiery flavors. But for an early twentieth century American manufacturer, mint oils would have been the cheapest and easiest breath-freshening flavor agent to obtain. Mint farms flourished in cool, damp regions near the Great Lakes and in the Pacific Northwest; some companies had already made a fortune distilling mint oils for export and medicinal use (peppermint was thought to ease digestive distress), and the addition of the manufacture of candies and toothpastes was a lucrative leap.

But it wasn't accessibility alone that made peppermint the most popular Lifesaver flavor for years and, over time, the preferred flavor for dental hygiene products. It's the sensation, more than the scent or the taste, that causes us to associate mint with clean mouths. Mint makes the mouth feel cold.

That "fresh" sensation is a thermal illusion: the actual temperature of your mouth doesn't change. Mouths contain particular cells that that activate in the presence of hot or cold: the condition of extreme temperature "turns on" the cell, which then sends a message to the brain that the mouth is rather hot or rather cold. But menthol also "turns on" these cells, which send their message to the brain as directed, and we experience a coolness in the mouth that isn't there. By itself, mint doesn't make the mouth a less suitable environment for germs; it's the abrasives in toothpastes or the alcohols in mouthwashes that do the dirty work. But it's easy to see how minty freshness became associated with cleanliness: the illusory change of temperature and the sharp, distinctive taste remind us more of cleaning agents than candy.

10 At the same time, the cool feeling of mint is more appealing and marketable than the taste of actual astringent solutions. Classic Listerine doesn't cool, it burns: that fiery sensation is not a thermal illusion but a mild irritation of the sensitive mouth tissues as the antiseptic solution goes about its germ-killing business. Effective, but it doesn't make a strong case for its own daily use. And so, in an intriguing reversal of the invented demand for antiseptic mouthwash, the market compelled Listerine to introduce a gentler, mint-flavored antiseptic for the first time in 1992. As the company president remarked to the *New York Times,* they'd done their research, and they knew that mint is what the market wanted.

In the toothpaste aisle, it certainly seemed that other dental care companies were acting on the same research, deviating from mintiness only for children, who perhaps haven't yet acquired the taste for the strong, astringent flavor. Adult toothpastes tend to come with a maximized mint punch. Because we associate that cool sensation with a clean sensation, toothpastes promise us more intense mint flavor to create the illusion of a more intensely clean mouth.

The promise is not so appealing if you associate mint oil with a puffy, swollen mouth and itchy face, however. My mint reaction subsided as I got older, as often happens with allergies, so I now enjoy mint tea and can withstand a mildly minted baking soda toothpaste. But without the daily exposure to concentrated mint oils, the tastes of "mint expressions" and "curiously strong mints" are repellent to me.

Analyze

1. In your own words, explain how "social insecurities" figured into the success of Listerine.
2. How did the American public buy into the idea of mint toothpaste?
3. How does Davis's personal experience with mint figure into her main idea?

4. What does Davis's article say about consumerism and culture?
5. Consider the article by Sharon Begley and Jean Chatzky in this chapter. How does Begley and Chatzky's point about neuroscience relate to Davis's explanation of ad campaigns and the illusion of "freshness"?

Explore

1. What oral hygiene products do you use? Why do you select one type or brand over others?
2. Davis explains how a particular ad campaign "exaggerates a social ailment and normalizes the cure." In your own words, explain how a cure becomes normalized.
3. How do ad campaigns, like those for Listerine or toothpaste, change history?
4. What other ad campaign (or type of campaign) has impacted the way Americans think of themselves, their bodies, or their families?
5. Why do you think illusions like the "fresh sensation" of mint toothpaste work so well? Why do consumers buy into them?

David E. Procter

The Rural Grocery Crisis

The author of two books on community building, David E. Procter is the director of the Center for Engagement and Community Development and the Institute for Civic Discourse and Democracy at Kansas State University, where he works to revive rural and local communities. The following article originally appeared in the *Daily Yonder,* whose motto is to "keep it rural." Here, Procter considers the demise of the rural grocery store and possible implications for our lives as consumers and citizens.

"We are one of your statistics, I'm afraid. We are losing our grocery store in Protection. The owner has an illness and she must sell or go out of business. It will be a sad situation for an already depressed town."

This e-mail, from an economic development director in Southwest Kansas, is one of many we've received at Kansas State University. Similar e-mails, letters, and phone calls are coming into non-profits, local governments, universities, and economic development offices, and all are making the same point.

Rural America's grocery stores are facing a crisis. These businesses are closing at an alarming rate. Almost daily another small-town, independently-owned store shuts its doors and closes up shop.

In Iowa, for example, 43% of grocery stores in towns with populations less than 1,000 have closed, while in Kansas, nearly one in five rural grocery stores has gone out of business since 2006. These disappearing businesses are creating a crisis, as rural grocery stores represent a critical piece of the infrastructure that sustains rural America.

5 Rural grocery stores are part of the economic engine that sustains rural communities. They are a significant source of local taxes, powering the creation and maintenance of civic services and amenities. They provide essential, stable jobs—butchers, cashiers, managers, and stockers—at a time when we are desperate for employment opportunities.

Dollars spent at a local, independently-owned grocery store cycle through the local economy more than do dollars spent in national chain stores at the edge of town, and certainly more so than when those dollars are spent at an out-of-town big-box market.

Rural grocery stores are also a vital source for nutrition and health, providing a supply of fresh fruits, vegetables, dairy and protein. Where no grocery store exists, rural citizens are living in a "food desert." Citizens in these food-deprived areas struggle simply to find healthy and nutritious food for their families and themselves.

From initial investigations out of our office at the Center for Engagement and Community Development at Kansas State University, it has become clear that many parts of rural America are facing a crisis of access to healthy foods. Research indicates that millions of rural Americans live in food deserts.

A majority of the land area in several states of the Midwest and Mountain West could be described as food desert. "Severe" food desert counties—area where citizens have to drive more than 10 miles to a grocery store—are still apparent in the western portions of the Great Plains states. Approximately 40% of Kansas counties are "severe food desert" counties, and a significant portion of the population in half of Oklahoma's 77 counties live in severe food deserts. The following map displays the food deserts

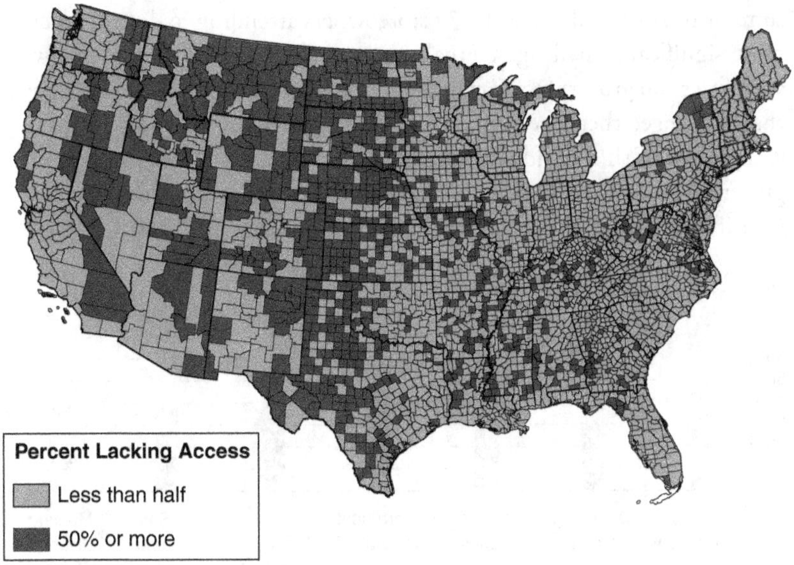

throughout the U.S. and illustrates the severity of this problem in the central plains.

Grocery stores are also important vehicles for community development. 10
They serve as gathering places, where folks see one another, talk about the latest issues affecting their towns, and dream together about what their communities could be. Just like our local schools, cafes, and post offices, rural grocery stores are important community assets, providing tangible evidence of local strength and stability.

So, the question is, why are these rural stores closing? Certainly, there are difficult economic and demographic trends that hurt rural grocery stores' chances to remain profitable. These include rural population decline, increased competition from larger chain stores, new shopping patterns, and changing food distribution models.

But we wanted to understand the crisis from the perspective of the rural grocery store owner and work to address those challenges. To understand the significant challenges rural grocery stores face, Kansas State mailed a survey to all rural grocery stores in Kansas communities with populations of 2,500 or less. Eighty-six of the 213 grocery stores responded.

Kansas State University and the Kansas Sampler Foundation—a Kansas non-profit dedicated to preserving rural Kansas—hosted a rural grocery summit in 2008 and asked the 70 storeowners attending to describe their most significant challenges. Finally, we conducted in-depth interviews with five rural grocery store owners and again asked them about the issues that challenged them the most.

From all of this, we identified the "Big Seven Challenges" facing rural grocery store owners. These challenges and the percentage of store owners identifying them as significant are illustrated in the graph below.

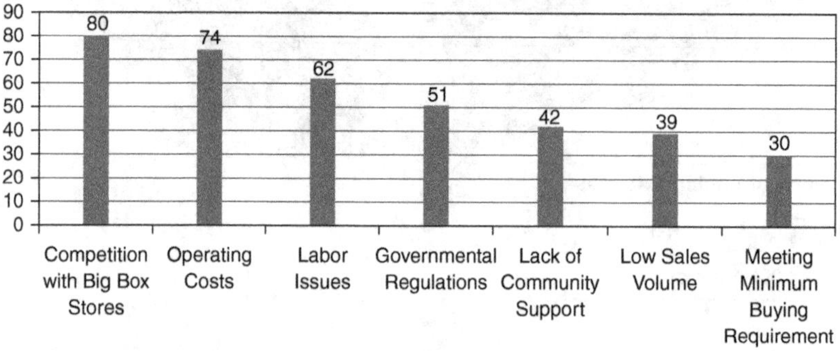

The most frequent, significant challenge identified by our rural grocers was competition with big box grocery stores.

In the past twenty years, we have seen a tremendous rise in the number of big-box, national-chain markets. In addition, big-box wholesalers have moved into the grocery business, and now many offer large food sections as part of their stores. Rural store owners view these stores as competition that threatens their very survival.

We also heard about the challenges of building maintenance, insurance, and shipping costs in the grocery business. The most significant operating expense is utilities, particularly energy. The costs of heating and cooling any store are significant.

By far, though, the operating cost of refrigeration is the greatest challenge. Many store owners struggle with outdated and inefficient coolers. A broken cooler could ruin a significant percentage of a grocery's inventory.

Many rural grocery stores struggle to find an adequate supply of reliable workers. Besides the challenge of finding "good help," in many small towns there is also the problem of finding any employees at all. In many rural communities, there is simply a lack of available folks to hire. This can be a real problem, because if the store owner and family are the only workers, they are likely to burn out or wear out.

Rural grocers must abide by a variety of regulations, such as those governing alcohol sales, food handling, WIC and SNAP participation, proper labeling, workers' comp, and federal and state wage laws.

Some grocers feel these government regulations are overly intrusive, but 20
for others the problem regulations pose is a matter of time and labor.

Lack of community support is one of the most frustrating challenges faced by rural grocers. Grocers say that they are asked to support a variety of community projects—the local ball team, church youth groups, the 4-H Club. They are frustrated when they notice adult sponsors and parents of these community groups traveling to distant big-box stores to do their grocery shopping.

This challenge of low sales volume is related to several others, and of course poses a basic problem. Nearly all rural grocery stores—certainly those in Kansas—are required to purchase a minimum dollar-amount of food each week from wholesale distributors. For small stores and especially those struggling with low sales volumes, this is a significant challenge.

If stores cannot meet the minimum, food distributors simply won't deliver food to their stores; they will literally drive right past and onto a store in the next town where the minimum can be met.

Analyze

1. Explain how Procter supports his statement: "Rural grocery stores are part of the economic engine that sustains rural communities."
2. According to this article, what is the biggest threat to rural grocery stores?
3. How does Procter make this about communities rather than stores?
4. How is the rural grocery store crisis about American culture? What does the disappearance of these stores say about change and resistance?
5. Compare Procter's article to Charles Kenny's "Haiti Doesn't Need Your Old T-Shirt" (in this chapter). What beliefs or assumptions do they share?

Explore

1. Explore "food deserts." What have other scholars and writers said about them?
2. In your area, what are the signs of community strength? What buildings, places, and events suggest cohesion and support?

3. In your area, what are the signs of community decay or weakness? Again, consider buildings, places, and events.
4. Why do you think sociologists and economists are interested in (and often concerned about) the decline of local stores?
5. How are consumers, rather than businesses, the main threat to local businesses?

Dan Heath and Chip Heath
How to Pick the Perfect Brand Name

Brothers Dan Heath and Chip Heath have coauthored several books, including, most recently, *Decisive: How to Make Better Choices in Life and Work* (2013). They are columnists for *Fast Company* magazine, which seeks to "inspire readers and users to think beyond traditional boundaries, lead conversations, and create the future of business." In the following article, the Heaths examine what contributes to, and results from, a successful brand name.

Even more than the crazy wigs and high-protein clothing, it's the name that makes Lady Gaga. If her name were Bethany Cranston (or, say, Stefani Germanotta), forget about it.

Everybody wants a Gaga name for their new product/website/startup. But if you've ever brainstormed about names, you know how deflating the process can be. The URLs for every four-letter word in the English language have long since been snatched up. Yet you crave something unique, something legally protectable. So here come the artful misspellings ("Gene-yus") and the syllable mashups ("TechnoRiffic"). Later, as you review your whiteboard full of gawky names, someone walks by with a BlackBerry and you seethe with envy. That's how it's done. (*Hey, has anyone trademarked Graype?*)

No one in the naming world has generated more envy than a boutique firm called Lexicon. You may not recognize the name. But Lexicon has created 15 billion-dollar brand names, including BlackBerry, Dasani, Febreze,

OnStar, Pentium, Scion, and Swiffer. Lexicon's steady success shows that great names do not come from lightning-bolt moments. (Nobody gets struck 15 times.) Rather, Lexicon's magic is its creative process.

Consider its recent work for Colgate, which was preparing to launch a disposable mini toothbrush. The center of the brush holds a dab of special toothpaste, which is designed to make rinsing unnecessary. So you can carry the toothbrush with you, use it in a cab or an airplane lavatory, and then toss it out.

Lexicon founder and CEO David Placek's first insight came early. 5
When you first see the toothbrush, Placek says, what stands out is its small size. "You'd be tempted to start thinking about names that highlight the size, like Petite Brush or Porta-Brush," he says. As his team began to use the brush, what struck them was how unnatural it was, at first, not to spit out the toothpaste. But this new brush doesn't create a big mass of minty lather—the mouthfeel is lighter and more pleasant, more like a breath strip. So it dawned on them that the name of the brush should not signal smallness. It should signal lightness, softness, gentleness.

Armed with that insight, Placek asked his network of linguists—70 of them in 50 countries—to start brainstorming about metaphors, sounds, and word parts that connote lightness. Meanwhile, he asked another two colleagues within Lexicon to help. But he kept these two in the dark about the client and the product. Instead, he gave this team—let's call them the excursion team—a fictional mission. He told them that the cosmetics brand Olay wanted to introduce a line of oral-care products and it was their job to help it brainstorm about product ideas.

Placek chose Olay because he believed that beauty was an implicit selling point for the new brush. "Good oral care means white teeth, and white teeth are better looking," Placek says. So the excursion team began to come up with intriguing ideas. For instance, they proposed an Olay Sparkling Rinse, a mouthwash that would make your teeth gleam.

In the end, it was the insight about lightness, rather than beauty, that prevailed. The team of linguists produced a long list of possible words and phrases, and when Placek reviewed it, a word jumped out at him: *wisp*. It was the perfect association for the new brushing experience and it tested well; it's not something heavy and foamy, it's barely there. It's a wisp. Thus was born the Colgate Wisp.

Notice what's missing from the Lexicon process: the part when everyone sits around a conference table, staring at the toothbrush and brainstorming names together. ("Hey, how about ToofBrutch—the URL is available!") Instead, Lexicon's leaders often create three teams of two, with each group pursuing a different angle. Some of the teams, blind to the client and the product, chase analogies from related domains. For instance, in naming Levi's new Curve ID jeans, which offer different fits for different body types, the excursion team dug into references on surveying and engineering.

Necessarily, this often leads to wasted work—in the case of the Wisp, the excursion team found themselves at a dead end with the Olay project. But it's precisely this willingness to work in parallel, to endure some inefficiency, that often leads to a break in the case, as with the BlackBerry.

When Research in Motion engaged Lexicon, Placek and his team knew that they were fighting negative associations with PDAs: They buzz, they vibrate, they irritate us and stress us out. So he challenged the excursion team—again, unfamiliar with the actual client—to catalog things in the world that bring joy to people, that slow us down, that relax us. In other words, the antidotes to those negative PDA associations.

The list grew quickly. Camping, riding a bicycle, having a martini on Friday night. Taking a bubble bath, fly-fishing, cooking. Having a martini on Thursday night. Later, someone added "picking strawberries" to the list. Someone else plucked out the word *strawberry*. But one of Lexicon's linguists said, "No, strawberry sounds slow." (Think of the similar vowels in *drawl, dawdle, stall.*) Soon it was crossed out and replaced with the word blackberry underneath. *Hey, wait, the keys on the PDA look just like the seeds on a blackberry.* Epiphany!

Actually, no. "Most clients feel that they're going to know the perfect name as soon as they see it, but it doesn't happen that way," Placek says. Even "BlackBerry" was not easy to sell. The client had been leaning toward more descriptive names such as "EasyMail." (Interestingly, the same was true of past blockbuster names: Some at Intel had wanted to call the Pentium "ProChip," and some at P&G had wanted to call the Swiffer "EZMop." And no doubt someone wanted to call Budweiser "EZGut.")

As Lexicon's success demonstrates, a great name can make a big difference. When some smart marketer renamed the Chinese gooseberry a kiwi, the fruit became a huge hit. But we shouldn't overheroicize names. After all, we live in a world where some of the most powerful brands are called Microsoft, Walmart, and General Electric. Clearly, a mediocre name isn't destiny. For every Lady Gaga, there's a Katy Perry. So maybe there's hope for you after all, Bethany Cranston.

Analyze

1. What's so special about Lady Gaga—not the singer, but the name? Why is her name used in the introduction of the article?
2. Explain how the story of the *Wisp* functions in this article: why is the story told in detail? What does it help to show?
3. Explain how the point about kiwis, in the concluding paragraph, relates to the author's main point.
4. The title of the article promises to tell readers how to pick a perfect product name. In your own words, explain the brainstorming processes that the authors celebrate and one they seem to condemn.
5. The authors also make a subtle case against "lightning-bolt moments." Explain their case—and how they make it. Describe what examples or situations help to show their point.

Explore

1. Why is Katy Perry a worse name than Lady Gaga for a pop singer? And why is Bethany Cranston worse yet? How do the syllables, the vowels, and the word associations play into the effect of the names?
2. The authors suggest that BlackBerry, as a product name, is and should be envied. Why? How does *BlackBerry* function? Why do you think experts in the field of marketing would praise the name?
3. Name a product that you personally dislike but that also has a perfect name. Explain why the name, despite the product itself, is effective.
4. Companies spend millions of dollars every year on names and slogans. They carefully tweak words, fonts, and images to attract the target audience or primary consumer group. By and large, the process works. Americans respond very well to advertising. Explain how you have been part of this process. Tell of a specific product and how you were quietly attracted to its name, its slogan, or its packaging.

Charles Kenny
Haiti Doesn't Need Your Old T-Shirt

A development economist, Charles Kenny examines social and political trends related to growth and corruption. He is the author of numerous journal and magazine articles, books, and blog posts. The following article originally appeared in *Foreign Policy* magazine, which seeks to "combine original thinking with real-world illustrations of ideas in action." Here, Kenny questions the value of certain donated goods.

The Green Bay Packers this year beat the Pittsburgh Steelers to win Super Bowl XLV in Arlington, Texas. In parts of the developing world, however, an alternate reality exists: "Pittsburgh Steelers: Super Bowl XLV Champions" appears emblazoned on T-shirts from Nicaragua to Zambia. The shirt wearers, of course, are not an international cadre of Steelers die-hards, but recipients of the many thousands of excess shirts the National Football League produced to anticipate the post-game merchandising frenzy. Each year, the NFL donates the losing team's shirts to the charity World Vision, which then ships them off to developing countries to be handed out for free.

Everyone wins, right? The NFL offloads 100,000 shirts (and hats and sweatshirts) that can't be sold—and takes the donation as a tax break. World Vision gets clothes to distribute at no cost. And some Nicaraguans and Zambians get a free shirt. What's not to like?

Quite a lot, as it happens—so much so that there's even a Twitter hashtag, #SWEDOW, for "Stuff We Don't Want," to track such developed-world offloading, whether it's knit teddy bears for kids in refugee camps, handmade puppets for orphans, yoga mats for Haiti, or dresses made out of pillowcases for African children. The blog *Tales from the Hood*, run by an anonymous aid worker, even set up a SWEDOW prize, won by Knickers 4 Africa, a (thankfully now defunct) British NGO set up a couple of years ago to send panties south of the Sahara.

Here's the trouble with dumping stuff we don't want on people in need: What they need is rarely the stuff we don't want. And even when they do need that kind of stuff, there are much better ways for them to get it than for a Western NGO to gather donations at a suburban warehouse, ship everything off to Africa or South America, and then try to distribute it to remote areas. World Vision, for example, spends 58 cents per shirt on shipping, warehousing, and distributing them, according to data reported by the blog *Aid Watch*—well within the range of what a secondhand shirt costs in a developing country. Bringing in shirts from outside also hurts the local economy: Garth Frazer of the University of Toronto estimates that increased used-clothing imports accounted for about half of the decline in apparel industry employment in Africa between 1981 and 2000. Want to really help a Zambian? Give him a shirt made in Zambia.

5 The mother of all SWEDOW is the $2 billion-plus U.S. food aid program, a boondoggle that lingers on only because of the lobbying muscle of agricultural conglomerates. (Perhaps the most embarrassing moment was when the United States airdropped 2.4 million Pop-Tarts on Afghanistan in January 2002.) Harvard University's Nathan Nunn and Yale University's Nancy Qian have shown that the scale of U.S. food aid isn't strongly tied to how much recipient countries actually require it—but it does rise after a bumper crop in the American heartland, suggesting that food aid is far more about dumping American leftovers than about sending help where help's needed. And just like secondhand clothing, castoff food exports can hurt local economies. Between the 1980s and today, subsidized rice exports from the United States to Haiti wiped out thousands of local farmers and helped reduce the proportion of locally produced rice consumed in the country from 47 to 15 percent. Former President Bill Clinton concluded that the food aid program "may have been good for some of my farmers in Arkansas, but it has not worked. . . . I had to live every day with the consequences of the lost capacity to produce a rice crop in Haiti to feed those people because of what I did."

Bottom line: Donations of cash are nearly always more effective. Even if there are good reasons to give stuff rather than money, in most cases the stuff can be bought locally. Economist Amartya Sen, for example, has conclusively shown that people rarely die of starvation or malnutrition because of a lack of food in the neighborhood or the country. Rather, it is because they can't afford to buy the food that's available. Yet, as Connie Veillette of the Center for Global Development reports, shipping U.S. food abroad in response to humanitarian disasters is so cumbersome it takes four to six months to get there after the crisis begins. Buying food locally, the U.S. Government Accountability Office has found, would be 25 percent cheaper and considerably faster, too.

In some cases, if there really is a local shortage and the goods really are needed urgently, the short-term good done by clothing or food aid may well outweigh any long-term costs in terms of local development. But if people donate SWEDOW, they may be less likely to give much-needed cash. A study by Aradhna Krishna of the University of Michigan, for example, suggests that charitable giving may be lower among consumers who buy cause-related products because they feel they've already done their part. Philanthrocapitalism may be chic: The company Toms Shoes has met with considerable commercial success selling cheap footwear with the added hook that for each pair you buy, the company gives a pair to a kid in the developing world (it's sold more than a million pairs to date). But what if consumers are buying Toms instead of donating to charity, as some surely are? Much better to stop giving them the stuff we don't want—and start giving them the money they do.

Analyze

1. Kenny opens his article by alluding to football T-shirts. How does the image of Haiti's citizens wearing NFL shirts relate to his main point?
2. Why is the food aid program, explained in paragraph 5, "the mother of all SWEDOW"?
3. In your own words, explain Kenny's subtle argument about people who send their T-shirts and underwear to poor counties. What do those people not understand? How are their assumptions flawed? Where are they going wrong?
4. Even if you've never seen the word before, what can you infer about *philanthropicapitalism?* Given Kenny's concluding paragraph, how would you define the term?
5. Explain how Kenny's argument relates to Dan Heath and Chip Heath's article, "How to Pick the Perfect Brand Name" (in this chapter).

Explore

1. Do you give to charity? Why or why not?
2. If everyone in America read Kenny's article, what might change? How might Kenny's words impact people's thinking, shopping habits, or charity donations?
3. Kenny argues, "Here's the trouble with dumping stuff we don't want on people in need: What they need is rarely the stuff we don't want."

Explain why this might be true. Consider a specific item that might be shipped to a poor country. Further, explain how sending that item might do more harm than good.

4. Consider the following response to Kenny's article—posted to the *Foreign Policy* website by William O' Keefe, the Senior Director of Advocacy for Catholic Relief Services. Explain why you accept or do not accept O'Keefe's response:

> Though Mr. Kenny makes valid points in his critique of giving items such as clothing in the name of international charity, his brush gets a bit too broad when he uses it to condemn the entire food aid program of the United States. Certainly that program has its flaws and can be improved, but food from the U.S. keeps many people alive and healthy throughout the world. Today, millions in East Africa rely on food from the U.S. to get them through a horrendous drought. This is not the same as giving people t-shirts. Nor is it "dumping stuff we don't want on people in need." It is giving much needed nutrition to people who have no way else to get it.

Drew Harwell

Honey Buns Sweeten Life for Florida Prisoners

A business reporter for the *Tampa Bay Times*, Drew Harwell explores the politics of place. His articles often focus on real estate, housing, and property tax. In the following, Harwell considers the large role of a small commodity in the Florida prison system.

The honey buns enter lockup the same way anyone else does: bound, escorted through halls and sally ports, and secluded in small boxes solely opened from the outside. From there the honey buns languish for days, maybe longer, until they're gone.

They are a lowly, sturdy food designed for desperate cravings and vending machine convenience. They can endure weeks of neglect and even a mild mashing in a coat pocket or backpack. They are, it should come as no surprise, especially beloved by a similarly hardy but disrespected population: Florida's prison inmates.

Inmates in the Florida prison system buy 270,000 honey buns a month. Across the state, they sell more than tobacco, envelopes and cans of Coke. And they're just as popular among Tampa Bay's county jails. In Pasco's Land O'Lakes Detention Center, they're outsold only by freeze-dried coffee and ramen noodles.

Not only that, these honey buns—so puffy!—have taken on lives of their own among the criminal class: as currency for trades, as bribes for favors, as relievers for stress and substitutes for addiction. They've become birthday cakes, hooch wines, last meals—even ingredients in a massive tax fraud.

5 So what is it about these little golden glazed snacks? Is it that they're cheap, which is big, since the prisoners rely on cash from friends and family? That their sugary denseness could stop a speeding bullet? That they're easy, their *mise en place* just the unwrapping of plastic? What gives?

Maybe considering the honey bun can help us understand life behind bars.

Jailhouse cuisine is a closely calculated science.

A day's meals inside the mess hall must be hearty enough to meet the 2,750-calorie count, healthy enough to limit fat and sodium, easy enough for prison cooks to prepare and cheap enough to meet the state's average grocery bill—about $1.76 per inmate per day.

With all criteria met, meals behind bars achieve an impressive level of mediocrity. The portions are reasonable, the nutritional content adequate, the taste ordinary, the presentation dull, the blandness as inescapable as the facilities themselves. The meals are made to guarantee very little except survival.

10 Problem inmates don't have it any easier. Their punishment: "special management meals" of Nutraloaf, a tasteless lump of carrots, spinach and grits that resembles a sad fruitcake. Compared to that, honey buns are a revolution. Honey buns are fried dough in a bag. Honey buns meet next to none of the human body's needs and are impressively unhealthy.

The 6 ounces of a Mrs. Freshley's Grand Honey Bun, the favored pastry of Florida's prisons, serve up 680 calories, 51 grams of sugar and 30 grams of fat. The icing is sticky and frost white, like Elmer's Glue. The taste bears all the subtlety of a freshly licked sugar cube.

"As you can imagine," said Janice Anderson, a spokeswoman for Flowers Foods, which owns the Mrs. Freshley's brand, "this product is for those folks that feel like having something very decadent."

Decadent!

Inmates at the Maryland Correctional Institution for Women used honey buns as the base for a Christmas apple pie. Inmates at the Robeson County Jail in Lumberton, N.C., mixed in honey buns to sweeten a wine they fermented from orange juice. During his two-month stay in an Illinois jail cell, NFL defensive tackle Tank Johnson gulped down, after hearty meals of beef sticks and summer sausages, 40 honey buns for dessert.

Prisoners on death row have even turned to the sweets for their last meals. Charles Roache, lethally injected in North Carolina in 2004, chose a sirloin steak, popcorn shrimp and a honey bun.

George Alec Robinson, an unemployed sanitation worker and father of three, paid his public defenders in honey buns after they saved him from Virginia's electric chair.

"He said, 'This is all in the world I can give you guys,'" attorney James C. Clark told the *Washington Post*. "They were good, too."

In September, the day after the New Orleans Saints beat the San Francisco 49ers in a Monday Night Football game, a fight broke out in the Alpha Pod of the Hernando County Jail. Inmate Ricardo Sellers, 21, had punched Brandon Markey, 23, in the face, sending Markey to a Brooksville hospital, according to Hernando deputies. Sellers was angry that Markey hadn't paid up after losing a bet over football.

His debt? Four honey buns.

For all their sweetness, honey buns have a history of involvement in prison violence. In 2006, at the Kent County Jail in Michigan, inmate Benny Rochelle dragged his cell mate off the top bunk, killing the man, when he could not find his honey bun. And last year, at the Lake Correctional Institution west of Orlando, two men were sentenced to life in prison for stabbing with crude shivs the man they thought had stolen shaving cream, cigarettes and a honey bun from their footlockers.

Yes, murder over honey buns. Was it their decadence, or their status as jailhouse currency?

In Texas and Pennsylvania, inmates bartered honey buns for tablets of Seroquel, an addictive antipsychotic abused on the street as a sleeping pill.

In Sarasota, a millionaire businessman charged with child abuse earned the nickname "Commissary King" after fashioning honey buns into birthday cakes for inmates he felt he could sway to his defense.

In Naples, a bail bondsman was accused of giving an inmate hundreds of dollars' worth of honey buns over 13 years as rewards for referring him business.

And at the Graceville Work Camp, in the Panhandle, a Jacksonville trucker known for sharing his faith called it one of his great joys to sneak honey buns under inmates' pillows. In some cases, honey buns have proven too seductive for inmates' own good. At the Stock Island Detention Center, outside Key West, scheming inmates offered overnight arrestees in the jail's drunk tank an irresistible deal: their Social Security numbers for a honey bun. Using the numbers, they filled out tax forms with phony information—a scam that cost the IRS more than $1 million in fraudulent refunds.

As a retired Monroe County sheriff told the *Miami Herald,* "They were eating a lot of honey buns on the taxpayer."

After Ryan Frederick took the stand last year during his capital murder trial in Virginia, prosecutor James Willett made a strange request.

Stand up. Open your jacket. Turn sideways.

When he had been arrested for shooting a detective during a drug raid, Frederick had weighed 120 pounds, according to the *Virginian-Pilot.* After a year in lockup, he ballooned to 185.

Exhibit A: Frederick's gut.

"You're not exactly wasting away from regret and remorse now, are you?" Willett said.

Frederick's behavior at the Chesapeake City Jail was central to prosecutors' argument that he had bragged of the killing. His weight gain, they said, further proved his shamelessness.

But during his testimony, Frederick said the extra pounds stemmed from something else.

To deal with the stresses of jail, he said, he ate.

"I have a bad habit of doughnuts and honey buns," he told the jury.

Some inmates use honey buns to combat cravings deeper than a sweet tooth. At the Hernando County Jail, where honey buns are regulars atop the bestsellers list, the sweets have served as substitutes for other vices.

"Many people in jail are addicts or abusers of substances," said jail administrator Maj. Mike Page. "Alcohol is based in sugars generally, and the human body will receive some satisfaction of cravings from the honey bun as a substitute for the sugar."

Armon Power, an inmate at Alabama's Holman Correctional Facility who earned 30 cents an hour stamping license plates at the prison tag plant, explained it to a TV crew in simpler terms: "I crave honey buns. I buy honey buns," he said. "I can't buy no wine."

Convicted murderer Michael Caruso is a canteen operator at the Zephyrhills state prison. His is a prestigious job. Of all the tedious prison work, his pays the most ($75 a month) and affords him the sweetest office: front and center to the boxes of honey buns.

He sells about 60 sweets a day at this sprawling, razor-wired campus of mostly elderly prisoners in east Pasco. The men like to smother the honey buns with peanut butter Squeezers packets. Some inmates, he said, try to "manipulate" him into handing them over for free, though most think their $1.08 price tags, cheaper than foods like the $2.75 Big AZ Bubba Twins chili cheese dogs, are easier to stomach.

"It's the same as on the street," Caruso said. "When you get paid you drink Budweiser. After that you drink Black Label."

In prison, as in life, thrift wins. In 2009, when Florida upped its canteen prices, 60 families called and wrote letters to complain. Most of the anger, according to the Associated Press, centered on the price of honey buns, raised from 66 cents to 99 cents. (To, now, $1.08.)

But something funny happens, Caruso said. On Fridays, inmates will buy up honey buns for the weekend, when they gather in the dayroom to watch football. The prisoners share. Seems to happen all the time.

Maybe that's what it is with honey buns. They're sweet, when nothing else is.

Analyze

1. On its surface, this article is about honey buns. On a deeper level, it's about prison life. And on a deeper level still, what is this article about?

2. Harwell explains that the honey buns sold in the prison are "impressively unhealthy." How does this point fit into the main idea of the article? Why is it important that the honey buns are devoid of nutritional value?
3. How does the fight between two inmates, Markey and Sellers, support Harwell's main idea?
4. Explain how the issue of alcoholism relates to Harwell's main idea.
5. Consider Harwell's choice for a one-word paragraph: "Decadent!" What purpose does that single word (with an exclamation point!) serve?

Explore

1. In your own words, why are honey buns so sought after in prison?
2. Does this article make prison inmates seem more ordinary or less ordinary? Point to specific passages that support your thinking.
3. How might having a family member or loved one in prison impact readers' understanding of this article?
4. The United States jails more of its citizens than any country in the world. And most of the inmates come from abject poverty or working-class families. How do these facts figure into your thinking about honey buns? Is there some correlation between honey buns and poverty? Honey buns and socioeconomic class?
5. Consider Sara Davis's history of mint or Begley and Chatzky's point about neuroscience and spending habits. How do their articles (both in this chapter) shed light on the prisoners' attraction to honey buns?

Sharon Begley and Jean Chatzky

The New Science Behind Your Spending Addiction

The senior health and science correspondent at Reuters, Sharon Begley writes on issues related to neuroscience and the brain's potential for change. She is the author of numerous magazine articles, blog posts, and books, including the 2012 book *The Emotional Life of Your Brain.* Jean Chatzky is the financial editor for NBC's *Today.* She writes and speaks on issues related to personal finance, debt, and wealth. Among her many publications is the 2012 book *Money Rules.* In the following article, Begley and Chatzky examine our consumer impulses, and how we can change them.

Like many colleges, Washington University in St. Louis offers children of its faculty free tuition. So Leonard Green, a professor of psychology there, did all he could to persuade his daughter to choose the school. He extolled its academic offerings, praised its social atmosphere, talked up its extracurricular activities—and promised that if Hannah chose Washington he would give her $20,000 each undergraduate year, plus $20,000 at graduation, for a nest egg totaling $100,000.

She went to New York University.

To many, this might seem like a simple case of shortsightedness, a decision based on today's wants (an exciting city, independence) versus tomorrow's needs (money, shelter). Indeed, the choice to spend rather than save reflects a very human—and, some would say, American—quirk: a preference for immediate gratification over future gains. In other words, we get far more joy from buying a new pair of shoes today, or a Caribbean vacation, or an iPhone 4S, than from imagining a comfortable life tomorrow. Throw in an instant-access culture—in which we can get answers on the Internet within seconds, have a coffeepot delivered to our door overnight, and watch movies on demand—and we're not exactly training the next generation to delay gratification.

"Pleasure now is worth more to us than pleasure later," says economist William Dickens of Northeastern University. "We much prefer current consumption to future consumption. It may even be wired into us."

5 As brain scientists plumb the neurology of an afternoon at the mall, they are discovering measurable differences between the brains of people who save and those who spend with abandon, particularly in areas of the brain that predict consequences, process the sense of reward, spur motivation, and control memory.

In fact, neuroscientists are mapping the brain's saving and spending circuits so precisely that they have been able to rev up the saving and disable the spending in some people (in the lab, alas; not at the cash register). The result: people's preferences switch from spending like a drunken sailor to saving like a child of the Depression. All told, the gray matter responsible for some of our most crucial decisions is finally revealing its secrets. Call it the "moneybrain." Psychologists and behavioral economists, meanwhile, are identifying the personality types and other traits that distinguish savers from spenders, showing that people who aren't good savers are neither stupid nor irrational—but often simply don't accurately foresee the consequences of not saving. Rewire the brain to find pleasure in future rewards, and you're on the path to a future you really want.

In one experiment, neuroeconomist Paul Glimcher of New York University wanted to see what it would take for people to willingly delay gratification. He gave a dozen volunteers a choice: $20 now or more money, from $20.25 to $110, later. On one end of the spectrum was the person who agreed to take $21 in a month—to essentially wait a month in order to gain just $1. In economics-speak, this kind of person has a "flat discount function," meaning he values tomorrow almost as much as today and is therefore able to delay gratification. At the other end was someone who was willing to wait a month only if he got $68, a premium of $48 from the original offer. This is someone economists call a "steep discounter," meaning the value he puts on the future (and having money then) is dramatically less than the value he places on today; when he wants something, he wants it now. The $21 person was, tellingly, an MD-PhD student. "If you're willing to go to grad school for eight years, you're really willing to delay gratification," says Glimcher.

More revealing was the reason for the differences. To measure brain activity while people considered whether to delay gratification, researchers slid their subjects into functional magnetic resonance imaging (fMRI) machines. The scientists found that activity in two regions—the ventral striatum, tucked deep in the brain, and the medial prefrontal cortex (PFC) right behind the forehead—closely tracked people's preferences. In someone who was offered a choice between $100 today or $100 next week, activity in these regions plunged when the next-week choice was considered, and fell even more as the payoff was postponed further and further into the future. These are spend-it-now, to-hell-with-tomorrow people who seek immediate gratification. In other people, however, activity in the ventral striatum and medial prefrontal cortex activity was the same whether they were thinking of having money today or down the road—indicating that they were just as happy either way.

For anyone who wants to save more but can't seem to do so, that raises the obvious question: how can I make my ventral striatum and medial prefrontal cortex as happy about rewards in the future as they are about rewards today?

It's something that scientists are actively studying. In one classic study from the late 1960s, fondly known as the marshmallow experiment, scientists at Stanford University led by psychologist Walter Mischel (now at Columbia University) offered 4-year-olds a marshmallow, and left it invitingly in front of them. The hitch: if the kids waited to eat the marshmallow until the experimenter, who stepped out of the room, returned in a few minutes, they could have two marshmallows. More than a decade later, the children who waited and got the second marshmallow scored much higher on the SAT, supporting the idea that impulse control and other aspects of "emotional intelligence" are linked to academic performance. The reward delayers were also less likely to be obese, to have become addicted to illegal drugs, and to be divorced—outcomes that are more likely in people who go for immediate gratification.

The marshmallow children were tested every dozen years or so, says Mischel, and are now in their 40s. In a study reported in August in the *Proceedings of the National Academy of Sciences,* scientists led by psychobiologist B. J. Casey of Weill Cornell Medical College gathered 59 of the original kids and gave them an adult version of the delayed-gratification test. Using fMRI, they analyzed differences in brain activity between those who were good at delaying gratification and those who opted for instant rewards, marshmallows or otherwise. In high delayers, the brain's thoughtful, rational prefrontal cortex was more active, as was the right inferior frontal gyrus, which inhibits the "I want it now" impulse. Poor delayers had less activity in both regions, but higher activity in regions of the limbic system that respond to instant gratification. Identifying the regions of the brain that control such impulses is a first step in learning how to strengthen them and, ultimately, to enjoy saving.

Other studies, too, have shown the key role the prefrontal cortex plays in making us willing to defer gratification today in favor of saving for retirement. The dorsolateral PFC, in particular, sends "calm down" signals to the midbrain's "I want it now" circuits. As a result, in studies that use strong magnets to temporarily disable the dorsolateral PFC on human volunteers, "people get more impulsive," says NYU's Glimcher. That is, they strongly prefer immediate gratification. "But if you artificially activate it," he says, people become perfectly content to save for tomorrow.

The noninvasive "zapping" technology, called transcranial magnetic stimulation (TMS), is currently being studied at Columbia University and NYU, among other places. The technology works by inducing a weak electric current in targeted regions of the brain. In the lab, that allows scientists to pinpoint regions of people's brains responsible for specific functions. In other words, if zapping an area disables that area, then anything the person can no longer do is presumably controlled by that spot.

So far, none of the researchers using TMS to map the brain have wheeled the device to a shopping mall and aimed it at people who buy $300 sunglasses and $150 T-shirts despite having contributed $0 to their savings, but the notion isn't preposterous. TMS has been successfully used to treat chronic pain, major depression, tinnitus, and some symptoms of schizophrenia, in each case by revving up or shutting down activity in specific brain circuits that underlie the condition.

15 Since zapping your brain to rev up the dorsolateral PFC is not ready for prime time, scientists have begun searching for more practical ways to develop a moneybrain that has a talent for saving. One hint comes from the discovery that the size of the dorsolateral PFC differs from one person to another, notes neuroeconomist Paul Zak of Claremont Graduate University, as does the number and strength of its connections to the midbrain's circuits. Everything that's been discovered about the plasticity of the adult brain suggests that it should be possible to increase the number or strength of these connections so that the midbrain receives more calming signals.

Research has also shown that having a good short-term (or "working") memory is associated with being able to project yourself into the future and plan for it, which is a prerequisite of saving. That's partly because achieving a goal requires keeping it in mind. Brain scans back this up: the dorsolateral PFC is responsible for both. In one recent study, psychologist Warren Bickel of Virginia Tech put people through training exercises that improved their memory, and found they also developed "longer time horizons," meaning they valued the future more. "We're only at the beginning of figuring out how to change people's temporal horizons," says Bickel. "But the preliminary data are encouraging."

That seems to be what some of those original marshmallow-experiment children accomplished. Although the kids who remained in the same category—good at delaying gratification as toddlers as well as adults, or bad at both ages—have received the lion's share of the media attention, Mischel points out that many of the kids who gobbled up the marshmallow at the age of 4 learned to resist the lure of immediate gratification by the time they were young adults. "Being unable to delay gratification is not something we're stuck with for life," says Mischel. And a public that is infatuated with brain scans should know that just because a brain behaves in a particular way does not mean that it is hard-wired to do so.

To the contrary: even children can train their brains to recognize that forgoing pleasure now can bring a greater payoff later, says Claremont's Zak: doing homework tonight can bring good grades next month; saving a small allowance to buy one nice thing later rather than cheap junk every week. "You develop willpower and patience through practice," he says. "If you defer gratification, the payoff can be greater than with immediate gratification," says Zak, "but your brain has to learn that." He also finds that a squirt of the hormone oxytocin—known as the "love hormone" because of the role it plays in pair bonding and maternal behavior—makes people more patient: when people with a shot of the hormone are offered $10 now or $12 later, they are willing to wait 43 percent longer for that "later" to arrive (14 days rather than 10, for instance). "This tells us that people who are happier and have greater social support save more," says Zak. "Oxytocin reduces anxiety, so we can make decisions that are better for us." Not that we should be shooting ourselves up—but the research does suggest that any way we can reduce anxiety might also help us save for a rainy day.

This is good news for a generation of young people whose odds appear to be stacked against them. Research shows this group typically isn't willing to delay gratification, in part because they tend to be more impulsive and less patient, but also because they think they have plenty of time to save when they're older. "A college student who expects to graduate and obtain a high-paying job, or a young professional who expects to gain significant annual raises, will be apt not to save because they expect to be able to make up for lost time by saving more later," says economist Antony Davies of Duquesne University. "Another factor is inexperience. Young people are inexperienced at being old. A 22-year-old will perceive 20 years as an eternity. To ask this person to save for retirement is like asking the person to give his money to someone else: he cannot picture himself as a retiree."

Economists are waiting to see how the entitled, indulged children of helicopter parents will behave. On the one hand, many of them have been showered with every conceivable largesse, from private music lessons and pricey soccer camps to the SAT tutoring that got them into a top college. For many of those raised in two-career households, "no" was a word they seldom heard from their parents, so eager were Mom and Dad to compensate for their lack of quantity time by providing quality time—and experiences and stuff—instead. Even if they are inclined to save, they're facing real obstacles: many emerged from college with significantly more student-loan debt than those who came before them and are entering a job market getting weaker by the month.

Science has yet to identify whether the brains of the Twitter generation are any different from the rest of ours, but today's culture of one-click shopping and instant messaging doesn't merely satisfy our desire for instant gratification, it encourages it. "If you grow up in an environment marked by such short time horizons, of course you're going to satisfy your desires as quickly as you can," says Virginia Tech's Bickel. "Unless you're trained to control your impulses, why would you? Instant gratification is fun, and that's what today's technology is teaching us." What life teaches us, however, is another matter. Five years after she graduated, Hannah Green admits that, although she loved NYU, maybe she should have accepted that $100,000 from her father instead.

Analyze

1. This article is part report and part argument. What main point about neurology do Begley and Chatzky report? What point about instant gratification do they argue?
2. In your own words, what is the *moneybrain?* How does the concept relate to Begley and Chatzky's main idea?
3. Explain how the famous marshmallow experiments at Stanford correspond to the more recent findings of neuroeconomists.

4. Neuroplasticity, a relatively recent idea, involves the brain's ability to change—to develop new patterns and modes of thinking. How important is this concept to Begley and Chatzky's main idea? How does it fit into their subtle argument about training one's brain?
5. In the last two paragraphs, Begley and Chatzky admit that scientists have not yet determined generational differences in brain function. Why is that admission important? How does it function in their argument?

Explore

1. Are you one of those kids who wants the extra marshmallow or not? Would you like to change your reflex? Why or why not?
2. What's so bad about instant gratification? How might it negatively impact the typical college student?
3. Begley and Chatzy claim that "today's culture of one-click shopping and instant messaging doesn't merely satisfy our desire for instant gratification, it encourages it." Explain how that works. In your own experience, how does one-click shopping encourage instant gratification? Even if you've never shopped online, how do you think the typical online interface stimulates people's reflexes?
4. This article suggests that going to college—and then graduate school—might train the brain away from instant gratification. In other words, those with advanced degrees might be more inclined to save, to control impulsive buying habits. Why might this be true? Might there be some neurological cause/effect to getting a college degree?
5. A researcher from Virginia Tech says, "If you grow up in an environment marked by such short time horizons, of course you're going to satisfy your desires as quickly as you can." In your experience, how does this play out? Have you witnessed this or the opposite of this?

Sharon Angel
Sorting Out Santa

A songwriter, illustrator, and writer, Sharon Angel is currently pursuing a degree in liberal studies. In the following essay, written for a first-semester writing course, she explains the origin of Santa Claus and his particular role in American consumer culture. She also borrows some sophisticated concepts—such as *postmodernity, hyper-reality,* and *simulacrum*—to link Santa to broader cultural trends.

It's Black Friday. Forget peace on Earth and good will to men. It's time to find a parking space and avoid getting slush on your pant leg. Hopefully, you do not suffer from migraines because here comes Santa Claus, the bell-ringer. He is in his second hour of charitable arthritis of the wrist and fully habituated to the drip . . . drip . . . drip of icicle water torture. Confined to his windy hollow under the Wal-Mart eaves, he is meek and fierce and wise—or at least patient and maybe even compassionate.

Compassion is the essence of a Santa long forgotten by most Americans, a quality that has survived a journey of a thousand years. The voyage from human being to the symbol began with a Christian philanthropist named Nicholas, Bishop of Myra ("Saint Nicholas"; Haladewicz-Grzelak). Before his veneration to sainthood came acts of kindness. As with many historic figures, most details died[1] along with him or were recorded, and perhaps distorted, through legend and iconography. St. Nicholas' feast day, set on the anniversary of his death is still celebrated as a holiday by people abroad and in select areas of the U.S., on December 6th ("Saint Nicholas").

The origins of the Santa 21st century Americans recognize are based in numerous cultures, some predating Christianity[2] ("Santa Claus"; Haladewicz-Grzelak). What sets St. Nicholas' influence apart from other champions of compassion is that his character originated from a living, breathing person: the Bishop of Myra. But even when we refer to Saint Nicholas as "Saint Nick" (such as in the Christmas song "Up on the House Top") a saintly image is not conjured. Instead, what might pop into one's head is a giant red-clad elf, poised to deliver a new flat-screen.

Americans make a conscious choice to display Santa, but the modern image of Santa reflects Americans' willingness to accept increasingly cheapened versions of Santa to which we become accustomed. For example, my family has an annual tradition of visiting a drive-through Christmas light display near Detroit, MI. It is five miles long and set up on a road that is especially closed-off for the exhibit. The entry fee is a modest five dollars, and each display along the route is marked with an advertisement for the business that sponsors it. After dark, vehicles line up and slowly cruise through archways of twinkle lights and rolling hillsides featuring sparkling characters such as dinosaurs, elves, a sea serpent and a series of Santas. Certainly, children are entertained by the blinking lights. However, they are also trapped in a car, and the vast majority of vehicles do not pull aside at the end of the exhibit where visitors can stretch their legs, buy cocoa, or chat with an actor in a Santa suit. The experience for most visitors includes no walking, no fresh air, no stars, no outside interaction—just some family time in an automobile, gliding like a gondola through a digitally timed, theme machine.

The passengers in these vehicles may not feel as though they are being 5
intentionally taught to value a symbol or an icon or an artificial holiday, but they are learning to value something complex—and they are participating in the substitution of a natural environment by an artificial reality. Exit Bishop of Myra; enter the lighted, slightly kinked inflatable all-American Santa bobbing like a massage bed in a cheap motel. I think it is safe to say that the Bishop of Myra has been obliterated. This lawn decoration is our new reality. It has strategic advantages: mass production, distribution, media campaigns, hoards of willing consumers and hostages, consumers who *are* hostages. We live among the plastic Santas and there's nothing to indicate that they won't be back next December, or should I say November—or why not October? That's the beauty of this artificial consumer world: whichever items are selected most often from the menu will be offered again, while those items that are not chosen often enough to be profitable will be dropped from the menu—which makes choosing easier—and makes deviation more difficult.[3]

The model for our current Santa, by which all plastic Santas are cast, is most directly derived from an anonymous poem, which we now know as *'Twas the Night before Christmas* (later attributed to Clement C. Moore). This poem was published in the New York *Sentinel* magazine in 1823. Forty years later, an artist named Thomas Nast (who is also known for introducing the elephant and donkey political party images) drew inspiration from this poem and illustrated it in an 1863 issue of *Harpers' Weekly*. The images Nast drew were a marked departure from the white-garbed bishop, or stern St. Nicholas—and portrayed a very secular Santa ("Know Thy

History"). This Santa was jolly, plump, wore a fur-trimmed coat, and had a workshop where he could make toys. Nast continued to produce Santa illustrations of this genre until 1866 (El Santo).

Then, in 1890, in Brockton Massachusetts, something surreal happened. Santa began making appearances in James Edgar's department stores. Santa had now completed the transition from a real bishop, to an icon, and then to a real person *playing* an icon (surrounded by goods) in his own Santa-world setting. This transition is something cultural theorists, such as Jean Baudrillard, call simulacrum, or more commonly, hyper-reality. In his book entitled *Postmodernism for Beginners,* Jim Powell writes about Baudrillard's theory of how simulacra impact culture: "We are now in the Third Order of Simulacra—the era of postmodernity—the era of models. No longer is the simulacrum a counterfeit . . . or an infinite series, like automobiles rolling off the assembly line—but simulacrum becomes reality itself" (Powell 51).

As Jayme Stayer illustrates so well in his essay "Whales R Us," if we replace our own sense of reality in favor of interacting in an artificial "reality," simulacrum can be dangerous. Stayer speaks to the inability of the artificial Sea World to teach its visitors a true appreciation for creatures of the sea.

> Too occupied with obscuring the real moral, environmental, and scientific issues at stake, Sea World is constitutionally incapable of teaching respect for nature. Love of nature is spiritually informed and politically assertive. It is not the kind of passive, sentimental quackery Sea World prefers, and it cannot be taught with the crude tools in Sea World's lesson plans: glib moralizing, base pandering, and clichés masquerading as insights (Stayer 217).

Most people know when they are being solicited by this disengaged mentality. In the case of Disney World, we go willingly—to play. I was too young to remember believing in Santa Claus, and maybe I never did. However, I do remember playing along with the game on Christmas Eve and morning. The sock-filling, cookie eating, gifts under the magically lit Christmas tree experience made for some family moments that I treasure.[4] But my senses alert me, sometimes quietly and sometimes in abhorrence, when I encounter the hyper-real attempting to seduce me—or force me to participate.

But there's something, still, that seems real and vital about the Santa at Wal-Mart. Although statues of Nicholas the philanthropist have not found their way into the Christmas lawn and garden section, his qualities of benevolence and compassion are still vibrant. They are still working in the world of real human interaction. Compassion and good will may find purpose in the simulacrum, but they are somehow free to operate outside of it as well. Examples of unconditional generosity do exist within and beyond the scheme of consumerism. Last Christmas the Salvation Army bell ringers raised a record 147.6 million dollars through their Red Kettle charity campaign ("Poor Economy"). And then we have the Santa of letters and of listening. He receives the woes and wonders of our 21st century, the letters of the hopeful who wish to tap into his abundance, the requests of the desperate who speak concerns that have no solution except the healing power of being received by an empathetic reader.

Enthroned in a shopping mall, some Santas are there for the paycheck, 10
and others are there to offer authentic Santa comfort—at least until they are exhausted due to the demands of our postmodern lifestyles. Inside these suits are "the real deal." They are the souls who dare to take on the children's hospitals, bringing the best they have to the terminally ill, and giving of themselves something priceless. If I were trapped on a hyper-real island, with several versions of Santa, this is the Santa I would choose.

Notes

1 The year of St. Nicholas' death varies from source to source. According to *Cultural Codes in the Iconography of St. Nicholas,* "The Bishop of Myra, St. Nicholas, died in Myra (Demre, Turkey) on the 6th of December (The year of his death is usually given within the span of 345–352 A.D.)" However, the online Wikipedia article "Saint Nicholas" entry gives the following dates; Born c. AD 270, died Dec. 6 343 (aged 73). Because of the ambiguity concerning the exact dates, I refer to St. Nicholas of Myra as having lived generally in the 4th century A.D.

2 The secularism of Santa is a natural result of his character's journey, from his pagan and pre-Christian folklore predecessors, through many significant cultural changes. The scope of this essay does not include details on (relatively recent) pertinent, historical events such as the Protestant Reformation (1517–1648) the Industrial "Revolution" (1750–1850) and the American Civil War (1861–1865). Further associations of interest would include the role of secularism as derived from the period of the Enlightenment.

3 These ideas refer to concepts introduced by J. Powell on pages 52 and 53 of *Postmodernism for Beginners:* "Thus our lives are controlled by a system of binary regulation—where the question/answer option of the test has been reduced to an either/or binary code. This system of binary choices acts as a 'deterrence model,' which suppresses radical change."

4 This essay addresses adults, focusing on the meaning and role of Santa Claus in Postmodern American "culture." This fact is not meant to downplay the impact of Santa Claus' role/folklore as it is passed down from parent to child. Janet Gill and Theodora Papatheodorou raise some interesting points regarding this parent-child interaction in their article "Perpetuating the Father Christmas Story: A Justifiable Lie?"

Works Cited

Dennis, Tami. "Poor economy? Yep, but red kettles set record for Salvation Army." *Los Angeles Times*. Tribune Company, 31 Jan. 2012. Web. 2 Feb. 2013.

Haladewicz-Grzelak, Malgorzata. "Cultural Codes in the Iconography of Saint Nicholas (Santa Claus)." *Sign Systems Studies* 39.1(2011): 105–45. *Ebscohost*. Web. 12 Nov. 2012.

"Know Thy History: Thomas Nast's Santa Claus." *Webcomicoverlook.com*, 14 Dec. 2010. Web. 10 Nov. 2012.

Powell, Jim. *Postmodernism for Beginners*. New York: Writers and Readers Publishing, Inc., 1998. Print.

"Saint Nicholas." *Wikipedia the Free Encyclopedia*. Web. 10 Nov. 2012.

"Santa Claus." *Wikipedia the Free Encyclopedia*. Web. 10 Nov. 2012.

Stayer, Jayme. "Whales R Us." *The Composition of Everyday Life: A Guide to Writing*, 4th ed. Ed. John Mauk and John Metz. Boston: Wadsworth Cengage Learning, 2013. 213–17. Print.

Analyze

1. Explain the function of Angel's opening paragraph. How does it relate to the rest of her essay?
2. What single sentence embodies Angel's main idea about Santa Claus?
3. Explain how the concept of "hyper-reality" relates to Angel's point about Santa Claus.
4. Explain the particular way the Stayer passage supports Angel's point about American consumerism.
5. How does Angel's point relate to one of the other works from this chapter? (For example, you might consider Begley and Chatzky or Charles Kenny's points about consumerism.)

Explore

1. Explain a time when you were "seduced by the hyper-real"—or, at least, beckoned by it.
2. Angel says that "Santa had now completed the transition from a real bishop, to an icon, and then to a real person *playing* an icon (surrounded by goods) in his own Santa-world setting." What other cultural figures have developed in this fashion—from real person, to icon, to person playing the icon?
3. Angel explains that compassion can, and does, exist outside of the hyper-real layer of everyday life. In your experience, what supports or opposes this idea?
4. Angel claims, "Most people know when they are being solicited by this disengaged mentality." Explain why you agree or disagree with her statement.
5. How is Santa Claus a representative figure of American consumer culture?

Fredrik deBoer

The Resentment Machine: The Immiseration of the Digital Creative Class

Fredrik deBoer is a doctoral student in rhetoric and composition at Purdue University and a self-professed "cranky lefty." The author of the political blog *L'Hôte,* he specializes in second language writing and inequality in higher education. His work has appeared in publications such as *Balloon Juice, Consider,* '*The League of Ordinary Gentlemen, The New Inquiry,* and *Wunderkammer Magazine.* In the following *New Inquiry* article, deBoer dissects the notion of cultural consumption.

The popular adoption of the Internet has brought with it great changes. One of the peculiar aspects of this particular revolution is that it has been historicized in real time—reported accurately, greatly exaggerated, or outright invented, often by those who have embraced the technology most fully. As impressive as the various changes wrought by the exponential growth of Internet users were, they never seemed quite impressive enough for those who trumpeted them.

In a strange type of autoethnography, those most taken with the internet of the late 1990s and early 2000s spent a considerable amount of their time online talking about what it meant that they were online. In straightforwardly self-aggrandizing narratives, the most dedicated and involved Internet users began crafting a pocket mythology of the new reality. Rather than regarding themselves as tech consumers, the most dedicated Internet users spoke instead of revolution. Vast, life-altering consequences were predicted for these rising technologies. In much the same way as those speaking about the importance of New York City are often actually speaking about the importance of themselves, so those who crafted the oral history of the Internet were often really talking about their own revolutionary potential. Not that this was without benefits; self-obsession became a vehicle for an intricate literature on emergent online technology.

Yet for all the endless consideration of the rise of the digitally connected human species, one of the most important aspects of Internet culture has gone largely unnoticed. The Internet has provided tremendous functionality, for facilitating commerce, communication, research, entertainment, and more. Yet for a comparatively small but influential group of its most dedicated users, its most important feature, the killer app, is its power as an all-purpose sorting mechanism, one that separates the worthy from the unworthy—and in doing so, gives some meager semblance of purpose to generations whose lives are largely defined by purposelessness. For the postcollegiate, culturally savvy tastemakers who exert such disproportionate influence over online experience, the Internet is above and beyond all else a resentment machine.

The modern American "meritocracy," the education/employment vehicle, prepares thousands of upwardly mobile young strivers for everything but the life they will actually encounter. The endlessly grinding wheel of American "success" indoctrinates young people with a competitive vision that most of them never escape. The numbing and frenetic socioacademic sorting mechanism compels most of the best and the brightest adolescents in our middle and upper class to compete for various laurels from puberty to adulthood. School elections, high school and college athletics, honors societies, finals clubs, dining clubs, the subtler (but no less real) social competitions—all make competition the natural habitus of American youth. Every aspect of young adult life is transformed into a status game, as academics, athletics, music and the arts, travel, hobbies, and philanthropy are all reduced to fodder for college applications.

This instrumentalizing of all of the best things in life teaches teenagers the unmistakable lesson that nothing is to be enjoyed, nothing experienced purely, but rather that each and every part of human life is ultimately subservient to what is less human. Competition exists as a vehicle to provide the goods, material or immaterial, that make life enjoyable. The context of endless competition makes that means into an end itself. The eventual eats the immediate. No achievement, no effort, no relationship can exist as an end in itself. Each must be ground into chum to attract those who confer status and success—elite colleges and their representatives, employers.

As has been documented endlessly, this process starts earlier and earlier in life, with elite preschools now requiring that students pass tests and get references, before they can read or write. Many have lamented the rise of competition and gatekeeping in young children. Little attention has been paid to what comes after the competitions end.

It is, of course, possible to keep running on the wheel indefinitely. There are those professions (think: finance) that extend the status contests of childhood and adolescence into the gray years, and to one degree or another, most people play some version of this game for most of their lives. But for a large chunk of the striving class, this kind of naked careerism and straightforward neediness won't do. Though they have been raised to compete and endlessly conditioned to measure themselves against their peers, they have done so in an environment that denies this reality while it creates it. Many were raised by self-consciously creative parents who wished for children who were similarly creative, in ethos if not in practice. These parents operated in a context that told them to nurture unique and beautiful butterflies while simultaneously reminding them, in that incessant subconscious way that is the secret strength of capitalism, that their job as parents is to raise their children to win. The conversion of the hippies into the yuppies has been documented endlessly by pop sociologists like David Brooks. What made this transformation palatable to many of those being transformed was the way in which materialist striving was wedded to the hippie's interest in culture, art, and a vague "nonconformist" attitude.

It is no surprise that the urge to rear winners trumps the urge to raise artists. But the nagging drive to preach the value of culture does not go unnoticed. The urge to create, to live with an aesthetic sense, is admirable, and if inculcated genuinely—which is to say, in defiant opposition to the competitive urge rather than as an uneasy partner to it—this romantic artistic vision of life remains the best hope for humanity against the deadening drift of late capitalism. Only to create for the sake of creation, to build something truly your own for no purpose and in reference to the work of no other person—perhaps there's a chance for grace there.

But in context of the alternative, a cheery and false vision of the artistic life, self-conscious creativity becomes sublimated into the competitive project and becomes twisted. Those raised with such contradictory impulses are left unable to contemplate the stocks-and-suspenders lifestyle that is the purest manifestation of the competitive instinct, but they are equally unable to cast off the social-climbing aspirations that this lifestyle represents. Their parentage and their culture teach them to at once hunger for the material goods that are the spoils of a small set of professions, but at the same time they distrust the culture of those self-same professions. They are trapped between their rejection of the means and an unchosen but deep hunger for the ends.

Momentum can be a cruel thing. High school culminates in college acceptance. This temporary victory can often be hollow, but the fast pace of life quickly leaves no time to reckon with that emptiness. As dehumanizing and vulgar as the high-school glass-bead game is, it certainly provides adolescents with a kind of order. That the system is inherently biased and riotously unfair is ultimately besides the point. In the many explicit ways in which high-school students are ranked emerges a broad consensus: There is an order to life, that order indicates value, and there are winners and losers.

10 Competition is propulsive and thus results in inertia. College students enjoy a variety of tools to continue to manage the competitive urge. Some find in the exclusive activities, clubs, and societies of elite colleges an acceptable continuation of high-school competition. Others never abandon their zeal for academic excellence and the laurels of high grades and instructor approval. Some pursue medical school, law school, an MBA, or (for the truly damned) a PhD. But most dull the urge by persisting in a four-or-five-year fugue of alcohol, friendship, and rarefied living.

The end of college brings an end to that order, and for many, this is bewildering. Educated but broadly ignorant of suffering, scattershot in their passions, possessed of verbal dexterity but bereft of the experience that might give their words meaning, culturally sensitive 20-somethings wander into a world that is supposed to be made for them, and find it inhospitable. Without the rigid ordering that grades, class rank, leadership, and office provide, the incessant and unnamed urge to compete cannot be easily addressed. Their vague cultural liberalism—a dedication to tolerance and egalitarianism in generally vague and deracinated terms—makes the careers that promise similar sorting unpalatable. The economic resentment and petty greed that they have had bred into them by the sputtering machine of American capitalism makes lower-class life unthinkable.

Driven by the primacy of the competitive urge and convinced that they need far more material goods than they do to live a comfortable life, they seek well-paying jobs. Most of them will find some gainful employment without great difficulty. Perhaps this is changing: As the tires on the Trans Am that is America go bald, their horror at a poor job market reveals their entitlement more than anything. But the numbers indicate that most still find their way into jobs that become careers. Many will have periods of arty unemployed urbanism, but after awhile the gremlin begins whispering, "You are a loser," and suddenly, they're placing that call to Joel from Sociology 205 who's got that connection at that office. Often, these office jobs will enjoy the cover of orbiting in some vaguely creative endeavor like advertising. One way or the other, these jobs become careers in the loaded sense. In these careers, they find themselves in precisely the position that they long insisted they would never contemplate.

The competitive urge still pulses. It has to; the culture in which students have been raised has denied them any other framework with which to draw meaning. The world has assimilated the rejection of religion, tradition, and other determinants of virtue that attended the 1960s and wedded it to a vicious contempt for the political commitments that replaced them in that context. Culture preempts the kind of conscious understanding that attends to conviction, that all traditional designations of meaning are uncool.

If straightforward discussion of virtue and righteousness is socially unpalatable, straightforward political engagement appears worse still. Pushed by an advertising industry that embraces tropes of meaning just long enough to render them meaningless (Budweiser Clydesdales saluting fallen towers) and buffeted by arbiters of hipness that declare any unapologetic embrace of political ideology horribly cliché, a fussy specificity envelops every definition of the self. Conventional accounts of the kids these days tend to revert to tired tropes about disaffection and irony. The reality is sadder: They are not passionless, but many have invested their passion in a shared cultural knowledge that denies the value of any other endeavor worthy of personal investment.

Contemporary strivers lack the tools with which people in the past have differentiated themselves from their peers: They live in a post-virtue, post-religion, post-aristocracy age. They lack the skills or inspiration to create something of genuine worth. They have been conditioned to find all but the most conventional and compromised politics worthy of contempt. They are denied even the cold comfort of identification with career, as they cope with the deadening tedium and meaninglessness of work by calling attention to it over and over again, as if acknowledging it somehow elevates them above it.

Into this vacuum comes a relief that is profoundly rational in context—the self as consumer and critic. Given the emptiness of the material conditions of their lives, the formerly manic competitors must come to invest the cultural goods they consume with great meaning. Meaning must be made somewhere; no one will countenance standing for nothing. So the poor proxy of media and cultural consumption comes to define the individual. In many ways, cultural products such as movies, music, clothes, and media are the perfect vehicle for the endless division of people into strata of knowingness, savvy, and cultural value.

These cultural products have no quantifiable value, yet their relative value is fiercely debated as if some such quantifiable understanding could be reached. They are easily mined for ancillary content, the TV recaps and record reviews and endless fulminating in comments and forums that spread like weeds. (Does anyone who watches *Mad Men* not blog about it?) They are bound up with celebrity, both real and petty. They can inspire and so trick us into believing that our reactions are similarly worthy of inspiration. And they are complex and varied enough that there is always more to know and more rarefied territory to reach, the better to climb the ladder one rung higher than the person the next desk over.

There is a problem, though. The value-through-what-is-consumed is entirely illusory. There is no there there. This is what you can really learn about a person by understanding his or her cultural consumption, the movies, music, fashion, media, and assorted other socially inflected ephemera: nothing. Absolutely nothing. The Internet writ large is desperately invested in the idea that liking, say, *The Wire,* says something of depth and importance about the liker, and certainly that the preference for this show to *CSI* tells everything.

Likewise, the Internet exists to perpetuate the idea that there is some meaningful difference between fans of this band or that, of Android or Apple, or that there is a *Slate* lifestyle and a *This Recording* lifestyle and one for *Gawker* or *The Hairpin* or wherever. Not a word of it is true. There are no Apple people. Buying an iPad does nothing to delineate you from anyone else. Nothing separates a Budweiser man from a microbrew guy. That our society insists that there are differences here is only our longest con.

This endless posturing, pregnant with anxiety and roiling with class re- 20
sentment, ultimately pleases no one. Yet this emptiness doesn't compel people to turn away from the sorting mechanism. Instead, it draws them further and further in. Faced with the failure of their cultural affinities to define an authentic and fulfilling self, postcollegiate middle-class upwardly-oriented-if-not-upwardly-mobile Americans double down on the importance of these affinities and confront the continued failure with a formless resentment. The bitterness that surrounds these distinctions is a product of their inability to actually make us distinct.

The savviest of the media and culture websites tap into this resentment as directly as they dare. They write endlessly about what is overrated. They assign specific and damning personality traits to the fan bases of unworthy cultural objects. They invite comments that tediously parse microscopic distinctions in cultural consumption. They engage in criticism as a kind of preemptive strike against those who actually create. They glamorize pettiness in aesthetic taste. The few artistic works they lionize are praised to the point of absurdity, as various acolytes try to outdo each other in hyperbole. They relentlessly push the central narrative that their readers crave, that consumption is achievement and that creators are to be distrusted and "put in their place." They deny the frequently sad but inescapable reality that consumption is not creation and that only the genuinely creative act can reveal the self.

This, then, is the role of the resentment machine: to amplify meaningless differences and assign to them vast importance for the quality of individuals. For those who are writing the most prominent parts of the Internet—the bloggers, the trendsetters, the über-Tweeters, the tastemakers, the linkers, the creators of memes and online norms—online life is taking the place of the creation of the self, and doing so poorly.

This all sounds quite critical, I'm sure, but ultimately, this is a critique I include myself in. For this to approach real criticism I would have to offer an alternative to those trapped in the idea of the consumer as self. I haven't got one. Our system has relentlessly denied the role of any human practice that cannot be monetized. The capitalist apparatus has worked tirelessly to commercialize everything, to reduce every aspect of human life to currency exchange. In such a context, there is little hope for the survival of the fully realized self.

Analyze

1. What exactly is the "resentment machine"? Explain it as precisely as possible—and integrate specific phrases or terms from deBoer.
2. DeBoer argues that "cultural products such as movies, music, clothes, and media are the perfect vehicle for the endless division of people into strata of knowingness, savvy, and cultural value." In your understanding of this article, what is a cultural product? What does it do? How does it function? How are movies, music, clothes, and media cultural products?
3. According to deBoer, how are Americans being conned by the media? In what particular way are we being deceived about ourselves?
4. In his second paragraph, deBoer says, "In a strange type of autoethnography, those most taken with the Internet of the late 1990s and early 2000s spent a considerable amount of their time online talking about what it meant that they were online." Consider this term: *autoethnography*. What does it mean? How does it fit into the main point of deBoer's article?
5. Explain how Begley and Chatzky's "The New Science Behind Your Spending Addiction" (in this chapter) relates to or supports deBoer's argument.

Explore

1. How are you part of, influenced by, or resistant to the resentment machine?
2. DeBoer argues that "the capitalist apparatus has worked tirelessly to commercialize everything, to reduce every aspect of human life to

currency exchange." Give some examples of this process. What behaviors, acts, or practices have been reduced to currency exchange? Can you think of any that have not?

3. DeBoer argues that mainstream television programs can "trick" viewers into identifying with the characters, the situations, and the values sold along with the program. What in your experience supports or challenges this idea?
4. Consider the essay by Richard Lawson and Jen Doll, "Lies Hollywood Told Us: Love and Romance Edition," in Chapter 6. How do their claims relate to deBoer's? In what way is deBoer going beyond the argument made by Lawson and Doll?
5. DeBoer concludes that "there is little hope for the fully realized self." First, what do you think he means by "the fully realized self?" Second, do you agree with his conclusion? Why or why not?

Damien Walter

Sparks Will Fly

The course director of the Certificate in Creative Writing at University of Leicester, Damien Walter specializes in the genre of weird fiction. Currently at work on his first novel, he has published stories in various literary publications and writes the "Weird Things" column for the newspaper the *Guardian*. The following article originally appeared in *Aeon* magazine, which describes itself as "open to diverse perspectives and committed to progressive social change." Here, Walter explains why consumerism and creativity are at odds—and how this fissure impacts our culture.

I arrived in Leicester in the late '90s as a student, a year after losing my mother to cancer. Having little support, I worked my way through university as a street sweeper, a factory worker, a waiter, a barman, a door-to-door salesman, a cleaner, recycling operative and grill chef. I wanted to be a writer but that seemed like an unattainable dream at the time. A few years later I began working for Leicester's library service as a literature development worker.

The first initiative I ran was a project to gather the reminiscences of senior citizens. There I was, in my mid-20s, in the meeting room of an older persons' lunch club. I had a circle of plastic stacking chairs, paper, pens and a dozen volunteers, most of them past their 80th birthday. At the time, I could manage (as I still can) a good line in cocky arrogance. I told everyone how things were going to be and what the project was going to achieve. We were to capture voices from under-represented stakeholders in the local community, thereby encouraging social cohesion. I hadn't yet learnt that the language of Arts Council England funding bids doesn't mean much to normal people. Patient smiles greeted my words.

After a long pause, a woman in her 90s started to speak. She had grown up in a children's home in Leicester, she told us. She had been abused by her father and then by another man at the home. She had worked in factories when she was old enough. Her husband died young, and so did her son. It took her half an hour to say this much. At the end, she said she'd never told anyone about her life before.

I was, in retrospect, unprepared for that project in every possible way. I spent the next fortnight doing a lot of listening and transcribing. The other stories were no easier to hear. Child abuse, abhorred in today's media, was so prevalent in the industrial communities of England before the Second World War that it had passed almost without comment.

5 We published a small pamphlet of writing from the project. It seemed puny and easily ignored, but it meant a great deal to the group. There was even a small reception to launch it. A few friends and relatives and a dignitary from the local council came along to enjoy the municipally funded wine and nibbles. The storytellers themselves had all made new friends, and had kept busy instead of sitting idle in care homes. They had had a chance to speak. And a few people had listened.

It would take me the best part of a decade to really understand why that was important.

In dozens of projects and hundreds of workshops, I tried to help people to develop everything from basic literacy to advanced creative writing skills. I worked with teenagers from local schools, who loved vampire novels and wrote their own hip-hop lyrics but said they didn't like English, until you told them that Mary Shelley was the first goth and 'rap' stood for

'Rhythmic American Poetry.' I worked with groups of factory workers and people caught in mind-numbing call-centre jobs who just wanted to find something, anything, to show that they were worth more than that. I sat in on daylong symposia of Urdu verse and learnt what it is to have Hindu and Muslim communities talk to each other through poetry. I ran projects with drug users and mental health service users, often the same people. A lot of these people were young men, my own age, from roughly the same background as me. I started to see how real the gaps in society are, and how easy they are to fall through.

This all happened in a midlands city of 330,000 people. Leicester now has the third-largest Hindu community in England and Wales, as well as substantial Muslim, Black African, Somali, Polish and Chinese populations. In the late 1800s it was an industrial powerhouse, the hosiery capital of Europe. By the start of the 20th century, it was home to some of the poorest wards in Britain. Throughout the industrial revolution, it had sucked in thousands of rural labourers to man its factories. When the factories closed, that population, lacking any history of education or development, was abandoned, left to subsist on state benefits and lower-than-minimum-wage jobs on huge sink estates. Decades later, many are still there.

I honestly have no idea, beyond individual stories, if the creativity work I did had any real effect. I still get e-mails from one or two of the school kids I worked with: they've gone on to write their own sci-fi books. But there's a guilt trap in almost any job where the aim is to help other people. Human need is infinite, and you quickly learn the limits of what can be achieved, or else you break from the pressure of attempting the impossible.

Even so, what I did see again and again was the real difference that a 10
sliver of creative life can make, even to people in the worst circumstances. I saw it most often through the discipline of writing, and I think that the written word makes a good route for many people. But any act that helps to empower a person creatively can ignite the imaginative spark without which life of any kind struggles—and in many senses fails—even to begin.

Between the years of 1914 and 1930 the psychiatrist and founder of analytical psychology Carl Gustav Jung undertook what he later termed a "voluntary confrontation with his unconscious." Employing certain techniques of active imagination that became part of his theory of human development, Jung incited visions, dreams and other manifestations of his imagination, which he recorded in writing and pictures. For some years, he kept the results of this process secret, though he described them to close friends and family as the most important work of his life. Late in his career, he set about collecting and transcribing these dreams and visions.

The product was the "Liber Novus" or "New Book," now known simply as *The Red Book.* Despite requests for access from some of the leading thinkers and intellectuals of the 20th century, very few people outside of Jung's close family were allowed to see it before its eventual publication in 2009. It has since been recognised as one of the great creative acts of the century, a magnificent and visionary illuminated manuscript equal to the works of William Blake.

It is from his work on *The Red Book* that all of Jung's theories on archetypes, individuation and the collective unconscious stem. Of course, Jung is far from alone in esteeming human creativity. The creative capacity is central to the developmental psychology of Jean Piaget and the constructivist theory of learning, and creativity is increasingly at the heart of our models of economic growth and development. But Jung provides the most satisfying explanation I know for why the people I worked with got so much out of discovering their own creativity, and why happiness and the freedom to create are so closely linked.

Jung dedicated his life to understanding human growth, and the importance of creativity to that process. It seems fitting that the intense process that led to *The Red Book* should also have been integral to Jung's own personal development. Already well into his adult life, he had yet to make the conceptual breakthroughs that would become the core of his model of human psychology. In quite a literal sense, the process of creating *The Red Book* was also the process of creating Carl Jung. This simple idea, that creativity is central to our ongoing growth as human beings, opens up a very distinctive understanding of what it means to make something.

15 Anyone who has performed any significant creative feat, whether writing a novel or founding a business, will acknowledge the element of inner transformation inherent in the act. The person who attends a writing class in her 20s isn't the same person who completes a great novel in her 50s, and it isn't only day-to-day life that shapes her in the meantime: the creative process itself will have been at work. The growth that comes from progress through the stages of any artistic discipline provides a backbone for our

intellectual and emotional development as human beings. And it is as a framework for growth that our creative endeavours should be judged. Commercial success more often than not follows growth, but it can become a fatal distraction from it, as we see in the trajectories of celebrities who ape creativity to achieve fame but remain stunted as human beings.

This point raises difficult questions about our society. Much about the way we have chosen to organise our lives, often with the goal of maximising material comfort, is bad for creativity. These problems are most pronounced for the bulk of the population who work inside the structures that support the creativity of others: the factories, offices, shops and other parts of the system of consumer capitalism.

If you are a production line worker at a Foxconn factory in China, a retail operative at Walmart or a call-centre assistant at the Next offices in Leicestershire, the chances of finding any measure of creativity in your work are slim. They are sure to be less than those of the graphic designer using the Apple iPad, the billionaire inheritors of the Walmart fortune, or me sitting here typing this essay on my laptop. As much as our social hierarchies are about limiting and controlling access to wealth, they are also about limiting and controlling access to creativity. Increasingly, the real benefit that money buys is the time, freedom and power to act creatively.

And yet, perhaps internal factors are the greatest barrier to creative fulfilment for most people. We are driven creatures. While our lust for status, money, power and sex can be harnessed towards creative ends, it is more likely to block any spark we might have had. Our consumer culture is happy to cater to these drives. We lose decades of our lives chasing money to buy luxury goods and climbing through artificial hierarchies in the workplace. We struggle with the health problems caused by high-calorie, high-fat diets. We become caught in webs of addiction, trying to distract our minds from the emptiness left by our lost creativity. The novelist Don DeLillo wrote that "longing on a large scale is what makes history." Our longings shape our lives and they shape the world around us. But it is our longing to create that is our deepest drive, and the one that makes us the most human. We ignore it at our own cost.

Albert Einstein once said that "every child is born a genius." Educationalists ask: "What if every child could be made an Einstein?" The key to unlocking our full human potential lies in our creative drive. As a writer and critic of science fiction, I am fascinated by the prospect of a world where our full human potential has been realised, and I believe that a "creator culture" is the necessary next step on the path to achieving that vision. We are already well on the way; it might arrive much sooner than many of us expect. Moreover, some of our most pressing societal concerns—from economic decline to environmental collapse—exist because we are resisting the natural evolution of a more creative society.

What might a creator culture look like?

Firstly, it is not a utopia. It is much like the developed world today, with governments, businesses, financial systems, political parties, cities, nations and many other elements of modern, post-industrial life. But it is a society where human creativity has been made the first priority.

The arts and sciences are at the heart of a creator culture, but so are many other kinds of human creativity. Entrepreneurialism, community work, industry; there are many paths. The economic system will have been rebalanced to distribute wealth more fairly to all, permitting the 10–15 hour working week that John Maynard Keynes predicted nearly a century ago. While some people will still be richer than others, wealth will no longer be hoarded by a tiny minority. Poverty as we know it will no longer exist. A more equal society will allow everyone the time and freedom to follow their creative passions, without the paralysing question of whether they produce wealth.

The rise of automation in the workplace will have continued, and the physical work that remains will be distributed more fairly across society. Otherwise, employment in a creator culture will consist almost entirely of knowledge work. The rise of the knowledge worker was among the most remarkable developments of the 20th century, ushering in an era in the developed world that would already seem semi-utopian to the people of the 19th century. For software engineers, graphic designers, data analysts, writers, doctors, lawyers and a huge range of other kinds of worker, the key asset is knowledge rather than any capacity for physical labour. That will be the norm in a creator culture.

Most workers will be freelancers, and to earn a living wage, they will have to work an average of two days a week. Nevertheless, many people will work tirelessly on projects and jobs that relate to their creative interests. Networks will subsume hierarchical organisational structures. As has already happened with open-source software development, many business models will be challenged by networks of knowledge workers providing better products and services at better prices.

Technology is foundational to a creator culture. The focus of the networked, knowledge-based workforce will be the invention and application of new technologies. The automation of most routine work tasks will provide the base of production that allows such a culture to flourish in the first place. But instead of allowing the wealth created by automation to accumulate in the hands of a few, it must be distributed to the many. We need the right technologies, implemented for the benefit of society; progress can't be driven by purely commercial imperatives. And to turn the disruptive effects of technology into positive social change we need to think far beyond the currently limited scope of our education system.

Education is the lubricant that allows a creator culture to function. Basic education will often continue into one's late 20s and early 30s. Most people will return to education many times between spells of employment. There will no longer be an artificial divide between the sciences, humanities and arts: all contribute holistically to a full education. The utilitarian demand for education that only leads to specific jobs will be as frowned upon in a creator culture as behavioural conditioning and corporal punishment are in our own society. The singular aim of education will be human development. Every person should be freed to achieve their full creative potential.

For many people, a creator culture will appear far from utopian. It will demand exceptional levels of independence and self-reliance from its citizens. Creativity, moreover, is always uncertain, always accompanied by the risk of failure. A creator culture will require universal lifelong education, the explicit redistribution of wealth and the deconstruction of many existing hierarchies and authority structures. These will be difficult ideas for political conservatives to accept. But it will also demand that the structures of government, education and social care that exist to support the bottom of society are continually reformed, and that they ultimately make themselves redundant, as the poverty they serve is eliminated. That, in practice, may be equally difficult for the political left to embrace.

Such a society would also change the shape of certain environmental issues. The climb out of poverty inevitably places demands on the natural resources of our planet. Yet consumerism is built on ever-increasing demand for goods, which fuels economic growth. A creator culture would lead to a plateau in demand and a levelling of growth. The energy we invest in buying consumer goods would instead go towards our creative activities. And though it is very unlikely that our demand for resources will do anything but increase over time, a creator culture might also help us to reach beyond the limits of our own planet.

That's because, though it isn't a utopia itself, a creator culture might eventually let us bring about the utopian visions of science fiction. Imagine our planet populated by billions of humans, educated to the standard of the greatest scientists and given the freedom to cultivate their full measure of creativity. At our disposal is any technology we can conceive and create. Within our reach is a universe of unlimited resources. In the whole of that universe, humans are the only beings we know with the power of creation. And there are only a few billion of us—a large number on a small planet perhaps, a vanishingly small one in an infinite cosmos. We're going to need the wondrous creativity of every single human being to knock this universe in to shape. I wonder, what will we create?

30 We are *Homo faber*, "Humankind the Creator." God did not create us in his image, we created god in our image. We might only be an insignificant species orbiting an insignificant star in an infinite and impassive universe. But we have, perhaps uniquely, the power of creation. Why, then, are we trapped on this ball of rock, repeating the same patterns of self-destructive behaviour, instead of fulfilling our creative potential?

We are caught in a consumer culture that works against our innate creativity. The economic crisis of 2008 might have heralded the collapse of that culture. The consumerist economic model—itself a set of ad hoc compromises following the death of the industrial model—has reached the end of its useful existence. It evolved for a world where technology placed creativity in the hands of the few and television communicated their message to the masses, in what the entrepreneur Seth Godin has called the TV-industrial complex. Today, the Internet has decentralised communications, and computers the size of an iPhone place vast creative resources in the hands of broad swathes of the population. The ongoing financial crisis is a symptom of an economy that has fallen behind its own technological capacities.

The instinctive response of our leaders is to reconstruct our consumer culture. The generation holding the reins of society is trained to think of us as passive consumers. It might take a generational shift before a world leader addresses a speech, not to the world's consumers, but to its creators.

Yet a creator culture is emerging from the ground up, driven by creators themselves. The crowd-funding platform Kickstarter is only three years old and last year it significantly outfunded the U.S. National Endowment for the Arts. It has allowed artists and entrepreneurs of all kinds to sidestep traditional forms of investment. Crowd-funded creativity is not driven by the commercial imperative of business or the political priorities of government, but by the creative passions of the crowd. "Maker" culture resurrects the spirit of craftsmanship and combines it with technologies, such as 3D printing, that promise to do for manufacturing what the Internet did for communication. The principles of "open source" are now being applied far beyond the software development community, invigorating academic and scientific research, politics and government, the media and education. Notice how many of the new voices that are emerging through social media—the cultural curator Maria Popova, an "interestingness hunter-gatherer" who started the Brain Pickings blog; the New York-based Big Think project to sift the "best thinking on the planet"; many TED talks—make creativity their central concern. All articulate our new understanding of creativity.

But the green shoots of a creator culture are only just bursting through the rubble of consumerism. Most of us are still plugged in to a mass media that equates creativity with branding and marketing and ignores its potential for human development. Businesses are still afraid of the ideas of their own employees, missing the fact that this creativity is their only hope of adapting to changing times. And our political landscape, dominated by a Left-Right dialogue that only engages with creativity as a source of economic growth, seems incapable of making the changes needed to bring about a creator culture.

In years of working with people struggling to reclaim their creativity, I learnt one very important lesson. Creation is the start, not the end, of the process of growth. We do not escape our tedious jobs, our oppressive social hierarchies, our addictive and self-destructive behaviour, and then become creative. We begin to create; then the process of growth it sets in train helps to free us from the traps that life sets.

We need to learn this lesson as a culture. We have to place the human capacity to create at the very centre of our social and political life. Instead of treating it as a peripheral benefit of economic growth, we need to understand that our wealth only grows at the speed that we can develop our creative capacities. And we must realise that we can no longer afford to empower the creativity of the few at the cost of the many. Our systems of government, business and education must make it their mission to support the creative fulfilment of every human being.

Analyze

1. What single sentence in Walter's article best captures his main idea?
2. Explain how Walter's experience with the seniors in the Leicester home relates to his main idea.
3. Early in his article, Walter references the twentieth-century psychologist Carl Jung. Explain how Jungian thought matters here. How does Jung support Walter's main idea?
4. Walter argues, "As much as our social hierarchies are about limiting and controlling access to wealth, they are also about limiting and controlling access to creativity." Explain this point. What does he mean by "social hierarchies" and how do they limit access to creativity?
5. Articulate the specific differences between a consumer culture and a creative culture.

Explore

1. Are you free to create? Why or why not? What forces, processes, or people figure into your freedom (or lack thereof)?
2. Walter argues, "Increasingly, the real benefit that money buys is the time, freedom and power to act creatively." What have you experienced, witnessed, or read that supports this idea?
3. Walter also says that "Most of us are still plugged in to a mass media that equates creativity with branding and marketing and ignores its potential for human development." Consider your own life. How might you or your friends be plugged in to the system described here? How might your favorite attractions or pastimes be part of that system?
4. What are the obstacles to Walter's proposal? Who or what would stand in the way of moving toward a creative culture?
5. How does Walter's article impact your thinking about college—your chosen academic major, your potential career, even the classes you might take in the future?

Forging Connections

1. Marketers try to fuse consumer products to identity. Everything from pickup trucks to mascara is pitched to reinforce a type of man, woman, or child—the gruff outdoorsy type, the well-groomed metropolitan type, or even the edgy hipster who resists labels and types. Consider a particular product in your life, one that is important to you practically, and explain how it has become part of your identity, part of your understanding of yourself. Resist the urge to say that you are beyond the influence of marketing and consumption trends. Be honest. Try to probe the subtle ways that the product has nestled up close to your identity—and vice versa. Borrow insights from Fredrik deBoer ("The Resentment Machine"), Mike Rose ("Blue-Collar Brilliance," Chapter 1), or even James Gleick ("What Defines a Meme?," Chapter 4).
2. How is consumerism related to work? How do our jobs invite us to adopt a lifestyle and, therefore, buy particular products? How does working in a specific field prompt people to adopt some consumer reflexes? Consider your own job or career choice—or those among your family members. Develop an essay that forges a connection between work and consumption. Also, you might borrow insights from writers in the Work chapter. For instance, Elizabeth Dwoskin ("Why Americans Won't Do Dirty Jobs," Chapter 1) might shed light on this subtle connection.

Looking Further

1. Being a consumer means belonging to a group—not consciously buying products but behaving in a pattern: buying the same types of shirts as others in your demographic, eating at the same restaurants as others in your age range, and so on. Examine your own consumer patterns—where you eat, what you eat, what you drink, or what you wear. Write an ethnographic essay that examines your own consumption patterns. Describe yourself as part of a particular demographic: single college students under 25, married students with no children, 50+ college students returning for a second career, and so on. Borrow insights from the writers in this chapter to help explain how your peer group gets identified as consumers. Integrate images and specific advertisements to illustrate the types of products and services that are pitched to you.

2. Begley and Chatzky make reference to the work of the neuroeconomist Paul Glimcher. What is neuroeconomics? Research the field and find out its focus. Try to understand the trends, the claims, and even the debates within the field. In an analytical essay, explain what the work of neuroeconomics means for American culture. Use the information you discover to help generate insights about the state of consumerism in modern American life.

Chapter 3

Social Media: How We Communicate

When it launched in 2003, MySpace introduced the era of online social networking. By 2006, it was the most accessed website in the world. Millions of people on every continent signed up to post intimate details about their lives. And then along came Facebook, whose popularity dwarfed MySpace. On its way to one billion users, Facebook currently serves three times the number of people in the United States. In short, social media are normal. They now operate at the center of culture, in the daily routine of millions. People of different countries, age groups, religions, and entirely different worldviews convene in the same social media. Business owners, artists, politicians, and even religious leaders now see Facebook and Twitter as necessary. However, it hasn't been a quiet process. From the moment they first came along, social media have been debated. They have been blamed and celebrated, condemned and defended. For instance, some media scholars credited Twitter for the civic uprising in Egypt—and even more broadly for the Arab Spring, which saw democratic protests in Saudi Arabia, Egypt, Libya, Iran, and Syria. Others have blamed Twitter for the end of the English language. Still others have said that Twitter and Facebook have doomed civilization to a future of teenage silliness and shallow self-involvement.

The readings in this chapter take on a range of issues related to social media. In her essay, "What It Means Today To Be 'Connected,'" Lucy P. Marcus celebrates networking technology. She argues that relationships forged across huge distances can be deeper and more profound than those confined by traditional boundaries. As the chapter proceeds, the articles introduce doubts. In "Lying, Cheating, and Virtual Relationships," Cynthia Jones examines the way multiplayer online games enable, even cultivate, dishonesty. Michael Erard explores the real effects of social media addiction in "What I Didn't Write About When I Wrote About Quitting Facebook." When he tries to quit Facebook, he finds himself pulled back, face-to-face with his own yearning. Both Jones and Erard see a definite tension between real (nondigital) life and the allure of an online identity. Toward the end of the chapter, writers pose even tougher questions: Roger Scruton claims in "Hiding Behind the Screen" that online identity—a life of avatars—lacks "risk, embarrassment, suffering, and love." And in "What Defines a Meme?" James Gleick explains how the rise of social media is cultivating a new kind of human—a new step in the very nature of the species.

Lucy P. Marcus
What It Means Today To Be "Connected"

Lucy P. Marcus was named one of the most influential voices on Twitter in 2011 and 2012. An expert on global economic trends and business ethics, Marcus is the founder and CEO of Marcus Ventures, whose mission is "to build strong funding businesses." She writes frequently for *BusinessWeek*, *CSRWire*, *Harvard Business Review*, the *Huffington Post*, and *Reuters*. In the following *Harvard Business Review* blog post, Marcus explores the value of online relationships and the meaning of "real" connections.

> *Only connect! That was the whole of her sermon. Only connect the prose and the passion, and both will be exalted, and human love will be seen at its height. Live in fragments no longer. Only connect, and the beast and the monk, robbed of the isolation that is life to either, will die.*
>
> —*E.M. Forster, Howards End (1910)*

I was recently selected as one of Britain's "best connected" women by *Director*, a business magazine. This prompted me to reflect on what it actually means to be "connected." I began to explore the meaning of connectedness, both in person, and in an ever more virtual world, and to consider whether the two forms are so different. I considered it both in my role as a board director, but also in a wider framework of building relationships and gathering, synthesizing and sharing knowledge.

Connecting with people and innovative ideas is more important than ever. To my mind, in a world where new and interesting ideas can come from anywhere, true value is found by breaking through the silos of sector-only or country-only knowledge and relationships. In such a world, it is not about the number of people you know or the mountain of business cards you collect, but rather about the depth and authenticity of the relationships you build and sustain, the depth and maturity of the connection you have with one another, and about valuing and nurturing the free flow of ideas.

The integration of social media tools, like Twitter, LinkedIn, Google Plus, and Facebook, and the use of technologies like video Skype means that when used to best effect, the online and offline exchange of ideas can be seamless and without the restrictions of distance and time. We need only keep an open mind and be on both "transmit" and "receive" to be able to find new, dynamic ways to work together and make the most of the synergies thus created. One of the most exciting developments that technological advances have facilitated is the breaking down of the hierarchy of ideas, allowing great ideas to bubble to the surface from virtually anywhere. This means that it matters little whether an idea originates from a young woman entrepreneur in Japan or an elder statesman in Africa.

> "For me, the insight is more important than the size of the input."

I have found myself asking a question via Twitter, sending the query out into the ether, only to have some of the most creative and interesting solutions coming back in very short order. I am struck by the fact that some of the best, most considered answers can come from unlikely sources, and I'm encouraged that oftentimes the most compelling answers do not come from "experts" but rather from someone I had not heard of before. More and more I look at the answer or the new idea before I look to see who sent it. This marks an extraordinary and complete shift in power to the idea, and away from the source. Ideas are increasingly judged on their merit, no longer requiring "validation" on the basis of their source before they are taken seriously. This opportunity for innovation to flourish and for talent to shine will only reach its full potential if connectedness is based on authenticity, depth and continuity.

5 Why? To me authenticity is the key to building relationships both online and offline. It is easy to see, either in person or over social media, when someone is putting on an act, or is genuinely interested in a particular issue. Connectedness is not an end in itself. It is not about the number of connections you have on LinkedIn, the number of followers on Twitter or the number of friends on Facebook, but about the relationship that you have with them. The real measure of connectedness is both how much you give and how much you get, and how much anyone cares or trusts what you say. It is that relationship that PeerIndex and Klout try, in part, to measure. As the kind of connectedness that social media and technologies like Skype facilitate crosses and blurs the boundaries between social and professional networks, the depth of the relationships that result is often profound. For me, the insight is more important than the size of the input: a light-hearted quip is often more helpful and insightful than a long post or link to a book, or more often now, an e-book. It is about sharing ideas,

developing them together, and putting them jointly to good use—this depth increases with the degree of connectedness you have, and in turn sustains it over time.

The most interesting part of social media is how it enables more meaningful connections with friends, colleagues, and advisers. Connectedness in this sense is also about the seamless way in which our communication continues, irrespective of whether we are meeting over a cup of tea or meeting over Skype, sending each other direct messages on Twitter or writing on each other's Facebook walls, or sharing links and holding conversations in LinkedIn or Google Plus.

When done well, with authenticity, depth and continuity, being connected, both online and offline, facilitates constant learning, synthesizing, evolving, and sharing that is, for me, the most exciting and rewarding part of being "connected."

Analyze

1. For Marcus, authenticity is a key dimension of a connected life. What do you think she means by *authenticity*?
2. Marcus also says that depth and continuity are key qualities of a connected life. What do you think she means by *depth* and *continuity*?
3. Marcus uses quotation marks around the word *connected*. What might those quotation marks mean? Why are there no quotation marks around other words, such as *connectedness* or *communication*?
4. An epigraph is a statement or quotation that comes at the beginning of an article and connects to the article's main idea. Writers use them to establish a way of thinking—a perspective or overall vision for their work. Explain the relationship between Marcus's epigraph, which comes from the novel *Howards End,* and her main idea.
5. Explain the overall purpose of this article. Is Marcus defending, celebrating, or familiarizing social media? Is she doing something else? Point out particular passages that support your answer.

Explore

1. Marcus says that "true value is found by breaking through the silos of sector-only or country-only knowledge and relationships." What are "the silos of sector-only or country-only knowledge?" Explain how you might exist in such silos.

2. Give an example of an authentic and an inauthentic online relationship.
3. Explain a relationship that hovers between authentic and inauthentic—that is not clearly one or the other. Explain, then, how this gray area might pose problems in professional or personal life.
4. Marcus mentions PeerIndex and Klout—companies that measure and manage online influence. Check out both of these companies online. What are the plusses and minuses of such companies? Why might they be crucial in a connected age? What questions do they raise?
5. In "Hiding Behind the Screen" (later in this chapter), Roger Scruton explains that social media such as Facebook diminish the real complexity of friendship. He argues that "by placing a screen between yourself and the friend, while retaining ultimate control over what appears on that screen, you also hide from the real encounter—denying the other the power and the freedom to challenge you in your deeper nature and to call on you here and now to take responsibility for yourself and for him." Do you think Scruton's point about Facebook challenges anything in Marcus's article? Does Scruton make you think differently about Marcus's characterization of social media?

Steven D. Krause
Living Within Social Networks

An English professor at Eastern Michigan University, Steven D. Krause studies the intersection between writing and technology. An avid blogger, he has written articles for such publications as the *Chronicle of Higher Education, College Composition and Communication Online, Computers and Composition,* and *Kairos.* In the following essay, Krause considers the social impact of social media.

In 2011, Toyota ran an amusing commercial that played off of the worst fears we have about social media sites like Facebook. The commercial opens with a college-aged woman sitting at a tidy desk in front of her laptop and speaking directly to the camera about an article (or "part of an article") she read online about how older people were becoming more antisocial. She explains that this was the reason why she was "really aggressive with my parents about joining Facebook," and while she speaks, the scene turns to her parents: smiling, attractive and active 50-somethings driving their Toyota Venza Sports Utility Vehicle down a dirt road into the wilderness. The couple parks and takes the mountain bikes off the roof of the sporty car. The scene goes back to the young woman who proclaims aloud her parents are up to "19 friends now," though she immediately mouths silently into the camera "*so sad*" since that is such a pathetically small number of Facebook friends. We jump back to her parents who are now on their bikes in the real world, joining real friends for a real bike ride through real nature. The scene switches back to our Facebook enthusiast a final time. "I have 687 friends," she says in a deadpan tone. "*This* is living."[1]

Of course, the intention of the commercial is the exact opposite: that is, sitting in front of your laptop looking at pictures of puppies on Facebook all day is decidedly *not* living. Rather, "living" means getting out in nature and being active with others in a real—not virtual—space. And it helps to do all this in a stylish new Toyota, too.

The ad works well because it plays humorously off of some of the greatest fears of Facebook and other social media, that they leave us alone and inactive, involved in what is at best superficial "friendships" in a pretend space. Stephen Marche presumes we know the answer to the question "Is Facebook Making Us Lonely?" in his May 2012 *The Atlantic* article of the same name:

> We are living in an isolation that would have been unimaginable to our ancestors, and yet we have never been more accessible. Over the past three decades, technology has delivered to us a world in which we need not be out of contact for a fraction of a moment.... Yet within this world of instant and absolute communication, unbounded by the limits of time or space, we suffer from unprecedented alienation. We have never been more detached from one another, or lonelier. (61–2)

It's a dramatic claim, but is it a claim that is broadly supported by evidence and experiences? There's a fairly good chance that you the reader has a Facebook account—after all, almost a billion people have one, and most college students and fellow professors that I encounter use Facebook and social media to some extent. Do *you* feel detached and lonely because of it?

Facebook is but one of the many Internet services that have been called social media, software tools and websites that make it easy for anyone with access to write content for the Internet, something that wasn't nearly as simple just a few years ago. Facebook allows its users to write original updates about anything, to share web links—serious stories about the anti-social behavior of senior citizens or humorous pictures of puppies—and to "like" the postings and sharings of the people users know on Facebook, their "friends." Readers who have a Facebook account already know what I'm talking about.

But in considering social media as a whole, it's important to not think of only Facebook but rather to think about the rise of the many ways we quickly add and share content online and its likely importance in the way that we will interact into the foreseeable future. As Steven Johnson points out in his 2009 *Time* magazine article about one of Facebook's rivals, "How Twitter Will Change the Way We Live," "Social networks are notoriously vulnerable to the fickle tastes of teens and 20-somethings. . . ." Johnson asks, "Remember Friendster?" And I would add, "Remember MySpace?" or, maybe in the not so distant future, perhaps even, "Remember Facebook?"

But tools *like* Facebook are not going away. The shift to social media—tools and online spaces which allow anyone to easily create, share, and comment on the content created by others—shifts the paradigm as to how we understand and relate to the things we read and watch online, and indeed, how we "read" and "watch" each other.

Is this new wave of Internet interaction, social media, ironically making us more apart, lonely, or unproductive? There's been a fair amount of research on these questions and the results are often surprising and contradictory. For example, in their *First Monday* essay "Facebook and Academic Performance: Reconciling a Media Sensation with Data," Josh Pasek, eian more, and Ester Hargittai follow and replicate the claims of an earlier study by Aryn Karpinski called "A Description of Facebook Use and Academic Performance Among Undergraduate and Graduate Students." In that study, Karpinski found that Facebook use had a negative impact on students' grades, and even though Karpinski's was a small study, it became a bit of a "media sensation" in 2009. Pasek, moore, and Hargittai repeated Karpinski's study with a larger and more diverse group of students, and they found just the opposite. Not only was there no evidence of a negative relationship between Facebook and grades, Pasek and his colleagues found that Facebook use was more common among students with higher grades.

Even the answer to the question asked by Marche's *Atlantic* article, "Is Facebook Making Us Lonely?" is less than clear. According to John Cacioppo, who is the director of the Center for Cognitive and Social Neuroscience at the University of Chicago and is called by Marche "the world's leading expert on loneliness," it depends. Facebook is merely a tool, he says, and like any other tool, its effectiveness will depend on its user. "If you use Facebook to increase face-to-face contact," he says, "it increases social capital." So if social media let you organize a game of football among your friends, that's healthy. If you turn to social media instead of playing football, however, that's unhealthy. To extend this example a bit: the college student who uses Facebook as a way of connecting with her professor about assignments, follows useful research sources via Twitter, and collaborates with classmates on a Blogger site seems to me to be making the most of the power of social media. On the other hand, the obsessive Facebook-er who uses it and similar tools to *escape* connections between him and his classmates and professors is being victimized by social media.

So, to turn back to my opening example for a moment: paradoxically, I'd 10
suggest that *both* the older couple with their snazzy SUV and the college-aged woman with her laptop are indeed "living," depending on what we don't know about what their lives beyond the commercial entail. Assuming that college-aged Facebook fan does indeed leave her apartment to interact with at least *some* of her 687 "Friends"—people who probably range from actual and "real life" friends to mere acquaintances to the famous who make their fans Facebook friends—then yes, this *is* living. And if those retired parents are obsessed with their mountain biking and otherwise cut off from the day-to-day world and the interactions of those around them—including things like Facebook—well, maybe they aren't living to their potential after all.

Note

1 See "2011 Toyota Venza Commercial—Social Network," http://www.youtube.com/watch?v=TUGmcb3mhLM

Works Cited

Johnson, Steven. "How Twitter Will Change the Way We Live." *Time Magazine.* 5 June 2009. Web. 20 Sept. 2012.

Marche, Stephen. "Is Facebook Making Us Lonely?" *The Atlantic.* May 2012, 60–69. Print.

Pasek, Josh, eian more, and Hargittai, Eszter. "Facebook and Academic Performance: Reconciling a Media Sensation with Data." *First Monday* 14. 4 May 2009. Web. 20 Sept. 2012.

Analyze

1. Explain how the Toyota ad works in Krause's argument: how does it support, develop, or shape his ideas?
2. Krause says, "The shift to social media . . . shifts the paradigm as to how we understand and relate to the things we read and watch online, and indeed, how we 'read' and 'watch' each other." Explain why Krause uses quotation marks around *read* and *watch.* What is he suggesting?
3. Krause offers a range of insights and answers to the question: Is Facebook making us lonely? What is his answer? (Note: It's more complicated than "it depends.")
4. For Krause, what is living? What does it mean?
5. How does Krause's position align with or oppose claims made by Roger Scruton ("Hiding Behind the Screen")?

Explore

1. Is Facebook making us lonely? Does social media make you lonely?
2. How do you use social media? As a way to connect with professors, family, and friends or as a way to hide away from the relationships that may benefit you?
3. Is Facebook merely a tool—like a hammer or a saw? Or is it more like a car? Or is it something altogether different than a tool?
4. How do you think the shift to online social media has shifted the way you (or others) think?
5. Are Facebook and Twitter forms of consumption? Why or why not?

Cynthia Jones

Lying, Cheating, and Virtual Relationships

A professor of philosophy at the University of Texas, Pan American, Cynthia Jones is the director of the Pan American Collaboration for Ethics in the Professions (PACE), which seeks to "promote interdisciplinary research and engagement on issues in diverse fields of professional ethics." The author of several scholarly and popular articles, she co-edited the book *A Future for Everyone: Innovative Social Responsibility and Community Partnerships* (2004) with David Maurrasse. In this article from *Global Virtue Ethics Review*, Jones explores the ethical questions surrounding virtual dating.

Gem and Zupy were married earlier this year in a beautiful ceremony atop a snow-covered mountain with a breathtaking view. They met last year and dated for seven months before officially taking the plunge. Theirs is a fairly common story, except the couple has never been in the same city together or even in the same state. And Gem and Zupy are both married to other people irl (in real life). Their wedding ceremony, and their entire relationship, is virtual, having taken place in the virtual world of *Second Life*. How does virtual dating compare to traditional face-to-face dating? Since they are both legally married to other people, does Gem and Zupy's virtual relationship and marriage count as cheating or even as polygamy?

Continually improving technology has made virtual dating more attractive than in the past. The advent of social virtual worlds like *Second Life*, and the popularity of other kinds of virtual worlds such as MMORPGs (massively multiplayer online role-playing games) like the immensely popular *World of Warcraft*, have made purely virtual relationships and dating more appealing than in the past when the available options were online chat rooms and dating websites. And not all virtual dating remains purely virtual as some online relationships later turn into "real-world" relationships. Virtual dating offers a host of perks that dating in real life cannot, such as: sexual encounters without fear of disease or pregnancy, anonymity, and, for some, a chance to "cheat" on a partner without ever leaving home. This paper will explore the ethical and prudential aspects of virtual dating, focusing on moral issues like lying and on prudential issues like satisfying urges for different partners within a committed relationship without ever touching another person.

Dating, Cybersex, and Virtual Worlds

Virtual dating, online relationships, and online sexual encounters (which I will group under the category *cybersex*) can take place in a number of ways and in a number of virtual venues, but perhaps the easiest places for such encounters to take place in are virtual worlds. Virtual dating, online relationships and cybersex are in no way restricted to virtual worlds, however virtual worlds like the popular *Second Life* and *World of Warcraft* offer subscribers far more visual stimulation, as well as more potential partners, than most other online venues. Having spent over four years playing *World of Warcraft* and a few months wandering around some very interesting places in *Second Life*, I can say that both worlds are far more "social" than one might suspect. While online dating experiences and cybersex encounters surely can vary greatly, a look at these two most popular virtual worlds can offer some insight into purely virtual relationships.

For those who have never encountered a virtual or online world, the idea of dating in one may be strange indeed. But virtual worlds have amassed a huge number of subscribers and their popularity only continues to grow. Linden Lab's *Second Life* (SL, for short) and Blizzard's *World of Warcraft* (commonly known as WoW) each claim to have more than 12 million subscribers worldwide, and WoW has servers in many different countries.

5 The difference, in general, between social virtual worlds like SL and MMORPGs like WoW is the general purpose of the worlds: social vs. gaming. Most people initially log on to WoW to play the game, although the social aspect is often significant for subscribers as well. *Second Life*, on the other hand, is not a game, even though one can find some games to play within the world, and it did not begin its life as a computer game like WoW did, before the online aspect became popular. From personal experience, I can say that if I create a new character in WoW, one whose name is unknown to any of my online friends, I can be online for hours without anyone talking to me. If I don't want to be bothered and ignore anyone who talks to me in chat, probably no one would care. Logging in to SL, on the other hand, as a new avatar (the name given the virtual characters of the subscribers) you will find your virtual self greeted by many other avatars before you even figure out how to walk forward. Other avatars may follow you around and talk to

you, even if you try to ignore them. As such, SL is purely intended to be a social enterprise, so to speak, and those who log on should expect the social aspect. Everyone in SL is in the same world, although the world is huge, and individuals can buy virtual space and modify and add to the world itself. WoW, on the other hand, has a large number of servers in many different countries, each is identical and each supports approximately 20K–50K users.

There is a cost difference between SL and WoW as well. One cannot log on to WoW without paying the monthly subscription fees (roughly $15 a month, although a free short-term trial is possible) and without purchasing the software. SL, on the other hand, can be accessed without purchasing anything, although some subscribers pay real money to have enhanced graphics, in-game money, and more "bling" for their avatars. This makes SL more accessible to the general public since it is free to join and log on.

Both virtual worlds have their own currency. The currencies of WoW and SL can be purchased online—the Linden of SL and virtual gold from WoW. The main difference here is that Blizzard's rules forbid the buying and selling of WoW gold outside of the game, an offense which is punishable, if discovered, by having one's account banned. In contrast, SL encourages its subscribers to buy and sell Lindens outside of and inside of SL and Linden Labs sells virtual land in SL for real money to individuals, companies, schools, and even countries to be developed and populated.

But what about dating? Independently-run websites exist for both SL and WoW subscribers interested in "hooking up"[1] although the SL sites seem more popular, which is perhaps not surprising given that SL is social rather than game-based. The upshot is that SL is far more popular for dating. SL avatars and the world itself can be significantly modified by users in a manner that WoW does not permit. Although character movement in virtual worlds is of course scripted, SL subscribers can write scripts or buy them for their avatars to allow them to have sex—an aspect utilized by many SL subscribers. Avatars can thus move and gyrate and appear to have sex in ways that WoW toons or characters cannot. There are even whole areas for sexual encounters in SL and specific "mature" zones dedicated to fetishisms and other kinds of sex-related activities like bondage and discipline, S & M, and dominance and submission. But dating and sex in SL has its critics, even amongst people who admittedly engage in virtual dating and cybersex. One such critic argues that a significant attraction of cybersex, the imagination and creativity of the participants, is compromised in a virtual world like SL, especially since one can use pre-written "canned" lines while engaged in the act. (Welles, 2007)

Real Virtual Couples

Reports in the media of couples who met online, had online relationships, were married online, or found their partners "cheating" online are easy enough to find.[2] There are even books in print about virtual dating and infidelity. A few stories about virtual couples have received large amounts of publicity, like the story of Dave Barmy and Laura Skye (David and Amy Pollard irl). (Cable, 2008) In real life, the couple is an unemployed and rather overweight British pair who met in SL, married in SL and irl, and not long after divorced in both worlds after Amy caught David's SL avatar in compromising positions with other women. Both Amy and David have moved on, Amy to a beau from WoW and David to a hostess at the club he operates in SL. Comparing Amy and David's irl personas to their handsome, fit, successful, and trendy online personas has afforded the media a chance to poke fun at and generalize virtual relationships, making them seem absurdly fake and made-up.

10 But despite the media's interest appearing to lie solely in exploiting the "freak factor" involved in virtual dating and relationships, a large number of people choose to not only flirt and date virtually but to become sexually and emotionally involved in a purely virtual manner. And the number grows daily. Some people move from virtual dating to a "normal" relationship with a former virtual partner, but many others prefer to keep it virtual. So what's the attraction, you may ask?

The Perks and the Problems of Virtual Dating

There are obvious advantages to virtual dating. First, one can engage in a heavy dose of fantasy if dating virtually. Even those who choose to cyber (engage in cybersex) via webcams where they can actually see their partners can still remain considerably removed from the reality of messy real-world relationships and feel free to role-play. (One cannot help but wonder if virtual daters would choose to go back into the Matrix after being freed if they were promised great bodies, well-endowed organs, and wealth and success . . .)

A second attractive perk of online dating is the cost. Anyone with a computer and Internet access can engage in a virtual relationship for little to no cost. Going out with your best girl in SL is considerably cheaper than the irl counterpart. But the lower costs of virtual dating aren't just financial. You can extend less of yourself in a virtual relationship and so the emotional costs can be quite lower. I remember an interview with a very attractive young woman on the popular HBO show *Real Sex,* detailing her numerous online relationships and sexual encounters. She argued that a cost/benefit analysis of virtual dating and cybersex vs. their irl counterparts had led her to date exclusively online. Virtual dating is free from most emotional and financial costs, fear of physical abuse, and the chance of contracting STDs and unwanted pregnancy. It also offered her the chance to engage with multiple partners without the baggage of jealousy, messy entanglements, and the ties that an irl relationship carried.

The anonymity aspect of virtual dating and cybersex can clearly be counted as a third appealing perk. Anonymity can free a person to do things they would never dream of doing irl. For those who wish to explore lifestyles that are not socially accepted or are even illegal, virtual dating, online relationships, and cybersex offer them the freedom to explore their desires anonymously. One can only hope that some of these illicit desires can be satisfied virtually, especially if they involve harm to unwilling others. (Of course anonymity can unquestionably have a serious moral component as well, but we'll come to that in the next section.)

A final obvious perk of virtual dating and cybersex over real-life relationships and sex the old-fashioned way is the freedom to disengage. It is considerably easier to walk away from a relationship in which you never have to look your partner in the eye and say "It's over." And there is less fear of being stalked by crazy ex's if they don't have your personal information. What about problems or potential costs of virtual dating, online relationships, and cybersex, in comparison to the "real deal?" Most of the benefits we have just discussed have another side. The costs of virtual dating may be considerably lower than irl dating, but the satisfaction gained from such relationships may be considerably lower as well. It is fun to role-play, but having a partner who knows you for who you really are carries an immeasurable benefit. One downside of anonymity is that if you never see or speak to the person on the other end of the ravishingly handsome avatar with whom you're flirting or cybering, you have no idea of the gender, age, attractiveness, or mental health of said individual. Although the costs may be lower, the potential payoffs are lower as well. The old adage "nothing ventured, nothing gained" comes to mind.

One prudential question we can ask of virtual marriages in particular, apart from the other aspects of these relationships, is whether a virtual marriage legally counts as polygamy if one or both partners happen to be married irl to someone else. Virtual marriages do not, of course, currently count as "real" in terms of polygamy, however, virtual adultery or infidelity has begun to be cited as a reason for divorce. The divorce laws in the U.S. vary, but I wouldn't be surprised if virtual infidelity was soon counted among the plausible grounds for divorce in some places.

Many relationships end due to infidelity. Virtual relationships seem to some to offer a way to technically remain monogamous, if monogamy and sex are defined in physical terms, while having guilt-free virtual relations with a variety of partners. Have we finally found a way to have the best of both worlds? Can you cheat on your partner without ever touching someone else? This raises related but distinct questions regarding the moral aspects of virtual dating and cyber [dating].

Two Ethical Aspects of Virtual Dating: Lying and Cheating

I believe the two most compelling ethical questions arising from virtual dating and virtual relationships are as follows. First, is it permissible to lie to one's virtual partners, given that role-playing and taking on virtual identities which are quite distinct from one's irl persona are generally assumed to be the norm in an online environment? Second, do virtual relationships and cybersex count as cheating, assuming the existence of real-world partners who are unaware of the virtual hanky-panky?

Let's discuss lying first. What can one expect in virtual dating, online relationships, and cybersex in terms of truth-telling? It seems that any reasonable person in a virtual world should expect to doubt the absolute honesty of potential virtual partners. However, anyone who has been in a successful and meaningful relationship would probably say that honesty and communication are integral components of a healthy relationship. Where does this leave virtual dating and online relationships? This is surely a problem if one expects to find a satisfying relationship, in terms of honesty and communication, in a virtual world. And the anonymity that we counted as a perk in the previous section is not without moral implications. Anonymity affords virtual partners certain protections and perks, but it also makes it exceedingly easy to lie. Nonetheless, honest encounters are possible in virtual worlds, if one is careful. Assuming that it is morally problematic to lie to a partner irl, is it wrong to lie to a virtual partner?

What do ethicists say about lying in general? Some ethicists argue that lying is always wrong, regardless of the circumstances or the consequences. (Rachels, 2009) Kantian ethics, for example, argues that lying to a person treats that person as merely a means to an end, or uses them—and that is wrong. (Rachels, 2009) Undoubtedly, lying is usury. But what if lying is expected? Is lying morally problematic in virtual dating, virtual relationships, and cybersex if it is generally acknowledged that people are lying about themselves? Let's look at a different ethical theory.

Utilitarian ethics, which focuses on maximizing benefit and avoiding harm, would argue that lying is typically morally problematic because it has the potential to harm others in a significant way. (Rachels, 2009) Lying, however, is not always wrong on utilitarian grounds. Lying may be justified if the circumstances and consequences warrant not telling the truth. Benefiting others and avoiding harm are central to morality on utilitarian grounds. If virtual partners expect that the individuals with whom they are virtually interacting are likely not being completely truthful, then they are less apt to be harmed. Further, if virtual partners tell tall tales to heighten the sexual experience and the role-playing involved for both partners, and this is expected, then lying in such a scenario wouldn't seem to be problematic on this account.

Notice that the issue of lying, as we've discussed it, differs from the issue of cheating in an important way. The worry in lying is directed towards not harming the person on the other end of the computer connection, whereas the issue of cheating involves possible harm caused to a person outside of the virtual relationship, namely the irl partners of those engaging in virtual dating, virtual relationships, and cybersex. Of course cheating involves a component of lying as well, but the issues involved in lying to one's irl partner can be delineated from lying to virtual partners.

We now turn to the issue of cheating. So what really counts as cheating? It may plausibly count as cheating if one engages in multiple online relationships without informing one's multiple virtual partners, however the cheating I would like to address is cheating on irl partners with virtual partners. Do I have to physically touch another person in order to count as cheating on my husband, for example? (I can't help but be reminded of the amusing debate during the Clinton presidency when pundits debated whether intercourse was required for sex.)

From what I can tell, more women than men think that engaging in online relationships is morally problematic, when one has a partner irl who is unaware of the virtual relationships. Perhaps an important component here is honesty as well; that is, if one's partner irl is aware of and has no problems with their partner engaging in virtual relationships, it would be harder to argue that cheating occurred. But what about those who engage in online dating, virtual relationships, or cybersex without informing their irl partners?

It is reasonable to assume that virtual dating and cybersex can be damaging to a real-world relationship, especially if lying to one's irl partner plays a role. It is easy enough to find media accounts of husbands and wives who argue that their spouses neglected them for a virtual partner or partners. Even if virtual sex isn't grounds for divorce per se, neglect is.

Cheating is typically much more complex than just sex. And sex may not have to be involved for one to cheat on a partner. If this is the case, then virtual relationships can clearly count as cheating on irl partners. Again, lying or betrayal plays a role. The sense of betrayal involved in cheating is complicated. An irl partner can find their position and their time usurped by a virtual partner, and this usurping can be just as real if the relationship is virtual. Further, the intimacy involved in many virtual relationships can be just as intense as irl. Intimacy with a partner outside of a committed relationship surely seems to be cheating, especially if we take cheating to encompass emotional infidelity. It may reasonably be argued that emotional infidelity is more harmful to a relationship than physical infidelity. For example, just like finding out in the real world that your partner has engaged in "meaningless" sex with a prostitute, finding out that your partner has engaged in "meaningless" cybersex with a virtual partner whose real name is unknown seems to me at least to be less worrisome than finding out that your partner has decided he or she is in love with and desires to commit to and marry someone else, even if it is "only virtual."

Real or Not?

So what can we conclude from our foray into the world of virtual dating, online relationships, and cybersex? Perhaps that these are as real as you allow them to be and that the emotions involved in virtual relationships can be seriously detrimental to irl partners, if you have them. Lying is clearly a worry, as is emotional attachment and emotional infidelity, if one is juggling a virtual partner and an irl partner.

Virtual dating offers a host of perks that irl relationships may not, and virtual dating may be a springboard to an irl relationship, if that's your cup of tea, but use with caution.

Notes

1 www.avmatch.com and www.datecraft.com, respectively.

2 For examples, see http://www.time.com/time/world/article/0,8599,1859231,00.html and http://online.wsj.com/article/SB118670164592393622.html.

References

Cable, A. (2008). *Divorced from Reality: All Three Accounts of the Second Life Love Triangle that Saw a Woman Separate from Her Husband for Having a Cyber-Affair.* July 30; http://www.dailymail.co.uk/femail/article-1085915/Divorced-reality-All-accounts-Second-Life-love-triangle-saw-woman-separate-husband-having-cyber-affair.html

Rachels, J. and Rachels, S. (2009). *The Elements of Moral Philosophy* (6 ed.). New York: McGraw-Hill.

Welles, D. (2007). *The Ins and Outs of a Second Sex Life.* July 30; http://www.theregister.co.uk/2007/01/09/good_sex_in_second_life/

Analyze

1. According to Jones's analysis, what are the primary ethical questions about virtual dating?
2. Much of this article analyzes the ethical tensions related to virtual dating. But Jones also makes some direct claims about those tensions. Identify passages that demonstrate Jones's stance on virtual dating.
3. Jones explains that virtual communities such as *World of Warcraft* and *Second Life* "are far more 'social' than one might suspect." Why is this statement crucial to her examination of virtual relationships?

4. Jones explains several dimensions to *World of Warcraft* and *Second Life,* such as the infrastructure, the currency, and even the real estate. Why are these dimensions important to her analysis of virtual dating?
5. Compare Jones's writing style to that of Lucy B. Marcus in "What It Means Today To Be 'Connected.'" Beyond the different ideas each has about the Internet and connectedness, how are the two articles different? How does Jones approach the issues in a way that's different from Marcus?

Explore

1. How is cybersex different from sex?
2. If you have cybersex with someone other than your significant other, is it cheating? Why or why not?
3. How is falling in love in virtual reality similar to or different from falling in love with someone you meet at a bar or in a college classroom?
4. Jones says that "Cheating is typically much more complex than just sex. And sex may not have to be involved for one to cheat on a partner." What, then, constitutes cheating on a significant other? How is it more than sex? How are issues such as betrayal and intimacy involved?
5. How does Jones's analysis of virtual dating relate to Roger Scruton's claims in "Hiding Behind the Screen" about online friendship? What tensions or questions seem to be operating in both articles?

Michael Erard
What I Didn't Write About When I Wrote About Quitting Facebook

As a linguist, Michael Erard studies the slips, stumbles, and elegant performances of daily language. He has written for a range of newspapers and magazines, including *Psychology Today*, the *Atlantic*, the *New York Times*, *Reason*, *Science*, *Slate*, and *Wired*. For this article, he set out to examine and even dramatize the way people quit social media such as Facebook. The article first appeared on *The Morning News*, which describes itself as "an online magazine of essays, art, humor, and culture published weekdays since 1999." According to its website, the editors of *The Morning News* "believe in good writing, tight editing, wit, curiosity, making mistakes, and solving them with tequila."

The first thing I didn't write about quitting Facebook was a status update to my friends saying, I'm quitting Facebook.

I also did not write a proposal for the nonfiction book I imagined, which was about quitting Facebook. In the book, I would indulge the conceit that my Facebook friends are, actually, my good friends, and that the social network comprises a sort of community when taken as a whole. Then, as one does with one's friends, I would call each person up or visit them and tell them I was leaving Facebook, which would create an opportunity to talk about Facebook and this whole social media thing, but mainly it would be to get to know something about who they actually were and why we were linked in the first place and what it all might have meant.

Eighteen weeks of five interviews a day would get me through my friend list, I calculated. Friends from high school and college and grad school. Friends of friends. Editors. Siblings and a couple of cousins, my in-laws. Random admirers and hangers-on. The resulting book would reflect our conversations about how much Facebook had enhanced our friendships and our lives in general, or maybe it hadn't, and we'd talk about that, too. And we'd exchange info, and say goodbye, and then linger, and wave, and wave, until we couldn't see each other any more—one of those departures where you look away out of exhaustion with the moment, then when you look up find they've gone, vanished, as if they hadn't been there at all.

At the end of the book, I would actually unplug from Facebook, and I would write about that, too, and the heartwarming account of the ties that bind us would inspire you to hold your Facebook friends close, so close, because the time we pass in this mortal coil is so fleeting; we are truly encountering only the passing of the person, not the person in themselves.

5 But I didn't write this, nor did I write a status update about leaving. When I quit, there were no goodbyes. No interviews. Just, I'm outta here.

Another thing I did not write about quitting Facebook was that one of the great social pleasures in my life has been to leave gatherings or parties unannounced. You know, when the party is socked in solid from the front door to the kitchen, and the conversation is drying up like old squeezed limes, it's easiest to keep heading out the back. How cool the night. How open and unquestioning the darkness. "French leave," we English speakers say. ("English leave," the French say.) Often I went to parties to be able to vanish from them. But the disappearing act rarely happens any more; I could never get away with it. Such pleasures one has to give up because they're so unsuited to middle-aged life. You get trained, after a while, to going to every person in the room. Hey, great to see you again. See you later. Send me a note about that thing. Yes, let's do that. Goodbye, bye. The book idea was, in a way, testing out the durability of that social grace. But I didn't write about either topic.

I did, however, start an essay that could have been about why I quit Facebook, except that I got distracted by the emergence of a genre you could call the Social Media Exile essay, and I wondered whether I could meet the conventions of that genre if I ever tried to write about why I quit Facebook, though the truth is, I didn't really want to write another version of the Social Media Exile Essay, dramatizing the initial promise of this or that social media or network, the enthusiastic glow of online togetherness, then the disillusionment, the final straw, the wistful looking back. I did write that it seems like so many people have had their crack at "The Day I Quit Blogging" or "Why I Tweet No More," which aren't real essay titles but could have been, also like "How Google Broke My Heart" or "Farewell MySpace" or "*Je Ne Regrette Rien,* Friendster." So this essay never got written.

I was also writing e-mails to former Facebook friends who had noticed that I was gone from their friend list and who were taking my disappearance personally, all because of what I hadn't written about quitting Facebook—which I didn't start writing, because I had to placate my friends. Really, it wasn't because of you, it was because of the whole enterprise, I wrote, which had begun to throw salt on my misanthropy. I went no farther than that—I feared offending them if I wrote about how difficult it became to have peaceable face-to-face relationships with people who projected unlikeability online.

I did tweet the observation that Facebook isn't going to pay you a pension or 401k for all the time you spent there, and quite a lot of people liked this. So that was one veiled thing I wrote about why I quit Facebook.

I didn't write about the shock of finding out that the two dear sons of one of my Facebook "friends" had been tragically killed in an auto accident, not recently but two years ago. Somehow I had missed this fact, until an anniversary post by one of the grieving parents—the status update elliptical, scourged by grief—pointed me toward the incident. I do not know what I would have done or written if I had known before. I did not write anything to them now because I felt so ashamed of my ignorance amidst a wealth of things to click on and know about. A wealth of things that may not matter so much. It's always been a world in which you can lose your children or your parents in an instant, but somehow I have made it this far without knowing that in my gut.

Instead of writing about any of this, once I was not on Facebook anymore, I found myself sending e-mails with some witty insights or photos of my baby, but it just wasn't the same; a request for housing help for a friend via e-mail got no responses. However, I was now *talking* a lot about quitting Facebook, and this for a time became the most interesting thing about me. Fueled by how interesting I now was, I wrote a draft of an essay about writing about why I quit Facebook, which was clever but did not contain any of the things I have already said I didn't write about. Plus, as the editor pointed out, I didn't actually explain why I had quit. I hadn't written about feeling like Facebook was a job. Like I was running on a digital hamster wheel. But a wheel that someone else has rigged up. And a wheel that's actually a turbine that's generating electricity for somebody else. That's how I felt, which is what I should have written.

I thought about how I didn't want to write about why I quit, only about how great it feels to be free, because how often do you get to leave a job? Something along the lines of, you stand up at your desk, you un-pin the photo of your dog or loved one from the cubicle wall, and you walk right out the door, don't take the elevator because it's slower than the stairs, and you bid the thrumming hive adios. Leaving Facebook felt like that. The sun singing on your face like springtime. The birds all whistling your theme song.

In the standard Social Media Exile essay, one doesn't mention or announce when one returns to blogging or Twitter. For each platform or network one leaves, there's another one to return to. Sometimes they're the same. So I'm going to close this piece by breaking that convention and mentioning how easy it turns out to be to reactivate Facebook. When you sign back in, all your stuff is there, as if you'd never left. It's like coming back to your country after a month in a foreign land, and it makes one feel that the whole reason for leaving is to make the place seem strange again. Being away from Facebook was certainly that. But I had to come back. That's where all the people are. I've got a book coming out, and I need to let my friends know. Anyway, you know where to find me and what to talk about when you do. I'll have some cookies baked.

Analyze

1. In one sentence, try to articulate Erard's point about Facebook and the process of quitting.
2. Throughout the article, Erard repeats the phrase "what I didn't write about." What effect does this repetition have on you? What point might that repetition make?
3. Much of this article is *confessional*. Erard is telling us a good deal about his personal struggle. Explain the function of his confessions: How do they relate to or help support the main idea?
4. In paragraph 6, Erard describes the way he would leave parties unannounced. How does this information support his main idea? How does it relate to the point about Facebook and the struggle to leave it?
5. This article might be considered *parody*. In other words, Erard might be spoofing or mocking the way people sound (what they say, what they don't say) when they try to quit Facebook. Identify passages that make you think the article might, in part, be a parody.

Explore

1. Do you know anyone addicted to Facebook? Are you addicted? What is it like? Does Erard capture the feeling? Which passages or comparisons from the article seem accurate to you? Which don't?
2. What do you think is worse for people: Facebook or Twitter? What particular qualities or reflexes does each bring out?

3. Apparently, enough people have tried to quit Facebook that Erard discovered an entire genre (or category) of writing that he calls the Social Media Exile essay. What do you think this says about Facebook itself, people's daily lives in 21st-century America, or people's inabilities?
4. It's easy to defend Facebook against naysayers. After all, it connects people who might otherwise lose track of one another. It allows shy people to have a voice. It makes people feel better about their days. But what else does Facebook do for people? What other, less acknowledged, value does it have?
5. Erard's article drew a range of comments—both sympathetic to and condemning of chronic Facebookers. Consider the following three comments. What do they say about Facebook and its role in public life?
   - "I just didn't like what I was hearing about snooping by employers or even prospective employers. And FB's policy of making unannounced changes compromising user privacy really bites. I simply don't trust FB."—banshee
   - "Got all Facebook'ed up and quit within the month because of no self discipline—it was taking over my life. Went back several months later and stayed longer this time, but still quit the scene—again, too much time spent with too little actual benefit."—Guest
   - "Quitting Facebook is so 2009."—Jungberg

Robert Fulford

How Twitter Saved the Octothorpe

A columnist for the *National Post* and *Toronto Life*, Robert Fulford is a Toronto-based journalist, editor, and broadcaster. His work focuses on art, entertainment, and culture, often through a Canadian lens. He is the author of numerous articles, reviews, and books, including the 1999 book *The Triumph of Narrative: Storytelling in the Age of Mass Culture*. In the following article, Fulford considers the value of the octothorpe.

When punctuation geeks assembled earlier this month at Punctuacon, our annual convention, we spent the usual two or three hours whining about the pathetic size of our gathering, compared to Comic-Con International in San Diego, Dragon*Con in Atlanta or any of those tiresome Star Trek conventions that draw multitudes to worship at the shrine of William Shatner.

We have no heroes like Shatner, just ourselves and our proud tradition of judging and promoting the images and ideograms of language—and our totally imaginary convention.

That should be enough, but a love for punctuation, signage and graphic symbols remains a lonely passion. It's hard not to be bitter.

Why can't the rest of the world understand that a well-designed semicolon or an expertly made STOP sign is every bit as enthralling as a mint *Batman* first edition, an early sketch of the Jedi, or a photograph signed by Margot Kidder herself? Why can't they care about the tragically missing apostrophe on the logo of a certain coffee-shop chain?

5 Still, Punctuacon was happier this year than usual, mostly because we could forget about what had become at previous conventions the most melancholy issue on the agenda: Who will save the octothorpe?

The Big O is a sign with deep historical and cultural roots, part of our heritage. It didn't deserve the neglect it suffered in recent times. It's lived under many names: the hash, the crunch, the hex (that's in Singapore), the flash, the grid. In some circles it's called tic-tac-toe, in others pig-pen. From a distance it looks like the sharp sign on a musical score. Whether you call it a pound sign or a number sign or anything else, it retains its identity. It's so majestically simple that it always looks good, even if drawn by someone utterly without graphic talent. Good old #. It can't go wrong.

Even so, it was in decline for years. After generations of vigorous life everywhere in the retailing world where numbers were written, it lost out to computerized invoices and receipts that simply ignored its value. In literature, after centuries showing printers where to put spaces, it was abolished by computers that do the same job with the touch of a keyboard.

It lost its proud place alongside the & and the @, on a shelf higher than both the © and the ®. After a while # appeared mostly in a cameo role on touch-tone phones, a serious comedown.

But lately the pendulum has swung again. On Twitter, the home of microbloggers, the octothorpe has a new career, reborn as the "hashtag."

Tweeters use hashtags to catalogue their tweets. Someone writing about Miles Davis, for instance, will tag his name #Miles. Anyone coming after will be able to find all the tweets dealing with Miles. (You don't have to wade through phrases like "miles to go before I sleep" or "I'd go a million miles for one of your smiles.")

Tech for Luddites, a valuable online resource ("Providing tips, tricks, and 10
techniques for navigating the digital world"), says hashtags allow tweeters to build interest-based communities. It's heartening that this function has been created spontaneously, unplanned by the Twitter hierarchy—just as, long ago, copyist monks in monasteries invented their own working language.

This year *GQ* magazine, a major arbiter of the cool, has anointed # "symbol of the year." *GQ* explains: "Hashtags have changed the way we think, communicate, process information. # is everywhere." What we have here is one of the great comeback stories in the history of competitive punctuation. Today, & © and ® have been left in the dust (of course @ retains its status in e-mail).

And what about the name, octothorpe? It's been replaced, obviously, but there's no reason to be upset. Change is the law of usage. That term now becomes, at least for the immediate future, a historical artifact. Its own history will be the subject of discussion for generations to come, whenever punctuation geeks gather.

It was born somewhere in the Bell system in the 1970s, when touchtone became established. The first half of the name was easy, though rich in cultural reference. Since the # has eight points the name fell within the order of eight, where an eight-sided figure is an octagon, a sea creature with eight suckered arms is an octopus, eight notes are an octave and octopush (an underwater game played by two teams of scuba divers pushing a lead puck on the bottom of a swimming pool) originally had eight players a side.

And where did "thorpe" come from? The *American Heritage Dictionary* says it honours James Edward Oglethorpe, the 18th-century British general who helped found the colony of Georgia in 1732. A more popular story has an engineer at Bell Labs deciding to honour Jim Thorpe, an Indian athlete who won the pentathlon and decathlon for the U.S. at the 1912 Olympics; he had his gold medals taken from him when his background as a professional athlete was disclosed, a decision that was reversed three decades after his death.

A third explanation was endorsed in 1996 by the *New Scientist,* an ex- 15
cellent journal in Britain. On ancient maps you can sometimes find the #

used to indicate the presence of a village; it looks like a primitive plan of eight fields of identical size, with a village square in the middle. It's possible that octothorpe derives from the Old Norse word for village, which survives today in some British town names, such as Scunthorpe in North Lincolnshire.

The fourth story, backed by evidence as strong as the sources for the other three, emerged in 2006, a year after an earlier column I wrote on the octothorpe. It blames a weird form of anonymous malice perpetrated by Bell Labs engineers (people named Schaak, Uthlaut, Asplund and Eby) who devised a sound that speakers of various languages would find difficult to pronounce. Probably this etymological mystery will go unsolved and we'll never know the truth.

Through all these troubled times, we octothorpe supporters remained loyal, like hockey fans who wear Maple Leafs sweaters despite all the years of pain. Even though Punctuacon is a fictional organization (though metaphorically vibrant), you can understand why the members of our little band were pleased to raise a glass to the hash mark in its new life on Twitter.

Analyze

1. Explain the effect of Fulford's first four paragraphs. What idea do they establish? How does that idea serve the rest of the article?
2. Consider Fulford's characterization of the hashtag on Twitter: "It's heartening that this function has been created spontaneously, unplanned by the Twitter hierarchy—just as, long ago, copyist monks in monasteries invented their own working language." Why do you think he's heartened by the spontaneous role? Why is it good that the Twitter hierarchy didn't plan on the function of #?
3. Fulford gives several versions of the octothorpe's history. What is the purpose of the different versions? What idea do they serve or support?
4. Fulford values the tradition of language but he also seems to value change. Identify a passage that shows Fulford's values—a place where he accepts change yet celebrates the history of language.
5. Explain what assumptions or beliefs Fulford's article shares with Steven D. Krause's, "Living Within Social Networks."

Explore

1. Do you tweet? Why or why not?
2. Are you a "tech Luddite?" Why or why not?
3. Fulford says, "Change is the law of usage." What other linguistic change has occurred in your lifetime or at least recently enough that your parents recall a different usage? Explain the change—and why you think it happened.
4. What is the role of punctuation in a culture? What does it do besides regulate language? What quieter, more subtle, functions does it have?
5. What's your personal role in the maintenance of English punctuation? Are you obedient, transgressive, unconcerned, dismissive, ignorant, or passive? Explain your role in detail.

Roger Scruton
Hiding Behind the Screen

A philosopher, essayist, critic, novelist, and poet, Roger Scruton serves as a scholar at the American Enterprise Institute, a visiting professor at both Oxford University and at the University of St. Andrews in Scotland. The author of numerous books, including *The Face of God: The Gifford Lectures* and *How to Think Seriously About the Planet: The Case for an Environmental Conservatism* (both 2012), he is currently exploring the influence of neuroscience on culture. In the following essay, which was adapted from a lecture, Scruton considers the limitations of human development in online contexts.

Human relations, and the self-image of the human being, have been profoundly affected by the Internet and by the ease with which images of other people can be summoned to the computer screen to become the objects of emotional attention. How should we conceptualize this change, and what is its effect on the psychic condition of those most given to constructing their world of interests and relationships through the screen? Is this change as damaging as many would have us believe, undermining our capacity for real relationships and placing a mere fantasy of relatedness in their stead? Or is it relatively harmless, as unproblematic as speaking to a friend on the telephone?

First, we should make some distinctions. We all now use the computer to send messages to our friends and to others with whom we have dealings. This sort of communication is not different in any fundamental respect from the old practice of letter writing, except for its speed. Of course, we should not regard speed as a trivial feature. The rapidity of modern communications does not merely accelerate the process whereby relationships are formed and severed; it inevitably changes how those relationships are conducted and understood. Absence is less painful with the Internet and the telephone, but it also loses some of its poignancy; moreover, e-mails are seldom composed as carefully as letters, since the very slowness with which a letter makes its way to its destination prompts us to put more of our feelings into the words. Still, e-mail is reality, not virtual reality, and the changes it has brought about are changes in real communication between real people.

Nor does the existence of social networks like Facebook, which are also for the most part real communication between real people, involve any attempt simply to substitute a virtual reality for the actual one. On the contrary, they are parasitic on the real relationships they foster, and which they alter in large part by encouraging people to put themselves on display, and in turn to become voyeurs of the displays of others. Some might claim that the existence of these networking sites provides a social and psychological benefit, helping those who shy away from presenting themselves directly to the world to gain a public place and identity. These sites also enable people to keep in touch with a wide circle of friends and colleagues, thereby increasing the range of their affections, and filling the world with goodwill and happy feelings.

Yet already something new is entering the world of human relations with these innocent-seeming sites. There is a novel ease with which people can make contact with each other through the screen. No more need to get up from your desk and make the journey to your friend's house. No more need for weekly meetings, or the circle of friends in the downtown restaurant or bar. All those effortful ways of making contact can be dispensed with: a touch of the keyboard and you are there, where you wanted to be, on the site that defines your friends. But can this be real friendship, when it is pursued and developed in such facile and costless ways?

Friendship and Control

Real friendship shows itself in action and affection. The real friend is the 5
one who comes to the rescue in your hour of need; who is there with comfort in adversity and who shares with you his own success. This is hard to do on the screen—the screen, after all, is primarily a locus of information, and is only a place of action insofar as communication is a form of action. Only words, and not hands or the things they carry, can reach from it to comfort the sufferer, to ward off an enemy's blows, or to provide any of the tangible assets of friendship in a time of need. It is arguable that the more people satisfy their need for companionship through relationships carried out on the screen, the less will they develop friendships of that other kind, the kind that offers help and comfort in the real trials of human life. Friendships that are carried out primarily on the screen cannot easily be lifted off it, and when they are so lifted, there is no guarantee that they will take any strain. Indeed, it is precisely their cost-free, screen-friendly character that attracts many people to them—so much so, students of mine tell me, that they fear addiction, and often have to forbid themselves to go to their Facebook account for days on end, in order to get on with their real lives and their real relationships.

What we are witnessing is a change in the *attention* that mediates and gives rise to friendship. In the once normal conditions of human contact, people became friends by being in each other's presence, understanding all the many subtle signals, verbal and bodily, whereby another testifies to his character, emotions, and intentions, and building affection and trust in tandem. Attention was fixed on the other—on his face, words, and gestures. And his nature as an embodied person was the focus of the friendly feelings that he inspired. People building friendship in this way are strongly aware that they appear to the other as the other appears to them. The other's face is a mirror in which they see their own. Precisely because attention is fixed on the other there is an opportunity for self-knowledge and self-discovery, for that expanding freedom in the presence of the other which is one of the joys of human life. The object of friendly feelings looks back at you, and freely responds to your free activity, amplifying both your awareness and his own. As traditionally conceived, friendship was ruled by the maxim "know thyself."

When attention is fixed on the other as mediated by the screen, however, there is a marked shift in emphasis. For a start, I have my finger on the button; at any moment I can turn the image off, or click to arrive at some new encounter. The other is free in his *own* space, but he is not really free in *my* space, over which I am the ultimate arbiter. I am not risking myself in the friendship to nearly the same extent as I risk myself when I meet the other face to face. Of course, the other may so grip my attention with his messages, images, and requests that I stay glued to the screen. Nevertheless, it is ultimately a *screen* that I am glued to, and not the face that I see in it. All interaction with the other is at a distance, and whether I am affected by it becomes to some extent a matter of my own choosing.

In this screenful form of conducting relationships, I enjoy a power over the other person of which he himself is not really aware—since he is not aware of how much I wish to retain him in the space before me. And the power I have over him he has too over me, just as I am denied the same freedom in his space that he is denied in mine. He, too, therefore, will not risk himself; he appears on the screen only on condition of retaining that ultimate control himself. This is something I know about him that he knows that I know—and vice versa. There grows between us a reduced-risk encounter, in which each is aware that the other is fundamentally *withheld,* sovereign within his impregnable cyber-castle.

But that is not the only way in which cyber-relationships are affected by the medium of their formation. For instance, while "messaging" is still very much alive on Facebook, much of it is depersonalized in nature: the use of private messages has for many been supplanted by posting messages on a friend's public "Wall," meaning that the entire network is now participant in the communiqué. And while the Wall post still maintains the semblance of interpersonal contact, probably the most common form of communication on Facebook is the "status update," a message that is broadcast from one person to everyone (or, put another way, to no one in particular).

10 All of these communications, along with everything on the screen, appear in competition with whatever else might be called up by the mouse. You "click on" your friend, as you might click on a news item or a music video. He is one of the many products on display. Friendship with him, and relationships generally, belong in the category of amusements and distractions, a commodity that may be chosen, or not, depending on the rival goods. This contributes to a radical demotion of the personal relationship. Your friendships are no longer special to you and definitive of your moral

life: they are amusements, things that have no real life of their own but borrow their life from your interest in them—what the Marxists would call "fetishes."

There is a strong argument to be made that the Facebook experience, which has attracted millions of people from all around the world, is an antidote to shyness, a way in which people otherwise cripplingly intimidated by the venture outwards into society are able to overcome their disability and enjoy the web of affectionate relationships on which so much of our happiness depends. But there is an equally strong argument that the Facebook experience, to the extent that it is supplanting the physical realm of human relationships, hypostatizes shyness, retains its principal features, while substituting an ersatz kind of affection for the real affection that shyness fears. For by placing a screen between yourself and the friend, while retaining ultimate control over what appears on that screen, you also hide from the real encounter—denying the other the power and the freedom to challenge you in your deeper nature and to call on you here and now to take responsibility for yourself and for him.

I was taught growing up that shyness (unlike modesty) is not a virtue but a defect, and that it comes from placing too high a value on yourself—a value that forbids you to risk yourself in the encounter with others. By removing the *real* risks from interpersonal encounters, the Facebook experience might encourage a kind of narcissism, a self-regarding posture in the midst of what should have been other-regarding friendship. In effect, there may be nothing more than the display of self, the others listed on the website counting for nothing in themselves.

Freedom Requires Context

In its normal occurrence, the Facebook encounter is still an encounter—however attenuated—between real people. But increasingly, the screen is taking over—ceasing to be a medium of communication between real people who exist elsewhere, and becoming the place where people finally achieve reality, the only place where they relate in any coherent way to others. This next stage is evident in the "avatar" phenomenon, in which people create virtual characters in virtual worlds as proxies for themselves, so enabling their controllers to live in complete self-complacency behind the screen, exposed to no danger and yet enjoying a kind of substitute affection through the adventures of their cyber-ego.

The game *Second Life* offers a virtual world and invites you to enter it in the form of an avatar constructed from its collection of templates. It has its own currency, in which purchases can be made in its own stores. It rents spaces to avatars as their homes and businesses. By late 2009, the company that created *Second Life* announced that its user base had collectively logged more than a billion hours in the system and had conducted business transactions worth more than a billion dollars.

Second Life also provides opportunities for "social" action, with social positions achieved by merit—or, at any rate, virtual merit. In this way people can enjoy, through their avatars, cost-free versions of the social emotions, and can become heroes of "compassion," without lifting a finger in the real world. In one notorious incident in 2007, a man attempted to sue an avatar for theft of his *Second Life* intellectual property. The property itself was an "adult entertainment" product—one among many such *Second Life* products now available that enable your cyber-ego to realize your wildest fantasies at no risk to yourself. There have been many reports of couples who have never met in person conducting adulterous affairs entirely in cyberspace; they usually show no guilt towards their spouses, and in fact proudly display their emotions as though they had achieved some kind of moral breakthrough by ensuring that it was only their avatars, and not they themselves, that ended up in bed together.

Most people probably would see this as an unhealthy state of affairs. It is one thing to place a screen between yourself and the world; it is another thing to inhabit the world on that screen as the primary sphere of your relationships. In vesting one's emotional life in the adventures of an avatar, one retreats completely from real relationships. Instead of being a means to augment relationships that exist outside of it, the Internet could become the sole arena of social life—but an unreal life involving unreal people. The thought of this reawakens all of those once-fashionable claims of alienation and the fetishism of commodities of which Marx and his followers accused capitalist society. The nerd controlling the avatar has essentially "placed his being outside of himself," as they would have put it.

The origin of those critiques lies in an idea of Hegel's, an idea of enduring importance that is constantly resurging in new guises, especially in the writings of psychologists concerned with mapping the contours of ordinary happiness. The idea is this: we human beings fulfill ourselves through our own free actions, and through the consciousness that these actions bring of our individual worth. But we are not free in a state of nature, nor do we, outside the world of human relations, have the kind of consciousness of self that allows us to value and intend our own fulfillment. Freedom is not reducible to the unhindered choices that even an animal might enjoy; nor is self-consciousness simply a matter of the pleasurable immersion in immediate experiences, like the rat pressing endlessly on the pleasure switch. Freedom involves an active engagement with the world, in which opposition is encountered and overcome, risks are taken and satisfactions weighed: it is, in short, an exercise of practical reason, in pursuit of goals whose value must justify the efforts needed to obtain them. Likewise, self-consciousness, in its fully realized form, involves not merely an openness to present experience, but a sense of my own existence *as an individual,* with plans and projects that might be fulfilled or frustrated, and with a clear conception of what *I* am doing, for what purpose, and with what hope of happiness.

All those ideas are contained in the term first introduced by the philosopher Johann Gottlieb Fichte to denote the inner goal of a free personal life: *Selbstbestimmung,* self-determination or self-certainty. Hegel's crucial claim is that the life of freedom and self-certainty can only be obtained through others. I become fully myself only in contexts which compel me to recognize that I am another in others' eyes. I do not acquire my freedom and individuality and then, as it were, try them out in the world of human relations. It is only by entering that world, with its risks, conflicts, and responsibilities, that I come to know myself as free, to enjoy my own perspective and individuality, and to become a fulfilled person among persons.

In the *Phenomenology of Spirit* and the *Philosophy of Right,* Hegel tells many pleasing and provocative parables about the way in which the subject achieves freedom and fulfillment through his *Entäusserung*—his objectification—in the world of others. The status of these parables—whether they are arguments or allegories, conceptual analyses or psychological generalizations—has always been a matter of dispute. But few psychologists now would dispute the fundamental claim that underpins them, which is that the freedom and fulfillment of the self come about only through the recognition of the other. Without others, my freedom is an empty cipher. And recognition of the other involves taking full responsibility for my own existence as the individual who I am.

In his efforts to "set Hegel on his feet," the young Marx drew an important contrast between the true freedom that comes to us through relationships with other subjects and the hidden enslavement that comes when our 20 ventures outwards are not towards subjects but towards objects. In other words, he suggested, we must distinguish the *realization* of the self, in free relations with others, from the *alienation* of the self in the system of things. That is the core of his critique of private property, and it is a critique that is as much bound up with allegory and storytelling as the original Hegelian arguments. In later writings the critique is transformed into the theory of "fetishism," according to which people lose their freedom through making fetishes of commodities. A fetish is something that is animated by a *transferred* life. The consumer in a capitalist society, according to Marx, transfers his life into the commodities that bewitch him, and so loses that life—becoming a slave to commodities precisely through seeing the market in goods rather than the free interactions of people; as the place where his desires are brokered and fulfilled.

These critiques of property and the market, it should be noted, do not merit endorsement. They are flamboyant offshoots of a Hegelian philosophy which, properly understood, endorses free transactions in a market as much as it endorses free relations between people generally—indeed, it sees the one as an application of the other. Rather, the crucial idea from which we may still learn is that of the *Entäusserung*, the realization of the self through responsible relations with others. This is the core contribution of German Romantic philosophy to the understanding of the modern condition, and it is an idea that has direct application to the problems that we see emerging in our new world of social life conducted on the Internet. In the sense in which freedom is a value, freedom is also an artifact that comes into being through the mutual interaction of people. This mutual interaction is what raises us from the animal condition to the personal condition, enabling us to take responsibility for our lives and actions, to evaluate our goals and character, and both to understand the nature of personal fulfillment and to set about desiring and intending it.

This process of raising ourselves above the animal condition is crucial, as the Hegelians emphasized, to the growth of the human subject as a self-knowing agent, capable of entertaining and acting from reasons, and with a developed first-person perspective and a sense of his reality as one subject among others. It is a process that depends upon real conflicts and real resolutions, in a shared public space where each of us is fully accountable for what he is and does. Anything that interferes with that process, by undermining the growth of interpersonal relations, by confiscating responsibility, or by preventing or discouraging an individual from making long-term rational choices and adopting a concrete vision of his own fulfillment, is an evil. It may be an unavoidable evil; but it is an evil all the same, and one that we should strive to abolish if we can.

Television and the Trend Toward Self-Alienation

Transferring our social lives onto the Internet is only one of the ways in which we damage or retreat from this process of self-realization. Long before that temptation arose (and preparing the way for it) was the lure of television, which corresponds exactly to the Hegelian and Marxist critique of the fetish—an inanimate thing in which we invest our life, and so lose it. Of course we retain ultimate control over the television: we can turn it off. But people don't, on the whole; they remain fixed to the screen in many of those moments when they might otherwise be building relationships through conversation, activities, conflicts, and projects. The television has, for a vast number of our fellow human beings, destroyed family meals, home cooking, hobbies, homework, study, and family games. It has rendered many people largely inarticulate, and deprived them of the simple ways of making direct conversational contact with their fellows. This is not a question of TV's "dumbing down" of thought and imagination, or its manipulation of people's desires and interests through brazen imagery. Those features are familiar enough, and the constant target of despairing criticism. Nor am I referring only to its addictive quality—though research by the psychologists Mihaly Csikszentmihalyi and Robert Kubey offers convincing evidence that TV is addictive in the same way as gambling and drugs.

The concern is rather the nature of television as a replacement for human relationships. By watching people interacting on TV sitcoms, the junkie is able to dispense with interactions of his own. Those energies and interests that would otherwise be focused on others—in storytelling, arguing, singing together, or playing games; in walking, talking, eating, and acting—are consumed on the screen, in vicarious lives that involve no engagement of the viewer's own moral equipment. And that equipment therefore atrophies.

We see this everywhere in modern life, but nowhere more vividly than 25
in the students who arrive in our colleges. These divide roughly into two

kinds: those from TV-sodden homes, and those who have grown up talking. Those of the first kind tend to be reticent, inarticulate, given to aggression when under stress, unable to tell a story or express a view, and seriously hampered when it comes to taking responsibility for a task, an activity, or a relationship. Those of the second kind are the ones who step forward with ideas, who go out to their fellows, who radiate the kind of freedom and adventurousness that makes learning a pleasure and risk a challenge. Since these students have had atypical upbringings, they are prone to be subjects of mockery. But they have a head start over their TV-addled contemporaries. The latter can still be freed from their vice; university athletics, theater, music, and so on can help to marginalize TV in campus life. But in many other public or semi-public spaces, television has now become a near necessity: it flickers in the background, reassuring those who have bestowed their life on it that their life goes on.

These criticisms of television parallel criticisms of the "fetishizing" nature of mass culture made by Max Horkheimer, Theodor Adorno, and other members of the neo-Marxist Frankfurt school. Interestingly enough, the Frankfurt school ideas have been recently put to use in criticizing another way in which we can now achieve instant and cost-free stimulation: the iPod. In his 2008 book *Sound Moves,* Michael Bull draws on the "cultural theory" of Horkheimer and Adorno to argue that, thanks to the iPod, urban space has in many ways ceased to be public space and has become fragmented and privatized, each person retreating into his own inviolable sphere and losing his dependency upon and interest in his fellows. This process not only alienates people from each other, it enables people to retain control over their sensations, and so shut out the world of chance, risk, and change.

Although there is good reason to be sympathetic with Bull's argument, as well as those original criticisms of the consumer economy made by Adorno and Horkheimer, their criticisms had the wrong target: namely, the system of capitalist production and the emerging culture industry which forms part of it. The object of Adorno and company's scorn was the substitution of risk-free and addictive pleasures for the pleasures of understanding, freedom, and relationship. They may have been right in thinking that the culture industry has a propensity to favor the first kind of pleasure, for this kind of pleasure is easily packaged and marketed. But take away the healthy ways of growing up through relationships and the addictive pleasures will automatically take over, even where there is no culture industry to exploit them—as we witnessed in communist Europe. And, just like the theater, the media of mass culture can also be used positively (by those with critical judgment) to enhance and deepen our real sympathies. The correct response to the ills of television is not to attack those who manufacture televisions or who stock them with rubbish: it is to concentrate on the kind of education that makes it possible to take a critical approach to television, so as to demand real insight and real emotion, rather than kitsch, Disney, or porn. And the same is true for the iPod.

To work towards this critical approach means getting clear about the virtues of *direct* rather than vicarious relations. Why, as Villiers de l'Isle-Adam said, do we go to the trouble of living rather than asking our servants to do it for us? Why do we criticize those who eat burgers on the couch, while life plays out its pointless drama on the screen? Get clear about these questions, and we can begin to educate children in the art of turning off the television. The avatar can therefore be seen as merely the latest point in a process of alienation whereby people learn to "put their lives outside of themselves," to make their lives into playthings over which they retain complete, though in some way deeply specious, control. (They control physically what controls them psychologically.) And this is why it is so tempting to look back to those old Hegelian and Marxist theories. For they were premised on the view that we become free only by "moving outwards," embodying our freedom in shared activities and mutually responsible relations. And the Hegelians distinguished a true from a false way of "moving outwards": one in which we gain our freedom by giving it real and objective form, as opposed to one in which we lose it by investing it in objects that alienate us from our inner life. Those theories show how the thing that we (or at any rate the followers of Hegel) most value in human life—self-realization in a condition of freedom—is separated by a thin dividing line from the thing which destroys us—self-alienation in a condition of bondage.

Impressive though they are, however, the Hegelian-Marxist theories are shot through with metaphor and speculation; they are not anchored in empirical research or explanatory hypotheses; they rely for their plausibility entirely on *a priori* thoughts about the nature of freedom, and about the metaphysical distinction between subject and object. If they are to be of use to us we will have to translate them into a more down-to-earth and practical language—one that will tell us how our children should be educated, if we are to bring them out from behind the screen.

The Necessary Risks of Life Off the Screen

30 We must come to an understanding, then, of what is at stake in the current worries concerning the Internet, avatars, and life on the screen. The first issue at stake is risk. We are rational beings, endowed with practical as well as theoretical reasoning. And our practical reasoning develops through our confrontation with risk and uncertainty. To a large extent, life on the screen is risk-free: when we click to enter some new domain, we risk nothing immediate in the way of physical danger, and our accountability to others and risk of emotional embarrassment is attenuated. This is vividly apparent in the case of pornography—and the addictive nature of pornography is familiar to all who have to work in counseling those whom it has brought to a state of distraught dependency. The porn addict gains some of the benefits of sexual excitement, without any of the normal costs; but the costs are part of what sex means, and by avoiding them, one is destroying in oneself the capacity for sexual attachment.

This freedom from risk is one of the most significant features of *Second Life,* and it is also present (to an extent) on social networking sites like Facebook. One can enter and leave relationships conducted solely via the screen without any embarrassment, remaining anonymous or operating under a pseudonym, hiding behind an avatar or a false photograph of oneself. A person can decide to "kill" his screen identity at any time, and he will suffer nothing as a consequence. Why, then, trouble to enter the world of real encounters, when this easy substitute is available? And when the substitute becomes a habit, the virtues needed for the real encounter do not develop.

It should not go unmentioned that the habit of reducing risk is one that is widespread in our society, and indeed encouraged by government. An unhealthy obsession with health and an unsafe craze for safety have confiscated many of the risks that previous generations have not merely taken for granted but incorporated into the process of moral education. From the padding of children's playgrounds and the mandating of helmets for skateboarders to the criminalization of wine at the family table, the health-and-safety fanatics have surrounded us at every point with a web of prohibitions, while encouraging the belief that risks are not the concern of the individual but a matter of public policy. Children are not, on the whole, encouraged to risk themselves in physical ways; and it is not surprising if they are reluctant, in consequence, to risk themselves in emotional ways either.

But it is unlikely that this is either the source of risk-avoidance in human relationships, or a real indication of the right and the wrong way to proceed. No doubt children need physical risk and adventure if they are to develop as responsible people, with their full quota of courage, prudence, and practical wisdom. But risks of the soul are unlike risks of the body; you don't learn to manage them by being exposed to them. As we know, children exposed to sexual predation do not learn to deal with it but, on the contrary, tend to acquire the habit of *not* dealing with it: of altogether closing off a genuine emotional engagement with their sexuality, reducing it to a raw, angry bargaining, learning to treat themselves as objects and losing the capacity to risk themselves in love. Much modern sex education, which teaches that the only risks of sex are medical, exposes children to the same kind of harm, encouraging them to enter the world of sexual relations without the capacity to give or receive erotic love, and so learning to see sex as lying outside the realm of lasting relationships—a source of pleasure rather than love.

In human relations, risk avoidance means the avoidance of *accountability*, the refusal to stand *judged* in another's eyes, the refusal to come *face to face* with another person, to give oneself in whatever measure to him or her, and so to run the risk of rejection. Accountability is not something we should avoid; it is something we need to learn. Without it we can never acquire either the capacity to love or the virtue of justice. Other people will remain for us merely complex devices, to be negotiated in the way that animals are negotiated, for our own advantage and without opening the possibility of mutual judgment. Justice is the ability to see the other as having a claim on you, as being a free subject just as you are, and as demanding your accountability. To acquire this virtue you must learn the habit of face-to-face encounters, in which you solicit the other's consent and cooperation rather than imposing your will. The retreat behind the screen is a way of retaining control over the encounter, while minimizing the need to acknowledge the other's point of view. It involves setting your will outside yourself, as a feature of virtual reality, while not risking it as it must be risked, if others are truly to be encountered. To encounter another person in his freedom is to acknowledge his sovereignty and his right: it is to recognize that the developing situation is no longer within your exclusive control, but that you are caught up by it, made real and accountable in the other's eyes by the same considerations that make him real and accountable in yours.

35 In sexual encounters it is surely obvious that this process of "going out" to the other must occur if there is to be a genuine gift of love, and if the sexual act is to be something more than the friction of body parts. Learning to "go out" in this way is a complex moral process, which cannot be simplified without setting sex outside the process of psychological attachment. And it seems clear—though it is by no means easy to give final proof of it—that attachment is increasingly at risk, and that the cause of this is precisely that sexual pleasure comes without justice or commitment. It is surely plausible to suggest that when we rely on the screen as the forum of personal development, we learn habits of relationship without the discipline of accountability, so that sex, when one arrives at it (as even the screen addict may eventually), will be regarded in the same narcissistic way as the vicarious excitements through which it has been rehearsed. It will occur in that indefinable "elsewhere" from which the soul takes flight, even in the moment of pleasure.

Perhaps we can survive in a world of virtual relations; but it is not a world into which children can easily enter, except as intruders. Avatars may reproduce on the screen: but they will not fill the world with real human children. And the cyber-parents of these avatar-children, deprived of all that makes people grow as moral beings—of risk, embarrassment, suffering, and love—will shrink to mere points of view, on a world in which they do not really occur.

Analyze

1. Scruton begins his article by making "some distinctions" (in paragraphs 2–4). Explain those distinctions and why they are critical to his argument about human relationships.
2. As best you can, summarize Scruton's claim in each section: Friendship and Control, Freedom Requires Context, Television and the Trend Toward Self-Alienation, and The Necessary Risks of Life Off the Screen. Try to capture the full dimension of his points.
3. In paragraph 10, Scruton explains the idea of a "fetish." Explain how this idea fits into his overall argument about social media.
4. In paragraph 11, Scruton describes an argument for the value of Facebook. Halfway through the paragraph, he then responds to that argument with an "equally strong argument." This move, often called a *turnabout paragraph*, allows Scruton to counter opposing positions. Find another turnabout paragraph and explain the opposing position that Scruton counters.

5. Scruton borrows some concepts from 19th- and 20th-century philosophers (such as Hegel, Marx, and Adorno). Focus on one of those philosophers and explain his role in Scruton's argument.

Explore

1. In his first sentence, Scruton explains that humans are used as "objects of emotional attention" on the Internet. Consider this phrase. What does it make you think or feel? What argument can you sense lurking inside of the phrase?
2. Scruton explains that Facebook removes "*real* risk" from friendship. How is this true or false? What have you witnessed or read that supports or contradicts this point?
3. Scruton claims that "e-mail is reality, not virtual reality." What does he mean? Why does he state it in this way?
4. In his conclusion, Scruton claims that "risk, embarrassment, suffering, and love" make people grow into "moral beings." Examine each of these phenomena: risk, embarrassment, suffering, and love. How do they prompt us to become moral beings?
5. Look up *phenomenology* online and then describe why it might be an important idea in discussions about virtual life.

James Gleick

What Defines a Meme?

Award-winning author and Pulitzer Prize finalist James Gleick has published numerous books, including *The Information: A History, a Theory, a Flood* (2011), from which the following essay was adapted. A former editor and reporter for *The New York Times*, he founded an Internet service in 1993 that launched the first full-featured graphical user interface to connect online. This article originally appeared in *Smithsonian* magazine, which was "created for modern, well-rounded individuals with diverse interests." Here, Gleick considers the ways in which culture reproduces itself, both biologically and virtually.

"What lies at the heart of every living thing is not a fire, not warm breath, not a 'spark of life.' It is information, words, instructions," Richard Dawkins declared in 1986. Already one of the world's foremost evolutionary biologists, he had caught the spirit of a new age. The cells of an organism are nodes in a richly interwoven communications network, transmitting and receiving, coding and decoding. Evolution itself embodies an ongoing exchange of information between organism and environment. "If you want to understand life," Dawkins wrote, "don't think about vibrant, throbbing gels and oozes, think about information technology."

We have become surrounded by information technology; our furniture includes iPods and plasma displays, and our skills include texting and Googling. But our capacity to understand the role of information has been sorely taxed. "TMI," we say. Stand back, however, and the past does come back into focus.

The rise of information theory aided and abetted a new view of life. The genetic code—no longer a mere metaphor—was being deciphered. Scientists spoke grandly of the *biosphere:* an entity composed of all the earth's life-forms, teeming with information, replicating and evolving. And biologists, having absorbed the methods and vocabulary of communications science, went further to make their own contributions to the understanding of information itself.

Jacques Monod, the Parisian biologist who shared a Nobel Prize in 1965 for working out the role of messenger RNA in the transfer of genetic information, proposed an analogy: just as the biosphere stands above the world of nonliving matter, so an "abstract kingdom" rises above the biosphere. The denizens of this kingdom? Ideas.

5 "Ideas have retained some of the properties of organisms," he wrote. "Like them, they tend to perpetuate their structure and to breed; they too can fuse, recombine, segregate their content; indeed they too can evolve, and in this evolution selection must surely play an important role."

Ideas have "spreading power," he noted—"infectivity, as it were"—and some more than others. An example of an infectious idea might be a religious ideology that gains sway over a large group of people. The American neurophysiologist Roger Sperry had put forward a similar notion several years earlier, arguing that ideas are "just as real" as the neurons they inhabit. Ideas have power, he said:

> Ideas cause ideas and help evolve new ideas. They interact with each other and with other mental forces in the same brain, in neighboring

> brains, and thanks to global communication, in far distant, foreign brains. And they also interact with the external surroundings to produce in toto a burstwise advance in evolution that is far beyond anything to hit the evolutionary scene yet.

Monod added, "I shall not hazard a theory of the selection of ideas." There was no need. Others were willing.

Dawkins made his own jump from the evolution of genes to the evolution of ideas. For him the starring role belongs to the replicator, and it scarcely matters whether replicators were made of nucleic acid. His rule is "All life evolves by the differential survival of replicating entities." Wherever there is life, there must be replicators. Perhaps on other worlds replicators could arise in a silicon-based chemistry—or in no chemistry at all.

What would it mean for a replicator to exist without chemistry? "I think that a new kind of replicator has recently emerged on this very planet," Dawkins proclaimed near the end of his first book, *The Selfish Gene,* in 1976. "It is staring us in the face. It is still in its infancy, still drifting clumsily about in its primeval soup, but already it is achieving evolutionary change at a rate that leaves the old gene panting far behind." That "soup" is human culture; the vector of transmission is language, and the spawning ground is the brain.

For this bodiless replicator itself, Dawkins proposed a name. He called 10
it the meme, and it became his most memorable invention, far more influential than his selfish genes or his later proselytizing against religiosity. "Memes propagate themselves in the meme pool by leaping from brain to brain via a process which, in the broad sense, can be called imitation," he wrote. They compete with one another for limited resources: brain time or bandwidth. They compete most of all for *attention.* For example:

> *Ideas.* Whether an idea arises uniquely or reappears many times, it may thrive in the meme pool or it may dwindle and vanish. The belief in God is an example Dawkins offers—an ancient idea, replicating itself not just in words but in music and art. The belief that Earth orbits the Sun is no less a meme, competing with others for survival. (Truth may be a helpful quality for a meme, but it is only one among many.)
>
> *Tunes.* This tune has spread for centuries across several continents.
>
> *Catchphrases.* One text snippet, "What hath God wrought?" appeared early and spread rapidly in more than one medium. Another,

"Read my lips," charted a peculiar path through late 20th-century America. "Survival of the fittest" is a meme that, like other memes, mutates wildly ("survival of the fattest"; "survival of the sickest"; "survival of the fakest"; "survival of the twittest").

Images. In Isaac Newton's lifetime, no more than a few thousand people had any idea what he looked like, even though he was one of England's most famous men. Yet now millions of people have quite a clear idea—based on replicas of copies of rather poorly painted portraits. Even more pervasive and indelible are the smile of Mona Lisa, *The Scream* of Edvard Munch and the silhouettes of various fictional extraterrestrials. These are memes, living a life of their own, independent of any physical reality. "This may not be what George Washington looked like then," a tour guide was overheard saying of the Gilbert Stuart portrait at the Metropolitan Museum of Art, "but this is what he looks like now." Exactly.

Memes emerge in brains and travel outward, establishing beachheads on paper and celluloid and silicon and anywhere else information can go. They are not to be thought of as elementary particles but as organisms. The number three is not a meme; nor is the color blue, nor any simple thought, any more than a single nucleotide can be a gene. Memes are complex units, distinct and memorable—units with staying power.

Also, an object is not a meme. The hula hoop is not a meme; it is made of plastic, not of bits. When this species of toy spread worldwide in a mad epidemic in 1958, it was the product, the physical manifestation, of a meme, or memes: the craving for hula hoops; the swaying, swinging, twirling skill set of hula-hooping. The hula hoop itself is a meme vehicle. So, for that matter, is each human hula hooper—a strikingly effective meme vehicle, in the sense neatly explained by the philosopher Daniel Dennett: "A wagon with spoked wheels carries not only grain or freight from place to place; it carries the brilliant idea of a wagon with spoked wheels from mind to mind." Hula hoopers did that for the hula hoop's memes—and in 1958 they found a new transmission vector, broadcast television, sending its messages immeasurably faster and farther than any wagon. The moving image of the hula hooper seduced new minds by hundreds, and then by thousands, and then by millions. The meme is not the dancer but the dance.

For most of our biological history memes existed fleetingly; their main mode of transmission was the one called "word of mouth." Lately, however, they have managed to adhere in solid substance: clay tablets, cave walls, paper sheets. They achieve longevity through our pens and printing presses, magnetic tapes and optical disks. They spread via broadcast towers and digital networks. Memes may be stories, recipes, skills, legends or fashions. We copy them, one person at a time. Alternatively, in Dawkins' meme-centered perspective, they copy themselves.

"I believe that, given the right conditions, replicators automatically band together to create systems, or machines, that carry them around and work to favor their continued replication," he wrote. This was not to suggest that memes are conscious actors; only that they are entities with interests that can be furthered by natural selection. Their interests are not our interests. "A meme," Dennett says, "is an information-packet with attitude." When we speak of *fighting for a principle* or *dying for an idea*, we may be more literal than we know.

Tinker, tailor, soldier, sailor. . . . Rhyme and rhythm help people remember bits of text. Or: rhyme and rhythm help bits of text get remembered. Rhyme and rhythm are qualities that aid a meme's survival, just as strength and speed aid an animal's. Patterned language has an evolutionary advantage. Rhyme, rhythm and reason—for reason, too, is a form of pattern. *I was promised on a time to have reason for my rhyme; from that time unto this season, I received nor rhyme nor reason.*

Like genes, memes have effects on the wide world beyond themselves. In some cases (the meme for making fire; for wearing clothes; for the resurrection of Jesus) the effects can be powerful indeed. As they broadcast their influence on the world, memes thus influence the conditions affecting their own chances of survival. The meme or memes comprising Morse code had strong positive feedback effects. Some memes have evident benefits for their human hosts ("Look before you leap," knowledge of CPR, belief in hand washing before cooking), but memetic success and genetic success are not the same. Memes can replicate with impressive virulence while leaving swaths of collateral damage—patent medicines and psychic surgery, astrology and Satanism, racist myths, superstitions and (a special case) computer viruses. In a way, these are the most interesting—the memes that thrive to their hosts' detriment, such as the idea that suicide bombers will find their reward in heaven.

Memes could travel wordlessly even before language was born. Plain mimicry is enough to replicate knowledge—how to chip an arrowhead or start a fire. Among animals, chimpanzees and gorillas are known to acquire behaviors by imitation. Some species of songbirds learn their songs, or at least song variants, after hearing them from neighboring birds (or, more recently, from ornithologists with audio players). Birds develop song repertoires and song dialects—in short, they exhibit a birdsong culture that predates human culture by eons. These special cases notwithstanding, for most of human history memes and language have gone hand in glove. (Clichés are memes.) Language serves as culture's first catalyst. It supersedes mere imitation, spreading knowledge by abstraction and encoding.

Perhaps the analogy with disease was inevitable. Before anyone understood anything of epidemiology, its language was applied to species of information. An emotion can be infectious, a tune catchy, a habit contagious. "From look to look, contagious through the crowd / The panic runs," wrote the poet James Thomson in 1730. Lust, likewise, according to Milton: "Eve, whose eye darted contagious fire." But only in the new millennium, in the time of global electronic transmission, has the identification become second nature. Ours is the age of virality: viral education, viral marketing, viral e-mail and video and networking. Researchers studying the Internet itself as a medium—crowdsourcing, collective attention, social networking and resource allocation—employ not only the language but also the mathematical principles of epidemiology.

One of the first to use the terms "viral text" and "viral sentences" seems to have been a reader of Dawkins named Stephen Walton of New York City, corresponding in 1981 with the cognitive scientist Douglas Hofstadter. Thinking logically—perhaps in the mode of a computer—Walton proposed simple self-replicating sentences along the lines of "Say me!" "Copy me!" and "If you copy me, I'll grant you three wishes!" Hofstadter, then a columnist for Scientific American, found the term "viral text" itself to be even catchier.

> Well, now, Walton's own viral text, as you can see here before your eyes, has managed to commandeer the facilities of a very powerful host—an entire magazine and printing press and distribution service. It has leapt aboard and is now—even as you read this viral sentence—propagating itself madly throughout the ideosphere!

Hofstadter gaily declared himself infected by the *meme* meme. 20

One source of resistance—or at least unease—was the shoving of us humans toward the wings. It was bad enough to say that a person is merely a gene's way of making more genes. Now humans are to be considered as vehicles for the propagation of memes, too. No one likes to be called a puppet. Dennett summed up the problem this way: "I don't know about you, but I am not initially attracted by the idea of my brain as a sort of dung heap in which the larvae of other people's ideas renew themselves, before sending out copies of themselves in an informational diaspora. . . . Who's in charge, according to this vision—we or our memes?"

He answered his own question by reminding us that, like it or not, we are seldom "in charge" of our own minds. He might have quoted Freud; instead he quoted Mozart (or so he thought): "In the night when I cannot sleep, thoughts crowd into my mind. . . . Whence and how do they come? I do not know and I have nothing to do with it."

Later Dennett was informed that this well-known quotation was not Mozart's after all. It had taken on a life of its own; it was a fairly successful meme.

For anyone taken with the idea of memes, the landscape was changing faster than Dawkins had imagined possible in 1976, when he wrote, "The computers in which memes live are human brains." By 1989, the time of the second edition of *The Selfish Gene,* having become an adept programmer himself, he had to amend that: "It was obviously predictable that manufactured electronic computers, too, would eventually play host to self-replicating patterns of information." Information was passing from one computer to another "when their owners pass floppy discs around," and he could see another phenomenon on the near horizon: computers connected in networks. "Many of them," he wrote, "are literally wired up together in electronic mail exchange. . . . It is a perfect milieu for self-replicating programs to flourish." Indeed, the Internet was in its birth throes. Not only did it provide memes with a nutrient-rich culture medium, it also gave wings to the *idea* of memes. *Meme* itself quickly became an Internet buzzword. Awareness of memes fostered their spread.

A notorious example of a meme that could not have emerged in pre- 25
Internet culture was the phrase "jumped the shark." Loopy self-reference characterized every phase of its existence. To jump the shark means to pass a peak of quality or popularity and begin an irreversible decline. The phrase

was thought to have been used first in 1985 by a college student named Sean J. Connolly, in reference to an episode of the television series "Happy Days" in which the character Fonzie (Henry Winkler), on water skis, jumps over a shark. The origin of the phrase requires a certain amount of explanation without which it could not have been initially understood. Perhaps for that reason, there is no recorded usage until 1997, when Connolly's roommate, Jon Hein, registered the domain name jumptheshark.com and created a web site devoted to its promotion. The web site soon featured a list of frequently asked questions:

> *Q. Did "jump the shark" originate from this web site, or did you create the site to capitalize on the phrase?*
>
> *A. This site went up December 24, 1997, and gave birth to the phrase "jump the shark." As the site continues to grow in popularity, the term has become more commonplace. The site is the chicken, the egg and now a Catch-22.*

It spread to more traditional media in the next year; Maureen Dowd devoted a column to explaining it in *The New York Times* in 2001; in 2002 the same newspaper's "On Language" columnist, William Safire, called it "the popular culture's phrase of the year"; soon after that, people were using the phrase in speech and in print without self-consciousness—no quotation marks or explanation—and eventually, inevitably, various cultural observers asked, "Has 'jump the shark' jumped the shark?" Like any good meme, it spawned mutations. The "jumping the shark" entry in Wikipedia advised in 2009, "See also: jumping the couch; nuking the fridge."

Is this science? In his 1983 column, Hofstadter proposed the obvious memetic label for such a discipline: *memetics.* The study of memes has attracted researchers from fields as far apart as computer science and microbiology. In bioinformatics, chain letters are an object of study. They are memes; they have evolutionary histories. The very purpose of a chain letter is replication; whatever else a chain letter may say, it embodies one message: *Copy me.* One student of chain-letter evolution, Daniel W. VanArsdale, listed many variants, in chain letters and even earlier texts: "Make seven copies of it exactly as it is written" (1902); "Copy this in full and send to nine friends" (1923); "And if any man shall take away from the words of the book of this prophecy, God shall take away his part out of the book of life" (Revelation 22:19). Chain letters flourished with the help of a new 19th-century technology: "carbonic paper," sandwiched between sheets of writing paper in stacks. Then carbon paper made a symbiotic partnership with another technology, the typewriter. Viral outbreaks of chain letters occurred all through the early 20th century. Two subsequent technologies, when their use became widespread, provided orders-of-magnitude boosts in chain-letter fecundity: photocopying (c. 1950) and e-mail (c. 1995).

Inspired by a chance conversation on a hike in the Hong Kong mountains, information scientists Charles H. Bennett from IBM in New York and Ming Li and Bin Ma from Ontario, Canada, began an analysis of a set of chain letters collected during the photocopier era. They had 33, all variants of a single letter, with mutations in the form of misspellings, omissions and transposed words and phrases. "These letters have passed from host to host, mutating and evolving," they reported in 2003.

> Like a gene, their average length is about 2,000 characters. Like a potent virus, the letter threatens to kill you and induces you to pass it on to your "friends and associates"—some variation of this letter has probably reached millions of people. Like an inheritable trait, it promises benefits for you and the people you pass it on to. Like genomes, chain letters undergo natural selection and sometimes parts even get transferred between coexisting "species."

Reaching beyond these appealing metaphors, the three researchers set out to use the letters as a "test bed" for algorithms used in evolutionary biology. The algorithms were designed to take the genomes of various modern creatures and work backward, by inference and deduction, to reconstruct their phylogeny—their evolutionary trees. If these mathematical methods worked with genes, the scientists suggested, they should work with chain letters, too. In both cases the researchers were able to verify mutation rates and relatedness measures.

Still, most of the elements of culture change and blur too easily to qual- 30
ify as stable replicators. They are rarely as neatly fixed as a sequence of DNA. Dawkins himself emphasized that he had never imagined founding anything like a new science of memetics. A peer-reviewed *Journal of Memetics* came to life in 1997—published online, naturally—and then faded away after eight years partly spent in self-conscious debate over status, mission

and terminology. Even compared with genes, memes are hard to mathematize or even to define rigorously. So the gene-meme analogy causes uneasiness and the genetics-memetics analogy even more.

Genes at least have a grounding in physical substance. Memes are abstract, intangible and unmeasurable. Genes replicate with near-perfect fidelity, and evolution depends on that: some variation is essential, but mutations need to be rare. Memes are seldom copied exactly; their boundaries are always fuzzy, and they mutate with a wild flexibility that would be fatal in biology. The term "meme" could be applied to a suspicious cornucopia of entities, from small to large. For Dennett, the first four notes of Beethoven's Fifth Symphony (quoted above) were "clearly" a meme, along with Homer's *Odyssey* (or at least the idea of the *Odyssey*), the wheel, anti-Semitism and writing. "Memes have not yet found their Watson and Crick," said Dawkins; "they even lack their Mendel."

Yet here they are. As the arc of information flow bends toward ever greater connectivity, memes evolve faster and spread farther. Their presence is felt if not seen in herd behavior, bank runs, informational cascades and financial bubbles. Diets rise and fall in popularity, their very names becoming catchphrases—the South Beach Diet and the Atkins Diet, the Scarsdale Diet, the Cookie Diet and the Drinking Man's Diet all replicating according to a dynamic about which the science of nutrition has nothing to say. Medical practice, too, experiences "surgical fads" and "iatro-epidemics"—epidemics caused by fashions in treatment—like the iatro-epidemic of children's tonsillectomies that swept the United States and parts of Europe in the mid-20th century. Some false memes spread with disingenuous assistance, like the apparently unkillable notion that Barack Obama was not born in Hawaii. And in cyberspace every new social network becomes a new incubator of memes. Making the rounds of Facebook in the summer and fall of 2010 was a classic in new garb:

> *Sometimes I Just Want to Copy Someone Else's Status, Word for Word, and See If They Notice.*

Then it mutated again, and in January 2011 Twitter saw an outbreak of:

> *One day I want to copy someone's Tweet word for word and see if they notice.*

By then one of the most popular of all Twitter hashtags (the "hashtag" being a genetic—or, rather, memetic—marker) was simply the word "#Viral."

In the competition for space in our brains and in the culture, the 35
effective combatants are the messages. The new, oblique, looping views of genes and memes have enriched us. They give us paradoxes to write on Möbius strips. "The human world is made of stories, not people," writes the novelist David Mitchell. "The people the stories use to tell themselves are not to be blamed." Margaret Atwood writes: "As with all knowledge, once you knew it, you couldn't imagine how it was that you hadn't known it before. Like stage magic, knowledge before you knew it took place before your very eyes, but you were looking elsewhere." Nearing death, John Updike reflected on

> *A life poured into words—apparent waste intended to preserve the thing consumed.*

Fred Dretske, a philosopher of mind and knowledge, wrote in 1981: "In the beginning there was information. The word came later." He added this explanation: "The transition was achieved by the development of organisms with the capacity for selectively exploiting this information in order to survive and perpetuate their kind." Now we might add, thanks to Dawkins, that the transition was achieved by the information itself, surviving and perpetuating its kind and selectively exploiting organisms.

Most of the biosphere cannot see the infosphere; it is invisible, a parallel universe humming with ghostly inhabitants. But they are not ghosts to us—not anymore. We humans, alone among the earth's organic creatures, live in both worlds at once. It is as though, having long coexisted with the unseen, we have begun to develop the needed extrasensory perception. We are aware of the many species of information. We name their types sardonically, as though to reassure ourselves that we understand: urban myths and zombie lies. We keep them alive in air-conditioned server farms. But we cannot own them. When a jingle lingers in our ears, or a fad turns fashion upside down, or a hoax dominates the global chatter for months and vanishes as swiftly as it came, who is master and who is slave?

Analyze

1. In your own words, define a meme and explain how it works.
2. Gleick gives a range of examples to illustrate the nature and function of memes. Which example in this article is most helpful to you? Which helps you to best understand?
3. This article begins with a statement about information technology and then progresses along a chain of connected ideas (often called a *line of reasoning*). Trace the line of reasoning. Explain how Gleick goes from the nature of information technology to the concept of an infosphere.
4. According to Gleick, why is the Internet such a vital step in the evolution of the meme?
5. Gleick says that "Language serves as culture's first catalyst. It supersedes mere imitation, spreading knowledge by abstraction and encoding." As best you can, explain this point in your own language. (Imagine that you're explaining this point to someone who hasn't read the article.)

Explore

1. How have you, or people you know, participated in the spreading a meme?
2. Gleick suggests that humans do not choose language but that language chooses us—that it works through us to pollinate others. Clearly, this idea runs contrary to most people's thinking. What have you experienced that either supports or opposes Gleick's suggestion?
3. Gleick explains, "Ideas have 'spreading power.' An example of an infectious idea might be a religious ideology that gains sway over a large group of people." Give another example of an infectious idea, one that takes hold of many people and maintains control of thought and behavior.
4. What social or political forces get in the way of memes? Can you think of any specific situations in which a policy, law, group, or organization hindered the replication (or spreading) of a meme?
5. In his conclusion, Gleick boldly claims, "Most of the biosphere cannot see the infosphere; it is invisible, a parallel universe humming with ghostly inhabitants. But they are not ghosts to us—not anymore." After reading this article, do you think people are developing the "extrasensory perception" that he describes? Explain why you accept or do not accept Gleick's claim.

Forging Connections

1. How do social media influence users' relationship to nature? Do social media make people more distant from the patterns and complexities of the natural world? Does life in virtual reality somehow undermine or enrich human understanding of their place in the ecosystem? Consider articles in Chapter 7, "Nature: How We Share the Planet," specifically those by Rob Dunn ("Fly on Wall Sees Things It Wishes It Hadn't"), David P. Barash ("Two Cheers for Nature"), or Michael Shellenberger and Ted Nordhaus ("Evolve"). How do their claims make you think about life on social media sites? Develop your thinking in a written essay. Integrate photos or graphics from social media sites to illustrate your claims.
2. How do social media influence people's identities? For instance, how might Facebook impact the way individual users identify themselves according to gender, ethnicity, or sexual orientation? Or how might MMORPGs like WoW stretch, reinforce, or shatter players' identities? Consider Sameer Pandya ("The Picture for Men: Superhero or Slacker") or other writers in Chapter 5 and the points they make about the role of media in maintaining identity. Develop your thinking in a written essay and integrate specific references to social media. Consider specific scenes, gaming rules, or even direct player exchanges.

Looking Further

1. Explore a particular feature on a social media site. For instance, you might focus on the way Facebook organizes friends or how it sends notifications to an e-mail account. In an essay, explain how that feature enhances or deepens the virtual experience. Explain the subtle effects, the quiet ways in which people are influenced or impacted. Try to avoid selling the feature or just flatly condemning it. Instead, try to *understand how it operates* in the broader culture of social media, how it works to reinforce the virtual world. Borrow insights from the writers in this chapter to help explain the subtle effects.
2. James Gleick concludes "What Defines a Meme?" with a profound note on human nature: "Most of the biosphere cannot see the infosphere; it is invisible, a parallel universe humming with ghostly inhabitants. But they are not ghosts to us—not anymore. We humans, alone among the earth's organic creatures, live in both worlds at once. It is as

though, having long coexisted with the unseen, we have begun to develop the needed extrasensory perception." To what extent do you think social media is changing human nature? How is the *infosphere* changing how humans operate, even what humans are? Make your case in an argumentative project that employs both written passages and images. Integrate photos or graphics from social media sites to illustrate your claims.

Chapter 4

Identity: Who We Are

In America, identity is and always has been a tough issue. On one hand, we are anxious to identify with a group. We openly call ourselves Democrats, Republicans, conservatives, liberals, Spartans, Falcons, Phoenixes, Texans, flatlanders, gangsters, cheeseheads, hipsters, or Jeep owners. We are glad not simply to join a group, but also to adopt that group's history, present, and future. We get flags, bumper stickers, particular shoes, t-shirts, hats, and even body paint to make sure that everyone else knows how to label us. When our favorite team loses to the dreaded archrival, we take it personally. And when the candidate from another political party gets into office, some of us even argue that the world is ending. But Americans also buy into the idea that we are each individuals with no shared identity. Consider some clichés that circulate in everyday language:

Everyone is different. Everyone is an individual. I'm my own person. Such statements eclipse the ongoing practice of managing our group identities and affiliations. In short, Americans are serious but also unsure about identity. Is it personal or shared? The answer seems to be both.

Identity also has a dark side. Once we figure out "who we are," we also tend to figure out who isn't us—who doesn't belong, who shouldn't have power, who should stay away or be silenced. Our struggle is nothing new. For hundreds of years, slavery was an official institution. In the 1800s, Irish and Dutch immigrants were condemned as inherently dirty, unintelligent, and naturally immoral. Similar statements were made, at different times, about Chinese, Jews, Africans, Arabs, and homosexual and transgendered people. And if you've attended high school or watched how Congress works, you know that such identity politics still thrive.

The readings in this chapter explore the tensions of identity—the conflict and cleavage created by change. Sameer Pandya and Cristina Black deal with shifts in gender. Doug LaForest examines popular culture and race. S. Alan Ray and Eboo Patel discuss identity conflicts on college campuses, and Leila Ahmed examines the intersection of gender and religious identity.

Sameer Pandya

The Picture for Men: Superhero or Slacker

A lecturer in the Department of Asian-American Studies at the University of California, Santa Barbara, Sameer Pandya writes the Research of Culture blog for *Pacific Standard* magazine, where the following post first appeared. A writer of fiction and nonfiction, he has published works on cultural topics such as education, sports, religion, race, and entertainment. Here, Pandya examines the restrictive nature of American masculine identity.

At the end of the fourth season of the critically loved and chronically underwatched *Friday Night Lights*, the former football star Tim Riggins martyrs himself for the sake of his brother and newborn nephew.

For much of the season, he and his brother Billy have been stripping down stolen cars and making the type of fast cash they cannot make legitimately. Tim wants the quick cash to fund his desire to buy a bit of sun-drenched Texas countryside, and Billy needs it for his new duties as a father.

As the season finale starts, the brothers are talking to a lawyer and working through their options after they have both been arrested and released. Through the duration of the television hour, it becomes clear that Tim is going to take the fall so that his brother can be a present father to his new son. Their own father had run out on the brothers early in their lives. In a couple of truly emotionally stirring scenes, Tim tells his brother of his decision and then heads into the sheriff's office to turn himself in.

In the show, the character of Tim Riggins is a poster child for what Hanna Rosin has provocatively referred to, in a recent *Atlantic* cover story, as "The End of Men." Rosin argues that in our postindustrial society, women are succeeding in a way in which men cannot keep up. Women are attending and graduating from college and professional schools at a higher rate, and women are entering and ascending in the work force in greater numbers and more successfully.

And in the recession we are living through, men have been hit the hardest. "The worst-hit industries were overwhelmingly male and deeply identified with macho: construction, manufacturing, high finance."

Riggins had plenty going for him: handsome, athletically gifted, a full 5
scholarship at a state university to play football. But in line with the self-destructive behavior the character has displayed—quick to throw punches, quiet on verbal communication—he throws much of this away. A year after the end of high school, he has abandoned college and returned home to open a mechanics shop with his brother, where business is quite slow.

In contrast, his love interest has long abandoned the small Texas town where the show takes place and moved on to her new life at Vanderbilt.

If the makers of *Friday Night Lights* and Rosin are to be believed, there is a simple message being transmitted: Men are screwed. Or to put it another way, for a large subsection of American men, their options in life have become severely limited.

The possible reasons for this are layered and complicated. But recent research points to one possible culprit: traditional forms of masculinity.

In two different studies presented Aug. 16 at the American Psychological Association meetings in San Diego, researchers examined the lives of boys.

10 Sharon Lamb, a distinguished professor of mental health at the University of Massachusetts–Boston along with her co-authors Lyn Mikel Brown and Mark Tappan of Colby College, found that media images, particularly of superheroes, severely limit the models of boys' behavior. Today's movie superheroes offer a basic template for superhero behavior: nonstop violence when in costume, and the exploitation of women, the flaunting of money, and wielding guns when not.

In the past, Lamb argues, comic book heroes "were heroes the boys could look up to and learn from because outside of their costumes, they were real people with real problems and many vulnerabilities."

"Today's movie superheroes offer a basic template for superhero behavior: nonstop violence when in costume, and the exploitation of women, the flaunting of money, and wielding guns when not."

Now, boys between the ages of 4 and 18 have only two choices.

"In today's media, superheroes and slackers are the only two options boys have. Boys are told if you can't be a superhero, you can always be a slacker. Slackers are funny, but slackers are not what boys should strive to be; slackers don't like school and they shirk responsibility. We wonder if the message boys get about saving face through glorified slacking could be affecting their performance in school."

Lamb suggests teaching boys to distance themselves from these images by helping them recognize the problems with them.

15 Lamb's fellow researcher on the panel, Carlos Santos of Arizona State University, offers another set of questions and solutions to this larger question of masculinity. Santos examined 426 middle school boys and posed a series of sharp research questions. Are middle school boys able to resist being emotionally stoic, autonomous, and physically tough—the traditional, stereotypical markers of masculinity—as they moved from the sixth to the eighth grade? What difference does ethnicity make? Do relationships with families and peers foster resistance? Does resistance affect psychological health?

His conclusions provide a certain amount of hope, given the right type of influences. Santos found that boys who remained close to their mothers, siblings, and peers did not act as tough or shut down emotionally. However, close relationships with fathers encouraged greater autonomy and detachment from friendships.

One assumes that these fathers had learned how to be men from their own fathers, thus maintaining a certain cycle of traditional masculinity.

How can the cycle be broken? "If the goal is to encourage boys to experience healthy family relationships as well as healthy relationships, clinicians and interventionists working with families may benefit from having fathers share with their sons on the importance of experiencing multiple and fulfilling relationships in their lives," Santos said.

Santos also found that boys from diverse ethnic and racial backgrounds were able to resist masculine stereotypes, thus breaking another type of stereotype about the hyper-masculinity of certain ethnic minorities.

20 Time is of the essence in resistance. Santos suggests that the ability to resist internalizing macho images declines as the boys grow older.

And what happens to these boys when they grow older is that they encounter Hanna Rosin announcing their end even before they have had an opportunity to begin.

Certainly, changing media images and encouraging broad-ranging relationships are both important in subverting traditional, and often socially harmful, markers of masculinity. But there is another factor that might also contribute to broadening the choices beyond gun-slinging superhero and slacker: the availability and variety of work.

Of course, making work available now and in the future is no simple task. Among the bad job and unemployment numbers that seem to come out every week, it is clear that there is a bumpy road ahead not only for men, but also for the economy as a whole.

As much as I am worried about my two young boys being bombarded by superhero-slacker images, I am even more worried about the jobs that might not be available to them when they hit adulthood.

25 And here the studies by Lamb and Santos come back into play. Rethinking certain masculine traits for boys—stoic, autonomous, tough—may be the key for the men they will become to survive in a postindustrial economy. Rosin writes, "The attributes that are most valuable today—social intelligence, open communication, the ability to sit still and focus—are, at a minimum, not predominantly male."

We may not be able to control the availability of jobs, but we can control how boys prepare for them.

Analyze

1. In your own words, explain the problem with the superhero and slacker male images in the media.

2. How does the scene from *Friday Night Lights* figure into this article? What point does it help to establish?
3. What is the postindustrial economy? How might it relate to gender and to jobs?
4. What do you think Pandya means by "traditional masculinity"? What are the negative or positive qualities that this article attributes to traditional masculinity?
5. Explain how the Lamb and Santos study figures into Pandya's article. What points does the study help to make?

Explore

1. Which image, superhero or slacker, has had more impact on you or the men you know?
2. What other identifiers, beyond superhero or slacker, can you imagine? Make a list of terms that characterize the type of men, fictional or real, in your life.
3. What popular culture texts (films, songs, or television shows) support the slacker image that Pandya explains?
4. What popular culture text (film, song, or television show) might push against or complicate the slacker image? Explain how the text works—what it does to make the slacker image unattractive or somehow different than what the audience might expect.

Cristina Black

Bathing Suit Shopping with Annette Kellerman, the Australian Mermaid

The entertainment editor for *Foam* magazine, Cristina Black writes on various pop culture topics ranging from surfing to fashion. Her work has appeared in such publications as *Dazed & Confused, Nylon, Time Out New York,* and the *Village Voice.* The following blog post originally appeared in *The Hairpin*, a website that targets a primarily female readership. In it, Black explores the changing nature of women's swimsuit fashion, and what it might mean for female identity.

It's the same thing every spring: You peruse the magazines, grit your teeth, and go bathing suit shopping. But when you get into the dressing room, it's a big old mess. Your limbs are pale, lumpy, mottled, and large-looking. You shouldn't have eaten so much pasta/drunk so much wine. You should have started around mid-February cutting out carbs/going to the gym. So you head home empty handed, in a haze of disgust and frustration.

Before you get fitted for a burqa, though, think of this: A hundred years ago, you wouldn't have been in this position, shopping for a bathing suit, because there was no such thing. You would be rummaging through your summer storage trunk for your stockings, bloomers, and sailor dress, which would be made of wool, because that's actually what women wore to the beach until one lady came along and changed all that. Annette Kellerman, known in her time as "the Australian Mermaid," was a competitive swimmer, diver, model, actress, stuntwoman, fitness guru, and, yes, professional mermaid in vaudeville and movies, who originally sewed stockings onto a man's racing suit for less drag in the water. Then, one day, circa 1908, she forewent those old leg coverings and appeared on a Boston beach in a skin-tight onesie with the legs cut off mid-thigh. She was arrested. Later, in court, she explained she was not a provocateur but a pragmatist. She simply wanted to swim freely, and was that so wrong? "I may as well be swimming in chains," she complained. Before long, she had created her own line of women's swimwear, when there really was no such thing, and long before celebrities regularly leveraged their fame to sell clothes. The "Annette Kellerman" was the first modern swimsuit for women. And, in many ways, its namesake was one of the first modern women.

By the time of her famous beach arrest, Kellerman, still in her early 20s, was already a world-class swimmer. She had beaten dozens of men in long distance races; swum the Thames, the Seine, and the Danube; and had attempted to cross the English Channel three times—then the only woman who had dared to try—making it three-quarters of the way before succumbing to frigid temperatures and seasickness. "The men wore no clothes, but I was compelled to put on a bathing suit," she recalled of her first Channel swim. "Small as it was, it chafed me. When I finished, the flesh under my arms was raw and hurt fearfully."

When long distance swimming failed to pull her and her father-manager out of poverty, Kellerman turned to high-diving in Chicago and quickly became the highest paid act on the vaudeville circuit. Meanwhile, she invented the sport of synchronized swimming with a water ballet performance in a glass tank at the New York Hippodrome. After a 1908 study of 3,000 female figures, a Harvard University faculty member named Kellerman "the Perfect Woman" because of the similarity of her physical attributes to the Venus de Milo. She was uncomfortable with the label. "I don't want to be just a pretty fish," she complained.

5 It's worthwhile to note that Kellerman was not particularly thin by today's standards. At 5′ 4″, she measured 33 inches in the chest, 26 at the waist. Her hip measurement was never recorded, but from photos, it looks like it never dipped too far south of 40. Most of the bathing-beauty pinups she spawned had similar figures, round-butted and full-thighed, but for a long time, Kellerman was considered the prettiest fish of them all. When she tired of flopping into the water like a trick seal, she parlayed her rising star into a silent film career, becoming the first major actress to do a nude scene (in *A Daughter of the Gods* in 1916). Later in life, Kellerman became a celebrity fitness guru when there was no such thing, and opened a health food store in Long Beach when everybody still drank whole cow's milk and ate steak for dinner. She was a vegetarian many decades before it stopped seeming strange. And right up to her death at age 88, she bragged that she could still bend over and touch her toes, a picture of perfect health until the end.

Well into the '70s, Annette Kellerman swam every day. "There is nothing more democratic than swimming," she wrote. "Bathing is a society event but swimming out beyond the surf line is just plain social. Everyone is happy and young and funny. No one argues. No one scolds. There is no time and no place where one may so companionably play the fool and not be called one." When she puts it that way, it seems a little silly to think that bathing suit shopping is excruciating for women because we are frightened at the thought of baring so much skin. We forget how fragile is the freedom to go swimming and sunning in clothes that let us feel the water and wind and sun on our skin. Ladies, relish the skimpiness of today's suits! If it makes you more comfortable, go ahead and wear a maillot cut low on the legs, high in the neck. Just be glad you have a choice.

Analyze

1. For whom is this article written? What gender, age group, or race? Everyone? Anyone in particular? What specific passages support your answer?
2. What is Black's main idea? Is this article about gender? Fashion changes? Body size? Sports? In your own words, explain Black's main idea.

3. Black explains that Kellerman was a "picture of perfect health until the end." Why is this point important to the article? How does it help to support Black's main idea?
4. Kellerman once described swimming as democratic. In your understanding, what does that mean? How is swimming democratic?
5. Compare Black's point about women to the point Sameer Pandya makes in "The Picture for Men: Superhero or Slacker" about young men. How are these articles similar? How do they point to similar cultural tensions?

Explore

1. Black's article shows how cultures change. What attitudes or beliefs changed or faded so that Kellerman's one-piece bathing suit went from scandalous to normal to modest?
2. What is the biggest change in fashion you've seen in your lifetime? What attitudes or beliefs were behind that change? What ideas about men, women, sex, and freedom might have spurred that change?
3. Compare Kellerman to a contemporary female celebrity. Are there any women in today's media who have served a similar function?
4. People like Annette Kellerman have helped to create choices for us today. She established a broader range of possible behaviors and options. Name another person in history who did this. Explain the choices that he or she made available to others.

Doug LaForest

Undocumented Immigrants

Douglas LaForest is pursuing a degree in computer information technology. In the following essay, developed for a second-semester writing course, he examines the role of language in shaping cultural notions of *other.* With a range of sources, personal testimony, and appeals, he argues against the use of a common phrase.

Language is power. This is especially true of language which maligns a person. A friend of my family is aware of this. She hands out pamphlets asking that people consider the language they use when discussing Down's syndrome. She has championed local projects that advocate for people living with Down's syndrome, which includes her daughter. Her volunteer work reminds people that her daughter is a person first. She's not a "Down's child." It does not define her. This is not merely a matter of semantics; it's validating an individual's humanity. My friend understands that this issue is a cornerstone to building upon issues of justice and quality of life for her daughter as well as other individuals who live with Down's syndrome.

I think of my friend's work when I hear of the current debates over immigration. Immigration laws are outdated and unjust. But before any changes can be made to the system, we have to begin to use language which acknowledges the humanity of the individuals who are affected by the immigration system. We cannot begin to have just conversations and make legal changes within the immigration system without taking action regarding the language we use. One of the primary reasons we have not been able to justly reform our immigration system is based on our inability to use language which validates the humanity of individuals who are also undocumented immigrants.

Not too long ago, I heard another friend mention a local incident which involved an "illegal alien." Apparently, the man was to be deported to Mexico after his home was swarmed by armed policeman. My friend's description of the man, the "illegal alien," shocked me. This is a friend whom I think of as tolerant and thoughtful of others. When I suggested he use the phrase "undocumented immigrant" rather than "illegal alien," he agreed. He confessed that his poor choice was simply a result of the jargon he was accustomed to hearing and therefore using.

The conversation between my friend and me is precisely the reason why Jose Antonio Vargas, a Pulitzer Prize–winning journalist, decided to "come out." He wanted to draw attention to the need for just immigration reform, and to insist that we begin using language in conversations and media that validates an individual's humanity. Vargas was tired of hearing all of the pejorative language used to describe individuals in immigrant communities: "illegal aliens," "illegal immigrants" or simply "illegals." Working in journalism, he had heard these derogatory descriptions used in writing and in political campaigns. But at some point, he was done with it all and was willing to take personal risk. What was the personal risk? He himself struggles in a complicated life which includes the experience of being an undocumented immigrant.

In this summer's June 6th issue of *The New York Times*, Vargas shared 5
his life story, and ever since, he has risked being deported. Filipino born, Vargas was put on a plane at the age of twelve to join his grandparents in California. His grandparents, like many families, wanted for their grandson a good education and a better life as a United States citizen. Though Vargas didn't know it for many years, he was an undocumented immigrant. Unable to find a legal route to obtain citizenship for their grandson, his grandparents hoped that he would one day marry a citizen and thereby obtain a green card. But, as it turns out, Vargas is gay and did not want to live with the lie of a fraudulent marriage.

Vargas bravely revealed his life story. He was compelled to do it when time after time he was suffering and realizing that there was an "undeniable" consensus that the media framing around illegal immigration was "stuck in simplistic, us-versus-them, black-or-white, conflict-driven narrative." As he had hoped, by sharing his life story, a debate once again emerged surrounding immigration, but this time there was an urgency to humanize the issue. Furthermore, the media has responded to Vargas's insistence that the phrase undocumented immigrant be used (Ly). Currently, television networks and newspapers are engaged in a debate as to how to describe the individuals struggling within the immigration system. Vargas has argued fervently that the media needs to lead the way in using the phrase undocumented immigrant, and nothing else.

Again, this is not simply a matter of semantics. What comes to mind when reading text that defines the person in the article as an illegal immigrant or simply illegal? The word "criminal" comes to mind, right? Some newspapers are responding to Vargas's request. They're beginning to discontinue such negative descriptions. For example, *The Cornell Daily Sun* wrote an editorial underlying the humanity of this community. "No human being is illegal." And though the "first person to coin the phrase may have done so out of convenience, naivety or xenophobia," *The Cornell Daily Sun* agreed that the term conveyed criminality. The editorial concludes by saying that "it is the action of entering the United States without permission that is illegal, not the immigrant him or herself ("What Does It Mean?").

Claudia Melendez Salinas, an education reporter at the *Monterey County Herald* convinced her newspaper to change its wording to "undocumented immigrant." How? "I told them 'illegal' was offensive and compared it to other offensive labels like 'spic.' That's how people use it, if you think about it" (qtd. in Ly).

So what might be one of the reasons for derogatory language? Perhaps there's an anti-immigrant sentiment that is especially fearful of the changing demographics of our nation; there's a growing Hispanic population. Vargas notes in his June *Time Magazine* article that the Hispanic population is growing. The Pew Hispanic Center reports that 56% of the nation's growth from 2000–2010 was Hispanic (Rubio 52). Some of that percentage, as Vargas reports, is the percentage of undocumented immigrants: 59% of the undocumented immigrants being from Mexico. He writes, "Whites represent a shrinking share of the total U.S. population." And he goes on to argue that "The immigration debate is impossible to separate from America's unprecedented and culture-shifting demographic make-over."

10 Could it be that our nation's resistance to using respectful language is wrapped in a "white" vs. "Hispanic" sentiment? My sense is that as a nation, this is true and based on fear of diverse peoples. Vargas writes about "white conservatives" who would quickly complain to him of "other" people joining their schools and churches and the discomfort of overhearing Spanish in Wal-Mart (Vargas 42).

Consider the following experience: The Leelanau Children's Center, where my three-year-old son attends, had a parenting night. It was early in the fall and new families were coming together to share an evening of introductions and to create community. I think of the Children's Center as being progressive—progressive in the sense that community building is emphasized and everyone is welcome, regardless of race, economic status and any other potential category of differences. Many of the parents were first generation immigrants from Mexico. To start off the evening, the directors of the Children's Center requested parents sit in a circle with one another and introduce ourselves. It seemed friendly enough. Like any introductory circle, there were plenty of shy folks and some nervous laughter. Circle participants would often respond with welcoming words or gestures in response to a parent's introduction. As the introductions progressed, there was a growing sense of comfort. Then, one Hispanic man began to introduce himself and speak of his children. Only he spoke in Spanish. The minute he finished sharing, there was silence. You could have heard a pin drop. I realized that no one knew how to respond. Or was it that there was a general discomfort in the room with his choice of language? Had he just crossed the line of an unspoken rule? I left thinking about that exchange and a general "tolerance" of immigration that might have been tested. Did I witness and perhaps participate in a very subtle anti-immigration sentiment?

Language is power. As a nation we have only begun to reconsider language that respects an individual's humanity when speaking about the lives of people in immigrant communities. Using the phrase "undocumented immigrants" instead of derogatory phrases such as "illegal immigrant," "illegal alien," and "illegal" is fundamental to validating a person's life. It's not just a matter of semantics. Perhaps one of the reasons that derogatory language continues is that, as a nation, we are struggling to accept the shifting demographics of the population: In the U.S. Hispanics will soon outnumber folks from European descent.

Vargas urges us to challenge ourselves to get beyond the fear. He insists that we look at the issue of immigration, the language we use in describing immigrant communities and the changing demographics of this nation in a holistic light. Vargas concludes his personal coming out story in *Time Magazine* with a question: "when will you realize that we are one of you?"(43).

Works Cited

Ly, Phuong. "Vargas' Essay Renews Attention to Media's Use of 'Illegal' and 'Undocumented.'" *Poynter.org.* The Poynter Institute, 6 July 2011. Web. 6 Apr. 2013.

Rubio, Angelica. "Undocumented, Not Illegal: Beyond the Rhetoric of Immigration Coverage." *NACLA Report on the Americas* 44.6 (2011): 50–52. *Academic Search Elite.* Web. 15 May 2013.

Vargas, Jose Antonio. "Just Not Legally." *Time* 179.25 (2012): 34–44. Print.

———. "My Life as an Undocumented Immigrant." *The New York Times.* n. p. New York Times, 22 June 2011. Web. 25 May 2013.

"What Does it Mean to be 'Illegal?'" Editorial. *The Cornell Daily Sun* [Ithaca]. n. p. Cornell Daily Sun, 16 Oct. 2012. Web. 8 Apr. 2013.

Analyze

1. Explain why LaForest begins and ends his essay with the point that "language is power." Why is this statement so critical to his main idea?

2. LaForest devotes much of his essay to analyzing the cause of certain phrases. In your words, explain LaForest's conclusion. What is behind the persistence of phrases such as *illegal alien*?
3. Near the end of his essay, LaForest connects derogatory language to fear. Explain how that connection supports his main idea.
4. LaForest argues that this discussion is "not merely a matter of semantics." Why does he make this point? What assumption or belief is countering?
5. LaForest uses a range of support strategies throughout his essay. He relies on personal testimony and on the testimony of journalists. Which passage do you think is most powerful? What situation seems most supportive or revealing?

Explore

1. Why might *undocumented immigrant* be more humane than *illegal alien*?
2. Of the two phrases, *undocumented immigrant* and *illegal alien*, do you think one is more accurate? Or if both are accurate, why would one be used more than the other?
3. Throughout American history, language has been central to issues of race, gender, and sexual orientation. Why? Why are the labels and terms we assign to others so important? Why do they generate concern and even outrage?
4. Are you part of a community that has been labeled by others? What is the label? What power does it have in your life?

S. Alan Ray

Despite the Controversy, We're Glad We Asked

President of Elmhurst College, S. Alan Ray is a professor of religion and society. In describing Elmhurst, he explains, "We think about how the things we learn can be related to the world beyond college. . . . We don't have the problem of reconciling reflection and action. Here, reflection and action have always gone hand in hand." In the following *Chronicle of Higher Education* article, Ray describes the effects of a college application question that asks about students' sexual orientation.

When we decided this year to make one of our routine annual revisions in the application for undergraduate admission at Elmhurst College, we weren't expecting to make national headlines as a result. But we did. What landed Elmhurst in the media spotlight last month was a new application question. Like some others, the question was optional. It asked: "Would you consider yourself a member of the LGBT (lesbian, gay, bisexual, transgender) community?"

Like many other institutions, our private liberal-arts college in Chicago's western suburbs, long affiliated with the United Church of Christ, has included optional questions on our admission applications for many years. They ask about matters like ethnic identity, religious affiliation, and languages spoken at home. But this new question generated levels of interest and controversy that those other questions never did.

Our revised application became news when the national organization Campus Pride sent out a press release congratulating us for "setting the bar" by becoming the first college in the United States to ask prospective undergraduates about sexual orientation and gender identity on its application. The Campus Pride release was quickly followed by articles in newspapers, segments on national radio shows, and stories on major news-media Web sites. We hadn't sought this wave of publicity, but we were proud to have so much attention focused on our efforts to build a campus that is diverse, open, and affirming to all students.

Of course, the coverage also occasioned some commentary that challenged our wisdom and motivation. That the new application question produced some controversy will not surprise anyone familiar with online comment strings and call-in radio, which too often are more about heat than light. The application question had placed us in the middle of a national discussion about diversity and sexual identity—one that continues to stir passions and challenge established beliefs.

Perhaps the most common question I heard from our supportive but 5
surprised friends was simply this: Why did we do it? One way of explaining is simply to quote our application, which notes that Elmhurst is "committed to diversity and connecting underrepresented students with valuable resources on campus." For years we have asked students about their personal interests, high-school activities, and faith traditions, among other things, so we can connect them with campus support and gauge their eligibility for certain opportunities, including scholarships.

This year we decided to include self-identified LGBT students in the process. We wanted them to know that they, like all our students, would find abundant resources at Elmhurst to enable them to succeed. We wanted them to know that they would not feel isolated on our campus because of their sexual orientation or gender identity. On the contrary: We clearly, openly, emphatically want them here.

Beyond that, there are substantive reasons to reach out directly to LGBT students, who still experience hostility and discrimination on some campuses. Studies show that they are at significantly higher risk for harassment compared with their heterosexual peers, and many have reported experiencing a difficult or hostile campus climate or actual harassment. A recent survey found that 13 percent of gay students said they feared for their physical safety; the number rises to 43 percent for transgender students.

Media coverage of our decision was overwhelmingly positive, but the public's reaction ran the gamut from grateful praise to harsh criticism, clearly reflecting the sharp divisions over this issue. Most of the negative response was based on a misunderstanding of what the application question says and how responses to the question will be used. One sticking point for some critics was the availability of scholarship money for students who identified themselves as lesbian, gay, bisexual, or transgender. Over the years, Elmhurst has awarded what we call Enrichment Scholarships to talented students whose presence would add to the diversity and richness of campus life. Now gay and transgender students are eligible for these scholarships, too. That does not, as some uninformed commentators suggested, deprive another deserving student of a scholarship. We offer scholarships of varying kinds to all qualifying admitted students; they are not capped at a certain number. Thus one student's gain is not another student's loss.

It is becoming ever more clear to educators that students learn best when they engage with a wide spectrum of individuals, both like and unlike themselves—that is, if they are part of a campus community that resembles our diverse society and multicultural world. That's why Elmhurst and many other colleges and universities make an extra effort to recruit students of color, international students, first-generation students, and many others. Encouraging talented, self-identified gay and transgender students to come to Elmhurst enhances the education of every one of our students.

10 It is also the right thing to do. The United Church of Christ, with which Elmhurst is affiliated, is a Protestant denomination with a long and proud history of shattering our society's color and gender barriers. The tradition

that made the church the first mainstream American denomination to ordain an African-American minister, the first to ordain a female minister, and the first to ordain an openly gay minister is one that resonates with our own core values. The church describes itself as "extravagantly welcoming." Elmhurst is, too.

It is possible, as some people have suggested, that students will misrepresent themselves as gay or lesbian on applications solely to qualify for a scholarship. I think it also is unlikely. There have always been opportunities for fraud in the application process, but I have seen no evidence that this happens much at Elmhurst or elsewhere.

It is also possible that some students will object to the question as intrusive or inappropriate. But we hope that many more students will recognize it as part of our sincere effort to meet them, and understand them, as they really are. After all, one of the great aims of higher education is to help students to attain—as Elmhurst's sixth president, the theologian H. Richard Niebuhr, put it—an "effective individuality." That can happen only if students and educators alike are willing to take on the deepest matters of identity with unflinching honesty and open minds.

One of the unanticipated benefits of this episode is the opportunity it has afforded Elmhurst to clearly communicate two of its core values—its unyielding commitment to diversity and profound respect for individuals—to people who previously were unfamiliar with us. I think that those around the country who read or heard about Elmhurst for the first time as a result of our application question encountered a principled institution in the process of uncovering new ways to do right by its students. We are hoping the discussion that resulted from our action encourages other colleges and universities to follow our lead.

Analyze

1. Consider Ray's opening strategy. How does it impact your entry into the article—and the issue it raises?
2. How does Ray address positions or claims that might oppose the Elmhurst College application questions? Focus on a specific passage and explain how Ray deals with opposition.
3. Much of Ray's article focuses on the reason Elmhurst asked the question. In one or two sentences, summarize the reason.

4. Ray explains that online commentary and radio talk shows often generate “more about heat than light.” How does this point help his case?
5. Read “Is Your Campus Diverse?” by Eboo Patel (later in this chapter). What underlying belief or value do Ray and Patel share? Explain how that shared belief functions in each article.

Explore

1. Do you think your campus is welcoming to LGBT students? Why or why not?
2. Do you think an application question about sexual orientation is intrusive, inappropriate, or inviting? What’s your reasoning? What beliefs are behind your answer?
3. According to Ray, the United Church of Christ has played a critical role in “shattering our society’s color and gender barriers.” How does this point impact your thinking about religion, gender equality, or race?
4. Why do you think policy issues related to sexual orientation generate so much controversy? What fears, beliefs, or assumptions are driving that controversy?

Eboo Patel

Is Your Campus Diverse? It's a Question of Faith

Named one of America's Best Leaders of 2009 by *U.S. News & World Report*, Eboo Patel focuses on advancing the interfaith movement across colleges worldwide. He has published three books on issues related to religious identity and frequently contributes to CNN, The Huffington Post, National Public Radio, *USA Today*, and the *Washington Post*. In the following *Chronicle of Higher Education* article, Patel considers the importance of religious diversity on college campuses.

It came as no surprise to me to read the recent *New York Times* article indicating that Muslim students feel particularly welcome on Roman Catholic campuses—precisely because of their faith. "Here people are more religious, even if they're not Muslim, and I'm comfortable with that," a Muslim student said of her experience at the University of Dayton.

That was my father's experience at the University of Notre Dame 35 years ago. He was a Muslim immigrant from India in the land of gray snow and white Catholics. While the priests didn't always understand his faith, they always respected it, and he felt that the broader environment nurtured it. When he missed home, he'd go to the Grotto of Our Lady of Lourdes, where the flickering candles reminded him of the line in the Koran that God is light upon light.

When I went to the University of Illinois at Urbana-Champaign, in the mid-1990s, we were focused on other forms of identity. The Rodney King beating and its aftermath had sparked a rise in campus activism around race. You couldn't walk 10 feet in any direction without seeing a copy of Cornel West's *Race Matters* or running into a heated discussion about the role of black women in the feminist movement. Freshman orientation, resident-adviser training, speeches by the football coach at pep rallies—race was a theme in all of these.

Part of the rationale for 1990s-era campus multiculturalism was to remedy the racial bias in the broader society: to lift up underrepresented narratives, to remind people that many communities have contributed to the American project, to ensure that our perceptions of race were not driven by the crime reports on the evening news. Gender, sexuality, class, and ethnicity all got some airtime, but mostly we talked about race. And one form of identity was almost totally excluded: faith.

Now that the evening news is full of stories of faith-based violence, and 5
our public discourse has a constant undercurrent of religious prejudice (Barack Obama is a Muslim! Mitt Romney isn't a Christian!) colleges can no longer ignore faith identity. For many of the same reasons that they actively engaged race, so should they now actively and positively engage faith identity.

That Catholic colleges are welcoming places for people from other religions is very good news on one front. It means that Samuel Huntington's "clash of civilizations" thesis—the idea that people of different faith backgrounds are inherently in conflict with one another—is not inevitable, at least not everywhere. On American Catholic campuses, it appears, the clear and proud expression of one faith identity isn't a barrier that separates people of different faiths, it's a bridge that invites them in.

And it's not just Catholic colleges. A few years ago, I was invited to speak at Berea College, a nondenominational Christian college, and my podium was set up right in front of a large cross. The minister asked if I would feel more comfortable if it was covered. Not at all, I told him. Berea's understanding of that cross was the key reason the college had such a diverse student body, and precisely why they had invited a Muslim speaker to address the community. I was proud to speak in front of that cross. In fact, its presence allowed me to open my talk with a Muslim prayer.

But interfaith work is not just for religious campuses, and creating a "safe space" for different faiths cannot be the ultimate goal. In the most religiously diverse nation in human history and the most religiously devout nation in the West at a time of global religious conflict, how people from different faith backgrounds get along and what they do together is a crucial question. And so it must be a central question for our public universities as well.

Robert Putnam, who teaches American politics at Harvard, emphasizes that faith communities are the single largest repository of social capital in America, but that they operate mainly within their own restrictive networks. Certainly faith groups can continue to work in isolation. The tension among religions in America can grow, faith can become a weapon, and we can move directly into the open conflict we see in other religiously diverse societies. Or we can encourage more social capital among faith communities (and between them and philosophically secular ones), and help them cooperate to serve the common good. Colleges are miniature civil societies that can nurture that vision of interfaith respect and cooperation, and train a critical mass of leaders to help achieve it.

10 What if campuses took religious diversity as seriously as they took race? What if recruiting a religiously diverse student body, creating a welcoming environment for people of different faith and philosophical identities, and offering classes in interfaith studies and co-curricular opportunities in interfaith leadership became the norm? What if university presidents expected their graduates to acquire interfaith literacy, build interfaith relationships, and have opportunities to run interfaith programs during their four years on campus? What impact might a critical mass of interfaith leaders have on America over the course of the next generation?

I'm pretty convinced that one reason Barack Obama is president is because of the 1990s-era multiculturalism movement on campuses. A generation of college students caught a vision of what a multicultural nation should look like—and those were the people who staffed the moonshot Obama campaign. Imagine the impact a 21st-century campus interfaith movement could have on the nation over the course of the next 30 years. Perhaps we won't be Googling "Sikh" when we hear of a hate-fueled murder in Milwaukee; perhaps we'll be electing a Sikh president.

Analyze

1. What single sentence best captures Patel's main idea?
2. Explain how Patel uses current events to develop his point about college campuses.
3. Patel invites readers to encourage "more social capital among faith communities." What does he mean by this? What is social capital and how can it function among communities?
4. According to Patel, what is the relationship between the culture of college campuses and the politics of the nation? How do college campuses figure into cultural change?
5. Patel uses the phrase "underrepresented narrative." If narrative is a story, what is an underrepresented narrative? And how is the concept important to this article?

Explore

1. Is your campus diverse? In what specific ways? In what ways is it not diverse?
2. Patel compares religious diversity and racial diversity. How are these concepts similar? What do race and religious affiliation have in common? How are they different?
3. Look up Samuel Huntington's "clash of civilizations" thesis online. What have you seen, read, or experienced that supports or challenges Huntington's thesis?
4. Should diversity among groups always be encouraged? Why is diversity helpful?
5. When is diversity unhelpful, dangerous, or ruinous?

Leila Ahmed
Reinventing the Veil

A professor at Harvard Divinity School, Leila Ahmed studies Islam's role in constructing female identity. She is the author of numerous articles and books, including the 2011 book *A Quiet Revolution: The Veil's Resurgence, from the Middle East to America.* In the following *Financial Times* article, Ahmed examines the cultural impact of a particular Islamic tradition.

I grew up in Cairo, Egypt. Through the decades of my childhood and youth—the 1940s, 1950s and 1960s—the veil was a rarity not only at home but in many Arab and Muslim-majority cities. In fact, when Albert Hourani, the Oxford historian, surveyed the Arab world in the mid-1950s, he predicted that the veil would soon be a thing of the past.

Hourani's prophecy, made in an article called *The Vanishing Veil: A Challenge to the Old Order*, would prove spectacularly wrong, but his piece is nevertheless a gem because it so perfectly captures the ethos of that era. Already the veil was becoming less and less common in my own country, and, as Hourani explains, it was fast disappearing in other "advanced Arab countries," such as Syria, Iraq and Jordan as well. An unveiling movement had begun to sweep across the Arab world, gaining momentum with the spread of education.

In those days, we shared all of Hourani's views and assumptions, including the connections he made between unveiling, "advancement" and education (and between veiling and "backwardness"). We believed the veil was merely a cultural habit, of no relevance to Islam or to religious piety. Even deeply devout women did not wear a hijab. Being unveiled simply seemed the modern "advanced" way of being Muslim.

Consequently the veil's steady "return" from the mid-1980s, and its growing adoption, disturbed us. It was very troubling for people like me who had been working for years as feminists on women and Islam. Why would educated women, particularly those living in free Western societies where they could dress as they wished, be willing (apparently) to take on this symbol of patriarchy and women's oppression?

5 The appearance of the hijab in my own neighbourhood of Cambridge, Massachusetts, in the late 1990s was the trigger that launched my own

studies into the phenomenon. I well remember the very evening that generated that spark. While I was walking past the common with a friend, a well-known feminist who was visiting from the Arab world, we saw a large crowd with all the women in hijab. At the time, this was still an unusual sight and, frankly, it left us both with distinct misgivings.

While troubling on feminist grounds, the veil's return also disturbed me in other ways. Having settled in the U.S., I had watched from afar through the 1980s and 1990s as cities back home that I had known as places where scarcely anyone wore hijab were steadily transformed into streets where the vast majority of women now wore it.

This visually dramatic revolution in women's dress changed, to my eyes, the very look and atmosphere of those cities. It had come about as a result of the spread of Islamism in the 1970s, a very political form of Islam that was worlds away from the deeply inward, apolitical form that had been common in Egypt in my day. Fuelled by the Muslim Brotherhood, the spread of Islamism always brought its signature emblem: the hijab.

Those same decades were marked in Egypt by rising levels of violence and intellectual repression. In 1992, Farag Foda, a well-known journalist and critic of Islamism, was gunned down. Nasr Hamid Abu Zayd, a professor at Cairo University, was brought to trial on grounds of apostasy and had to flee the country. Soon after, Naguib Mahfouz, the Egyptian novelist and Nobel Laureate, was stabbed by an Islamist who considered his books blasphemous. Such events seemed a shocking measure of the country's descent into intolerance.

The sight of the hijab on the streets of America brought all this to mind. Was its growing presence a sign that Islamic militancy was on the rise here too? Where were these young women (it was young women in particular who wore it) getting their ideas? And why were they accepting whatever it was they were being told, in this country where it was entirely normal to challenge patriarchal ideas? Could the Muslim Brotherhood have somehow succeeded in gaining a foothold here?

My instinctive readings of the Cambridge scene proved correct in some 10
ways. The Brotherhood, as well as other Islamist groups, had indeed established a base in America. While most immigrants were not Islamists, those who were quickly set about founding mosques and other organisations. Many immigrants who grew up as I did, without veils, sent their children to Islamic Sunday schools where they imbibed the Islamist outlook—including the hijab.

The veiled are always the most visible, but today Islamist-influenced people make up no more than 30 to 40 per cent of American Muslims. This is also roughly the percentage of women who veil as opposed to those who do not. This means of course that the majority of Muslim American women do not wear the veil, whether because they are secular or because they see it as an emblem of Islamism rather than Islam.

My research may have confirmed some initial fears, but it also challenged my assumptions. As I studied the process by which women had been persuaded to veil in Egypt in the first place, I came to see how essential women themselves had been in its promotion and the cause of Islamism. Among the most important was Zainab al-Ghazali, the "unsung mother" of the Muslim Brotherhood and a forceful activist who had helped keep the organisation going after the death of its founder.

For these women, adopting hijab could be advantageous. Joining Islamist groups and changing dress sometimes empowered them in relation to their parents; it also expanded job and marriage possibilities. Also, since the veil advertised women's commitment to conservative sexual mores, wearing it paradoxically increased their ability to move freely in public space—allowing them to take jobs in offices shared with men.

My assumptions about the veil's patriarchal meanings began to unravel in the first interviews I conducted. One woman explained that she wore it as a way of raising consciousness about the sexist messages of our society. (This reminded me of the bra-burning days in America when some women refused to shave their legs in a similar protest.) Another wore the hijab for the same reason that one of her Jewish friends wore a yarmulke: this was religiously required dress that made visible the presence of a minority who were entitled, like all citizens, to justice and equality. For many others, wearing hijab was a way of affirming pride and rejecting negative stereotypes (like the Afros that flourished in the 1960s among African-Americans).

15 Both Islamist and American ideals—including American ideals of gender justice—seamlessly interweave in the lives of many of this younger generation. This has been a truly remarkable decade as regards Muslim women's activism. Perhaps the post-9/11 atmosphere in the West, which led to intense criticism of Islam and its views of women, spurred Muslim Americans into corrective action. Women are reinterpreting key religious texts, including the Koran, and they have now taken on positions of leadership

in Muslim American institutions: Ingrid Mattson, for example, was twice elected president of the Islamic Society of North America. Such female leadership is unprecedented in the home countries: even al-Ghazali, vital as she was to the Brotherhood, never formally presided over an organisation which included men.

Many of these women—although not all—wear hijab. Clearly here in the West, where women are free to wear what they want, the veil can have multiple meanings. These are typically a far cry from the old notions which I grew up with, and profoundly different from the veil's ancient patriarchal meanings, which are still in full force in some countries. Here in the West—embedded in the context of democracy, pluralism and a commitment to gender justice—women's hijabs can have meanings that they could not possibly have in countries which do not even subscribe to the idea of equality.

But things are changing here as well. Interestingly, the issue of hijab and whether it is religiously required or not is now coming under scrutiny among women who grew up wearing it. Some are re-reading old texts and concluding that the veil is irrelevant to Islamic piety. They cast it off even as they remain committed Muslims.

It is too soon to tell whether this development, emerging most particularly among intellectual women who once wore hijab, will gather force and become a new unveiling movement for the 21st century: one that repeats, on other continents and in completely new ways, the unveiling movement of the early 20th century. Still, in a time when a number of countries have tried banning the hijab and when typically such rules have backfired, it is worth noting that here in America, where there are no such bans, a new movement may be quietly getting under way, a movement led this time by committed Muslim women who once wore hijab and who, often after much thought and study, have taken the decision to set it aside.

Occasionally now, although less so than in the past, I find myself nostalgic for the Islam of my childhood and youth, an Islam without veils and far removed from politics. An Islam which people seemed to follow not in the prescribed, regimented ways of today but rather according to their own inner sense, and their own particular temperaments, inclinations and the shifting vicissitudes of their lives.

I think my occasional yearning for that now bygone world has abated 20
(not that it is entirely gone) for a number of reasons. As I followed, a little like a detective, the extraordinary twists and turns of history that brought

about this entirely unpredicted and unlikely "return" of the veil, I found the story itself so absorbing that I seemed to forget my nostalgia. I also lost the vague sense of annoyance, almost of affront, that I'd had over the years at how history had, seemingly so casually, set aside the entirely reasonable hopes and possibilities of that brighter and now vanished era.

In the process I came to see clearly what I had long known abstractly: that living religions are by definition dynamic. Witness the fact that today we have women priests and rabbis—something unheard of just decades ago. As I followed the shifting history of the veil—a history which had reversed directions twice in one century—I realised that I had lived through one of the great sea changes now overtaking Islam. My own assumptions and the very ground they stood on had been fundamentally challenged. It now seems absurd that we once labelled people who veiled "backward" and those who did not "advanced" and that we thought that it was perfectly fine and reasonable to do so. Seeing one's own life from a new perspective can be unsettling, of course—but it is also quite bracing, and even rather exciting.

Analyze

1. What does Ahmed mean by "reinventing" the veil?
2. In several passages, Ahmed draws attention to her own thinking—and how it changed during her research. Consider, for instance, paragraphs 12 through 14. How do these passages function in the article? How do they show something crucial? How do they support her main idea?
3. Explain Ahmed's point about context and the meaning of hijab. Which single sentence best characterizes her point?
4. Ahmed calls religions "dynamic." What does she mean? And how does that meaning figure into her main idea?
5. People often imagine that society advances through history—that civilizations move forward in some collective way toward a more enlightened or more free state. Explain how Ahmed's conclusion complicates or challenges the idea of such progress.

Explore

1. Why do you think hijab generates so many questions or concerns? Why does the veil carry so much cultural weight?

2. Can something as old as hijab be reinvented? What cultural forces keep something from being reinvented?
3. How do religious traditions figure into cultural change or cultural stasis? Consider a religious practice or ritual other than Islamic dress to develop your point.
4. *Cultural context* is key to Ahmed's analysis of hijab. Broadly speaking, what is the relationship between meaning and context—between the meaning of a specific act and the culture surrounding it?
5. Have you ever been able to view your own life from a new perspective? If so, what happened? What prompted the new vision? If not, what forces or habits or social patterns have kept you from a new perspective?

Forging Connections

1. How does identity get used to sell products and services? Explain how a particular advertisement or advertising campaign targets a specific demographic: young heterosexual men, middle-aged white women, young Hispanic women, gender-neutral teens, older rural or suburban white men, and so on. Explain how specific elements in the ad appeal to the target audience. To help explain the relationship between marketing and identity, borrow insights from Robert Moor, "Mother Nature's Sons" (Chapter 7) and Fredrik deBoer, "The Resentment Machine" (Chapter 2).
2. What happens to identity on social media? How does it get complicated or simplified? In what ways does identity flatten out or change? In an essay, argue that social media either enriches or diminishes personal identity. Make a case that relies on your own experience and your research of specific social media. Integrate quotations, descriptions, even terms of agreement between users and social media providers. Borrow insights from any of the writers in Chapter 4, "Social Media: How We Communicate."

Looking Further

1. How are personal identity and culture related? How do the two concepts influence one another? Does one cause the other? Does one fold into the other? Does one challenge or animate the other? In an analytical essay, explain the relationship. Although you are dealing with

concepts, try to ground your ideas with specific examples and situations. Use your own life experience to dramatize ideas. Allude to popular culture or history to illustrate your thinking. Integrate images and photographs to flesh out especially abstract points.

2. Eboo Patel and S. Alan Ray deal with identity issues on college campuses. Explore the demographics of your own campus. Research changes in one specific category: race, gender, religion, or sexual orientation. In an essay, explain how the student body has changed, in that one respect, over the past decade, and over several decades. Explain what institutional or social forces may have influenced that change, and finally, explore the relationship between your college campus and the surrounding culture. Is your campus a microcosm—a representation of the broader American culture? Or is it distinct in some way?

Chapter 5

Entertainment: What We Watch, How We Listen

If we want to understand the intellectual trends of a culture, we would do well to explore its schools, colleges, and universities. But if we want to understand a culture's emotional reflexes, we should study its entertainment. What a culture reads, watches, and listens to says something about its collective desires, hopes, and fears. After all, when we're listening to music or watching our favorite programs, we are not simply escaping daily life; we are escaping *into* something—into an invented reality that resonates with how we feel or how we want to feel for a while.

Entertainment is a form of escape, but it is also a reflection of shared fears and hopes. Consider, for instance, how many thousands of films and novels focus on the horrors of technology gone wrong—humanity's own creation taking over. From *Frankenstein* to the *Matrix* films, plenty of works dramatize the fear of our own creations. Or consider the many happy endings in Hollywood movies, those that show peace between races, reconciliation of enemies, the utter destruction of evil, or the discovery of true love. Such works dramatize what millions of people quietly yearn for in their own lives. In other words, entertainment gives shape to and reflects a range of deep emotions. It embodies what people hate, love, need, crave, and fear.

It is no wonder, then, that scholars, writers, and everyday citizens want the most popular forms of entertainment to reflect their lives. They want to see themselves—or people like themselves—on the screen and inside of the drama. They want to escape into someone else's life, but they also want that life to resemble their own. This is the tension of contemporary entertainment, and the writers in this chapter deal with it directly. Whether it's a need for community, a hope for realism, or a longing to see men and women who resemble those in our lives, the articles and blogs in this chapter examine specific works from popular culture and explain how they reveal or resemble parts of our own identities.

Laura Bennett

Fallon and Letterman and the Invisible Late Show Audience

A staff writer at *The New Republic*, Laura Bennett explores issues related to TV and film entertainment. She is the author of numerous magazine articles, book reviews, and blog posts. In the following magazine article, Bennett examines the ways late-night TV audiences build a sense of community.

Last night both Jimmy Fallon and David Letterman sent their studio audiences home for the storm and did their shows for an empty theater. The result was an eerie kind of performance art: all those rows of empty chairs, the coughs and cleared throats from crew members, the strange clarity of each single peal of laughter from someone backstage. Both shows opened with their respective hosts standing outside in the whipping rain like weathermen, explaining that the show would go on. "There's no audience tonight," Fallon said into the camera. "So you are the audience. So imagine laughter. Imagine fun. Imagine excitement."

The bands had clearly been instructed to play extra loudly to cover up the silence as the hosts jogged on stage. "Please, please, keep it down," Fallon joked as the studio echoed with straggling claps from cameramen and producers. Letterman had a crew member hold up hand-written cards with alternate names for Hurricane Sandy that included "Trumpical Storm" and "Oprah Windy," a gag that called attention to just how far this comedy landscape has drifted from the analog world. (Fallon read from a list of viewer submissions to the hashtag #halloweendisaster.) "You're performing as if there was an audience," said announcer Steve Higgins to Fallon as he paused between jokes. "I'm assuming that people at home will be watching either on their laptops or with their generators out, and they'll want to leave room for laughs," he said.

Both *Late Night* and *The Late Show* highlighted just how much the studio audience has become ingrained in the format—the way Fallon occasionally hands cue cards for failed jokes to people in the crowd, or dispenses high-fives as he leaves the theater, and how Letterman is a master of playing up the casual one-on-one chat with an audience member for laughs. It was hard not to miss that classic moment when Letterman stands and smiles and soaks up the applause before his monologue. Or the way he pauses and rides out a joke, riffing over the laughter, letting it sink in. And watching Letterman and Fallon was to become newly attuned to the art of the segue: the sudden, uneasy emptiness of between-joke pauses, accompanied by an impulse to doubt whether the thing you heard was as funny as it seemed since it felt so newly strange that no other voices were laughing.

Todd VanDerWerff of The AV Club wrote last year that the "illusion of community," especially for TV comedy, is becoming less and less important. He attributed this to the fact that audiences have increasingly been raised on "setup-punchline humor" that makes it hard for us to be surprised by anything, and the way the Internet "provides an instant community for viewers." "We don't need ghost voices to laugh with us," he wrote, "when we have our friends online spitting out LOLs." In the era of TV blogs and Twitter we have substituted reliance on the arbitrary tastes of the studio audience for a curated, engaged, and informed community of our own making.

Granted, both shows last night were hilarious. Fallon was absurdist and 5
fidgety; Letterman was calm and resolute—the joke was his pretending that nothing was different at all. Both used shots of the empty seats to great comic effect. And generally speaking both shows made for excellent

television, offering up a totally new angle on the late-night experience that hinged on the thrill of being privy to behind-the-scenes dynamics: the particular jokes the crew laughed at, the amped-up rapport between Letterman and wingman Shaffer and the crew, and between Fallon and announcer Steve Higgins and the Roots and everyone else on set. But instead of convincing me that the live studio audience is a bygone trick, a vestigial limb of the late-night format, it reminded me why the on-set community is still key to the experience of these shows.

> "In the era of TV blogs and Twitter we have substituted reliance on the arbitrary tastes of the studio audience for a curated, engaged, and informed community of our own making."

Watching *The Late Show,* I thought of a great old clip from 1986 when Letterman led his whole audience in an enthusiastic rendition of "O, Canada," an off-key chorus of random voices filling the small studio. It was a display of rowdy, impromptu, human-to-human community, and it was so much fun to watch. Today the illusion of community is everywhere, but the late night show is the one place where it does not unfurl in a sidebar of piecemeal commentary but in the midst of the action, in a way that allows the host to participate and respond. So last night's Letterman and Fallon were ultimately a reminder that the talk show still relies on in-person community—even in the age of hashtags, there is something weirdly comforting about that filled-up room.

Analyze

1. Bennett suggests that live studio audiences have an inherent value—something, perhaps, beyond entertainment. What is that value? And what passage or sentence from the article best characterizes that value?
2. Explain how *community* figures into Bennett's main idea. What does she mean by *community?* How is it connected to live studio audiences?
3. Explain how Todd VanDerWerff's point in paragraph 4 fits into Bennett's overall point. How does VanDerWerff's description of prevailing trends in entertainment support or reinforce something critical in Bennett's article?
4. Analyze Bennett's final statement. What does "weirdly comforting" suggest? How does it relate to the rest of the article?

5. The chapter introduction claims that entertainment "embodies what people hate, love, need, crave, and fear." How does Bennett's article speak to this claim?

Explore

1. Bennett explains that "illusion of community is everywhere." What does she mean by "illusion" and how does that contrast with something more real or genuine?
2. Point to other situations in the media—or in daily life—that support or conjure the illusion of community.
3. What is your favorite hosted television program? Explain its particular qualities or values—what it does for viewers, what kind of entertainment it provides.
4. How does community "unfurl in a sidebar of piecemeal commentary?" What do you think Bennett is describing?
5. The chapters of this book argue that culture is filled with, and even defined by, the tension between tradition and change. What cultural tensions does Bennett describe in her article? What do you think is the most important or critical tension related to late-night television shows?

Richard Lawson and Jen Doll

Lies Hollywood Told Us: Love and Romance Edition

Writers for *The Atlantic Wire*, Richard Lawson and Jen Doll explore the quirky underside of popular culture and entertainment news. In the following article, they dissect several romantic myths that Hollywood films perpetuate.

Love is hard. Romantic movies make it harder. We've lived through lifetimes of rom-coms and romances and the occasional dramas that make relationships seem ever so simple or sometimes complicated but still beautiful. . . . If you only wait it out and sleep in your makeup and make sure to attend weddings with your gay best friend, and love dogs and do the right thing and are fully aware of when he or she is or is not just that into you. And we are tired. Tired of the lies. Tired of the misleading details. Tired of being fooled into thinking that real life works this way, and therefore our expectations are completely and totally reasonable and why hasn't anyone flown a plane overhead explaining how devoted they are to us? Sure, *The Five-Year Engagement* may have been a flop, but that doesn't mean it didn't imperil thousands of Americans with unrealistic romantic expectations, and, further, continue a long tradition of movies cementing bad habits and relationship turmoil. Let's put a stop to it, here and now. Here are the ways in which Hollywood lies. It probably cheats, too.

You will never have to choose between two amazing men (or women) who love you equally and utterly but in completely opposite ways. One will not be a brunette, and one will not be a blonde, because you either like blondes or you like brunettes. One will also not be a hunter while the other is a bread-maker, and one will not be courageous and strong and your best friend while the other loves you unconditionally, even, maybe, after he's been driven mad by corrupt governmental forces. Neither of them will want to kill you, unless you're complaining about taking out the garbage again, and in that case, it's only figuratively. Nor will you have to choose between your adoring, perfect boyfriend or girlfriend and his/her annoying, perfect best friend. More likely, you will tolerate the annoying best friend who's always making the dumb jokes or talking about shopping because your beloved adores that person, foul piece of humanity he or she may be, and, more importantly, when you make fun of the BFF your beloved tends to get really annoyed and denies you sex.

You will not find someone ten years after you met them but did not give them your number because you were being weird or whimsical and, at the time, coyly believed in fate. You will not be able to track them down using old receipts and half-disappeared memories, they will not appear magically at a skating rink when it has just begun to snow. And even if they do, even if you and your wacky friend do somehow manage to track this person down, it will have been ten years and you only met them the once so it will be awkward and you will very quickly realize that the connection you felt all those years ago was just a quick, passing thing, a ribbon of lightning gone as quick as it came. You're both older now and you have different values and you live all the way across the country and this whole adventure will suddenly feel sad and strange instead of exciting and romantic. You will realize that if you were interested a decade ago you should have just given them your stupid phone number and he or she would have called and you would have gone on some dates and maybe it would have worked out and maybe it wouldn't have, but at least it would be then, and you would know, rather than wasting all this money on airplanes to New York ten long years later.

Your hook-up buddy will never be more than your hook-up buddy. Same with your sperm donor.

There will never be a last-minute chase scene as you board the plane 5
to Dubai/New York City/Los Angeles/Singapore/Iowa City, Iowa, in which your lover, former lover, or best friend not yet your lover has finally realized his or her grave mistake, and that he or she needs you desperately after all. This person will not stop you before you board and will certainly not board the plane himself, eyes wild, rushing through the seats to find you and ask for your hand in marriage. For one thing, in this day and age of air travel, that is impossible. Further: He will not be carrying flowers, or gifts, or even a bottle of water. There will be no grand gesture. More likely, if your lover does decide he wants to try again after you fly to Singapore, he will e-mail you and schedule a time in which you can Skype. It will probably be some months from the time you depart, around the same time that you start dating someone else, because former lovers have that sort of radar. Maybe he will convince you to come back, and maybe he won't. But he will not arrive at your doorstep, if you even have a doorstep, without telling you he's coming, and then get down on one knee and proffer a ring/a sign that says "To Me You Are Perfect"/a bottle of champagne/something important that only the two of you know about. If, on the very rare occasion, he actually does arrive, you will probably have to take out a restraining order, or, alternatively, pick him up at the airport.

You will never fall in love with a hooker with a heart of gold, or, if you are a hooker, your john will not fall in love with you and also happen to be a very wealthy businessman and a very nice person, too, who takes you on shopping sprees and cleans you up and makes you presentable and teaches you what fork to use at the dinner table and introduces you to high society. When you consider going back to your old ways, he will not climb a fire escape and rescue you and get down on one knee and promise to make you an honest woman. You will not watch Lucille Ball stomp on grapes together and congratulate yourselves on your good fortune in finding each other, and there will not be a kindly hotel manager who looks like Hector Elizondo to take anyone under his wing at the Regent Beverly Wilshire.

Your male friend will not suddenly realize he loves you. He will not have any romantic epiphany in which he remembers great, unwittingly sexy times you had together and realize suddenly that they make up a perfect patchwork quilt of love. If you have had this friend for years and years and he has not shown an interest then he is either a gay person or really just not into you. Either way, he will not show up at your house in the rain and tell you a story about something you two did when you were kids, he will not make an awkward, embarrassing speech at a party, in front of everyone. Your other friends will not nod and smile knowingly, because they thought you two would get together all along. (And if they did, wouldn't they be not very good friends for having never said anything to you?) There will not be a nice old jazz song that plays. There will be no end credits.

Your marriage will not be interrupted by the person who's actually right for you, at the altar, when the minister asks if anyone would like to speak out against said marriage. If anyone does disapprove of the marriage (and surely, someone, somewhere, will), they will never say anything until and unless your marriage ends, years later, possibly, and then that person will say something to the tune of, "I never liked him/her anyway." This person is more likely to be a relative than the person who has hidden away their love for you, like a locket underground, for many, many years because they only wanted you to be happy, even though you clearly weren't. Additionally, you will not be a wedding planner who falls in love with a client, or a client who falls in love with a wedding planner, or, for that matter, an escort who falls in love with a client, or a client who falls in love with an escort, and you will certainly not marry someone you meet when you are a bridesmaid at a wedding, or a guest at a funeral.

That slacker guy who got you pregnant? Chances are, he's not going to reform and suddenly become wonderful. But you never know!

You will not fall in love with someone you fight with all the time, be they neighbor or coworker or obnoxious magazine writer. If you fight with them all the time it means you do not like each other and do not get along and should not, will not, date. Why would you want to date the asshole across the hall anyway? Why would that smug jerk at the rival advertising company suddenly seem appealing? This will not happen. You are enemies, not future lovers. Stay away from this person because they make you mad and you do stupid things to get back at them, stupid wacky zany things that no one will find cute, they will just think you're annoying and you will probably get fired or evicted and it will all be because of this complete ass who you will never fall in love with.

There will not be a makeover montage. There just won't be.

You will not meet on a boat, or on a plane, or in a school or florist's shop or mall, or via a professional male matchmaker, and be of two different social and economic classes yet know from the minute your eyes meet that you are kindred spirits destined to be together despite the odds, despite impending tragedy. You will not save one another over and over again, from water, from fire, from certain death, from bad humans, from falling back into your own sad life. You will not, in the end, attempt to climb atop a board together—once, only once—and fail, and then stop trying. You will not freeze to death in the cold, cold sea waters after the *Titanic* has sunk.

There will not be a comedy of manners or tiny, insurmountable offenses, in which he says one thing and you take it the wrong way and then you say something else, and then other people stick their noses in and sway you in one way or the other, but then he saves your sister from ill repute, and you finally realize what a good man he is, and how he love-love-loves you.

There will not be a "happy ever after." There might be a happy sometimes. For best chances of such, stop believing what you see in romantic movies.

Analyze

1. Explain the function of Lawson and Doll's opening statement. How does their first claim relate to or support their main point?
2. Unlike many articles, especially more formal works written in an academic setting, this article uses the second-person pronoun *you* to address readers directly. How does that affect your understanding of the point? How does it influence the way you read it?
3. Lawson and Doll take on and refute a range of typical romance movie formulas—and *suggest* specific movies along the way. How does this strategy work for the overall success of the article? Why is it better or worse not to continue listing specific characters or plots throughout the article?

4. Lawson and Doll explain, to some degree, their purpose in writing the article. In your own words, what is their purpose? What are they trying to do with this article? What do they want for their audience?
5. What other article, book, or even television show has the same purpose as Lawson and Doll? Explain, as specifically as possible, how another author or person is aiming for the same effect.

Explore

1. Does a small part of you still cling to the romantic formulas that Lawson and Doll mention? Or do you know someone who still clings to these romantic ideals? If so, why? What's the attraction? Why can't some people (or most people) let these ideals go?
2. Lawson and Doll argue that Hollywood makes romantic relationships even harder than they naturally are. How does your experience support or challenge that claim?
3. What other unhealthy ideals do Hollywood movies project? (If you can, give specific movie titles or scenes.)
4. When people talk about movies, television, and influence, they often focus on children—on the way popular culture prompts feelings and behaviors in developing lives. But what about adults? Using your own experiences and observations, explain how popular entertainment may influence healthy and fully mature adults.
5. Do you think Americans are more able to resist the allure of popular entertainment than they were in previous eras? Why or why not?

Stefan Babich
The Fall of the Female Protagonist in Kids' Movies

Stefan Babich is a blogger for *Persephone Magazine*, which describes itself as "a daily blog focused on topics of interest for modern, intelligent, clever women." The blog's goal is to "give a voice to more women from a variety of backgrounds and with diverse interests." In the following post, Babich considers the role of female protagonists in animated children's films.

There was a time, not too long ago, when two-dimensional, hand-drawn animation and computer-generated cartoons existed side-by-side. Every fall, sometime around Thanksgiving, Pixar and Disney would collaborate and release a family comedy featuring anthropomorphic creatures or objects rendered with state-of-the-art computer graphics. Every summer, Disney would come out with another one of its more traditional pieces, an animated musical based on some hopelessly depressing classic story made kid-friendly by the addition of rousing songs and sidekicks with attention deficit hyperactivity disorder. It seemed a perfect arrangement, one built to last. The two types of films were different enough that there was room for both—the classic adventure/dramas that earned Disney its name, and the edgier, more tongue-in-cheek Pixar films that were designed to amuse adults as well as kids.

The alliance was not to last. Slowly but inexorably, the new, computer-animated films drove their hand-drawn cousins aside, until now, hand-drawn children's films are (at least in America) a relic of the past. All the major animated films of this year so far (*Rango, Rio, Gnomeo and Juliet*) have been made with computers.

It's not entirely clear what killed the hand-drawn animated movie. Maybe it was Disney's decision to abandon the musical format in its latest summer releases (*Atlantis* and *Lilo and Stitch* featured no songs, and *Tarzan,* while containing a fair number of songs, did not have any singing characters). Maybe it was the box-office triumphs of computer-animated films like *Shrek* and *Monsters, Inc.* over their hand-drawn counterparts (*Monsters, Inc.* trounced *Atlantis, The Lost Empire* in box offices worldwide). In any case, it soon became clear that the battle between the two forms of animation was over, and the victor clear.

In any battle, there are casualties, and the "animation war" was no exception. One of the most unfortunate (and surprising) side effects of the triumph of computer-generated animation was the death of the female protagonist in children's movies.

Think of all the female protagonists in Disney musicals. There are quite 5
a number, almost as many as there are males—Cinderella, Belle, Ariel, Pocahontas, Mulan . . . the list goes on. Now think of female protagonists in Pixar movies.

There aren't any. Not a single one.

In Dreamworks, the story isn't quite as bad. But it still took them until 2009 to release their first movie starring a female character in a leading role (*Monsters v. Aliens*).

In 2012, Pixar, maybe having noticed the troubling discrepancy in its numbers, is aiming to change its game by releasing its first female-centric film, titled *Brave.* One has to wonder what took them so long.

It's easy to cut Pixar a break. After all, they've made a lot of critically-acclaimed movies, the most recent of which (*Up* and *Toy Story 3*) were nominated for Best Picture at the Academy Awards. They've combined state-of-the-art technology with skillful and emotionally resonant storytelling. And, despite the shortage of female protagonists, they have had a number of strong, memorable female characters. Characters like Elastigirl from *The Incredibles,* and Eve, from *Wall-E.* Fernanda Diaz of FlavorWire argues: "For Pixar to have a gender 'problem,' it would have to systematically place women in subservient roles and make the male superior—something which none of the films actually do." But is this really the only definition of sexism? Arguably, Pixar—and other similar companies—do show male superiority by showing, time and again, that the most important figures in a story are always male.

10 The most confusing part is that most of the stories in these animated movies would work just as well with a female protagonist. Is there any reason the rat in *Ratatouille* couldn't have been a lady? Is there any reason *Wall-E* couldn't have been the story of a female-voiced robot who encounters a male-voiced love interest named ADAM? It's not as though the gender of these characters is their most important feature, or indeed, very relevant at all to their personalities or the stories they are a part of. As Linda Holmes writes for NPR:

> Russell, in *Up,* is Asian-American, right? And that's not a big plot point; presumably, he just is because there's no particular reason he shouldn't be. You don't need him to be, but you don't need him not to be, either. It's not politics; it's just seeing the whole big world. Well, the whole big world has a lot of little girls in it, too.

Just as it's easy to defend Pixar, it is fairly easy to criticize Disney films for being sexist. And to be fair, there's a lot about Disney's past portrayals of women that's deserving of criticism, beyond the fact that almost all its female characters happen to be princesses. A disturbingly large percentage of their female leads end up getting saved by a man at some point, usually the climax. Ariel is rescued from the villainess by heroic prince Eric; Jasmine is rescued from the villain by Aladdin. Furthermore, a pretty big percentage of the female leads in Disney musicals seem to have only one goal—to get the guy. Their desire to obtain a man seems to be the most important motivating force in their lives, and the drama of the films often revolve around that desire. There is Ariel, in *The Little Mermaid,* who gives away her voice in order to obtain the love of Prince Eric. There is Cinderella, whose escape from her family lies in getting the prince to fall in love with her. Is Disney portraying women as weak, dependent people dependent on a man's love for their happiness and well-being?

Well, Disney might not be quite as sexist as it first appears. After all, when it comes to the focus on finding romance above all else, it's pretty much the same deal with the male protagonists. Though the girls seem to be driven by a desire to get the guy, the guys also seem unable to find happiness unless they get the girl. A lot of the male-centric story lines mirror the female-centric ones in key respects. In place of Cinderella, we have Aladdin, who pretends to be a prince to get the princess just as she disguises herself in order to get the prince. We have Hercules, who gives up his godhood to be with a woman, just as Ariel gives up her kingdom under the sea to be with Eric. Tarzan is only really happy when he gets to be with Jane. Often, when we see a Disney princess pining over a man, it's not really sexism on display—it's just the romantic nature of Disney movies. The men are just as single-mindedly obsessed with romance as are the women.

Admittedly, this defense doesn't address the fact that so many females in Disney movies need rescuing during the big action scenes. Yes, Disney has a justified reputation for sexism. But it was improving with the times. Mulan and Pocahontas were certainly more proactive characters than Belle and Ariel, just as these characters were stronger than Cinderella and Sleeping Beauty. And the fact is that Disney had a much higher percentage of female protagonists than Hollywood as a whole. That has to count for something.

It's not that hard to argue Disney is no more sexist than Pixar or Dreamworks. After all, if little girls fifteen years ago were left with somewhat stereotypical princesses as their role models, girls today have to come to grips with the fact that the male character is almost always the center of attention.

Surely such a striking trend has to be due to more than coincidence. 15
So, what exactly, killed the female animated protagonist?

The answer may lie in the few female protagonists there have been since the rise of Pixar and Dreamworks. Susan Murphy of *Monsters vs. Aliens,*

Rapunzel of *Tangled,* and Mérida of the upcoming *Brave* all share a striking characteristic—they are human.

Whereas most of the Disney movies of the '80s and '90s focused on human characters taken from classic fairytales and from history (people like Tarzan, Pocahontas, Quasimodo and of course, the Little Mermaid), the vast majority of computer animated films these days tend to revolve around anthropomorphic animals and objects ranging from toys to penguins to cars. Maybe it's because humans are harder to animate realistically with computers than cute talking critters; maybe it's because early CGI animated films like *Toy Story* and *A Bug's Life* set a trend that later movies just happened to follow. But it's odd that when female protagonists do show up in modern animated films, it's almost always in the ones starring actual people. There are exceptions, like Mala in the somewhat lesser known *Battle for Terra.* But the statistics are still pretty striking—and pretty intriguing.

Why is it that anthropomorphic creatures are far more likely to be male? It seems to suggest that our conception of the heroine is somehow linked to the physical. Why is it so important that a heroine have an attractive human body, while a male hero can be a rat, penguin, or robot?

Though we'd all like to think we've taken strides forward in terms of sexism in children's movies, it seems filmmakers are having difficulty separating the concept of "heroine" from the concept of "sexiness." But if most kids' movies are going to be about animals and objects, rather than human beings, that's what needs to happen if the female protagonist is to finally be revived.

Analyze

1. In some passages, Babich defends Disney and Pixar for their sluggish progress on female protagonists. Explain how those passages function. What do they help Babich to do? How do they help to develop the main idea?
2. According to Babich, what particular ideas, forces, or trends are behind the lack of female protagonists in kids' movies?
3. In the middle of this article, Babich quotes Linda Holmes from NPR. Explain how the quotation functions. How does it support or develop Babich's main idea?
4. Babich's article was published in *Persephone Magazine*—"a daily blog for bookish and clever women." How does the publication influence your understanding of the specific claims or support used throughout the article?
5. Explain how Babich's article deals with or points to cultural change.

Explore

1. Babich explains that "In 2012, Pixar, maybe having noticed the troubling discrepancy in its numbers, is aiming to change its game by releasing its first female-centric film, titled *Brave.* One has to wonder what took them so long." What do you think took Pixar so long?
2. Read Amanda Marcotte's article, "The Shocking Radicalism of *Brave*" (in this chapter). Does Marcotte offer any answers to the previous question?
3. Consider the following questions from Babich's article: "Why is it that anthropomorphic creatures are far more likely to be male?" "Why is it so important that a heroine have an attractive human body, while a male hero can be a rat, penguin, or robot?" What answers can you provide?
4. Consider other recent mainstream movies that feature female protagonists. Explain how those characters, or a particular character, upholds or challenges the trend in kids' movies. Are the lead women sexy and strong? Are any simply strong, intelligent, or savvy?
5. Consider the following online comment to Babich's blog: "The thing with Disney is that generally they just re-hash old fairy tales, which did contain princess characters that needed rescuing etc. That's not Disney's fault, it's just how the story goes. It *is* their fault however that they end up bland and soul-less after being 'Disneyfied.'" The commenter, Martin, makes a fairly common charge about Disney's shallow or uncomplicated movies. How do you think Martin's charge relates to Babich's concern about gender? How might the two points overlap?

Amanda Marcotte
The Shocking Radicalism of *Brave*

A feminist writer, Amanda Marcotte offers a witty perspective on contemporary political issues. She is a blogger and the author of the books *It's a Jungle Out There: The Feminist Survival Guide to Politically Inhospitable Environments* (2007) and *Get Opinionated: A Progressive's Guide to Finding Your Voice (and Taking a Little Action)* (2010). In the following article, Marcotte analyzes Pixar's film *Brave* (2012) through a feminist lens.

The marketing for Pixar's new girl-centric film, *Brave,* suggests it is a movie in which a wild-haired heroine single-handedly conquers the monarchy, the patriarchy, and the myth that there are no attractive flat-heeled shoes. Feminists as much as anyone imagined that this would be the story, since so much of today's media aimed at girls is about "empowering" young women (as if the main obstacle to women's equality throughout most of history has been a lack of spunk, instead of eons of direct and indirect oppression based on the notion that women exist to be the trophies and helpmeets of men). Small wonder then that so many critics have emerged from the theater a bit befuddled by what they saw: the story of a young princess and her mother trying to understand each other despite their radically different approaches to life as a woman in medieval society.

Tom Carson, while praising the movie's effectiveness, argued that the filmmakers "seem to be playing by rules that don't interest them very much and not making an especially bright job of it." Jacyln Friedman also loved the movie but asked, "If the sparkling minds at Pixar can't imagine their way out of the princess paradigm, how can we expect girls to?" It's hard to blame these critics for feeling a bit let down. The movie fails to present any alternatives to stifling gender roles; the lead character, Merida, is all rebellion, but she never offers any ideas for how to fix things other than a speech denouncing arranged marriages.

Still, there's a danger in letting this disappointment blind us. For all its faults, *Brave* is shockingly radical for a mainstream movie. As with *Wall-E* before it, *Brave* is an example of what happens when Pixar gets political. We don't get much in the way of imaginative alternatives to our current problems, but we do get a scathing satire that doesn't hold back despite being in a children's movie. *Wall-E* turned its satirical eye on the problem of mass consumerism and environmental destruction; the laziness and greed of the human race allows our planet to become a landfill while we become formless blobs without any goals higher than being fed more sugary sodas. In the end, no real path to prevent this dystopia is suggested. *Wall-E* seems satisfied to go no further than biting commentary.

Brave turns that same satirical eye toward the patriarchy. In the imaginary medieval Scotland of Merida's world, unquestioned male dominance lets men be buffoons. They spend all their time puffing out their chests and bragging about how tough they are. These men know so little outside of violent competition that the smallest upset—Merida's unwillingness to be traded in marriage like a baseball card—nearly dissolves the kingdom in war. As in real life, men in *Brave* often tune out women telling them things they don't want to hear, and Merida's father's reluctance to listen to his daughter almost causes him to accidentally kill his beloved wife.

5 Even more interesting, the filmmakers take a critical look at the way women function under male dominance. Many patriarchal societies leave the stressful job of forcing girls to comply with degrading social norms to women, especially mothers. Unlike other movies such as *Real Women Have Curves,* where sexism-enforcing mothers are painted as villains, Merida's mother, Elinor, pushes her daughter to perform femininity out of love. As with mothers throughout history who have done everything from put young girls on diets to hold them down to have their clitorises removed at puberty, they are acting not out of hatred but out of a love that leads them to protect their daughters from the price of rebellion. In real life, that price is often exile; in this movie, it's war. With stakes this high, it's hard not to feel for a mother in such a bind.

In this grim world of male dominance, the fantasy of a single individual changing everything with a grand gesture of empowerment starts to look silly indeed. A lesser film would have made Merida's plot to out-man the men at archery the end of the story, but this more realistic portrayal shows how individual action can make the situation worse. Only when the female characters start to work together—to take the collective action so beloved by progressive organizers—does actual change occur. In the end, *Brave* doesn't have much to do with girl-power fantasies that imagine girls doing it for themselves without offering a real challenge to male privilege. But it tells a story that feels awfully familiar to those doing feminist work in the maddeningly complex real world.

Analyze

1. For Marcotte, *Brave* represents a significant cultural shift—at least in terms of entertainment. In your own words, explain that shift.
2. In Marcotte's introductory paragraph, she puts quotes around "empowering." Why? What is she suggesting? What idea or subtle debate might the quotation marks signal or suggest?
3. Explain the function of Marcotte's second paragraph. What purpose does it serve? How do the Carson and Friedman critiques of *Brave* help to support Marcotte's main idea?
4. Explain how Marcotte's title relates to her main idea.

5. Carefully examine Marcotte's concluding paragraph. Explain how the distinction between individual and collective action figures into Marcotte's point about *Brave*.
6. Consider Stefan Babich's argument in "The Fall of the Female Protagonist in Kids' Movies" in this chapter. What particular ideas or beliefs do you think Marcotte shares with Babich?

Explore

1. *Brave* is about cultural change in a medieval society. What other movies take on big cultural shifts related to gender, race, or sexuality?
2. Why do you think so many movies focus on princesses? What's the appeal?
3. What is "the patriarchy"? Look up the term online. How are you part of it? How are you outside it?
4. Marcotte argues that *Brave* is more sophisticated than a girl-power fantasy. Can you think of another movie that could be labeled a boy- or girl-power fantasy? What specific elements of the movie (such as the characters, storyline, setting) make you think that it deserves the label?
5. How does a movie like *Brave* support or undermine a sense of community?

Steve Yates
The Sound of Capitalism

Steve Yates is a writer for the British publication *Prospect,* which defines itself as "an entertaining, informative and open-minded magazine that mixes compelling argument and clear headed analysis with elegance and vitality in design." In the following article, Yates considers the cultural value of hip hop. (Note British spelling conventions throughout.)

The latest album by the twin titans of hip hop has been a record-breaking success. On its release, Jay-Z and Kanye West's *Watch the Throne* had the highest ever first week sales on iTunes of any new album. A total of 290,000 copies were downloaded that week, and when CDs are taken into account, the album's sales approached the 450,000 mark. Hip hop is big business.

Watch The Throne is symbolic of the status that hip hop, or rap, has now reached. Originating in the South Bronx in New York City in the late 1970s, when performers began rapping over looped beats taken from soul and funk records, hip hop has since journeyed right into the heart of mainstream culture.

Jay-Z is married to Beyoncé Knowles, queen of R&B, and together they form the most influential power couple in global music. His wealth is estimated by *Forbes* at around $450m, and he has had 12 U.S. number one albums (only the Beatles, with 19, have had more). Kanye West's fortune is around $70m. *Watch the Throne* is thick with references to wealth—even the sleeve is designed by Givenchy's Riccardo Tisci: "Luxury rap, the Hermès of verses," raps Kanye, giving the brand its French pronunciation, lest anyone should think he was mistaking the high-end goods manufacturer for a mythic Greek messenger.

But for its detractors, this materialism is one of rap's three deadly sins, along with its violence and misogyny. Casual fans of hip hop often see its materialistic side as something either to be played down or embraced "ironically." Some commentators judge it more harshly. When the riots broke out across Britain this summer, many saw hip hop's celebration of materialism as one of the key causes. Paul Routledge, writing in the *Mirror,* summarised this view when he said, "I blame the pernicious culture of hatred around rap music, which glorifies violence and loathing of authority . . . [and] exalts trashy materialism."

Routledge is not *entirely* wrong. The story of hip hop's journey into the 5
cultural mainstream is the story of its love affair with materialism, or, more accurately, capitalism. Its lead exponents, like Jay-Z and Kanye West, are brilliant entrepreneurs with vast fortunes (even if their music advocates a profligacy that is anathema to the savvy business operator). Hip hop's rise has been, at root, a straightforward process of free-market enterprise: an excellent product has been pushed with great skill and new markets opened up with real dynamism and flair.

Unsurprisingly, corporate brands have been keen to get involved. Darren Wright, creative director of the Nike account at advertising agency

Wieden+Kennedy explains the appeal: "With hip hop you're buying more than music. It isn't a genre—it's a lifestyle, encompassing fashion, break dancing, the clothes or the jewels you wear. . . . The lifestyle is worth its weight in gold because it's not just about one rap song, it's so much more."

The view of hip hop as a genre concerned only with the basest forms of materialism is a serious oversimplification. It misunderstands the way that rap's relationship with capitalism has fed its creativity and led to both its commercial and artistic success.

While modern hip hop is unashamedly materialistic, its ancestors were different. As far back as the 1960s, artists such as *The Last Poets* and Gil Scott-Heron combined African-American music with spoken word poetry. But Scott-Heron, like others of that generation, was critical of the passive materialism that he saw working its way into black culture. As he intoned on "The Revolution Will Not Be Televised": "The revolution will not go better with Coke/The revolution will not fight the germs that may cause bad breath/The revolution will put you in the driver's seat." This political consciousness was taken up in the 1980s by the extraordinary Public Enemy, a New York group that mixed incendiary politics with apocalyptic music, militaristic dress and cartoon humour. Gentler, but still political, takes on "Afrocentricity" were advanced by the brilliant Native Tongues collective including groups like De La Soul, A Tribe Called Quest and the Jungle Brothers.

But by the early 1990s, this "conscious" streak was being eclipsed by the giddy thrills of gangsta rap. Its motivation was pithily summarised by NWA (Niggaz With Attitude), the group who named and codified the subgenre, on their track "Gangsta Gangsta"—"life ain't nothin' but bitches and money." Despite this apparent nihilism, NWA embraced the American dream with relish. They set down the unapologetic "money-is-all" credo of the low-level street hustler, in which drug dealing, guns and the police swirl about in a ferocious urban storm. Like other popular representations of American gangsterism—*The Godfather, Scarface*—it was a vision of unfettered free market enterprise.

10 Slowly, the early political message was replaced by this focus on accumulation, both in the lyrics and also the business practice of those who were running the scene. One of hip hop's key entrepreneurs was Percy "Master P" Miller, who grew his No Limit empire from an L.A. record shop into a record label and then into a conglomerate. Miller spearheaded a new wave of hip hop business by entering into joint ventures with music companies.

He chose Priority, which was independent of the major record labels, and which had made a packet out of NWA and other leading artists. His deal brought all the benefits of working for major labels, such as distribution and marketing muscle, without the drawbacks—Master P was able to retain copyright control over the music and release records to his own schedule.

But not content with music, he diversified wildly: clothing, property, Master P dolls—even telephone sex lines. His debut film, the low-budget, straight-to-video *I'm Bout It* (1997) raked in sales that would have satisfied major studios. In 1998, Miller's companies grossed $160m.

In New York, the business interests of Sean "Puff Daddy" Combs developed along parallel lines: music, restaurants, a magazine, the inevitable clothing line, all name-stamped in a manner that led the consumer back to the man himself. Dan Charnas, in his masterful book *The Big Payback: The History Of The Business Of Hip Hop,* describes Miller and Combs as "the embodiment of the superpowered artist, two one-man brands, the fulfilment of [the] vision of self-determination and ownership—not just for hip hop artists, not just for black artists, but for all American artists." Having turned their art into business, they turned their business back into art. According to Charnas, their success "would mark the beginning of an unprecedented spike in black American entrepreneurship."

So while hip hop started off as an underground, and often political movement, it has for many years pursued an increasingly intimate relationship with business. Hip hop now has a materialist, acquisitive streak hard-wired into its identity. It is this embrace of capitalism that has taken hip hop from outsider status right to America's core. This ascent was neatly symbolised when Barack Obama, on the nomination campaign trail in 2008, dismissed criticisms from the Clinton camp by mimicking Jay-Z's famous "dirt off my shoulder" gesture. Asked which rappers were on his iPod, there was only one candidate.

British variants of rap music have been growing in success, too. Yet the contrast with America is marked. Maybe the conflicting attitudes are born of economic realism: the market is much smaller, and British hip hop has a limited international audience. That was perhaps why British rap's flirtation with outlandish "bling" materialism was comparatively short-lived. In the early 2000s, the south London group So Solid Crew emerged at the forefront of the "garage" scene. Its members imitated the flow, though not the accents, of American rap superstars over electronic dance rhythms that successfully merged influences ranging from American house and hip hop, to Jamaican dancehall and British drum 'n' bass. Instantly, they became the sound of young black London. "Proper [rap] songs started with So Solid," says Elijah Butterz, a 24-year-old DJ and label owner, over a pint of Guinness in a Walthamstow pub. "When they hit, *eeeeveryone* was into them. If you listened to garage you were cool. If you didn't you weren't."

So Solid, along with other British garage acts, brought American-style bling culture to Britain's clubs. Smart dress, diamonds and champagne became dancefloor staples. But this quickly generated a backlash. Wretch 32 is a 26-year-old from Tottenham who found fame this year with two number one singles and a top five album. He feels that the norms of American hip hop do not always translate well in Britain: "I think because of our culture, people don't go for stuff like that—someone making them feel like they're less of a person for having less money."

In response, east London rapidly developed its own sound, called grime—a rap-dominated genre with a harsh, electronic edge, and lyrics that sounded like a fight in a fried chicken shop. Chantelle Fiddy, 30, a journalist and label consultant, agrees: "Grime was the middle finger to [garage]. It was for those people who were either not old enough or didn't have the money to go to the [garage] raves. Someone like me, who came up through jungle and just danced like a dick in trainers, I never felt comfortable with garage."

Grime has had its triumphs. Dizzee Rascal scored a significant success with his 2003 debut *Boy In Da Corner.* Others, such as Tinchy Stryder, Tinie Tempah and now Wretch 32 have followed in Dizzee's wake, increasingly adapting the sound for the mainstream. But inflated claims of riches don't really fly. "In grime you can't really lie about it," says Sian Anderson, a 20-year-old writer, label consultant, PR and DJ for the influential radio station Rinse FM. "If you're talking about popping champagne and then you go out on [the] road and you haven't got an amazing car and you don't look that great, then everyone knows you're a liar and your music's not real, so you're back to square one."

Road rap is south London's counterpart to the east end's grime. Slower and meaner than grime, and with a closer resemblance to U.S. gangsta rap, it's shown little interest in winning mainstream acceptability. Its biggest name, Giggs, has served time on weapons charges—he started in the music business when he got out. But his career has been dogged by police interference. His shows have frequently been cancelled and contract talks with a major record company were curtailed, reputedly after a call to the label from Operation Trident, the unit in the Metropolitan Police dealing with black-on-black gun crime. Then came Form 696, a risk-assessment form requiring London promoters to submit extensive details about themselves, their performers and even, in the original version, the probable ethnic make-up of the audience. After this, grime and road rap often struggled to get live bookings. Although the Met denied racial profiling, senior music industry figures complained to the Equality and Human Rights Commission about this stringent requirement.

Denied a live platform, they've found a new one online, notably on SBTV, now confidently billed as Britain's biggest youth media channel. But not everyone cares about chasing the music mainstream anyway. "I don't want to be part of it," says Elijah Butterz. "Apart from Rinse, there's nothing there doing what I want to do. Everyone expects you to dig into the music industry, but as long as I can make money from bookings and merchandising, I'll continue doing what I'm doing." For Elijah, that means running the eponymous Butterz label, one of very few to still release vinyl records, Djing (for free) on Rinse and living off his DJ club bookings.

This quiet determination seems a long way from the hardheaded ambi- 20
tions of American hip hop, whose outlook has always been more expansive. "There's no protocol to the things I'm selling because I'm selling my culture," Jay-Z's partner Damon Dash, told me in 2003. Dash was the driving force behind the growth of Roc-A-Fella, their jointly-owned music business, whose name is an explicit reference to the capitalist heights they sought to scale.

The relationship between American hip hop and leading brands has always been strong. Adidas sales spiked after Run-DMC's 1986 track "My Adidas"; Tommy Hilfiger went from obscurity to being the highest-traded clothing company on Wall Street in 1996 after steady name-dropping by hip hop artists from 1992. Courvoisier reportedly received a 30 percent sales boost in the U.S. after Busta Rhymes released "Pass The Courvoisier"—the largest single rise since Napoleon III named it the official cognac of the imperial court. Its rival, Hennessy, the most popular brandy in hip hop, estimates that the majority of its customers are young black males.

British rappers are learning this lesson. Dizzee Rascal has had two Nike trainers of his own—an invaluable tie-in—and now owns his own label, Dirtee Stank. Tinie Tempah has a clothing range with Disturbing London, while Tinchy Stryder's Star In The Hood line looks a more durable bet than his records.

But this is still a far cry from the U.S., where rappers get to hobnob with the president. On *Watch The Throne*'s emblematic "Murder To Excellence," Kanye and Jay-Z contrast the black-on-black murder of American ghettoes with their lives of luxury. "Black tie, black Maybachs/Black excellence, opulence, decadence/Tuxes next to the President, I'm present," raps Jay-Z, before bemoaning how few black faces he sees at the pinnacle and calling on more to join him.

When critics zero in on hip hop's materialism, as they did this summer, they see just a fraction of the story—the fraction that talks about money, cars and glamour. But fixating on this element of hip hop ignores its limited appeal in Britain, where rappers have largely ditched the "bling" posturing of the early 2000s. When Wiley, the most influential man in grime after Dizzee Rascal, called his recent album *100% Publishing,* he was celebrating his bargaining power. It's a similar sentiment expressed by Margate rapper Mic Righteous, who, contrasting his homeless past with his present, raps, "I used to cherish every pound I got, now I cherish every pound I earn."

In the past 30-or-so years, hip hop has tried politics and it has tried gangsterism. But in the end it settled for capitalism, which energized it and brought it to a position of global dominance. American rappers like Puff Daddy and Master P, men who fought their way into the big time, did so by selling a vision of independence, empowerment and material success. That vision is also found, if less vividly, in Britain's rap music. And though hip hop retains unpleasant features, the core message, that people can have better lives, is incontestably a good one.

Analyze

1. How is this a pro-hip hop article?
2. Early in the article, Yates mentions hip hop's materialism. What does he mean by materialism?
3. Yates gives a brief history of hip hop in America and Britain. How does that history help to support his point about "the sound of capitalism"?
4. Toward the end of his article, Yates describes a relationship between cognac and a Busta Rhymes album. Explain how this passage relates to Yates's main idea.

5. How is this article about cultural change and resistance to change? If hip hop has become normal, a substantial phenomenon at the center of society, how did it happen? How does Yates's article help to make sense of the process?

Explore

1. Yates says that "Hip hop now has a materialist, acquisitive streak hard-wired into its identity." Give some examples that you know of to support or challenge this statement.
2. Yates explains, "In the past 30-or-so years, hip hop has tried politics and it has tried gangsterism. But in the end it settled for capitalism." How are politics and gangsterism fundamentally different from capitalism? Or how are they not different?
3. Yates discusses the relationship between American and British hip hop artists almost interchangeably. What does this say about the relationship between the U.S. and British cultures?
4. How do you think hip hop represents late 20th-century America? What particular values or beliefs does the musical style embody?
5. Make a case that Yates's article should have appeared in Chapter 2, "Consumerism: How We Spend." In other words, explain why his ideas are more related to how we consume than what we do to entertain ourselves.

Forging Connections

1. Consider the ways nature gets used to sell products and services. For example, in car commercials, vast desert landscapes often surround a family sedan, rushing mountain streams are used to market beer, and forest canopies help to sell sleeping pills. Write an essay that examines the America's relationship with nature through advertisement. What do our ads suggest about the purpose of the natural world? What do they suggest about its role in human life or our role in the world around us? What kinds of attitudes and beliefs about nature do our most common ads reinforce? Borrow insights from Robert Moor, "Mother Nature's Sons" (Chapter 7) and Freddie deBoer, "The Resentment Machine" (Chapter 2).
2. Examine the language of your favorite movie or television program. Study the characters' vocabulary, use, formality, and dialect. What

particular phrases get repeated or promoted? What do those phrases suggest about the shared values? Write an analytical essay—or what is sometimes called an *ethnography*—about the language and the way it shapes the community of characters. Before writing, consider the strategies of writers in Chapter 3, "Language: What We Mean," specifically Blake Gopnik ("Revolution in a Can"), Robert Lane Greene ("OMG, ETC"), and Autumn Whitefield-Madrano ("Thoughts on a Word: Fine"). Although these writers have different purposes, they explore language and its influence on communities. As you develop your essay, integrate specific quotations and phrases from the movie or program.

Looking Further

1. Whether we like or not, television programs have messages. They suggest politics, tension between genders, age groups, races, classes, and religious traditions. Even the absence of people reinforces a way of thinking. For example, until the 2009 appearance of Susan Boyle on *Britain's Got Talent,* such programs consistently reinforced the idea that superstar singers are, or should be, young and sexy. This wasn't an overt message, but it was suggested by a range of judgments, storylines, camera angles, and audience responses. Take on a specific television program and examine the social or political messages it suggests. Write an analytical essay that focuses on one of those messages. Explain how the program whispers, implies, and quietly reinforces the message. Integrate quotations, images, and scene descriptions—anything to help illustrate your point.
2. What is your favorite genre of music? Examine its role as an economic force. As Yates does with rap music ("The Sound of Capitalism"), explore the way another genre has become part of the broader culture of commerce. What particular artists, albums, or technological advances helped the genre to become a viable part of the economy? What musical qualities or marketing strategies (or both) developed the genre into something that generates revenue and sustains the art form? Develop an essay that explains its emergence and role in people's lives. Rather than making a case for or against the genre, try to analyze it. Try to uncover why it has thrived—or barely survived—in the marketplace.

Chapter 6

Politics: How We Govern

Politics is a cultural drama. In no other arena can we more directly witness the tensions of a culture—the friction between the past and future, hopes and fears, values and needs, and even reality and imagination. In a televised representative democracy like the United States, we get to watch these frictions performed. We get to see questions grow into issues, debates, and drawn-out battles. In short, we get to witness a civilization arguing with and sometimes screaming at itself.

In literal terms, politics is about the *polis* (Greek for *city* or *gathering place*). In practical terms, politics is the implementation of laws that govern all realms public and private life: commerce, work, education, language, entertainment, consumption, even sex and procreation. It's no wonder, then, that politics garners so many emotions and that people demonize their opponents so openly. Everything about people's lives, at some point, comes down to political decisions. From preschool to nursing homes, from birth to burial, from inheritance to estate planning, our entire lives are governed by decisions that other people make on our behalf. If you are a citizen, an immigrant, or even a fetus, you are a political entity. Even if you are not interested in politics, they are interested in you—and to a large degree, they govern your daily and nightly behavior.

The readings in this chapter focus on a range of political issues. Jeremy Brecher, David Korten, and Deanna Isaacs take on economic inequalities. Starhawk and David R. Dow deal with issues of health care. Janice Brewer and Katelyn Langdale explore the problems of immigration policy. As in other chapters, the authors do not necessarily take opposing views. In fact, they do not necessarily take on the same point of contention. For example, Janice Brewer argues about the problems of illegal immigration across the Mexican border while Katelyn Langdale explains the struggle of people trying to gain legal entry through the formal bureaucracy. As you read, then, try not to get caught up in contrary opinions about each topic. Avoid falling into the typical either/or political positions. Instead, read to better understand how your culture is managing these complex topics.

Jeremy Brecher

The 99 Percent Organize Themselves

A historian, social activist, and documentarian, Jeremy Brecher studies the human drives behind major cultural shifts. Focusing his work on issues related to labor, globalization, and social change, Brecher is the author of numerous articles and books, including the 2012 book *Save the Humans? Common Preservation in Action.* In the following magazine article, Brecher considers the cultural significance of the Occupy movement.

In mid-October I spent two days and a night with Occupy Wall Street in Zuccotti Park. Since then I've read a barrage of advice for what OWS and its companion movements around the world should be doing. But I've been haunted by another question: What should those of us who are sympathetic to OWS (according to polls, roughly two-thirds of Americans are), but are not going to relocate to a downtown park, be doing to advance the well-being of the 99 percent?

I got one part of my answer as I groggily logged on to the web at 5:30 the morning after I returned home from Zuccotti Park. When I left the park, its private owner Brookfield Properties had announced it would clear the park "for cleaning" and enforce rules preventing tarps, sleeping bags and lying down. Mayor Bloomberg said the NYPD would enforce those rules, effectively ending the encampment.

But a funny thing happened on the way to the eviction. When OWS put out a call for support, thousands of people began to converge on the park for nonviolent resistance to eviction. Unions called on their members to protect the encampment. The president of the AFL-CIO's Central Labor Council lobbied the city to cancel the crackdown. Lawyers prepared to bring suit to protect the occupiers' First Amendment rights. City council members and other New York politicians lobbied the mayor to halt the eviction. Against all expectation, Mayor Bloomberg announced that Brookfield was abandoning the "cleanup" plan and the company announced it would try to reach an accommodation with the occupiers. The mobilization of supporters had forced the mayor and the park owners to back down. I had my first answer to what the rest of the 99 percent can do: protect the occupations.

Since then, there have been similar mobilizations to protect occupations in cities from Atlanta to Oakland. Many have involved a similar combination of public officials, trade unions and rank-and-file 99 percenters just showing up to defend their rights. In one extraordinary case, law enforcement officials themselves were responsible for saving the Occupy Albany encampment in Academy Park across from the State Capitol and City Hall. As protests grew, Police Chief Steven Krokoff issued an internal memo stating, "I have no intention of assigning officers to monitor, watch, videotape or influence any behavior that is conducted by our citizens peacefully demonstrating in Academy Park" and that the department would respond "in the same manner that we do on a daily basis" to any reported crime.

According to the Albany *Times-Union,* Albany Mayor Jerry Jennings, 5
under pressure from the administration of Governor Andrew Cuomo, thereupon directed city police to arrest several hundred Occupy Albany protesters. The police refused. The *Times-Union* reported that "State Police supported the defiant posture of Albany police leaders to hold off making

arrests for the low-level offense of trespassing, in part because of concern it could incite a riot or draw thousands of protesters in a backlash that could endanger police and the public." According to the official, "The bottom line is the police know policing, not the governor and not the mayor." Meanwhile, Albany County District Attorney David Soares informed the mayor and police officials that, "Unless there is property damage or injuries to law enforcement we don't prosecute people for protesting."

A 99 Percent Movement?

I remember well how the movement against the Vietnam War, so powerful among the youth on America's campuses in the 1960s, was largely isolated from the rest of the country. Something very different is happening right now, however: the Occupy movements have been building alliances through direct action mutual aid. And 99 percenters are connecting with them and utilizing their spirit and methods to contest their own injustices. The result is that OWS, instead of becoming isolated, is morphing before our eyes into what some are calling the 99 Percent Movement.

When Rose Gudiel received an eviction notice for her modest home in La Puente, a working-class suburb of Los Angeles, she announced, "We're not leaving." She and her family hunkered down while dozens of friends and supporters camped in their yard, determined to resist. When thousands started to gather outside Los Angeles City Hall to launch Occupy LA, Rose Gudiel went down and told her story to one of its first General Assemblies. A group from Occupy LA joined the vigil at her home and some stayed to camp out. Next Rose Gudiel and an Occupy LA delegation protested in front of the $26 million dollar Bel Air mansion of Steve Mnuchin, CEO of OneWest, which serviced her mortgage. The next day they held a sit-in at the Pasadena regional office of Fannie Mae, where Rose Gudiel's 63-year-old disabled mother made an impassioned plea to save her home and nine protesters were arrested—all broadcast that night on the TV news. The next day Rose Gudiel received a letter from the bank saying her eviction had been called off and soon she had a deal for a renegotiated mortgage. Housing advocates are now considering a campaign called "Let a thousand Roses bloom." MSNBC commented that Rose Gudiel provides "an example of how the sprawling 'Occupy' movement—often criticized for its lack of focus—can lend muscle to specific goals pursued by organizations and individuals."

An alliance has been developing between the occupations around the country and many different layers of organized labor. In New York a group from OWS joined a march of 500 to a Verizon store held to support the contract campaign of Verizon workers. "We're all in this together," 53-year-old Steven Jackman, a Verizon worker from Long Island, said about Occupy Wall Street. In Albany, New York, Occupy Albany joined a protest outside the State Capitol featuring a roasted pig wearing a gold top hat, sporting a gold chain and chomping on a cigar. The adoption of OWS themes and language was apparent. A local union official said, "The corporate pig's been out there, taking a bite out of America, out of the 99 percent, for years and I'm inviting all of the 99 percent of America to come on down today and take a bite out of the corporate pig."

The collaboration of OWS and labor can take some unusual forms. To support art handlers of the Teamsters' union, activists from OWS started showing up at Sotheby's auctions, masquerading as clients. They would suddenly stand up and, instead of offering a bid, disrupt the proceedings with loud denunciations of the company's labor practices. OWS activists likewise went to a Manhattan restaurant owned by a prominent Sotheby's board member, clinked on glasses for silence, and then denounced the company as a union-buster. Jason Ide, president of the Teamsters local that represents the art handlers, told the *Washington Post* that the Occupy tactics surprised and inspired him and his members—so much so that the workers have become regulars at OWS. "Now is this rare opportunity for labor unions, and especially the union leadership, to take some pointers," for example by considering the civil-disobedience approach taken by Occupy demonstrations.

Meanwhile, a close working relationship has developed between climate 10
and environmental activists and the Occupy movement. A number of environmental activists, including Bill McKibben and Naomi Klein, were early endorses of the Occupy movement, and a delegation from Occupy DC marched to join a rally against the Keystone XL pipeline. Next a group of students and climate activists organized an "#OccupyStateDept" action and occupied the area outside the Ronald Reagan Building overnight to protest the Keystone XL pipeline—and to secure admission to a hearing on the pipeline the next day. Ethan Nuss, who had stood in line for fourteen hours, told the hearing, "Every day I wake up and work for a vision in this country of a 100 percent clean energy economy that will create jobs for my generation when my generation is facing the largest unemployment since the Great Depression." Bill McKibben urged pipeline opponents to join

the Occupy DC encampment and invited Occupy DC to join the upcoming anti-pipeline action at the White House.

Bringing It All Back Home

Just as workers, community residents, students, and even housewives in the 1930s adopted the "sit-down strike" to address their grievances, so the robust but nonviolent direct action of the Occupy movements is being adopted by diverse communities and constituencies to address their own concerns. For example, a hundred students and teachers recently occupied a New York Board of Education meeting to protest budget cutbacks, layoffs, large class sizes and overemphasis on standardized testing. After the city school chancellor and school board members fled the meeting, the crowd held an impromptu "general assembly." Her voice amplified by the echo of the "people's microphone," an elementary school student named Indigo told the assembly,

> "Mic check. I'm Indigo, and I am an 8-year-old third grader, and I'm sad Ms. Cunningham is doing work for free. I don't think it's fair that teachers are getting laid off. The thing that would help me learn more would be if we had smaller classes. My teacher, Ms. Lamar, has to shout to be heard."

99 percenters are also bringing the OWS message back into their own communities. For example, OWSers joined a protest in Harlem against "stop and frisk" racial profiling by law enforcement officials. Soon, activists began holding Occupy Harlem General Assemblies. And civil rights and labor groups, including the Coalition of Black Trade Unionists, the A. Philip Randolph Institute, the Labor Council for Latin American Advancement, the Asian Pacific American Labor Alliance, the National Action Network and the New York State and New York City chapters of the NAACP organized their own rally in City Hall Park and marched to the Zuccotti Park to show their support for the OWS movement.

Occupy College provides another example of how 99 percenters are taking the Occupy message—and mode of self-organization—into other arenas. It is organized both to support the occupations around the country and around the world, and to address the specific issues affecting college students like the cost of education and the burden of college debt that have been important themes of the Occupy movements. Occupy College has established a website and is initiating national solidarity teach-ins in early November at colleges around the country.

While there has been a lot of debate in recent years about face-to-face vs. 15
Internet organizing, in fact the Occupy and 99-percenter movements have brilliantly combined the two. While many Occupy groups and General Assemblies have been highly local, there is also widespread self-organization occurring on the web by groups such "Knitters for Occupy Wall St" and "Knitters for the 99 Percent" linking people all over the country who are making warm clothes for the occupiers. Here are some ways 99 percenters might want to think about organizing with their own real and virtual communities:

- Bring a speaker from your local Occupy group to a meeting in your living room or to whatever organizations you belong to.
- Organize a General Assembly in your neighborhood to discuss the issues of the 99 percent. Discuss what is upsetting people and decide on some concrete action to address it.
- If your PTA supports teachers' jobs and programs for low-income students, get them to visit their political representatives and also do a joint action with your local Occupy group.
- If your church's food pantry or homeless shelter needs money, hold an action at your local bank offices demanding that they feed the homeless in "their" community. If they won't, ask your elected officials to take a look at the benefits they receive from "their" community. (Remember, according to Mayor Bloomberg it was the threat of city council officials to look into benefits received by the owners of Zuccotti Park that led them to back off their efforts to shut down OWS.)
- Create a Facebook page for your own equivalent of "Knitters for the 99 Percent."
- Create a group to monitor local media and to protest when they favor the concerns of the 1 percent over those of the 99 percent.
- Organize public hearings in your town about what's really happening to the 99 percent and how the 1 percent's power is affecting them.
- Create your own temporary occupations in your own milieu addressing concerns about housing, jobs, media or whatever else concerns you and your fellow 99 percenters.

While the connections that have developed with unions are of great importance, we need to remember that the great majority of 99 percenters don't have unions. Self-organization of non-union workers is a crucial next step. Take some of your co-workers down to visit your local occupation. Invite someone from your local Occupy group to meet with people from your workplace. Discuss what support you can give each other and the 99 Percent movement.

The Power of the Powerless

There is clearly a bigger movement growing out of the Occupy movement. But how will it develop? Some expect it to become like the Tea Party, a pressure group within the political party system. Others imagine something like the Tahrir Square demonstrations that toppled the Mubarak regime in one concentrated upheaval.

Neither of these visions takes enough account of the role of "secondary institutions"—schools, religious congregations, workplaces, communities, ethnic groups, and subcultures—in American society. The cooperation and acquiescence of these institutions provide the "pillars of support" on which both the government and the corporations depend—and through which their power can be humbled. And they provide arenas in which people can make change that will genuinely affect their lives long before they are powerful enough to defeat corporate control of national politics.

"In our top-down, corporate-controlled political system, even our political parties and local governments can be considered secondary institutions."

In our top-down, corporate-controlled political system, even our political parties and local governments can be considered secondary institutions. Those who are active in political parties and organizations can play a role supporting the Occupy movements and addressing the needs of the 99 percent. You can invite a speaker from your local Occupation group; support them in the street; and insist your organization's leaders and the politicians it supports take a pro-Occupation stand. You can identify ways in which your organization and those it supports acquiesce in the interests of the 1 percent and demand that they stop.

The same is true of local governments. In Los Angeles, for example, the city council unanimously passed a resolution supporting "the continuation of the peaceful and vibrant exercise in First Amendment Rights" of the Occupy LA. 20

Beyond that, local governments and political parties can start pursuing the interests of the 99 percent and stop supporting those of the one percent. In Los Angeles, for example, the same night the city council voted to endorse Occupy LA, it also reaffirmed its support for a "Responsible Banking Initiative," which would leverage the city's over $25 billion in pension and cash investments to pressure banks to invest in the city. Moving city funds to nonprofit development banks is also being discussed.

In Brooklyn, Assemblyman Vito J. Lopez proposed a millionaire's tax to raise $4 billion to prevent the cutting of vital social services. Absent such a tax, he proposed a $4 billion fund to be voluntarily contributed by 400 companies in the financial sector each contributing $5 million to $10 million for three years to create jobs, fix infrastructure and build affordable housing. He did not say how the companies would be persuaded to contribute, but his proposal was made at the start of a march from the Brooklyn Borough Hall across the Brooklyn Bridge to Wall Street.

I remember when, during the Vietnam War millions of people joined the monthly demonstrations and "work breaks" known as the Vietnam Moratorium—only to have the national leadership shut it down and move into electoral politics. Although some politicians and labor leaders have called for OWSers to campaign for Obama or the Democratic Party, such a shift is unlikely to happen to the Occupy movement. For those who want that to happen, their best strategy will be to make Obama and the Democratic Party something the Occupy movement (and the rest of the 99 percent) believe is worth supporting. Start freezing foreclosures, taxing the rich, creating new public works jobs and housing the homeless. Build an alternative to corporate greed and they will come.

Winter Soldiers

The occupations have been incredibly successful. But nothing can fail like success. *Z* magazine founder Michael Albert, just returned from conversations with protest veterans in Greece, Turkey, London, Dublin and Spain, reports he was told that their massive assemblies and occupations at first were invigorating and uplifting. "We were creating a new community. We were making new friends. We were hearing from new people." But as days and weeks passed, "it got too familiar. And it wasn't obvious what more they could do."

25 Besides boredom (rarely a problem so far), winter is coming. I can testify just from sleeping out on one rainy night in October that, whatever the occupiers' determination, it's going to be tough. Some will need to create sturdier encampments better protected against the elements. Some will need to come inside.

When a threatened army successfully repositions itself it is a victory, not a defeat. What matters is that the social forces that have made OWS and its kin continue their feisty, imaginative, nonviolent reclaiming of public space by marches, occupations and other forms of direct action without getting pinned down in positions they can't sustain. That way they can continue their crucial role in inspiring the rest of us 99 percenters to organize ourselves.

For that, they need help right now from the rest of us 99 percenters. In New York, there is now a campaign to let the protesters stay and set up tents. Elsewhere possibilities for using indoor spaces where occupiers can "come in from the cold" (with or without official permission) are being explored. Occupiers need both material aid and political pressure from unions, religious groups and ordinary 99 percenters to make the transition to the next phase.

In 1932 at the pit of the Great Depression, labor journalist Charles R. Walker visited "Hoovervilles" and unemployed workers' organizations around the country. He predicted:

> There will be increasing outbursts of employed and unemployed alike—a kind of spontaneous democracy expressing itself in organized demonstrations by large masses of people. They will "march or meet in order, elect their own spokesmen and committees, and work out in detail their demands for work or relief. They will present their formulated needs to factory superintendents, relief commissions, and city councils, and to the government at Washington."

What Walker called a "rough and ready democracy" is what OWS and its progeny around the country are creating today.

30 The unemployed councils Walker described lasted only a few years, but from them sprang the Workers Alliance, a hybrid of a trade union for workers on government public works projects and a welfare rights organization. It in turn was a crucial springboard for the industrial union movement that would transform the U.S. economic and political system.

The Occupy movement is not unlikely to last forever, nor would it be a good thing if it did. It could be forgotten like so many movements of the past. But it instead it could be remembered as the progenitor of the 99 Percent Movement. That depends on the rest of us 99 percenters.

Analyze

1. Explain how Brecher's allusions to the Vietnam War help to support his main idea.
2. Subheadings help writers to organize ideas, but they also help to create subtlety and dimension in an essay. Examine Brecher's subheadings and explain how they add subtlety or dimension to his main idea.
3. How does the paragraph about Rose Gudiel (paragraph 7) support Brecher's main idea?
4. Brecher admits that "nothing can fail like success." Explain what he means by this and how it relates to the success of the 99 Percent Movement.
5. How is Brecher's argument about culture—about a process through which things become normal?

Explore

1. People in the top 1 percent earn nearly $400,000 per year. Chances are, you're in the 99 percent. What does this mean to you? How does it impact your decisions about college, loans, work, or voting?
2. Have you or do you know someone who has directly participated in an Occupy movement? How does your answer influence your thinking about the movement?
3. When should American citizens protest? What kinds of issues, systems, or events should prompt people to take to the streets (or parks) and be heard?
4. Brecher explains that police departments have had a complex and evolving response to the Occupy movement. Consider the role of police departments in protests. What should they do? To whom should they listen? What are the gray areas? What are the questions or complexities they have to consider?
5. According to a range of studies, the United States ranks far behind European countries in upward mobility (the ability to keep earning more throughout one's life). In other words, moving from working

class to middle class—and from middle class to upper middle class—is more difficult in the United States than many other places in the world. Why is this? What forces or beliefs or systems might be involved?

David Korten
When Bankers Rule the World

David Korten is a writer and speaker who is deeply involved in the efforts of public interest citizen action groups. After working for many years to transform political structures in Southeast Asia, he realized that to achieve "a positive human future, the United States must change." He is the author of numerous articles and books, including the 2010 book *Agenda for a New Economy: From Phantom Wealth to Real Wealth*. In the following magazine article, Korten examines the cultural impact of Wall Street.

The tell-all defection of Greg Smith, a former Goldman Sachs executive, provided an insider's view of the moral corruption of the Wall Street banks that control of much of America's economy and politics. Smith confirms what insightful observers have known for years: the business purpose of Wall Street bankers is to maximize their personal financial take without regard to the consequences for others.

Wall Street's World of Illusion

Why has the public for so long tolerated Wall Street's reckless abuses of power and accepted the resulting devastation? The answer lies in a cultural trance induced by deceptive language and misleading indicators backed by flawed economic theory and accounting sleight-of-hand. To shatter the trance we need to recognize that the deception that Wall Street promotes through its well-funded PR machine rests on three false premises.

1. We best fulfill our individual moral obligation to society by maximizing our personal financial gain.
2. Money is wealth and making money increases the wealth of the society.
3. Making money is the proper purpose of the individual enterprise and is the proper measure of prosperity and economic performance.

Wall Street aggressively promotes these fallacies as guiding moral principles. Their embrace by Wall Street insiders helps to explain how they are able to reward themselves with obscene bonuses for their successful use of deception, fraud, speculation, and usury to steal wealth they have had no part in creating and yet still believe, as Goldman CEO Lloyd Blankfein famously proclaimed, that they are "doing God's work."

The devastation created by Wall Street's failure affirms three truths that are the foundation on which millions of people are at work building a New Economy:

1. Our individual and collective well-being depends on acting with concern for the well-being of others. We all do better when we look out for one another.
2. Money is not wealth. It is just numbers. Sacrificing the health and happiness of billions of people to grow numbers on computer hard drives to improve one's score on the Forbes Magazine list of the world's richest people is immoral. Managing a society's economy to facilitate this immoral competition at the expense of people and nature is an act of collective insanity.
3. The proper purpose of the economy and the enterprises that comprise it is to provide good jobs and quality goods and services beneficial to the health and happiness of people, community and nature. A modest financial profit is essential to a firm's viability, but is not its proper purpose.

The critical distinction between making money and creating wealth is the 5
key to seeing through Wall Street's illusions.

Ends/Means Confusion

Real wealth includes healthful food, fertile land, pure water, clean air, caring relationships, quality education and health care, fulfilling opportunities for service, healthy and happy children, peace, time for meditation and spiritual reflection. These are among the many forms of real wealth to which we properly expect a sound economy to contribute.

Wall Street has so corrupted our language, however, that it is difficult even to express the crucial distinction between money (a facilitator of economic activity), and real wealth (the purpose of economic activity).

Financial commentators routinely use terms like wealth, capital, resources, and assets when referring to phantom wealth financial assets, which makes them sound like something real and substantial—whether or not they are backed by anything of real value. Similarly, they identify folks engaged in market speculation and manipulation as investors, thus glossing over the distinction between those who game the system to expropriate wealth and those who contribute to its creation.

The same confusion plays out in the use of financial indicators, particularly stock price indices, to evaluate economic performance. The daily rise and fall of stock prices tells us only how fast the current stock bubble is inflating or deflating and thus how Wall Street speculators are doing relative to the rest of us.

10 Once we are conditioned to embrace measures of Wall Street success as measures of our own well-being, we are easily recruited as foot soldiers in Wall Street's relentless campaign to advance policies that support its control of money and thus its hold on nearly every aspect of our lives.

Modern Enslavement

In a modern society in which our access to most essentials of life from food and water to shelter and health care depends on money, control of money is the ultimate instrument of social control.

Fortunately, with the help of Occupy Wall Street, Americans are waking up to an important truth. It is a very, very bad idea to yield control of the issuance and allocation of credit (money) to Wall Street banks run by con artists who operate beyond the reach of public accountability and who Greg Smith tells us in his *New York Times* op-ed view the rest of us as simple-minded marks ripe for the exploiting.

By going along with its deceptions, we the people empowered Wall Street to convert America from a middle class society of entrepreneurs, investors, and skilled workers into a nation of debt slaves. Buying into Wall

Street lies and illusions, Americans have been lured into accepting, even aggressively promoting, "tax relief" for the very rich and the "regulatory relief" and "free trade" agreements for corporations that allowed Wall Street to suppress wages and benefits for working people through union busting, automation, and outsourcing jobs to foreign sweatshops.

Once working people were unable to make ends meet with current income, Wall Street lured them into making up the difference by taking on credit card and mortgage debt they had no means to repay. They were soon borrowing to pay not only for current consumption, but as well to pay the interest on prior unpaid debt.

This is the classic downward spiral of debt slavery that assures an ever- 15
growing divide between the power and luxury of a creditor class and the powerless desperation of a debtor class.

Bust the Trusts, Liberate America

Before Wall Street dismantled it, America had a system of transparent, well-regulated, community-based, locally owned, Main Street financial institutions empowered to put local savings to work investing in building real community wealth through the creation and allocation of credit to finance local home buyers and entrepreneurs.

Although dismissed by Wall Street players as small, quaint, provincial, and inefficient, this locally rooted financial system created the credit that financed our victory in World War II, the Main Street economies that unleashed America's entrepreneurial talents, the investments that made us the world leader in manufacturing and technology, and the family-wage jobs that built the American middle class. It is a proven model with important lessons relevant for current efforts to restore financial integrity and build an economy that serves all Americans.

Two recent reports from the New Economy Working Group—*How to Liberate America from Wall Street Rule* and *Jobs: A Main Street Fix for Wall Street's Failure*—draw on these lessons to outline a practical program to shift power from Wall Street to Main Street, focus economic policy on real wealth creation, create a true ownership society, unleash Main Street's entrepreneurial potential, bring ourselves into balance with the biosphere, meet the needs of all, and strengthen democracy in the process.

For far too long, we have allowed Wall Street to play us as marks in a confidence scam of audacious proportion. Then we wonder at our seeming powerlessness to deal with job loss, depressed wages, mortgage foreclosures, political corruption and the plight of our children as they graduate into debt bondage.

20 Let us be clear. We will no longer play the sucker for Wall Street con artists and we will no longer tolerate public bailouts to save failed Wall Street banks.

Henceforth, when a Wall Street financial institution fails to maintain adequate equity reserves to withstand a major financial shock or is found guilty of systematic violation of the law and/or defrauding the public, we must demand that federal authorities take it over and break it up into strictly regulated, community-accountable, cooperative member-owned financial services institutions.

Occupy Wall Street has focused national and global attention on the source of the problem. Now it's time for action to bust the Wall Street banking trusts, replace the current Wall Street banking system with a Main Street banking system, and take back America from rule by Wall Street bankers.

Analyze

1. According to Korten, how has Wall Street (and the illusion it has perpetuated) threatened democracy?
2. Korten argues, "By going along with its deceptions, we the people empowered Wall Street to convert America from a middle class society of entrepreneurs, investors, and skilled workers into a nation of debt slaves." How does this statement support or relate to his main idea?
3. Korten also argues, "Real wealth includes healthful food, fertile land, pure water, clean air, caring relationships, quality education and health care, fulfilling opportunities for service, healthy and happy children, peace, time for meditation and spiritual reflection." How does this definitional statement support his main idea?
4. Explain what values or beliefs Korten shares with Jeremy Brecher ("The 99 Percent Organize Themselves").
5. How is Korten's article an examination of culture? In other words, beyond the economic issues, what is Korten pointing to and arguing about?

Explore

1. Korten explains that Americans are in a "cultural trance" when it comes to financial matters. What have you seen that supports or challenges this idea?
2. Korten uses the term "Wall Street" to suggest a broader system of banks, companies, and stock portfolios. He contrasts this to "Main Street." What do you think the latter refers to or includes? Who or what makes up "Main Street"?
3. Because of retirement policies and tax laws, most working Americans are now directly connected to Wall Street. Why should or shouldn't people be concerned about this?
4. What does the phrase "community-accountable" mean? What organizations or companies should be community-accountable?
5. Consider the next essay in this chapter, Deanna Isaacs's "The Transnational Economy," and explain how a "transnational economy" might be related to Korten's concerns or hopes.

Deanna Isaacs
The Transnational Economy

The culture columnist for the *Chicago Reader,* Deanna Isaacs writes on issues related to art and architecture, urban culture, education, and politics. In the following article, she examines the phenomenon of global capitalism, and what it means for our work and well-being.

Amid all the blather about V-shaped and U-shaped economic recoveries, it's become pretty clear that we don't have any recovery at all. And that there's none on the near horizon. It looks, in fact, like we're screwed. What's less clear is exactly what happened.

A housing bubble and bust? Sure, but DeVry University history professor Jerry Harris says that's only one piece of a much bigger picture. According to Harris, we're undergoing a change so profound it portends the decline not only of America, but of the nation-state as an institution.

This startling development is the rise of global capitalism, complete with a transnational ruling elite that operates through nondemocratic bodies like the World Trade Organization, the G-20, the IMF, and the World Bank, Harris said in an Open University of the Left lecture at the Lincoln Park branch of the Chicago Public Library last month. In other words, the escape of big money from its historic national anchors and the social obligations that went with them.

The enabler is our friend technology. Both the *Chicago Tribune* and *The New York Times* carried stories this week about how technological innovation is taking jobs away rather than increasing them, as many experts expected. But that's not news to Harris, who began studying the economy after he was laid off from U.S. Steel's South Works plant in 1982.

5 "We lost a lot of jobs to technology before we lost them to other countries," Harris says. At U.S. Steel, where he started out in the blast furnace and then became a machine-shop apprentice, he recalls that the skilled workers he was training with "came in one day and found computer boards attached to their machines." During that decade, in factories across America, skilled labor was replaced by microchips, middle management was eliminated, and productivity skyrocketed. "By 1988," Harris notes in his 2008 book, *Dialectics of Globalization: Economic and Political Conflict in a Transnational World,* "the U.S. required only 40 percent of its blue-collar labor force to produce an amount of manufactured goods equal to that produced in 1977."

And then, IT advances made it practical to manage production anywhere in the world, and—whoosh.

Democracy and capitalism had grown up together, rooted in the French and American revolutions and bound by a socioeconomic contract that balanced property rights with personal rights, Harris says. "For many decades we had a nation-centric economy," with companies that identified themselves as loyal corporate citizens. Remember the slogan 'What's good for General Motors is good for the country'? At that time, the majority of General Motors' employment, sales, and assets were all inside the United States. Now the reverse is true: a majority of their employment, sales, and assets are outside their home country. And that's the case for all the major corporations around the world."

This should not be confused with that quaint old thing we once knew as the "international economy," Harris cautions. That was based on the export of products made in one country and sold in another. "Today, companies produce, invest, and employ everywhere, so what you have is a transnational corporation and a global assembly line. And in that scenario, he adds, as production moves to whatever country offers the cheapest sweatshop, "we're seeing the economic and social contract ripped up."

Harris says he doesn't "want to overstate the case" (i.e., nations aren't dead yet), "but transnational corporations and those who run them have less and less invested in any one particular country. They can make money anywhere, and the logic of capitalism itself drives them to lower their cost of production and increase their efficiency. If they don't do that, they become less competitive. They're driven to globalize, and as they do, they're less invested, for example, in the education system at home. They don't need as many engineers and scientists coming out of the United States when they can use Chinese, Indian, and Brazilian graduates at lower cost. The same logic drives their tax strategies. There are more corporate headquarters in the Cayman Islands than there are people there."

Meanwhile, we have a shrinking middle class here and growing poverty. 10
"That has political implications that we're seeing, for example, in the Occupy protests," Harris says. "There's a feeling of alienation, a sense that the national government is controlled by corporations. We gave billions to the banks (including foreign-owned banks), which they used to increase their own bonuses. What if that money went into infrastructure development, hiring people to build bridges, sewer systems, roads?

"We're not in the same situation as the southern European countries, but when you see the inability of the Obama administration to get the jobs bill through, and the whole discussion at the congressional level goes toward debt rather than stimulus, I think that's totally ass-backwards. About 76 percent of the people in polls say, yeah, raise the taxes on the wealthy and superrich, and yet not one Republican will do it. So where's the democracy in that?"

Analyze

1. What is the difference between an international and a transnational economy?
2. Why is a transnational economy a potential problem for or challenge to democracy?
3. Isaacs explains that "Democracy and capitalism had grown up together, rooted in the French and American revolutions and bound by a socioeconomic contract that balanced property rights with personal rights." How is this point related to her main idea?
4. Explain how Isaacs's parenthetical statement "nations aren't dead yet" functions in her overall argument.

5. Like David Korten ("When Bankers Rule the World"), Isaacs is arguing about more than economic issues. Explain how she is dealing with the culture—with broader processes surrounding any particular regulation or policy.

Explore

1. Why is a "shrinking middle class" a concern for so many economists?
2. What is the profound change that Isaacs references in her opening paragraphs? Have you seen evidence of it in your life?
3. Isaacs argues that the U.S. economy experienced no recovery, but most analysts have concluded the opposite: that the United States has been, since the recession of 2007, gaining momentum. So is Isaacs simply wrong? Or is she arguing about something bigger than the current situation?
4. This article was published at the end of 2011. Do you think anything significant has changed since then? Has anything happened to slow or shift the trend that Isaacs describes?
5. One commenter, "Pelham," to Isaacs's article on the *Chicago Reader* website suggested a proposal: "Mandate that all Fortune 500 companies' charters be put up for nationwide vote every four years. Let's all have a hand in deciding whether companies that offshore and outsource American jobs and technology should continue to function under their current management or be handed over to their workers or nationalized. This would also have the ancillary effect of establishing, for the first time in human history, truly representative democracy." Respond to Pelham's suggestions.

Starhawk

A Pagan Response to the Affordable Care Act

A social activist and religious leader, Starhawk (www.starhawk.org) examines political issues from a Neo-Pagan perspective, which emphasizes a feminine, earth-based spirituality. Named an *Utne Reader* Visionary in 1995, she is a blogger, a contributor to the *Washington Post,* and the author of numerous books of nonfiction, fiction, and children's literature. In the following blog post, Starhawk considers the spiritual and political dimensions of health care.

Jason Pitzi-Waters, of the Pagan Newswire Collective, asked a few of us to respond to the Supreme Court's decision that the Affordable Care Act is constitutional. Here's mine:

A Pagan response—or rather, this Pagan's response for there is no universal agreement among Pagans on any issue—to the upholding of the Affordable Care Act has two aspects: is it good for us, individually and as a community, and is it in concert with our Pagan values.

While the Act is not as good for me, individually or many of us as a single-payer system would be, it is definitely an improvement over the callous and greed-ridden system we've got. Like many other Pagan writers and teachers, I'm self-employed and have been pretty much all my adult life. I've had health insurance since my mother brow-beat me into getting it in my twenties, with the same company. While I'm pretty healthy for my age, I've seen my premiums go up and up every year, to the point that they were costing me more than my mortgage, more than my food budget, more than anything else. Now, if I were being taxed for a single-payer system, when my income went down my payments would go down. But with private insurance, the price just keeps going up and up and up! When it finally reached over $1200 a month, I started looking for other options. I tried switching companies, but I'm now over sixty, overweight (not alone among Pagans in being so!) and with minor but irritating health problems that somehow drove my projected premiums up even higher! So I switched to a lower-cost plan that has a $6000 deductible. That would keep me from losing my house should I get a serious illness, and having lost five friends in the last five months, mostly to cancer, I can't ignore that possibility. I'm still trying to save up the $6000 to have ready in the bank should I need it suddenly—because if I do get sick, I won't be able to travel and teach which provides the bulk of my income.

Meanwhile, I encountered the dreaded Socialized Medicine when I was in England and needed a new asthma inhaler. I was able to get an appointment at the local clinic in Totnes—the same day I asked for one. I saw a doctor, who gave me a new prescription. He very apologetically informed me that I would have to pay for it, he was so sorry, because I'm not on National Health. I said that was okay, as an American, I was used to it. The clinic had a pharmacy on the premises, and the pharmacist filled the prescription, also expressing regret and embarrassment that I had to pay. He then charged me just over 5 English pounds—less than $10, for two inhalers, each of which costs me about $35 in the US!

I left, infuriated—not at the National Health, but at our own rip-off 5
system. Why should we pay two, four, seven times as much if not to enrich

somebody at our expense? Since I shifted my insurance, and since my own trusted doctor retired, I haven't been to see a doctor since, except for a couple of weeks ago when I had a serious bout with asthma after camping out in the desert. I went to the clinic at the University of California. I had to fill out a form before I saw anyone, stating my financial qualifications to be seen. The form informed me that the visit would like cost something in the neighborhood of $450! But they couldn't tell me how much, ahead of time. No one tells you what any specific treatment costs, before you have it—yet you are expected to pay. I know there are many preventive things I should be doing, at my age—like keeping a watch on my blood sugar levels, but when money is short, as it often is, I hesitate to make an appointment or sign up for tests that might break the budget. And I think many others, Pagans and not-Pagans, are in the same situation.

So for me personally, the ACA will help. The insurance exchanges may allow me to get a better policy at lower cost. Some of the provisions of the act assure more justice and fairness for everyone. And while it's not the National Health or Canada's public insurance, I believe we are in a better position to push for more when we build on success than we would be if we had to recover from failure.

I didn't mean to write quite this much. Do I have feelings about this? Evidently I do!

Now, as for the ethics. Our traditions tell us that we Witches were the village healers, the wise women and cunning men who offered herbs and treatment and magic to the sick, especially to the poor. As such we have a special interest in assuring access to health care for all.

I believe the core value in Pagan ethics is the understanding that we are interconnected and interdependent. On that basis, health care is an important right and everyone should have access to it. My personal health is not separate from your well-being. Health is partly a matter of personal responsibility, but all of us are subject to forces beyond our control. If we suffer illness or injury or sheer bad luck, we shouldn't be left alone to suffer the consequences unaided. We live in a more and more toxic environment, and the constant assaults on our health from pollutants and radiation and the degradation of our food supply are our collective responsibility. No one should be left alone to bear the consequences of our collective failure to protect the life-support systems around us. Rather, it is to all of our benefit to share a public responsibility for our mutual well being, because every single one of us, at some point in life, will need that help. No one gets through life unscathed, and in the end we die. If we truly accept death as part of life, with its attendant break-downs of the body and the many sorts of mischance that befall us along the way, then we do well to offer one another solidarity and succor.

To sum up, universal access to health care is consonant with our core 10
Pagan values of interconnection and interdependence. The Affordable Care Act is a small step toward that end, flawed but better than no change at all. As Michael Moore has said, it should spur us to keep working for a better, more equitable system. But I believe we'll do better building on a small success than we would have trying to recover from an abject failure. I hope as Pagans we can help to lead the way.

Analyze

1. How is Starhawk's Paganism central to her position?
2. Starhawk says, "No one gets through life unscathed, and in the end we die." How does this point relate to her main idea? Explain the intellectual steps required to go from this bold and general statement to her point about health care.
3. Explain how Starhawk's experience in England supports her main idea.
4. How is Starhawk's position related to Katelyn Langdale's essay "The Illogical World of U.S. Immigration"? Despite the topics and specific policy positions, what beliefs or assumptions might they share?
5. How does Starhawk's post show or dramatize the tension between tradition and cultural change?

Explore

1. You might be accustomed to hearing politicians and news channel pundits explain their views on health care policy. How has this text, written by a tax-paying citizen and Pagan, impacted your thinking?
2. Where did you derive your opinions about health care? From what people, channels, programs, or texts?
3. What principle or concept should be at the center of health care policy? Profit? Individual responsibility? Public responsibility? Unity? Something else?
4. It's a well-published fact that U.S. citizens pay dramatically more than most European countries for health care. What do you think is the cause? What causes have you heard or read about?
5. Why do you think positions on health care policy are often dependent on people's loyalty to the Republican and Democratic parties?

David R. Dow

We Stop the Next Aurora Not with Gun Control but with Better Mental Health Treatment

A professor at the University of Houston Law Center and Rice University, David R. Dow is a death penalty lawyer whose work focuses on capital punishment, justice, and jurisprudence. He is the author of numerous articles and books, including the forthcoming book *Things I've Learned from Dying* (2014). In the following *Daily Beast* article, Dow considers the phenomenon of mass shootings as a mental health issue.

I've been a gun-control advocate for thirty years, but when I received two e-mails Friday afternoon advocating gun control while the bodies in Aurora, Colo. were still warm, the solicitations left me cold. It's not just because the exploitation of a tragedy to achieve a political objective is obscene; it's because we've had this argument before, we know it by heart, and it doesn't matter a whit.

Gun-control advocates say if we had more rigorous laws, Columbine and Virginia Tech, and now Aurora, would not have happened. The NRA says if more people at the scene of the tragedy had been packing heat, they could have taken the shooter down.

Both arguments are equally absurd. If reports are accurate, James Holmes, the accused shooter in Aurora, was wearing body armor head to toe. Nobody carrying a .38 or a .45 was going to stop him. If ten people had been carrying guns with 10 rounds each, another hundred people would have been wounded, some probably mortally.

More important, what these mass slaughters have in common has less to do with the ease of getting weapons than with our society's reaction to monstrous acts perpetrated by those with mental illness. The key word is reaction; we do not do anything until it is too late.

5 In his magisterial book about Columbine, Dave Cullen exposes the broken brains of Eric Harris and Dylan Klebold, and the portrait that emerges, in my view, is one that strict gun laws could not have altered. I suspect we'll learn the same of Jared Lee Loughner, who shot Rep. Gabrielle Giffords and killed six others, if he ever goes on trial. All three are

psychological siblings of Anders Breivik, the diseased Norwegian who murdered 77 men and women last year. And Breivik in turn is the psychological cousin of our own Timothy McVeigh, who murdered 168 people without any guns at all. (Norway, by the way, has a higher rate of gun ownership than any other country in Western Europe, but gun-control advocates in America would be thrilled for even a watered-down version of the country's restrictions.)

Some people are talking about mental illness today who were not talking about it Thursday, and that's good, but most people are talking about gun control and capital punishment. A friend asked me on my Facebook page whether Aurora is a good reason for the death penalty.

If you are talking about the death penalty now, you are talking about closing the barn door after the mare is a mile down the road, and if you are talking about gun control, you're bringing a knife to a gun fight. The problem we have in America is a deep cultural denial that there are thousands of damaged human beings whom we ignore until they explode, and who get worse while—and because—we ignore them.

Here's what we should have learned by now: You do not mend broken people by trying to close off their access to guns, because they will get them online or use homemade bombs instead, and you do not deter other broken people by killing the ones who crack. If you were to ask Jared Loughner or James Holmes about Timothy McVeigh, your answer would probably be a blank stare.

Gun control is good for a lot of things. It will keep kids from killing themselves with their dads' unsecured guns. It will make it harder for drug dealers to kill each other, and it will save lives in ordinary robberies. It might even prevent wildfires in the West. But it will not stop the mentally ill from reaping carnage because the proximate cause of their carnage is disease, not hardware.

If you say that a ten-round clip would have limited the damage in 10
Aurora, you might be right. But you also might be wrong, because Holmes might have walked in instead with a bomb. Either way, here we are arguing about how to limit the damage broken people do rather than talking about how to mend broken people.

Of course nobody needs an AK-47 or a twenty-round clip, and the Supreme Court ruling making it more difficult for communities to restrict access to guns was deeply unsound. But before we get sidetracked for the umpteenth time talking about limiting access to certain calibers, or muzzle velocities, or clip size, we should perhaps start talking about how we can identify broken people—not just when they walk into a gun store to purchase a weapon (although certainly there as well), but also when they apply to college, or for a driver's license, or do anything else that might call them to the attention of people who are trained to look.

Prisons, homeless shelters, and highway underpasses are teeming with mentally ill human beings because our society thinks harsh punishment will solve most of the problem, and restrictions to the implements of crime will solve the rest. Wrong and wrong again. Nobody is responsible for the unspeakable tragedy James Holmes unleashed besides James Holmes. But all of us share responsibility for ignoring the James Holmeses of our world until they force us to learn their infamous names.

Analyze

1. Dow calls the two most common policy positions on mass shootings "equally absurd." In your own words, explain those two positions and Dow's criticism of each.
2. Explain the function of Dow's references to other mass shootings. How do they serve his main idea?
3. Dow says, "If you are talking about the death penalty now, you are talking about closing the barn door after the mare is a mile down the road." Articulate his point without the interesting metaphor. Explain why he thinks the death penalty is an irrelevant issue when it comes to mass shootings.
4. In his conclusion, Dow argues that "all of us share responsibility for ignoring the James Holmses of the world." Explain how this point relates to his main idea.
5. Explain how Dow's argument relates to culture. (How is his main idea related to the way people grapple with or resist change?)

Explore

1. This article was written before the December 2012 mass shooting of schoolchildren in Newtown, CT. How do you think Dow's argument might change with news of that shooting, which took the lives of 20 children, several of their teachers, and the gunman's mother?
2. Consider Starhawk's blog post in this chapter about the Affordable Care Act ("A Pagan's Response to the Affordable Healthcare Act").

How is her point related to Dow's? What is the relationship between health care policy and homicidal behavior?

3. Some people argue that mass shootings are a natural, or at least inevitable, consequence of living in a free society. What do you think?
4. One commenter, "robwriter," responded to Dow's article with the following point about mental illness. How would you respond to robwriter?

> I have no argument against the premise of this piece; it seems clear that the problem is mental illness, not weaponry per se. However, we've had this conversation before too and it turns out that advocating for the mentally ill is a long row to hoe. As a healthcare worker who has had occasional to frequent contacts with the mentally ill I can assure you that as a group they are not very sympathetic. In short, they are mostly difficult to relate to at best, a pain in the ass generally, extremely dangerous at worst. AIDS and breast cancer have their nationally recognized ribbons. People with degenerative neurological diseases like Lou Gehrig's are objects of pity. People with Down's Syndrome are typically open and affectionate. The mentally ill, not so much. So basically, the mentally ill aren't getting a ribbon any time soon.
>
> The U.S. has quietly divested itself of the responsibility to care for the mentally ill. The national wave of state hospital closures in decades past was an abdication excused with the specious argument that the severely incompetent would be managed as outpatients. Instead they ended up off their meds, sleeping in doorways, rummaging for food in dumpsters, mumbling to themselves as they wander the streets, covered in filth and stinking to high heaven for lack of bathing. In a word, no one we want to cuddle with.
>
> America will massively incarcerate pot smokers in for-profit prisons, but not drunk drivers who commit vehicular homicide. America will pursue corporate welfare schemes like Romneycare, but won't commit to any form of a single payer system that might extend basic healthcare to all its citizens at sustainable cost. Apology in advance to Mr. Dow, but the notion that the U.S. will get serious about mental health just because some sicko guns down a few score people every six months or so is nearly delusional.

Janice Brewer

Letter from Governor Janice Brewer to President Barack Obama

A member of the Republican Party, Janice Brewer is Arizona's 22nd governor. In the wake of her anti-illegal immigration measures as governor, Brewer has been at the center of national debate about immigration law, reform, and rights. She is the author of the 2011 book *Scorpions for Breakfast: My Fight Against Special Interests, Liberal Media, and Cynical Politicos to Secure America's Border.* In 2010, Brewer corresponded with President Obama about the problem of illegal immigration in Arizona. The following letter was part of the exchange between the White House and the governor's office.

STATE OF ARIZONA

JANICE K. BREWER
GOVERNOR

EXECUTIVE OFFICE

JUNE 23, 2010

The Honorable Barack Obama
The President of the United States
The White House
1600 Pennsylvania Avenue
Washington, DC 20500

Dear Mr. President:

Thank you for the opportunity to visit with you in person during my recent trip to Washington, D.C. As you know, the issue of border security is foremost in the thoughts of many Arizonans and Americans alike, and I appreciated the chance to personally relate to you my concerns and outline my proposed solutions.

Mr. President, the need for action to secure Arizona's border could not be clearer. Recently, my office received a number of calls from constituents concerned at reports of new sign postings in interior counties of Arizona warning residents not to access federal lands due to criminal activity associated with the border. These warnings signal to some that we have handed over portions of our border areas to illegal immigrants and drug traffickers. This is unacceptable. Instead of warning Americans to stay out of parts of our own country, we ought to be warning international lawbreakers that they will be detained and prosecuted to the fullest extent of the law. We ought to be establishing measures to ensure that illegal traffic of any sort is kept to an absolute minimum, and that Americans are safe and secure within our own borders.

When we visited, you committed to present details, within two weeks of our meeting, regarding your plans to commit National Guard troops to the Arizona border and expend $500 million in additional funds on border security matters. You also discussed sending members of your senior staff to Arizona to discuss your plans. While I am pleased the 28th has been set for a meeting time and we have reviewed a copy of the Department of Homeland Security's "Southwest Border Next Steps" press release, I am still awaiting details on National Guard deployments and how the proposed additional border security funding will specifically affect Arizona (and the other Border States). As I mentioned to you on June 3rd, it is very difficult to have much of a dialogue without specific details regarding your proposals. I strongly urge you to request your staff provide us with missing details of your proposals prior to the meeting on the 28th.

While we await the specific details of your border security plans, I wanted to take the time to reemphasize some of what I shared with you and respond further to some of what we discussed. In essence, I have proposed a four-point Border Surge strategy, as outlined in my recent letter to Senator Charles Schumer, summarized as follows:

1. National Guard Personnel and Aviation

I believe a significant number of troops operating with a legitimate mission set is an essential part of any strategy to secure the border. I appreciate your commitment of 1,200 troops and the promise that Arizona would receive the largest contingent. I am concerned, however, that more is required, such as the deployment of 6,000 personnel proposed by Senators Jon Kyl and John McCain for the entire southwestern border.

In addition, I want to make sure that these troops have legitimate missions that:

- Support federal, state and local law enforcement—all three!
- Serve as a blocking force to stop illegal crossing activities.
- Employ the troops in a way that speaks loudly to all—both north and south of the border—that the U.S. is serious about this matter.

As part of your commitment, I also hope that you order a significant increase in aviation resources supporting border security operations on the ground. After meeting and talking to various experts, I am persuaded that aviation support is critical to the effort on the ground. Any effort will fail absent the ability to coordinate ground assets from the air, particularly given the nature of much of Arizona's border region terrain. I respectfully ask that you give serious consideration to my May 20, 2010 correspondence, which makes a very reasonable request for a reallocation of National Guard OH-58 helicopter assets in order to make a Border Surge effective. Your support of this request can make a significant difference between a winning effort versus a losing effort.

2. Border Fence

In short Mr. President, we need to complete, reinforce and then maintain the border fence. In my April 6, 2010 letter to you I proposed inmate labor and other methods (i.e., purchasing instead of leasing equipment) as a means to bring down construction/maintenance costs. I certainly support efficient and effective Ports of Entry where both American and Mexican border officials can allow legal traffic and crossings. Everywhere else along the border, though, I strongly believe we must have fencing and barriers that are both substantial and monitored if the illegal crossings are to be minimized.

3. Enforce Federal Law and Appropriately Fund the Effort

The United States must be prepared to detain, prosecute and then incarcerate convicted violators of United States laws. The current "no consequences policy" has resulted in a border security failure. I appreciate your general proposal to commit additional resources, but it is very difficult for me to comment without any details. It is without doubt, though, that the current border policy will continue to fail the State of Arizona without additional resources committed to the Border Patrol, Immigration and Customs Enforcement (ICE) personnel and detention facilities; prosecution; public defense; and federal prisons.

4. Reimburse States for the Additional Burden of Illegal Immigration

As I mentioned the very first time we met last year, I must continue the calls for Arizona to be reimbursed for expenses we are forced to carry because of our porous southern border. Arizona and a few other states are at a terrible disadvantage in good times, and an even worse position during bad times, because of the additional costs of illegal immigration. Just in terms of state prison costs, we estimate ongoing expenses at approximately $150 million to incarcerate criminal aliens. While substantial on its own, this figure does not include law enforcement, prosecution and defense costs, or the enormous societal costs of the criminal behavior of those who are not even legally entitled to be here.

We are hundreds of millions of dollars short of what we should receive to relieve the disproportionate law enforcement/jail/prison, health care and education burdens we face due to our porous southern border and rampant illegal immigration. It is simply unfair for the federal government to force Border State taxpayers to carry these burdens.

Immigration Reform

You shared with me your thoughts about the matter of immigration reform and I am grateful you listened to mine. As I mentioned in our meeting, the phrase "comprehensive immigration reform" is code for "amnesty" to many in Arizona and elsewhere in our Nation. Many Americans are still waiting for the reforms that were promised by the federal government in the 1980s when amnesty was granted to thousands of illegal immigrants. Until we establish a secure border, and reestablish trust with the public that our international borders are meaningful and important, and enforcement of federal immigration law is not an idle threat, any discussion of "comprehensive reform" is premature.

Let's first block illegal entry into the United States and enforce current law, and then other discussions, including immigration reform, might then, and only then, make sense to the public. I am committed to a serious discussion of legitimate reform—but not any false front for amnesty—when the federal government halts the free flow of illegal immigrants and illegal drugs across the southwestern border.

Arizona's Law

You also shared some concerns about a "patchwork" approach to policy. This makes sense to me, but the failure of the federal government has driven frustration levels to the point that tolerating the status quo is no longer acceptable for Arizona. From my perspective, the single most significant factor behind the passage this year of SB 1070 and HB 2162 (the follow-up bill with amendments to SB 1070) was the frustration of Arizona elected officials, and the public we serve, regarding the failure of the federal government over the years to effectively address the problem of illegal immigration.

The growing concerns over spillover violence, the increased awareness of kidnappings, the spread of drop houses in neighborhoods throughout metropolitan areas, the scourge of the drug trade and the oppressive financial burdens posed by illegal immigration—burdens even more difficult to shoulder in this economic downturn—all contributed to accelerating the public's frustration.

I am 100% committed to fair and just enforcement of the new Arizona law. I have made it clear that civil rights will not be compromised. The first step has been educating and training law enforcement, as well as the public, on the details of the law—a step I have already ordered in Arizona.

Instead of any discussion about suing Arizona and not cooperating with the efforts of local Arizona law enforcement to address illegal immigration, the federal government should reassure Arizona (and other states) that securing the border and enforcing federal immigration laws are duties to which the federal government will make a renewed and sincere commitment.

When the public sees consistent evidence of federal commitment, I am convinced the demand for state actions will wane. State and local governments have plenty to do and will be happy to stay out of border security and immigration law enforcement—along with the expenses of such work—if the federal government takes a firm and effective grip on the problem.

Conclusion

In closing, I want to assure you that I am looking to develop a solution, not have a standoff, with you and the federal government. Illegal immigration is a serious problem and I am sincerely committed to seeing something done to curb it. The real challenges at hand are about violent crime, huge taxpayer burdens, the rule of law and ensuring that our southern border does not become an open door for radical terrorists. Commerce with other countries is important to me and Arizonans—I truly want a vibrant and positive relationship with Sonora, other Mexican States and the rest of the world. Federal immigration law, however, must be honored and enforced, and our border must represent an effective means to help ensure our sovereignty and security.

I remain eager to receive the specific details of your proposals and to have the follow-up meeting with your senior staff. It is disappointing that we are such a short time away from the meeting and Arizona and the other Border States still are awaiting the specific details of what you are proposing. There is still time, however, to ensure the meeting next week is productive.

Finally, I want to re-extend the invitation I made to you to come to Arizona yourself, visit with families living along the southwestern border and see the situation firsthand. My prior visits to the border and the air survey of the Cochise County region have been very important to shaping my perspectives and thinking. Governor Richardson joined me for one trip and I believe you would also benefit from such an experience.

And when you do come, lunch is on me!

Yours in service to the great state of Arizona,

Janice K. Brewer
Governor

Analyze

1. Identify passages in which Brewer is deferential or conciliatory to President Obama. How do these passages function in her argument? What do they accomplish or help to establish?
2. Brewer refers several times to her visit with President Obama. Why? What do these references do for her argument?
3. In her section on Immigration Reform, Brewer explains that "comprehensive immigration reform" is code for "amnesty." What does she mean here? What is her subtle argument?
4. Explain how Brewer addresses concerns about racial profiling.
5. How is Brewer's letter about the tension between state government and federal government? What passages most dramatize that tension?

Explore

1. Should the National Guard protect the border between Arizona and Mexico? Why or why not?
2. Should the federal government reimburse Arizona (and other border states) for the costs incurred from border protection, incarceration, and health care related to illegal immigration? Why or why not?
3. Why do Mexican citizens continue immigrating to the United States despite the perils?
4. Where do you place illegal immigration as a national priority? Consider other national issues such as education, economic stimulus, environmental protection, banking regulation, and terrorism. Where is illegal immigration? Why would you give it high or low priority?
5. Consider Katelyn Langdale's argument in this chapter ("The Illogical World of U.S. Immigration") about immigrating to the United States. How does her argument relate to Brewer's? How does it complicate the immigration issue?

Katelyn Langdale
The Illogical World of U.S. Immigration

Katelyn Langdale is pursuing a degree in computer science. In the following essay, developed for a first-semester writing course, she questions the effectiveness of U.S. immigration policy in promoting cultural diversity. She relies on personal testimony and several outside sources to make her case.

I was minutes away from talking to the man or woman who was about to change my life. For the past thirty minutes, I had been sitting on hold, waiting to speak to a Global Visas representative about the possibility of moving to the United States and starting a new life. I envisioned myself working, enjoying all the sights and sounds that the country had to offer, and finally being able to live with my boyfriend. My heart leapt into my throat as I heard the call being transferred through, and found myself shocked by the gruff, abrupt man on the other end. "Yeah, hello. Global Visas." I stated my case and heard an audible sigh at the other end. "Are you a doctor or a highly trained professional? Do you have immediate relatives in the United States? Are you wealthy?" My answer to all of his questions was a big, resounding "no." The representative did not sound enthused and simply told me, "You won't get in. Move to Canada, they let all sorts of people live in their country. Goodbye."

The world of immigration is an interesting one, with the policies being so perplexing and mind-bending that many seek the help of immigration lawyers. With a lawyer's assistance, I discovered that I had two choices: The first was to apply for a fiancé visa and marry my boyfriend within three months of arriving in the United States, and the second was to obtain a student visa and go to school. The first would have been easier, but I didn't want to be forced into a rushed marriage. Because of such restrictive immigration laws, it looked as though school was my only chance to enter the country for an extended period of time.

Immigration debates stir up emotions. Plenty of politicians and organizations link immigration to population control and unemployment. One such organization, FAIR (The Federation for American Immigration Reform), claims that "Immigration is directly responsible for over sixty percent of population growth in America" (7) and that "An estimated

1,880,000 American workers are displaced from their jobs every year by immigration" (7). With the U.S. population standing at a projected 314,913,484 as of December 2012 (United States Census Bureau), it seems unreasonable and maybe a little far-fetched for FAIR to make such a bold claim in regards to the role of immigrants in population increase. In terms of employment, while FAIR'S evidence against immigrants is damning, *New York Times* writer Eduardo Porter suggests otherwise:

> The most recent empirical studies conclude that the impact is slight: they confirm earlier findings that immigration on the whole has not led to fewer jobs for American workers. More significantly, they suggest that immigrants have had, at most, a small negative impact on the wages of Americans who compete with them most directly, those with a high school degree or less.

In "Immigration's Impact on U.S. Workers," writer Steven Camarota comments that "the overall impact of immigration is almost certainly very small," and he states that "arguments for or against immigration are as much political and moral as they are economic." In addition to these facts, jobs have technically been lost due to talented, skilled international students having their next round of visas denied. Snapdeal.com founder Kunal Bahl is an Ivy League–educated student who found himself unable to stay in the United States after his visa application was rejected. Back in his home country of India, Bahl's online-based business flourished, to the point where he had to hire 300 employees in order to cope with the massive workload. If his visa application to stay in the United States had been accepted, Bahl would have hired U.S. citizens to fill these roles ("Strict U.S.").

As an international student, I feel as though my days are numbered 5
unless I choose to get married within the next two years. But even if this is the case, I will still find myself stuck in the visa war. I viewed the United States as a free, welcoming country, but now I live in fear that one mistake at school will cost me my newfound American life. Failing a subject results in a violation of my visa terms and I will be told to leave the country. I can work, but only on-campus for a maximum of 20 hours. I pay almost three times as much for tuition as a regular in-state student and I do not get offered any kind of payment plan. Once I am finished with my education, I don't get to stay here and put my skills into practice in the United States.

Some people may argue that I should just accept the visa the way it is, and I honestly do. When my student visa got approved, I knew exactly what to expect in terms of employment limitations, the costs involved and the strict academic requirements. However, as someone who loves this country, and as someone who wants to start a family here, I find it nonsensical that literally no other options exist for individuals like me. Of course, there is the controversial Diversity Visa Lottery Program to take into consideration, but the chance of me "winning" an immigration visa is few and far between.

For the uninitiated, the Diversity Visa Lottery Program is a United States Government-based initiative that encourages diversity by handing out 50,000 immigration visas each year to anyone from an "underrepresented" country who enters their name (Krikorian). 50,000 visas sounds like a generous amount, but take into consideration the millions of people who submit their name every year. Since its conception, the program's rules and guidelines have no doubt become more refined and strict, but the number of entries is still immense.

Some would argue that this is diversity at its finest, but how can the United States even justify this program when so many individuals have been genuinely battling the immigration system for years? As if the whole idea of the lottery isn't ridiculous enough, past visa winners have even been involved in terrorist activity, which brings the program's integrity and filtering methods into question. According to Mark Krikorian, executive director of the Center for Immigration Services, there is one man in particular who was able to take complete advantage of the lottery system:

> The most notorious lottery winner is Hesham Mohamed Ali Hedayet, the Egyptian immigrant who went to Los Angeles International Airport to kill Jews on July 4, 2002. Hedayet came to this country on a temporary visa, became illegal when he overstayed his welcome, then applied for asylum, was denied, again becoming an illegal alien, and finally got a green card when his wife won the lottery.

While I oppose FAIR's stance on completely slashing immigration numbers, I do agree with the organization's wish to have the lottery abolished. Such a warped system is an insult to anyone who has been, or is currently, tied up in the legalities of the immigration system. In some cases, the whole immigration and citizenship process can take up to 28 years for an individual (Flynn and Dalmia 33). How can this be justified?

So, let me break it down: The United States upholds the strictest of immigration policies in order to keep the country safe, yet it allows thousands of relatively unchecked, unfiltered, potentially dangerous people into the country each year with the childlike belief that it creates diversity. This leads me to believe that the immigration process is flawed. And it is infuriating to think that the path to citizenship can be as hard as waiting 28 years or as easy as submitting a name to the lottery and winning. 10

I want nothing more than to prove myself to the people of the United States. I promise that I will be a good, valuable citizen. I want to work hard, help support the economy and eventually start a family, and so do many others stuck in the immigration system. Unfortunately though, a promise alone is not enough to satisfy the United States government and its policies. In a country so concerned with the safety, security, and livelihood of its citizens, I can understand why many may still oppose immigration—even the idea—but Edwin Yohnka, the chair of the ABA Pro Bono Immigration Project makes a plea: "If we're concerned about protecting our way of life, we have to start by respecting it. Part of that is recognizing that we welcome people to come here" (qtd. in Tebo 47).

Works Cited

Camarota, Steven A. "Immigration's Impact on U.S. Workers." Center for Immigration Studies, 19 Nov. 2009. Web. 4 Dec. 2012.

Flynn, Mike, and Shikha Dalmia. "What Part of Legal Immigration Don't You Understand?" *Reason.org* Reason Foundation, Oct. 2008. Web. 19 Nov. 2012.

Federation for American Immigration Reform. "Immigration 101: A Primer on Immigration and the Need for Reform." *FAIR*. Federation for American Immigration Reform, 2000. Web. 4 Dec. 2012.

Krikorian, Mark. "Gambling with Visas." *The American Enterprise* 15.3: 52–56. *Academic OneFile*. Web. 4 Dec. 2012.

Porter, Eduardo. "Immigration and American Jobs." *The New York Times*, 19 Oct. 2012. Web. 4 Dec. 2012.

"Strict U.S. immigration policies contribute to high unemployment." *RT*. Autonomous Non-Profit Organisation (ANO) "TV-Novosti," 4 Aug. 2012. Web. 4 Dec. 2012.

Tebo, Margaret Graham "The Closing Door: U.S. Policies Leave Immigrants Separate and Unequal." *ABA Journal* 88.9: 43–47. Web. 19 Nov. 2012.

United States Census Bureau, Dec. 2012. Web. 9 Dec. 2012.

Analyze

1. What is Langdale's point about immigration policy?
2. Explain how Langdale's personal testimony functions in this essay. What specific idea does it help to flesh out or support?
3. How does the allusion to Hedayet, the Egyptian immigrant arrested in Los Angeles, help to support Langdale's argument?
4. In her conclusion, Langdale appeals directly to the people of the United States. What is the effect? How does this support her main idea?
5. What assumptions or beliefs do you think Langdale shares with Governor Janice Brewer ("Letter from Governor Janice Brewer to President Barack Obama")?

Explore

1. What do you think of the Diversity Visa Lottery Program? Should the United States continue the program? Why or why not?
2. What is the inherent value of diversity to a civilization like the United States of America? What does ethnic and racial diversity do for the culture?
3. Beyond the two options available to immigrants like Langdale (get married or attend school), what else can you imagine? If immigrants want to move here through all the legal channels, what else could they do on the road to full citizenship?
4. When did your family emigrate to the United States? Under what conditions? What country did they leave behind? What were they hoping for?
5. How will racial and ethnic diversity figure into your future professional life? For example, in what capacity will you interact with people of different racial backgrounds? What languages will help you to thrive in your work?

Forging Connections

1. Are you in the 99 percent? The top 5 percent? The bottom 50 percent? How has your socioeconomic class impacted your decisions as a college student? Did you consider, for instance, applying to the Ivy League, a local community college, or a state school in your region? Even if you didn't consciously weigh your own or your parents' income level, how might it have played a role in your present situation? Write a reflective essay that explores answers to these questions. Borrow insights from Jeremy Brecher ("The 99 Percent Organize Themselves") or David Korten ("When Bankers Rule the World"), or authors in Chapter 1, "Work: What We Do" such as Mike Rose ("Blue-Collar Brilliance"), Christian Williams ("This, That, and the American Dream"), or Jason Storms ("In the Valley of the Shadow of Debt").
2. How is entertainment or consumerism related to politics? More specifically, how have television programs like *The Daily Show, The Colbert Report,* and *The O'Reilly Factor* impacted political views in this country? Research one of these shows and explore its demographic. Examine how the viewing audience tends to vote or what political positions it champions. Or you might take a less direct path. Consider, for example, how football and advertisements surrounding it have suggested a kind of worldview or a certain set of values. Or imagine how prime time sitcoms have prompted a way of thinking about socioeconomic class. Write an analytical essay that makes connections between a particular program (or type of program) and some broader political trend. Borrow insights from writers such as Fredrik deBoer ("The Resentment Machine," Chapter 2), James Gleick ("What Defines a Meme?," Chapter 4), or Sameer Pandya ("The Picture for Men: Superhero or Slacker," Chapter 5).

Looking Further

1. Research the Affordable Care Act and examine, specifically, how the new health care laws within it affect you as a college student. Write an analytical essay that traces specific provisions to your living situation. In addition to financial issues, explore the indirect impact on your decisions. For example, one provision allows college students to remain on their parent or legal guardian's health care plan without taking a full

load of courses. Students can take six or eight credit hours and still retain health care. How might this provision, or others, impact your life?

2. What kind of political creature are you? Are you socially liberal and fiscally conservative or the opposite? Are you moderate in all things or do you veer dramatically to the left or right? Are you a secular humanist who seeks further separation of church and state or a neo-conservative pushing for prayer in public schools? Before answering, research some political party platforms: the Republican, Democratic, Libertarian, Socialist, and Green. Try to understand some of the common tensions and positions on issues related to taxes, education, the environment, immigration, and women's rights. In a personal essay, describe which principles from these parties seem most appealing to you. If you do not subscribe to one party entirely, make up your own. Give it a name, a motto, and even a symbol. Integrate images to help express the nature of your political party platform.

Chapter 7

War: How We Fight

War can be seen as the end of culture—its apex, ultimate conclusion, and most direct expression. In this perspective, war and culture are bound together. The soldiers, bombs, and machinery are natural extensions of shared beliefs. The whole society, in fact, culminates in military force. Serving as a signof this union, the national flag announces no difference between the soldier and an elementary school student, between a tank and a church back home, or between a bomb dropped on an enemy and the town where the bomb was made. In this perspective, citizens have duties: to sacrifice their children's lives, to pay taxes, or even to protest policies that seem out of line with shared beliefs. But war can also be seenas separate from culture, as a necessary reflex to keep culture alive. In this perspective, war is the sacrificial lamb. As Donald

Rumsfeld argued after the administration of President George W. Bush invaded Iraq in 2003, "We fight them over there so we don't have to fight them here."

These two perspectives are always in conflict. A country at war can never maintain one exclusively. When we hear monstrous stories (soldiers urinating on dead bodies, shooting a roomful of children, or raping a young woman), the connection between war and mainstream culture seems impossible. But we also elect, celebrate, and cling to the soldiers who fight in our name. Even if the front lines are halfway around the world, we know the people on those lines. Some are our children, spouses, parents, and dear friends. And maybe their return best dramatizes our ongoing inability to reconcile culture and war: in our communities, towns, and national policies, we always seem ill-equipped to help veterans come all the way home. The writers in this chapter wrestle with the relationship between war and culture. Doug Stanton begins with a meditation on the distance of war and its quiet invasion of his hometown. Benjamin Busch argues that war is the opposite of culture. Chris Hedges, Nick Turse, and Tom Malinowski, Sarah Holewinski, and Tammy Schultz suggest a close relationship. They point out subtle and explicit overlap between U.S. institutions and its military force. And Emily Chertoff reminds us that war, sometimes, happens within our own borders.

Doug Stanton

What the Water Dragged In

Doug Stanton is a political, travel, and adventure writer whose work focuses on war and insurgency. The author of two books, he has written numerous articles for magazines such as *Esquire, Men's Journal, Outside,* and *Sports Afield.* In the following *New York Times* article, Stanton considers the local effects of global crises.

It's strange having your own oil spill.

What we have, of course, is a blip compared to the one in the Gulf of Mexico, which this week formally broke all records for offshore spills. But after watching the gulf catastrophe unfold from afar, the news that oil was gushing from a pipeline just three hours south of here into a small creek that flows into the Kalamazoo River and, eventually, into Lake Michigan, came as a surprise.

Until last week, I wasn't aware that a pipeline even existed, though I must have driven over or past it hundreds of times. The leak is now under control, but a good storm could still blow some of the estimated one million gallons of spilled oil into the lake, and maybe even north along its sandy coast, past numerous resort towns and into the Grand Traverse Bay, to a place called Clinch Park, where I've been swimming most mornings from June to October since I was a kid.

It's hard enough to try to capture oil floating in an ocean. But oil moving downstream in a swift river? Forget about it. As the pre-Socratic philosopher Heraclitus said, you can't step into the same river twice.

But despite the danger to the lake, many people here, busy enjoying their 5
summer vacations, haven't paid much attention to the spill. After all, Lake Michigan has lived through worse. It may be near the center of the continent, but it's not immune to the outside world, as we've learned over and over.

First there were the invasive Asian carp, swimming around the Chicago River a mere six miles from the mouth of the lake. These voracious eaters get excited by the sound of boat motors and can leap by the hundreds into the air all at once, in some hellish version of a water ballet. An oil spill seems almost benign in comparison.

We've also had to contend with an invasion of gobies—small, bug-eyed fish you're supposed to kill if you catch. They disrupt the food chain that normally supports native lake trout, perch and bass. They entered the lake in the ballast water of international shipping traffic, along with zebra mussels, which filter micro-organisms—also food for native fish—out of the water.

As a result of the zebra mussel infestation, the lake, several summers ago, was often as clear as a Bahamian bay. When I swam, I could see 50 feet in any direction. This extra sunlight fed more algae at deeper depths, which created algal blooms that floated up on the beach in smelly heaps. Now that the mussels have died off, the lake has returned to something like normal.

So for now, I swim. Winters are so long in northern Michigan, nearly nine months of gray skies and deep snow, that summer comes as a fresh burst. Amnesia sets in—you forget that winter will ever return. Friends from other parts of the country descend. The days ripen perfectly, the air no warmer or colder than your skin so that the edges of your body seem to extend beyond you, up and down the tree-lined streets.

Traverse City sits halfway between the North Pole and the Equator, and our summer days are long. The light seems to take forever to vanish from the sky and, when it does, it goes out like someone folding a white sheet in the dark. A flare on the horizon. Then a rustle: Goodnight.

"No zebra mussels, no carp, no oil spill headed my way. No politicians, no bloggers."

I swim in the midst of bad news to stay sane. I crawl over the sand bottom in six feet of water, which is cold and green, and nothing has changed in my life—I'm a kid again. No zebra mussels, no carp, no oil spill headed my way. No politicians, no bloggers. Every day I step refreshed and clean from the water, and go up to the bookstore, Horizon's, and order a coffee and stand on the street in flip-flops in the chill air, feeling the hot cup in my hand, the fine texture of its paper, feeling as if I've just come awake from a dream.

And what I carry around in my head is this, the image of the water, of looking around 20 feet in any direction, and beyond my periphery the lake darkening to the color of light in a storm. Sometimes I see fish slicing around my field of vision—silver missiles headed to deeper water. The work day is about to begin; traffic pours past on the four-lane parkway. I wonder what the people driving by think of me, when I'm swimming out there along the buoys; and in a time when there is too much news to think about, I hope they think nothing at all.

When the oil spill in Michigan began, I heard about a memorial service for Paul Miller, a 22-year-old Marine corporal from the nearby village of Lake Ann, who was killed on July 19 in Afghanistan. Later in the week, I stood in the funeral home, not far from the beach where I swim, and stared at Corporal Miller's flag-draped coffin.

I thought this: that the world's troubles can be nearer to us than we think, flowing in our direction, flowing toward *home.*

And while it's true that we used to live in Lake Ann, and our son may have played summer baseball with Corporal Miller years earlier, I don't remember meeting him. Maybe I passed him on the street, a tyke headed over to the ice cream shop with his parents, where we were standing in line, too, with our children, all of us oblivious to the news to come, the depth and coldness of the water ahead.

Analyze

1. How are an oil spill, invasive species, and the death of a soldier related?
2. What single sentence do you think embodies Stanton's main idea?
3. Explain the role of swimming in this essay. How is it related to Stanton's main idea?
4. How are the small towns (Traverse City and Lake Ann) important to Stanton's main idea?
5. Compare Stanton's article to "Throwing the Last Stone" by Benjamin Busch (in this chapter). What beliefs or assumptions do you think they might share?

Explore

1. Explain how a national or global problem manifests in your everyday life.
2. How do you forget about the troubles of the world beyond your own town?
3. Stanton's essay was published during the BP oil spill in the Gulf of Mexico in 2010. How did this crisis reach into your community?
4. How has the war in Afghanistan reached into or influenced your community? Explain the degree to which people discuss, ignore, or avoid the issue.

Benjamin Busch
Throwing the Last Stone

Benjamin Busch is a writer, filmmaker, actor, photographer, and illustrator. As a U.S. Marine Corps infantry officer, he served two combat tours in Iraq and was awarded the Bronze Star. In his memoir *Dust to Dust*, Busch tells of a rambunctious and often reckless boyhood that seemed inevitably "drawn to conflict." In the following *Daily Beast* article, published in March 2012 after a U.S. soldier gunned down sixteen Afghan civilians, Busch examines our collective responsibilities related to war.

Sixteen Afghan civilians have been killed, in their homes, under our protection. One man acting alone we are quick to say. And it's probably true. An Army of one. But that one man is one of us.

There will be official statements, medical conjecture, military analysis, political showmanship, and protest. We will learn the facts over time, everyone hurrying to rule out abject senselessness with a justification of one kind or another. Posttraumatic stress and brain injury will be broadly blamed and we will hope that it is only something as terrible as that. We will become procedural in order to avoid being emotional. This will happen because this is how we respond to world events, but what is important now is what this one stunning occurrence means to our national soul.

The Taliban, our enemies, the group that justified our invasion of Afghanistan by harboring Bin Laden and al Qaeda, have vowed revenge. The very men who have a brutal record of torture, barbarous treatment of women, murder, and terrorism have found in this massacre of families a way to claim righteous indignation. It is here where we have no defense. Our moral character is built on the emphatic claim that we defend the innocent, that we and our allies are just. We have tried with tremendous sacrifice to prove it: 1,787 Americans brought home from the valleys of Afghanistan to be buried, 15,460 wounded there . . . and now this.

In a land where trust is hard won, this betrayal will echo. Our president and commanders have apologized. The military necessarily speaks with humble resignation when civilians are killed because it knows that when villages are battlefields, collateral casualties are unavoidable. Afghans have simply come to expect tragedy. But these fatalities were not the result of an official operation, not an accident justified by the presence of an enemy. President Obama has said that "This incident does not represent the exceptional character of our military," which is true except that our military *is* represented by this incident. The killer wore an American flag on his shoulder, a soldier of the rank and file, and by that symbol our military is colored by his act, and so are we. We cannot distance ourselves from him because we sent him there.

5 These Afghan children, the oldest being 12, were born into uncertainty and had lived their whole lives in a war we brought upon them, killed finally by a soldier we sent to protect them. This man, an American, was able to seek them in their sleep, shoot and stab them, and burn them in their blankets. Children the age of his own. Murderers exist without war, but because this act took place in war it makes him a war criminal, and it

indicts the nation he serves. We know who threw the first stone, but history will judge us by how we throw the last one.

I commanded Marines in Iraq and I was responsible for every bullet my unit fired. The war was fought in villages, on farmland, in cities, and through homes. We endangered ourselves by how carefully we tried to avoid causing harm to noncombatants, but they lived in the crossfire and I have seen people cry for sorrows I had a hand in delivering. I cannot restore the dead, and I will not forget them.

Our wars have long haunted veterans who have survived their survival. I was born in the year of the Tet offensive, my parents protestors, but we have learned few lessons from that conflict. Civilian casualties were staggering. 700,000 men were drafted, most sent against their will to fight in the jungles, returning home to be vilified for serving the nation that sent them. Many have taken their own lives in part because of the lives they've taken and for those they've seen lost. The conflict is now known as a taxing lost cause, a mistake, the sufferings of our soldiers pointless, our view of the enemy never sensible. It was a war made by the generation that prides itself on its clean moral victory over fascism in World War II, but that war was ended by dropping atomic bombs on families.

We seem not to notice how linear our world perspective is. What we call the Vietnam War the Vietnamese call the American War. Veterans of Vietnam see all the same signs in Afghanistan and have long been vocal opponents of our deepening involvement. We would do well to ask them how we should feel right now.

In their oath of vengeance, the Taliban called us "sick-minded American savages." We will be afraid to call our soldier mad, to admit that he lost his mind in war. This allows for the possibility that any one of us could go insane at any time, and that every veteran poisoned by their combat experience could be on edge for life. And some will be. The mind keeps our morality in balance, reminds us of learned social consequences, keeps rage and other primal instincts civilized. In many ways our ethical stability is preserved by our sense of community, security, and home. War takes all of those elements away, immerses the military in danger, and makes its members vulnerable to an involuntary loss of self-control. What is truly surprising is how rarely these acts of madness occur and how powerfully most veterans preserve their humanity.

Experts will try to find a cause to blame: fatigue, injury, disassociation, 10
derangement, leadership, agreeing finally that all leave the act inexcusable,

but we have to believe that we are in some way responsible, and feel regret. The cause may be our mission in Afghanistan and we might ask if that is a noble cause, something we believe in enough to invest so much life and produce so much death. What happens in the lives of others has yet to upset us where we live, and that has made these wars something that somehow does not include us here. Therein lies the danger in national disinterest. Do we have an honest collective emotional reaction to efforts that do not reach deep into our days and take something from us? Distant events stir little public empathy and we are a people known more and more for our selfish distractions than for our awareness. We will want to say that war estranged this soldier from our society, but there is much evidence that our society is completely disconnected from his war. This rampage far from us is part of what should be a much larger discussion about who we are now and what our wars mean. This act of one man is not allowed the convenience of being isolated, unrepresentative of our "deep respect for the people of Afghanistan." President Karzai stated, "When Afghan people are killed deliberately by U.S. forces this action is murder and terror and an unforgivable action." He is careful not to mention *accidental* deaths which have been tolerated as inevitable. We might consider this as we think about why we keep sending service members into situations in which they cannot be forgiven for what could occur.

We will put our children to sleep in our homes tonight, safe from wars, free to dream. We might take a moment to imagine what it would be like to lose our entire family, tonight, to a policeman, and wonder aloud what apologies would be worth.

Analyze

1. Explain Busch's opening strategy. How does he use the Army's motto?
2. How does Busch not allow himself or readers (us) to dismiss the shooting in Afghanistan as an isolated incident? Identify specific passages and explain how they work to this end.
3. How does Busch's own role as a Marine function in the article?
4. In paragraph 7, Busch alludes to the Vietnam War. Why? What does the allusion accomplish? How does it relate to the main idea?
5. How is this an argumentative article? What particular point is Busch arguing? What idea or claim do you think he is arguing against?

Emily Chertoff

Occupy Wounded Knee: A 71-Day Siege and a Forgotten Civil Rights Movement

Emily Chertoff is a writer and producer for *The Atlantic*, which "is dedicated to equipping opinion leaders with breakthrough ideas and original insights." In her work, she explores issues related to national and international politics, education, and technology. Here, Chertoff reflects on a historical case of war at home.

On February 27, 1973, a team of 200 Oglala Lakota (Sioux) activists and members of the American Indian Movement (AIM) seized control of a tiny town with a loaded history—Wounded Knee, South Dakota. They arrived in town at night, in a caravan of cars and trucks, took the town's residents hostage, and demanded that the U.S. government make good on treaties from the 19th and early 20th centuries. Within hours, police had surrounded Wounded Knee, forming a cordon to prevent protesters from exiting and sympathizers from entering. This marked the beginning of a 71-day siege and armed conflict.

Russell Means, one of AIM's leaders, died yesterday. Means was a controversial figure within the movement and outside of it; as his *New York Times* obituary put it, "critics, including many Indians, called him a tireless self-promoter who capitalized on his angry-rebel notoriety." After getting his start in activism in the 1970s, Means went on to run for the Libertarian presidential nomination in 1987, and for governor of New Mexico in 2002. He also acted in scores of films, most famously in a lead role in the 1992 version of *The Last of the Mohicans.*

For all the contradictions of his life, he was no less controversial than AIM itself. The Wounded Knee siege was both an inspiration to indigenous people and left-wing activists around the country and—according to the U.S. Marshals Service, which besieged the town along with FBI and National Guard—the longest-lasting "civil disorder" in 200 years of U.S. history. Two native activists lost their lives in the conflict, and a federal agent was shot and paralyzed. Like the Black Panthers or MEChA, AIM was a militant civil rights and identity movement that sprung from the political and social crisis of the late 1960s, but today it is more obscure than the latter two groups.

The Pine Ridge reservation, where Wounded Knee was located, had been in turmoil for years. To many in the area the siege was no surprise. The Oglala Lakota who lived on the reservation faced racism beyond its boundaries and a poorly managed tribal government within them. In particular, they sought the removal of tribal chairman Dick Wilson, whom many Oglala living on the reservation thought corrupt. Oglala Lakota interviewed by PBS for a documentary said Wilson seemed to favor mixed-race, assimilated Lakota like himself—and especially his own family members—over reservation residents with more traditional lifestyles. Efforts to remove Wilson by impeaching him had failed, and so Oglala Lakota tribal leaders turned to AIM for help in removing him by force. Their answer was to occupy Wounded Knee.

5 Federal marshals and National Guard traded heavy fire daily with the native activists. To break the siege, they cut off electricity and water to the town, and attempted to prevent food and ammunition from being passed to the occupiers. Bill Zimmerman, a sympathetic activist and pilot from Boston, agreed to carry out a 2,000-pound food drop on the 50th day of

the siege. When the occupiers ran out of the buildings where they had been sheltering to grab the supplies, agents opened fire on them. The first member of the occupation to die, a Cherokee, was shot by a bullet that flew through the wall of a church.

To many observers, the standoff resembled the Wounded Knee Massacre of 1890 itself—when a U.S. cavalry detachment slaughtered a group of Lakota warriors who refused to disarm. Some of the protesters also had a more current conflict in mind. As one former member of AIM told PBS, "They were shooting machine gun fire at us, tracers coming at us at nighttime just like a war zone. We had some Vietnam vets with us, and they said, 'Man, this is just like Vietnam.'" When PBS interviewed federal officials later, they said that the first death in the conflict inspired them to work harder to bring it to a close. For the Oglala Lakota, the death of tribe member Buddy Lamont on April 26 was the critical moment. While members of AIM fought to keep the occupation going, the Oglala overruled them, and, from that point, negotiations between federal officials and the protesters began in earnest. The militants officially surrendered on May 8, and a number of members of AIM managed to escape the town before being arrested. (Those who were arrested, including Means, were almost all acquitted because key evidence was mishandled.) Even after the siege officially ended, a quiet war between Dick Wilson and the traditional, pro-AIM faction of Oglala Lakota continued on the reservation—this despite Wilson's re-election to the tribal presidency in 1974. In the three years following the stand-off, Pine Ridge had the highest per capita murder rate in the country. Two FBI agents were among the dead. The Oglala blamed the federal government for failing to remove Wilson as tribal chairman; the U.S. retorted that it would be illegal for them to do so, somewhat ironically citing reasons of tribal self-determination.

Today, the Pine Ridge reservation is the largest community in what may be the poorest county in the entire United States. (Per capita income in 2010 was lower in Shannon County, South Dakota, where Pine Ridge is located, than in any other U.S. county.) Reports have the adult unemployment rate on the reservation somewhere between 70 and 80 percent. AIM—and Means—drew a lot of attention to the treatment of indigenous people in the U.S. But perhaps more than any other civil rights movement, its work remains unfinished.

Analyze

1. A eulogy is a speech or text that honors the memory of someone who has passed away. How is this article a eulogy? What other genre is at work?
2. Chertoff's title borrows a phrase from more recent civil disturbances. How does the title support or relate to her main idea about Means?
3. How is this article about cultural change, tradition, or resistance to change? In your answer, consider the role of eulogy and the particular memory of Russell Means.
4. What is the most detailed or graphic passage in the article? How does it support or relate to the main idea?
5. How does Chertoff collapse the difference between war and civil disorder?

Explore

1. When we think of war, at least in the United States, we might imagine military operations in other countries—places far beyond our own borders. We use phrases like "civic unrest" or "civil disorder" to characterize a country at war with itself. How would you describe the events at Wounded Knee? As war, civil unrest, or something else?
2. Research the Wounded Knee Massacre. How does it fit into U.S. history? What do you think it means in the story of American culture?
3. Find out more about the Pine Ridge reservation. What do you think its presence—and its particular economic condition—means to American culture? How does it fit into a description of the United States?
4. American Indian reservations are technically sovereign countries. They are, literally, countries within a country. How does this impact your understanding of the Wounded Knee siege and standoff?
5. Explain how Chertoff's article relates to Chris Hedges's essay in this chapter, "War Is Betrayal."

Nick Turse
A Six-Point Plan for Global War

A journalist and historian, Nick Turse studies the cultural effects of our propensity for war. The author of numerous articles and three books, he is the managing editor for *TomDispatch*, a website that considers itself "a regular antidote to the mainstream media." In the following blog post, Turse examines the intersection between war and culture.

It looked like a scene out of a Hollywood movie. In the inky darkness, men in full combat gear, armed with automatic weapons and wearing night-vision goggles, grabbed hold of a thick, woven cable hanging from a MH-47 Chinook helicopter. Then, in a flash, each "fast-roped" down onto a ship below. Afterward, "Mike," a Navy SEAL who would not give his last name, bragged to an Army public affairs sergeant that, when they were on their game, the SEALs could put 15 men on a ship this way in 30 seconds or less.

Once on the aft deck, the special ops troops broke into squads and methodically searched the ship as it bobbed in Jinhae Harbor, South Korea. Below deck and on the bridge, the commandos located several men and trained their weapons on them, but nobody fired a shot. It was, after all, a training exercise.

All of those ship-searchers were SEALs, but not all of them were American. Some were from Naval Special Warfare Group 1 out of Coronado, California; others hailed from South Korea's Naval Special Brigade. The drill was part of Foal Eagle 2012, a multinational, joint-service exercise. It was also a model for—and one small part of—a much publicized U.S. military "pivot" from the Greater Middle East to Asia, a move that includes sending an initial contingent of 250 Marines to Darwin, Australia, basing littoral combat ships in Singapore, strengthening military ties with Vietnam and India, staging war games in the Philippines (as well as a drone strike there), and shifting the majority of the Navy's ships to the Pacific by the end of the decade.

That modest training exercise also reflected another kind of pivot. The face of American-style war-fighting is once again changing. Forget full-scale invasions and large-footprint occupations on the Eurasian mainland; instead, think: special operations forces working on their own but also training or fighting beside allied militaries (if not outright proxy armies) in hot spots around the world. And along with those special ops advisors, trainers, and commandos expect ever more funds and efforts to flow into the militarization of spying and intelligence, the use of drone aircraft, the launching of cyber-attacks, and joint Pentagon operations with increasingly militarized "civilian" government agencies.

5 Much of this has been noted in the media, but how it all fits together into what could be called the new global face of empire has escaped attention. And yet this represents nothing short of a new Obama doctrine, a six-point program for 21st-century war, American-style, that the administration is now carefully developing and honing. Its global scope is already breathtaking, if little recognized, and like Donald Rumsfeld's military lite and David Petraeus's counterinsurgency operations, it is evidently going to have its day in the sun—and like them, it will undoubtedly disappoint in ways that will surprise its creators.

The Blur-ness

For many years, the U.S. military has been talking up and promoting the concept of "jointness." An Army helicopter landing Navy SEALs on a Korean ship catches some of this ethos at the tactical level. But the future, it seems, has something else in store. Think of it as "blur-ness," a kind of organizational version of war-fighting in which a dominant Pentagon fuses its forces with other government agencies—especially the CIA, the State Department, and the Drug Enforcement Administration—in complex, overlapping missions around the globe.

In 2001, Secretary of Defense Donald Rumsfeld began his "revolution in military affairs," steering the Pentagon toward a military-lite model of high-tech, agile forces. The concept came to a grim end in Iraq's embattled cities. A decade later, the last vestiges of its many failures continue to play out in a stalemated war in Afghanistan against a rag-tag minority insurgency that can't be beaten. In the years since, two secretaries of defense and a new president have presided over another transformation—this one geared toward avoiding ruinous, large-scale land wars which the U.S. has consistently proven unable to win.

Under President Obama, the U.S. has expanded or launched numerous military campaigns—most of them utilizing a mix of the six elements of 21st-century American war. Take the American war in Pakistan—a poster-child for what might now be called the Obama formula, if not doctrine.

Beginning as a highly-circumscribed drone assassination campaign backed by limited cross-border commando raids under the Bush administration, U.S. operations in Pakistan have expanded into something close to a full-scale robotic air war, complemented by cross-border helicopter attacks, CIA-funded "kill teams" of Afghan proxy forces, as well as boots-on-the-ground missions by elite special operations forces, including the SEAL raid that killed Osama bin Laden.

The CIA has conducted clandestine intelligence and surveillance missions in Pakistan, too, though its role may, in the future, be less important, thanks to Pentagon mission creep. In April, in fact, Secretary of Defense Leon Panetta announced the creation of a new CIA-like espionage agency within the Pentagon called the Defense Clandestine Service. According to the *Washington Post,* its aim is to expand "the military's espionage efforts beyond war zones."

Over the last decade, the very notion of war zones has become remark- 10
ably muddled, mirroring the blurring of the missions and activities of the CIA and Pentagon. Analyzing the new agency and the "broader convergence trend" between Department of Defense and CIA missions, the *Post* noted that the "blurring is also evident in the organizations' upper ranks. Panetta previously served as CIA director, and that post is currently held by retired four-star Army Gen. David H. Petraeus."

Not to be outdone, last year the State Department, once the seat of diplomacy, continued on its long march to militarization (and marginalization) when it agreed to pool some of its resources with the Pentagon to create the Global Security Contingency Fund. That program will allow the Defense Department even greater say in how aid from Washington will flow to proxy forces in places like Yemen and the Horn of Africa.

One thing is certain: American war-making (along with its spies and its diplomats) is heading ever deeper into "the shadows." Expect yet more clandestine operations in ever more places with, of course, ever more potential for blowback in the years ahead.

Shedding Light on "the Dark Continent"

One locale likely to see an influx of Pentagon spies in the coming years is Africa. Under President Obama, operations on the continent have accelerated far beyond the more limited interventions of the Bush years. Last year's war in Libya; a regional drone campaign with missions run out of airports and bases in Djibouti, Ethiopia, and the Indian Ocean archipelago nation of Seychelles; a flotilla of 30 ships in that ocean supporting regional operations; a multi-pronged military and CIA campaign against militants in Somalia, including intelligence operations, training for Somali agents, a secret prison, helicopter attacks, and U.S. commando raids; a massive influx of cash for counterterrorism operations across East Africa; a possible old-fashioned air war, carried out on the sly in the region using manned aircraft; tens of millions of dollars in arms for allied mercenaries and African troops; and a special ops expeditionary force (bolstered by State Department experts) dispatched to help capture or kill Lord's Resistance Army leader Joseph Kony and his senior commanders, operating in Uganda, South Sudan, the Democratic Republic of the Congo, and the Central African Republic (where U.S. Special Forces now have a new base) only begins to scratch the surface of Washington's fast-expanding plans and activities in the region.

Even less well known are other U.S. military efforts designed to train African forces for operations now considered integral to American interests on the continent. These include, for example, a mission by elite Force Recon Marines from the Special Purpose Marine Air Ground Task Force 12 (SPMAGTF-12) to train soldiers from the Uganda People's Defense Force, which supplies the majority of troops to the African Union Mission in Somalia.

15 Earlier this year, Marines from SPMAGTF-12 also trained soldiers from the Burundi National Defense Force, the second-largest contingent in Somalia; sent trainers into Djibouti (where the U.S. already maintains a major Horn of Africa base at Camp Lemonier); and traveled to Liberia where they focused on teaching riot-control techniques to Liberia's military as part of an otherwise State Department spearheaded effort to rebuild that force.

The U.S. is also conducting counterterrorism training and equipping militaries in Algeria, Burkina Faso, Chad, Mauritania, Niger, and Tunisia. In addition, U.S. Africa Command (Africom) has 14 major joint-training exercises planned for 2012, including operations in Morocco, Cameroon, Gabon, Botswana, South Africa, Lesotho, Senegal, and what may become the Pakistan of Africa, Nigeria.

Even this, however, doesn't encompass the full breadth of U.S. training and advising missions in Africa. To take an example not on Africom's list, this spring the U.S. brought together 11 nations, including Cote d'Ivoire, The Gambia, Liberia, Mauritania, and Sierra Leone to take part in a maritime training exercise code-named Saharan Express 2012.

Back in the Backyard

Since its founding, the United States has often meddled close to home, treating the Caribbean as its private lake and intervening at will throughout Latin America. During the Bush years, with some notable exceptions, Washington's interest in America's "backyard" took a backseat to wars farther from home. Recently, however, the Obama administration has been ramping up operations south of the border using its new formula. This has meant Pentagon drone missions deep inside Mexico to aid that country's battle against the drug cartels, while CIA agents and civilian operatives from the Department of Defense were dispatched to Mexican military bases to take part in the country's drug war.

In 2012, the Pentagon has also ramped up its anti-drug operations in Honduras. Working out of Forward Operating Base Mocoron and other remote camps there, the U.S. military is supporting Honduran operations by way of the methods it honed in Iraq and Afghanistan. In addition, U.S. forces have taken part in joint operations with Honduran troops as part of a training mission dubbed Beyond the Horizon 2012; Green Berets have been assisting Honduran Special Operations forces in anti-smuggling operations; and a Drug Enforcement Administration Foreign-deployed Advisory Support Team, originally created to disrupt the poppy trade in Afghanistan, has joined forces with Honduras's Tactical Response Team, that country's most elite counternarcotics unit. A glimpse of these operations made the news recently when DEA agents, flying in an American helicopter, were involved in an aerial attack on civilians that killed two men and two pregnant women in the remote Mosquito Coast region.

Less visible have been U.S. efforts in Guyana, where Special Operations 20
Forces have been training local troops in heliborne air assault techniques. "This is the first time we have had this type of exercise involving Special Operations Forces of the United States on such a grand scale," Colonel Bruce Lovell of the Guyana Defense Force told a U.S. public affairs official earlier this year. "It gives us a chance to validate ourselves and see where we are, what are our shortcomings."

The U.S. military has been similarly active elsewhere in Latin America, concluding training exercises in Guatemala, sponsoring "partnership-building" missions in the Dominican Republic, El Salvador, Peru, and Panama, and reaching an agreement to carry out 19 "activities" with the Colombian army over the next year, including joint military exercises.

Still in the Middle of the Middle East

Despite the end of the Iraq and Libyan wars, a coming drawdown of forces in Afghanistan, and copious public announcements about its national security pivot toward Asia, Washington is by no means withdrawing from the Greater Middle East. In addition to continuing operations in Afghanistan, the U.S. has consistently been at work training allied troops, building up military bases, and brokering weapons sales and arms transfers to despots in the region from Bahrain to Yemen.

In fact, Yemen, like its neighbor, Somalia, across the Gulf of Aden, has become a laboratory for Obama's wars. There, the U.S. is carrying out its signature new brand of warfare with "black ops" troops like the SEALs and the Army's Delta Force undoubtedly conducting kill/capture missions, while "white" forces like the Green Berets and Rangers are training indigenous troops, and robot planes hunt and kill members of al-Qaeda and its affiliates, possibly assisted by an even more secret contingent of manned aircraft.

The Middle East has also become the somewhat unlikely poster-region for another emerging facet of the Obama doctrine: cyberwar efforts. In a category-blurring speaking engagement, Secretary of State Hillary Clinton surfaced at the recent Special Operations Forces Industry Conference in Florida where she gave a speech talking up her department's eagerness to join in the new American way of war. "We need Special Operations Forces who are as comfortable drinking tea with tribal leaders as raiding a terrorist compound," she told the crowd. "We also need diplomats and development experts who are up to the job of being your partners."

Clinton then took the opportunity to tout her agency's online efforts, aimed at websites used by al-Qaeda's affiliate in Yemen. When al-Qaeda recruitment messages appeared on the latter, she said, "our team plastered the same sites with altered versions . . . that showed the toll al-Qaeda attacks have taken on the Yemeni people." She further noted that this information-warfare mission was carried out by experts at State's Center for Strategic Counterterrorism Communications with assistance, not surprisingly, from the military and the U.S. Intelligence Community.

These modest online efforts join more potent methods of cyberwar being employed by the Pentagon and the CIA, including the recently revealed "Olympic Games," a program of sophisticated attacks on computers in Iran's nuclear enrichment facilities engineered and unleashed by the National Security Agency (NSA) and Unit 8200, Israeli's equivalent of the NSA. As with other facets of the new way of war, these efforts were begun under the Bush administration but significantly accelerated under the current president, who became the first American commander-in-chief to order sustained cyberattacks designed to cripple another country's infrastructure.

From Brushfires to Wildfires

Across the globe from Central and South America to Africa, the Middle East, and Asia, the Obama administration is working out its formula for a new American way of war. In its pursuit, the Pentagon and its increasingly militarized government partners are drawing on everything from classic precepts of colonial warfare to the latest technologies.

The United States is an imperial power chastened by more than 10 years of failed, heavy-footprint wars. It is hobbled by a hollowing-out economy, and inundated with hundreds of thousands of recent veterans—a staggering 45% of the troops who fought in Afghanistan and Iraq—suffering from service-related disabilities who will require ever more expensive care. No wonder the current combination of special ops, drones, spy games, civilian soldiers, cyberwarfare, and proxy fighters sounds like a safer, saner brand of war-fighting. At first blush, it may even look like a panacea for America's national security ills. In reality, it may be anything but.

The new light-footprint Obama doctrine actually seems to be making war an ever more attractive and seemingly easy option—a point emphasized recently by former Chairman of the Joint Chiefs of Staff General Peter Pace. "I worry about speed making it too easy to employ force," said Pace when asked about recent efforts to make it simpler to deploy Special Operations Forces abroad. "I worry about speed making it too easy to take the easy answer—let's go whack them with special operations—as opposed to perhaps a more laborious answer for perhaps a better long-term solution."

As a result, the new American way of war holds great potential for un- 30
foreseen entanglements and serial blowback. Starting or fanning brushfire wars on several continents could lead to raging wildfires that spread unpredictably and prove difficult, if not impossible, to quench.

By their very nature, small military engagements tend to get larger, and wars tend to spread beyond borders. By definition, military action tends to have unforeseen consequences. Those who doubt this need only look back to 2001, when three low-tech attacks on a single day set in motion a decade-plus of war that has spread across the globe. The response to that one day began with a war in Afghanistan, that spread to Pakistan, detoured to Iraq, popped up in Somalia and Yemen, and so on. Today, veterans of those Ur-interventions find themselves trying to replicate their dubious successes in places like Mexico and Honduras, the Central African Republic and the Congo.

History demonstrates that the U.S. is not very good at winning wars, having gone without victory in any major conflict since 1945. Smaller interventions have been a mixed bag with modest victories in places like Panama and Grenada and ignominious outcomes in Lebanon (in the 1980s) and Somalia (in the 1990s), to name a few.

The trouble is, it's hard to tell what an intervention will grow up to be—until it's too late. While they followed different paths, Vietnam, Afghanistan, and Iraq all began relatively small, before growing large and ruinous. Already, the outlook for the new Obama doctrine seems far from rosy, despite the good press it's getting inside Washington's Beltway.

What looks today like a formula for easy power projection that will further U.S. imperial interests on the cheap could soon prove to be an unmitigated disaster—one that likely won't be apparent until it's too late.

Analyze

1. This article chronicles change in military culture. In your own words, describe that change.
2. What does Turse mean by the "blurring" of military operations?
3. Turse explains that military operations will become "more clandestine," or more secretive in coming years. He also says that we should expect "ever more potential for blowback." What do you think he means? And why is a more secretive military apt to generate more blowback?
4. Turse says that President Obama was "the first American commander-in-chief to order sustained cyberattacks designed to cripple another country's infrastructure." Explain how this point supports Turse's main idea.
5. In Turse's understanding, why might cyberwar be an especially dangerous turn?

Explore

1. Turse argues that America has primarily been losing small-scale wars for the past sixty years. Why, then, do you think we continue to launch or maintain military operations?

2. What does Turse's point about newer and more agile military operations make you think about the future of war?
3. What is the relationship between a country's culture and its war making? Are they opposite? Do they overlap? Is one the cause of the other?
4. Reread Turse's final paragraph. What do you think he's predicting—or at least suggesting?
5. Compare Turse's article to Neal Whitman's ("'Kinetic' Connections"). How do they overlap?

Neal Whitman
"Kinetic" Connections

Neal Whitman is a linguist who studies the impact of words on our daily lives. A columnist for *Visual Thesaurus* magazine, he writes scripts for the *Grammar Girl* podcast and blogs for *Literal-Minded.* In the following magazine article, Whitman dissects the word *kinetic* in the context of war.

I stayed up late on the night of May 1 to hear President Obama's stunning announcement: A special-forces mission, which could have gone humiliatingly wrong, had instead succeeded in killing Osama bin Laden, the man behind the worst terrorist attack on American soil. I watched until the news reporters ran out of things to say, when they began to fill airtime by repeating things and asking the opinions of people in the streets while waiting for something else to happen.

I had to wait until the next morning to read more about how U.S. forces had actually managed to achieve this victory, when I read this article in the *National Journal* online. The team of Navy SEALs that carried out the mission, I learned, were part of a special group of special-missions units and task forces known as the Joint Special Operations Command. The article went on to explain some more about JSOC, saying:

> Recently, JSOC built a new Targeting and Analysis Center in Rosslyn, Va. Where the National Counterterrorism Center tends to focus on threats to the homeland, TAAC, whose existence was

> first disclosed by the Associated Press, focuses outward, on active "kinetic"—or lethal—counterterrorism missions abroad.

The definition of *kinetic* caught my eye. It was in quotation marks, followed by a gloss to explain its meaning. Apparently the author, Mark Ambinder, didn't expect his readers to be familiar with this specialized meaning of *kinetic.* But people have been getting familiar with it for several months now. My introduction to it was during the annual meeting of the American Dialect Society in January, when the term *kinetic event* won the "Most Euphemistic" category in the ADS's 2010 Word of the Year vote. A kinetic event is "a violent action in the field of battle," according to the definition Ben Zimmer is writing in the "Among the New Words" column in next month's issue of *American Speech,* the journal of the ADS. The term had been in the news from Afghanistan in reports like this one from September (to appear in Ben's entry):

> The coalition is reporting . . . that in August, just last month, there were more than 4,900 kinetic events. That's an attack, mortars, rockets, small arms, IEDs.

In March, the public awareness of this new sense of *kinetic* was raised further by the phrase *kinetic military action,* the widely ridiculed term used by Ben Rhodes, the Deputy National Security Advisor in describing the United States' role in the ongoing conflict in Libya. Jonathan Allen wrote an article on *Politico.com:*

> Police action, conflict, hostilities and now "kinetic military action." They're all euphemisms for that word that this White House and many before it have been so careful not to say: War.
>
> Administration officials told congressional aides in a closed briefing earlier this week that the United States is not at war with Libya, and Deputy National Security Adviser Ben Rhodes danced around the question in a Wednesday exchange with reporters aboard Air Force One.
>
> "I think what we are doing is enforcing a resolution that has a very clear set of goals, which is protecting the Libyan people, averting a

> humanitarian crisis, and setting up a no-fly zone," Rhodes said. "Obviously that involves kinetic military action, particularly on the front end. But again, the nature of our commitment is that we are not getting into an open-ended war, a land invasion in Libya."

Although the military sense of *kinetic* seeped into public consciousness 5
in 2010 and 2011, as with many seemingly new words, it turns out to have spent a number of years paying its dues before getting its big break.

The euphemistic feel of *kinetic* comes from its association with scientific inquiry. Unless you're a teacher (who deals with visual, auditory, and kinesthetic learning styles) or an artist (who might create kinetic sculptures), the word *kinetic* probably brings to mind high-school physics class, and lectures about potential and kinetic energy. In fact, in its first uses relating to the military or national defense, *kinetic* did mean "relating to kinetic energy." In the 1978 edition of the *Code Name Handbook: Aerospace Defense Technology* the acronym *SKEW* is defined as a "shoulder-fired kinetic energy weapon." A kinetic-energy weapon, as opposed to a chemical-energy weapon, is one that does its damage with the simple kinetic energy of the projectiles it fires. A gun with ordinary, non-exploding bullets would be one example of a kinetic energy weapon.

Alternatively, a kinetic energy weapon could be a missile or other heavy object hurled from space, as long as it isn't equipped with, say, a nuclear warhead. A 1983 article in the *Boston Globe* quotes a brochure for a weapons conference as mentioning missiles as kinetic energy weapons. One part of Ronald Reagan's proposed Strategic Defense Initiative/"Star Wars" missile-defense system was the "kinetic kill vehicle" (KKV). The term starts appearing in news reports from 1985, and continues to do so even now, though these days the focus is more on destroying Chinese rather than Russian missiles or satellites.

A year after the proposal of SDI, the phrase *kinetic energy penetrator* as a synonym/euphemism for *bullet* was in circulation, and five years after that, it got a real workout during Operation Desert Storm, when U.S. tanks were equipped with kinetic energy penetrators made of depleted uranium—a good conveyor of kinetic energy because of its high density. (I have to say, though, that using DU as a weapon by turning it into a really heavy piece of ammunition is like using a barometer to determine the height of a building by throwing it over the edge and timing how long it takes to hit the ground.)

These uses of *kinetic* seem to have paved the way toward its broader meaning of military attacks, which had become well-established by the time of the September 11 terrorist attacks. In a 2002 article in *Slate,* Timothy Noah introduces his readers to the term *kinetic warfare:* "Retronym" is a word coined by Frank Mankiewicz, George McGovern's campaign director, to delineate previously unnecessary distinctions. Examples include "acoustic guitar," "analog watch," "natural turf," "two-parent family," and "offline publication." Bob Woodward's new book, *Bush at War,* introduces a new Washington retronym: "kinetic" warfare.

Noah then quotes from page 150 of *Bush at War,* in which President Bush and his advisors talk about "going kinetic" against al Qaeda after 9/11. Noah continues:

> In common usage, "kinetic" is an adjective used to describe motion, but the Washington meaning derives from its secondary definition, "active, as opposed to latent." Dropping bombs and shooting bullets—you know, killing people—is kinetic. But the 21st-century military is exploring less violent and more high-tech means of warfare, such as messing electronically with the enemy's communications equipment or wiping out its bank accounts. These are "non-kinetic." . . . Asked during a January [2002] talk at National Defense University whether "the transformed military of the future will shift emphasis somewhat from kinetic systems to cyber warfare," Donald Rumsfeld answered, "Yes!" (Rumsfeld uses the words "kinetic" and "non-kinetic" all the time.)

In addition to *kinetic warfare* and *kinetic systems,* there is a host of other 21st-century *kinetic* terms, including *kinetic operations, kinetic capability, kinetic engagements, kinetic strike, kinetic activity,* and *kinetic targeting,* i.e., bombing. These days the bombs don't have to be non-explosive; the opposite of kinetic targeting is *soft targeting:* dropping leaflets. Areas where fighting is going on are *kinetic areas. Kinetic* can be a predicate adjective, too, i.e., one that comes after a linking verb. An army unit might *go kinetic,* and an article from 2006 tells how British soldiers in Iraq believed their American counterparts were "too kinetic." (Kinetic Yankees, if you will.) There is even an adjective, *post-kinetic,* to describe reconstruction, or places where battles have taken place.

Commander Philip Thrash, an old high-school friend and former field artillery officer in the U.S. Army, served in Afghanistan in 2007 and 2008. He confirms that it isn't just the top brass who use *kinetic*. He started to hear it among his superiors in 2003 or 2004, and during his service, he and his peers and subordinates used it often. As he explained: You hear your superiors use it, and if you want to communicate effectively with them, you use the words they use, and then it just becomes part of your lexicon. *Kinetic* is useful because it can cover a lot of more specific verbs, such as *engage, acquire (a target), move to contact, destroy, neutralize*. Summing up, Philip used an unsettling but soberingly accurate turn of phrase that has been in print since at least the late 1970s, and that some veterans remember from the Vietnam War. Basically, he said, *kinetic* is "a polite way of saying 'kill people and break things.'"

Analyze

1. What does "kinetic" mean in terms of the military? Why do you think kinetic is used rather than some other terms?
2. What is Whitman's point? What subtle argument does he make about "kinetic" as a term for military operation?
3. How does Whitman's introduction function in the article? What mood or idea does it help to establish?
4. Whitman says, "I have to say, though, that using DU [depleted uranium] as a weapon by turning it into a really heavy piece of ammunition is like using a barometer to determine the height of a building by throwing it over the edge and timing how long it takes to hit the ground." What does he mean and what is he suggesting about depleted uranium?
5. How is Whitman's essay about culture? How does he draw out the process through which acts, words, or concepts become normal?

Explore

1. Whitman finds "kinetic" to be a *euphemism*. What other euphemisms are used in times of war?
2. What nonmilitary euphemisms do you use on daily basis? What unpleasant qualities or acts are you trying to conceal?

3. Why do you think the term *kinetic* is not widely used among nonmilitary personnel?
4. What is a retronym? How is it important to Whitman's article?
5. How would you say military culture and nonmilitary culture overlap? Are they the same? Does one promote or support the other?

Chris Hedges
War Is Betrayal

A Pulitzer Prize–winning journalist and cultural critic, Chris Hedges writes about cultural myths related to war, progress, and religion. Named Online Journalist of the Year by the Los Angeles Press Club in 2009 and 2011, he is the author of numerous books and a column for the news website Truthdig, which strives to "challenge conventional wisdom." In the following magazine article, Hedges considers the morality of war.

We condition the poor and the working class to go to war. We promise them honor, status, glory, and adventure. We promise boys they will become men. We hold these promises up against the dead-end jobs of small-town life, the financial dislocations, credit card debt, bad marriages, lack of health insurance, and dread of unemployment. The military is the call of the Sirens, the enticement that has for generations seduced young Americans working in fast food restaurants or behind the counters of Walmarts to fight and die for war profiteers and elites.

The poor embrace the military because every other cul-de-sac in their lives breaks their spirit and their dignity. Pick up Erich Maria Remarque's *All Quiet on the Western Front* or James Jones's *From Here to Eternity*. Read *Henry IV*. Turn to the *Iliad*. The allure of combat is a trap, a ploy, an old, dirty game of deception in which the powerful, who do not go to war, promise a mirage to those who do.

I saw this in my own family. At the age of ten I was given a scholarship to a top New England boarding school. I spent my adolescence in the schizophrenic embrace of the wealthy, on the playing fields and in the dorms and classrooms that condition boys and girls for privilege, and came back to my working-class relations in the depressed former mill towns in Maine. I traveled between two universes: one where everyone got chance after chance after chance, where connections and money and influence almost guaranteed that you would not fail; the other where no one ever got a second try. I learned at an early age that when the poor fall no one picks them up, while the rich stumble and trip their way to the top.

Those I knew in prep school did not seek out the military and were not sought by it. But in the impoverished enclaves of central Maine, where I had relatives living in trailers, nearly everyone was a veteran. My grandfather. My uncles. My cousins. My second cousins. They were all in the military. Some of them—including my Uncle Morris, who fought in the infantry in the South Pacific during World War II—were destroyed by the war. Uncle Morris drank himself to death in his trailer. He sold the hunting rifle my grandfather had given to me to buy booze.

He was not alone. After World War II, thousands of families struggled 5
with broken men who, because they could never read the approved lines from the patriotic script, had been discarded. They were not trotted out for red-white-and-blue love fests on the Fourth of July or Veterans Day.

The myth of war held fast, despite the deep bitterness of my grandmother—who acidly denounced what war had done to her only son—and of others like her. The myth held because it was all the soldiers and their families had. Even those who knew it to be a lie—and I think most did—were loath to give up the fleeting moments of recognition, the only times in their lives they were told they were worth something.

"For it's Tommy this, an' Tommy that, an' 'Chuck him out, the brute!'" Rudyard Kipling wrote. "But it's 'Saviour of 'is country' when the guns begin to shoot."

Any story of war is a story of elites preying on the weak, the gullible, the marginal, the poor. I do not know of a single member of my graduating prep school class who went into the military. You could not say this about the high school class that graduated the same year in Mechanic Falls, Maine.

Geoff Millard was born in Buffalo, New York, and lived in a predominately black neighborhood until he was eleven. His family then moved to Lockport, a nearby white suburb. He wrestled and played football in high school. He listened to punk rock.

10 "I didn't really do well in classes," he says. "But that didn't seem to matter much to my teachers."

At fifteen he was approached in school by a military recruiter.

"He sat down next to me at a lunch table," Millard says. "He was a Marine. I remember the uniform was crisp. All the medals were shiny. It was what I thought I wanted to be at the time.

"He knew my name," Millard adds. "He knew what classes I was taking. He knew more about me than I did. It was freaky, actually."

Two years later, as a senior, Millard faced graduation after having been rejected from the only college where he had applied.

15 "I looked at what jobs I could get," he says. "I wasn't really prepared to do any job. I wasn't prepared for college. I wasn't prepared for the workforce. So I started looking at the military. I wanted to go active duty Marine Corps, I thought. You know, they were the best. And that's what I was going to do.

"There were a lot of other reasons behind it, too," he says. "I mean, growing up in this culture you envy that, the soldier."

Any story of war is a story of elites preying on the weak, the gullible, the marginal, the poor.

His grandfather, in the Army Air Corps in World War II, had died when he was five. The military honor guard at the funeral had impressed him. As a teenager, he had watched the burial of his other grandfather, also with military honors. Millard carried the folded flag to his grandmother after receiving it from the honor guard.

The pageantry has always been alluring. "We marched a long time," Louis-Ferdinand Céline, who fought in World War I, writes in *Journey to the End of the Night:*

> There were streets and more streets, and they were all crowded with civilians and their wives, cheering us on, bombarding us with flowers from café terraces, railroad stations, crowded churches. You never saw so many patriots in all your life! And then there were fewer patriots. . . . It started to rain, and then there were still fewer and fewer, and not a single cheer, not one.

20 And nearly a century later it is the same.

When Millard told his mother he wanted to be a Marine, she pleaded with him to consider the National Guard. He agreed to meet with the

Guard recruiter, whose pitch was effective and simple: "If you come here, you get to blow shit up."

"I'm seventeen," Millard says. "I thought being in the military was the pinnacle of what coolness was. I was just like, oh, I get to blow up stuff! I signed up right then and there on the spot. But the interesting thing he didn't tell me was that the 'shit' that he referred to would be kids.

"They don't teach you when you're in land mine school that the overwhelming percentage of victims of land mines are little kids. Because, like, in the States, a little kid will chase a soccer ball in the streets. And overseas, a little kid will chase a soccer ball into a minefield. Whether, you know, it happens in Korea or Bosnia or Iraq, kids get killed all the time by land mines. They get maimed by them. And that's just a reality of our military industrial complex. We put out these mines. We have no concern for what they do."

Not that this reality intruded on his visions of life in the military when he began.

"I just thought of it like this stuff you see on TV where cars blow up and stuff like that," he says.

For Anthony Swofford—author of *Jarhead,* a memoir about being a Marine in the first Gulf War—the tipping point came when the recruiter, who assured him he would be "a fine killer," told him he could book a threesome for $40 in Olongapo in the Philippines. "I'd had sex three times and been the recipient of five blow jobs and fourteen hand jobs," he writes. "I was sold."

But sometimes there's no need for a recruiting pitch. The culture does enough to make war, combat, and soldiering appealing.

Ali Aoun was born in Rochester, New York. His father is Lebanese. His mother is from the Caribbean. He says he wanted to be a soldier from the age of nine. He was raised watching war films. But even antiwar films such as *Platoon* and *Full Metal Jacket* celebrate the power and seductiveness of violence. He wanted this experience as his own. He says no one pushed him into it.

"I enlisted," he explains. "It was something I always wanted to do, although I got more than I bargained for. You never really know a woman until you jump in bed with her. It's just like the Army: you never really know about it until you enlist. It's not about defending the country or serving our people. It's about working for some rich guy who has his interests."

30 At first Millard liked the National Guard. He was able to enroll in Niagara County Community College as a business major, where he signed up for an African American studies class thinking it would be an easy A. He read *The Autobiography of Malcolm X.* He read Howard Zinn's *A People's History of the United States.* He read Frederick Douglass.

"It was the first time I'd really started to read," he says.

He was in the African American studies class when the attacks of 9/11 occurred. His wrestling coach came into the room to tell him he had been activated. He went home. He packed his bags. He thought about combat.

"I was pissed," he says. "I was like, they attacked us. I was ready to go to war."

But he was confused from the start.

35 "I really wanted to go to war with somebody, because we were attacked," he says. "But the one question I couldn't answer was, who were we going to go to war with?"

At first he did military funerals. Then he was called up for Iraq. He was by then a sergeant and was assigned to work in the office of a general with the 42nd Infantry Division, Rear Operation Center. He became, in military slang, a REMF—a rear echelon motherfucker. He was based in Tikrit, where he watched the cynical and cold manipulation of human life.

"It's not about defending the country or serving our people. It's about working for some rich guy who has his interests."

He relates the story of a traffic-control mission gone awry when an eighteen-year-old soldier made a bad decision. He was sitting atop an armored Humvee monitoring a checkpoint. An Iraqi car approached, and the soldier, fearing it might be carrying a suicide bomber, pressed the butterfly trigger on his .50 caliber machine gun. He put two hundred rounds into the car in less than a minute, killing a mother, a father, a four-year-old boy, and a three-year-old girl.

"They briefed this to the general," Millard says. "They briefed it gruesome. I mean, they had pictures. And this colonel turns around to this full division staff and says: 'If these fucking Hadjis learned to drive, this shit wouldn't happen.'

40 "If you lift your rifle and you look through the sights and you see a person, you can't pull the trigger," Millard says. "But if you lift your rifle and you look through the sights and you see a fucking Hadji, then what's the difference.

"That's a lot of what I saw in Iraq," he says. "These officers, high-ranking officers, generals, colonels, you know, the complete disregard. They knew all the stuff that happened. They got all the briefings. They knew what happened. And they either didn't speak up, they didn't say anything about it or they openly condoned it. When Iraqis got killed, to them, it was one less fucking Hadji around."

Millard's thirteen months in Iraq turned him into a passionate antiwar activist. He is the cofounder of the Washington, D.C., chapter of Iraq Veterans Against the War and served as its president for three years. He has taken part in numerous antiwar demonstrations around the country, was one of the organizers of the Winter Soldier hearings, returned to Iraq on a humanitarian aid mission in 2011, and now directs a homeless veterans initiative.

The briefing that Millard and his superiors received after the checkpoint killing was one of many. Sergeant Perry Jeffries, who served in the Fourth Infantry Division in Iraq after being called out of retirement, said the killing of Iraqi civilians at checkpoints was routine.

"Alpha troop and Balad Ruz shot somebody at least once," he says, referring to a troop detachment and to the soldiers manning a checkpoint in a small Diyala Province village. "Somebody else on what we called the Burning Oil Checkpoint, they shot somebody with a .50 cal, shot a guy once, and then several times."

Killing becomes a job. You do it. Sometimes it unnerves you. But the 45
demons usually don't hit until you come home, when you are lying alone in bed and you don't dare to tell your wife or your girlfriend what you have become, what you saw, what you did, why you are drinking yourself into a stupor, why you so desperately want to forget your dreams.

The disillusionment comes swiftly. It is not the war of the movies. It is not the glory promised by the recruiters. The mythology fed to you by the church, the press, the school, the state, and the entertainment industry is exposed as a lie. We are not a virtuous nation. God has not blessed America. Victory is not assured. And we can be as evil, even more evil, than those we oppose. War is venal, noisy, frightening, and dirty. The military is a vast bureaucratic machine fueled by hyper-masculine fantasies and arcane and mind-numbing rules. War is always about betrayal—betrayal of the young by the old, of idealists by cynics, and of soldiers and Marines by politicians.

"The biggest misconception about the war is that the soldiers care about politics," Jeffries says. "The right thinks the soldiers want support. They want to feel good. They want everybody to fly their flag and have a bumper sticker and go, 'Rah! Rah! Rah! I support the troops. Yay, thank you! Thank you! Thank you!' The left thinks the soldiers all want to run off and get out of there, that they're dying in a living hell. I think that most of the soldiers are young people that are having a decent adventure."

But, he goes on, "They may be having a very hard time. They're frustrated about the amount of resources they have been provided—how many hours of sleep they get, how nice their day is, whether they get to play their PlayStation or read their book at night or whatever. Like any human, you'd like to have some more of that."

Yet, while soldiers don't want to be forgotten, the support-the-troops brigade only maintains the mythology of war on the home front by pretending that we're actually all in it together, when in fact it's overwhelmingly the poor, powerless, and adrift who suffer.

Jeffries has little time for lawn chair warriors: "I remember hearing that somebody said, 'Oh, we're going to have a barbecue to support the troops.' I heard about this when I was in Iraq. I said, how the hell is that going to support me? It's not doing anything. Don't drink beer. Send me the beer. It's not doing me any good to have you drink it. I still don't like the yellow ribbons."

It is no surprise that soldiers sometimes come to despise civilians who chant patriotic mantras. Those soldiers may not be fans of the remote and rarely seen senior officers who build their careers on the corpses of others, including comrades, either. But to oppose the machine and risk being cast out of the magic circle of comradeship can be fatal. Fellow soldiers are the only people who understand the psychological torment of killing and being shot at, of learning to not think at all and instead be led as a herd of animals. Those ostracized in war have a hard time surviving, mentally and physically, so most service members say and do nothing to impede the madness and the killing.

Jessica Goodell came to understand that torment only too well, as she relates in her 2011 memoir *Shade it Black: Death and After in Iraq*. Goodell wasn't poor. She grew up in a middle-class home near Chautauqua Lake in upstate New York. Her father was a lawyer, and her mother worked at home. But her "universe fractured" when she was sixteen and her parents divorced. She could barely continue "the motions of everyday existence."

She was accepted at Ithaca College her senior year, but just before graduation a uniformed Marine came to her high school. He told her he had come to find "tough men."

"What about tough women?" she asked.

By that afternoon she was in the Marine recruiting office. She told the recruiter she wanted to be part of a tank crew but was informed that women were prohibited from operating tanks. She saw a picture of a Marine standing next to a vehicle with a huge hydraulic arm and two smaller forklift arms. She signed up to be a heavy equipment mechanic, although she knew nothing about it.

Three years later, while stationed at the Marine Corps Air Ground 55
Combat Center in the desert town of Twentynine Palms, California, she volunteered to serve in the Marine Corps' first official Mortuary Affairs unit, at Al Taqaddum Airbase in Iraq. Her job, for eight months, was to "process" dead Marines—collect and catalog their bodies and personal effects. She put the remains in body bags and placed the bags in metal boxes. Before being shipped to Dover Air Force Base, the boxes were stored, often for days, in a refrigerated unit known as a "reefer."

Her unit processed six suicides. The suicide notes, she told me in an interview, almost always cited hazing. Marines who were overweight or unable to do the physical training were subjected to withering verbal and physical abuse. They were called "fat nasties" and "shit bags." They were assigned to other Marines as slaves. Many were forced to run until they vomited or to bear-crawl—walk on all fours—the length of a football field and back. This would be followed by sets of monkey fuckers—bending down, grabbing the ankles, crouching like a baseball catcher, and then standing up again—and other exercises that went on until the Marines collapsed.

Goodell's unit was sent to collect the bodies of the Marines who killed themselves. They usually blew their faces off with assault rifles in port-a-johns or in the corners of abandoned bunkers or buildings. She and the other members of the Mortuary Affairs unit would have to scrape the flesh and brain tissue from the walls.

Goodell fell into depression when she returned home. She abused drugs and alcohol. And she watched the slow descent of her comrades as they too tried to blunt the pain with narcotics and self-destructive behavior. She details many of her experiences in *Shade It Black,* a term that refers to the missing body parts of dead Marines, which she colored black on diagrams of the corpses.

In a poignant passage, she talks about what it was like for her and a fellow Marine named Miguel to come home and see all those yellow ribbons:

> We'd frequently pass vehicles displaying the yellow ribbon "support-our-troops decal," but we never once mentioned it. We probably passed a hundred or more decals—two hundred if you count the multiple decals decorating the cars of the more patriotic motorists—and yet neither of us even once said, "Look, more support from the citizenry. Let's give the 'thumbs up' as we pass.'" . . . I knew that these people on their way to work or home or dinner had no idea what it was they were supporting. They did not have a clue as to what war was like, what it made people see, and what it made them do to each other. I felt as though I didn't deserve their support, or anyone's, for what I had done. . . . No one should ever support the people who do such things.

60 Stateside "support" not only reflects the myths of war, but it also forces Goodell and her comrades to suppress their own experiences:

> Here we were, leaving the ribbons behind us as we sped up on our way to Hell, probably, where we would pay for the sins these magnetic decals endorsed. There was an irony of sorts shaping the dynamic between our ribbon decal supporters and us. They were uninformed but good people, the kind whose respect we would welcome—if it were based upon something true. It was when we were around them that we had to hide the actual truth most consciously.

Those who return to speak this truth, like Goodell or Millard, are our contemporary prophets. They struggle, in a culture awash in lies, to tell what few have the fortitude to digest. The words these prophets speak are painful.

As a nation we prefer to listen to those who speak from the patriotic script. We prefer to hear ourselves exalted. If veterans speak of terrible wounds visible and invisible, of lies told to make them kill, of evil committed in our name, we fill our ears with wax. Not our boys and girls, we say, not them, bred in our homes, endowed with goodness and decency. For if it is easy for them to murder, what about us? It is simpler and more comfortable not to hear, to wish only that they would calm down, be reasonable, get some help, and go away. We brand our prophets as madmen. We cast them into the desert. This is why so many veterans are estranged and enraged. This is why so many succumb to suicide or addictions. Not long ago Goodell received a text message from a Marine she had worked with in Mortuary Affairs after he tried to commit suicide. "I've got $2,000 in the bank," the message read. "Let's meet in NYC and go out with a bang."

War comes wrapped in patriotic slogans; calls for sacrifice, honor, and heroism; and promises of glory. It comes wrapped in the claims of divine providence. It is what a grateful nation asks of its children. It is what is right and just. It is waged to make the nation and the world a better place, to cleanse evil. War is touted as the ultimate test of manhood, where the young can find out what they are made of. From a distance it seems noble. It gives us comrades and power and a chance to play a bit part in the great drama of history. It promises to give us identities as warriors, patriots, as long as we go along with the myth, the one the war-makers need to wage wars and the defense contractors need to increase their profits.

But up close war is a soulless void. War is about barbarity, perversion, and pain. Human decency and tenderness are crushed, and people become objects to use or kill. The noise, the stench, the fear, the scenes of eviscerated bodies and bloated corpses, the cries of the wounded all combine to spin those in combat into another universe. In this moral void, naïvely blessed by secular and religious institutions at home, the hypocrisy of our social conventions, our strict adherence to moral precepts, becomes stark. War, for all its horror, has the power to strip away the trivial and the banal, the empty chatter and foolish obsessions that fill our days. It might let us see, although the cost is tremendous.

Analyze

1. Look up "call of the Sirens" online. Try to find the mythological origin and then explain how the reference works in Hedges's introduction.
2. How is this article about socioeconomics?
3. Explain how Jessica Goodell's testimony supports Hedges's main idea.
4. Hedges says that in war, "the hypocrisy of our social conventions, our strict adherence to moral precepts, becomes stark." What does he mean? In your own words, explain this idea.
5. How is Hedges's article about American culture?

Explore

1. Hedges says, "War comes wrapped in patriotic slogans; calls for sacrifice, honor, and heroism; and promises of glory." List some specific and recent patriotic slogans that have been associated with war.
2. What do you think about the yellow ribbons in support of soldiers? How does Hedges's article—Goodell's words specifically—influence your thinking?
3. How does Hedges's article relate to "Throwing the Last Stone" by Benjamin Busch (in this chapter)? What specific claims, ideas, or values do the two writers share? Identify specific passages to support your answer.
4. Hedges argues that war is betrayal. How is war also a form of truth or honesty?
5. What's the connection between soldiers and politics?

Tom Malinowski, Sarah Holewinski, and Tammy Schultz

Post-Conflict Potter

Specializing in U.S. foreign policy and human rights policy, Tom Malinowski is the Washington director for Human Rights Watch. His articles have appeared in *Foreign Policy, The New Republic,* and the *Washington Post.* Sarah Holewinski is the executive director of the Campaign for Innocent Victims in Conflict (CIVIC), which seeks to "make warring parties more responsible to civilians before, during, and after armed conflict." Her articles have appeared in the *International Herald Tribune, USA Today,* and the *Washington Post.* Tammy Schultz is the director of national security and joint warfare at Marine Corps University. She writes for newspapers such as *Defense News,* the *Washington Post,* and the *Washington Times.* In the following *Foreign Policy* article, Malinowski, Holewinski, and Schultz use J. K. Rowling's fantasy world, and its terminology, as a lens for examining international policy.

At last, the long war against Voldemort and his army of Death Eaters has been brought to a responsible end. A short time ago, just a small band of brave witches and wizards at Hogwarts School stood between the dark forces and their ascension to power. Now their evil leader is dead, his armies are scattered, and the wizarding world can begin to recover from the terror they inflicted.

At such a moment of deliverance, it is natural to feel elation and closure—to allow ourselves the brief comfort of imagining that the drama, so meticulously documented by J.K. Rowling, is over. But if history teaches us anything (consider the bitter legacy still lingering from the 17th-century Goblin Wars or the recent experience of American Muggles in Iraq and Afghanistan), it is that the defeat of Voldemort by Harry Potter may have been the easy part. Indeed, one might even say it was child's play. The hard work of postwar stabilization still lies ahead.

Former U.S. Deputy Defense Secretary John Hamre and retired Gen. Gordon Sullivan have described four pillars of post-conflict reconstruction: security, governance and participation, urgent social and economic needs, and justice and reconciliation. Of these pillars, the magical world can currently afford to feel complacent about only one—social and economic needs. After all, with the proper application of scouring, mending, and engorgement charms, much of the physical damage wrought by the war can be repaired, and food can be multiplied to meet the needs of the population. But with respect to the other imperatives, critical challenges remain.

Surviving Death Eaters will have to be brought to justice or reintegrated into magical society. Long-standing rifts among magical communities that the war widened must be healed. Most of all, we must ensure that the values that triumphed in the final battle—tolerance, pluralism, and respect for the dignity of all magical and non-magical creatures alike—are reflected in the institutions and arrangements that emerge from the conflict. What ultimately matters is not just whether something evil was defeated, but whether something good is built in its place.

As experts on human rights, civilian protection, and national security, 5
we were recently asked by officials in the British Ministry of Magic to suggest lessons from the Muggle world that might apply to challenges facing post-Voldemort magical society. Our recommendations are summarized below.

Transitional Justice and Reconciliation

Thousands of Death Eaters fought with or provided material support to Voldemort, including prominent members of key magical institutions. It will be impossible to move forward unless we come to terms with the abuses they committed and meet legitimate demands for redress. In the magical world, after all, the ghosts of the past can literally haunt future generations.

Members of Voldemort's inner circle and others guilty of the worst crimes—the unforgivable curses of killing ("Avada Kedavra"), torture ("Crucio"), and mind control ("Imperio")—should be prosecuted before a court of law. We should reject calls by Order of the Phoenix hard-liners like Joe Lieberbottom, John "Mad Eye" McCain, and Lindsey Gramger to instead detain them without charge as "unlawful enemy spell-casters" for as long as the "war" against dark magic continues (though all three men deserve our thanks for their early warnings about the Dark Lord's return).

A more difficult dilemma arises with respect to the thousands of other wizards and witches who aided the Dark Lord's cause in less obvious ways. We cannot sweep their complicity under an invisibility cloak. At the same time, it would be impractical and unwise to prosecute all of them. For every wizard who willingly committed crimes for the Death Eaters, another was blackmailed, threatened, or coerced while under the Imperius Curse. Some actively participated in hostilities against other wizards and Muggles; others merely provided financing or shelter. A campaign to punish everyone would get out of hand, creating a climate of suspicion and score-settling in which innocents are snared. The last thing the wizarding world needs is a witch hunt.

A legitimate process must hold the victors to account as well. Remember, under the ruthless Barty Crouch, the Ministry of Magic's Department of Magical Law Enforcement was itself formally authorized to use unforgivable curses, including torture, against suspected Death Eaters, and innocent suspects were imprisoned after what were essentially show trials. When the ministry came under Voldemort's sway, how many of its employees went along with the abuses it committed? What about the controversial decisions made by those who are widely seen as heroes, like Hogwarts headmaster Albus Dumbledore—for, say, his use of child soldiers? What of Harry Potter himself, who once used the torture curse?

One way to address these challenges would be to establish a Truth and Reconciliation Commission modeled on the experience of Muggle South Africa. Rank-and-file Death Eaters and collaborators—as well as those who fought against them—would be given the opportunity to testify about their actions and be forgiven for those less serious offenses to which they fully and honestly confessed. Such a process would not only be cathartic, but would also help establish a more accurate and complete version of these traumatic events and could, in turn, become part of Hogwarts's curriculum. It would be important to ensure, however, that those who testify to such a commission tell the truth voluntarily, and not under the influence of Veritaserum. 10

Victims should also have their day in court. The Ministry of Magic should provide amends, in the form of gold or perhaps a bottle of Felix Felicis, to all those civilian wizards and witches harmed by either side during the war. Meanwhile, a property claims commission should be established to gather unlawfully amassed assets and return them to their rightful owners. The goblins in charge of Gringotts Bank should be required to question and report suspiciously large deposits of gold, especially by Politically Exposed Wizards. Some seized assets should be used to help wounded and cursed warriors and loved ones of the fallen, like the Weasley family. This year's Quidditch World Cup should be dedicated to their memory; it will be a chance to heal.

Finally, true reconciliation in the magical world must involve its nonhuman inhabitants as well. For complicated historical reasons, some magical creatures such as giants, trolls, and spiders fought alongside the Death Eaters during the final battle at Hogwarts. Given the anger felt by the wizarding community toward those who aided Voldemort, some might try to inflict collective punishment on these beings, as well as on those, like centaurs and merpeople, whose loyalties were uncertain or who remained neutral in the face of mass atrocities. In the short term, the International Confederation of Wizards (a consortium of magical lands, often meeting by a river in New York) should deploy a mission of peacekeeping Aurors with a mandate to protect vulnerable communities of magical creatures from revenge attacks. In the longer term, the International Confederation of Wizards should initiate a multistakeholder dialogue with these creatures and negotiate a compact that addresses the long-standing grievances that led them, tragically, to side with the Dark Lord.

Governance Reform

In their aptly named essay, "Dealing with Demons," Michèle Flournoy and Michael Pan argue that the reconciliation pillar of post-conflict reconstruction requires more than just dealing with past abuses and grievances. It also calls for "(1) law enforcement instruments that are effective and respectful of human rights; (2) an impartial, open, and accountable judicial system; (3) a fair constitution and body of law; (4) mechanisms for monitoring and upholding human rights; [and] (5) a humane corrections system." The wizarding world will need to implement fundamental reforms in each of these areas.

Members of the anti-Voldemort Order of the Phoenix will presumably form the core of a transitional governing authority, which would then organize elections for a permanent government. As democratic forces in Muggle Egypt and Libya have recently discovered, the legitimacy of post-revolutionary but pre-election transitional governments can be tenuous. This problem could be minimized in the magical world by having the Hogwarts Sorting Hat assign ministerial positions in the transitional authority.

15 The new government should rapidly draw up and submit to a referendum a new legal framework establishing checks and balances on its powers, as well as a Charter on the Rights of Witches and Wizards. We would also recommend that the Wizengamot, the high council of Magical Great Britain, be split into separate legislative and judicial bodies. The wizards who conjure the laws should not be the ones who interpret them.

The use of any form of torture should be banned, whether by the infamous Cruciatus Curse or methods euphemistically known as "enhanced hexation." We welcome J.K. Rowling's report that soul-sucking dementors will be banished from the prison at Azkaban, but we do not think this measure goes far enough. The next Minister of Magic should close Azkaban on day one of his administration. It is a symbol of abuse and a recruiting tool for future Death Eaters. (We recognize the practical difficulties in closing Azkaban so quickly, but believe that the prisoners could initially be moved to penal facilities in enchanted caves or castles as secure as Azkaban, but without the baggage. A judicial panel could then review each prisoner's case to determine whether he should be given a new trial, transferred to another magical state, or allowed to disapparate. As U.S. President Barack Obama will surely confirm when his magical counterpart next drops into the Oval Office, delay could be fatal. All it will take is one more attempted Death Eater attack and scaremongers in the Wizengamot will start calling for the return of dementors, making the closure of Azkaban politically impossible.)

In parallel, legitimate law enforcement measures should be stepped up. Merchants should be required to report bulk sales of magical supplies that could be combined for dark purposes. Lawful surveillance of dark alleys and curse-tracing spells on wands should be permitted, with a judicial warrant. Full body and Polyjuice Potion scanners should also be installed for international travelers across the Floo Network.

One of the great weaknesses of magical institutions is that they function top down, with little input from ordinary wizards and witches. And yet the war against Voldemort was won almost entirely bottom up, by grassroots organizations such as Dumbledore's Army and the Order of the Phoenix. The legal and political reforms we advocate depend on the growth of civil society (we assume a charm can be developed to make magical civil society especially vibrant).

Another urgent priority should be media diversification. A single wizarding newspaper—the *Daily Prophet*—cannot maintain its independence and hold government officials accountable when it has no competition (especially given the rumor, first published in the tabloid the *Quibbler,* that the *Prophet* may soon be bought by dark wizard Rupert Murdoch). New media should also be promoted in the magical world. Right now, for example, wizards and witches stay in touch by sending letters of any length by the slow, reliable method of owl post. A new system could be developed employing faster, lighter sparrows, which could distribute shorter messages—say under 140 characters—to larger numbers of people.

Finally, the Ministry of Magic must become more transparent to the 20
public and press. Fewer documents should be protected by the Fidelius Charm, and the budget of the Department of Mysteries should be declassified. Too much secrecy will only invite more WizenLeaks scandals.

International Magical Security

The great question remaining now is whether Voldemort's death means that the threat posed by dark magic has passed. Some might be tempted to believe so. After all, for ages many witches and wizards have let themselves believe that if they ignore the phenomenon entirely, if they lock it in the restricted section of the library or refrain from uttering the names of dark wizards, it will somehow go away. But as renowned defense-against-the-dark-arts expert Marc Sageman argued in his incisive book, *Leaderless Maleficium,* most dark wizards, while originally inspired by Voldemort, have over time transitioned to membership in an amorphous "social movement" organized into small cells and networked through Legilimency, a system likely to survive the demise of its leader and of "Death Eater Central." This view may be exaggerated (see Bruce Hoffman's response to Sageman, "The Myth of Grass-Roots Dark Magic"). But it would be unrealistic to assume that Voldemort's death will mark the end of magical extremism or that no other leader will emerge to unite his followers. For one thing, the House of Slytherin still remains.

The overall reform of states that already have strong institutions, such as Magical Great Britain, would help prevent the resurgence of new security threats and enshrine the values for which Voldemort's opponents fought. Resuming international events like the Triwizard Tournament could help spread those values and forge bonds among the established states. But none of this will suffice so long as dark wizards can find refuge in failed magical states where lawlessness reigns, as Voldemort did in Albania for over a dozen years. Far deeper international magical cooperation will be needed to deal with these ungoverned spaces.

For a start, new standards must be agreed upon. We suggest that the International Confederation of Wizards negotiate a Comprehensive Curse Ban Treaty, forbidding use or testing of certain forms of dark magic anywhere on the planet. The treaty should be enforced by deploying a ground-based network of sensors, or Sneakoscopes, throughout the world to detect unlawful spells.

Each sovereign magical state should be seen as having a responsibility to protect its citizens from dark magic. But if they fail to meet their responsibility, it should be the duty of the international magical community to step in. And when that community does act to pacify an unstable area, it should not try to do so on the cheap, by targeting dark wizards (or unruly trolls, giants, or dragons) with stunning spells deployed from unmanned aerial brooms. Stabilization Aurors will need to deploy to these places, employing a "clear, hold, and conjure" strategy designed to win hearts, minds, and souls.

We trust that these preliminary recommendations will be helpful to all magical persons as they recover from their recent conflict. If we have been of service to the community of witches and wizards, we humbly hope they might render us Muggles a service or two in return. For starters, we would very much appreciate it if they could lift the Petrificus Totalus curse someone has clearly placed on the U.S. Congress.

Analyze

1. In this article, the world of Harry Potter is used as an extended metaphor to help make sense of modern military policy. What is the main idea? What point do the authors make?
2. In the world of Harry Potter, Muggles are everyday, nonmagical humans. In this extended metaphor, explain who the Muggles are.
3. Who are "all magical persons"?
4. The authors assert, "The legal and political reforms we advocate depend on the growth of civil society (we assume a charm can be developed to make magical civil society especially vibrant)." Explain this point. What are they saying about legal and governmental institutions in the United States?
5. This article describes a major shift in international policy. Explain how it describes a change in culture.

Explore

1. What is postconflict reconstruction? See what others have said about it.
2. Why is a free media—one not owned by major political figures or parties—a vital part of democracy?
3. The authors argue, "The wizards who conjure the laws should not be the ones who interpret them." How does this point translate into modern U.S. institutions?
4. The authors reference a dark wizard at work in Albania. Who was this person?
5. The article calls for international collaboration to bring down evil dictators and to balance out bad international policy. What body or group in our world offers such collaboration?

Forging Connections

1. How does warfare get used to sell products and services in mainstream culture? Even beyond video games such as *Medal of Honor,* how has military conflict and armed battle become part of marketing? What are some terms, phrases, references, or even images that marketers now rely on to create a message? Focus on specific ads or ad campaigns. What do these ads suggest about war? What do they suggest about the relationship between war and everyday life? What kinds of attitudes and beliefs about war or patriotism do the ads reinforce? Borrow insights from Dan Heath and Chip Heath ("How to Pick the Perfect Brand Name," Chapter 2), Juliette Kayyem ("Never Say 'Never Again,'" Chapter 3), and James Gleick ("What Defines a Meme?," Chapter 4).
2. Explore the relationship between film and war. Focus on a specific film such as *The Deer Hunter, Full Metal Jacket, The Hurt Locker, Inglourious Basterds,* or a miniseries such as *Generation Kill.* Write an essay that explains how specific features (such as plot, character development, direction, or cinematography) make a point about war. For instance, what does the focus on Robert DeNiro's character in *The Deer Hunter* say about the relationship between the battlefield and home? What does the plot of *Inglourious Basterds* say about the way we learn about the history of war? What do the characters in *Generation Kill* say about the generation of U.S. soldiers that served after 9/11?

Looking Further

1. How will warfare change in the future? Consider the claims and descriptions made in this chapter and write an essay that describes a detailed future. Focus your ideas by narrowing on a specific branch of the military or a specific defense policy. Finally, consider the implications for American culture. What does this future suggest about mainstream culture? What will Americans tolerate, accept, or support? What kinds of conflict or loss will they accept? Integrate images, charts, or graphs to help illustrate your vision of the future.
2. Hedges claims that the military appeals to poor and working-class young people—those with few options in life. Research this claim. Try to find the average income of new recruits or their families. Seek out information about military recruiting strategies—the schools, colleges, and neighborhoods they designate as prime locations. Explain your findings in a thorough explanatory essay.

college

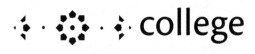

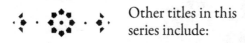

Other titles in this series include:

Language: A Reader for Writers
Gita DasBender
(ISBN: 9780199947485)

Community: A Reader for Writers
Nancy Enright
(ISBN: 9780190277079)

Sustainability: A Reader for Writers
Carl Herndl
(ISBN: 9780199947508)

Food: A Reader for Writers
Deborah Holdstein and Danielle Aquiline
(ISBN: 9780199385683)

Globalization: A Reader for Writers
Maria Jerskey
(ISBN: 9780199947522)

Culture: A Reader for Writers
John Mauk
(ISBN: 9780199947225)

Technology: A Reader for Writers
Johannah Rodgers
(ISBN: 9780199340736)

Identity: A Reader for Writers
John Scenters-Zapico
(ISBN: 9780199947461)

Queer: A Reader for Writers
Jason Schneiderman
(ISBN: 9780190277109)

Poverty/Privilege: A Reader for Writers
Connie Snyder Mick
(ISBN: 9780199361250)

Gender: A Reader for Writers
Megan Titus and Wendy Walker
(ISBN: 9780190298852)

Creativity: A Reader for Writers
Ryan Van Cleave
(ISBN: 9780190279929)

Humor: A Reader for Writers
Kathleen Volk Miller and Marion Wrenn
(ISBN: 9780199362684)

college

A READER *for* WRITERS

Todd James Pierce
California Polytechnic State University

New York Oxford
Oxford University Press

Oxford University Press is a department of the University of Oxford.
It furthers the University's objective of excellence in research,
scholarship, and education by publishing worldwide.

Oxford New York
Auckland Cape Town Dar es Salaam Hong Kong Karachi
Kuala Lumpur Madrid Melbourne Mexico City Nairobi
New Delhi Shanghai Taipei Toronto

With offices in
Argentina Austria Brazil Chile Czech Republic France Greece
Guatemala Hungary Italy Japan Poland Portugal Singapore
South Korea Switzerland Thailand Turkey Ukraine Vietnam

For titles covered by Section 112 of the US Higher Education Opportunity Act, please visit www.oup.com/us/he for the latest information about pricing and alternate formats.

Published by Oxford University Press
198 Madison Avenue, New York, New York 10016
http://www.oup.com

Library of Congress Cataloging-in-Publication Data
Names: Pierce, Todd James, 1965- author.
Title: College : a reader for writers / Todd Pierce, California Polytechnic State University.
Description: New York : Oxford University Press, [2016]
Identifiers: LCCN 2015037602| ISBN 9780190279950 | ISBN 9780190279974
Subjects: LCSH: College readers. | English language--Rhetoric--Problems, exercises, etc. | Report writing--Problems, exercises, etc. | Readers--Education. | College students--Conduct of life.
Classification: LCC PE1417 .P473 2016 | DDC 808/.0427--dc23
LC record available at http://lccn.loc.gov/2015037602

Printing number: 9 8 7 6 5 4 3 2 1

Printed in the United States of America
on acid-free paper

Chapter 8

Academic Life

Twenty years ago, professors took attendance by calling roll from the front of the class and recording those present in a grade book. Today professors can take roll with clickers and iPhone apps. Students sign in to an online page or complete a quiz—that doubles for attendance—on their laptops. In some cases, students don't even share physical space with the professor but log in remotely on a computer. They are present because the educational software logs their username as "active."

But attendance is only one way that academic life is changing to meet the desires and expectations of current students.

In this section, Eric Hoover explores the concept of "trigger warnings" on class syllabi, those brief descriptions some professors employ to prepare students for potentially distressing content; he also explores how trigger warnings have changed students' expectations for the college experience in general. Jacques Steinberg discusses electronic devices that professors are using to engage students raised on iPhones and handheld video games. Trip Gabriel visits a college that streams live lecture video to the dorm room, even though the lecture is occurring on the other side of the campus. And Douglas Belkin examines ways that geofencing and movement tracking technology might improve graduation rates at many colleges.

But this chapter doesn't simply explore new cultural and technological challenges shaping academic life; it also explores traditional problems faced by many students. Cecilia Capuzzi Simon examines how to pick a major. The problem of note taking—or rather of note taking as a small business—is analyzed by Laura Pappano. And Marcia Y. Cantarella offers advice on perhaps the oldest of all college problems: how to engage a course when the subject doesn't engage you.

The readings in this section, together, explore a variety of college experiences, placing traditional challenges shoulder to shoulder with ones that have emerged in the past decade. Together, these experiences define contemporary academic life.

Eric Hoover
The Comfortable Kid

Eric Hoover is a senior writer for *The Chronicle of Higher Education*, where he has written about standardized testing, the process of college admissions, and social media and gender issues within universities.

Go ahead, laugh at them. Call them thin-skinned, lily-livered, self-righteous. They always find a way to take offense. That's just how—as you've surely heard—today's college students roll.

Consider the evidence. Recently students have expressed many concerns that their elders describe as hypersensitivity gone haywire. In March, *The*

New York Times reported on campus discussions of "microaggressions," subtle slights of one's race, ethnicity, gender, or sexual orientation. This spring, commencement speakers at several prominent institutions withdrew amid students' opposition to their views or affiliations. By then the nation had heard all about "trigger warnings": Students on various campuses have called for alerts about assigned texts (yes, old sport, even *The Great Gatsby*) that might upset or traumatize them.

So when something awful happened this past May, perhaps nobody should've been surprised by how a student newspaper at the University of California at Santa Barbara reacted. After the fatal shootings of six students near the campus, *The Bottom Line*'s editors opted against immediately publishing an article, to protect student journalists from "emotional harm."

These developments raise a question. Are the future caretakers of civilization made of marshmallows?

Yes, say the pundits. Lately commentators have ridiculed students for an array of sins ("overreaching sensitivity," "longing for an 'offenseless' society"). The Daily Beast's jab at undergraduates ("The Oh-So-Fragile Class of 2014 Needs to STFU and Listen to Some New Ideas") bore this blunt conclusion: "Young people are the worst."

But the kids-these-days diss simplifies the complexity of 21st-century students. They are a diverse bunch with varying needs and wants, some more serious than others. They carry immense expectations through higher education's gates, and in the name of compassion and competition, colleges strive to serve. If students are soft, campuses help make them so.

"What happens on college campuses has as much to do with the institution and the adults within it as anything that the students bring," says Richard Arum, a professor of sociology and education at New York University. "There's a dynamic in place where colleges are catering to them as consumers and clients. They are increasingly making decisions to keep students happy."

That means trade-offs. The rise of the consumer ethos has sapped colleges' commitment to learning, argue Mr. Arum and Josipa Roksa, an associate professor of sociology at the University of Virginia, in *Academically Adrift: Limited Learning on College Campuses.* Yet the "delivery of elaborate and ever-expanding services," the authors concede, might also have positive consequences. Generally colleges have become more responsive to students, which hardly spells doom.

Just how responsive an institution should be, however, is debatable. The line between care and coddling can be blurry. Critiques of the college experience often mention the physical comforts that students now enjoy. The high-rise dorm. The fancy gym. The cafeteria featuring omelets with your choice of 17 locally sourced ingredients.

Those amenities are tangible expressions of a broader goal. Colleges continue to grapple with many dimensions of comfort—intellectual, cultural, social—and how much of it to provide. The challenge, some administrators and professors say, is making students uncomfortable in some ways but comfortable in others. Challenge their ideas and assumptions here, support their identities and interests there.

On an increasingly diverse campus, striking that balance is difficult. Some students stroll in, convinced that they own the place; others slink along, lugging problems and doubts. So, go ahead, laugh at college students. But maybe, just maybe, not all of them deserve it.

When colleges first entered the business of tending to students' personal needs, the streets were full of Model Ts. During the 1920s, the problems that students experienced as they adjusted to campus life became a widespread concern. Then, as now, those problems included frustration with large, impersonal classes, and depression.

Previously, college leaders had assumed that participation in extracurricular activities worked against students' academic performance. That notion faded as more and more research suggested a connection between personality development and achievement. Gradually a host of academic, social, and psychological programs grew. In 1924 the American College Personnel Association was founded to lead the burgeoning student-affairs profession.

Its purpose? To reduce the "psychic dislocation of college" by giving students more individualized attention, says Christopher P. Loss, an associate professor of public policy and higher education at Vanderbilt University, who describes the rise of student services in *Between Citizens and the State: The Politics of American Higher Education in the 20th Century*. Eventually educators were focused on the "whole student."

At least half of all students who enrolled in college in the 1920s left without earning a degree, typically in their first year. Although attrition then had many causes, Mr. Loss has found, colleges embraced extracurricular programs as the primary solution to the dropout problem (then known as "student mortality"). So began freshman week, orientation classes, clubs, honors programs, social events—myriad ways to make students feel at home.

"There's been an ongoing tension between being efficient and effective in handling this massive student body on the one hand," Mr. Loss says, "and providing personalized instruction and care on the other."

The influx of veterans on the original GI Bill cemented student services as a primary function of colleges. And long after the erosion of *in loco parentis* as the basis for discipline and social control, Mr. Loss writes in a forthcoming essay, the doctrine continued to compel colleges "to care for and nurture their students in order to help them steer clear of the innumerable academic and emotional challenges of going to school."

In the 1960s and 1970s, as institutions enrolled more and more black students, "diversity" was the key word in student affairs. Later, cultural programs and support services designed for students of various racial and ethnic backgrounds became the norm. Conceptions of diversity today go well beyond demographics. Many colleges now try to accommodate the broad spectrum of a student's identity: sexual orientation, religious beliefs, and political views, for instance, or hardships faced as a combat soldier or a victim of sexual assault.

"There's an almost infinite array of personal experiences, traumas, and tragedies that can shape or condition your capacities to be a member of a college community," says Mr. Loss. "What role does the college have to play in order to ensure that all students are treated fairly?"

An increasingly large one. Generally, educators believe they have a moral responsibility to develop students beyond the classroom. Those who are happy and "engaged" are more likely to succeed and graduate, which is also good for the bottom line. So colleges are canvassing students and alumni to gauge their satisfaction.

To that end, Augustana College, in Illinois, is trying to determine whether it inadvertently "privileges" extroverted students, making it easier for them to find a niche. In surveys of freshmen, the college includes a three-item scale, "Comfort With Social Interaction," which asks how they feel about meeting new people and interacting in unfamiliar settings. Researchers use the scores, along with responses to other questions, to determine how personality might affect students' sense of belonging on the campus. "We're asking, have we created this environment where we suck the oxygen out of the introverts in the room?" says Mark Salisbury, assistant dean and director of institutional research and assessment.

Such sophisticated inquiry suggests a level of concern that once would have seemed outlandish. In the age of Starbucks, where each cup bears a name, students—and the parents they call and text daily—expect a lot more than they used to. "It's part of the movement for individualization," says Jean Twenge, a professor of psychology at San Diego State University and author of *Generation Me: Why Today's Young Americans Are More Confident, Assertive, Entitled—and More Miserable Than Ever Before.* "On many campuses, there's this idea, 'I paid my money, thus I want this customized experience.'"

Customization means more options. But how many aspects of college should be optional?

Philip Wythe, a junior at Rutgers University, has thought carefully about that. In February, Mr. Wythe wrote a column for the New Brunswick campus newspaper in which he described trigger warnings on syllabi as "psychological protection for those who need it." Such warnings originated in feminist forums online, where they flag content that victims of sexual abuse might find distressing. Recently students on several campuses—Rutgers, UC-Santa Barbara, the University of Michigan—have called for their use in academic courses. A panel of students and faculty members at Oberlin College is weighing the issue.

Importing trigger warnings to the classroom, Mr. Wythe argues, would help students prepare themselves for emotionally hazardous material and avoid it if necessary. A trigger warning for *The Great Gatsby,* he suggests, might include the words "suicide" and "domestic abuse."

Mr. Wythe recounts in an email the experience of a close friend, a young woman at Rutgers, who suffered a panic attack in class. While watching a film in which the protagonist describes being sexually abused, Mr. Wythe writes, his friend started shaking and crying. Eventually she ran out of the room.

By his description, the woman had been "triggered," or reminded of a past trauma. Colleges have an obligation, he says, to try to prevent that, by warning students about material that deals with violence and sexual assault. "Trigger warnings aren't for able-minded students who are prone to sensitivity," he writes. "It's about individuals with disabilities, such as PTSD or severe anxiety disorder, which can disrupt daily life." More such students are going to college than ever before.

Mr. Wythe's views are informed by his experience in a high-school health class. During discussions of sensitive topics like depression and suicide, he explained in a recent interview on Huff Post Live, students were assured that if they felt uneasy at any point, they could approach the teacher and request "an alternate plan."

So Mr. Wythe has come to see the issue as a matter of transparency. "These are students trying to change the course of their own education, as in saying what they would like in the classroom, what they're comfortable with in the classroom," he said in the interview. In other words, they're consumers, making buying decisions. A trigger warning, he says, can help a student decide whether to skip a class on a given day—or whether to take that course in the first place.

That idea frustrates many professors who see an overstated problem. It's not as if students are always blindsided, as if instructors never preview assignments or contextualize them. One psychology professor who plans to assign a book about sexual abuse this fall says he will first discuss why reading it might be difficult. "Is that a trigger warning?" he asks. "Partly, it's being a good teacher."

The notion that a book, like a pack of cigarettes, needs a warning label strikes many professors as preposterous. Where to draw the line? Instructors aren't counselors, nor could they begin to anticipate all of the things that might traumatize someone.

Orange juice, for instance, triggers Mariah Woelfel, a student at DePaul University. She associates it with visiting her brother in the hospital after a car accident left him severely disabled. She opposes trigger warnings, however, because, as she wrote in *The DePaulia,* they go against "the main purpose of higher-level learning: to explore diversity in ideas, and challenge the ones that you already hold."

Trigger warnings are evidence that political correctness has given way to something broader, says Karen Swallow Prior, an English professor at Liberty University. "Now, instead of challenging the status quo by demanding texts that question the comfort of the Western canon," she wrote in *The Atlantic* this spring, "students are demanding the status quo by refusing to read texts that challenge their own personal comfort." She calls this "empathetic correctness."

Empathy is tricky. Where it exists, students may feel secure, and understanding might flow. But it's hard to cultivate.

Still, colleges should try, says Charles W. Green, a psychology professor at Hope College. Fifteen years ago, Mr. Green, who studies race and racism, helped start a residential academic program, or learning community, for freshmen interested in racial and cultural issues. The goal: to promote inclusion as the predominantly white campus diversified (today 15 percent of its students are nonwhite, up from 4 percent about a decade ago).

"If you're in the majority and it's all working for you, it's hard to see that other people might not be having this lovely time," he says. "Some people don't realize how common it is for students to have experiences that leave them feeling as if they are unwelcome on their own campus."

Mr. Green recalls a black student who was carrying a pizza back to the campus one evening when a group of teenagers surrounded her. When she refused to hand over her dinner, they called her the N-word. The next day, the young woman and several other black students came to his office. They were shaken.

Most incidents he hears about are more subtle. A white student tells a black student not to "play the race card" during a class discussion. A black woman reports that when professors ask students to discuss a topic in pairs, the white classmates to her left and right always turn away from her.

Whether a particular insult is also a microaggression—a subtle conveyance of bias or stereotype—is subjective ("No, where are you *really* from?" or "I have trouble telling Asians apart"). Some students say hurtful things because they're bigoted jerks; others, naïve or socially clumsy, don't mean to offend. The term "microaggression," like "trigger warning," comes from the realm of social justice, which increasingly informs discussions of diversity on campuses.

This is especially true at Emory University, where freshmen now discuss microaggressions during orientation. Throughout the year, students in the Issues Troupe write and perform skits to increase awareness of racial stereotypes and cultural differences.

Ajay Nair, senior vice president and dean of campus life at Emory, believes that the modern campus must move beyond traditional multicultural programs. "With multiculturalism, the destination is tolerance, not understanding," he says. "Our students are pushing back and saying, 'This doesn't work; tolerance doesn't lead to understanding.' Multiculturalism focuses on celebration instead of social justice and activism."

Mr. Nair envisions a "polycultural" model that acknowledges multiple identities. A student might be gay and Hispanic, or Asian-American and Christian. The dean has begun restructuring his entire division to reflect that model (think more collaboration, less compartmentalization). The shift serves another goal as well: persuading all students that they have a stake in diversity.

"A straight, white male student has a lot to offer, a particular way of understanding the world," says Mr. Nair. "As we think about a deeper understanding of diversity, the dialogue can't just be with certain parts of the community that have been marginalized."

Talking about microaggressions is a helpful way to frame that dialogue, Mr. Nair believes (as an Indian-American, he recalls being told that his English was "so good," even though he was born and raised in Philadelphia). Whether such discussions promote understanding, however, is complicated.

Jovonna Jones, a senior at Emory, says the term "microaggression" can help minority students describe their feelings to others. "There are many things my peers have experienced, but we didn't have a name for it before," says Ms. Jones, who is black. "It's another way of trying to explain how racism works to people who still don't want to hear it exists."

Sometimes, for instance, her peers call her "sassy," which she hears as a code word for the stereotype that black women have an attitude. Now and then, students ask to touch her hair; some have just gone ahead without asking. Framing her objections in terms of microaggressions, she says, can be empowering and productive.

But it's not always easy. When she hears someone say, "Oh, that's ghetto," she says, she has to decide whether to explain why that might offend not just her, but many black students. "It can become a very toxic position to be put in," she says. "What happened to it just mattering that you hurt someone's feelings?"

Some white students, meanwhile, have complained that diversity discussions shovel guilt down their throats. "Check your privilege," some are told, meaning that they should acknowledge their advantages in life, and maybe think twice about the views they're sharing. In April, Tal Fortgang, a white student at Princeton University, wrote a column describing the phrase as a rebuke that "threatens to strike down opinions without regard for their merits, but rather solely on the basis of the person that voiced them."

Exposing students to unfamiliar ideas has long been a core purpose of higher education. From temporary discomfort comes an essential struggle, writes Tricia A. Seifert, an assistant professor at the Ontario Institute for Studies in Education, at the University of Toronto. "Disequilibrium, cognitive dissonance, challenge—these are the building blocks of learning."

But is that still in vogue? A national survey of freshmen conducted annually by the Higher Education Research Institute at the University of California at Los Angeles suggests that many students wrestle with the concept. Generally, freshmen say they work well with others and tolerate those with different beliefs. Yet they rate themselves low on their "openness to having their own views challenged."

These days Netflix recommends a film based on those you like. Spotify suggests a band based on your listening habits. And curated news feeds deliver the political opinions you choose.

"As we have a greater expectation of physical comfort, of an ability to choose what media we want to see, what sources we want to read, it does cultivate, almost inevitably, seeking intellectual comfort," says Greg Lukianoff, president of the Foundation for Individual Rights in Education. "You want people to agree with you. It's part of human nature."

There's one problem, though. "It's just not intellectually healthy," he says.

Kathleen McCartney also thinks "ideological echo chambers" have diminished the appetite for true dialogue on campuses. She is president of Smith College, where some students and faculty members objected to the selection of Christine Lagarde, managing director of the International Monetary Fund, as this spring's commencement speaker, which they saw as an implicit endorsement. An online petition urging Smith to reconsider the invitation said the IMF had helped strengthen "imperialist and patriarchal systems that oppress and abuse women worldwide." A few students wrote to Ms. Lagarde, asking her not to come. A week before graduation, she withdrew.

Ms. McCartney insists that she wouldn't have minded if students had protested during the speech. "That's fair game," she says. What troubled her was the impulse to prevent anyone at Smith from hearing Ms. Lagarde. "They had many options between acquiescing and urging her to stay away," the president says.

Since the episode, Ms. McCartney has heard from members of the Class of 1964, recalling their objections to that year's commencement speaker, Dean Rusk, then the U.S. secretary of state, who supported the American role in the Vietnam War. Although many students wore black armbands in protest, they sat and listened to his speech.

What might explain why two generations responded so differently? Ms. McCartney cites social media, for one. "Before, you had to walk a petition around campus. Now you can put it online in a millisecond," immediately attracting like-minded classmates and a broader audience. But there's something deeper, too. "Maybe in 1964, students felt like the power to say 'don't come' wasn't there," she says. "Students are empowered today, and that's mostly good."

Mostly. Discussions of microaggressions and trigger warnings often flow from some wish, however vague, to make the world kinder, to make life easier for one's neighbor. And the pushback against commencement speakers challenges the notion that today's students are politically apathetic.

But there's a troubling side to those trends, all of which boil down to scrutiny of words—which words students should say, read, hear. "All these things," Ms. McCartney says, "can threaten free speech."

The attention to finely tuned sensitivities, the relentless delivery of more options, more alternatives can also convince students that the world stops for them. The comfortable kid can get far too comfortable.

Recently, Ms. McCartney heard a radio report about how younger students perceive criticism as especially harsh when their teachers grade assignments in red pen. Just for a moment, she imagined Smith students demanding that professors use only black or blue ink. "I hope," she says, "we don't have a red-pen movement."

Indeed, a national campaign about the harm caused by ink colors would be absurd. Life, we know, marks us up in whatever colors it wants. With wisdom drawn from our many years of experience, we tend to laugh at the kids, scoff at their ideas. But we should at least consider the possibility that old people are the worst.

Analyze

1. Do trigger warnings for college material protect students from potentially harmful experiences? Or do they harmfully shield students from the realities of the world around them?
2. How might a marketplace consumerism ethos at college—the desire to keep students happy—ultimately prevent them from receiving the best education possible? How might this same ethos play out in terms of course subjects, grades, and even graduation requirements?
3. Would you rather attend (a) a college with a modern, high-rise dorm, an elaborate gym, and a cafeteria that features "omelets with your choice of 17 locally sourced ingredients," but offers only mediocre courses that are not too difficult to pass or (b) a college with old-style,

cinderblock dorms, no fancy gym, and a cafeteria with food options no better than at an average food court, but with excellent courses that are challenging to pass?

4. Would you be willing to give up some comforts at college if it (a) reduced your tuition bill, (b) lowered your college debt, (c) allowed you better college resources for job placement, (d) allowed you more plentiful and varied class offerings, or (e) allowed you to take more small seminar-style courses instead of large hall lectures?

Explore

1. If you could pick only one area of comfort to receive at college, which would you pick: social (i.e., activities to foster friendships), educational (i.e., courses that support your individual learning needs), physical (i.e., comfortable beds), culinary (i.e., excellent food), recreational (i.e., modern gym), or entertainment (i.e., speakers and musicians performing on campus)? Why?
2. SHORT WRITING PROMPT: Write an opinion paper in which you argue for or against the use of syllabus-oriented trigger warnings on your campus. If you believe trigger warnings should be implemented at your college, what subject material should be covered under them?
3. FULL WRITING PROMPT: Write an essay about an experience—in class, on a sports team, in music or art, or while pursuing a hobby—that might have made you a better person if only the requirements were more stringent and difficult to achieve.

Trip Gabriel

Learning in Dorm, Because Class Is on the Web

Trip Gabriel, a journalist for the *New York Times*, primarily covers American politics, style, and higher education, including articles on college lifestyles and academic dishonesty.

Like most other undergraduates, Anish Patel likes to sleep in. Even though his Principles of Microeconomics class at 9:35 a.m. is just a five-minute stroll from his dorm, he would rather flip open his laptop in his room to watch the lecture, streamed live over the campus network.

On a recent morning, as Mr. Patel's two roommates slept with covers pulled tightly over their heads, he sat at his desk taking notes on Prof. Mark Rush's explanation of the term "perfect competition." A camera zoomed in for a close-up of the blackboard, where Dr. Rush scribbled in chalk, "lots of firms and lots of buyers." The curtains were drawn in the dorm room. The floor was awash in the flotsam of three freshmen—clothes, backpacks, homework, packages of Chips Ahoy and Cap'n Crunch's Crunch Berries.

The University of Florida broadcasts and archives Dr. Rush's lectures less for the convenience of sleepy students like Mr. Patel than for a simple principle of economics: 1,500 undergraduates are enrolled and no lecture hall could possibly hold them.

Dozens of popular courses in psychology, statistics, biology and other fields are also offered primarily online. Students on this scenic campus of stately oaks rarely meet classmates in these courses.

Online education is best known for serving older, nontraditional students who cannot travel to colleges because of jobs and family. But the same technologies of "distance learning" are now finding their way onto brick-and-mortar campuses, especially public institutions hit hard by declining state funds. At the University of Florida, for example, resident students are earning 12 percent of their credit hours online this semester, a figure expected to grow to 25 percent in five years.

This may delight undergraduates who do not have to change out of pajamas to "attend" class. But it also raises questions that go to the core of a college's mission: Is it possible to learn as much when your professor is a mass of pixels whom you never meet? How much of a student's education and growth—academic and personal—depends on face-to-face contact with instructors and fellow students?

"When I look back, I think it took away from my freshman year," said Kaitlyn Hartsock, a senior psychology major at Florida who was assigned to two online classes during her first semester in Gainesville. "My mom was really upset about it. She felt like she's paying for me to go to college and not sit at home and watch through a computer."

Across the country, online education is exploding: 4.6 million students took a college-level online course during fall 2008, up 17 percent from a year earlier, according to the Sloan Survey of Online Learning. A large majority—about three million—were simultaneously enrolled in face-to-face courses, belying the popular notion that most online students live far from campuses, said Jeff Seaman, co-director of the survey. Many are in community colleges, he said. Very few attend private colleges; families paying $53,000 a year demand low student–faculty ratios.

Colleges and universities that have plunged into the online field, mostly public, cite their dual missions to serve as many students as possible while remaining affordable, as well as a desire to exploit the latest technologies.

At the University of Iowa, as many as 10 percent of 14,000 liberal arts undergraduates take an online course each semester, including Classical Mythology and Introduction to American Politics.

At the University of North Carolina at Chapel Hill, first-year Spanish students are no longer offered a face-to-face class; the university moved all instruction online, despite internal research showing that online students do slightly less well in grammar and speaking.

"You have X amount of money, what are you going to do with it?" said Larry King, chairman of the Romance languages department, where budget cuts have forced difficult choices. "You can't be all things to all people."

The University of Florida has faced sweeping budget cuts from the State Legislature totaling 25 percent over three years. That is a main reason the university is moving aggressively to offer more online instruction. "We see this as the future of higher education," said Joe Glover, the university provost.

"Quite honestly, the higher education industry in the United States has not been tremendously effective in the face-to-face mode if you look at national graduation rates," he added. "At the very least we should be experimenting with other modes of delivery of education."

A sampling of Florida professors teaching online found both enthusiasm and doubts. "I would prefer to teach classes of 50 and know every student's name, but that's not where we are financially and space-wise," said Megan Mocko, who teaches statistics to 1,650 students. She said an advantage of the Internet is that students can stop the lecture and rewind when they do not understand something.

Ilan Shrira, who teaches developmental psychology to 300, said that he chose his field because of the passion of a professor who taught him as an undergraduate. But he thought it unlikely that anyone could be so inspired by an online course.

Kristin Joos built interactivity into her Principles of Sociology course to keep students engaged. There are small-group online discussions, and students join a virtual classroom once a week using a conferencing software called WiZiQ.

"Hi, everyone, welcome to Week 9. Hello!" Dr. Joos said in a peppy voice recently to about 60 students who had logged on. She sat at a desk in her home office; a live video feed she switched on at one point showed her in black librarian's glasses and a tank top.

Ms. Hartsock, the senior psychology major, followed the class from her own off-campus home, her laptop open on the dining room table. As Dr. Joos lectured, a chat box scrolled with students' comments and questions.

The topic was sexual identity, which Dr. Joos defined as "a determination made through the application of socially agreed-upon biological criteria for classifying persons as females and males."

She asked students for their own definitions. One, bringing an online-chat sensibility to an academic discussion, typed: "If someone looks like a chick and wants to be called a chick even though they're not, now they can be one."

Ms. Hartsock, 23, diligently typed notes. A hard-working student who maintains an A average, she was frustrated by the online format. Other members of her discussion group were not pulling their weight, she said. The one test so far, online, required answering five questions in 10 minutes—a lightning round meant to prevent cheating by Googling answers.

In a conventional class, "I'm someone who sits toward the front and shares my thoughts with the teacher," she said. In the 10 or so online courses she has taken in her four years, "it's all the same," she said. "No comments. No feedback. And the grades are always late."

As her attention wandered, she got up to microwave some leftover rice.

Analyze

1. If you had a choice between attending a lecture in person or watching it in your dorm, which would you choose? And why?
2. The essay asks readers to consider the connection between personal contact and learning. How much better do you learn material in an environment with "face-to-face contact with instructors and fellow students" than in a virtual environment of streaming video and pixels?
3. What is lost when learning shifts from classrooms and lecture halls to online environments? And what is gained?

Explore

1. One concern about online lecture classes is that they limit student involvement and discussion. In one model of education the professor is the expert who delivers information to an audience. In another model the professor is a facilitator who offers information in an attempt to create meaningful discussion between students. What are the pros and cons of each model?
2. Public universities often explain their interest in online education as an attempt to both (a) keep tuition costs low and (b) deliver classes to as many students as possible. Both of these goals are partially accomplished by limiting the face-to-face in-class time that students share with professors. In your opinion, for public universities, is this a good trade?
3. SHORT WRITING PROMPT: The article explains that some colleges ballooned lecture courses out to 1,500 students as a cost-savings measure, most likely designed to keep other classes small. To save money at your college, assuming its budget was cut, where would you reduce or change funding? Lower funding to health or fitness centers? Increase small discussion classes by five seats each? Increase lecture hall classes by offering video-streaming options? Reduce the quality of food on campus? Cut landscaping budgets? Cut student activities budgets? Cut funding to sports programs? After you have made your decisions, consider one more thing: what would be the social, educational, or institutional costs of these cuts?

Douglas Belkin

Cracking Down on Skipping Class: High-Tech Trackers Aim to Boost Attendance, as Colleges Seek Higher Graduation Rates

Douglas Belkin, a resident of Chicago, is a reporter who writes about higher education for *The Wall Street Journal*.

Skipping class undetected for a game of ultimate Frisbee might become a thing of the past as more universities adopt mandatory-attendance policies and acquire high-tech trackers that snitch when students skip.

At Villanova University, student ID cards track attendance at some lectures. Administrators at University of Arkansas last semester began electronically monitoring the class attendance of 750 freshmen as part of a pilot program they might extend to all underclassman. And at Harvard, researchers secretly filmed classrooms to learn how many students were skipping lectures.

The moves reflect the rising financial consequence of skipping too many classes and, consequently, dropping out. More than four in 10 full-time college students fail to graduate in six years. Many are stuck with crippling student debt and no credentials to help them pay it back. Graduation rates also figure into closely watched school rankings.

In response, schools are under pressure from taxpayers and parents to increase retention and graduation rates, said Mike Reilly, executive director of the American Association of Collegiate Registrars and Admissions Officers. Schoolwide policies on attendance are fairly rare but growing, Mr. Reilly said.

Many colleges are using "retention alert systems" that monitor behaviors that can lead to dropping out—including playing hooky. "There's just so much more at stake now than there was 20 years ago and parents want to protect their investment; they want to make sure their kids are in class," said Rosalind Alderman, who leads the retention effort at St. Mary's University in San Antonio. If professors report a student is skipping class at St. Mary's the student's "risk level" elevates from green to yellow to red in the school's monitoring system.

The latest entrant into the market of tracking student's whereabouts: Class120, a $199-a-year notification service that tracks a student through the GPS in their smartphone and alerts their parents (or another third party) in real time if their child isn't within a geofence mapped around the classroom where they are scheduled to be.

"For most students, if they miss too many classes, there is no safety net," said Jeff Whorley, whose company, Core Principle, has mapped about 2,000 college campuses to create the system. "Just three days of missed classes can completely unravel a semester."

The app's reminder was jarring for Caleb Hiltunen, a sophomore at Columbia College in Chicago who was a beta tester for Class120. One morning last semester he was sick in bed when the app pinged to alert him he missed class—a notification that would go to a student's parents once the app is live.

"I think it's good stuff," Mr. Hiltunen said. "I had a roommate freshman year kicked out of college for not attending enough classes. This kid was smart but he was lazy and had no motivation. I think something like this could have helped him."

Attendance is the best known predictor of college grades, even more so than scores on standardized admissions tests, said Marcus Crede, a professor of psychology at Iowa State University who studies the subject. The correlation is particularly high in science, engineering and math. And grades, in turn, seem linked to graduation rates, he said.

Mandatory attendance has long been a staple in high schools. At community colleges, such as Stark State in Ohio, financial aid is tied to attendance, a policy that dates back decades. At some Christian schools, such as Abilene Christian University in Texas, chapel attendance has been tracked with assigned seats since the 1980s.

At most four-year colleges, attendance policy has been left to the professors' discretion. Until recently, taking roll was especially tough in large lecture halls. But new technologies using chips in student IDs and interactive software that allows students to engage with professors through their laptops make the job easier.

At Villanova, student monitoring of some form has been in place in some form since 2007.

As online interactions have grown, schools have realized they have a trove of new data to look at, such as how much a student is accessing the syllabus, taking part in online discussions with classmates and reading assigned material. Such technology "shows faculty exactly where students are interacting outside as well inside the classroom," said Stephen Fugale, Villanova's chief information officer.

Not all such technology is foolproof. Dartmouth College accused 64 students of cheating in a sports-ethics class last semester when students used a clicker—individually linked to each student—for classmates who were absent.

At Harvard, Vice Provost Peter Bol said the lecture halls were filmed without student consent to gauge attendance without skewing the results by making students aware they were being measured. Many on campus were angered when the results were made public in November, but the test provided some insight into class attendance.

Among 10 lectures monitored, attendance averaged 60%, declining from 79% as the semester began to 43% as it ended. Attendance also fell more than 10 percentage points over an average week. Courses that incorporated attendance into the final grade averaged 87%, compared with 49% for those that didn't.

University of Arkansas began experimenting with mandatory attendance as a way to boost its 62% six-year graduation rate, said Provost Sharon Gaber. "We talk about helicopter parents," she said. "Well, some of these kids haven't learned how to get out of bed on their own yet."

Analyze

1. What would be gained and what would be lost if your college implemented an electronic attendance system by using ID cards or some other means?
2. College has traditionally been considered a place where teenagers have the freedoms and responsibilities of legal adults. A high-tech tracking system would suggest that college students today are less responsible than those of previous generations. Do you believe that college students today need more supervision to successfully manage college?
3. Previous generations have considered college an experience where students investigate ideas that matter, find themselves, prepare for life as adults, and explore cultural and scientific interests from a variety of academic disciplines. In this article, college is viewed primarily as an "investment," a training program designed to elevate students' earnings potential. Do you feel this is the best way to view the college experience?
4. Would you be more or less likely to attend a college with a "geofence" grid mapped over its campus? Why?

Explore

1. What would best motivate you to attend all class sessions—a system that rewards you with additional financial aid, a system that rewards you with a higher course grade, a system that threatens you with notifying your parents, or some other system?
2. In general, do you feel that poor class attendance is more closely tied to situation-specific problems (work schedules, poor sleep habits, late-night

studying) or to the overall general motivation of a student? That is, for most students, does a situation need to be changed or does the responsibility level of the student need to be improved?

3. FULL WRITING PROMPT: In an essay, propose an attendance policy and tracking system that would improve freshman attendance at your college. Your policy should tie good attendance to some benefit or punishment for students. Your policy should also take into account what you feel is a reasonable level of freedom and responsibility for college freshmen, most of whom are eighteen years old. The tracking system itself—such as roll call, ID cards, smartphone apps, and so forth—must be reasonable to implement and not place an unusual cost burden on the school or students. Most of all, it must be structured in a way to encourage students to better engage college learning.

Jacques Steinberg

More Professors Give Out Hand-Held Devices to Monitor Students and Engage Them

Jacques Steinberg spent 25 years as a reporter at the *New York Times* reporting on education. He is the author of *The Gatekeepers: Inside the Admissions Process of a Premier College* and now works with Say Yes to Education, a nonprofit that seeks to improve educational opportunities for children in the inner city.

If any of the 70 undergraduates in Prof. Bill White's "Organizational Behavior" course here at Northwestern University are late for class, or not paying attention, he will know without having to scan the lecture hall.

Their "clickers" will tell him.

Every student in Mr. White's class has been assigned a palm-size, wireless device that looks like a TV remote but has a far less entertaining purpose. With their clickers in hand, the students in Mr. White's class automatically clock in as "present" as they walk into class.

They then use the numbered buttons on the devices to answer multiple-choice quizzes that count for nearly 20 percent of their grade, and that always begin precisely one minute into class. Later, with a click, they can signal to their teacher without raising a hand that they are confused by the day's lesson.

But the greatest impact of such devices—which more than a half-million students are using this fall on several thousand college campuses—may be cultural: they have altered, perhaps irrevocably, the nap schedules of anyone who might have hoped to catch a few winks in the back row, and made it harder for them to respond to text messages, e-mail and other distractions.

In Professor White's 90-minute class, as in similar classes at Harvard, the University of Arizona and Vanderbilt, barely 15 minutes pass without his asking students to "grab your clickers" to provide feedback

Though some Northwestern students say they resent the potential Big Brother aspect of all this, Jasmine Morris, a senior majoring in industrial engineering, is not one of them.

"I actually kind of like it," Ms. Morris said after a class last week. "It does make you read. It makes you pay attention. It reinforces what you're supposed to be doing as a student."

Inevitably, some students have been tempted to see clickers as "cat and mouse" game pieces. Noshir Contractor, who teaches a class on social networking to Northwestern undergraduates, said he began using clickers in spring 2008—and, not long after, watched a student array perhaps five of the devices in front of him.

The owners had skipped class, but their clickers had made it.

Professor Contractor said he tipped his cap to the students' creativity—this was, after all, a class on social networking—but then reminded them that there "are other ways to count attendance," and that, by the way, they were all signatories to the school's honor principle. The practice stopped, he said.

Though the technology is relatively new, preliminary studies at Harvard and Ohio State, among other institutions, suggest that engaging students in class through a device as familiar to them as a cellphone—there are even applications that convert iPads and BlackBerrys into class-ready clickers—increases their understanding of material that may otherwise be conveyed in traditional lectures.

The clickers are also gaining wide use in middle and high schools, as well as at corporate gatherings. Whatever the setting, audience responses are received on a computer at the front of the room and instantly translated into colorful bar graphs displayed on a giant monitor.

The remotes used at Northwestern were made by Turning Technologies, a company in Youngstown, Ohio, and are compatible with PowerPoint. Depending on the model, the hand-helds can sell for $30 to $70 each. Some colleges require students to buy them; others lend them to students.

Tina Rooks, the chief instructional officer for Turning Technologies, said the company expected to ship over one million clickers this year, with roughly half destined for about 2,500 university campuses, including community colleges and for-profit institutions. The company said its higher-education sales had grown 60 percent since 2008, and 95 percent since 2006.

At Northwestern, more than three dozen professors now use clickers in their classrooms. Professor White, who teaches industrial engineering, was among the first here to adopt them about six years ago.

He smiled knowingly when asked about some students' professed dislike of the clickers.

"They should walk in with them in their hands, on time, ready to go," he said.

Professor White acknowledged, though, that the clickers were hardly a silver bullet for engaging students, and that they were just one of many tools he employed, including video clips, guest speakers and calling on individual students to share their thoughts.

"Everyone learns differently," he said. "Some learn watching stuff. Some learn by listening. Some learn by reading. I try to mix it all into every class."

Many of Professor White's students said the highlight of his class was often the display of results of a survey-via-clicker, when they could see whether their classmates shared their opinions. They also said that they appreciated the anonymity, and that while the professor might know how they responded, their peers would not.

Last week, for example, he flashed a photo of the university president, Morton Schapiro, onto the screen, along with a question, "Source of power?" followed by these possible answers:

"1. Coercive power" (sometimes punitive).
"2. Reward power."
"3. Legitimate power" (typically by virtue of one's office).

"4. Expert power" (more typically applied to someone like an electrician or a mechanic).

"5. Referent power" (usually tied to how the leader is viewed personally).

To Professor White's seeming relief, a clear majority, 71 percent, chose No. 3, a sign that they considered his ultimate boss to be "legitimate."

And then, to his delight, the students emerged from their electronic veils to register their opinions the old-fashioned way.

"They can be very reluctant to speak when they think they're in the minority," he said. "Once they see they're not the only ones, they speak up more."

Analyze

1. Do you believe an electronic method of tracking attendance would improve the level of education students receive at your college?
2. Are clickers or other monitoring devices an invasion of students' privacy—or an affront to their perceived levels of responsibility?
3. Are electronic tracking systems more likely to turn students into responsible adults or turn them into individuals who have difficulty managing their schedule without supervision?

Explore

1. The article suggests that electronic clickers—or similar iPhone or iPad apps—may help engender discussion in some lecture hall classes. Do you believe that electronic clickers or apps would better engage students at your college?
2. Clickers are used, primarily, to increase interest in lecture classes. What other methods might professors use to deepen student interest in a lecture hall environment without using hand-held electronics?
3. SHORT WRITING PROMPT: Clickers, in effect, crowd source opinions from a lecture hall class. Propose a plan, either with or without electronics, that would increase participation by *individual* students, with *individual* opinions, in a large lecture hall environment. In what situations might electronic opinion polls be valuable, and in what situations might individual discussion be valuable to a student's development?

Cecilia Capuzzi Simon
Major Decisions

Cecilia Capuzzi Simon is a regular contributor to *The New York Times*, where her articles often focus on education, psychology, and media. At present she teaches writing at American University's School of Communication.

What's your major? It's the defining question for college students—and the cliché that's launched a thousand friendships and romances. It's also a question that has become harder for students to answer.

Blame it on the growing number of possibilities. Colleges and universities reported nearly 1,500 academic programs to the Department of Education in 2010; 355 were added to the list over the previous 10 years as colleges, to stay competitive and current, adopted new disciplines like homeland security and global studies, cyberforensics and agroecology.

At the University of Michigan and Arizona State University, students choose from a dizzying 251 and 250 majors, respectively. DePaul University in Chicago offers 24 more majors than it did in 2002, for a total of 98.

And graduating with a double (or triple) major, minor or concentration as a way to hedge bets in an uncertain job market has become increasingly popular; the number of bachelor's degrees awarded with double majors rose 70 percent between 2001 and 2011, according to the Education Department.

Some students go to college knowing exactly what they want to do. But most don't. At Penn State, 80 percent of freshmen—even those who have declared a major—say they are uncertain about their major, and half will change their minds after they declare, sometimes more than once. How to decide?

The New Explorer

Colleges and universities have vested interests in students declaring early. Retention rates for declared students are better, and they are more likely to graduate in four years. But college officials also recognize that deciding on a major can be overwhelming, especially when coupled with the fear that a wrong choice will result in added semesters and tuition.

"Students no longer have the luxury of stumbling into a major or making mistakes," says Neeta P. Fogg, a research professor at Drexel University's Center for Labor Markets and Policy, and a co-author of "College Majors Handbook With Real Career Paths and Payoffs."

"Exploratory" is the new undeclared. Colleges have moved away from the negative-sounding "undecided" label to encourage students to experiment with unfamiliar disciplines and, perhaps, discover a passion and career path. "We want to remind them that they have an active role" in their academic choices, says Mary Beth Collier, the dean of academic advising at the State University of New York at New Paltz. At SUNY, exploratory students are urged to try new subjects using general education electives.

Ms. Collier tells students: "You've taken the same six subjects since kindergarten. If you don't know your major, don't come here and take the same subjects expecting to figure it out." That can mean fulfilling a U.S. studies requirement with a political science or black studies course instead of a rehash of U.S. history that you should have learned in high school.

Some schools have made exploration official. At the University of Florida, where 61 percent of students change their majors by the end of their second year, there are three exploratory tracks—engineering and science, humanities and letters, and social and behavioral—that students can declare for three semesters before choosing a specialized major. At the University of Cincinnati, undecided students can enroll in an exploratory studies program.

When in Doubt, Take It

Advisers caution: Don't abandon subjects that you may need later. Students often don't realize that many popular majors—psychology, social sciences, business—have math and science requirements. You might have to forgo majoring in economics, for example, if come junior year you have to make up courses in calculus and statistics.

This requires thinking ahead, says Fritz Grupe, the creator of MyMajors.com and an emeritus professor of computer science at the University of Nevada. You may not know what to do with the rest of your life at age 18, but you can cover your bases with prudent planning. Some majors have a curriculum that follows a tight sequence of courses. It's easier to switch out of engineering than it is to take it up (if that's possible at all) later in your college career.

The "biggest mistake" students make, Dr. Grupe adds, is failing to research what's required of the major, and the profession. Nursing may sound attractive because "you like to help people," he says, but nursing students take the same demanding math and science curriculum as pre-med students, and the work is often technical and not for every kindhearted soul.

The Bottom Line

Colleges "do not make decisions in a vacuum," Dr. Fogg says. They are constantly tweaking their offerings. The Department of Education's list shows clusters of new programs in established fields of study that mirror scientific, cultural and societal developments. Some are cross-disciplinary or specializations, like biosystems engineering, clinical nurse leadership, computational biology and international policy analysis.

Quirkier additions to the list obviously reflect marketplace trends and student demand, like culinary science/culinology, digital arts, casino management and sports communication. At Montclair State University in New Jersey, which offers 300 majors, minors and concentrations, a new fashion studies major has been hugely popular, thanks to the university's proximity to Manhattan; with Madison Square Garden and Giants Stadium in sight, it also saw opportunity in a sports industry and event-planning major within its business school.

Still, it's difficult to predict the employment market, says Michele Campagna, the executive director of the Center for Advising and Student Transitions at Montclair State. Many students choose majors they think will lead to jobs, but "four years from now," she says, "freshmen will be applying for jobs that don't even exist today."

Most employers are looking for transferable skills—the ability to problem solve, work in teams, write and communicate, and think critically, says Ms. Collier of SUNY New Paltz. These can be developed in any liberal arts discipline. It makes no sense, she says, to "suffer through a major" because you think it will lead to employment. "We tell students, 'Find a major that makes you intellectually engaged, that expands your brain and deepens your understanding of the world.' "

At the same time, cautions Dr. Fogg, the stakes for college students today couldn't be higher: 41 percent of graduates are employed in jobs that don't require a college degree. Many employers today lack the resources and patience for on-the-job training, she says, and are looking for college graduates who are "shelf-ready employees." So pick up professional direction, job-related skills and work experience, she says, and of course follow your heart.

Analyze

1. What was—or *is*—the most difficult aspect in deciding on your major?
2. "What's your major?" is often the first question that two students ask each other. What would be a different question that would reveal more meaningful information about students you meet at college? In your opinion, why are American students so focused on "majors" when they meet new people?
3. In your opinion, which would serve students better in the long run: a traditional major, such as history or math, or a newly developed, highly specialized major, such as international policy analysis? Why?
4. If you were to exclude career considerations from selecting a major—that is, if you were to study only a major that interested you in terms of your own curiosity and personal development—what would you study? And why? Would it be different than your current major or majors you are actively considering?

Explore

1. At most high schools, students do not have a major or even a declared major area of study. Discuss the pros and cons of colleges offering this model to *some* students: a four-year general education focused on transferable skills, such as writing, critical thinking, and creative problem solving. Assume students would obtain breadth in their education, taking multiple courses in math, science, social science, literature, arts, writing, humanities, business, and so forth, rather than an education focused primarily in one discipline.
2. SHORT WRITING PROMPT: With the help of the web, a career counselor, a school adviser, and/or a research librarian, answer the following questions: What are the long-term social and workplace benefits to majoring in engineering, English, and biology? Which of these majors, for you, would yield the highest personal satisfaction? Which

would give you broad skills to change careers as you move through life? Which would offer the highest potential salary for new graduates? Which would offer the highest potential salary for graduates twenty years after graduation? With which major do students express the highest degree of satisfaction?

3. FULL WRITING PROMPT: In the article: Dr. Grupe advises that "the 'biggest mistake' [students make when picking a major] . . . is failing to research what's required of the major, and the profession." In a full essay, chart your future path through a major on your campus. You choose the major. Identify the classes that will be most difficult for you to complete, and identify resources on campus (the math lab, peer tutoring, etc.) that will help you succeed. Use the web to explore possible entry-level jobs for new graduates in this major. Look at job ads to see if certain minors, certificate programs, or internships will be helpful in obtaining a job. Note starting salaries. Ask seniors or recent graduates how difficult jobs are to obtain in this field. Your final paper should be a road map through one major, noting projected difficulties and their solutions, leading to one or two possible entry-level jobs after college.

Laura Pappano
Take Notes from the Pros

Laura Pappano is the author of *Inside School Turnarounds* and *The Connection Gap*, as well as the co-author of *Playing with Boys*. Her articles on education regularly appear in *The New York Times*, *The Harvard Education Letter*, and *The Boston Globe*.

When it comes to taking lecture notes, Laura Gayle, a sophomore at Florida State University, has her methods. A smiley face connotes an important person. If the professor says, "Make sure you know this," she uses an asterisk. A triangular button signals a video clip played in class. Later, she will organize the notes, write a video summary and check uncertainties against the textbook or with the professor. For "Introduction to Classical Mythology," she'll even alphabetize a list of Greek gods and goddesses.

Then, a few days before the exam, she puts it all up for sale.

Since last fall, when she uploaded her macroeconomics notes onto Flashnotes.com to pay for a birthday gift for her mother, Ms. Gayle has sold more than 500 copies of the study guides that she's put together for her courses, made over $3,285 and tapped into a growing, if controversial, online marketplace.

In describing her approach, Ms. Gayle, a human resources major with a 3.8 grade-point average, sounds aggressive in the best way. "I sit in the front row center for every single class, whether I am selling notes or not," she says. "For me it is a matter of paying attention, being detail-oriented and," if something is unclear, "taking the initiative to go out and find the answer." Her study guides are rated five stars by users.

While borrowing, bartering and selling class notes is nothing new, the online market is just getting organized. Amazon-like sites matching note sellers and buyers have come and gone in recent years as students who started them graduate. NerdyNotes at Stony Brook University is surviving the graduation of a founder, but bigger players are arriving.

Flashnotes started up last fall on five campuses—Kent State, Ohio State, Florida State, Rutgers and University of Maryland—with 30,000 registered users. There are now about 100,000 at 100 campuses, and the company just bought Moola-guides, a Florida State start-up. The sites let student sellers set prices for notes (average is $9) but take a cut. Flashnotes gets 30 percent; NerdyNotes takes 50.

The marketplace has annoyed some professors, who bar their students from buying or selling notes. In 2010, California State University banned students on its 23 campuses from using NoteUtopia.com (since bought by Flashnotes), citing a little-known state education code prohibiting the selling of class notes for commercial purposes. Some argue that lectures are professors' intellectual property, including notes recording their ideas; others warn that notes are a student's interpretation of a class. Some say that selling them promotes laziness by enticing students to skip lectures.

Still others encourage it. "I want them to use any resource they can to do well on my tests," says Lora Holcombe, an economics professor at Florida

State. "It's not like with the notes you sleep on them and they'll go into your head. You have to do some heavy studying."

Michael Matousek, who graduated from Kent State in 2010, dreamed up Flashnotes during a statistics class in his senior year. He had switched majors twice so was taking a required class that covered topics he had previously studied. Students found the professor confusing, but Mr. Matousek "knew *how* they were confused."

After classmates repeatedly sought his help, he compiled and sold his notes to a friend. Soon others wanted copies, so Mr. Matousek collected $10 for each emailed copy, netting more than $1,000 for the semester. The experience showed him the power of peer education—and not necessarily led by brainiacs. "The 4.0 kids, they can't explain," he says. "The 3.5, the 3.6 kids understand what it takes to learn something." Mr. Matousek graduated with a 3.67 G.P.A. and now heads a staff of 22 at Flashnotes headquarters in Faneuil Hall in Boston.

The demand is not surprising. "Students are notoriously poor note-takers," says Kenneth Kiewra, professor of educational psychology at the University of Nebraska, Lincoln. They tend to record only a third of the important lecture points.

What makes notes great? "Completeness," Dr. Kiewra says.

Research shows that having detailed, comprehensive notes raises test performance. In his oft-cited 1985 study, published in *Human Learning*, Dr. Kiewra randomly assigned 100 students to one of seven groups. Forty-eight hours after a lecture, the groups had 25 minutes to review before a test. Each group was assigned a learning method: *Take your own notes and review* (1) your notes, (2) your notes as well as instructor notes, (3) without any notes. *Don't take notes but review* (1) instructor notes, (2) without any notes. *Skip the lecture but review* (1) instructor notes, (2) without any notes.

Groups that reviewed instructor notes performed best. "It didn't matter so much what you did during the lecture," Dr. Kiewra explains. "It mattered what notes you had." Even those who didn't attend the lecture but reviewed instructor notes did better than those who attended and "reviewed their own crummy notes."

He concludes: "The real value of note-taking is not so much in the taking as in the having."

Getting down details along with main points is easier said than done. Average lecture speed is 100 to 125 words a minute, but college students listening to a lecture write 22 words a minute by hand; they type just 33 words a minute. In his latest research Dr. Kiewra has found that when the professor pauses three times to let students catch up and fill in missing information, they have more "original, additional and total notes" than those who waited to revise immediately after a lecture. If a student fails to note a particular point, Dr. Kiewra says, there is only a 5 percent chance of recalling it later.

Videotaped lectures help. When students viewed a video twice, they recorded 53 percent of the details, up from 38 percent, Dr. Kiewra says. Watching three times raised it to 60 percent.

Memory is a weak tool, but thinking about the information—paraphrasing rather than writing everything verbatim—improves retention, according to a series of studies at Princeton, published last April in *Psychological Science*. Students who took notes by hand rather than laptop wrote less but performed better. Laptop users tended to merely transcribe a lecture "rather than processing and reframing it in their own words"; they scored strikingly lower on conceptual tests.

Alexandra E. Hadley, a Boston College junior who has posted 29 different offerings on Flashnotes in the last year, uses paper for small discussion classes and a laptop for lectures. An English and communications major, she says she thinks hard about points the professor stresses. "I try to be very present in all of my classes," she says. "That is key—focusing on what I am doing." That means considering points as you take notes and connecting new ideas with information from earlier lectures. "I was taking notes in my research methods class and we were talking about pop culture," she says. "We touched on two theories, but it reminded me of another one, so I threw that in my notes."

Umar Zaidi, a Stony Brook senior from Queens double-majoring in political science and sociology, prefers to grab a seat near a power outlet and tap away. "When you are typing you can look at your professor," he says. He reads over the syllabus before class, "so when the professor mentions something that rings a bell, I type it up." While typing he organizes material into sections with main ideas, bullet points and asterisks.

Mr. Zaidi uploaded a semester's worth of lecture notes for "Urban Politics," an upper-level course, when NerdyNotes started up last spring. Sales, at $10 a packet, were slow at first. (Biology notes are the most in demand on campus.) Classmates didn't take notes, he says, because they thought political science was a breeze—until the midterm. After, he netted $150. "If they're too lazy to make notes," he says, "then I'll make notes and take advantage."

But Mr. Zaidi won't sell the study guides he makes for himself. One doesn't want to make it too easy for classmates. Indeed, some campuses are not good note-selling territory because students don't want to help competitors. In other words, at Flashnotes, Mr. Matousek says, "we're not putting a huge emphasis on Harvard."

Analyze

1. Do online class note sources do more to help students or harm students? Consider those who use the notes, those who make and receive payment for the notes, and the ways that the class environment is changed by having a note option available.
2. Do professional notes, with complete lecture outlines, help students to learn more efficiently or undercut a student's education?
3. In your opinion, who owns the content of a lecture class: the college, the professor, the students, or some combination of all three?

Explore

1. Is it a better learning experience to write down exactly what a professor says in your class notes? Or is it better to rephrase the professor's ideas into your own language? That is, do you learn better through the language of an expert or by digesting information and assimilating it into your own vocabulary? What are the pros and cons of each approach?
2. In terms of using notes to engage difficult material, when is your optimal time to review notes: before each class, at the end of each week, or in the days leading up to a test? How does your mind best absorb new concepts in a way that you understand them with depth and familiarity?
3. SHORT WRITING PROMPT: Identify a class subject where professional notes might deepen your understanding of the course material. How would professional notes accomplish this? Likewise, identify a class subject where professional notes might lessen your own engagement with the course material.

Marcia Y. Cantarella
Just Not Feeling It—Or When You Don't Love a Subject You Have to Take

Marcia Y. Cantarella is the president of Cantarella Consulting, where she explores issues of college access, diversity, and student success. She has worked at Hunter College, Princeton University, New York University, and Metropolitan College of New York, where she has served as a dean and a vice president of student affairs.

I had a great email when I got back to a work focus after the holidays. The topic was what to do when you are just not loving the subject you have to take. It was from a student I had met when I did a workshop this past summer for students heading off to college for the first time. I usually give out cards and tell students that the winners will reach out to me. And generally a few do. And Timothy did. And he wanted "to ask you for your opinion on the best way to consistently absorb information that you have no interest in or that doesn't challenge you much. What did you/do you do when you need to memorize/learn things that don't interest you much?" A really great question.

We have all been there—the A+ students and those of us who struggled more. Some courses we naturally loved because the subject just spoke to us and some because we were blessed with a fabulous professor who could make reading the phone book fascinating. But there was always the one (or more) course that was meeting a requirement and just did not work for us. Today students are focused on the relationship of what they study to the jobs they see themselves having. So everything is also seen through the lens of relevance. Given that perspective a course won't be interesting if it does not relate to the perceived future career goal. There is the reality too that every professor does not teach like a rock star. I had one in graduate school who would literally doze off reading his yellowing notes and on a hot summer evening that meant most of the class wanted to doze off too.

But there are ways to approach this problem of not loving a subject. And it is a problem because lack of interest leads to less focus and attention to the class and maybe then to a lower grade. Readings do not get read. Dozing or texting in class happens. Hands do not go up when questions are asked. GPAs can be damaged. Think of 25 percent of your grade for class participation being shot because of boredom.

So here is what I told Timothy. First unpack the course. What are the skills you are going to get from it? Does it push you to read, research, write, collaborate with others, and solve problems? Which of these skills are you likely to need in the workplace where you see yourself? Your motivation can be to really perfect those skills because they will be useful to you for achieving your dreams.

Second, what might you learn about the world that could be good to know? Does it help to know something about how the body fights disease when you have a sick grandmother? Does it help to know something about the political process when the outcome of an election can change your quality of life? How does this subject relate to your life?

Does it help to know enough of literature or the arts that you don't feel like a dummy when your work colleagues are talking about books or a joke has a reference to Shakespeare and you don't get it? Or you are the idiot who does not know who Paul McCartney is when collaborating with Kanye and gets laughed at all over the internet. Some of what you learn just helps you be part of the conversation but those who are part of the conversation get ahead. Again it is tied to your dreams of success. You are keeping your eyes on the prize.

A magic way to become engaged and, maybe the most important, is to ask your professor what drew them to the subject in the first place. They have spent their lives deeply immersed in a field. They do it for the love of the subject. I know from my own experience that I had to love my field (American Studies focused on Business) in order to spend the 6+ years it took to earn my doctorate and then to teach it for several years after. They want you to love it too. They can get excited talking about it. Getting to know your professors is always a smart strategy. And so getting them going on what they love will endear you and also maybe turn on the light bulb for you. Both outcomes are good for your grades. And a strong GPA is good for your goals.

Similarly talk to upperclassmen who are doing this as a major. I remember assembling a panel of students of different majors to share with underclassmen what they liked about their chosen fields. And each was wildly enthusiastic about their own major. So use the experience of those who are immersed in the subject but closer to your own goals and life experience to see what they see through their eyes. How do they study? What professors do they love? What questions excite them?

Finally maybe you are not studying effectively. The struggle to get a subject can also be because you are not approaching the study effectively. Study groups can energize a subject because you have several minds and skill sets being brought to bear. Figure out how you learn best—if you are a visual learner then charts and pictures may help, for example. Learning social sciences is not the same as studying poetry or the memorization Bio requires. Use your school's tutoring centers to learn how to best approach each subject so you have a better chance of getting it.

One thing you may not realize is that you need to learn how to read for college. Yes, you might make it to college, but that does not mean you know how to read. With a heavy reading load—more than in high school—you learn that different kinds of reading work for different classes. Some academic disciplines require close reading, some require memorizing key concepts, and still others involve a process of skimming and comprehending. Some sciences, like biology, may require a lot of memorization, but you also have to understand what you are memorizing. So reading with access to a glossary or dictionary is wise. It is easy to be "bored" when the issue is really not understanding.

If reading in the humanities (history, philosophy, art) or social sciences (psychology, sociology, economics), look for themes or key concepts and evidence to support them. Once you know what you're looking for, it is easy to skim or read faster. A key skill in learning is to argue with evidence, so note where you disagree with the author's premises and why. Having that kind of debate can also get your interest up in a subject.

Sometimes it helps get interested if you have to explain material to those who are not familiar with it as a way of testing your own understanding. Students who tutor younger kids find it helps them too.

And finally do what Timothy did. Ask someone for help! So smart! Love may follow and bring success with it.

Analyze

1. The central question for this article is a good one for new college students: "What did you/do you do when you need to memorize/learn things that don't interest you much?" What advice can you contribute beyond those answers offered in the essay?

2. Many experts believe that college should serve a larger purpose than simple career training. How can students move beyond a career-readiness understanding of college—"study to the jobs they see themselves having"—to one that speaks to a model in which college helps students improve in many areas of life?
3. The article suggests that this is a good way to better engage the fullness of the college experience: "Getting to know your professors is always a smart strategy." Can you think of other strategies that would likely help students get more out of the college classroom experience in general?

Explore

1. Some employers see college as a process in which students learn to pursue long-term goals with focus and passion, while struggling through difficult classes or classes that merely meet "a requirement." This skill—sometimes called grit or drive—shows that a student has developed perseverance, which is a marker of future career success. Aside from technical and academic abilities, what other life skills, such as perseverance, do students often develop while completing a college degree?
2. Most colleges have multiple committees and substantial oversight when developing both general education and major requirements. Review the list of classes for your major—or a major that interests you—to identify a class for which you don't immediately understand its value. Either through email or in a brief meeting, ask an advisor how this class will help you develop as a student. Many students find that understanding the rationale for requiring a class—or how a class fits into a larger educational program—helps them to better engage the material.
3. SHORT WRITING PROMPT: Develop a complete list of tutoring centers and study-skills programs offered on your campus. Most colleges have a writing center and a math lab. Many offer occasional (and often free) short classes in speed-reading, note taking, test taking, and essay research. Lasting only a single evening or two, these classes are usually not offered for college credit but informally, as a means to help students succeed in college. To develop this list, review your college's website, ask juniors and seniors, and visit the writing center and various student support areas at your school.

Paul Fain
Competent at What?

Paul Fain, a journalist, writes for *Inside Higher Ed*. His work has also appeared in *The New York Times*, *Washington City Paper*, and *Mother Jones*.

Competency-based education appears to be higher education's "next big thing." Yet many academics aren't sure what it is. And that goes double for lawmakers and journalists.

A new group is stepping in to try to clear up some of the confusion. The nascent Competency-Based Education Network (C-BEN) will include up to 20 institutions that offer competency-based degrees or are well on their way to creating them.

The Lumina Foundation is funding the three-year effort. Public Agenda, a nonprofit research organization, is coordinating the work.

The group's overarching goals are to share intelligence and discuss "best practices" on competency-based education, while also influencing the national conversation, according to the invitation for applications, which are due at the end of next month.

"This national network will consist of representatives from colleges and universities willing to commit time and effort to solving common challenges around developing quality competency-based models capable of scaling or spreading to affordably serve more students," the invitation document said.

The reason for the project's creation, said several officials who are working on it, is a growing need for shared guiding principles. Interest in online education is high, and many college leaders want competency-based education to avoid the hype, misconceptions and resulting backlash massive open online courses have received.

"There's really a danger of people just repackaging what they're doing and calling it competency-based education because it's the buzzword du jour," said Amy Laitinen, a former Education Department and White House official who is deputy director of the New America Foundation's higher education program.

Network and Incubator

Laitinen is a consultant for the project. Joining her is Mike Offerman, an expert on competency-based education, and Sally Johnstone, vice president for academic advancement at Western Governors University.

The group will focus on the nitty-gritty details of building a new program, including how to design sound assessments, comply with financial aid policies and make tweaks to business processes and information technology systems.

Participants will also discuss how to talk about and market their new degrees. Everything will be on the table, said several officials, even the term "competency."

A separate Lumina grant will help pay for a website that will make public much of the network's work and research. Southern New Hampshire University is responsible for creating the website.

"We're going to share as much of that as possible," said Paul LeBlanc, the university's president.

Southern New Hampshire, which has moved aggressively into competency-based education, will also host quarterly meetings at its campus for the group's members.

The network will be limited to colleges that are at least close to creating competency-based degrees. However, a separate, somewhat similar new effort is aimed at institutions that are interested in getting into the space.

That project is an "incubator" that the Bill and Melinda Gates Foundation is funding through its Next Generation Learning Challenges grant, which is managed by Educause. To participate, colleges will need to submit a plan to begin creating a competency-based program by January 2015, according to a draft document about the grant.

"C-BEN and the incubator share the goals of developing and advancing competency-based business models capable of scaling and serving many more students from all backgrounds," the document said. "Both will offer exposure to subject matter experts and will encourage the development and testing of relevant tools for institutions."

Carol Geary Schneider, president of the Association of American Colleges and Universities, welcomed the deepening conversation over competency-based education. She said she hopes the network can provide some clarity on the emerging delivery model, which the association has viewed warily.

The competency-based movement does have promise, she said. Ideally, Schneider said, competency-based programs share goals with the Degree Qualifications Profile (DQP), a Lumina-funded effort that attempts to define what degree holders should know and be able to do. Schneider helped author the profile.

However, Schneider said competency-based education could also lead to degrees that are based on a haphazard grouping of one-off competencies rather than a holistic curriculum. And she said competency is "now being used to define so many experiments."

Defining Competency

Competency-based education's defining feature, experts said, is that it places a priority on the assessment of defined learning outcomes, regardless of where the learning occurs. That typically means breaking credit requirements into discrete "competencies" that indicate a student has mastered concepts.

The idea is hardly new. Decades ago pioneering institutions like Alverno College, Excelsior College, Thomas Edison State College and others with a focus on adult students began assessing competencies and issuing college credit for experiential learning. As with Advanced Placement tests, students could pass assessments and earn credit for knowledge and skills they gained outside the traditional classroom.

Western Governors offers a twist on this model. Created in 1997, the online university added the element of self-paced instruction. Students at Western Governors can work through automated, asynchronous online course material at their own speed. And the university's instructors act more like tutors than professors in a lecture hall.

A third style first hit the scene this year. This approach, which is called "direct assessment," drops the credit-hour standard and completely severs the link between competencies and the amount of time students spend mastering them.

Earlier this year the federal government and regional accreditors gave a green light to new direct assessment offerings from College for America, a subsidiary of Southern New Hampshire, and Capella University.

Northern Arizona University has also pursued a direct-assessment program. So has the University of Wisconsin System, with its growing

"Flexible Option." More are on the way, including one from Brandman University. The Western Association of Schools and Colleges (WASC), a regional accreditor, this week approved Brandman's new, competency-based, bachelor degree in business administration.

Even advocates for competency-based education say it raises plenty of questions.

For example, Laitinen, who is a prominent critic of the credit hour, has begun publicly worrying about moving too fast on competency-based education. She said lawmakers in particular might be overeager to help spur the creation of new programs by making changes to legislation before academics even know what changes might help.

The work around competency-based education "needs to be done responsibly and thoughtfully, and with the right motivation" said Laitinen, adding that "the right motivation is outcomes."

Schneider agreed. "We're in a long-term change from a higher education system organized around credit hours" to one based on "demonstrated achievements of capabilities."

That's a difficult undertaking, she said. "We're trying to invent something new."

The Lumina-funded group's creators want its members to help lead conversations around those big-ticket questions.

A steering committee composed of representatives from 10 or so colleges with experience on competency-based education will help set the network's agenda, said several officials who are involved in the effort.

The committee's first co-chairs are Laurie Dodge, vice chancellor of institutional assessment and planning and vice provost at Brandman University, and David Schejbal, dean of continuing education, outreach and e-learning at University of Wisconsin-Extension.

Dodge said the project will seek to create a set of shared guiding principles. "The big thing is quality and rigor," she said.

One key to the work being helpful, said Schneider, is whether colleges share meaningful details about their assessments. Competency-based education relies heavily on assessments, so it's important to know what they measure.

"Ultimately we're going to need to reach some ground rules," Schneider said.

The invitation for applications said institutions must commit to sharing information about assessments, such as details about testing principles and how to formulate good assessments. They will not, however, be required to share "trade secrets." Western Governors, for example, has taken some heat for allegedly not being open about its competencies and assessments.

Johnstone recently responded to that criticism by saying "there are few people that ask" about course-level competencies.

LeBlanc said he was confident that participants would get specific about the creation of quality assessment tools. "We have to have transparency."

In the meantime, LeBlanc has been busy discussing competency-based education with accreditors. In a recent span of five days he spoke at three meetings held by regional accrediting agencies.

No "Single Model"

Colleges will be asked to do a substantial amount of work to participate in the group. And just sending their president to quarterly meetings won't cut it.

To apply, institutions must identify a team of up to seven employees, including faculty members, academic leaders, business and financial aid officers, information technology leaders, institutional researchers and marketing officials.

Several of the project's leaders said they want a broad range of competency-based programs to be represented.

"It is not our intention to push for a single model or approach," said Alison Kadlec, a senior vice president at Public Agenda, who will help lead the project.

Schejbal said the group hopes to come up with some sort of "standard, working definition" for competency-based education. But that doesn't mean they will be prescriptive.

"We don't have any intention of being exclusionary or telling people how to do it," he said.

The effort grew out of an April meeting Lumina held with representatives of approximately 25 institutions that were working on competency-based degrees. During the planning of that meeting and other, related discussions there was controversy over whether or not to include for-profit institutions.

Some advocates of competency-based education worry that for-profits might create lower-quality programs that could hurt the movement.

However, it appears the group will be open to participation by at least some for-profits. Capella, for example, which is widely viewed as a leader on competency-based education, is planning to contribute, said officials from the university.

No group is ever big enough for everyone, however. And some college leaders have grumbled about Lumina's outsized role in organizing conversations about competency-based education. But the network's leaders said few colleges actually have competency-based programs up and running.

"A lot of the right players are around the table," said Deb Bushway, Capella's chief academic officer.

Analyze

1. One advocate of competency-based education sees college primarily as a set of knowledge and skills that graduates "should know and be able to do." What important aspects of your experience would not fit into this description of a college education? And which would?
2. Assuming you are enrolled in a traditional college, what would be lost or gained if you transferred to a "competency-based" program?
3. In competency-based education, students can "earn credit for knowledge and skills they gained outside the traditional classroom." What college-level skills have you learned outside the classroom? And how did you learn them?
4. This model of competency-based education acknowledges that some college subjects take more than a single term to master, others take less, yet all are fixed into semester-length (or quarter-length) courses. In your opinion, which subjects need more time to master and which less?

Explore

1. Competency-based education would reduce the time a student spends in college. It may lower the overall cost of tuition, and it would limit the time a student was removed from the workforce. Both of these outcomes have potential advantages. But what experiences or skill development would be lost if the overall college experience were shortened by a year or two?
2. SHORT WRITING PROMPT: Make two lists. On the first list, identify a set of college subjects with which you might engage well,

without a class, as a self-directed learner. On the second, list a set of college subjects with which you would likely not engage well, without a class, as a self-directed learner.

3. FULL WRITING PROMPT: In an essay, relate an experience in which you taught (or tried to teach) yourself a complex skill or engage in a difficult subject. How well were you able to accomplish this? What were the strengths of self-guided learning? And the shortcomings?

Forging Connections

1. In "The Comfortable Kid," the author suggests that trigger warnings infantilize college students—that is, trigger warnings deny college students the opportunity to gain maturity through challenging situations. In your experience at college so far, can you identify other areas where classes protect students from challenging or disturbing information? Is this protection helpful to students or does it delay their entry into the adult world?
2. Multiple articles in this chapter describe colleges acting with a "consumer ethos"—that is, colleges want to make the student (i.e., the consumer) happy, perhaps with slightly higher-than-average grades, professors who aren't too strict, and classes that aren't too challenging. This consumer ethos is reinforced with websites like Rate My Professors, which places a premium on easygoing instructors and interesting classes that don't require heavy workloads. As you consider your campus, where do you see evidence of this "consumer ethos"? In your opinion, is a consumer ethos a beneficial or detrimental force on a college campus?

Looking Further

1. Multiple articles in this chapter discuss ways that technology can be integrated into the college experience, such as with clickers or attendance devices. Technology, no doubt, will continue to be an important element at college. Which technology-related experiences in the classroom have helped you learn a subject with depth and complexity? And which technology-related experiences have placed more emphasis on the technology than on learning? How can colleges better focus on meaningful technology-related experiences?

2. A few articles in this chapter offer practical advice for students—on choosing a major, for example, and how to pass a class you don't love. As you look ahead into your career as a college student, what is the one area of concern for which you would most like useful advice, an area not covered in this book and also not yet covered in your class?

Chapter 9

The Ever-Changing Curriculum

If you had attended the University of Pennsylvania in the mid-1800s, your class list would likely have included courses in classical literature and classical languages (such as Latin and ancient Greek), religious studies, and various math subjects (such as geometry and calculus). Classes recently added to the curriculum included offerings in mechanics, constitutional law, electricity, and magnetism. But over time curriculums change. Most students today are not required to take courses in Latin or religion. If students explore magnetism, they likely explore it as part of a physics sequence.

The needs of students—and the expectations for higher education—change over time. In today's college, students are more likely to take Spanish or Chinese than they are ancient Greek, as skills of international business have a higher perceived value than skills relating to antiquity. In ways, it might be ideal if college lasted five or six years, allowing students to pursue both Spanish and ancient Greek. But for most programs, a college education is capped at four years of study, 120 semester hours, or 180 quarter hours. The curriculum debate always focuses on this: to best serve contemporary students, what subjects should be included in those four years, and to make room for new requirements, what old classes should fall away?

In the past decade or so, colleges have explored many new requirements: many of these classes carry official college credit, though some are non-credit requirements to cover social concerns. Laura Pappano explores the possibility of requiring a course in creativity or creative thinking, while Rajat Bhageria suggests that, in an age of iPhones and tablet computers, all students should take at least one course in programming code. Scott Carlson investigates what is lost when colleges remove physical education courses to make way for new requirements. Rich Barlow, Diana Divecha, and Robin Stern explore two new social courses, one on alcohol abuse, the other on emotional health. These articles discuss the ways in which the college experience is changing, removing some traditions to make way for new ones. Together, these authors point to what a college curriculum might look like in the near future and the way new classes help students adapt to our ever-changing world.

Laura Pappano

Learning to Think Outside the Box: Creativity Becomes an Academic Discipline

Laura Pappano is the author of *Inside School Turnarounds* and *The Connection Gap*, as well as the co-author of *Playing with Boys*. Her articles on education regularly appear in *The New York Times*, *The Harvard Education Letter*, and *The Boston Globe*.

It bothers Matthew Lahue and it surely bothers you: enter a public restroom and the stall lock is broken. Fortunately, Mr. Lahue has a solution. It's called the Bathroom Bodyguard. Standing before his Buffalo State College classmates and professor, Cyndi Burnett, Mr. Lahue displayed a device he concocted from a large washer, metal ring, wall hook, rubber bands and Lincoln Log. Slide the ring in the crack and twist. The door stays shut. Plus, the device fits in a jacket pocket.

The world may be full of problems, but students presenting projects for Introduction to Creative Studies have uncovered a bunch you probably haven't thought of. Elie Fortune, a freshman, revealed his Sneaks 'n Geeks app to identify the brand of killer sneakers you spot on the street. Jason Cathcart, a senior, sported a bulky martial arts uniform with sparring pads he had sewn in. No more forgetting them at home.

"I don't expect them to be the next Steve Jobs or invent the flying car," Dr. Burnett says. "But I do want them to be more effective and resourceful problem solvers." Her hope, she says, is that her course has made them more creative.

Once considered the product of genius or divine inspiration, creativity—the ability to spot problems and devise smart solutions—is being recast as a prized and teachable skill. Pin it on pushback against standardized tests and standardized thinking, or on the need for ingenuity in a fluid landscape.

"The reality is that to survive in a fast-changing world you need to be creative," says Gerard J. Puccio, chairman of the International Center for Studies in Creativity at Buffalo State College, which has the nation's oldest creative studies program, having offered courses in it since 1967.

"That is why you are seeing more attention to creativity at universities," he says. "The marketplace is demanding it."

Critical thinking has long been regarded as *the* essential skill for success, but it's not enough, says Dr. Puccio. Creativity moves beyond mere synthesis and evaluation and is, he says, "the higher order skill." This has not been a sudden development. Nearly 20 years ago "creating" replaced "evaluation" at the top of Bloom's Taxonomy of learning objectives. In 2010 "creativity" was the factor most crucial for success found in an I.B.M. survey of 1,500 chief executives in 33 industries. These days "creative" is the most used buzzword in LinkedIn profiles two years running.

Traditional academic disciplines still matter, but as content knowledge evolves at lightning speed, educators are talking more and more about "process skills," strategies to reframe challenges and extrapolate and transform information, and to accept and deal with ambiguity.

Creative studies is popping up on course lists and as a credential. Buffalo State, part of the State University of New York, plans a Ph.D. and already offers a master's degree and undergraduate minor. Saybrook University in San Francisco has a master's and certificate, and added a specialization to its psychology Ph.D. in 2011. Drexel University in Philadelphia has a three-year-old online master's. St. Andrews University in Laurinburg, N.C., has added a minor. And creative studies offerings, sometimes with a transdisciplinary bent, are new options in business, education, digital media, humanities, arts, science and engineering programs across the country.

Suddenly, says Russell G. Carpenter, program coordinator for a new minor in applied creative thinking at Eastern Kentucky University, "there is a larger conversation happening on campus: 'Where does creativity fit into the E.K.U. student experience?' " Dr. Carpenter says 40 students from a broad array of fields, including nursing and justice and safety, have enrolled in the minor—a number he expects to double as more sections are added to introductory classes. Justice and safety? Students want tools to help them solve public safety problems and deal with community issues, Dr. Carpenter explains, and a credential to take to market.

The credential's worth is apparent to Mr. Lahue, a communication major who believes that a minor in the field carries a message. "It says: 'This person is not a drone. They can use this skill set and apply themselves in other parts of the job.' "

On-demand inventiveness is not as outrageous as it sounds. Sure, some people are naturally more imaginative than others. What's igniting campuses, though, is the conviction that everyone is creative, and can learn to be more so.

Just about every pedagogical toolbox taps similar strategies, employing divergent thinking (generating multiple ideas) and convergent thinking (finding what works). The real genius, of course, is in the *how.*

Dr. Puccio developed an approach that he and partners market as FourSight and sell to schools, businesses and individuals. The method, which is used in Buffalo State classrooms, has four steps: clarifying, ideating, developing and implementing. People tend to gravitate to particular steps, suggesting their primary thinking style. Clarifying—asking the right question—is critical because people often misstate or misperceive a problem. "If you don't have the right frame for the situation, it's difficult to come up with a breakthrough," Dr. Puccio says. Ideating is brainstorming and calls for getting rid of your inner naysayer to let your imagination fly. Developing is building out a solution, and maybe finding that it doesn't work and having to start over. Implementing calls for convincing others that your idea has value.

Jack V. Matson, an environmental engineer and a lead instructor of "Creativity, Innovation and Change," a MOOC that drew 120,000 in September, teaches a freshman seminar course at Penn State that he calls "Failure 101." That's because, he says, "the frequency and intensity of failures is an implicit principle of the course. Getting into a creative mind-set involves a lot of trial and error."

His favorite assignments? Construct a résumé based on things that didn't work out and find the meaning and influence these have had on your choices. Or build the tallest structure you can with 20 Popsicle sticks. The secret to the assignment is to destroy the sticks and reimagine their use. "As soon as someone in the class starts breaking the sticks," he says, "it changes everything."

Dr. Matson also asks students to "find some cultural norms to break," like doing cartwheels while entering the library. The point: "Examine what in the culture is preventing you from creating something new or different. And what is it like to look like a fool because a lot of things won't work out and you will look foolish? So how do you handle that?"

It's a lesson that has been basic to the ventures of Brad Keywell, a Groupon founder and a student of Dr. Matson's at the University of Michigan. "I am an absolute evangelist about the value of failure as part of creativity," says Mr. Keywell, noting that Groupon took off after the failure of ThePoint.com, where people were to organize for collective action but instead organized discount group purchases. Dr. Matson taught him not just to be willing to fail but that failure is a critical avenue to a successful end. Because academics run from failure, Mr. Keywell says, universities are "way too often shapers of formulaic minds," and encourage students to repeat and internalize fail-safe ideas.

Bonnie Cramond, director of the Torrance Center for Creativity and Talent Development at the University of Georgia, is another believer in taking bold risks, which she calls a competitive necessity. Her center added an interdisciplinary graduate certificate in creativity and innovation this year. "The new people who will be creative will sit at the juxtaposition of two or more fields," she says. When ideas from different fields collide, Dr. Cramond says, fresh ones are generated. She cites an undergraduate class that teams engineering and art students to, say, reimagine the use of public spaces. Basic creativity tools used at the Torrance Center include thinking by analogy, looking for and making patterns, playing, literally, to encourage ideas, and learning to abstract problems to their essence.

In Dr. Burnett's Introduction to Creative Studies survey course, students explore definitions of creativity, characteristics of creative people and strategies to enhance their own creativity. These include rephrasing problems as questions, learning not to instinctively shoot down a new idea (first find three positives), and categorizing problems as needing a solution that requires either action, planning or invention. A key objective is to get students to look around with fresh eyes and be curious. The inventive process, she says, starts with "How might you . . ."

Dr. Burnett is an energetic instructor with a sense of humor—she tested Mr. Cathcart's martial arts padding with kung fu whacks. Near the end of last semester, she dumped Post-it pads (the department uses 400 a semester) onto a classroom desk with instructions: On pale yellow ones, jot down what you learned; on rainbow colored pads, share how you will use this learning. She then sent students off in groups with orders that were a litany of brainstorming basics: "Defer judgment! Strive for quantity! Wild and unusual! Build on others' ideas!"

As students scribbled and stuck, the takeaways were more than academic. "I will be optimistic," read one. "I will look at tasks differently," said another. And, "I can generate more ideas."

Asked to elaborate, students talked about confidence and adaptability. "A lot of people can't deal with things they don't know and they panic. I can deal with that more now," said Rony Parmar, a computer information systems major with Dr. Dre's Beats headphones circling his neck.

Mr. Cathcart added that, given tasks, "you think of other ways of solving the problem." For example, he streamlined the check-in and reshelving of DVDs at the library branch where he works.

The view of creativity as a practical skill that can be learned and applied in daily life is a 180-degree flip from the thinking that it requires a little magic: Throw yourself into a challenge, step back—pause—wait for brilliance to spout.

The point of creative studies, says Roger L. Firestien, a Buffalo State professor and author of several books on creativity, is to learn techniques "to make creativity happen instead of waiting for it to bubble up. A muse doesn't have to hit you."

Analyze

1. The article claims that though creativity was once considered part of an ethereal process called inspiration, "ability to spot problems and devise smart solutions—is being recast as a prized and teachable skill." In your opinion, how is "creativity" a teachable skill?
2. How is "creative thinking" different from "critical thinking"?
3. How is "creative thinking" different from "being imaginative"?
4. What is a "process skill"? How is the acquisition of a process skill different from the acquisition of a body of knowledge?

Explore

1. The article claims that universities encourage students to develop skills for which they already have an aptitude: university classes are "way too often shapers of formulaic minds," rewarding students with high grades for taking familiar subjects and punishing them with low grades for taking subjects in which they don't have much previous experience. If all college classes were ungraded—with students receiving full credit for a good faith effort on each assignment—what new or additional classes might you take that you would otherwise avoid?
2. The article suggests that creativity skills are particularly important at the intersection between two seemingly unrelated areas of study, such as engineering and visual arts. Why is creativity important in intersecting disciplines? The article also suggests that in the near future, many jobs will develop in interdisciplinary intersections. Do you agree?
3. SHORT WRITING PROMPT: Jack V. Matson, an environmental engineer at Penn State, suggests that there is value in failure. Relate a story in which you failed—and explore what you learned from the experience.
4. FULL WRITING PROMPT: Agree or disagree: your college should *require* all students to take one course in creative studies. This will add one course to your school's general education requirements and remove one course from free electives. What benefits do you believe students would receive from a course in creative studies? Is this benefit large enough to mandate that students take such a course as a general education requirement?

Rajat Bhageria
Should We Require Computer Science Classes?

Rajat Bhageria is an eighteen-year-old entrepreneur and engineer who is the author of *What High School Didn't Teach Me: A Recent Graduate's Perspective on How High School Is Killing Creativity*. He is also the inventor of ThirdEye, a Google Glass app that assists the sight impaired.

Computer science: most of us don't even know what it is. It may seem distant and even a bit threatening. What does it mean? How is it used? Indeed, most students—and even more adults—don't know anything about computer science. There are so many misconceptions that too many people are afraid to even *try* it.

Moreover, since computer science is a relatively recent field—at least compared to chemistry, English or history—administrators high in the schooling hierarchy are not willing to substitute it for a subject that has existed for some time and *works*. But it is precisely because we live in this modern world that this recent subject is so incredibly important; most everything around us was in some sense affected by code, and yet most of us cannot even write a simple program that calculates how much gas we use in a year.

Now, there is no doubt that some colleges do require all students to take one CS class. The problem: not enough do. This scenario is especially nonsensical considering that CS teaches problem solving like no other—even theoretical math and physics courses. Why? Computer science is all about finding the easiest way to do something—the method that is most efficient and requires the least lines of code.

So, let's say I want to create a program for my theoretical t-shirt business that tracks profits. It seems pretty easy, right? Find revenue and then subtract costs. But something you may not have realized is how many unique routes a programmer may take to create a program that accomplishes this task. Unlike a paper-and-pencil logbook, programs are dynamic since there are always many different ways of accomplishing the same thing.

Nevertheless, some methods are more practical than others. This is the programmer's job. He or she must identify the "easiest" method to implement a particular assignment. And thus, programming is "difficult," mainly because it requires a programmer to think deeply about how to do a particular task, locating the most efficient and economical approach. Once the programmer has this "algorithm"—just a fancy term for a series of instructions the computer follows, kind of like a recipe—most of the hard work is done. Actually typing the code into the computer is a fairly simple task.

Unlike many of those math and physics courses, computer science is an extremely versatile tool. Indeed, you can use programming to enhance your lifestyle for almost any situation. Want to create a business? You'll need a website. Want to do college research? Many labs around the world use MATLAB to assist in creating accurate data-tables and graphs. Want to create video games like *Halo, Call of Duty* or *Mario Brothers*? Programming is a must.

Furthermore, in terms of numbers, CS pays off; computer science majors make on average $60,000 right out of college. That's second only to engineering (and even that by only $3,000) and is significantly higher than business (at $54,000), math and sciences (at $42,000), and humanities & social sciences (at $37,000).

But not enough students even know what computer science is because their schools don't teach it to everyone. And thus, schools are discarding tremendous opportunities for their students. So what's the solution? The basic response after weighing the enormous number of positives over the small number of negatives of CS is to give the green light: go ahead add more CS classes; require some CS for everyone. But here's the problem: finding enough qualified instructors willing to teach can be a challenge.

Still, there is a simple solution to this problem—a way to help a few instructors teach CS to large numbers of students. Indeed, precisely because of computer science and the Internet revolution, there is a plethora of online resources focused on computer programming—many of which are free. These websites (e.g., CodeAcademy.com, Code.org, and Treehouse) cover basic concepts, offer tests, and help students apply the concepts to practical projects.

These classes are revolutionary as they help students to learn outside a traditional classroom. In fact, an instructor is only necessary to ensure that students are *doing* the work; the website takes care of the rest. Once the students start working, the addictive nature of programming usually entices them to more deeply explore the topic. Indeed, there is almost no reason *not* to teach students how to program with so little negatives to bear.

Even a study hall supervisor with a minimal background in CS can easily convert a study hall into an Intro to Computer Programming through these programming websites.

More and more, the ability to independently run a business (a club, an organization, a non-profit, or a team) is significantly more important than having a formal education in terms of earning and then succeeding in a job. And in any of these cases, having a programming background—especially in creating websites—is almost imperative in today's fast-changing business culture.

Analyze

1. What level, if any, of computer programing should all students with a college education possess?
2. What core skills in a CS course—apart from understanding and writing code—might translate well to other disciplines? That is, how might the intellectual skills acquired in a CS course, such as problem solving and critical thinking, help students in other majors, even if those students won't write code for a living?
3. The author believes that colleges might employ study hall monitors to supervise students in a self-directed CS course, with much of the class content provided by free online tutorials. Do you believe that this would be an effective or meaningful method of college study?

Explore

1. The author feels that computer programing, a relatively recent field of study at most colleges, is essential for all college graduates. Are there other relatively new fields of study that, in your opinion, should be arranged as introductory courses required for all students?
2. The author is a college student himself, who is interested in improving education. In your opinion, what role should students play in shaping educational experiences—especially considering that professors are usually considered experts within their disciplines? Is student input likely to make a class easier or more challenging; more or less career-focused; more lecture-oriented or discussion-centered? What opportunities exist at your college for students to shape its educational environment?

3. FULL WRITING PROMPT: Agree or disagree: your college should *require* all students to take one course in computer science, with an emphasis on programming. This will add one course to your school's general education requirements and remove one course from free electives. What benefits do you believe students would receive from a course in computer science? Is this benefit large enough to mandate that students take such a course as a general education requirement?

Diana Divecha and Robin Stern
Why College Freshmen Need to Take Emotions 101

Diana Divecha is a developmental psychologist and research affiliate of the Yale Center for Emotional Intelligence. **Robin Stern** is a psychoanalyst and associate director of the Yale Center for Emotional Intelligence.

You've dropped your kid off at college. You may feel sad and nostalgic in spite of newfound freedom, or even that parenting as you know it is behind you. Your child, at the same time, has a new roommate—or two or three—has started classes, and has received grades on her first set of assignments. You exhale, believing that she's well on her way.

But mid-autumn, when students get their first real feedback on their academic performance, is when college counselors see the first big spike in anxiety. And in general, anxiety on college campuses is on the rise. Why? There's a lot more going on for students than buying books, writing papers, playing sports, and pledging fraternities and sororities.

In fact, many college students are struggling, even suffering.

College life for most freshmen is emotionally challenging. The security and comfort of old relationships are interrupted, bringing feelings of grief, or loss, or of being at sea—in spite of being surrounded by hundreds (often thousands) of new peers. In the context of those ruptures, the desire to connect can lead kids to make unsatisfying or poor choices, perhaps even socializing with people they don't really like. Some freshmen bring with them unresolved interpersonal difficulties from high school or family life, which complicates their adjustment.

On a deeper level, at college there are new and often unexpected challenges to their identity and sense of efficacy: Perhaps the freshman was a high performer with career plans in high school and is shocked by the lower grades in college; or maybe it is her first time out of her community and she can't find people like herself. Many students have financial pressures, leading them to take too many classes at once, or to take on an extra job, or even to skimp on meal plans, leaving them hungry. Rising inequality in an increasingly competitive economy has raised all the stakes.

A 2013 survey of 380 college counseling departments across the country shows that anxiety is the most common presenting problem in their offices, followed by depression and relationship problems. A quarter of students seen in counselors' offices are on psychotropic medications, and though American students are famously medicated more than students from other countries, it still signals a problem for individuals. And many counselors privately say that their students are surprisingly lonely. Karen Gee, a health educator at UC Berkeley said that on a single day, she saw six students who were painfully, tearfully lonely. "Many have suffered in silence due to the stigma of loneliness," she said.

A 2013 survey of over 123,000 students across 153 campuses confirmed that over half of students feel overwhelming anxiety, and about a third experience intense depression, sometime during the year. Almost a third report that their stress has been high enough at some point to interfere with their academics—lowering their grades on exams or courses or projects—and 44% say that academic or career issues have been traumatic or difficult to handle. The majority of college students don't get enough sleep, and half say that they've felt overwhelmed and exhausted, lonely or sad sometime during the year. Colleges often blame parents, but the problem is likely more systemic: American children rank 26th out of 29 developed countries on overall measures of well-being.

Colleges are trying to meet students' emotional needs, but efforts and resources vary. Many universities report upping their budgets, adding staff, increasing their outreach to students, and/or experimenting with innovative programs. This fall, Gee started a "friendliness" campaign at UC Berkeley to help students connect in healthy ways—and when one lonely freshman posted that he wanted to make friends, he received 180 "likes" and ten offers to "hang out." For those that do take advantage of counseling, the majority say it helps with academic difficulties. But data show that the reach is constrained: Counseling centers serve only about 10 percent of students on campus, and there is an inverse relationship between the size of the college and the ratio of mental health workers to students (in other words, larger campuses have proportionally fewer resources available). According to students, it's not unusual to experience long wait times (even two to three months) and inconsistent, insufficient meetings.

We can do better.

Students need real emotional skills. There is a large and growing body of research that suggests that the skills of emotional intelligence—the ability to reason with and about emotions to achieve goals—are correlated with positive outcomes across the entire age spectrum, from preschool through adulthood. Emotions affect learning, decision-making, creativity, relationships, and health, and people with more developed emotion skills do better. Among college students, skills of emotional intelligence are linked to engaging in fewer risky behaviors whereas self-esteem is not.

And, our research at the Yale Center for Emotional Intelligence with children in classrooms shows us that these abilities can be taught. In classrooms where children learn to recognize, understand, label, express, and regulate their emotions, they are rated as having a greater range of skills: they have better relationships and social skills and are more connected to each other and their teachers; they are better at managing conflict; they are more autonomous and show more leadership skills; and they perform better in academic subjects (it's easier to concentrate when they feel better).

Colleges would do well to go beyond the therapeutic model and integrate positive emotional skill-building into their orientations, their freshman seminars, and their dormitory lives. Pace University and McCaulay Honors College in New York City are already experimenting with this: Pace is incorporating a short course in emotion skills into their freshman seminar, and McCaulay purchased a mobile app for all of their freshmen to help them recognize their feelings, make decisions about how to regulate them, and track them over time. Many graduate schools are beginning to recognize that emotion skills are necessary to their students' future success. Our neighbor, the Yale School of Management, has incorporated into their program a standardized test of emotional intelligence and a mobile app that teaches emotional skills. Several medical schools have approached us for advice on how to incorporate emotional intelligence into their training of doctors.

When college students are aware of what they're feeling, they can make conscious decisions about how to manage those emotions, rather than escalate, act out, or medicate. When they identify emotional patterns and clearly see preceding triggers, they can reflect on how and with whom they spend that time and employ strategies to manage the things that "set them off." When students are anxious and pressured, they can use strategies to calm themselves and proceed on tasks with lowered anxiety. When they inevitably discover new aspects of themselves in college, e.g., sexual or religious or political orientations, they can share these discoveries with trusted family or friends so they don't feel alone in their journey. When they are more masterful at reading others' cues, they'll be better able to resolve interpersonal conflicts. They might not be able to solve the problem, but they can have empathy for the other person, de-escalate, and take care of themselves.

And what about parents?

Parenting is an ongoing renegotiation of the balance between expectations and supports, and parents can recognize that college kids need them in different ways from before. College personnel say that kids' confidence is undermined when parents intervene on their behalf. Instead, when a campus issue arises, it is better to be a coach from the sidelines and encourage kids to "work the system," seek out resources, and advocate for themselves. At the same time, kids need to draw on their attachments to parents—and research shows that in families where parents offer it, kids do better in the long run.

Of course, it can take real emotional skills to figure out how to best support a student who is growing and changing away from home. Parents can listen carefully for cues that a student may be struggling. Then parents can set the stage for a successful conversation by "putting on their own oxygen mask first"—that is, pausing, checking in with themselves, and regulating their own—possibly intense—emotions. Without that personal "check-in," strong feelings of parental anxiety, disappointment, or anger will likely interfere with clear thinking and the outcome of helping the student.

It's easy to think that once kids go off to college, they are fully-launched and independent adults who no longer need our help. But the needle on adulthood has inched up the age range since medieval times, when children were considered adults as soon as they could dress, feed and toilet themselves. These days, based on brain, psychological, and social development, the field of developmental science considers adulthood to begin at around age 25-30.

Of course parents already invest a lot in their children's education. But investing in their emotional lives by teaching real skills is an important foundation to their success and can yield great returns. While it certainly won't solve all of our kids' problems, we can certainly keep an intentional focus on teaching them skills that they will need to successfully negotiate their freshman experience . . . and every year of their lives.

Imagine trying to solve complex mathematical problems without the tools of algebra or calculus. Emotions are constantly at play—you're probably having some right now—but every day we ask our children, ourselves, and each other to solve complex emotional problems with few real tools. An ongoing education in emotions from preschool through college, based on the emerging field of emotion science, will go a long way toward equipping our youth for adulthood—and easing the journey along the way.

Analyze

1. How is the emotional experience of college different than that of high school?
2. Aside from grades, in your experience, what factors contribute to a heightened sense of anxiety for most students at your college?
3. Many students experience tremendous personal change during the first term of college—so much so that many first-year students see their "college identity" as distinct from their "high school identity." What elements of the college experience most strongly contribute to this change in identity?
4. Describe one activity or new service that your college could provide that would make students feel more connected to each other on your campus.

Explore

1. The article claims "the needle on adulthood has inched up the age range since medieval times." With this in mind, when do you believe

that college students are emotionally independent (though perhaps not financially independent) from their parents?

2. For whom is the college journey more difficult—assuming it's a journey *away* from home—students or their parents?
3. SHORT WRITING PROMPT: In an annotated list, name the top seven sources of anxiety for freshman/sophomore students at your college as you understand them.
4. FULL WRITING PROMPT: Agree or disagree: your college's orientation program should require a one-day seminar on emotional skills for all new students, even if this adds one day to the orientation program.

Rich Barlow

BU Mandates Online Alcohol Course for First-Year Students

Rich Barlow, a graduate of Dartmouth College and a former reporter for *The Boston Globe*, is a staff writer for *BU Today*.

More than a third (35 percent) of first-year BU students don't drink alcohol. But many students may not know that, misled by urban myth about universal, *Animal House* imbibing on college campuses.

This year, the University is requiring first-year students to take an online alcohol course to separate truthful wheat from mythic chaff, starting before they even arrive on campus.

Those students will receive log-in instructions midsummer for AlcoholEdu for College. The course includes two parts: the first, featuring educational material and surveys before and after the material is studied, takes between one and a half and two and a half hours to complete. (It needn't all be done in one sitting.) Part 2 is a third, 15-minute survey.

In recent years, the University has offered students another online survey, iHealth, to dispel misconceptions, but has not required it. The hope is that through the mandatory course, students will be more responsible about alcohol use.

"It is used by most of our peer institutions as a prevention-level intervention for first-year college students" to curb dangerous drinking, says Elizabeth Douglas, manager of wellness and prevention services at Student Health Services. "We are using AlcoholEdu because it has the capacity to track student completion, in addition to having evidence of its being an effective intervention."

That evidence comes from a three-year, 30-campus study that found reduced frequency of drinking, including binge drinking, and related problems among students who participated in AlcoholEdu, as compared with students who did not.

Part 1 must be completed before students arrive on campus for the academic year. They will be required to finish Part 2 sometime in October; the University will send them a reminder email. AlcoholEdu is designed to be taken by both drinkers and nondrinking students. The surveys and intersecting information touch on such topics as how many drinks are in a bottle of wine or beer, factors influencing whether people drink, exaggerated notions of heavy drinking on campuses, alcohol's effects on the body and mind, and tactics students can use to protect themselves and friends from harm in a variety of drinking situations.

The course also provides information for parents about discussions they should have with their children: about alcohol, about its possible effects on schoolwork, and about drinking laws. It asks their views on college alcohol policies, issues they deem important to discuss with their kids, and demographic information about their families.

The new program follows a drop in alcohol-related violations and hospital runs on campus last year, which officials attribute to their recent alcohol enforcement program, entering its third academic year this fall. That program features increased police patrols of known party neighborhoods, dispersing parties, issuing citations, and publishing fall's enforcement statistics on *BU Today*.

Meanwhile, a city ordinance allows Boston police to arrest landlords and tenants in so-called problem properties—rentals with four documented complaints of loud parties or alcohol violations.

Douglas says the University likely will use AlcoholEdu in coming years, since BU chooses responsible drinking programs "based on research and evidence of effectiveness."

Analyze

1. The article suggests that *Animal House*–style parties are a "myth" at many universities—that is, disorderly, drunken house parties are events that new students often associate with the college experience but rarely happen in real life. In your opinion, why are images of drunken house parties so closely associated with college life? Consider how movies, TV shows, books, and magazines might contribute to this myth.
2. Why do you think that Boston University (BU) requires students to complete part of the alcohol education program *before* arriving at college?
3. The AlcoholEdu program, according to the article, helps educate students on alcohol consumption (such as how many servings are in a bottle of wine) and the effects of alcohol use (such as the effects of alcohol on the body). How successful do you believe an online program would be on your campus in reducing problem drinking among students?

Explore

1. AlcoholEdu is an online program. On your campus, do you believe an online program (one that allows students to participate anonymously, without peer engagement) would be more or less effective than a face-to-face program (a student discussion group led by a counseling professional)? In what type of environment, private or semi-public, would students on your campus be more likely to participate honestly?
2. The BU program strongly advises parents to initiate discussions about alcohol use with their college-age children, even though these "children" are legal adults. In your opinion, what is the best role parents can play in their children's life when it comes to issues of drinking, sexual experimentation, and financial responsibility?
3. FULL WRITING PROMPT: Agree or disagree: your college should require a non-credit online alcohol education program for all incoming students.

Scott Carlson
When Colleges Abandon Phys Ed, What Else Is Lost?

Scott Carlson is a senior writer for *The Chronicle of Higher Education,* where he writes on college management, the cost of higher education, and sustainability.

It's warm-up time at 7:45 a.m., with sunlight just starting to stream into a mat room in the kinesiology building at Los Angeles City College. A dozen students—most of them Latinas, all dressed in thick, white judo uniforms—stand at one end of the room, breathing hard, their hands over their heads or resting heavily on their hips. It's too early to be up, their faces say, and way too early to bear crawl, somersault, or drag yourself across the room using only your arms.

"Ready," comes a new command, "let's shrimp!" It's like a sit-up, combined with scooting butt-first along the mat. One young woman curses under her breath, while the rest bend to the floor in resignation. This is only the beginning: Later this morning, they will repeatedly toss one another to the ground, wrestle a partner into submission, or escape from a heavy pin.

Hayward Nishioka stands quietly on one side of the room, looking for signs of a transformation he has seen in scores of judo students at LACC. Most had almost no physical education leading up to college, he says, speculating that if they had known what his judo course entailed, they would have quit. Now, midway through the semester, he sees grit.

"By the time they get out of here, they'll be different people," says Mr. Nishioka, a professor emeritus of physical education at LACC. "Just this type of movement says to them: 'I can move, I can roll. I can also go against somebody. These people are trying really hard to try to beat me up, but I am able to survive this.'"

Decades ago, Mr. Nishioka used judo in his own bid to survive. It was an escape route from a rough East LA neighborhood, to travel the world as an international judo champion. After his competitive career was over, he spent 40 years here at LACC—eight years as chair of the physical-education department—helping students with backgrounds much like his own discover the vitality of their bodies, the connection of that body to the mind, and the new confidence, character, and life lessons that might come from a little soreness and sweat.

"We are physical creatures, first and foremost," he says. "Everything we do in education is about improving the brain. But how do we improve the brain? Through our physical acts. Our physical senses are our antennae."

Mr. Nishioka's focus on the body runs counter to prevailing trends, from kindergarten through college, where recess and physical education have been given up in favor of more sit-down classroom time. Although colleges have built lots of swanky recreation centers in recent years, studies indicate that college physical-education requirements are at an all-time low. Meanwhile, researchers have seen alarming trends among the college-aged population: significant rates of obesity, hypertension, depression, anxiety.

Paradoxically, colleges are cutting back on physical education just as a growing body of research indicates that regular physical activity is key to cognitive development and helps people focus, process information faster, and remember things more easily. John J. Ratey, an associate clinical professor of psychiatry at Harvard Medical School, has called exercise "Miracle-Gro for the brain."

Bradley J. Cardinal, a professor of public health and human sciences at Oregon State University, has researched the decline of physical education at colleges. "There is definitely a point of irony with schools saying we want to focus on academics, so we are going to cut back on physical activity or physical education," he says. "We do research showing the benefits of physical activity, and the federal government funds this stuff, and we don't use it."

Moreover, Mr. Nishioka, reaching back to the idealistic founders of judo, says physical educators are losing the opportunity to teach life lessons that go beyond fitness and health. The field or the judo mat, for example, can be a place to learn about loyalty, resolve, or courage in the face of sure defeat—a lesson rarely conveyed so effectively in a classroom. "Physical education should be more about teaching values, morals, losing with honor, friendship," he says. "Even physical educators these days don't think about these things."

Mr. Nishioka made his fame through combat on the judo mat, and he seems to have spent his whole life fighting. He was born in 1942 to a single mother and never knew his father, whom he suspects was a criminal. He spent the first few years of his life in a Japanese internment camp before returning to East LA, where he was always in one scrap or another. Kids would hunt him down after school and call him a "Jap."

"That was a war cry," he says. They'd gang up on him. But the young Nishioka adhered to a Japanese principle of *kataki-uchi,* or blood revenge. He would follow kids home from school or go looking for them at their houses, when they'd be alone, and he'd give a licking right back.

When he was about 12, Dan Oka, the man who would become Mr. Nishioka's stepfather, took the boy to watch a judo contest. "I was taken by their throws and flying through the air," he says. "When we got back to the house, I said, 'What's that like? I want to try that.'" Mr. Oka put an old army jacket on the boy, grabbed him by the collar, and tossed him onto the wood floor several times. Despite the bumps and bruises, Mr. Nishioka was hooked.

Judo is a Japanese form of wrestling. Two fighters try to hurl each other to the mat. A perfect throw, landing a player flat on his back, will end the match. An imperfect throw might bring the fight to the ground, where the fighters try to pin their opponents or make them submit using strangleholds or potentially bone-breaking armlocks.

Compared with street fighting, Mr. Nishioka says, judo seemed easy. It had rules—and beauty in turning an opponent's force into a sailing throw. But Mr. Nishioka went out on the mat with the same primal instinct for survival he'd carried to the streets. From 1965 to 1970, he won three national championships and a gold medal in the Pan-American Games. Judo took him around the world—on a goodwill tour of Europe with teammates like Ben Nighthorse Campbell, who would later become a U.S. senator, and to Japan, where he studied with Shigeru Egami, a legendary karate instructor.

As his competitive career waned in the 1970s, he began teaching judo at Los Angeles City College. It was a transition that put Mr. Nishioka more firmly on a path set by judo's founder, Jigoro Kano.

Kano, who studied philosophy and economics under Western professors, was a director in Japan's Ministry of Education and is now considered the country's "father of physical education." Trained in samurai jiujitsu from his teenage years in the 1870s to early adulthood, Kano was strongly influenced by the philosopher Herbert Spencer, who described the ideal education as one that blends mind, morals, and body. In 1908,

Kano's judo, a recreational form of jiujitsu, became a requirement in Japanese schools.

John Stevens, a former professor of Buddhist studies at Tohoku Fukushi University who wrote a biography of Kano, says the ideal person of the samurai era—which lasted into Kano's childhood—was a physical force on the battlefield as well as an accomplished statesman, poet, or philosopher. After the Meiji Restoration, "scholarly people became kind of wimpy," Mr. Stevens says. "When Kano was teaching high school, he was appalled at how weak the students were—a lot of them had servants that would carry their books to class." When Kano visited the legislature, he would stop officials and tell them they looked ill and should exercise more.

"You cannot be a well-rounded person if you don't know your body, or be confident, or be aware of your surroundings—all of those things you get from judo training." Mr. Stevens says. "Ideally, that's what he wanted."

At the grade-school level in the United States, parents and teachers have lamented how schools have shortened recess and gym classes to make room for written exercises and testing. After-school entertainment, meanwhile, has become more sedentary: gaming, surfing the Internet, texting friends. That has led to what some physical educators call a "pipeline problem" for college P.E programs.

"A lot of these students were not physically active as kids," says Jared A. Russell, an associate professor of kinesiology at Auburn University. "We have students coming to campus who have never swung a tennis racket or a baseball bat, or who can't swim at all."

The trend among grade-school physical-education programs has been seen in college programs, too. Mr. Cardinal, of Oregon State, was a co-author of a 2012 study showing that among 354 institutions, fewer than 40 percent had maintained any physical-education requirement, down from 67 percent in 1993 and 87 percent in 1968. Public institutions were more likely than private ones to have dropped the requirement.

Mr. Cardinal points to several possible explanations. For one, physical-education departments might be politically weaker than other departments on campus, and lose ground as administrators shift more resources and emphasis to science, math, and other academic subjects. PE programs are also professionalizing—as they rebrand under the more scientifically oriented "kinesiology," the departments focus more on sending students into health fields like physical therapy or nutrition, and less on "service" courses like swimming or basketball.

The departments' facilities have also, to some extent on campuses across the country, been replaced by opulent recreation centers. Administrators look at those rec centers and wonder why they need to spend money on physical-education departments.

Some of those factors seem to have gone into a decision earlier this year at the University of Notre Dame to eliminate the physical-education department and requirements to take two PE courses and pass a swimming test. Next year the requirements will be replaced by two courses that spend more time on university orientation, community standards, strategies for academic success, and spiritual life, as well as helping students set goals for physical activity.

Hugh R. Page Jr., dean of the First Year of Studies program, says the new courses are "placing a greater degree of the onus for wellness on the shoulders of individual students" by encouraging them to take "ownership of their physical well-being." Notre Dame, he says, is not diminishing its emphasis on physical activity. He points out that three-quarters of the students played on varsity teams in high school and will play some intramural, club, or intercollegiate sport during their time at the university. "You don't necessarily have to require students to take a volleyball course or a tennis course to generate their involvement" in physical activity, he says.

It's a different story at Los Angeles City College. As chair of the PE department, Mr. Nishioka spent the past several years fighting for more prominence for physical education, only to see administrators cut the square footage of a new kinesiology building by half. When Mr. Nishioka started at LACC, in the 1970s, students were required to take one PE class every semester; today they're required to take only one during their time at the college.

And over the years, the "pipeline problem" in Los Angeles has become just as challenging as in any other city. In 2013, student advocates sued 37 California school districts for not providing the physical-education hours mandated by state law. Some critics have highlighted the condition of PE at the Los Angeles Unified School District as particularly egregious. Studies found that 25 to 40 percent of students from the district were obese, and 75 percent failed state fitness standards.

Under pressure to jam more math, reading, social studies, and science into each semester with fewer resources, schools and colleges have found room by cutting back on exercise time. "All of my research flies in the face of that, and that is actually contrary and counterproductive to normal growth and development," says Darla M. Castelli, an associate professor of physical-education pedagogy at the University of Texas at Austin, who studies the connection between exercise and brain health.

Her studies and others show that regular exercise allows people to process information more accurately, allocate more working memory to a given task, and improve attention span—even among people in their cognitive peak years, from age 21 to 27.

There are several competing theories to explain those effects: Aerobic activity might help oxygenate the brain through increased blood flow, stimulating the growth of new brain cells or helping to maintain neuroplasticity, or the connection of synapses. Physical activity might also activate the production of "brain-derived neurotropic factor," or BDNF, a protein that stimulates the growth of the hippocampal region, which is responsible for memory.

Ms. Castelli says one study suggests that people get cognitive benefits from coordinated movements—as in, say, dance, where a person has to work off of and respond to a partner. And there are new theories that active people can build up a cognitive "reserve" that will stave off decline as they head into their 30s and beyond.

Unfortunately, her studies of people in the peak college years show nearly 50 percent with signs of cardiometabolic risk factors, like high glucose or high blood-lipid levels. "They're at risk and they don't even know it, and they're largely inactive," she says. Most believe that they are getting all the exercise they need by walking to class.

There is an ancient ideal that goes beyond brain or bodily health: The classroom instructs in one way, but the field, judo mat, and dance floor hold other invaluable lessons, especially as educators emphasize the importance of collaboration. Mr. Cardinal often discusses the topic with his wife, who teaches dance at Western Oregon University: Dance harnesses creativity in the moment, working in space and time to challenge an individual in a whole new way—to say nothing of the courage it takes to cut loose in front of an audience.

Or he mentions times when he has seen groups of colleagues take on a ropes course: There, the person who is a leader in the office or classroom often becomes a follower. "And someone who is not typically the leader now has to be in the leadership position," he says, "and people see him in a new light."

That is what Kano intended when he created judo, more than 100 years ago. Old samurai fighting techniques, through a marriage of mind and body, would teach principles that people could use everywhere. "Judo began with the study of martial arts, and then it gradually became clear that it could be applied to physical education, intellectual training, moral education, social interaction, management, and people's everyday lives," Kano wrote. "It is wrong to assume that judo ends in the dojo."

At judo practice in Los Angeles, as tangled bodies roll on the ground, it's clear that the close contact, aggression, pain—and, occasionally, the unexpectedly graceful throws—push some students to discover things about themselves. For Marilyn Hernandez, who is studying biochemistry, the class was her first experience with a contact sport. "I really fell in love with it," she says. Every tussle on the mat gave her lessons in improvisation and determination, and she lost 30 pounds to boot. "You have to say, I can do this. You are the person who is going to win. It's mental." She dreams of transferring to San Jose State University, which has a top-ranked judo team.

Sintia Diaz, who is studying early-childhood education, has decided that she wants to become a professional fighter, and she was thrilled to land in a class led by a martial-arts luminary. She's tiny, about five feet tall and slight. Yet she's a pit bull—walking up to men a foot taller than her and challenging them to fight. She says she once lacked self-esteem, in part because of her size. "Judo gave me a totally different perspective about myself," she says. Now if she makes a mistake or fails at something, she shrugs it off. "It's about how did I grow, or what did I learn? It's crazy to take a class for a few months and feel totally empowered. I had never felt that before."

Mr. Nishioka observes all of this from the sidelines or while walking through the grappling bodies, stopping now and then to adjust a pin or a cranking arm. At the end of the class, he tells the students to encircle the mat, and he reminds them why they are here. "What is judo about? Is it just technique?" he prods. No. "Small judo" is just the throws and pins and how they work.

"But 'large judo' is taking the techniques and concepts and applying them to your everyday lives," he says. To meet a challenge, to do the impossible, to have courage. "This is one of the few activities at City College that will teach you about bravery," he says, gesturing to the mat, "because you have to be brave to get out here."

Analyze

1. What role, if any, should your college play in combating obesity and promoting physical well-being in its students?
2. The article suggests that physical education classes might offer students a unique learning experience (promoting values, morals, honor, and friendship) that are more difficult to acquire in traditional "sit-down" classes. Aside from activity skills (such as how to throw a football or how to swim freestyle), what lessons, in your opinion, might be best learned in a physical education class?
3. The article claims that at many colleges the responsibility of physical education has shifted from the school (through required PE classes) to the individual (through voluntary participation at a student gym or activity center). In your opinion, are the majority of college students mature enough to take full responsibility for their physical well-being by the age of 18?

Explore

1. The article takes the position that colleges should participate in a student's moral education—an education that exceeds academic exploration, technical training, and career preparation. In your opinion, what is a college's obligation to help develop a student's sense of morals and values?
2. Most colleges cap programs of study at 120 semester credit hours or 180 quarter credit hours for a bachelor's degree—or half of that for an associate's degree. Adding one required class often means removing a different requirement—or reducing free electives. Most colleges revise their general education requirements every few years. Assuming you wish to add three or four units of physical activity to the general education requirements of your college, what three- or four-unit current requirement (or free electives) would you remove?
3. FULL WRITING PROMPT: Agree or disagree: your college should increase the number of required physical education classes, a decision that will lower the number of free electives available to students.

Forging Connections

1. Writers in this section take note of ways that college can change to serve both professional goals and personal development. Laura Pappano and Rajat Bhageria, respectively, recommend courses in creativity and coding (professional skills), while Scott Carlson advocates for physical education (personal development). Beyond those courses discussed in this chapter, name one class not currently required at your college that you believe all students should take for career readiness in the twenty-first century. Also identify one course, not currently required, that all students should take for personal development. Be prepared to discuss your rationale.
2. With required courses on emotional health and drinking, some colleges are taking on a parental role, particularly with freshmen and sophomores. Explore your campus to find examples of paternalism in how the college relates to younger students—that is, how it guides students toward responsible, respectful, and moral behavior, a duty that was once centered inside the family. Do you believe that paternalism within a college setting is helpful or detrimental to students?

Looking Further

1. The author of "When Colleges Abandon Phys Ed, What Else Is Lost?" suggests that American colleges have relinquished physical activities "in favor of more sit-down classroom time." That is, colleges place a premium on sedentary activities, such as reading, writing, and studying. Through this, colleges increase the value of the mind and decrease the value of the body. Do you believe that this is a positive trend, to so heavily privilege mental development for four years? Has college, with its emphasis on learning as opposed to doing, changed how we think about the human experience in general, to place a higher premium on mental activity than physical activity?
2. The article "Learning to Think Outside the Box" suggests that creativity—once thought to be the domain of genius and inspiration—can to some extent be a teachable process skill. What other areas, once thought to be the domain of genius and inspiration, might someday be offered as a class?

Additional Readings

identity

Other titles in this series include:

Culture: A Reader for Writers,
John Mauk
(ISBN: 9780199947225)

Language: A Reader for Writers,
Gita DasBender
(ISBN: 9780199947485)

Sustainability: A Reader for Writers,
Carl Herndl
(ISBN: 9780199947508)

Globalization: A Reader for Writers,
Maria Jerskey
(ISBN: 9780199947522)

identity

A READER *for* WRITERS

John Scenters-Zapico
University of Texas at El Paso

New York Oxford
Oxford University Press

Oxford University Press publishes works that further Oxford University's objective of excellence in research, scholarship, and education.

Oxford New York
Auckland Cape Town Dar es Salaam Hong Kong Karachi
Kuala Lumpur Madrid Melbourne Mexico City Nairobi
New Delhi Shanghai Taipei Toronto

With offices in
Argentina Austria Brazil Chile Czech Republic France Greece
Guatemala Hungary Italy Japan Poland Portugal Singapore
South Korea Switzerland Thailand Turkey Ukraine Vietnam

Published by Oxford University Press.
198 Madison Avenue, New York, New York 10016
http://www.oup.com

Library of Congress Cataloging-in-Publication Data
Scenters-Zapico, John.
Identity : a reader for writers / John Scenters-Zapico, University of Texas at El Paso.
pages cm
Includes bibliographical references and index.
ISBN 978-0-19-994746-1 (pbk.)
1. College readers. 2. English language--Rhetoric--Handbooks, manuals, etc. 3. English language--Grammar--Handbooks, manuals, etc. 4. Report writing--Handbooks, manuals, etc. 5. Identity (Philosophical concept) in literature. I. Title.
PE1417.S357 2014
808'.0427--dc23

2013037246

Printing number: 9 8 7 6 5 4 3 2 1

Printed in the United States of America
on acid-free paper

Keith Dorwick
"Getting Called Fag"

The author of this literacy narrative shares a story about getting called "fag" in the 1970s when he was around fifteen years old. Despite the hurt the event caused him, he maturely contemplates the process of naming things and of others naming us as an act of rhetoric. This story comes from the Digital Archives of Literacy Narratives (DALN) and is available for open-access download in video, audio, text, or all three at the Digital Archive of Literacy Narratives at Ohio State University (http://daln.osu.edu/). If you read the text below first and then listen to the audio of it, you will find that you pick up on different points.

While this narrative has the potential to appear negative or even sad, how does Dorwick make it into a story of growth and strength?

Ok, so I'm maybe 15, maybe 16 at the time of the story and I'm living out in Glendale Heights, Illinois, and Crane's Chicago Business once described it as a hardscrabble factory town, but it wasn't. It was a bedroom community, kinda working class I guess, yeah. Certainly my parents were, certainly I am, I consider myself that way anyway. And I'm walking down the street, all of a sudden this car goes screeching past me. And then as in lots of small towns I guess, you kind of drive

"I didn't know anybody who was gay, and I was worried that I was the only one."

around. You drive around a lot, go back and forth here and there. Anyway, there were maybe 8, 9, maybe 10 kids, crammed, all guys, into this car. It made me kind of think of one of those cars in the circus with all the clowns. Well I laughed, and when I laughed, they got kind of upset on one of their passes. And so they zoomed around again just so they could yell: "Faggot! Fag!" "Queer!" Now, at the time I hadn't really dealt with the fact that I was gay, I kinda sorta was wondering it, and I knew I was kinda intrigued, and interested in men. But I didn't really know what to do about it, or even if I wanted to do anything about it. So, so I was kind of appalled, like, "How did they know?" "How do they know? I haven't said anything about this to anybody? How do they know?" But then the other thing is that I kinda was feeling pretty liberated. Because I had been worried, this is 1975, there wasn't any Will and Grace, you know. There weren't a whole lot of media role models for young gay guys, and I didn't know anybody who was gay, and I was worried that I was the only one. And the minute that they called me those names, I started to think "Oh my God, I'm not the only one." "There are people out here, there are people like me." And that was totally cool, that was in fact liberating. And so I kinda started trying to figure out where I could run into guys, and I kinda figured out where I could run into guys. And one thing led to another and it was all pretty fun. Well years later, years and years later. I think it was maybe even in one of my courses, at the University of North Chicago, where I did my MA and my PHD. So maybe it was Bill Cavino, or maybe it was David (. . .). And anyway we got onto the subject of naming and what people are called and the implications for naming, as an act of rhetoric. And I thought back to that story, at that moment, and I connected to that story right then. And I realized that that was the first act that I consider myself as a Rhetorician, because it's the first time that I thought of that language in that way. Not as something solid, where this word means that word, but I had actually thought about what the language means and how it operates. And what it's implications were. And if there were names for these things, then there must be things connected to these things, to these concepts. And so that's it, the more I . . . The older I get, you know, the more I think that it's naming, and language that makes us who we are. I mean, you know, there's an old Biblical story, that one of Adam's gifts and tasks and duties, was to name everything that hadn't yet had a name. It came straight out of God's mind into being, and now it needed to be called something, and that was Adam's job. So you know, we've been called The Human, one of the definitions is the Man who Laughs, another is the Man who Plays, another is Homosapiens, The Wise Ones, all those names. Some sexist, some not. For me it's those who name. That's really what we do. And that's what we do as artists, that's what we do in our lives, with metaphor. So, so I think we are the ones who name. Thanks.

Analyze

1. What lesson does Dorwick draw from his encounter with the young men in the car?
2. The young men in the car use the derogatory word *fag* to label the author. At the time, he was trying to figure out his sexuality, so how did being named this actually help him?
3. The writer uses the rhetorical mode description to share how he saw the carload of young men. How does he use this mode to show where the event took place as well as to criticize the young men?

Explore

1. By using compare and contrast, make a list of the ways that Dorwick presents the positive and negative of his experience as a young man. Share these in class.
2. The author takes a highly insensitive comment about his sexuality and seems to make us forget about the negative connotations of the experience. He turns the occurrence around and shows us the power of words and language to lead us to new understandings of the dimensions of language. Using the power of language, he took something that was intended to be destructive and turned it into something constructive in his life. Have you ever been called something negative that you turned into a positive? Or have you ever read, heard, or watched an event from a book, short story, newspaper, blog, Facebook, or movie that was intended to cause one reaction—positive or negative—and ended up causing the opposite?
3. Using Dorwick's talk as an example, and keeping in mind the fact that names have the power to bring up many emotions, argue why it is so important to be aware of the multiple ways in which words can have power.

Amy Tan
"Mother Tongue"

Tan was born in California and is the daughter of Chinese immigrants who had fled China's Cultural Revolution in the 1940s. While at one point in her life she worked to separate herself from her ethnicity, she came to realize that a combination of experiences and things make us who we are. In her case, she came to accept her Chinese side. This is embraced in her well-known novel, *The Joy Luck Club*. Below, Tan shares her language experiences growing up in an immigrant household. Through the differences of language in her home, she becomes sensitive to language manifested in different ways.

From the ways that language was used around her, how does Tan come to understand that identity and language interconnect and make us who we are?

I am not a scholar of English or literature. I cannot give you much more than personal opinions on the English language and its variations in this country or others.

I am a writer. And by that definition, I am someone who has always loved language. I am fascinated by language in daily life. I spend a great deal of my time thinking about the power of language—the way it can evoke an emotion, a visual image, a complex idea, or a simple truth. Language is the tool of my trade. And I use them all—all the Englishes I grew up with.

Recently, I was made keenly aware of the different Englishes I do use. I was giving a talk to a large group of people, the same talk I had already given to half a dozen other groups. The nature of the talk was about my writing, my life, and my book *The Joy Luck Club.* The talk was going along well enough, until I remembered one major difference that made the whole talk sound wrong. My mother was in the room. And it was perhaps the first time she had heard me give a lengthy speech, using the kind of English I have never used with her. I was saying things like "The intersection of memory upon imagination" and "There is an aspect of my fiction that relates to thus-and-thus"—speech filled with carefully wrought grammatical phrases, burdened, it suddenly seemed to me, with nominalized forms, past perfect tenses, conditional phrases, all the forms of standard English that

I had learned in school and through books, the forms of English I did not use at home with my mother.

Just last week, I was walking down the street with my mother, and I again found myself conscious of the English I was using, the English I do use with her. We were talking about the price of new and used furniture and I heard myself saying this: "Not waste money that way." My husband was with us as well, and he didn't notice any switch in my English. And then I realized why. It's because over the twenty years we've been together, I've often used that same kind of English with him, and sometimes he even uses it with me. It has become our language of intimacy, a different sort of English that relates to family talk, the language I grew up with.

5 So you'll have some idea of what this family talk I heard sounds like, I'll quote what my mother said during a recent conversation which I videotaped and then transcribed. During this conversation, my mother was talking about a political gangster in Shanghai who had the same last name as her family's, Du, and how the gangster in his early years wanted to be adopted by her family, which was rich by comparison. Later, the gangster became more powerful, far richer than my mother's family, and one day showed up at my mother's wedding to pay his respects. Here's what she said in part:

"Du Yusong having business like fruit stand. Like off the street kind. He is Du like Du Zong—but not Tsung-ming Island people. The local people call putong, the river east side, he belong to that side local people. That man want to ask Du Zong father take him in like become own family. Du Zong father wasn't look down on him, but didn't take seriously, until that man big like become a mafia. Now important person, very hard to inviting him. Chinese way, came only to show respect, don't stay for dinner. Respect for making big celebration, he shows up. Mean gives lots of respect. Chinese custom. Chinese social life that way. If too important won't have to stay too long. He come to my weddings. I didn't see, I heard it. I gone to boy's side, they have YMCA dinner. Chinese age I was nineteen."

You should know that my mother's expressive command of English belies how much she actually understands. She reads the *Forbes* report, listens to *Wall Street Week,* converses daily with her stockbroker, reads all of Shirley McLain's books with ease—all kinds of things I can't begin to understand. Yet some of my friends tell me they understand 50 percent of what my mother says. Some say they understand 80 to 90 percent. Some say they understand none of it, as if she were speaking pure Chinese. But to me, my mother's English is perfectly clear, perfectly natural. It's my mother tongue. Her language, as I hear it, is vivid, direct, full of observation and imagery. That was the language that helped shape the way I saw things, expressed things, made sense of the world.

Lately, I've been giving more thought to the kind of English my mother speaks. Like others, I have described it to people as "broken" or "fractured" English. But I wince when I say that. It has always bothered me that I can think of no way to describe it other than "broken," as if it were damaged and needed to be fixed, as if it lacked a certain wholeness and soundness. I've heard other terms used, "limited English," for example. But they seem just as bad, as if everything is limited, including people's perceptions of the limited English speaker.

I know this for a fact, because when I was growing up, my mother's "limited" English limited my perception of her. I was ashamed of her English. I believed that her English reflected the quality of what she had to say. That is, because she expressed them imperfectly her thoughts were imperfect. And I had plenty of empirical evidence to support me: the fact that people in department stores, at banks, and at restaurants did not take her seriously, did not give her good service, pretended not to understand her, or even acted as if they did not hear her.

My mother has long realized the limitations of her English as well. 10
When I was fifteen, she used to have me call people on the phone to pretend I was she. In this guise, I was forced to ask for information or even complain and yell at people who had been rude to her. One time it was a call to her stockbroker in New York. She had cashed out her small portfolio and it just so happened we were going to New York the next week, our very first trip outside California. I had to get on the phone and say in an adolescent voice that was not very convincing, "This is Mrs. Tan."

And my mother was standing in the back whispering loudly, "Why he don't send me check, already two weeks late. So mad he lie to me, losing me money."

And then I said in perfect English, "Yes, I'm getting rather concerned. You had agreed to send the check two weeks ago, but it hasn't arrived."

Then she began to talk more loudly. "What he want, I come to New York tell him front of his boss, you cheating me?" And I was trying to calm her down, make her be quiet, while telling the stockbroker, "I can't tolerate any more excuses. If I don't receive the check immediately, I am going to have to speak to your manager when I'm in New York next week." And sure enough, the following week there we were in front of this astonished stockbroker, and I was sitting there red-faced and quiet, and my mother, the real Mrs. Tan, was shouting at his boss in her impeccable broken English.

We used a similar routine just five days ago, for a situation that was far less humorous. My mother had gone to the hospital for an appointment, to find out about a benign brain tumor a CAT scan had revealed a month ago. She said she had spoken very good English, her best English, no mistakes. Still, she said, the hospital did not apologize when they said they had lost the CAT scan and she had come for nothing. She said they did not seem to have any sympathy when she told them she was anxious to know the exact diagnosis, since her husband and son had both died of brain tumors. She said they would not give her any more information until the next time and she would have to make another appointment for that. So she said she would not leave until the doctor called her daughter. She wouldn't budge. And when the doctor finally called her daughter, me, who spoke in perfect English—lo and behold—we had assurances the CAT scan would be found, promises that a conference call on Monday would be held, and apologies for any suffering my mother had gone through for a most regrettable mistake.

15 I think my mother's English almost had an effect on limiting my possibilities in life as well. Sociologists and linguists probably will tell you that a person's developing language skills are more influenced by peers. But I do think that the language spoken in the family, especially in immigrant families which are more insular, plays a large role in shaping the language of the child. And I believe that it affected my results on achievement tests, IQ tests, and the SAT. While my English skills were never judged as poor, compared to math, English could not be considered my strong suit. In grade school I did moderately well, getting perhaps B's, sometimes B-pluses, in English and scoring perhaps in the sixtieth or seventieth percentile on achievement tests. But those scores were not good enough to override the opinion that my true abilities lay in math and science, because in those areas I achieved A's and scored in the ninetieth percentile or higher.

This was understandable. Math is precise; there is only one correct answer. Whereas, for me at least, the answers on English tests were always a judgment call, a matter of opinion and personal experience. Those tests were constructed around items like fill-in-the-blank sentence completion, such as "Even though Tom was ---, Mary thought he was ---." And the correct answer always seemed to be the most bland combinations of thoughts, for example, "Even though Tom was shy, Mary thought he was charming," with the grammatical structure "even though" limiting the correct answer to some sort of semantic opposites, so you wouldn't get answers like "Even though Tom was foolish, Mary thought he was ridiculous." Well, according to my mother, there were very few limitations as to what Tom could have been and what Mary might have thought of him. So, I never did well on tests like that.

The same was true with word analogies, pairs of words in which you were supposed to find some sort of logical, semantic relationship—for example, "*Sunset* is to *nightfall* as --- is to ---." And here you would be presented with a list of four possible pairs, one of which showed the same kind of relationship: *red* is to *stoplight, bus* is to *arrival, chills* is to *fever, yawn* is to *boring*. Well, I could never think that way. I knew what the tests were asking, but I could not block out of my mind the images already created by the first pair, "*sunset* is to *nightfall*"—and I would see a burst of colors against a darkening sky, the moon rising, the lowering of a curtain of stars. And all the other pairs of words—*red, bus, stoplight, boring*—just threw up a mass of confusing images, making it impossible for me to sort out something as logical as saying: "A sunset precedes nightfall" is the same as "a chill precedes a fever." The only way I would have gotten that answer right would have been to imagine an associative situation, for example, my being disobedient and staying out past sunset, catching a chill at night, which turns into feverish pneumonia as punishment, which indeed did happen to me.

I have been thinking about all this lately, about my mother's English, about achievement tests. Because lately I've been asked, as a writer, why there are not more Asian Americans represented in American literature? Why are there few Asian Americans enrolled in creative writing programs? Why do so many Chinese students go into engineering? Well, these are broad sociological questions I can't begin to answer. But I have noticed in surveys—in fact, just last week—that Asian students, as a whole, always do significantly better on math achievement tests than in English. And this makes me think that there are other Asian American students whose English spoken in the home might also be described as "broken" or "limited." And perhaps they also have teachers who are steering them away from writing and into math and science, which is what happened to me.

Fortunately, I happen to be rebellious in nature and enjoy the challenge of disproving assumptions made about me. I became an English major my first year in college, after being enrolled as pre-med. I started writing non-fiction as a freelancer the week after I was told by my former boss that writing was my worst skill and I should hone my talents towards account management.

20 But it wasn't until 1985 that I finally began to write fiction. And at first I wrote using what I thought to be wittily crafted sentences, sentences that would finally prove I had mastery over the English language. Here's an example from the first draft of a story that later made its way into *The Joy Luck Club,* but without this line: "That was my mental quandary in its nascent state." A terrible line, which I can barely pronounce.

Fortunately, for reasons I won't get into today, I later decided I should envision a reader for the stories I would write. And the reader I decided upon was my mother, because these were stories about mothers. So with this reader in mind—and in fact she did read my early drafts—I began to write stories using all the Englishes I grew up with: the English I spoke to my mother, which for lack of a better term might be described as "simple"; the English she used with me, which for lack of a better term might be described as "broken"; my translation of her Chinese, which could certainly be described as "watered down"; and what I imagined to be her translation of her Chinese if she could speak in perfect English, her internal language, and for that I sought to preserve the essence, but neither an English nor a Chinese structure. I wanted to capture what language ability tests can never reveal: her intent, her passion, her imagery, the rhythms of her speech and the nature of her thoughts.

Apart from what any critic had to say about my writing, I knew I had succeeded where it counted when my mother finished reading my book and gave me her verdict: "So easy to read."

Analyze

1. What are the Englishes Tan speaks of?
2. What made Tan realize that her Englishes make her who she is and make her a better writer? How does she compare/contrast the Englishes in her life?
3. How did imagining an audience change Tan's approach to writing? Who was her audience?

Explore

1. What Englishes do you speak? Share some examples in the form of a story.
2. Have you ever felt uncomfortable because of the way you talk, or someone in your family? Describe the experience to your classmates and why you felt this way.

3. While growing up, Tan felt embarrassed by her mother's English, what she called broken and fractured. She also includes other labels that make her sound limited. Write about an experience you have had where you felt limited because of your way of talking, or share an experience where you made someone else feel like this, or of an example of this from something you have read or seen such as a novel, short story, or movie.

Taylor Garcia
"Could Have Done Better"

Cindy Selfe video interviewed Taylor Garcia for the Digital Archive of Literacy Narratives project, which is an online research site dedicated to collecting all sorts of literacy narratives, ranging from views about the impact of reading and writing, like this one, to music and digital literacy learning experiences. In this interview at Garcia's graduation he admits he never liked reading or writing and, in hindsight, he could have put more effort into his studies. For more on this story, go to http://daln.osu.edu/. In our selection, Taylor Garcia describes his narrative as "a story about growing up fast."

What do you think are the most important skills to have for college and your intended career?

INTERVIEWER: Can you tell me your name?

TAYLOR: Taylor Garcia.

INTERVIEWER: Talk to me about what's happening to you today and how you, you know, feel on this day.

TAYLOR: I am going through my graduating ceremony for getting my GED. And, it's exciting.

INTERVIEWER: How old are you?

TAYLOR: Seventeen

INTERVIEWER: Ok, tell me what role reading and writing has played in your life. Do you read a lot? Are you a reader or a writer?

TAYLOR: No, I actually don't like reading or writing.

INTERVIEWER: Tell me about why.

TAYLOR: I don't know. I'm good at reading and writing both, real good. I just don't like those. I'm more of a math and science guy.

INTERVIEWER: How did you come to be a math and science guy and not a reading and writing guy?

TAYLOR: I don't know. I just, ever since I started school in kindergarten, I liked math and science a lot more than reading and writing.

INTERVIEWER: Can you tell us a story about that? Like, something that happened in school or something that made you like that?

TAYLOR: I guess, I just, I like, I like excel really, really, well, really fast in math and science and I was interested in, you know, doing different things in numbers and money and just stuff like that.

INTERVIEWER: Can you tell us a story about something that you did that made you interested in math and science?

TAYLOR: No, there's not really a story.

INTERVIEWER: Ok. Can you talk to us about maybe a story about how you grew up and something that you did at home?

TAYLOR: I grew up, I like, used to play outside a lot and I never really liked school all that much. I did good but I didn't like going there, except for friends and stuff.

INTERVIEWER: Why didn't you like school?

TAYLOR: It was boring. 'Cause none of my classes were high enough for me to where, like I was always more advanced than the classes I was in. So, I got bored and I acted up and that's what led to me having to get my GED in the end.

INTERVIEWER: Did, um, so when you were bored in class, it was just too slow for you?

TAYLOR: Yeah.

INTERVIEWER: Can you remember any particular teacher or class that made you make up your mind to drop out or not to go?

TAYLOR: Uh, well no, I got in trouble in the ninth grade, well trouble started in the eighth grade. I had a drug and alcohol problem and that carried on for a while. Then I went to the ninth grade and ended up leaving that school and I had to go, I went to an in-patient treatment, and then I came out of that and went to a different school, and I ended up getting in trouble there and had to leave there too and went to a computer school, and it just wasn't cutting it for me, so I decided to leave.
INTERVIEWER: Why? How come? What was the computer school? Was that not what you wanted to do?
TAYLOR: It was just, I was not very good at, like, working on computer just sitting there and then doing something like that. It was just boring and there was no push forward or anything like that. And I had to catch the bus an hour and a half to get there. And then to work on a computer which is something that I could have done at home if I wanted to. So, I quit that and decided to get my GED.

"So, I quit that and decided to get my GED."

INTERVIEWER: And now what do you want to do with your life after graduation?
TAYLOR: Uh, I plan on going to college in the fall and getting a business degree. Or a degree in political science.
INTERVIEWER: Where do you want to go to college?
TAYLOR: Uh, I'm going to start out at Columbus State and hopefully transfer to OSU.
INTERVIEWER: And what is it that you want to study? Talk to me about why you want to study business or political science.
TAYLOR: Well I've always loved politics and what's going on in the world. I have very strong views and opinions about that. And business, like I said in the beginning, I love math and I like money and different stuff like that. I've always thought about doing realty or owning my own business or just something like that since I was a little kid.
INTERVIEWER: And can you tell me what you think of the current political state of the world?
TAYLOR: It's not good, I don't, uh, agree with the war, I don't agree with where our soldiers are and how they're being used, and how everything is going on in this world. All our money problems are all wrong.
INTERVIEWER: Do you read a lot of newspapers or listen to the news?
TAYLOR: Yeah. I listen to the news just about every day.
INTERVIEWER: And if you were president what would you do?
TAYLOR: Uh, if I were president there would be tons of different things. Um, I don't know, I can't really say. But, I would do whatever I can do to

fix the economy and put our troops in the right places, help our own country more than, I mean we've got people here starving in our own country that don't have clothes on their backs and I don't see why we send money to other countries when we have all those problems right here; diseased kids with no homes or families.

INTERVIEWER: How about funding for education?

40 **TAYLOR:** Education is important, I feel, I feel bad that I didn't go through with whole, my whole high school career because, you know, there's a lot of things you learn, not just book wise, but social wise and other things just from being in high school and what-not and, you know, going to school, it's a good thing. We need funding for school 'cause there's so many classes getting cut like art classes and music classes and those are essential, you know, growing up and getting smarter too.

INTERVIEWER: What kinds of classes do you look forward to taking in college?

TAYLOR: Um, I don't know, I don't really know. College has so many different classes to offer, I don't, I don't know; a lot of 'em.

INTERVIEWER: What kinds of things do you look forward to in college just generally?

TAYLOR: Just, college life, I am glad that I am going to be out on my own soon and trying something different. I've always heard college is so much more different than grade school. It's a lot funner. The work's harder, but it's also more interesting and all that. And that's what I've heard and that's what I look forward to.

45 **INTERVIEWER:** Tell me about, do you have any stories about your GED program and how you did in the GED program? What's that been like for you?

TAYLOR: I did real well in the GED program, and, like I said, I've been real smart really my whole life. I was the class clown, and I got in trouble and stuff, so. But the GED, I went and took the pre-test and I passed that, so I came back and took the actual GED test and I passed that in, like, half the time they gave me to do so. I don't know, I just, I actually, I didn't find the GED test hard at all.

INTERVIEWER: Do you think that the GED program is one that should be continued and supported?

TAYLOR: Oh, of course. I mean, because everybody has their own troubles, you know, inside the home, outside the home at school or somewhere else and people make mistakes and they mess up and, you know, without the GED program there's a lot of people who wouldn't be able to move on to college, you know, or have their high school diploma.

INTERVIEWER: So, you think it's pretty worthwhile?
TAYLOR: Yeah, it's worthwhile. It's a good thing that should be funded by the state.
INTERVIEWER: Thank you very much! That's excellent!
TAYLOR: Thank you!

Analyze

1. Why is Taylor averse to reading or writing, preferring math and science?
2. What was Taylor's view about school when he was growing up?
3. How does Taylor see the current state of the political world?

Explore

1. Interview two of your classmates about a literacy experience they have had. Some areas you can ask them about include the following: Who taught them to read or write, and where? How did they achieve this? Who taught them to use their first computer and software? Report your findings to the class. You might also think about recording your interviews and sharing them on the Digital Archives site.
2. The GED seems to have served as a pressure valve for Taylor; that is, he realizes he was not focused or ready in high school. In groups, discuss the pros and cons of the GED. Do you think it is a fair exam, considering the fact that most students attend four years of high school in order to earn their degree? Look into the requirements for a GED in your area so you can compare a traditional high school degree with it.
3. Taylor seems to shift focus in the interview about what his strengths and interests are and what he eventually wants to earn a degree in. Is the shifting focus of interests common among your peers in class? Based on the responses you come up with, create a Classification and Division chart of what your peers' strengths and interests are and what they eventually want to earn a degree in.

Mike Rose
"I Just Want to Be Average"

Rose, a professor in the School of Education at UCLA, is a prolific writer and has won numerous awards for his work. In his essay below, we find that his start in high school was anything but successful. From his own experience, he shows us what happens to students who are placed in classes with low expectations. "I Just Want to Be Average" comes from his book *Lives on the Boundary* (1989), a book examining the educationally underprivileged.

How do your educational experiences contrast with Rose's?

It took two buses to get to Our Lady of Mercy. The first started deep in South Los Angeles and caught me at midpoint. The second drifted through neighborhoods with trees, parks, big lawns, and lot of flowers. The rides were long but were livened up by a group of South L.A. veterans whose parents also thought that Hope had set up shop in the west end of the country. There was Christy Biggars, who, at sixteen, was dealing and was, according to rumor, a pimp as well. There were Bill Cobb and Johnny Gonzales, grease-pencil artists extraordinaire, who left Nembutal-enhanced swirls of "Cobb" and "Johnny" on the corrugated walls of the bus. And then there was Tyrrell Wilson. Tyrrell was the coolest kid I knew. He ran the dozens like a metric halfback, laid down a rap that outrhymed and outpointed Cobb, whose rap was good but not great—the curse of a moderately soulful kid trapped in white skin. But it was Cobb who would sneak a radio onto the bus, and thus underwrote his patter with Little Richard, Fats Domino, Chuck Berry, the Coasters, and Ernie K. Doe's mother-in-law, an awful woman who was "sent from down below." And so it was that Christy and Cobb and Johnny G. and Tyrrell and I and assorted others picked up along the way passed our days in the back of the bus, a funny mix brought together by geography and parental desire.

Entrance to school brings with it forms and releases and assessments. Mercy relied on a series of tests . . . for placement, and somehow the results of my tests got confused with those of another student named

Rose. The other Rose apparently didn't do very well, for I was placed in the vocational track, a euphemism for the bottom level. Neither I nor my parents realized what this meant. We had no sense that Business Math, Typing, and English-Level D were dead ends. The current spate of reports on the schools criticizes parents for not involving themselves in the education of their children. But how would someone like Tommy Rose, with his two years of Italian schooling, know what to ask? And what sort of pressure could an exhausted waitress apply? The error went undetected, and I remained in the vocational track for two years. What a place.

My homeroom was supervised by Brother Dill, a troubled and unstable man who also taught freshman English. When his class drifted away from him, which was often, his voice would rise in paranoid accusations, and occasionally he would lose control and shake or smack us. I hadn't been there two months when one of his brisk, face-turning slaps had my glasses sliding down the aisle. Physical education was also pretty harsh. Our teacher was a stubby ex-lineman who had played old-time pro ball in the Midwest. He routinely had us grabbing our ankles to receive his stinging paddle across our butts. He did that, he said, to make men of us. "Rose," he bellowed on our first encounter; me standing geeky in line in my baggy shorts. "'Rose'? What the hell kind of name is that?"

"Italian, sir," I squeaked.

"Italian! Ho. Rose, do you know the sound a bag of shit makes when it 5
hits the wall?"

"No, sir."

"*Wop!*"

Sophomore English was taught by Mr. Mitropetros. He was a large, bejeweled man who managed the parking lot at the Shrine Auditorium. He would crow and preen and list for us the stars he'd brushed against. We'd ask questions and glance knowingly and snicker, and all that fueled the poor guy to brag some more. Parking cars was his night job. He had little training in English, so his lesson plan for his day work had us reading the district's required text, *Julius Caesar,* aloud for the semester. We'd finished the play way before the twenty weeks was up, so he'd have us switch parts again and again and start again: Dave Snyder, the fastest guy at Mercy, muscling through Caesar to the breathless squeals of Calpurnia, as interpreted by Steve Fusco, a surfer who owned the school's most envied paneled wagon. Week ten and Dave and Steve would take on new roles, as would we all, and render a water-logged Cassius and a Brutus that are beyond my powers of description.

Spanish I—taken in the second year—fell into the hands of a new recruit. Mr. Montez was a tiny man, slight, five foot six at the most, soft-spoken and delicate. Spanish was a particularly rowdy class, and Mr. Montez was as prepared for it as a doily maker at a hammer throw. He would tap his pencil to a room in which Steve Fusco was propelling spitballs from his heavy lips, in which Mike Dweetz was taunting Billy Hawk, a half-Indian, half-Spanish, reed-thin, quietly explosive boy. The vocational track at Our Lady of Mercy mixed kids traveling in from South L.A. with South Bay surfers and a few Slavs and Chicanos from the harbors of San Pedro. This was a dangerous miscellany: surfers and hodads and South-Central blacks all ablaze to the metronomic tapping of Hector Montez's pencil.

10 One day Billy lost it. Out of the corner of my eye I saw him strike out with his right arm and catch Dweetz across the neck. Quick as a spasm, Dweetz was out of his seat, scattering desks, cracking Billy on the side of the head, right behind the eye. Snyder and Fusco and others broke it up, but the room felt hot and close and naked. Mr. Montez's tenuous authority was finally ripped to shreds, and I think everyone felt a little strange about that. The charade was over, and when it came down to it, I don't think any of the kids really wanted it to end this way. They had pushed and pushed and bullied their way into a freedom that both scared and embarrassed them.

Students will float to the mark you set. I and the others in the vocational classes were bobbing in pretty shallow water. Vocational education has aimed at increasing the economic opportunities of students who do not do well in our schools. Some serious programs succeed in doing that, and through exceptional teachers . . . students learn to develop hypotheses and troubleshoot, reason through a problem, and communicate effectively—the true job skills. The vocational track, however, is most often a place for those who are just not making it, a dumping ground for the disaffected. There were a few teachers who worked hard at education; young Brother Slattery, for example, combined a stern voice with weekly quizzes to try to pass along to us a skeletal outline of world history. But mostly the teachers had no idea of how to engage the imaginations of us kids who were scuttling along at the bottom of the pond.

And the teachers would have needed some inventiveness, for none of us was groomed for the classroom. It wasn't just that I didn't know things—didn't know how to simplify algebraic fractions, couldn't identify different kinds of clauses, bungled Spanish translations—but that I had developed various faulty and inadequate ways of doing algebra and making sense of Spanish. Worse yet, the years of defensive tuning out in elementary school had given me a way to escape quickly while seeming at least half alert. During my time in Voc. Ed., I developed further into a mediocre student and a somnambulant problem solver, and that affected the subjects I did have the wherewithal to handle: I detested Shakespeare; I got bored with history. My attention flitted here and there. I fooled around in class and read my books indifferently—the intellectual equivalent of playing with your food. I did what I had to do to get by, and I did it with half a mind.

But I did learn things about people and eventually came into my own socially. I liked the guys in Voc. Ed. Growing up where I did, I understood and admired physical prowess, and there was an abundance of muscle here. There was Dave Snyder, a sprinter and halfback of true quality. Dave's ability and his quick wit gave him a natural appeal, and he was welcome in any clique, though he always kept a little independent. He enjoyed acting the fool and could care less about studies, but he possessed a certain maturity and never caused the faculty much trouble. It was a testament to his independence that he included me among his friends—I eventually went out for track, but I was no jock. Owing to the Latin alphabet and a dearth of Rs and Ss, Snyder sat behind Rose, and we started exchanging one-liners and became friends.

There was Ted Richard, a much-touted Little League pitcher. He was chunky and had a baby face and came to Our Lady of Mercy as a seasoned street fighter. Ted was quick to laugh and he had a loud, jolly laugh, but when he got angry he'd smile a little smile, the kind that simply raises the corner of the mouth a quarter of an inch. For those who knew, it was an eerie signal. Those who didn't found themselves in big trouble, for Ted was very quick. He loved to carry on what we would come to call philosophical discussions: What is courage? Does God exist? He also loved words, enjoyed picking up big ones like *salubrious* and *equivocal* and using them in our conversations—laughing at himself as the word hit a chuckhole rolling off his tongue. Ted didn't do all that well in school—baseball and parties and testing the courage he'd speculated about took up his time. His textbooks were *Argosy* and *Field and Stream,* whatever newspapers he'd find on the bus stop—from the *Daily Worker* to pornography—conversations with uncles or hobos or businessmen he'd meet in a coffee shop, *The Old Man and the Sea.*

With hindsight, I can see that Ted was developing into one of those rough-hewn intellectuals whose sources are a mix of the learned and the apocryphal, whose discussions are both assured and sad.

15 And then there was Ken Harvey. Ken was good-looking in a puffy way and had a full and oily ducktail and was a car enthusiast . . . a hodad. One day in religion class, he said the sentence that turned out to be one of the most memorable of the hundreds of thousands I heard in those Voc. Ed. years. We were talking about the parable of the talents, about achievement, working hard, doing the best you can do, blah-blah-blah, when the teacher called on the restive Ken Harvey for an opinion. Ken thought about it, but just for a second, and said (with studied, minimal affect), "I just wanna be average."

That woke me up. Average? Who wants to be average? Then the athletes chimed in with the clichés that make you want to laryngectomize them, and the exchange became a platitudinous melee. At the time, I thought Ken's assertion was stupid, and I wrote him off. But his sentence has stayed with me all these years, and I think I am finally coming to understand it.

Ken Harvey was gasping for air. School can be a tremendously disorienting place. No matter how bad the school, you're going to encounter notions that don't fit with the assumptions and beliefs that you grew up with maybe you'll hear these dissonant notions from teachers, maybe from the other students, and maybe you'll read them. You'll also be thrown in with all kinds of kids from all kinds of backgrounds, and that can be unsettling—this is especially true in places of rich ethnic and linguistic mix, like the L.A. basin. You'll see a handful of students far excel you in courses that sound exotic and that are only in the curriculum of the elite: French, physics, trigonometry. And all this is happening while you're trying to shape an identity, your body is changing, and your emotions are running wild. If you're a working-class kid in the vocational track, the options you'll have to deal with this will be constrained in certain ways: you're defined by your school as "slow"; you're placed in a curriculum that isn't designed to liberate you but to occupy you, or, if you're lucky, train you, though the training is for work the society does not esteem; other students are picking up the cues from your school and your curriculum and interacting with you in particular ways. If you're a kid like Ted Richard, you turn your back on all this and let your mind roam where it may. But youngsters like Ted are rare. What Ken and so many others do is protect themselves from such suffocating madness by taking on with a vengeance the identity implied in the vocational track. Reject the confusion and frustration by openly defining yourself as the Common Joe. Champion the average. Rely on your own good sense. Fuck this bullshit. Bullshit, of course, is everything you—and the others—fear is beyond you: books, essays, tests, academic scrambling, complexity, scientific reasoning, philosophical inquiry.

The tragedy is that you have to twist the knife in your own gray matter to make this defense work. You'll have to shut down, have to reject intellectual stimuli or diffuse them with sarcasm, have to cultivate stupidity, have to convert boredom from a malady into a way of confronting the world. Keep your vocabulary simple, act stoned when you're not or act more stoned than you are, flaunt ignorance, materialize your dreams. It is a powerful and effective defense—it neutralizes the insult and the frustration of being a vocational kid and, when perfected, it drives teachers up the wall, a delightful secondary effect. But like all strong magic, it exacts a price.

My own deliverance from the Voc. Ed. world began with sophomore biology. Every student, college prep to vocational, had to take biology, and unlike the other courses, the same person taught all sections. When teaching the vocational group, Brother Clint probably slowed down a bit or omitted a little of the fundamental biochemistry, but he used the same book and more or less the same syllabus across the board. If one class got tough, he could get tougher. He was young and powerful and very handsome, and looks and physical strength were high currency. No one gave him any trouble.

I was pretty bad at the dissecting table, but the lectures and the textbook 20
were interesting: plastic overlays that, with each turned page, peeled away skin, then veins and muscle, then organs, down to the very bones that Brother Clint, pointer in hand, would tap out on our hanging skeleton. Dave Snyder was in big trouble, for the study of life—versus the living of it—was sticking in his craw. We worked out a code for our multiple-choice exams. He'd poke me in the back: once for the answer under *A*, twice for *B*, and so on; and when he'd hit the right one, I'd look up to the ceiling as though I were lost in thought. Poke: cytoplasm. Poke, poke: methane. Poke, poke, poke: William Harvey. Poke, poke, poke, poke: islets of Langerhans. This didn't work out perfectly, but Dave passed the course, and I mastered the dreamy look of a guy on a record jacket. And something else happened. Brother Clint puzzled over this Voc. Ed. kid who was racking up 98s and 99s on his tests. He checked the school's records and discovered the error. He recommended that I begin my junior year in the College Prep program.

According to all I've read since, such a shift, as one report put it, is virtually impossible. Kids at that level rarely cross tracks. The telling thing is how chancy both my placement into and exit from Voc. Ed. was; neither I nor my parents had anything to do with it. I lived in one world during spring semester, and when I came back to school in the fall, I was living in another.

Switching to College Prep was a mixed blessing. I was an erratic student. I was undisciplined. And I hadn't caught onto the rules of the game: why work hard in a class that didn't grab my fancy? I was also hopelessly behind in math. Chemistry was hard; toying with my chemistry set years before hadn't prepared me for the chemist's equations. Fortunately, the priest who taught both chemistry and second-year algebra was also the school's athletic director. Membership on the track team covered me; I knew I wouldn't get lower than a C. U.S. history was taught pretty well, and I did okay. But civics was taken over by a football coach who had trouble reading the textbook aloud—and reading aloud was the centerpiece of his pedagogy. College Prep at Mercy was certainly an improvement over the vocational program—at least it carried some status—but the social science curriculum was weak, and the mathematics and physical sciences were simply beyond me. I had a miserable quantitative background and ended up copying some assignments and finessing the rest as best I could. Let me try to explain how it feels to see again and again material you should once have learned but didn't.

You are given a problem. It requires you to simplify algebraic fractions or to multiply expressions containing square roots. You know this is pretty basic material because you've seen it for years. Once a teacher took some time with you, and you learned how to carry out these operations. Simple versions, anyway. But that was a year or two or more in the past, and these are more complex versions, and now you're not sure. And this, you keep telling yourself, is ninth- or even eighth-grade stuff.

Next it's a word problem. This is also old hat. The basic elements are as familiar as story characters: trains speeding so many miles per hour or shadows of buildings angling so many degrees. Maybe you know enough, have sat through enough explanations, to be able to begin setting up the problem: "If one train is going this fast . . ." or "This shadow is really one line of a triangle . . ." Then: "Let's see . . ." "How did Jones do this?" "Hmmmm." "No." "No, that won't work." Your attention wavers. You wonder about other things: a football game, a dance, that cute new checker at the market. You try to focus on the problem again. You scribble on paper for a while, but the tension wins out and your attention flits elsewhere. You crumple the paper and begin daydreaming to ease the frustration.

The particulars will vary, but in essence this is what a number of students go through, especially those in so-called remedial classes. They open their textbooks and see once again the familiar and impenetrable formulas and diagrams and terms that have stumped them for years. There is no excitement here. *No* excitement. Regardless of what the teacher says, this is not a new challenge. There is, rather, embarrassment and frustration and, not surprisingly, some anger in being reminded once again of long-standing inadequacies. No wonder so many students finally attribute their difficulties to something inborn, organic: "That part of my brain just doesn't work." Given the troubling histories many of these students have, it's miraculous that any of them can lift the shroud of hopelessness sufficiently to make deliverance from these classes possible.

25 Through this entire period, my father's health was deteriorating with cruel momentum. His arteriosclerosis progressed to the point where a simple nick on his shin wouldn't heal. Eventually it ulcerated and widened. Lou Minton would come by daily to change the dressing. We tried renting an oscillating bed—which we placed in the front room—to force blood through the constricted arteries in my father's legs. The bed hummed through the night, moving in place to ward off the inevitable. The ulcer continued to spread, and the doctors finally had to amputate. My grandfather had lost his leg in a stockyard accident. Now my father too was crippled. His convalescence was slow but steady, and the doctors placed him in the Santa Monica Rehabilitation Center, a sun-bleached building that opened out onto the warm spray of the Pacific. The place gave him some strength and some color and some training in walking with an artificial leg. He did pretty well for a year or so until he slipped and broke his hip. He was confined to a wheelchair after that, and the confinement contributed to the diminishing of his body and spirit.

I am holding a picture of him. He is sitting in his wheelchair and smiling at the camera. The smile appears forced, unsteady, seems to quaver, though it is frozen in silver nitrate. He is in his mid-sixties and looks eighty. Late in my junior year, he had a stroke and never came out of the resulting coma. After that, I would see him only in dreams, and to this day that is how I join him. Sometimes the dreams are sad and grisly and primal: my father lying in a bed soaked with his suppuration, holding me, rocking me. But sometimes the dreams bring him back to me healthy: him talking to me on an empty street, or buying some pictures to decorate our old house, or transformed somehow into someone strong and adept with tools and the physical.

Jack MacFarland couldn't have come into my life at a better time. My father was dead, and I had logged up too many years of scholastic indifference. Mr. MacFarland had a master's degree from Columbia and decided, at twenty-six, to find a little school and teach his heart out. He never took any credentialing courses, couldn't bear to, he said, so he had to find employment in a private system. He ended up at Our Lady of Mercy teaching five sections of senior English. He was a beatnik who was born too late. His teeth were stained, he tucked his sorry tie in between the third and fourth buttons of his shirt, and his pants were chronically wrinkled. At first, we couldn't believe this guy, thought he slept in his car. But within no time, he had us so startled with work that we didn't much worry about where he slept or if he slept at all. We wrote three or four essays a month. We read a book every two to three weeks, starting with the *Iliad* and ending up with Hemingway. He gave us a quiz on the reading every other day. He brought a prep school curriculum to Mercy High.

MacFarland's lectures were crafted, and as he delivered them he would pace the room jiggling a piece of chalk in his cupped hand, using it to scribble on the board the names of all the writers and philosophers and plays and novels he was weaving into his discussion. He asked questions often, raised everything from Zeno's paradox to the repeated last line of Frost's "Stopping by Woods on a Snowy Evening." He slowly and carefully built up our knowledge of Western intellectual history—with facts, with connections, with speculations. We learned about Greek philosophy, about Dante, the Elizabethan world view, the Age of Reason, existentialism. He analyzed poems with us, had us reading sections from John Ciardi's *How Does a Poem Mean?,* making a potentially difficult book accessible with his own explanations. We gave oral reports on poems Ciardi didn't cover. We imitated the styles of Conrad, Hemingway, and *Time* magazine. We wrote and talked, wrote and talked. The man immersed us in language.

Even MacFarland's barbs were literary. If Jim Fitzsimmons, hung over and irritable, tried to smartass him, he'd rejoin with a flourish that would spark the indomitable Skip Madison—who'd lost his front teeth in a hapless tackle—to flick his tongue through the gap and opine, "good chop," drawing out the single "0" in stinging indictment. Jack MacFarland, this tobacco-stained intellectual, brandished linguistic weapons of a kind I hadn't encountered before. Here was this *egghead,* for God's sake, keeping some pretty difficult people in line. And from what I heard, Mike Dweetz and Steve Fusco and all the notorious Voc. Ed. crowd settled down as well when MacFarland took the podium. Though a lot of guys groused in the schoolyard, it just seemed that giving trouble to this particular teacher was a silly thing to do. Tomfoolery, not to mention assault, had no place in the world he was trying to create for us, and instinctively everyone knew that. If nothing else, we all recognized MacFarland's considerable intelligence and respected the hours he put into his work. It came to this: the trouble-maker would look foolish rather than daring. Even Jim Fitzsimmons was reading *On the Road* and turning his incipient alcoholism to literary ends.

There were some lives that were already beyond Jack MacFarland's ministrations, but mine was not. I started reading again as I hadn't since elementary school. I would go into our gloomy little bedroom or sit at the dinner table while, on the television, Danny McShane was paralyzing Mr. Mota with the atomic drop, and work slowly back through *Heart of Darkness,* trying to catch the words in Conrad's sentences. I certainly was not MacFarland's best student; most of the other guys in College Prep, even my fellow slackers, had better backgrounds than I did. But I worked very hard, for MacFarland had hooked me. He tapped my old interest in reading and creating stories. He gave me a way to feel special by using my mind. And he provided a role model that wasn't shaped on physical prowess alone, and something inside me that I wasn't quite aware of responded to that. Jack MacFarland established a literacy club, to borrow a phrase of Frank Smith's, and invited—invited all of us—to join.

There's been a good deal of research and speculation suggesting that the acknowledgment of school performance with extrinsic rewards—smiling faces, stars, numbers, grades—diminishes the intrinsic satisfaction children experience by engaging in reading or writing or problem solving. While it's certainly true that we've created an educational system that encourages our best and brightest to become cynical grade collectors and, in general, have developed an obsession with evaluation and assessment, I must tell you that venal though it may have been, I loved getting good grades from MacFarland. I now know how subjective grades can be, but then they came tucked in the back of essays like bits of scientific data, some sort of spectroscopic readout that said, objectively and publicly, that I had made something of value. I suppose I'd been mediocre for too long and enjoyed a public redefinition. And I suppose the workings of my mind, such as they were, had been private for too long. My linguistic play moved into the world; . . . these papers with their circled, red B-pluses and A-minuses linked my mind to something outside it. I carried them around like a club emblem.

One day in the December of my senior year, Mr. MacFarland asked me where I was going to go to college. I hadn't thought much about it. Many of the students I teach today spent their last year in high school with a physics text in one hand and the Stanford catalog in the other, but I wasn't even aware of what "entrance requirements" were. My folks would say that they wanted me to go to college and be a doctor, but I don't know how seriously I ever took that; it seemed a sweet thing to say, a bit of supportive family chatter, like telling a gangly daughter she's graceful. The reality of higher education wasn't in my scheme of things: no one in the family had gone to college; only two of my uncles had completed high school. I figured I'd get a night job and go to the local junior college because I knew that Snyder and Company were going there to play ball. But I hadn't even prepared for that. When I finally said, "I don't know," MacFarland looked down at me—I was seated in his office—and said, "Listen, you can write."

My grades stank. I had A's in biology and a handful of B's in a few English and social science classes. All the rest were C's—or worse. MacFarland said I would do well in his class and laid down the law about doing well in the others. Still, the record for my first three years wouldn't have been acceptable to any four-year school. To nobody's surprise, I was turned down flat by USC and UCLA. But Jack MacFarland was on the case. He had received his bachelor's degree from Loyola University, so he made calls to old professors and talked to somebody in admissions and wrote me a strong letter. Loyola finally accepted me as a probationary student. I would be on trial for the first year, and if I did okay, I would be granted regular status. MacFarland also intervened to get me a loan, for I could never have afforded a private college without it. Four more years of religion classes and four more years of boys at one school, girls at another. But at least I was going to college. Amazing.

In my last semester of high school, I elected a special English course fashioned by Mr. MacFarland, and it was through this elective that there arose at Mercy a fledgling literati. Art Mitz, the editor of the school newspaper and a very smart guy, was the kingpin. He was joined by me and by Mark Dever, a quiet boy who wrote beautifully and who would die before he was forty. MacFarland occasionally invited us to his apartment, and those visits became the high point of our apprenticeship: we'd clamp on our training wheels and drive to his salon.

He lived in a cramped and cluttered place near the airport, tucked away in the kind of building that architectural critic Reyner Banham calls a *dingbat.* Books were all over: stacked, piled, tossed, and crated, underlined and dog eared, well worn and new. Cigarette ashes crusted with coffee in saucers or spilling over the sides of motel ashtrays. The little bedroom had, along two of its walls, bricks and boards loaded with notes, magazines, and oversized books. The kitchen joined the living room, and there was a stack of German newspapers under the sink. I had never seen anything like it: a great flophouse of language furnished by City Lights and Cafe Ie Metro. I read every title. I flipped through paperbacks and scanned jackets and memorized names: Gogol, *Finnegans Wake,* Djuna Barnes, Jackson Pollock, *A Coney Island of the Mind,* F. O. Matthiessen's *American Renaissance,* all sorts of Freud, *Troubled Sleep,* Man Ray, *The Education of Henry Adams,* Richard Wright, *Film as Art,* William Butler Yeats, Marguerite Duras, *Red-burn, A Season in Hell, Kapital.* On the cover of Alain-Fournier's *The Wanderer* was an Edward Gorey drawing of a young man on a road winding into dark trees. By the hotplate sat a strange Kafka novel called *Amerika,* in which an adolescent hero crosses the Atlantic to find the Nature Theater of Oklahoma. Art and Mark would be talking about a movie or the school newspaper, and I would be consuming my English teacher's library. It was heady stuff. I felt like a Pop Warner athlete on steroids. 35

Art, Mark, and I would buy stogies and triangulate from MacFarland's apartment to the Cinema, which now shows X-rated films but was then L.A.'s premier art theater, and then to the musty Cherokee Bookstore in Hollywood to hobnob with beatnik homosexuals—smoking, drinking bourbon and coffee, and trying out awkward phrases we'd gleaned from our mentor's bookshelves. I was happy and precocious and a little scared as well, for Hollywood Boulevard was thick with a kind of decadence that was foreign to the South Side. After the Cherokee, we would head back to the security of MacFarland's apartment, slaphappy with hipness.

Let me be the first to admit that there was a good deal of adolescent passion in this embrace of the avant-garde: self-absorption, sexually charged pedantry, an elevation of the odd and abandoned. Still it was a time during which I absorbed an awful lot of information: long lists of titles, images from expressionist paintings, new wave shibboleths, snippets of philosophy, and names that read like Steve Fusco's misspellings—Goethe, Nietzsche, Kierkegaard. Now this is hardly the stuff of deep understanding. But it was an introduction, a phrase book, a [travel guide] to a vocabulary of ideas, and it *felt* good at the time to know all these words. With hindsight I realize how layered and important that knowledge was.

It enabled me to do things in the world. I could browse bohemian bookstores in far-off, mysterious Hollywood; I could go to the Cinema and see events through the lenses of European directors; and, most of all, I could share an evening, talk that talk, with Jack MacFarland, the man I most admired at the time.

Knowledge was becoming a bonding agent. Within a year or two, the persona of the disaffected hipster would prove too cynical, too alienated to last. But *for* a time it was new and exciting: it provided a critical perspective on society, and it allowed me to act as though I were living beyond the limiting boundaries of South Vermont.

Analyze

1. What was Rose's bus ride like on the way to Our Lady of Mercy Catholic School?
2. What type of jobs does he mention as dead ends and why was he targeted for them?
3. What high school class caused a turning point in Rose's life and why?

Explore

1. Rose makes the comment that "Students will float to the mark you set." What does he mean by this? Apply the idea in a positive and negative way to someone you know, a character on a TV show, or to your own life.
2. Have you or someone you know ever seemed to, as Rose says, "Reject the confusion and frustration by openly defining yourself as the Common Joe"? What does this mean in terms of how we see ourselves and how others see us? Start with a list of definitions for Common Joe and how the term has been used. From the definitions and examples, create a PowerPoint (or something similar) showing the examples. Be sure to make a main point about how a label like Common Joe can serve to limit what we think we are capable of doing and being (or how we think of others).

3. Have you ever had a Mr. McFarland, someone who went that extra yard with you, who saw something in you that others did not? Or, to the contrary, have you ever had a teacher or authority figure who insisted on bringing down your sense of your abilities and your drive? Write an essay like Rose's that shows your experiences, positive or negative, while also making a point about the educational system.

Bureau of Labor Statistics, Current Population Survey (Chart)
"Education Pays: Education Pays in Higher Earnings and Lower Unemployment"

This chart from the Bureau of Labor Statistics graphically argues our earned income rises with the amount of education and number of degrees we receive.

If you printed out this chart and posted it in different places, where are some locations that it would be most effective? Least effective? Why?

Education pays in higher earnings and lower unemployment rates.

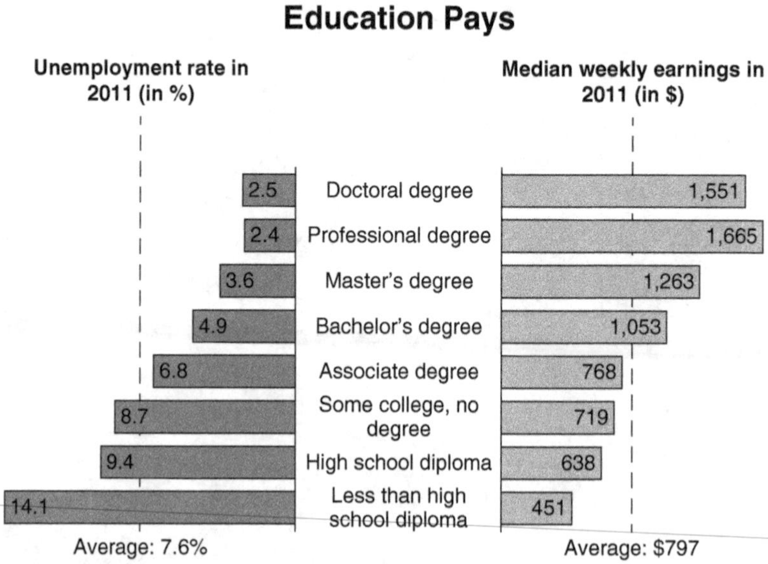

Figure 3.1 Note: Data are for persons age 25 and over. Earnings are for full-time wage and salary workers.

Source: Bureau of Labor Statistics, Current Population Survey.

Analyze

1. If you wanted to make the least amount of money you could, what degree would you strive for? How about the most money possible?
2. How effective would this chart be on the students in Rose's Vocational Education Class? How about his College Preparatory classes?
3. Run an informal survey in class to see what level of degree students in your class would like to earn. Discuss whether you want to earn a particular degree for the money or for personal interests.

Explore

1. This chart encourages earning college degrees. How do you think the salaries for technical workers, such as electricians and plumbers, and professional careers, such as firemen and policemen, fit in this chart? Research their salaries and place their earnings in a new chart that combines the Bureau of Labor Statistics findings with yours. Make sure you document your sources.
2. In addition to education, what do you think are factors that determine the income we make?
3. Using the Education Pays chart, create a poster or PowerPoint with images of people who you think fit each educational category. Also include images of their homes, cars, and lifestyles. Make sure to explain your reasons for placing the images in the categories.

Malcolm X
"Learning to Read"

Malcolm X (Malcolm Little) was convicted of robbery in 1946 and served seven years in prison. While there, he educated himself and began to follow the teachings of Elijah Muhammad. During the Civil Rights movement of the 1960s in the United States, he became one of the leading spokespersons for the Black Power movement. He was assassinated in 1965. Our excerpt, in which he describes his self-education, is from his 1965 autobiography.

What are some of the factors that made Malcolm X push for blacks to separate from whites?

It was because of my letters that I happened to stumble upon starting to acquire some kind of a homemade education.

I became increasingly frustrated. At not being able to express what I wanted to convey in letters that I wrote, especially those to Mr. Elijah Muhammad. In the street, I had been the most articulate hustler out there—I had commanded attention when I said something. But now, trying to write simple English, I not only wasn't articulate, I wasn't even functional. How would I sound writing in slang, the way I would *say* it, something such as, "Look, daddy, let me pull your coat about a cat, Elijah Muhammad—"

Many who today hear me somewhere in person, or on television, or those who read something I've said, will think I went to school far beyond the eighth grade. This impression is due entirely to my prison studies.

It had really begun back in the Charlestown Prison, when Bimbi first made me feel envy of his stock of knowledge. Bimbi had always taken charge of any conversations he was in, and I had tried to emulate him. But every book I picked up had few sentences which didn't contain anywhere from one to nearly all of the words that might as well have been in Chinese. When I just skipped those words, of course, I really ended up with little idea of what the book said. So I had come to the Norfolk Prison Colony still going through only book-reading motions. Pretty soon, I would have quit even these motions, unless I had received the motivation that I did.

5 I saw that the best thing I could do was get hold of a dictionary—to study, to learn some words. I was lucky enough to reason also that I should

try to improve my penmanship. It was sad. I couldn't even write in a straight line. It was both ideas together that moved me to request a dictionary along with some tablets and pencils from the Norfolk Prison Colony School.

I spent two days just riffling uncertainly through the dictionary's pages. I'd never realized so many words existed! I didn't know *which* words I needed to learn. Finally, just to start some kind of action, I began copying.

In my slow, painstaking, ragged handwriting, I copied into my tablet everything printed on that first page, down to the punctuation marks.

I believe it took me a day. Then, aloud, I read back, to myself, everything I'd written on the tablet. Over and over, aloud, to myself, I read my own handwriting.

I woke up the next morning, thinking about those words—immensely proud to realize that not only had I written so much at one time, but I'd written words that I never knew were in the world. Moreover, with a little effort, I also could remember what many of these words meant. I reviewed the words whose meanings I didn't remember. Funny thing, from the dictionary first page right now, that "aardvark" springs to my mind. The dictionary had a picture of it, a long-tailed, long-eared, burrowing African mammal, which lives off termites caught by sticking out its tongue as an anteater does for ants.

I was so fascinated that I went on—I copied the dictionary's next page. 10
And the same experience came when I studied that. With every succeeding page, I also learned of people and places and events from history. Actually the dictionary is like a miniature encyclopedia. Finally the dictionary's A section had filled a whole tablet—and I went on into the B's. That was the way I started copying what eventually became the entire dictionary. It went a lot faster after so much practice helped me to pick up handwriting speed. Between what I wrote in my tablet, and writing letters, during the rest of my time in prison I would guess I wrote a million words.

I suppose it was inevitable that as my word-base broadened, I could for the first time pick up a book and read and now begin to understand what the book was saying. Anyone who has read a great deal can imagine the new world that opened. Let me tell you something: from then until I left that prison, in every free moment I had, if I was not reading in the library, I was reading on my bunk. You couldn't have gotten me out of books with a wedge. Between Mr. Muhammad's teachings, my correspondence, my visitors, . . . and my reading of books, months passed without my even thinking about being imprisoned. In fact, up to then, I never had been so truly free in my life.

The Norfolk Prison Colony's library was in the school building. A variety of classes was taught there by instructors who came from such places as Harvard and Boston universities. The weekly debates between inmate teams were also held in the school building. You would be astonished to know how worked up convict debaters and audiences would get over subjects like "Should Babies Be Fed Milk?"

Available on the prison library's shelves were books on just about every general subject. Much of the big private collection that Parkhurst had willed to the prison was still in crates and boxes in the back of the library—thousands of old books. Some of them looked ancient: covers faded, old-time parchment-looking binding. Parkhurst . . . seemed to have been principally interested in history and religion. He had the money and the special interest to have a lot of books that you wouldn't have in a general circulation. Any college library would have been lucky to get that collection.

As you can imagine, especially in a prison where there was heavy emphasis on rehabilitation, an inmate was smiled upon if he demonstrated an unusually intense interest in books. There was a sizable number of well-read inmates, especially the popular debaters. Some were said by many to be practically walking encyclopedias. They were almost celebrities. No university would ask any student to devour literature as I did when this new world opened to me, of being able to read and *understand*.

15 I read more in my room than in the library itself. An inmate who was known to read a lot could check out more than the permitted maximum number of books. I preferred reading in the total isolation of my own room.

When I had progressed to really serious reading, every night at about ten P.M. I would be outraged with the "lights out." It always seemed to catch me right in the middle of something engrossing. Fortunately, right outside my door was a corridor light that cast a glow into my room. The glow was enough to read by, once my eyes adjusted to it. So when "lights out" came, I would sit on the floor where I could continue reading in that glow.

At one-hour intervals at night guards paced past every room. Each time I heard the approaching footsteps, I jumped into bed and feigned sleep. And as soon as the guard passed, I got back out of bed onto the floor area of that light-glow, where I would read for another fifty-eight minutes until the guard approached again. That went on until three or four every morning. Three or four hours of sleep a night was enough for me. Often in the years in the streets I had slept less than that.

The teachings of Mr. Muhammad stressed how history had been "whitened"—when white men had written history books, the black man simply had been left out. Mr. Muhammad couldn't have said anything that would have struck me much harder. I had never forgotten how when my class, me and all of those whites, had studied seventh-grade United States history back in Mason, the history of the Negro had been covered in one paragraph, and the teacher had gotten a big laugh with his joke, "Negroes' feet are so big that when they walk, they leave a hole in the ground."

This is one reason why Mr. Muhammad's teachings spread so swiftly all over the United States, among *all* Negroes, whether or not they became followers of Mr. Muhammad. The teachings ring true to every Negro. You can hardly show me a black adult in America—or a white one, for that matter—who knows from the history books anything like the truth about the black man's role. In my own case, once I heard of the "glorious history of the black man," I took special pains to hunt in the library for books that would inform me on details about black history.

I can remember accurately the very first set of books that really impressed me. I have since bought that set of books and I have it at home for my children to read as they grow up. It's called *Wonders of the World*. It's full of pictures of archeological finds, statues that depict, usually, non-European people.

I found books like Will Durant's *Story of Civilization*. I read H. G. Wells' *Outline of History*. *Souls of Black Folk* by W. E. B. Du Bois gave me a glimpse into the black people's history before they came to this country. Carter G. Woodson's *Negro History* opened my eyes about black empires before the black slave was brought to the United States, and the early Negro struggles for freedom.

J. A. Rogers' three volumes of *Sex and Race* told about race-mixing before Christ's time; and Aesop being a black man who told fables; about Egypt's Pharaohs; about the great Coptic Christian Empire; about Ethiopia, the earth's oldest continuous black civilization, as China is the oldest continuous civilization.

Mr. Muhammad's teaching about how the white man had been created led me to *Findings in Genetics*, by Gregor Mendel. (The dictionary's G section was where I had learned what "genetics" meant.) I really studied this book by the Austrian monk. Reading it over and over, especially certain sections, helped me to understand that if you started with a black man, a white man could be produced; but starting with a white man, you never could produce a black man—because the white chromosome is recessive. And since no one disputes that there was but one Original Man, the conclusion is clear.

During the last year or so, in the *New York Times,* Arnold Toynbeell used the word "bleached" in describing the white man. His words were: "White (i.e., bleached) human beings of North European origin . . ." Toynbee also referred to the European geographic area as only a peninsula of Asia. He said there was no such thing as Europe. And if you look at the globe, you will see for yourself that America is only an extension of Asia. (But at the same time Toynbee is among those who have helped to bleach history. He has written that Africa was the only continent that produced no history. He won't write that again. Every day now, the truth is coming to light.)

I never will forget how shocked I was when I began reading about slavery's total horror. It made such an impact upon me that it later became one of my favorite subjects when I became a minister of Mr. Muhammad's. The world's most monstrous crime, the sin and the blood on the white man's hands, are almost impossible to believe. Books like the one by Frederick Olmsted opened my eyes to the horrors suffered when the slave was landed in the United States. The European woman, Fanny Kemble, who had married a Southern white slaveowner, described how human beings were degraded. Of course I read *Uncle Tom's Cabin.* In fact, I believe that's the only novel I have ever read since I started serious reading.

Parkhurst's collection also contained some bound pamphlets of the Abolitionist Anti-Slavery Society of New England. I read descriptions of atrocities, saw those illustrations of black slave women tied up and flogged with whips; of black mothers watching their babies being dragged off, never to be seen by their mothers again; of dogs after slaves, and of the fugitive slave catchers, evil white men with whips and clubs and chains and guns. I read about the slave preacher Nat Turner, who put the fear of God into the white slave master. Nat Turner wasn't going around preaching pie-in-the-sky and "non-violent" freedom for the black man. There in Virginia one night in 1831, Nat and seven other slaves started out at his master's home and through the night they went from one plantation "big house" to the next, killing, until by the next morning 57 white people were dead and Nat had about 70 slaves following him. White people, terrified for their lives, fled from their homes, locked themselves up in public buildings, hid in the woods, and some even left the state. A small army of soldiers took two months to catch and hang Nat Turner. Somewhere I have read where Nat Turner's example is said to have inspired John Brown to invade Virginia and attack Harpers Ferry nearly thirty years later, with thirteen white men and five Negroes.

I read Herodotus, "the father of History," or, rather, I read about him. And I read the histories of various nations, which opened my eyes gradually, then wider and wider, to how the whole world's white men had indeed acted like devils, pillaging and raping and bleeding and draining the whole world's non-white people. I remember, for instance, books such as Will Durant's *The Story of Oriental Civilization,* and Mahatma Gandhi's accounts of the struggle to drive the British out of India.

Book after book showed me how the white man had brought upon the world's black, brown, red, and yellow peoples every variety of the suffering of exploitation. I saw how since the sixteenth century, the so-called "Christian trader" white man began to ply the seas in his lust for Asian and African empires, and plunder, and power. I read, I saw, how the white man never has gone among the non-white peoples bearing the Cross in the true manner and spirit of Christ's teachings—meek, humble, and Christlike.

I perceived, as I read, how the collective white man had been actually nothing but a piratical opportunist who used Faustian machinations to make his own Christianity his initial wedge in criminal conquests. First, always "religiously," he branded "heathen" and "pagan" labels upon ancient non-white cultures and civilizations. The stage thus set, he then turned upon his non-white victims his weapons of war.

I read how, entering India—half a *billion* deeply religious brown 30
people—the British white man, by 1759, through promises, trickery, and manipulations, controlled much of India through Great Britain's East India Company. The parasitical British administration kept tentacling out to half of the sub-continent. In 1857, some of the desperate people of India finally mutinied—and, excepting the African slave trade, nowhere has history recorded any more unnecessary bestial and ruthless human carnage than the British suppression of the non-white Indian people.

Over 115 million African blacks—close to the 1930's population of the United States—were murdered or enslaved during the slave trade. And I read how when the slave market was glutted, the cannibalistic white powers of Europe next carved up, as their colonies, the richest areas of the black continent. And Europe's chancelleries for the next century played a chess game of naked exploitation and power from Cape Horn to Cairo.

Ten guards and the warden couldn't have torn me out of those books. Not even Elijah Muhammad could have been more eloquent than those books were in providing indisputable proof that the collective white man had acted like a devil in virtually every contact he had with the world's collective non-white man. I listen today to the radio, and watch television, and read the headlines about the collective white man's fear and tension concerning China. When the white man professes ignorance about why the Chinese hate him so, my mind can't help flashing back to what I read, there in prison, about how the blood forebears of this same white man raped China at a time when China was trusting and helpless. Those original white "Christian traders" sent into China millions of pounds of opium. By 1839, so many of the Chinese were addicts that China's desperate government destroyed twenty thousand chests of opium. The first Opium war was promptly declared by the white man. Imagine! Declaring *war* upon someone who objects to being narcotized! The Chinese were severely beaten, with Chinese-invented gunpowder.

The Treaty of Nanking made China pay the British white man for the destroyed opium; forced open China's major ports to British trade; forced China to abandon Hong Kong; fixed China's import tariffs so low that cheap British articles soon flooded in, maiming China's industrial development.

After a second Opium War, the Tientsin Treaties legalized the ravaging opium trade, legalized a British-French-American control of China's customs. China tried delaying that Treaty's ratification; Peking was looted and burned.

"Kill the foreign white devils!" was the 1901 Chinese war cry in the Boxer Rebellion. Losing again, this time the Chinese were driven from Peking's choicest areas. The vicious, arrogant white man put up the famous signs, "Chinese and dogs not allowed."

Red China after World War II closed its doors to the Western white world. Massive Chinese agricultural, scientific, and industrial efforts are described in a book that *Life* magazine recently published. Some observers inside Red China have reported that the world never has known such a hate-white campaign as is now going on in this non-white country where, present birth-rates continuing, in fifty more years Chinese will be half the earth's population. And it seems that some Chinese chickens will soon come home to roost, with China's recent successful nuclear tests.

Let us face reality. We can see in the United Nations a new world order being shaped, along color lines—an alliance among the non-white nations. America's U.N. Ambassador Adlai Stevenson complained not long ago that in the United Nations "a skin game" was being played. He was right. He was facing reality. A "skin game" is being played. But Ambassador Stevenson sounded like Jesse James accusing the marshal of carrying a gun. Because who in the world's history ever has played a worse "skin game" than the white man?

Mr. Muhammad, to whom I was writing daily, had no idea of what a new world had opened up to me through my efforts to document his teachings in books.

When I discovered philosophy, I tried to touch all the landmarks of philosophical development. Gradually, I read most of the old philosophers, Occidental and Oriental. The Oriental philosophers were the ones I came to prefer; finally, my impression was that most Occidental philosophy had largely been borrowed from the Oriental thinkers. Socrates, for instance, traveled in Egypt. Some sources even say that Socrates was initiated into some of the Egyptian mysteries. Obviously Socrates got some of his wisdom among the East's wise men.

I have often reflected upon the new vistas that reading opened to me. I knew right there in prison that reading had changed forever the course of my life. As I see it today, the ability to read awoke inside me some long dormant craving to be mentally alive. I certainly wasn't seeking any degree, the way a college confers a status symbol upon its students. My homemade education gave me, with every additional book that I read, a little bit more sensitivity to the deafness, dumbness, and blindness that was afflicting the black race in America. Not long ago, an English writer telephoned me from London, asking questions. One was, "What's your alma mater?" I told him, "Books." You will never catch me with a free fifteen minutes in which I'm not studying something I feel might be able to help the black man.

Yesterday I spoke in London, and both ways on the plane across the Atlantic I was studying a document about how the United Nations proposes to insure the human rights of the oppressed minorities of the world. The American black man is the world's most shameful case of minority oppression. What makes the black man think of himself as only an internal United States issue is just a catch-phrase, two words, "civil rights." How is the black man going to get "civil rights" before first he wins his *human* rights? If the American black man will start thinking about his *human* rights, and then start thinking of himself as part of one of the world's great peoples, he will see he has a case for the United Nations.

I can't think of a better case! Four hundred years of black blood and sweat invested here in America, and the white man still has the black man begging for what every immigrant fresh off the ship can take for granted the minute he walks down the gangplank.

But I'm digressing. I told the Englishman that my alma mater was books, a good library. Every time I catch a plane, I have with me a book that I want to read—and that's a lot of books these days. If I weren't out here every day battling the white man, I could spend the rest of my life reading, just satisfying my curiosity—because you can hardly mention anything I'm not curious about. I don't think anybody ever got more out of going to prison than I did. In fact, prison enabled me to study far more intensively than I would have if my life had gone differently and I had attended some college. I imagine that one of the biggest troubles with colleges is there are too many distractions, too much panty-raiding, fraternities, and boola-boola and all of that. Where else but in a prison could I have attacked my ignorance by being able to study intensely sometimes as much as fifteen hours a day?

Analyze

1. What motivated Malcolm X to learn to read and write?
2. What pedagogy does he use to increase his vocabulary and penmanship?
3. What does Malcolm X mean when he says from his prison cell that "I never had been so truly free in my life"?

Explore

1. Rodriguez tells us that reading and the scholarly world seemed to be full of alienation and conflict. How does Malcolm X's experience differ from his?
2. We have all doubted and struggled with school and life at times like Malcolm X. Write about some of your experiences of these times, making sure to discover and share what helped you or motivated you to get through your tough stretch.

3. Malcolm X's journey and motivation to self-education is inspirational, considering he was in jail. Make a list of five intellectual things you would like to be better at or learn and the reasons why. Pick one of the items on the list and write an essay on how you are going to become better at it through self-education.

Studs Terkel
"Stephen Cruz"

Studs Terkel was well known on many fronts, but he was best known as an author of oral histories of common Americans, from which he published many books, including *Working, Division Street,* and *Hard Times.* This excerpt is an example of one of his oral histories focused on working life in America. In this piece we learn about the negative effects workplace racial profiling can have.

How do you feel about this Mexican-American worker's experiences? Do you feel we all need to modify our definitions and notions of what success means?

He is thirty-nine.

"The family came in stages from Mexico. Your grandparents usually came first, did a little work, found little roots, put together a few bucks, and brought the family in, one at a time. Those were the days when controls at the border didn't exist as they do now."

You just tried very hard to be whatever it is the system wanted of you. I was a good student and, as small as I was, a pretty good athlete. I was well liked, I thought. We were fairly affluent, but we lived down where all the trashy whites were. It was the only housing we could get. As kids, we never understood why. We did everything right. We didn't have those Mexican accents, we were never on welfare. Dad wouldn't be on welfare to save his soul. He woulda died first. He worked during the depression. He carries that pride with him, even today.

Of the five children, I'm the only one who really got into the business world. We learned quickly that you have to look for opportunities and add things up very quickly. I was in liberal arts, but as soon as Sputnik went up, well, golly, hell, we knew where the bucks were. I went right over to the registrar's office and signed up for engineering. I got my degree in '62. If you had a master's in business as well, they were just paying all kinds of bucks. So that's what I did. Sure enough, the market was super. I had fourteen job offers. I could have had a hundred if I wanted to look around.

5 I never once associated these offers with my being a minority. I was aware of the Civil Rights Act of 1964, but I was still self-confident enough to feel they wanted me because of my abilities. Looking back, the reason I got more offers than the other guys was because of the government edict. And I thought it was because I was so goddamned brilliant (Laughs). In 1962, I didn't get as many offers as those who were less qualified. You have a tendency to blame the job market. You just don't want to face the issue of discrimination.

I went to work with Procter & Gamble. After about two years, they told me I was one of the best supervisors they ever had and they were gonna promote me. Okay, I went into personnel. Again, I thought it was because I was such a brilliant guy. Now I started getting wise to the ways of the American Dream. My office was glass-enclosed, while all the other offices were enclosed so you couldn't see into them. I was the visible man.

They made sure I interviewed most of the people that came in. I just didn't really think there was anything wrong until we got a new plant manager, a southerner. I received instructions from him on how I should interview blacks. Just check and see if they smell, okay? That was the beginning of my training program. I started asking: Why weren't we hiring more minorities? I realized I was the only one in a management position.

I guess as a Mexican I was more acceptable because I wasn't really black. I was a good compromise. I was visibly good. I hired a black secretary, which was *verboten*. When I came back from my vacation, she was gone. My boss fired her while I was away. I asked why and never got a good reason.

Until then, I never questioned the American Dream. I was convinced if you worked hard, you could make it. I never considered myself different. That was the trouble. We had been discriminated against a lot, but I never associated it with society. I considered it an individual matter. Bad people, my mother used to say. In '68 I began to question.

10 I was doing fine. My very first year out of college, I was making twelve thousand dollars. I left Procter & Gamble because I really saw no opportunity. They were content to leave me visible, but my thoughts were not really solicited. I may have overreacted a bit, with the plant manager's attitude, but I felt there's no way a Mexican could get ahead here.

I went to work for Blue Cross. It's 1969. The Great Society is in full swing. Those who never thought of being minorities before are being turned on. Consciousness raising is going on. Black programs are popping up in universities. Cultural identity and all that. But what about the one issue in this country: economics? There were very few management jobs for minorities, especially blacks.

The stereotypes popped up again. If you're Oriental, you're real good in mathematics. If you're Mexican, you're a happy guy to have around, pleasant but emotional. Mexicans are either sleeping or laughing all the time. Life is just one big happy kind of event. *Mañana.* Good to have as part of the management team, as long as you weren't allowed to make decisions.

I was thinking there were two possibilities why minorities were not making it in business. One was deep, ingrained racism. But there was still the possibility that they were simply a bunch of bad managers who just couldn't cut it. You see, until now I believed everything I was taught about the dream: The American businessman is omnipotent and fair. If we could show these turkeys there's money to be made in hiring minorities, these businessmen—good managers, good decision makers—would respond. I naïvely thought American businessmen gave a damn about society, that given a choice they would do the right thing. I had that faith.

I was hungry for learning about decision-making criteria. I was still too far away from top management to see exactly how they were working. I needed to learn more. Hey, just learn more and you'll make it. That part of the dream hadn't left me yet. I was still clinging to the notion of work your ass off, learn more than anybody else, and you'll get in that sphere.

During my fifth year at Blue Cross, I discovered another flaw in the 15
American Dream. Minorities are as bad to other minorities as whites are to minorities. The strongest weapon the white manager had is the old divide and conquer routine. My mistake was thinking we were all at the same level of consciousness.

I had attempted to bring together some blacks with the other minorities. There weren't too many of them anyway. The Orientals never really got involved. The blacks misunderstood what I was presenting, perhaps I said it badly. They were on the cultural kick: a manager should be crucified for saying "Negro" instead of "black." I said as long as the Negro or the black gets the job, it doesn't mean a damn what he's called. We got into a huge hassle. Management, of course, merely smiled. The whole struggle fell flat on its face. It crumpled from divisiveness. So I learned another lesson. People have their own agenda. It doesn't matter what group you're with, there is a tendency to put the other guy down regardless.

The American Dream began to look so damn complicated, I began to think: Hell, if I wanted, I could just back away and reap the harvest myself.

By this time, I'm up to twenty-five thousand dollars a year. It's beginning to look good, and a lot of people are beginning to look good. And they're saying: "Hey, the American Dream, you got it. Why don't you lay off?" I wasn't falling in line.

My bosses were telling me I had all the "ingredients" for top management. All that was required was to "get to know our business." This term comes up all the time. If I could just warn all minorities and women whenever you hear "get to know our business," they're really saying "fall in line." Stay within that fence, and glory can be yours. I left Blue Cross disillusioned. They offered me a director's job at thirty thousand dollars before I quit.

All I had to do was behave myself. I had the "ingredients" of being the Chicano, the equivalent of the good nigger. I was smart. I could articulate well. People didn't know by my speech patterns that I was of Mexican heritage. Some tell me I don't look Mexican, that I have a certain amount of Italian, Lebanese, or who knows. (Laughs.)

20 One could easily say: "Hey, what's your bitch? The American Dream has treated you beautifully. So just knock it off and quit this crap you're spreading around." It was a real problem. Every time I turned around, America seemed to be treating me very well.

Hell, I even thought of dropping out, the hell with it. Maybe get a job in a factory. But what happened? Offers kept coming in. I just said to myself: God, isn't this silly? You might as well take the bucks and continue looking for the answer. So I did that. But each time I took the money, the conflict in me got more intense, not less.

Wow, I'm up to thirty-five thousand a year. This is a savings and loan business. I have faith in the executive director. He was the kind of guy I was looking for in top management: understanding, humane, also looking for the formula. Until he was up for consideration as executive V.P. of the entire organization. All of a sudden everything changed. It wasn't until I saw this guy flip-flop that I realized how powerful vested interests are. Suddenly he's saying: "Don't rock the boat. Keep a low profile. Get in line." Another disappointment.

Subsequently, I went to work for a consulting firm. I said to myself: Okay, I've got to get close to the executive mind. I need to know how they work. Wow, a consulting firm.

Consulting firms are saving a lot of American businessmen. They're doing it in ways that defy the whole notion of capitalism. They're not allowing these businesses to fail. Lockheed was successful in getting U.S. funding guarantees because of the efforts of consulting firms working on their behalf, helping them look better. In this kind of work, you don't find minorities. You've got to be a proven success in business before you get there.

The American dream, I see now, is governed not by education, opportu- 25
nity, and hard work, but by power and fear. The higher up in the organization you go, the more you have to lose. The dream is *not losing*. This is the notion pervading American today: Don't lose.

When I left the consulting business, I was making fifty-five thousand dollars a year. My last performance appraisal was: You can go a long way in this business, you can be a partner, but you gotta know our business. It came up again. At this point, I was incapable of being disillusioned any more. How easy it is to be swallowed up by the same set of values that governs the top guy. I was becoming that way. I was becoming concerned about losing that fifty grand or so a year. So I asked other minorities who had it made. I'd go up and ask 'em: "Look, do you owe anything to others?" the answer was: "We owe nothing to anybody." They drew from the civil rights movement but felt no debt. They've quickly forgotten how it happened. It's like I was when I first got out of college. Hey, it's really me, I'm great. I'm as angry with these guys as I am with the top guys.

Right now, it's confused. I've had fifteen years in the business world as "a success." Many Anglos would be envious of my progress. Fifty thousand dollars a year puts you in the one or two top percent of all Americans. Plus my wife making another thirty thousand. We had lots of money. When I gave it up, my cohorts looked at me not just as strange, but as something of a traitor. "You're screwing it up for all of us. You're part of our union, we're the elite, we should govern. What the hell are you doing?" So now I'm looked at suspiciously by my peer group as well.

I'm teaching at the University of Wisconsin at Platteville. It's nice. My colleagues tell me what's on their minds. I got a farm next-door to Platteville. With farm prices being what they are (laughs), it's a losing proposition. But with university work and what money we've saved, we're going to be all right.

The American Dream is getting more elusive. The dream is being governed by a few people's notion of what the dream is. Sometimes I feel it's a small group of financiers that gets together once a year and decides all the world's issues.

30 It's getting so big. The small-business venture is not there anymore. Business has become too big to influence. It can't be changed internally. A counterpower is needed.

Analyze

1. What kind of degree did Cruz get and why?
2. What types of discrimination does Cruz feel he has experienced?
3. What did Cruz do that was *verboten?*

Explore

1. In several of the essays in this chapter the writers are looking for a version of the American Dream. Some "make it," and some are still trying. Write a letter to Cruz telling him two of the other stories from this chapter (or if you know of another include it) so that he will see that others have had his challenges and have learned to cope with them.
2. Interview someone who is in a position that you would like to have when you are done with your degree. Find out what they experienced on their path toward that position and how they feel now that they are there. See whether they experienced any of the types of discrimination that Cruz experienced. Write up your results in the form of a story like Terkel did with Cruz.
3. Many people dream of the successes that Cruz had in his career. Of course, he has had challenges and issues that have tapered the effect of his successes. Write an essay about what Cruz's concerns are and suggest what might be done to eliminate some of these concerns in the future, or produce a PowerPoint telling of the negative effects of job profiling. Your audience is a room full of corporate human resources employees.

Stephen Marche
"We Are Not All Created Equal: The Truth about the American Class System"

Marche is a novelist and mainstream writer. His first novel, *Raymond and Hannah*, was published in 2005, and his second, *Shining at the Bottom of the Sea*, in 2007. His *Esquire* monthly column, "A Thousand Words about Our Culture," was a finalist for columns and commentary award by the American Society of Magazine Editors. His articles can also be read in the *New York Times* and the *Atlantic*. *We Are Not All Created Equal* argues that some of the old factors that determined wealth, such as race and gender, are now clearly determined by class.

Marche's argument is a sobering one. Was his intent to merely inform us, make us angry, wake us up from our delusion of the American Dream, or something else?

There are some truths so hard to face, so ugly and so at odds with how we imagine the world should be, that nobody can accept them. Here's one: It is obvious that a class system has arrived in America—a recent study of the thirty-four countries in the Organization for Economic Cooperation and Development found that only Italy and Great Britain have less social mobility. But nobody wants to admit: If your daddy was rich, you're gonna stay rich, and if your daddy was poor, you're gonna stay poor. Every instinct in the American gut, every institution, every national symbol, runs on the idea that anybody can make it; the only limits are your own limits. Which is an amazing idea, a gift to the world—just no longer true. Culturally, and in their daily lives, Americans continue to glide through a ghostly land of opportunity they can't bear to tell themselves isn't real. It's the most dangerous lie the country tells itself.

More than anything else, class now determines Americans' fates. The old inequalities—racism, sexism, homophobia—are increasingly antiquated. Women are threatening to overwhelm men in the workplace, and the utter collapse of the black lower middle class in the age of Obama—a catastrophe for the African-American community—has little to do with prejudice and everything to do with brute economics. Who wins and who loses has become simplified, purified: those who own and those who don't. Meanwhile Great Britain, the source of the class system, has returned, plain and simple, to its old aristocratic masters. Reverting to type, the overlords and the underclass seem little removed from their eighteenth-century predecessors. The overlords preach shared sacrifice from their palaces and the underclass riots and the middle classes quietly judge. Everybody knows where he stands.

Not in America. In the United States, the emerging aristocracy remains staunchly convinced that it is not an aristocracy, that it's the result of hard work and talent. The permanent working poor refuse to accept that their poverty is permanent. The class system is clandestine. And yet the most cherished dreams are the hardest to awaken from. The best-made shows on television now—some of the most beautifully shot, most beautifully articulated television shows ever made—capture in achingly precise detail the era that economists call the Great Compression, that shimmering, virtuous period before the 1970s when the middle class swelled so much that it came to believe it could never stop swelling—the original dangerous illusion. *Pan Am* is an unlikely parable of American fluidity. Being stuck in a tube in the air, serving coffee, and having your ass grabbed achieves glamour by virtue of the characters' ease of movement. Don Draper is a new Gatsby—he transforms himself from penniless vet to salesclerk to partner in an ad firm. Meanwhile, in Sitcomland, *Modern Family* has replaced working-class heroes like Homer Simpson and Ralph Kramden with the top 1 percent, and yet everyone, including the audience, seems to accept them as representative.

Meaningful, substantive approaches to class are going to have to come from elsewhere. This month, the second season of *Downton Abbey* returns to PBS, and we may as well all have a look, because if we are going to have a European-style class system, we better begin to import their values. The scenery is extremely lovely. The arrangements are very cozy. British aristocrats always look like they're daring the world to line them all up against a wall and erase the entire parasitical group of them, but at Downton, at least, the ruling class is somewhat aware of the arbitrary nature of its status. The American ruling class could learn from their humility. At Downton Abbey, where everyone has a place, at least the boy who cleans the boots and knives isn't a bad person because his job.

Herman Cain's comment in a recent interview on the Occupy Wall 5
Street movement, which is by no means an uncommon opinion, was this: "If you're not rich, blame yourself." The old Calvinist strain that connects prosperity to divine election runs deep. Work hard and stay late and you get to be a banker or doctor; drop out of high school or start using drugs and you'll end up at McDonald's. Even among liberals, the new trend toward behavioral economics demonstrates how poor people fare worse on tests requiring self-control, how their personal weaknesses create cycles of poverty. You don't have to be on talk radio to believe that the poor must be doing something wrong.

The Great Outcry that has filled the country with inchoate rage is the bloody mess of this fundamental belief in the justice of American outcomes crashing headfirst into the new reality. The majority of new college grads in the United States today are either unemployed or working jobs that don't require a degree. Roughly 85 percent of them moved back home in 2011, where they sit on an average debt of $27,200. The youth unemployment rate in general is 18.1 percent. Are these all bad people? None of us—not Generation Y, not Generation X, and certainly not the Boomers—have ever faced anything like it. The Tea Partiers blame the government. The Occupiers blame the financial industry. Both are really mourning the arrival of a new social order, one not defined by opportunity but by preexisting structures of wealth. At least the ranters are mourning. Those who are not screaming or in drum circles mostly pretend that the change isn't happening.

Post-hope, it is hard to imagine even any temporary regression back to the days of the swelling American middle class. The forces of inequality are simply too powerful and the forces against inequality too weak. But at least we can end the hypocrisy. In ten years, the next generation will no longer have the faintest illusion that the United States is a country with equality of opportunity. The least they're entitled to is some honesty about why.

Analyze

1. What two countries have less social mobility than the United States?
2. What percent of college graduates moved back home in 2011, and what is their average debt?
3. What are three of the television shows Marche mentions and how does he use them as examples?

Explore

1. Marche says, "In the United States, the emerging aristocracy remains staunchly convinced that it is not an aristocracy, that it's the result of hard work and talent. The permanent working poor refuse to accept that their poverty is permanent. The class system is clandestine." Create a comic that develops this argument.
2. In groups pick a few TV shows you watch or a couple recent movies and create a taxonomy of how rich and poor people are characterized, in the ways they behave and how they got where they are (rich or poor). Once done with the taxonomy, survey the class to see if they feel the characters from the classes reflect how they see them, that is, as representative.
3. Marche's argument is that if we are born rich, we stay that way, and if born poor, we remain this way. Write a researched essay in which you agree or disagree with him.

Devon W. Carbado and Miti Gulati
"Working Identity"

Carbado is a law professor at UCLA. He is the recipient of the Law School's Rutter Award for Excellence in Teaching, the Eby Award for the Art of Teaching, and the inaugural recipient of the Fletcher Foundation Fellowship, awarded to scholars whose work supports the goals of *Brown v. Board of Education*. He is coeditor of *Race Law Stories* and is coauthor of *Acting White? Rethinking Race in Post-Racial America*. Gulati is a law professor at Duke University. He has authored articles in journals such as the *Tulane Law Review*, the *University of Missouri Law Review*, the *Maine Law Review*, *Law and Contemporary Problems*, *Law and Social Inquiry*, *European Business Organization Law Review*, and *International Review of Law & Economics*. He is coauthor of two books, *The 3 1/2 Minute Transaction: Boilerplate and the Limits of Contract Design*, and *Acting White? Rethinking Race in Post-Racial America*. In our reading from *Acting White?* the authors argue blacks play secondary roles in a play—their workplaces/school admissions, politics—to avoid social hardships and to gain something from it.

From the readings from this chapter, do you think any of the writers' experiences fit what Carbado and Gulati describe?

Being an African American in a predominantly white institution is like being an actor on stage. There are roles one has to perform, storylines one is expected to follow, and dramas and subplots one should avoid at all cost. Being an African American in a predominantly white institution is like playing a small but visible part in a racially specific script. The main characters are white. There are one or two blacks in supporting roles. Survival is always in question. The central conflict is to demonstrate that one is black enough from the perspective of the supporting cast and white enough from the perspective of the main characters. The "double bind" racial performance is hard and risky. Failure is always just around the corner. And there is no acting school in which to enroll to rehearse the part.

Yet, blacks working in white institutions act out versions of this "double bind" racial performance every day. It is part of a broader phenomenon that we call "Working Identity." Working Identity is constituted by a range of racially associated ways of being, including how one dresses, speaks, styles one's hair; one's professional and social affiliations; who one marries or dates; one's politics and views about race; where one lives; and so on and so forth. The foregoing function as a set of racial criteria people can employ to ascertain not simply whether a person is black in terms of how she looks but whether that person is black in terms of how she is perceived to act. In this sense, Working Identity refers both to the perceived choices people make about their self-presentation (the racially associated ways of being listed above) and to the perceived identity that emerges from those choices (how black we determine a person to be).

Paying attention to Working Identity is important. Few institutions today refuse to hire any African Americans. Law expressly prohibits that form of discrimination and society frowns upon it. Indeed, most institutions profess a commitment to diversity, so much so that "diversity is good for business" is now a standard corporate slogan. Companies that invoke that mantra will have at least one black face on the company brochure or website. Moreover, employers want to think of themselves as "colorblind." That perception is hard to sell if all the employees are white. Finally, to the extent that there are some blacks in the workplace, the employer can use them as a shield against charges of racism or racial insensitivity: "How can you say we are racist. Obviously, we wouldn't adopt a policy that would hurt our African American colleagues."

The reality today, therefore, is that most firms want to hire *some* African Americans. The question is, which ones? Working Identity provides a basis upon which they can do so. Employers can screen their application pool for African Americans with palatable Working Identities. These African Americans are not "too black"—which is to say, they are not racially salient as African Americans. Some of them might even be "but for" African Americans—"but for" the fact that they look black, they are otherwise indistinguishable from whites. From an employer's perspective, this subgroup of African Americans is racially comfortable in part because they negate rather than activate racial stereotypes. More generally, the employer's surmise is that these "good blacks" will think of themselves as people first and black people second (or third or fourth); they will neither "play the race card" nor generate racial antagonism or tensions in the workplace; they will not let white people feel guilty about being white; and they will work hard to assimilate themselves into the firm's culture. The screening of African Americans along these lines enables the employer to extract a diversity profit from its African American employees without incurring the cost of racial salience. The employer's investment strategy is to hire enough African Americans to obtain a diversity benefit without incurring the institutional costs of managing racial salience.

5 At least ten implications flow from what we have just said.

1. Discrimination is not only an inter-group phenomenon, it is also an intra-group phenomenon. We should care both about employers preferring whites over blacks (an inter-group discrimination problem) and about employers preferring racially palatable blacks over racially salient ones (an intra-group discrimination problem).
2. The existence of intra-group discrimination creates an incentive for African Americans to work their identities to signal to employers that they are racially palatable. They will want to cover up their racial salience to avoid being screened out of the application pool.
3. Signaling continues well after the employee is hired. The employee understands that she is still black on stage; that her employer is watching her racial performance with respect to promotion and pay increases. Accordingly, she becomes attuned to the roles her Working Identity performs. She will want the employer to experience her Working Identity as a diversity profit, not a racial deficit.
4. Working Identity requires time, effort, and energy—it is work, "shadow work." The phenomenon is part of an underground racial economy in which everyone participates and to which almost everyone simultaneously turns a blind eye.

5. Working Identity is not limited to the workplace. Admissions officers can screen applicants based on their Working Identity. Police officers can stop, search, and arrest people based on Working Identity. The American public can vote for politicians based on their Working Identity. Here, too, there are incentives for the actor—to work her identity to gain admissions to universities, to avoid unfriendly interactions with the police, and to gain political office.
6. Working Identity is costly. It can cause people to compromise their sense of self; to lose themselves in their racial performance; to deny who they are; and to distance themselves from other members of their racial group. Plus, the strategy is risky. Staying at work late to negate the stereotype that one is lazy, for example, can confirm the stereotype that one is incompetent, unable to get work done within normal work hours.
7. Working Identity raises difficult questions for law. One can argue that discrimination based on Working Identity is not racial discrimination at all. Arguably, it is discrimination based on behavior or culture rather than race. Therefore, perhaps the law should not intervene. And even assuming that this form of discrimination is racial discrimination, it still might be a bad idea for the law to get involved. Do we really want judges deciding whether a person is or isn't "acting white" or "acting black"—and the degree to which they might be doing so? It is difficult to figure out what role, if any, law should play.
8. Working Identity transcends the African American experience. Everyone works their identity. Everyone feels the pressure to fit in, including white, heterosexual men. But the existence of negative racial stereotypes increases those pressures and makes the work of fitting in harder and more time consuming. African Americans are not the only racial minority that experiences this difficulty, though our focus in the book is primarily on this group.
9. Nor is race the only social category with a Working Identity dimension. Women work their identities as feminine or not. Men are expected to act like men. Gays and lesbians are viewed along a continuum of acting straight or not. Racial performance is but part of a broader Working Identity phenomenon.
10. We all have a Working Identity whether we want to or not. Working Identity does not turn on the intentional, strategic behavior of the actor.

Analyze

1. How do Carbado and Gulati define "working identity"?
2. How does working identity play a role in hiring in America?
3. What do Carbado and Gulati mean when they say employers want to hire blacks who look black but are indistinguishable from whites?

Explore

1. The authors present black employees as having to perform secondary roles in a play (their workplace). From the ten points Carbado and Gulati list, write an essay supporting or disagreeing with their argument.
2. Write an essay drawing from Carbado and Gulati's arguments about another race in America that also has the same challenges. You can draw from personal experience, from the essays in our book, or from experiences you have heard others talk about.
3. In point 5 Carbado and Gulati talk about the ways black Americans work their identity to avoid certain social hardships and to exact some sort of gain (e.g., college admissions, politics, etc.). In point 8 they say we all work our identity to fit in. How do the people in this chapter work their identity to fit in and why is this so common?

Forging Connections

1. Write a six-word description for each of the readings in this chapter.
2. When it comes to work, the American Dream is a myth that is ingrained in our lives, native born and immigrant alike, from birth to death. Write an essay exploring this myth: discuss whether it still exists, and if so for whom, and why it has worked for some and not for others.
3. In a collaborative group, focus on 3–4 types of jobs, ranging from low-wage to high-wage. Locate one person from each of these job types and interview them. Create one questionnaire that you will use for these interviews. If you can, record and take notes of the interviews so you can capture everything the interviewee says. Write an essay about your findings and how they relate to the forms of work and identity in this chapter.

Looking Further

1. Do our names and other identity-forming aspects of our lives affect the opportunities we have? How so?
2. Explore how last names, cultural identity, places of nationality, and education affect where we work and what our economic identity is in the context of this chapter's themes.
3. Apply the concept of working identity from this chapter to 3–5 movie or TV series characters with which you are familiar. Write an essay arguing how they do or do not fit the concept.

Peggy Orenstein

"The Way We Live Now: I Tweet, Therefore I Am"

Peggy Orenstein is the author of several books, including the best-selling *School Girls: Young Women, Self-Esteem and the Confidence Gap*, and her recent best-seller, *Cinderella Ate My Daughter: Dispatches from the Front Lines of the New Girlie-Girl Culture*. She also is a writer for *The New York Times Magazine* and has written for such publications as *The Los Angeles Times, Mother Jones, Discover, USA Today*, and *Vogue*. She has appeared on talk shows such as NPR's *Fresh Air* and *Morning Edition, Nightline, Good Morning America*, and *The Today Show*. In Orenstein's essay she shares how tweeting has become a "normal" part of her life; she describes this as if it were a normal appendage of her body and psyche responding to life.

If you have a Twitter account, how close do your tweets reflect your life at the moment?

On a recent lazy Saturday morning, my daughter and I lolled on a blanket in our front yard, snacking on apricots, listening to a download of E. B. White reading "The Trumpet of the Swan." Her legs sprawled across mine; the grass tickled our ankles. It was the quintessential summer moment, and a year ago, I would have been fully present for it. But instead, a part of my consciousness had split off and was observing the scene from the outside: this was, I realized excitedly, the perfect opportunity for a tweet.

I came late to Twitter. I might have skipped the phenomenon altogether, but I have a book coming out this winter, and publishers, scrambling to promote 360,000-character tomes in a 140-character world, push authors to rally their "tweeps" to the cause. Leaving aside the question of whether that actually boosts sales, I felt pressure to produce. I quickly mastered the Twitterati's unnatural self-consciousness: processing my experience instantaneously, packaging life as I lived it. I learned to be "on" all the time, whether standing behind that woman at the supermarket who sneaked three extra items into the express check-out lane (you know who you are) or despairing over human rights abuses against women in Guatemala.

Each Twitter post seemed a tacit referendum on who I am, or at least who I believe myself to be. The grocery-store episode telegraphed that I was tuned in to the Seinfeldian absurdities of life; my concern about women's victimization, however sincere, signaled that I also have a soul. Together they suggest someone who is at once cynical and compassionate, petty yet deep. Which, in the end, I'd say, is pretty accurate.

Distilling my personality provided surprising focus, making me feel stripped to my essence. It forced me, for instance, to pinpoint the dominant feeling as I sat outside with my daughter listening to E.B. White. Was it my joy at being a mother? Nostalgia for my own childhood summers? The pleasures of listening to the author's quirky, underinflected voice? Each put a different spin on the occasion, of who I was within it. Yet the final decision ("Listening to E.B. White's 'Trumpet of the Swan' with Daisy. Slow and sweet.") was not really about my own impressions: it was about how I imagined—and wanted—others to react to them. That gave me pause. How much, I began to wonder, was I shaping my Twitter feed, and how much was Twitter shaping me?

Back in the 1950s, the sociologist Erving Goffman famously argued that 5
all of life is performance: we act out a role in every interaction, adapting it based on the nature of the relationship or context at hand. Twitter has extended that metaphor to include aspects of our experience that used to be

considered off-set: eating pizza in bed, reading a book in the tub, thinking a thought anywhere, flossing. Effectively, it makes the greasepaint permanent, blurring the lines not only between public and private but also between the authentic and contrived self. If all the world was once a stage, it has now become a reality TV show: we mere players are not just aware of the camera; we mug for it.

The expansion of our digital universe—Second Life, Facebook, MySpace, Twitter—has shifted not only how we spend our time but also how we construct identity. For her coming book, *Alone Together*, Sherry Turkle, a professor at M.I.T., interviewed more than 400 children and parents about their use of social media and cellphones. Among young people especially she found that the self was increasingly becoming externally manufactured rather than internally developed: a series of profiles to be sculptured and refined in response to public opinion. "On Twitter or Facebook you're trying to express something real about who you are," she explained. "But because you're also creating something for others' consumption, you find yourself imagining and playing to your audience more and more. So those moments in which you're supposed to be showing your true self become a performance. Your *psychology* becomes a performance." Referring to "The Lonely Crowd," the landmark description of the transformation of the American character from inner- to outer-directed, Turkle added, "Twitter is outer-directedness cubed."

The fun of Twitter and, I suspect, its draw for millions of people, is its infinite potential for connection, as well as its opportunity for self-expression. I enjoy those things myself. But when every thought is externalized, what becomes of insight? When we reflexively post each feeling, what becomes of reflection? When friends become fans, what happens to intimacy? The risk of the performance culture, of the packaged self, is that it erodes the very relationships it purports to create, and alienates us from our own humanity. Consider the fate of empathy: in an analysis of 72 studies performed on nearly 14,000 college students between 1979 and 2009, researchers at the Institute for Social Research at the University of Michigan found a drop in that trait, with the sharpest decline occurring since 2000. Social media may not have instigated that trend, but by encouraging self-promotion over self-awareness, they may well be accelerating it.

None of this makes me want to cancel my Twitter account. It's too late for that anyway: I'm already hooked. Besides, I appreciate good writing whatever the form: some "tweeple" are as deft as haiku masters at their craft. I am experimenting with the art of the well-placed "hashtag" myself (the symbol that adds your post on a particular topic, like #ShirleySherrod, to a stream. You can also use them whimsically, as in, "I am pretending not to be afraid of the humongous spider on the bed. #lieswetellourchildren").

At the same time, I am trying to gain some perspective on the perpetual performer's self-consciousness. That involves trying to sort out the line between person and persona, the public and private self. It also means that the next time I find myself lying on the grass, stringing daisy chains and listening to E. B. White, I will resist the urge to trumpet about the swan.

Analyze

1. How did Orenstein become an active tweeter?
2. Do you agree with Orenstein's observation about people who tweet, that they're "at once cynical and compassionate, petty yet deep"?
3. What does Orenstein mean when she asks, "How much, I began to wonder, was I shaping my Twitter feed, and how much was Twitter shaping me?" Do you think that her concern is the same as people who videotape everything happening around them, even if others are being hurt in the process?

Explore

1. Orenstein states that "all of life is performance: we act out a role in every interaction, adapting it based on the nature of the relationship or context at hand. Twitter has extended that metaphor to include aspects of our experience that used to be considered off-set: eating pizza in bed, reading a book in the tub, thinking a thought anywhere, flossing." Whether you use Twitter, Facebook, Tumblr, or some other social media, write an essay or a comic book depicting the life the author projects from either a positive, negative, or "just the way it is" viewpoint.
2. Conduct an informal interview, like the one Orenstein says Sherry Turkle conducted, in class on the class's use of social media and cellphones. State your findings and how they conform with, dispute, or go beyond what Turkle found, for example, "Among young people especially she found that the self was increasingly becoming externally manufactured rather than internally developed: a series of profiles to be sculptured and refined in response to public opinion."

3. Write an argument either in agreement or disagreement with this claim from the essay: "performance culture, of the packaged self, is that it erodes the very relationships it purports to create, and alienates us from our own humanity. Consider the fate of empathy: in an analysis of 72 studies performed on nearly 14,000 college students between 1979 and 2009, researchers at the Institute for Social Research at the University of Michigan found a drop in that trait, with the sharpest decline occurring since 2000. Social media may not have instigated that trend, but by encouraging self-promotion over self-awareness, they may well be accelerating it."

Hanni Fakhoury, Kurt Opsahl, and Rainey Reitman

"When Will Our Email Betray Us? An Email Privacy Primer in Light of the Petraeus Saga"

Hanni Fakhoury writes and speaks on subjects involving technology, criminal law, privacy, and free speech. He is a staff attorney with the Electronic Frontier Foundation and in this role has argued before the Fifth Circuit Court of Appeals on warrantless cell tracking. Kurt Opsahl focuses on civil liberties, free speech, and privacy law as senior staff attorney with the Electronic Frontier Foundation. He is the coauthor of the *Electronic Media and Privacy Law Handbook*. Rainey Reitman studies the effects of technology on personal privacy, especially with social networking. At Electronic Frontier Foundation, she heads the activism team. She is a steering committee member for the Internet Defense League and on the board of directors for the Bill of Rights Defense Committee. While e-mail almost seems like an antique communication technology, it can, as scandals still regularly unfold, create powerful digital footprints, as the growing number of scandals make us aware.

Should law enforcement be allowed to trace all electronic information we share and post, such as e-mail and pictures?

The unfolding scandal that led to the resignation of Gen. David Petraeus, the Director of the Central Intelligence Agency, started with some purportedly harassing emails sent from pseudonymous email accounts to Jill Kelley. After the FBI kicked its investigation into high gear, it identified the sender as Paula Broadwell and, ultimately, read massive amounts of private email messages that uncovered an affair between Broadwell and Petraeus (and now, the investigation has expanded to include Gen. John Allen's emails with Kelley). We've received a lot of questions about how this works—what legal process the FBI needs to conduct its email investigation. The short answer? It's complicated.

The Electronic Communications Privacy Act (ECPA) is a 1986 law that Congress enacted to protect your privacy in electronic communications, like email and instant messages. ECPA provides scant protection for your identifying information, such as the IP address used to access an account. While Paula Broadwell reportedly created a new, pseudonymous account for the allegedly harassing emails to Jill Kelley, she apparently did not take steps to disguise the IP number her messages were coming from. The FBI could have obtained this information with just a subpoena to the service provider. But obtaining the account's IP address alone does not establish the identity of the emails' sender.

Broadwell apparently accessed the emails from hotels and other locations, not her home. So the FBI cross-referenced the IP addresses of these Wi-Fi hotspots "against guest lists from other cities and hotels, looking for common names." If Broadwell wanted to stay anonymous, a new email account combined with open Wi-Fi was not enough. The ACLU has an in-depth write-up of the surveillance and security lessons to be learned from this.

After the FBI identified Broadwell, they searched her email. According to news reports, the affair between Petraeus and Broadwell lasted from November 2011 to July 2012. The harassing emails sent by Broadwell to Jill Kelley started in May 2012, and Kelley notified the FBI shortly thereafter. Thus, in the summer of 2012, when the FBI was investigating, the bulk of the emails would be less than 180 days old. This 180 day old dividing line is important for determining how ECPA applies to email.

Compared to identifying information, ECPA provides more legal 5
protection for the contents of your email, but with gaping exceptions. While a small but increasing number of federal courts have found that the Fourth Amendment requires a warrant for all email, the government claims ECPA only requires a warrant for email that is stored for 180 days or less.

But as the Department of Justice Manual for searching and seizing email makes clear, the government believes this only applies to unopened email. Other email is fair game with only a subpoena, even if the messages are less than 180 days old. According to reports, Patraeus and Broadwell adopted a technique of drafting emails, and reading them in the draft folder rather than sending them. The DOJ would likely consider draft messages as "opened" email, and therefore not entitled to the protection of a search warrant.

In a nutshell, although ECPA requires a warrant for the government to obtain the contents of an email stored online for less than 180 days, the government believes the warrant requirement doesn't apply for email that was opened and left on the server—the typical scenario for webmail systems like Gmail—even if the messages are less than 180 days old. So, under the government's view, so long as the emails had been opened or were saved in the "drafts" folder, only a subpoena was required to look at contents of Broadwell's email account.

Confused? Well, here's where things get really complicated. The government's view of the law was rejected by the Ninth Circuit Court of Appeals, the federal appellate court that covers the western United States, including California, and the home to many online email companies and the servers that host their messages. As a result, the DOJ Manual notes that "Agents outside of the Ninth Circuit can therefore obtain such email (and other stored electronic or wire communications in "electronic storage" more than 180 days) using a subpoena . . ." but reminds agents in the Ninth Circuit to get a warrant.

News reports show that the FBI agents involved in the Petraeus scandal were in Tampa, Florida. Thus, according to the DOJ Manual, they did not need to get a warrant even if the email provider was in California (like, for example, Gmail): "law enforcement elsewhere may continue to apply the traditional narrow interpretation of 'electronic storage,' even when the data sought is within the Ninth Circuit."

A subpoena for email content would generally require notice to the subscriber, though another section of ECPA allows for delayed notice, for up to 90 days. The FBI interviewed Broadwell for the first time in September, about 90 days after the investigation began in June.

However, many providers nevertheless protect their users by following the Ninth Circuit rule, and insist upon a warrant for the contents of all email. In EFF's experience, the government will seek a warrant rather than litigate the issue. Thus, assuming the service provider stepped up, it is likely that the government used a warrant to obtain access to the emails at issue.

10 If a warrant was used, note that a warrant is often quite broad, and the government may well have obtained emails from other accounts under the same warrant. And as result, there's no telling how much email the FBI actually read.

The government is required to "minimize" its collection of some electronic information. For example, under the Wiretap Act, the government is supposed to conduct its wiretapping in a way that "minimize[s] the interception of communications not otherwise subject to interception." This ensures the government isn't listening to conversations unrelated to their criminal investigation.

But when it comes to email, such minimization requirements aren't as strong. The DOJ Manual suggests that agents "exercise great caution" and "avoid unwarranted intrusions into private areas," when searching email on ISPs but is short on specifics. *The New York Times* reported that FBI agents obtained access to Broadwell's "regular e-mail account." They could have read every e-mail that came through as they investigated the affair. Possibly, the FBI could have read an enormous amount of email from innocent individuals not suspected of any wrongdoing.

And while the Fourth Amendment requires search warrants to be specific and particular, as noted earlier, it's not entirely clear whether the FBI got a search warrant to search Broadwell's email. Even if it did get a warrant, the government has argued that broad warrants are needed in electronic searches because evidence could be stored anywhere. While some courts have pushed back on this broad search authority when it comes to email, many courts still give the government wide access to email and other forms of electronic content.

Sound confusing? It is. ECPA is hopelessly out of date, and fails to provide the protections we need in a modern era. Your email privacy should be simple: it should receive the same protection the Fourth Amendment provides for your home.

So why hasn't Congress done anything to update the law? They've tried a few times but the bills haven't gone anywhere. That's why EFF members across the country are joining with other advocacy groups in calling for reform. This week, we're proud to launch a new campaign page to advocate for ECPA reform. And we're asking individuals to sign EFF's petition calling on Congress to update ECPA for the digital era so that there can be no question that the government is required to go to a judge and get a warrant before it can rummage through our email, online documents, and phone location histories.

We know that major privacy scandals can prompt Congress to get serious 15
about updating privacy law. The Video Privacy Protection Act was inspired by the ill-fated Supreme Court nomination of Judge Robert Bork, after a local Washington reporter obtained Bork's video rental records. And the Foreign Intelligence Surveillance Act was inspired by the findings of the Church Committee, which showed that the FBI had warrantlessly surveilled Dr. Martin Luther King, Jr. and many other activists. If we learn nothing else from the Petraeus scandal, it should be that our private digital lives can become all too public when over-eager federal agents aren't held to rigorous legal standards.

Congress has dragged its feet on updating ECPA for too long, resulting in the confusing, abuse-prone legal mess we're in today. Join EFF in calling on Congress to fix the law.

Analyze

1. What is the 1986 Electronic Communications Privacy Act (ECPA)?
2. What led the FBI to Broadwell and how did they track her?
3. What is the 180-day guideline the ECPA applies to e-mail?

Explore

1. Petraeus and Broadwell would write e-mails to each other but not send them. They would post them to the draft folder of a shared e-mail account. The Department of Justice, according to this essay, would likely consider draft messages as "opened" e-mail and would therefore not consider them to be entitled to the protection of a search warrant. In groups, research and discuss this rule and take a stand on whether you agree with it or not.
2. Explore what the Fourth Amendment is and write an essay explaining why e-mail privacy should fall under the same protections that the Fourth Amendment protects.
3. A few of the essays in this chapter have argued that we need to be careful with what we put up and send out in our digital worlds. Create a visual or video that educates people to the personal, social, professional, and legal dangers of putting too much information out there.

Alan Norton
"10 Reasons Why I Avoid Social Networking Services"

Norton writes for *TechRepublic* primarily creating practical "10 Reasons" columns of advice on how to survive and succeed in the business world. In this essay he lists ten reasons why we should avoid online social networking.

Of the ten reasons Norton lists, which ones do you dis/agree with and why?

I have a confession to make. I don't do social networking. That's not *that* unusual for someone my age. Just 8% of all Facebook users fall into my age group. Nonetheless, according to the Pew Internet & American Life

Project, social networking is popular and still growing. While only 8% of adult Internet users used social networking sites in 2005, that number had grown to 65% by 2011. Why then do some people in general and older Internet users in particular avoid social networking services? I can give you 10 reasons why this experienced ancient one doesn't use them.

1. I have privacy concerns

   The recent IPO of Facebook wasn't as successful as its backers wanted. But it was successful bringing to the public's attention Facebook's privacy concerns. I, like many others, don't fully understand how serious those concerns are. It does make for a great excuse though to avoid Facebook altogether. Putting your personal information in the care of others, no matter how diligent their stewardship, increases your risk of that information getting into the hands of third parties.

   Our image is, in part, defined by our words. Each of us should ask how much of ourselves we want to give to people we don't even know. Once gone, that private piece of our lives can never be retrieved.

2. Ownership of content is unclear

   Who actually owns and who controls "your" intellectual content that you post is not as clear as you might think. Terms vary by social networking service, but typically you give up control of how your content may be used. Which raises the question: If you don't control it, do you really own it? It *isn't* clear who legally owns your content. The Twitter Terms of Service as of July 4, 2012, clearly states that you own the content you post:

   "You retain your rights to any Content you submit, post or display 5
   on or through the Services.... But what's yours is yours—you own your Content (and your photos are part of that Content)."

   According to a New York judge, however, Twitter owns your Tweets. That should at least cause you to pause before posting *anything* at any site other than your own. I am not a lawyer, but it appears that the legal ownership of your Tweets and other posted content may not be fully determined for years.

3. It's too impersonal

   Social networking offers an easy way to meet people—perhaps too easy. No commitment is required, and you can invest as much or as little of your time as you wish. Social networking services can be a great way to keep people at a distance: Interact only when and where you want with whom you want. That may be great for some people. I prefer more meaningful ways to interact, like face-to-face and over the phone.

People value your full attention and time. Social interaction is only as rewarding as you are willing to make it, whether in person or online.

4. I want to minimize online gaffes

There is that risqué limerick you shared while in high school or those embarrassing statements you made about a former employer that can be found with a simple Web search. Pity the poor job interviewee grilled by an interviewer who did his homework and found your ignorance, or worse, the bad information you posted about a topic for which you are supposed to be an expert. If you must post, practice safe posting. Of course, abstinence means never having to say you're sorry.

5. I want to minimize data points for possible data mining

Make a spelling mistake or grammatical error and you can be dinged for it forever. For me, it would be embarrassing as a writer and a blow to my ego but not a great loss. To a younger person interviewing for a job, consider what this report would do for a first impression:

10 It's not likely that you will run across this level of detail at your next job interview. But it isn't that difficult to collect such data—and you can bet that if it can be done, it will be done. Never mind the fact that such data is fraught with problems.

6. I don't subscribe to social fads

Call me a rebel, please. I don't like following the sheep to gain their acceptance. Clothing from Sears has always been my fashion statement, though the local thrift store has of late been getting my business. Twitter and Facebook may just be another fad that comes and goes, like AIM and MySpace.

7. I don't like being pressured to join

The sinister way that social networking services sneak into even the most ardent holdout's daily life is through invitations from friends and family members. Yes, I am now a lousy brother in law because I ignored an invitation from my brother's wife to join her inside circle at Facebook. I became a rotten friend when I politely turned down a request to be in a friend's LinkedIn professional network. Thank goodness my nephews and nieces have yet to ask me to "join up." I would hate to be a terrible uncle too.

8. I don't need the abuse

I used to think that posting at services like Usenet was something akin to self flagellation. Why would I risk being verbally flogged for posting what others might perceive as flame bait? I still don't need the abuse but, thankfully, I no longer take name calling like "idiot" or

User Name - Alan Norton For the period Jul-01-11 to Jun-30-12	Average # of posts per month	Average # of words per month	Avg #/% of misspellings per month	Avg #/% of grammatical errors per month
Facebook	0	0	0/0%	0/0%
Twitter	52	520	18/3.5%	4/0.8%
Google+	0	0	0/0%	0/0%
Usenet - alt.comp.hardware	11	506	22/4..3%	12/2.4%
Usenet - alt.support.depression	28	980	59/6.0%	33/3.4%
Other	76	2204	76/3.4%	62/2.8%
Totals	167	4210	175/4.2%	111/2.6%

"nimrod" as personally as I once did. Being flamed has instead become part of the profession "writer" and a badge of honor. Those who post on TechRepublic are a class act by comparison—people who disagree with me here call me "Mr. Norton."

9. It's more work

If your work is anything like my experiences in the cubicle, you already spend enough time typing when you answer emails, update status reports, and write code. It's just no fun coming home to more of the same.

This may not apply to you, but when you write for a living, it's not a 15
lot of fun interacting socially with the written word. After calculating the amount of wisdom I spew forth per dollar received, I have to tell you, I am working cheap (1:51—2:23). I just can't afford to give away my wisdom for free.

The Bottom Line . . .

Is that it's just not me (**#10**). Some of us prefer to keep ourselves to our self. I have heard about certain sites that cater to the courtship rituals of modern *Homo sapiens,* but every day that goes by I become less modern than the day before. Neither do I need to network for a job, though I *used* to believe that getting published was far better than social networking when it came to that big job interview. My notoriety, or lack thereof, has me now questioning the accuracy of that belief. Then there's the fact that I have yet to find a reason why I should tell countless others how totally devoid of meaning my life really is.

According to an analysis of tweets by Pear Analytics, 40% of all tweets are pointless babble. I have better ways to atrophy my brain, better ways to slowly turn my gray matter into mush. Is it possible that we will prefer communicating via machine rather than one on one? Personal social interaction could become a lost art. And it would be a shame for humanity to become so impersonal.

I can guess that some of you more analytical thinkers are saying, "Hold on there just a minute, Alan. You participate in the forums at TechRepublic. Doesn't that make you a hypocrite?" I believe that every writer should be available to answer any questions that you, the patient reader, might have. What you may perceive as hypocrisy is merely *relativistic disingenuous behavioral prioritization*. I would be hypocritical if I didn't participate. Besides, sometimes you've just gotta throw 10 silly reasons to the wind and risk acting the goat so you can help someone.

Analyze

1. What percent of Tweets are pointless babble?
2. What is "relativistic disingenuous behavioral prioritization"?
3. The author shares with us a statistic about his age: "Just 8% of all Facebook users fall into my age group." How old does that make him?

Explore

1. Norton argues that "Our image is, in part, defined by our words. Each of us should ask how much of ourselves we want to give to people we don't even know. Once gone, that private piece of our lives can never be retrieved." Drawing from the essays in this chapter and from your own experience on social networking sites, write an essay agreeing or disagreeing with this view.
2. In the following quote from the essay, does Norton contradict himself? "Social networking services can be a great way to keep people at a distance: Interact only when and where you want with whom you want. That may be great for some people. I prefer more meaningful ways to interact, like face-to-face and over the phone. People value your full attention and time. Social interaction is only as rewarding as you are willing to make it, whether in person or online." Think about what makes face-to-face interaction rewarding, and what makes social network interactions rewarding.

3. At the end of the essay Norton invites us to dialogue with him: "Do you share some of these objections and concerns? Or have you come to rely on social networking as a means of enriching your life and advancing your career?" To do so we can sign up with *TechRepublic's* 10 Things Newsletter. Create your own List of 10 Reasons Why I Love or Hate Social Networking (or a combination of the two, Why I Have a Love-Hate Relationship with Social Networking).

Forging Connections

1. How has the Internet changed the way we find out more about ourselves through our names (e.g., ancestry.com), about how important places are in relation to our notions of ourselves, about the schooling we receive and what we learn, how we become our jobs (I am a teacher, accountant, etc.), the investments we place in our relationships in defining our happiness or sadness or stability, and how we share all this indelible information, unfiltered, to the Internet with everyone?
2. Using essays from this chapter, prepare a letter to Latoya Peterson and Eric Sheninger ("Don't Trip over Your Digital Footprint") easing their worries about safety and privacy on the Internet.
3. Pick a recent situation from the news where someone's Internet identity became public and this resulted in arrest, exposure, criminal prosecution, or jail time. Gather as much information as you can about the story you select. Write an essay describing why, based on your focus, the "open" Internet where all information is available is working the way it should, or use the case as an example of why it needs to be protected more.

Looking Further

1. In the last chapter, Orenstein stated, "When friends become fans, what happens to intimacy? The risk of the performance culture, of the packaged self, is that it erodes the very relationships it purports to create, and alienates us from our own humanity." She is arguing that our personality and our way of behaving change us. Create a comic that shows the evolution or metamorphosis that you perceive humans undergoing as a result of sharing everything about themselves on social networking and cell phones.

2. Write a letter, a tweet, a text, and a six-word description to someone telling them about the various identities you have, how they evolve, and how they simply change based on where you are. Draw from the understandings of identity that you learned throughout the chapters. Do you see a different identity emerge based on the form you put your message in?
3. Going back to Chapter 1 with a focus on our names, Chapter 2 with a focus on where we are from, Chapter 3 with a focus on where we went to school, Chapter 4 with a focus on where we work, Chapter 5 with a focus on whom we love, and Chapter 6 with a focus on our Internet identities, we have explored many ways to think about how we think of ourselves and how others think of us, in good and bad ways. Write an essay that uses ideas from all of the chapters in which you reflect on the many nuanced ways that your identity is important to you on personal and social levels.

poverty/ privilege

Other titles in this series include:

Food: A Reader for Writers,
Danielle Aquiline and Deborah Holdstein
(ISBN: 9780199385683)

Technology: A Reader for Writers,
Johannah Rodgers
(ISBN: 9780199340743)

Humor: A Reader for Writers,
Kathleen Volk Miller and Marion Wrenn
(ISBN: 9780199362691)

Culture: A Reader for Writers,
John Mauk
(ISBN: 9780199947225)

Language: A Reader for Writers,
Gita DasBender
(ISBN: 9780199947485)

Sustainability: A Reader for Writers,
Carl Herndl
(ISBN: 9780199947508)

Identity: A Reader for Writers,
John Scenters-Zapico
(ISBN: 9780199947461)

Globalization: A Reader for Writers,
Maria Jerskey
(ISBN: 9780199947522)

poverty/ privilege

A READER *for* WRITERS

Connie Snyder Mick
University of Notre Dame

New York Oxford
Oxford University Press

Oxford University Press publishes works that further Oxford University's objective of excellence in research, scholarship, and education.

Oxford New York
Auckland Cape Town Dar es Salaam Hong Kong Karachi
Kuala Lumpur Madrid Melbourne Mexico City Nairobi
New Delhi Shanghai Taipei Toronto

With offices in
Argentina Austria Brazil Chile Czech Republic France Greece
Guatemala Hungary Italy Japan Poland Portugal Singapore
South Korea Switzerland Thailand Turkey Ukraine Vietnam

For titles covered by Section 112 of the US Higher Education Opportunity Act, please visit www.oup.com/us/he for the latest information about pricing and alternate formats.

Published by Oxford University Press
198 Madison Avenue, New York, New York 10016
http://www.oup.com

Library of Congress Cataloging-in-Publication Data
Poverty/privilege : a reader for writers / [edited by] Connie Snyder Mick.
pages cm
ISBN 978-0-19-936125-0
1. Poverty. 2. Wealth. 3. Social stratification. I. Mick, Connie Snyder. II. Title: Poverty, privilege.
HC79.P6P687 2014
305.5'12--dc23

2014033950

Printing number: 9 8 7 6 5 4 3 2 1

Printed in the United States of America
on acid-free paper

Vivyan Adair

"Reclaiming the Promise of Higher Education: Poor Single Mothers in Academe"

Vivyan Adair is a professor of women's studies, the Elihu Root Peace Fund Chair, and the director of the ACCESS Project at Hamilton College, which aims to help single parents remain in college and finish their degrees. She has published various scholarly articles and authored two books: *Reclaiming Class: Women, Poverty, and the Promise of Higher Education in America*, and *From Good Ma to Welfare Queen: A Genealogy of the Poor Woman in American Literature, Photography, and Culture*. In the following testimony delivered before the U.S. Senate Committee on Finance, Adair argues that higher education should be an option for people on welfare because it helps them overcome long-term welfare dependence and make positive contributions to society.

Should single mothers on welfare be encouraged to seek higher education instead of working?

Testimony Submitted to the U.S. Senate Committee on Finance

Hearing on Welfare Reform: A New Conversation on Women and Poverty

Submitted by Vivyan Adair, The Elihu Root Peace Fund Chair, Associate Professor of Women's Studies at Hamilton College

September 21, 2010

As children, my siblings and I were marked by poverty, our lives punctuated by bouts of homelessness, hunger, lack of medical and dental care, fear and despair. My young mother, a single parent of four, was a hard worker and an intelligent and honest woman who did her best to bring order, grace, and dignity to our lives. Yet, she was trapped in dead-end and demeaning jobs with which she could not support, nurture, and provide security for the children she loved. Perhaps not too surprisingly, I followed suit as a young woman, dropping out of school and becoming a single mother involved with a string of men who neglected and abused me, leaving me hurt, frustrated, despondent, and profoundly impoverished.

I know the desperation and hopelessness that shape the lives of poor women in the United States today. Yet, I was fortunate to have been poor and broken and verging on irredeemable hopelessness in an era when education could provide a lifeline for poor single mothers, as it has historically done for so many in our country, but fails to do today. Because of my interaction with a pre-reform welfare system, with superb educational institutions, and with instructors who supported and guided me, I was able to transform my life and that of my child through the life-altering pathway of higher education.

Access to Higher Education Prior to Welfare Reform

I entered college in the summer of 1987, as a single mother and welfare recipient without the skills, self-esteem, or vision necessary to succeed in school. My passage was guided by patient and able teachers whose classrooms became places where I built bridges between my own knowledge of the world and crucial new knowledge, skills, and methodologies. Dedicated faculty created exciting and engaging exercises and orchestrated challenging discussions that enabled me to use my newfound skills to re-envision my gifts, strengths, and responsibilities to the world around me. Little by little the larger social, creative, political, and material world exposed itself to me in ways that were resonant and urgent, inviting me to analyze, negotiate, articulate, and reframe systems, histories, and pathways that had previously seemed inaccessible. The process was invigorating, restorative, and life altering.

As a result, today I have a PhD and am employed as a tenured faculty member at a wonderful college in central New York State. My life and experience are certainly not anomalous. In "Together We Are Getting Freedom," Noemy Vides recalls that her life as a poor immigrant welfare mother began anew when she was encouraged to seek an education. She confides that it was through higher education that she was "born as a new woman with visions, dreams, hopes, opportunities, and fulfillment," adding that a college education is "the key ingredient in poor women's struggles to survive."

5 One of my own former students—a young, Latina, single mother of three—now a chemical engineer in California, recently wrote of a similar transformation through higher education. Valuing both the products and the processes of higher education, she reflected:

> "School gave me the credentials to pull my three daughters and me permanently out of poverty. After being raised in dire and painful poverty and then watching my own children suffer as I worked for minimum wage [at a fast food restaurant], this is so important to me. Today we own a home, a car, and pay taxes. I have a great paying job, my children excel in school and I can afford to care for them properly. But what is really revolutionary is what education did to our heads. I think differently now, I act differently and my girls relate to our world differently. My mother died broke, an alcoholic living in public housing. My younger sister is in jail and her children in foster care. We have broken that cycle through education once and for all. We are so grateful for this journey."

Indeed, in 1987, the year that I entered college, around the nation almost half a million welfare recipients were similarly enrolled in institutions of higher education as a route out of poverty. Prior to welfare reform in 1996, tens of thousands of poor single mothers quietly accessed postsecondary education to become teachers, lawyers, social service providers, business and civic leaders, and medical professionals. While education is important to all citizens, my experience and my research convinces me that it is essential for those who will face the continued obstacles of racism, classism, sexism, and homophobia; to those who have been distanced and disenfranchised from U.S. mainstream culture; and to those who have suffered generations of oppression and marginalization.

Closing Education's Doors to Women on Welfare

Despite a large number of reputable studies confirming the relationship between higher education and increased earnings (and thus financial stability), in 1996, Congress enacted the Personal Responsibility and Work Opportunity and Reconciliation Act (PRWORA) as a part of welfare reform. This act was composed of a broad tangle of legislation that "devolved" responsibility for assistance to the poor from the federal to the state level, and through a range of block grants, sanctions, and rewards, encouraged states to reduce their welfare rolls by developing stringent work requirements, imposing strict time limits, discouraging "illegitimacy," and reducing the numbers of applicants eligible for services. The act also promoted the development of programs and requirements that had the effect of discouraging—and in many cases prohibiting—welfare recipients from entering into or completing educational programs, mandating instead that they engage in "work first."

Specifically, the Temporary Assistance for Needy Families (TANF) work requirements, part of the 1996 PRWORA, drastically limited poor women's opportunities to participate in postsecondary education programs while receiving state support. Unlike previous provisions in Aid to Families with Dependent Children (AFDC) and JOBS, education training programs in existence when I first went to college, TANF restrictions from 1996 did not allow higher education to be counted as "work" and required a larger proportion of welfare recipients to engage in full-time recognized work activities. This work-first philosophy emphasized rapid entry into the labor force and penalized states for allowing long-term access to either education or training.

As a result of the dramatic overhaul of welfare policy in 1996, welfare recipient students left college for low-wage jobs in record numbers. Even as the nation began to embrace the conviction that access to education is the pathway to social and economic mobility, poor women were denied access to education that could have positively altered the course of their lives and those of their children. According to the Center on Budget and Policy

Priorities, in the first year of welfare reform, tens of thousands of poor women were forced to drop out of school. Across the nation, the decrease in enrollments among welfare recipients ranged from 29 percent to 82 percent.

In 1998, the Center for Law and Social Policy (CLASP) conducted a preliminary survey of key policy advocates in the fifty states and Washington, D.C., regarding welfare recipients' abilities to enter into and complete educational degrees. The study found that in 1995, almost 649,000 students across the nation were receiving AFDC benefits while enrolled in full-time educational programs; by the 1998–1999 school year, that figure had dropped by 47.6 percent, to fewer than 340,000 students. Today the number is estimated to have been reduced again by over 93 percent, with a national enrollment of less than 35,000 students.

The Personal Cost of Work-First Policies

A few years later, the prospects for these students remain dismal. One former computer science major with a ten-year-old son now earns $7.90 per hour. Recently she described changes in her family's quality of life as a result of the 1996 reform: "I call it welfare deform. Things are so much harder now. We can barely pay our rent. My son is alone all the time when I work. I just don't see a future anymore. With school there was hope. I was on my way to making a decent living for us. Now it is just impossible to survive day to day. Usually I can't pay my rent. I don't have a cent saved for emergencies. I don't know what I'm [going to] do."

A second student, who was a gifted and dedicated education major, returned to welfare after being forced to leave the university and then losing several minimum-wage jobs because she could not afford reliable childcare and was denied child-care assistance from the state for failing to name her child's father. She described the nightmare of losing job after minimum-wage job in order to care for her child, emphasizing that this was a "choice no mother should be forced to make." She added:

> It came down to, if I want to keep this job at [the fast-food restaurant] I have to leave my three-year-old daughter alone or maybe with a senile neighbor. And I couldn't even really afford that! Or we could go back to her dad who is a drunk. If I don't do that, we could both end up hungry or homeless. The choice they are making me make is to either abandon or hurt my daughter, and for what?

Similarly, Tonya Mitchell, the single mother of twins and a very successful pre-nursing major committed to providing health care for low-income and minority populations, was forced to drop out of a nursing program and assigned a "work first position" in a nursing home. She reminds us, "All I wanted was to be a nurse and help care for people. I had a very high grade point average and was on my way to a nursing degree with jobs that pay over $25 an hour in addition to benefits." Today, after over six years as a nursing aid, Mitchell makes $8 per hour. In an interview she told me:

> "I still need help from the state with childcare and food stamps and life is so much harder for us now than it was before. Clearly welfare reform and the Personal Responsibility Act changed our lives. I do not have the money I need to pay my rent and bills, my twins are in an awful daycare for about ten hours a day while I work in a job I hate, and we have little hope. If we survive it will be despite welfare reform!"

The experiences of students who had worked diligently to become responsible workers, taxpayers, and parents capable of providing their families with financial security, and who were forced to drop out of school to live in perpetual poverty, illustrates one startling failure of 1996 "welfare reform." Certainly not all low-income single mothers are able or willing to go to college. However, to prevent women who can do so from completing postsecondary degrees is the mark of shortsighted and fiscally-irresponsible policy.

Analyze

1. What is PRWORA? What aspects of welfare reform concern Adair?
2. Name three facts from the testimony that interest you.
3. What does Adair want her audience to think or do based on her testimony?

Explore

1. How does Adair build her ethos (character or credibility)?
2. Who are the stakeholders on the issue of women and welfare? Who would argue for supporting education and not just work as a condition

for public support? Who would argue against this? Where is the common ground?

3. Research welfare reform and write your own testimony for a U.S. Senate hearing on an aspect of this topic. Follow the format for the genre (type) of testimony.

Kai Wright
"Young, Black, and Buried in Debt: How For-Profit Colleges Prey on African-American Ambition"

Kai Wright is a professional writer and editor for *Colorlines* and *The Investigative Fund*. An investigative reporter and news commentator, he has also authored books and published in such periodicals as *The Nation* and *The American Prospect*. In the following article, Wright argues that for-profit educational institutions often prey upon black students, crippling them with student loan debt.

Should lenders and universities be responsible for providing loans that students can't afford to pay back?

There are a few dictums that have enjoyed pride of place in black American families alongside "Honor your parents" and "Do unto others" since at least Emancipation. One of them is this: The road to freedom passes through the schoolhouse doors.

After all, it was illegal even to teach an enslaved person to read in many states; under Jim Crow, literacy tests were used for decades to deny black voters their rights. So no surprise that from Reconstruction to the first black president, the consensus has been clear. The key to "winning the future," in one of President Obama's favorite phrases, is to get educated. "There is no surer path to success in the middle class than a good education," the president declared in his much-discussed speech on the roots of gun violence in black Chicago.

Rarely has that message resounded so much as now, with nearly one in seven black workers still jobless. Those who've found work have moved out of the manufacturing and public sectors, where good jobs were once available without a higher ed degree, and into the low-wage service sector, to which the uncredentialed are now relegated. So while it has become fashionable lately to speculate about middle-class kids abandoning elite colleges for adventures in entrepreneurship, an entirely different trend has been unfolding in black America—people are going back to school in droves.

It's true at all levels of education. Yes, black college enrollment shot up by nearly 35 percent between 2003 and 2009, nearly twice the rate at which white enrollment increased. But we're getting all manner of schooling as we seek either an advantage in or refuge from the collapsed job market. As I've reported on the twin housing and unemployment crises in black neighborhoods in recent years, I've heard the same refrain from struggling strivers up and down the educational ladder: "I'm getting my papers, maybe that'll help." GEDs, associates degrees, trade licenses, certifications, you name it, we're getting it. Hell, I even went and got certified in selling wine; journalism's a shrinking trade, after all.

5 But this headlong rush of black Americans to get schooled has also led too many down a depressingly familiar path. As with the mortgage market of the pre-crash era, those who are just entering in the higher ed game have found themselves ripe for the con man's picking. They've landed, disproportionately, at for-profit schools, rather than at far less expensive public community colleges, or at public universities. And that means they've found themselves loaded with unimaginable debt, with little to show for it, while a small group of financial players have made a great deal of easy money. Sound familiar? Two points if you hear troublesome echoes of the subprime mortgage crisis.

Between 2004 and 2010, black enrollment in for-profit bachelor's programs grew by a whopping 264 percent, compared to a 24 percent increase in black enrollment in public four-year programs. The two top producers of black baccalaureates in the class of 2011 were University of Phoenix and Ashford University, both for-profits.

These numbers mirror a simultaneous trend in eroding security among ambitious black Americans with shrinking access to middle-class jobs. It's true that the country's middle class is collapsing for everyone, but that trend is most profound among African-Americans. In 2008, as black folks flocked into higher ed, the Economic Policy Institute found that 45 percent of African-Americans born into the middle class were living at or near poverty as adults.

For too many, school has greased the downward slide. Nearly every single graduate of a for-profit school—96 percent, according to a 2008 Department of Education survey—leaves with debt. The industry ate 25 percent of federal student aid in the 2009–2010 school year. That's debt its students can't pay. The loan default rate among for-profit college students is more than double that of their peers in both public and nonprofit private schools, because the degrees and certificates the students are earning are trap doors to more poverty, not springboards to prosperity.

There's been growing, positive attention to this problem, and the Obama administration's ongoing efforts to rein in the excesses of for-profit schools are arguably among its most progressive policy goals. But few have understood the for-profit education boom as part of the larger economic challenge black America faces today. The black jobs crisis stretches way back to the 2001 recession, from which too many black neighborhoods never recovered. Workers and families have been scrambling ever since, trying to fix themselves such that they fit inside a broken economy. And it is that very effort at self-improvement, that same American spirit of personal re-creation and against-all-odds ambition that has so often led black people into the jaws of the 21st century's most predatory capitalists. From subprime credit cards through to subprime home loans and now on into subprime education, we've reached again and again for the trappings of middle-class life, only to find ourselves slipping further into debt and poverty.

Kiesha Whatley is an example. The 31-year-old mom in Queens, N.Y., has always done hair on the side to help make ends meet, so in 2006 she decided to go for her cosmetology certificate. She was in the city's welfare-to-work program, but was able to fill her work requirement by going to school. She figured what she needed most was to get a credential—to get legit. So she enrolled at a small, mom-and-pop for-profit in Brooklyn that her cousin had attended years before, but which had since changed ownership. Over what Whatley says was a seven-month program, she racked up more than $7,500 in debt, much of which she thought was actually a grant. She has still not passed the state cosmetology exam and she's back to doing hair on her own, now with debt she can't dream of paying back.

The subprime mortgage crisis was fueled by a similar mix of economic 10
desperation, financial illiteracy and aspirational ideology. For a generation, working-class people who hoped to achieve more permanent economic stability were told, loudly and repeatedly, that buying a home would validate them as legitimate participants in American life, not just as people with an asset, but as true neighbors and community members and citizens. Prosperity preachers and presidents alike sung the praises of the "ownership society," as George W. Bush so often called it, in which "more Americans than ever will be able to open up their door where they live and say, welcome to my house, welcome to my piece of property." Homeownership was understood then—just as higher education is now—as good no matter what. Just don't read the fine print.

All it took was one devastating downturn for those doors to slam shut, forcing millions of Americans into foreclosure. That still unfolding crisis has been particularly devastating for African-Americans, who have lost more than half of their collective assets after being targeted with subprime mortgage products. The black-white wealth gap is larger today than it's been since economists began recording it in 1984. And according to a recent analysis from the Alliance for a Just Society, ZIP codes with majority people of color populations saw 60 percent more foreclosures than white neighborhoods and these homeowners lost 69 percent more wealth.

Now, to make matters worse, expensive, nearly useless degrees may be to the bust years what expensive, totally useless refinance loans were to the boom: too-good-to-be-true golden tickets to the American Dream, sold in an unregulated market and targeted at the people for whom that dream is most elusive.

Last year, Garvin Gittens became a literal poster child for why that market is so dangerous. For several months, his face was plastered all over the New York City subway system as part of a city-led campaign to warn would-be students about debt scams. When we met last summer, Gittens laid out for me how he racked up more than $57,000 in public and private debt in pursuit of a two-year associate's degree in graphic design at the for-profit Katharine Gibbs School, in Midtown Manhattan. Like subprime mortgages, the debt didn't appear so intimidating at first, but just as balloon payments capsized so many tenuous family finances, a cascading series of loans, a few thousand dollars at a time, eventually caught up with Gittens. In the end, his degree proved as meaningless as it was expensive. When he went to apply for bachelor's programs, no legitimate college would recognize his credits because the school's shoddy performance had finally led the state to sanction it.

So Gittens has started over from scratch—but with tens of thousands of dollars in loans hanging over his head. As I listened to him recount his tale, just as he was about to once again begin his freshman year of college, what struck me most was how insistently the 27-year-old was holding on to his goal of getting credentialed. Even without a degree, he'd built a modestly successful graphic design business of his own. He'd landed fancy internships with hip-hop clothing designers and made smart choices like offsetting his design work with more reliable income from printing jobs. Yet a college degree remained such a coveted treasure for him that, even having [wasted] tens of thousands of dollars and two years of his life, he was prepared to do it all again.

"It's more of an emotional thing," Gittens explained, citing a graduate degree as his ultimate goal. "I'd like to say, 'I have a master's in design.' That would make me feel good." And the sky's the limit when you're buying self-worth.

Of course, the industry that's been turning fast profit off of ambitions like Gittens' is finally seeing tough times of its own. Take Gittens' alma mater, the now-closed Katharine Gibbs School. It was owned by Illinois-based Career Education Corp., a publicly traded firm that still runs dozens of schools across the country and in Europe, and which is among the industry's largest players. Career Ed booked $1.49 billion in revenue in 2012, but it faces steadily declining stock values as a series of investigations and scandals have limited its ability to pull in new students. Its "student starts"—as enrollment is called in the for-profit sector—dropped 23 percent last year. That comes after attorneys general in both New York and Florida launched probes in 2011 of the company for falsifying job placement rates. Career Ed has also had to answer to two national accrediting bodies for its job placement reporting in the past two years.

The company responded to these probes by launching its own investigation and revealing that barely a quarter of its health and design schools actually placed enough graduates in jobs to maintain accreditation. So Chairman Steve Lesnik, who also runs a company that develops golf facilities and athletic clubs, took over as CEO and overhauled the way Career Ed reports job placements, adding independent verification. He stresses Career Ed's newfound compliance with regulators and called 2012 a "year of renewal." "It's a simple thought: students first," he said last February, as he addressed investors for the first time as CEO and sought to calm nerves over the regulatory probes. "That idea permeates every action we take."

But while the company reassures regulators and investors that its education is sound, it's failing starkly by another blunt measure. Nearly 28 percent of students at Career Ed's health services school in New York City, the Sanford Brown Institute, default on their loans after three years. That rate's outstanding even among for-profits, and it is a sure sign that these degrees aren't leading to jobs with decent salaries—if they're leading to jobs at all.

Big for-profits like Career Ed—often run by financiers, not educators—are eager to differentiate themselves from small, independent trade schools like the one Whatley attended, where they argue the bad behavior is concentrated. But what all of the industry's players have in common is a business model that targets desperate people who have been pushed out of the workforce in overwhelming numbers over the past decade.

You needn't look further than these schools' ad campaigns to discover who's in their target demographic. They're a model of diversity. It's tough to find a marketing image that doesn't picture a happy person of color or a young woman, or both. One Sanford Brown online ad features a verbal montage of emotional touchstones that seem tailor-made to speak to working-class frustrations. “Before I contacted Sanford Brown I was working second shift,” says one woman’s voice. “I needed a career for myself and my family,” says another woman. “They empowered me to be a better person,” another declares. Watching the ads reminds me of one Atlanta woman’s explanation when I asked her why she signed off on such a bad deal as the subprime refinance that put her home at risk of foreclosure. She talked about the “nice young man” who came and sold it to her. He was well-dressed and clean cut and black. He seemed successful. He seemed to remind her of her ambitions for the young black men in her own life. Then he stole from her on behalf of his bank.

In this respect, for-profit schools function less like traditional educational institutions and more like payday lenders, rent-to-own businesses, pawn shops and the like—they all offer products that churn customers through debt for years on end. And, like the rest of the subprime market, selling for-profit degrees is especially good business in the worst of times. Career Ed’s previous CEO left his post just as the New York attorney general’s probe sent the company’s stock into free fall; he departed with a reported $5.1 million parachute. According to a Senate report last July, which used data from 2009, three-quarters of students at for-profit schools attended institutions that were owned by publicly traded corporations or private equity firms. The former had an average profit margin of nearly 20 percent—and their CEOs made an average of $7.3 million.

20 Regulators at both the federal and state level have begun working furiously to rein all of this in. Among other things, the Obama administration has tightened rules for schools to participate in the federal student aid program upon which for-profits depend. Last year, the Department of Education instituted a rule that disqualifies any school at which 30 percent of students or more have defaulted on their loans within three years of graduation. The first sanctions under the new rule won’t come until next fall, but according to the department’s tally, for-profits accounted for nearly three-quarters of the schools that would have been forced out in 2012.

There is significant evidence that schools were gaming the feds’ previous system for monitoring default rates. The Senate report from last July revealed aggressive machinations to push struggling graduates into forbearance—a costly way to escape delinquency—just long enough to push their defaults beyond the oversight window. At Career Ed, for instance, employees called students with delinquent loans an average 46 times to nudge them to file for forbearance, regardless of whether that was in the students' best interest financially. Gittens, Whatley and thousands of other unemployed or underemployed African-American strivers have been told again and again—by elected officials, by community leaders, by their own optimistic families—that they hold their economic destiny in their own hands. That they must pick up new skills, get more training, earn more credentials, adapt or die. One day the jobs will come, we're told, and we'd all better be ready to fill them. They're earnestly heeding that message, but the only thing an awful lot of them are earning is another lesson in just how expensive it is to be both poor and ambitious in America.

Analyze

1. What was the difference in enrollment in public four-year schools and for-profit schools between black and white Americans? Explain the difference.
2. List Wright's references, including statistical data and personal interviews. Did he miss any important perspectives? What one part of this essay would you share with someone else? Why?
3. Referring to himself, Wright writes: "Hell, I even went and got certified in selling wine; journalism's a shrinking trade, after all." How do the self-references construct Wright's ethos (character and credibility)? Do his personal and professional references add to or detract from the argument?

Explore

1. Education has typically been viewed as a means for building resilience, a safety net that increases employment possibilities and earning potential over a lifetime. However, Wright claims: "For too many, school has greased the downward slide." He continues, "The loan default rate among for-profit college students is more than double that of their peers in both public and nonprofit private schools, because the degrees and certificates the students are earning are trap doors to more poverty, not springboards to prosperity." Cite cases you know that support or challenge this claim. Is any education worthwhile no matter the cost? Write a researched letter to a parent, child, or friend considering college in which you explain your view on the link between the cost of education and the potential return on that investment.

2. Wright uses analogy to sound the alarm about education debt: "From subprime credit cards through to subprime home loans and now on into subprime education, we've reached again and again for the trappings of middle-class life, only to find ourselves slipping further into debt and poverty." Is his analogy convincing? How is the education crisis he describes similar to or different from the subprime mortgage crisis that surfaced in 2008? What do illiteracy and aspiration have to do with both?
3. Wright does a rhetorical analysis of the ad campaign for a for-profit school, analyzing how, for example, race and aspiration are represented in their pictures and dialogue. Choose two post-secondary institutions and do a rhetorical analysis of their recruiting materials, attending carefully to how each institution taps into narratives of *hope* (aspiration toward the American Dream) and narratives of *fear* (e.g., escape from financial uncertainty). Do the approaches seem fair or manipulative?

Michelle Alexander

"The New Jim Crow: How the War on Drugs Gave Birth to a Permanent American Undercaste"

Michelle Alexander is a civil rights lawyer and a professor of law at Ohio State University. She also writes freelance pieces concerning the mass incarceration of black Americans. The following is an argument about the continued effects of racial discrimination caused by targeting black Americans as criminals. Her claims are based on her book *The New Jim Crow: Mass Incarceration in the Age of Colorblindness*, which has earned much critical acclaim and spent over a year on the *New York Times* best-seller list.

In what ways does incarceration increase the likelihood of future poverty?

Ever since Barack Obama lifted his right hand and took his oath of office, pledging to serve the United States as its 44th president, ordinary people and their leaders around the globe have been celebrating our nation's "triumph over race." Obama's election has been touted as the final nail in the coffin of Jim Crow, the bookend placed on the history of racial caste in America.

Obama's mere presence in the Oval Office is offered as proof that "the land of the free" has finally made good on its promise of equality. There's an implicit yet undeniable message embedded in his appearance on the world stage: this is what freedom looks like; this is what democracy can do for you. If you are poor, marginalized, or relegated to an inferior caste, there is hope for you. Trust us. Trust our rules, laws, customs, and wars. You, too, can get to the promised land.

Perhaps greater lies have been told in the past century, but they can be counted on one hand. Racial caste is alive and well in America.

Most people don't like it when I say this. It makes them angry. In the "era of colorblindness" there's a nearly fanatical desire to cling to the myth that we as a nation have "moved beyond" race. Here are a few facts that run counter to that triumphant racial narrative:

- There are more African American adults under correctional control today—in prison or jail, on probation or parole—than were enslaved in 1850, a decade before the Civil War began.
- As of 2004, more African American men were disenfranchised (due to felon disenfranchisement laws) than in 1870, the year the Fifteenth Amendment was ratified, prohibiting laws that explicitly deny the right to vote on the basis of race.
- A black child born today is less likely to be raised by both parents than a black child born during slavery. The recent disintegration of the African American family is due in large part to the mass imprisonment of black fathers.
- If you take into account prisoners, a large majority of African American men in some urban areas have been labeled felons for life. (In the Chicago area, the figure is nearly 80%.) These men are part of a growing undercaste—not class, caste—permanently relegated, by law, to a second-class status. They can be denied the right to vote, automatically excluded from juries, and legally discriminated against in

employment, housing, access to education, and public benefits, much as their grandparents and great-grandparents were during the Jim Crow era.

Excuses for the Lockdown

5 There is, of course, a colorblind explanation for all this: crime rates. Our prison population has exploded from about 300,000 to more than 2 million in a few short decades, it is said, because of rampant crime. We're told that the reason so many black and brown men find themselves behind bars and ushered into a permanent, second-class status is because they happen to be the bad guys.

The uncomfortable truth, however, is that crime rates do not explain the sudden and dramatic mass incarceration of African Americans during the past 30 years. Crime rates have fluctuated over the last few decades—they are currently at historical lows—but imprisonment rates have consistently soared. Quintupled, in fact. A main driver has been the War on Drugs. Drug offenses alone accounted for about two-thirds of the increase in the federal inmate population, and more than half of the increase in the state prison population between 1985 and 2000, the period of our prison system's most dramatic expansion.

The drug war has been brutal—complete with SWAT teams, tanks, bazookas, grenade launchers, and sweeps of entire neighborhoods—but those who live in white communities have little clue to the devastation wrought. This war has been waged almost exclusively in poor communities of color, even though studies consistently show that people of all colors use and sell illegal drugs at remarkably similar rates. In fact, some studies indicate that white youth are significantly more likely to engage in illegal drug dealing than black youth. Any notion that drug use among African Americans is more severe or dangerous is belied by the data. White youth, for example, have about three times the number of drug-related visits to the emergency room as their African American counterparts.

That is not what you would guess, though, when entering our nation's prisons and jails, overflowing as they are with black and brown drug offenders. Human Rights Watch reported in 2000 that, in some states, African Americans comprised 80%–90% of all drug offenders sent to prison. Rates of black imprisonment have fallen since then, but not by much.

This is the point at which I am typically interrupted and reminded that black men have higher rates of violent crime. *That's* why the drug war is waged in poor communities of color and not middle-class suburbs. Drug warriors are trying to get rid of those drug kingpins and violent offenders who make ghetto communities a living hell. It has nothing to do with race; it's all about violent crime.

Again, not so. President Ronald Reagan officially declared the current drug war in 1982, when drug crime was declining, not rising. President Richard Nixon was the first to coin the term "a war on drugs," but it was President Reagan who turned the rhetorical war into a literal one. From the outset, the war had relatively little to do with drug crime and much to do with racial politics. The drug war was part of a grand and highly successful Republican Party strategy of using racially coded political appeals on issues of crime and welfare to attract poor and working class white voters who were resentful of, and threatened by, desegregation, busing, and affirmative action. In the words of H. R. Haldeman, President Richard Nixon's White House Chief of Staff: "[T]he whole problem is really the blacks. The key is to devise a system that recognizes this while not appearing to."

A few years after the drug war was announced, crack cocaine hit the 10
streets of inner-city communities. The Reagan administration seized on this development with glee, hiring staff who were to be responsible for publicizing inner-city crack babies, crack mothers, crack whores, and drug-related violence. The goal was to make inner-city crack abuse and violence a media sensation, bolstering public support for the drug war which, it was hoped, would lead Congress to devote millions of dollars in additional funding to it.

The plan worked like a charm. For more than a decade, black drug dealers and users would be regulars in newspaper stories and would saturate the evening TV news. Congress and state legislatures nationwide would devote billions of dollars to the drug war and pass harsh mandatory minimum sentences for drug crimes—sentences longer than murderers receive in many countries.

Democrats began competing with Republicans to prove that they could be even tougher on the dark-skinned pariahs. In President Bill Clinton's boastful words, "I can be nicked a lot, but no one can say I'm soft on crime." The facts bear him out. Clinton's "tough on crime" policies resulted in the largest increase in federal and state prison inmates of any president in American history. But Clinton was not satisfied with exploding prison populations. He and the "New Democrats" championed legislation banning drug felons from public housing (no matter how minor the offense) and denying them basic public benefits, including food stamps, for life. Discrimination in virtually every aspect of political, economic, and social life is now perfectly legal, if you've been labeled a felon.

Facing Facts

But what about all those violent criminals and drug kingpins? Isn't the drug war waged in ghetto communities because that's where the violent offenders can be found? The answer is yes . . . in made-for-TV movies. In real life, the answer is no.

The drug war has never been focused on rooting out drug kingpins or violent offenders. Federal funding flows to those agencies that increase dramatically the volume of drug arrests, not the agencies most successful in bringing down the bosses. What has been rewarded in this war is sheer numbers of drug arrests. To make matters worse, federal drug forfeiture laws allow state and local law enforcement agencies to keep for their own use 80% of the cash, cars, and homes seized from drug suspects, thus granting law enforcement a direct monetary interest in the profitability of the drug market.

The results have been predictable: people of color rounded up en masse for relatively minor, non-violent drug offenses. In 2005, four out of five drug arrests were for possession, only one out of five for sales. Most people in state prison have no history of violence or even of significant selling activity. In fact, during the 1990s—the period of the most dramatic expansion of the drug war—nearly 80% of the increase in drug arrests was for marijuana possession, a drug generally considered less harmful than alcohol or tobacco and at least as prevalent in middle-class white communities as in the inner city.

In this way, a new racial undercaste has been created in an astonishingly short period of time—a new Jim Crow system. Millions of people of color are now saddled with criminal records and legally denied the very rights that their parents and grandparents fought for and, in some cases, died for.

Affirmative action, though, has put a happy face on this racial reality. Seeing black people graduate from Harvard and Yale and become CEOs or corporate lawyers—not to mention president of the United States—causes us all to marvel at what a long way we've come.

Recent data shows, though, that much of black progress is a myth. In many respects, African Americans are doing no better than they were when Martin Luther King, Jr. was assassinated and uprisings swept inner cities across America, particularly when it comes to the wealth gap and unemployment rates. Unemployment rates in many black communities rival those in Third World countries. And that's with affirmative action!

When we pull back the curtain and take a look at what our "colorblind" society creates without affirmative action, we see a familiar social, political, and economic structure: the structure of racial caste. The entrance into this new caste system can be found at the prison gate.

This is not Martin Luther King, Jr.'s dream. This is not the promised land. The cyclical rebirth of caste in America is a recurring racial nightmare.

Analyze

1. What is a "racial caste"?
2. Name at least two facts that counter the "triumphant racial narrative."
3. While crime rates have fluctuated over the past few decades, imprisonment rates have done what?

Explore

1. What do the data tell us about the disparities between white and black incarceration rates? Compare that to public perceptions.
2. How does Alexander describe the purpose and plan of the war on drugs? Find at least two outside sources that offer different perspectives. Compare and contrast those perspectives. Is there common ground on any facts, values, causes, or solutions?
3. Write a letter to Alexander in which you challenge and/or support her claim that we have a new Jim Crow. Research the original Jim Crow laws for support. Use your own examples of the presence or absence of colorblindness to support your perspective.

Gabriel Thompson
"Could You Survive on $2 a Day?"

Gabriel Thompson is an author and independent journalist whose work centers on social issues such as immigration and workers' rights. The author of three books, his writing has also been published in *The Nation*, the *New York Times*, *Colorlines*, and *Huffington Post*. In this piece, published in *Mother Jones*, Thompson recounts how Americans experience hardship living on incomes far below the poverty line.

How can people who work full-time still experience "deep poverty"?

Two years ago, Harvard professor Kathryn Edin was in Baltimore interviewing public housing residents about how they got by. As a sociologist who had spent a quarter century studying poverty, she was no stranger to the trappings of life on the edge: families doubling or tripling up in apartments, relying on handouts from friends and relatives, selling blood plasma for cash. But as her fieldwork progressed, Edin began to notice a disturbing pattern. "Nobody was working and nobody was getting welfare," she says. Her research subjects were always pretty strapped, but "this was different. These people had nothing coming in."

Edin shared her observations with H. Luke Shaefer, a colleague from the University of Michigan. While the income numbers weren't literally nothing, they were pretty darn close. Families were subsisting on just a few thousand bucks a year. "We pretty much assumed that incomes this low are really, really rare," Shaefer told me. "It hadn't occurred to us to even look."

Curious, they began pulling together detailed household Census data for the past 15 years. There was reason for pessimism. Welfare reform had placed strict time limits on general assistance and America's ongoing economic woes were demonstrating just how far the jobless could fall in the absence of a strong safety net. The researchers were already aware of a rise in "deep poverty," a term used to describe households living at less than half of the federal poverty threshold, or $11,000 a year for a family of four. Since 2000, the number of people in that category has grown to more than 20 million—a whopping 60 percent increase. And the rate has grown from 4.5 percent of the population to 6.6 percent in 2011, the highest in recent memory save 2010, which was just a tad worse (6.7 percent).

But Edin and Shaefer wanted to see just how deep that poverty went. In doing so, they relied on a World Bank marker used to study the poor in developing nations: This designation, which they dubbed "extreme" poverty, makes deep poverty look like a cakewalk. It means scraping by on less than $2 per person per day, or $2,920 per year for a family of four.

> "'[E]xtreme' poverty, makes deep poverty look like a cakewalk."

In a report published earlier this year by the University of Michigan's National Poverty Center, Edin and Shaefer estimated that nearly 1 in 5 low-income American households has been living in extreme poverty; since 1996, the number of households in that category had increased by about 130 percent. Among the truly destitute were 2.8 million children. Even if you counted food stamps as cash, half of those kids were still being raised in homes whose weekly take wasn't enough to cover a trip to Applebee's. (Figure 3.1 reflects their data.)

In the researchers' eyes, it was a bombshell. But the media barely noticed. "Nobody's talking about it," Edin gripes. Even during a presidential campaign focusing on the economy, only a few local and regional news

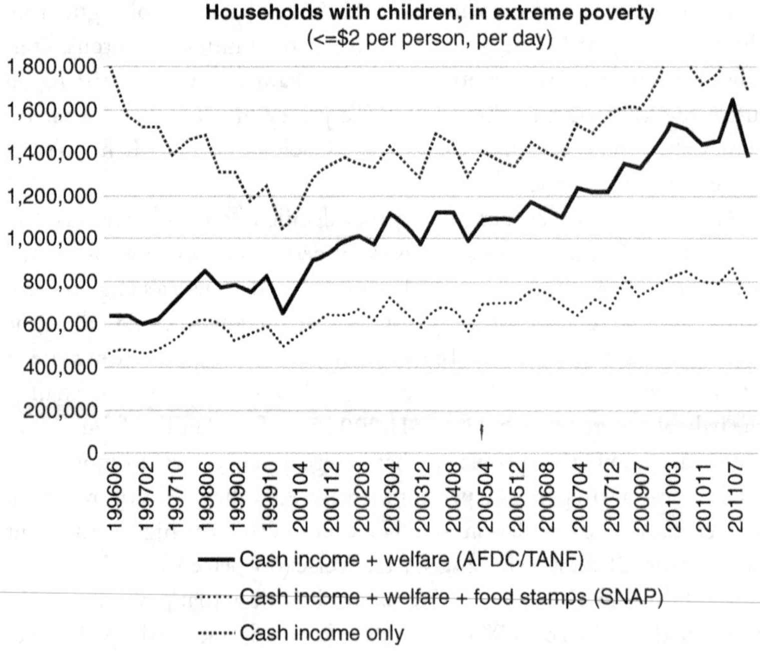

Figure 3.1

outlets took note of their report on the plight of America's poorest families. Mitt Romney told CNN that he wasn't concerned about the "very poor," who, after all, could rely on the nation's "very ample safety net." Even President Obama was reticent to champion any constituent worse off than the middle class. As journalist Paul Tough noted in the *New York Times Magazine* this past August, the politician who cut his teeth as an organizer in inner-city Chicago hasn't made a single speech devoted to poverty as president of the United States. (Paul Ryan has.)

If you want to explore the dire new landscape of American poverty, there's perhaps no better place to visit than Fresno, a sprawling, smoggy city in California's fertile Central Valley. Heading south on Highway 99, I pass acres of grapevines and newly constructed subdivisions before reaching the city limit, where a sign welcomes me to California's Frontier City. Ahead, no doubt, is a city, but all I see is brown haze. It's as if a giant dirt clod had been dropped from space. The frontier looks bleak.

In 2005, after Hurricane Katrina briefly focused the nation's attention on the plight of the poor, the Brookings Institution published a study looking at concentrated poverty. Only one city fared worse than New Orleans: You guessed it, Fresno. Earlier this year, the US Census identified Fresno County as the nation's second-poorest large metropolitan area. Its population has nearly doubled over the past three decades, which means more competition for minimum-wage farm and service-sector jobs, and a quarter of the county's residents fall below the federal poverty threshold. With fewer than 20 percent of adults 25 and up holding bachelors degrees, there's little prospect of better-paying industries flocking here.

For those living on the margins here, daily life can be a long string of emergencies. "There's this whole roiling of folks," says Edie Jessup, a long-time local anti-poverty activist. "They are homeless, move in someplace else, lose their jobs and are evicted, maybe end up in motels."

10 If I want to see how bad things are, Jessup advises, I should check out the area southwest of downtown. She gives me directions, and after crossing some train tracks near a pristine minor-league baseball stadium, I find myself in a virtual shantytown. Amid boarded up warehouses and vacant lots, the streets begin to narrow. They are filled with structures made of pallets, plywood, and upended shopping carts. A truck pulls up filled with bottles of water, and a long line of thirsty people forms.

Amid the makeshift shelters, one section of pavement has been cleaned up, fenced off, and filled with more than 60 Tuff Sheds—prefab tool sheds brought in to provide emergency housing for Fresno's growing street population. "It's not ideal," concedes Kathryn Weakland of the Poverello House, the nonprofit that oversees the encampment and doles out 1,200 hot meals a day. "But like one of the homeless told me, it beats sleeping in a cardboard box."

The collection of sheds even has a name: "Village of Hope."

In the wee hours of the following morning, I pay a visit to Josefa, a 37-year-old single mother from Mexico who lives in a low-slung apartment complex just north of downtown. She's awake and ready by 3 a.m. when the first family knocks on her door. A Latino couple hands off two children and a sleeping baby and then disappears into the dark, heading for fields outside of town. Over the next half hour, two more farmworker families do the same. The small living room is soon filled with kids in various states of somnolence. Some nestle together on couches; others spread out on blankets on the floor. Josefa heads down the hallway to her bedroom, cradling the baby girl and walking quietly to avoid waking her 10-year-old daughter in the next room.

Four hours later, she has accomplished the morning's major chores: Five of the six kids are awake, fed, and dressed. The only holdout is a feisty toddler who is waging a mighty fuss over the prospect of wearing a t-shirt. Josefa gives the edges of the boy's shirt a sharp downward tug and smiles, winning a small but important battle. After pulling her curly black hair into a ponytail she looks at her watch. "Let's go!" she calls, waving her hands toward the door. "We're going to be late."

The group heads down a dirt alleyway, led by a tiny girl wearing a 15
pink Dora the Explorer backpack that looks big enough to double as a pup tent. The school is three blocks away. Along the way, we pass modest but tidy single-family homes, a few shoddy apartment complexes, and two boarded-up buildings. On the surface, there's little to distinguish this neighborhood—known as Lowell—from other hardscrabble sections of Fresno. But Lowell is, in fact, the poorest tract in the city and among the poorest stretches of real estate in America. More than half of its residents, including nearly two-thirds of its children, live in poverty. One in four families earns less than $10,000 a year.

In a county where unemployment now hovers around 14 percent, Josefa is lucky to have work. Even better, she loves her job, and 10 minutes in her company is enough to realize she's got a gift with children. "They run up on the street and hug me," she says, beaming. "What could be better?"

What she lacks is money. Her farmworker clients are barely scraping by, so she only charges them $10 a day per child. At the moment it's late September, the heart of the grape season, so she's got a full house. But at times when there's less demand for farm work, or the weather is wet, she gets by largely on her monthly $200 allotment of food stamps. "I don't even have enough to pay for a childcare license," Josefa says. (Because of this, I've agreed to change her name for this story.)

Josefa estimates that her childcare business brings in $7,000 a year. She visits local churches for donated food and clothes, and has taken in relatives to help cover her $600 rent. Until earlier this year, Josefa and her daughter shared their small apartment with her niece's family. It was hardly ideal—some days, there were 12 people sardined in there. "Of course I need more money," Josefa tells me, pushing a stroller and holding the toddler's hand as we arrive back at her place. "But how can I charge more when no one has any more to give?"

Her niece, Guillermina Ramirez, is sitting in the apartment complex's small courtyard and overhears Josefa's last comment. "The key is to learn English," she announces. Guillermina, like Josefa, is undocumented, but she's married to a US citizen and says she will be a legal resident soon. She recently enrolled in English classes and anticipates securing "a really good job" once she's done. "That's what you need to get ahead."

Gary Villa and Jim Harper speak English and both are American citizens—as a member of the Northern Cheyenne Nation, Harper's lineage goes way back—but neither would say he's getting ahead. I run into the two men outside a temp agency three miles from Josefa's apartment. They've been waiting around since well before sunrise in hopes of finding something.

Villa, a stocky 23-year-old with a shaved head and goatee, tells me that he was pulling in a decent paycheck installing phone boxes for an AT&T subcontractor before he got laid off in 2008. He was evicted from his apartment and now lives with his mother—"It's kind of embarrassing," he mutters—while his girlfriend and two kids moved in with a relative. "You can't pay $800 in rent making $8 an hour."

Villa peers inside the job office, trying to discern any movement.

"At least we have family to fall back on," says Harper, 33, who keeps his long brown hair tucked beneath a red-and-blue Fresno State cap. After being let go from his job delivering radiators, he tried starting a handyman business called Jim's Everything Service. It didn't work out, so now he begins each day by calling seven temp agencies. But Fresno was slammed hard by the housing bust, and it remains a tough place for unemployed blue-collar workers. Harper, who is staying with his stepfather, says he's lucky to pull in more than $200 a month. His monthly food stamp allotment tacks on another $200, for an annual income of $4,800.

By now the sun is well above the horizon and it's shaping up to be yet another day without a paycheck. "The working class isn't the working class if there's no work, right?" says Harper, who is wearing paint-stained Dickies and a faded t-shirt. "We're getting pretty desperate out here."

"I like to joke that I'll take any job short of being a male whore," 25
he adds.

True enough, when the temp office clerk announces that there's a job available, Harper leaps at it even though the gig starts at 2 a.m. and he knows he'll have to arrive at the work site in the early evening, thanks to Fresno's limited bus service. He shrugs off the six hours he'll waste "twiddling his thumbs." What matters, Harper says, is to keep knocking on doors and making the calls, because "you never know when you might get your foot in the door."

Fleeing Fresno's hostile job market might seem like the logical solution, but it's never that simple. As frequently happens with the very poor—especially in light of the restrictions put in place with welfare reform—the informal safety nets that help keep people afloat also tend to keep them rooted in place. Losing his delivery job left Harper homeless. For a few months he lived out of his car or in a room in Fresno's "motel row," notorious for drugs and prostitution. But since moving into his stepfather's house, he's been able to use food stamps in lieu of rent. Leaving town would mean running the risk of being homeless again. And given Harper's income, there's no room for error.

Neither is there a clear path out of deep poverty for Josefa. She puts in twelve-hour days six days a week, so there's not much room to increase her workload. By allowing six other families to work, she plays a small but key role in making Fresno an agriculture powerhouse, but her cut is miniscule. "That's why it's so important for my daughter to study," she says.

The last time I speak to Harper, he tells me he's landed a stint working overnight at a series of grocery stores that are overhauling their freezer compartments. "It looks like it will be a 10-day job," he says, excited. In Fresno, that counts as a big success. I ask where he hopes to find himself in five years. He pauses and takes a deep breath. "Best case scenario, as sad as it sounds, is to be no worse off than I am right now," he says. "That's about all I can hope for."

Analyze

1. Use the text to define "deep poverty" and "extreme poverty."
2. What "bombshell" findings do researchers Edin and Shaefer discover?
3. What does Thompson write is one consequence of people relying on "informal safety nets" to stay afloat?

Explore

1. Why are people using "informal safety nets" as opposed to "formal" ones? What programs constitute the "formal" safety net in the U.S.? Use government sites to explore these programs. Use a timeline-producing tool such as dipity.com or tiki-toki.com to create a multimedia production showing when these programs were started.
2. This article includes two types of evidence: research data and original narratives based on personal interviews. Thompson quotes Edin as saying that the media barely noticed their shocking research. The workers profiled in this article—Josefa, Villa, and Harper—might feel that their shocking stories are equally overlooked. What does it take to get the public's attention and concern about poverty? Are we more likely to listen to research, personal testimonies, or articles like this one that combine both?
3. This article concludes with one of the day workers, Harper, stating that his greatest hope for his well-being in five years is that he's "no worse off." What tone does this set at the conclusion? Is it effective? Is it consistent with the rest of the article? How would you conduct research to find out if that attitude is representative of Americans at different levels of society? What sources could you use to find reliable data on public attitudes? Finally, how does his attitude compare to your attitude about life five years from now? Speculate about why your attitudes are the same or different.

Sonja Livingston
"Shame"

Sonja Livingston is a professor at the University of Memphis, teaching in the M.F.A. degree program and specializing in writing memoirs and women's nonfiction. The following excerpt is from her award-winning memoir *Ghostbread*, in which she details the physical, emotional, and mental hardships of growing up in poverty in the 1970s.

For what, if anything, should people living in poverty feel ashamed?

The thing is; it has a dent in it.

A scar runs across the face of the metal box. It's chipped and rusted in spots, pushes inward, and presses together whatever unfortunate food item has been placed inside.

There's nothing pretty about my lunchbox, nothing to see but the huge old head of Kwai Chang Caine, the crime-fighting monk from TV. If you look at it, that's all you'll see—Caine's bald head, cracked by the dent, looking like the shell of an overcooked egg.

The dent was there long before I ever got hold of it. It was a hand-me-down from my oldest brother, Bob, who is as quiet and strange as the box. And don't think I don't try covering Kung-Fu's rocky head with a carefully placed hand or two. I try. And try. But the head is hungry and wide and way too big for covering. Big, buttery, and unsmiling, Kung-Fu's head is the first thing people notice about me on the bus to Albion Primary School or at the Brownies. Having the head of Mohammed Ali or Evel Knievel hover on my box—even the entire Walton Family—would be far less painful.

I never tell my mother how much I hate it. I don't want to be seen as weak. 5
I prefer to look greedy, and so beg regularly for a Josie and the Pussycats Box. And when begging doesn't work, I bang my head against Kwai Chang's on the school bus; the first time on accident, but after that, for the easy laughs it earns me, and the chance of damaging it beyond repair. And finally, when knocking heads with Kwai Chang Caine fails to ruin the box, I simply leave it at home and hold off eating till after school.

On those autumn nights when flocks of Brownies gather in fidgety groups in the school gymnasium and open their sewing boxes in search of thread and needle to fashion dolls from empty Palmolive bottles, I look genuinely surprised that my own box had gone missing and ask my cousin Dori for a needle and some thread.

"Where's your sewing kit?" my mother asks when the troop leader reports that I'd forgotten it again and had to borrow from Dori, whose box is everything a sewing kit should be—clear plastic with powder-yellow handles, stuffed to capacity with yarn and thread and a rainbow of fabric scraps.

I shrug, keep to myself the fact that mine is not even a real sewing kit; that I'd prefer to pull needle and thread from a plain brown bag than carry around sewing supplies in Kung-Fu's big old head. I say nothing, and keep as a secondary source of shame the fact that I care about such things.

I decide to be rid of the subject once and for all by convincing my mother that I hate Brownies. And I must be a good liar because my mother somehow believes my aversion to singing and sewing and dipping peeled apples into brown sugar and cinnamon, pushing them onto the ends of broken branches, then turning them over an open fire. I hate the songs, the snacks, and the parades, I say while praying she doesn't look into my eyes.

10 "Just let me quit," I say.

And just like that, she does.

Analyze

1. In this text, what is the narrator supposed to use the Kung-Fu lunchbox for? What does this repurposing suggest to readers about her family's financial status?
2. How does the narrator try to get rid of the lunchbox?
3. Why doesn't the narrator come prepared for Brownies?

Explore

1. The narrator writes: "I never tell my mother how much I hate it. I don't want to be seen as weak. I prefer to look greedy, and so I beg regularly for a Josie and the Pussycats Box." Why does the narrator choose to project greed over weakness to her mother? What is the nature of that weakness? Explain.
2. When her mother asks why she didn't have her sewing kit at Brownies, the narrator shrugs and doesn't say what she's thinking, that hers "is not even a real sewing kit." Instead, she says nothing, "and keeps as a

secondary source of shame the fact that [she] care[s] about such things." If this is a secondary shame, what is the primary shame?

3. In this story, the lunchbox becomes a symbol for something larger, a visible sign of difference. What are the ultimate consequences (negative and positive) of the narrator's refusal to brand herself with the lunchbox?

Laura Sullivan-Hackley
"Speech Pathology: The Deflowering of an Accent"

Laura Sullivan-Hackley is a graphic designer who graduated with a degree in journalism from Western Kentucky University. She published the following prose in *Kalliope*, a literary magazine featuring poetry, nonfiction, fiction, and artwork. This piece also appears in the book *Reclaiming Class: Women, Poverty, and the Promise of Higher Education*, edited by Vivyan C. Adair and Sandra L. Dalhberg, a collection of essays written by women who sought higher education as an opportunity to overcome poverty. In her writing, Sullivan-Hackley conveys the pressure to erase unique and sometimes shaming marks of poverty, such as accents.

Has someone's criticism ever prompted you to want to mask unique characteristics that define a certain part of you?

Each schoolday was a raveling Pavlovian chain. First a flicker of naked bulb shocking us out of bed. Then Bus 64's engine grinding uphill, belching sour diesel exhaust in our path like a taunt, daring us in this chase. Once aboard, we watched the neighborhood's grey Etch-a-Sketch landscape scroll past our windows until it disappeared into fog behind us. We dreaded the air brake sighing that sigh of a tired old man, our cue to wade through Marlboro clouds toward the clatter and nag of homeroom bell.

When Bus 64 screeched and coughed to a stop in front of school one Tuesday, the driver refused to let us off. We sat, watching all other buses unload, spilling classmates into a new schoolday. At 8:01, a long sedan parked over our shadowed silhouettes in the bus lane. The county school superintendent thrust himself out of that black Lincoln, then boarded our bus two steps at a time. Grim like somebody had just died or egged his house, he appeared to be masturbating with his necktie, gripping and tugging and rearranging with one fist.

"Hogtrash." He flung the word out over us all like a Frisbee rimmed with mud for extra spin, then waited for it to settle.

"Every last one of you. Hogtrash. Never amount to nothing."

5 We would have searched each other's faces for clues, but our gazes drove forward, hard swizzlestick skewers this man might impale himself on. Bus 64 seemed to shrink, its brown vinyl closing around us like cupped hands of beggars until we were no longer passengers parked outside our destination; we were stepchildren bumming a ride.

The superintendent gave his tie one more fierce yank before spinning on his heels, knocking the door open with his fist. He tripped on the last step down, but his gaffe came too late to elicit even the slightest snag of an upper lip.

The slow stream of us snaked from Bus 64 to the linoleum school foyer. Stepping down to asphalt, my jaw clamped shut. By the ring of first-period bell, I had slated my own lesson plan: to master a new language, no matter how bitter or foreign its flavor on my tongue.

My words became bullets, severe and staccato. Rappelling the cliffs where *g*s and hard *o*s had always dropped off the ends of things, I fought past the *in*s and *uh*s my lips liked to rest upon. I stiffened against the easy lean of *ain't*, the lively rhythm of twang. I bit down on all the lacy fringe of my mother's words, the slurred segues between my father's syllables, that peppery patois of the neighborhood.

The prize I knew when I heard it pronounced, years and miles from Bus 64's shuttling: "You don't sound like you come from anywhere."

Analyze

1. Who is the unexpected visitor to Bus 64? What is his purpose?
2. What does the visitor call the students? What is the significance of that particular insult?
3. What self-directed "lesson plan" does the narrator write for herself after this incident?

Explore

1. Bus 64 becomes a character in this narrative. How does it symbolize its passengers before and after the incident?
2. The narrator describes her effort to erase her accent, deliberately fighting against the speech patterns she inherited from her mother and father. Why has the accent become a source of shame? Research this phenomenon, common to both rural and urban residents, of erasing an accent to conceal a heritage deemed socially undesirable. Write an academic essay or narrative on this issue using descriptive writing.
3. In the conclusion, the narrator claims that she has won the prize because she no longer has an accent that tells others where she comes from. Is she genuinely satisfied, or is there some regret in that accomplishment? What does it mean not to seem to come from anywhere? Think of economic disparities in your home region. Are the affluent areas and low-income areas clearly marked? What are the signs of that difference—verbal accents or physical amenities like parks, gates, and structures that inscribe those boundaries? Can people tell who is from "the wrong side of the tracks"? Census data show that some of the richest counties in the U.S. are next to the poorest. This is common around the world. Use a tool such as the Measure of America map (measureofamerica.org/map) to research your home region, or a region that interests you, to analyze local economic patterns. Now research causes for these sharp differences. What policies or practices (local, national, or global) contribute to this phenomenon of starkly unequal neighbors?

Sherman Alexie
"Why Chicken Means So Much to Me"

Sherman Alexie was raised on the Spokane Indian Reservation, and much of his writing, poetry, and filmmaking reflects his experience growing up as a Native American. The following excerpt is from his novel *The Absolutely True Diary of a Part-Time Indian*, which is based on events in Alexie's life. In it, the narrator confronts the many consequences of growing up as a poor Native American struggling with health problems and bullying.

Why do the poor need others to "pay attention to their dreams in order to have the chance to be something else"?

Okay, so now you know that I'm a cartoonist. And I think I'm pretty good at it, too. But no matter how good I am, my cartoons will never take the place of food or money. I wish I could draw a peanut butter and jelly sandwich, or a fist full of twenty dollar hills, and perform some magic trick and make it real. But I can't do that. Nobody can do that, not even the hungriest magician in the world.

I wish I were magical, but I am really just a poor-ass reservation kid living with his poor-ass family on the poor-ass Spokane Indian Reservation.

Do you know the worst thing about being poor? Oh, maybe you've done the math in your head and you figure:

$$\textit{Poverty} = \textit{empty refrigerator} + \textit{empty stomach}$$

And sure, sometimes, my family misses a meal, and sleep is the only thing we have for dinner, but I know that, sooner or later, my parents will come bursting through the door with a bucket of Kentucky Fried Chicken.

Original Recipe.

5 And hey, in a weird way, being hungry makes food taste better. There is nothing better than a chicken leg when you haven't eaten for (approximately) eighteen-and-a-half hours. And believe me, a good piece of chicken can make anybody believe in the existence of God.

So hunger is not the worst thing about being poor.

And now I'm sure you're asking, "Okay, okay, Mr. Hunger Artist, Mr. Mouth-Full-of-Words, Mr. Woe-Is-Me, Mr. Secret Recipe, what is the worst thing about being poor?"

So, okay, I'll tell you the worst thing.

Last week, my best friend Oscar got really sick.

10 At first, I thought he just had heat exhaustion or something. I mean, it was a crazy-hot July day (102 degrees with 90 percent humidity), and plenty of people were falling over from heat exhaustion, so why not a little dog wearing a fur coat?

I tried to give him some water, but he didn't want any of that.

He was lying on his bed with red, watery, snotty eyes. He whimpered in pain. When I touched him, he yelped like crazy.

It was like his nerves were poking out three inches from his skin.

I figured he'd be okay with some rest, but then he started vomiting, and diarrhea blasted out of him, and he had these seizures where his little legs just kicked and kicked and kicked.

And sure, Oscar was only an adopted stray mutt, but he was the only living thing that I could depend on. He was more dependable than my parents, grandmother, aunts, uncles, cousins, and big sister. He taught me more than any teachers ever did.

Honestly, Oscar was a better person than any human I had ever known.

"Mom," I said. "We have to take Oscar to the vet."
"He'll be all right," she said.

But she was *lying*. Her eyes always got darker in the middle when she lied. She was a Spokane Indian and a bad liar, which didn't make any sense. We Indians really should be better liars, considering how often we've been lied to.

"He's really sick, Mom," I said. "He's going to die if we don't take him to the doctor."

She looked hard at me. And her eyes weren't dark anymore, so I knew that she was going to tell me the truth. And trust me, there are times when the *last thing* you want to hear is the truth.

"Junior, sweetheart," Mom said. "I'm sorry, but we don't have any money for Oscar."
"I'll pay you back," I said. "I promise."
"Honey, it'll cost hundreds of dollars, maybe a thousand."
"I'll pay back the doctor. I'll get a job."

Mom smiled all sad and hugged me hard.

Jeez, how stupid was I? What kind of job can a reservation Indian boy get? I was too young to deal blackjack at the casino, there were only about fifteen green grass lawns on the reservation (and none of their owners outsourced the mowing jobs), and the only paper route was owned by a tribal elder named Wally. And he had to deliver only fifty papers, so his job was more like a hobby.

There was nothing I could do to save Oscar.

Nothing.

Nothing.

Nothing.

So I lay down on the floor beside him and patted his head and whispered his name *for hours.*

Then Dad came home from *wherever* and had one of those long talks with Mom, and they decided something *without me.*

And then Dad pulled down his rifle and bullets from the closet.

"Junior," he said. "Carry Oscar outside."

"No!" I screamed.

"He's suffering," Dad said. "We have to help him."

"You can't do it!" I shouted.

I wanted to punch my dad in the face. I wanted to punch him in the nose and make him bleed. I wanted to punch him in the eye and make him blind. I wanted to kick him in the balls and make him pass out.

I was hot mad. Volcano mad. Tsunami mad.

Dad just looked down at me with the saddest look in his eyes. He was crying. He looked *weak.*

I wanted to hate him for his weakness.

I wanted to hate Dad and Mom for our poverty.

I wanted to blame them for my sick dog and for all the other sickness in the world.

But I can't blame my parents for our poverty because my mother and father are the twin suns around which I orbit and my world would EXPLODE without them.

And it's not like my mother and father were born into wealth. It's not like they gambled away their family fortunes. My parents came from poor people who came from poor people who came from poor people, all the way back to the very first poor people.

Adam and Eve covered their privates with fig leaves; the first Indians covered their privates *with their tiny hands.*

Seriously, I know my mother and father had their dreams when they were kids. They dreamed about being something other than poor, but they never got the chance to be anything because nobody paid attention to their dreams.

Given the chance, my mother would have gone to college.

She still reads books like crazy. She buys them by the pound. And she remembers everything she reads. She can recite whole pages by memory.

Figure 3.5

She's a human tape recorder. Really, my mom can read the newspaper in fifteen minutes and tell me baseball scores, the location of every war, the latest guy to win the Lottery, and the high temperature in Des Moines, Iowa.

Given the chance, my father would have been a musician.

When he gets drunk, he sings old country songs. And blues, too. And he sounds good. Like a pro. Like he should be on the radio. He plays the guitar and the piano a little bit. And he has this old saxophone from high school that he keeps all clean and shiny, like he's going to join a band at any moment.

But we reservation Indians don't get to realize our dreams. We don't get those chances. Or choices. We're just poor. That's all we are.

It sucks to be poor, and it sucks to feel that you somehow *deserve* to be poor. You start believing that you're poor because you're stupid and ugly. And then you start believing that you're stupid and ugly because you're Indian. And because you're Indian you start believing you're destined to be poor. It's an ugly circle and *there's nothing you can do about it.*

Poverty doesn't give you strength or teach you lessons about perseverance. No, poverty only teaches you how to be poor.

So, poor and small and weak, I picked up Oscar. He licked my face because he loved and trusted me. And I carried him out to the lawn, and I laid him down beneath our green apple tree.

"I love you, Oscar." I said.

He looked at me and I swear to you that he understood what was happening. He knew what Dad was going to do. But Oscar wasn't scared. He was relieved.

But not me.

I ran away from there as fast as I could.

I wanted to run faster than the speed of sound, but nobody, no matter how much pain they're in, can run that fast. So I heard the boom of my father's rifle when he shot my best friend.

A bullet only costs about two cents, and anybody can afford that.

Analyze

1. The narrator offers to get a job and pay back his parents for the vet bill. Why won't that solution work?
2. Why does the narrator say he can't blame his parents for their poverty?
3. What does the narrator say his mother would do "if given the chance"? What would his father do "if given the chance"? What does that phrase mean here?

Explore

1. This story shows the excruciating sense of powerlessness when the poor can do "Nothing. Nothing. Nothing." Write an example similar to this story about a time when financial resources fell too short to provide an emotional or spiritual safety net for you or someone you know. Or write an example in which having financial resources provided someone with the ability to protect or expand vital capabilities, such as visiting a loved one at a critical time, going on a vacation or retreat to reenergize, or getting counseling.
2. The narrator names many emotional consequences of poverty: "It sucks to be poor, and it sucks to feel that you somehow *deserve* to be poor. You start believing that you're poor because you're stupid and ugly. And then you start believing that you're stupid and ugly because you're Indian. And because you're Indian you start believing that you're destined to be poor. It's an ugly circle and *there's nothing you can do about it.*" Analyze this passage drawing from the readings in this chapter and book that help you think about such issues as discrimination, shame, and the importance of emotional well-being.
3. The narrator writes: "Poverty doesn't give you strength or teach you lessons about perseverance. No, poverty only teaches you how to be poor." This seems to rebut arguments made outside the text that sometimes romanticize poverty, suggesting that suffering ennobles the poor. Analyze this passage in your own words, drawing from narratives of people in poverty (e.g., Sue in the Potts article) who reveal their own wavering sense of self-worth as they navigate life in poverty.

Tressie McMillan Cottom
"Why Do Poor People 'Waste' Money on Luxury Goods?"

Lecturing and publishing widely on the subjects of inequality, education, race, and gender, Tressie McMillan Cottom is a sociologist and regular columnist for *Slate*. Her work appears in academic journals and in mainstream publications including *The Atlantic*, *NPR*, *The Chronicle of Higher Education*, and many more. McMillan Cottom served as a fellow at the Center for Poverty Research at the University of California-Davis when she wrote this essay, originally published on *Talking Points Memo*, an online political news organization. In this essay, McMillan Cottom explains how investing in outward displays of wealth and education, such as professional clothing, can help low-income people get past the social gatekeepers who award mobility.

Have you ever desired—or purchased—something well beyond your budget in order to feel like you belong?

We hates us some poor people. First, they insist on being poor when it is so easy to not be poor. They do things like buy expensive designer belts and $2500 luxury handbags.

To be fair, this isn't about Errol Louis [McMillan Cottom is responding to Errol Louis's tweet: "I totally get that it's horrible and illegal to profile people. But still #SMFH over a not-filthy-rich person spending $2,500 on a handbag."]. His is a belief held by many people, including lots of black people, poor people, formerly poor people, etc. It is, I suspect, an honest expression of incredulity. If you are poor, why do you spend money on useless status symbols like handbags and belts and clothes and shoes and televisions and cars?

One thing I've learned is that one person's illogical belief is another person's survival skill. And nothing is more logical than trying to survive.

My family is a classic black American migration family. We have rural Southern roots, moved north and almost all have returned. I grew up watching my great-grandmother, and later my grandmother and mother, use our minimal resources to help other people make ends meet. We were those good poors, the kind who live mostly within our means. We had a little luck when a male relative got extra military pay when they came home a paraplegic or used the VA to buy a Jim Walter house. If you were really blessed when a relative died with a paid up insurance policy you might be gifted a lump sum to buy the land that Jim Walters used as collateral to secure your home lease. That's how generational wealth happens where I'm from: lose a leg, a part of your spine, die right and maybe you can lease-to-own a modular home.

5 We had a little of that kind of rural black wealth so we were often in a position to help folks less fortunate. But perhaps the greatest resource we had was a bit more education. We were big readers and we encouraged the girl children, especially, to go to some kind of college. Consequently, my grandmother and mother had a particular set of social resources that helped us navigate mostly white bureaucracies to our benefit. We could, as my grandfather would say, talk like white folks. We loaned that privilege out to folks a lot.

I remember my mother taking a next door neighbor down to the social service agency. The elderly woman had been denied benefits to care for the granddaughter she was raising. The woman had been denied in the genteel bureaucratic way—lots of waiting, forms, and deadlines she could not quite navigate. I watched my mother put on her best Diana Ross "Mahogany" outfit: a camel colored cape with matching slacks and knee high boots. I was miffed, as only an only child could be, about sharing my mother's time with the neighbor girl. I must have said something about why we had to do this. Vivian fixed me with a stare as she was slipping on her pearl earrings and told me that people who can do, must do. It took half a day but something about my mother's performance of respectable black person—her Queen's English, her Mahogany outfit, her straight bob and pearl earrings—got done what the elderly lady next door had not been able to get done in over a year. I learned, watching my mother, that there was a price we had to pay to signal to gatekeepers that we were worthy of engaging. It meant dressing well and speaking well. It might not work. It likely wouldn't work but on the off chance that it would, you had to try. It was unfair but, as Vivian also always said, "life isn't fair little girl."

I internalized that lesson and I think it has worked out for me, if unevenly. A woman at Belk's once refused to show me the Dooney and Burke purse I was interested in buying. Vivian once made a salesgirl cry after she ignored us in an empty store. I have walked away from many hotly desired purchases, like the impractical off-white winter coat I desperately wanted, after some bigot at the counter insulted me and my mother. But, I have half a PhD and I support myself aping the white male privileged life of the mind. It's a mixed bag. Of course, the trick is you can never know the counterfactual of your life. There is no evidence of access denied. Who knows what I was not granted for not enacting the right status behaviors or symbols at the right time for an agreeable authority? Respectability rewards are a crap-shoot but we do what we can within the limits of the constraints imposed by a complex set of structural and social interactions designed to limit access to status, wealth, and power.

I do not know how much my mother spent on her camel colored cape or knee-high boots but I know that whatever she paid it returned in hard-to-measure dividends. How do you put a price on the double-take of a clerk at the welfare office who decides you might not be like those other trifling women in the waiting room and provides an extra bit of information about completing a form that you would not have known to ask about? What is the retail value of a school principal who defers a bit more to your child because your mother's presentation of self signals that she might unleash the bureaucratic savvy of middle class parents to advocate for her child? I don't know the price of these critical engagements with organizations and gatekeepers relative to our poverty when I was growing up. But, I am living proof of its investment yield.

Why do poor people make stupid, illogical decisions to buy status symbols? For the same reason all but only the most wealthy buy status symbols, I suppose. We want to belong. And, not just for the psychic rewards, but belonging to one group at the right time can mean the difference between unemployment and employment, a good job as opposed to a bad job, housing or a shelter, and so on. Someone mentioned on Twitter that poor people can be presentable with affordable options from Kmart. But the issue is not about being presentable. Presentable is the bare minimum of social civility. It means being clean, not smelling, wearing shirts and shoes for service and the like. Presentable as a sufficient condition for gainful, dignified work or successful social interactions is a privilege. It's the aging white hippie who can cut the ponytail of his youthful rebellion and walk into senior management while aging black panthers can never completely outrun the effects of stigmatization against which they were courting a revolution. Presentable is relative and, like life, it ain't fair.

10 In contrast, "acceptable" is about gaining access to a limited set of rewards granted upon group membership. I cannot know exactly how often my presentation of acceptable has helped me but I have enough feedback to know it is not inconsequential. One manager at the apartment complex where I worked while in college told me, repeatedly, that she knew I was "Okay" because my little Nissan was clean. That I had worn a Jones New York suit to the interview really sealed the deal. She could call the suit by name because she asked me about the label in the interview. Another hiring manager at my first professional job looked me up and down in the waiting

room, cataloging my outfit, and later told me that she had decided I was too classy to be on the call center floor. I was hired as a trainer instead. The difference meant no shift work, greater prestige, better pay and a baseline salary for all my future employment.

I have about a half dozen other stories like this. What is remarkable is not that this happened. There is empirical evidence that women and people of color are judged by appearances differently and more harshly than are white men. What is remarkable is that these gatekeepers *told me the story*. They wanted me to know how I had properly signaled that I was not a typical black or a typical woman, two identities that in combination are almost always conflated with being poor.

I sat in on an interview for a new administrative assistant once. My regional vice president was doing the hiring. A long line of mostly black and brown women applied because we were a cosmetology school. Trade schools at the margins of skilled labor in a gendered field are necessarily classed and raced. I found one candidate particularly charming. She was trying to get out of a salon because 10 hours on her feet cutting hair would average out to an hourly rate below minimum wage. A desk job with 40 set hours and medical benefits represented mobility for her. When she left my VP turned to me and said, "did you see that tank top she had on under her blouse?! OMG, you wear a silk *shell*, not a tank top!" Both of the women were black.

The VP had constructed her job as senior management. She drove a brand new BMW because she "should treat herself" and liked to tell us that ours was an image business. A girl wearing a cotton tank top as a shell was incompatible with BMW-driving VPs in the image business. Gatekeeping is a complex job of managing boundaries that do not just define others but that also define ourselves. Status symbols—silk shells, designer shoes, luxury handbags—become keys to unlock these gates. If I need a job that will save my lower back and move my baby from Medicaid to an HMO, how much should I spend signaling to people like my former VP that I will not compromise her status by opening the door to me? That candidate maybe could not afford a proper shell. I will never know. But I do know that had she gone hungry for two days to pay for it or missed wages for a trip to the store to buy it, she may have been rewarded a job that could have lifted her above minimum wage. Shells aren't designer handbags, perhaps. But a cosmetology school in a strip mall isn't a job at Bank of America, either.

At the heart of these incredulous statements about the poor decisions poor people make is a belief that we would never be like them. We would know better. We would know to save our money, eschew status symbols, cut coupons, practice puritanical sacrifice to amass a million dollars. There is a regular news story of a lunch lady who, unbeknownst to all who knew her, died rich and leaves it all to a cat or a charity or some such. Books about the modest lives of the rich like to tell us how they drive Buicks instead of BMWs. What we forget, if we ever know, is that what we know now about status and wealth creation and sacrifice are predicated on who we are, i.e., not poor. If you change the conditions of your not-poor status, you change everything you know as a result of being a not-poor. You have no idea what you would do if you were poor until you are poor. And not intermittently poor or formerly not-poor, but born poor, expected to be poor and treated by bureaucracies, gatekeepers and well-meaning respectability authorities as inherently poor. Then, and only then, will you understand the relative value of a ridiculous status symbol to someone who intuits that they cannot afford to not have it.

Analyze

1. What specific incident prompts McMillan Cottom to write this article at this time?
2. What does McMillan Cottom mean when she describes her family as "good poors"?
3. What does the author say was perhaps her family's greatest resource? What "capability" does that lead to that becomes a "privilege" they loan out?

Explore

1. Referring to some of her mother's most expensive items of clothing, which were worn at all important social exchanges, McMillan Cottom writes: "I do not know how much my mother spent on her camel colored cape or knee-high boots but I know that whatever she paid it returned in hard-to-measure dividends." Explain. To what extent is this example relevant to the example that triggered the essay?
2. Write one sentence that explains how McMillan Cottom answers the question posed in her title.
3. What is "gatekeeping" and what does it have to do with poverty and social mobility? Cite observations and research.

James Webb
"Diversity and the Myth of White Privilege"

When this article was published in the *Wall Street Journal*, James Webb was serving in the U.S. Senate as a Democrat from Virginia. He previously served as the secretary of the Navy. He is the author of numerous books that draw on his military and historical interests, and he has written several articles published in the mainstream press that address wealth, race, and class struggles. In the following essay, Webb urges his audience to consider how white Americans are unfairly discriminated against by policies that attempt to correct for discrimination against minority groups.

Is it ever acceptable or desirable to consider race when awarding jobs, college admissions, or loans?

The NAACP believes the tea party is racist. The tea party believes the NAACP is racist. And Pat Buchanan got into trouble recently by pointing out that if Elena Kagan is confirmed to the Supreme Court, there will not be a single Protestant Justice, although Protestants make up half the U.S. population and dominated the court for generations.

Forty years ago, as the United States experienced the civil rights movement, the supposed monolith of White Anglo-Saxon Protestant dominance served as the whipping post for almost every debate about power and status in America. After a full generation of such debate, WASP elites have fallen by the wayside and a plethora of government-enforced diversity policies have marginalized many white workers. The time has come to cease the false arguments and allow every American the benefit of a fair chance at the future.

I have dedicated my political career to bringing fairness to America's economic system and to our work force, regardless of what people look like or where they may worship. Unfortunately, present-day diversity programs work against that notion, having expanded so far beyond their original purpose that they now favor anyone who does not happen to be white.

In an odd historical twist that all Americans see but few can understand, many programs allow recently arrived immigrants to move ahead of similarly situated whites whose families have been in the country for generations. These programs have damaged racial harmony. And the more they have grown, the less they have actually helped African-Americans, the intended beneficiaries of affirmative action as it was originally conceived.

How so?

Lyndon Johnson's initial program for affirmative action was based on the 13th Amendment and on the Civil Rights Act of 1866, which authorized the federal government to take actions in order to eliminate "the badges of slavery." Affirmative action was designed to recognize the uniquely difficult journey of African-Americans. This policy was justifiable and understandable, even to those who came from white cultural groups that had also suffered in socio-economic terms from the Civil War and its aftermath.

The injustices endured by black Americans at the hands of their own government have no parallel in our history, not only during the period of slavery but also in the Jim Crow era that followed. But the extrapolation of this logic to all "people of color"—especially since 1965, when new immigration laws dramatically altered the demographic makeup of the U.S.—moved affirmative action away from remediation and toward discrimination, this time against whites. It has also lessened the focus on assisting African-Americans, who despite a veneer of successful people at the very top still experience high rates of poverty, drug abuse, incarceration and family breakup.

Those who came to this country in recent decades from Asia, Latin America and Africa did not suffer discrimination from our government, and in fact have frequently been the beneficiaries of special government programs. The same cannot be said of many hard-working white Americans, including those whose roots in America go back more than 200 years.

Contrary to assumptions in the law, white America is hardly a monolith. And the journey of white American cultures is so diverse (yes) that one strains to find the logic that could lump them together for the purpose of public policy.

The clearest example of today's misguided policies comes from examining the history of the American South.

The old South was a three-tiered society, with blacks and hard-put whites both dominated by white elites who manipulated racial tensions in order to retain power. At the height of slavery, in 1860, less than 5% of whites in the South owned slaves. The eminent black historian John Hope Franklin wrote that "fully three-fourths of the white people in the South had neither slaves nor an immediate economic interest in the maintenance of slavery."

The Civil War devastated the South, in human and economic terms. And from post-Civil War Reconstruction to the beginning of World War II, the region was a ravaged place, affecting black and white alike.

In 1938, President Franklin Roosevelt created a national commission to study what he termed "the long and ironic history of the despoiling of this truly American section." At that time, most industries in the South were owned by companies outside the region. Of the South's 1.8 million sharecroppers, 1.2 million were white (a mirror of the population, which was 71% white). The illiteracy rate was five times that of the North-Central states and more than twice that of New England and the Middle Atlantic (despite the waves of European immigrants then flowing to those regions). The total endowments of all the colleges and universities in the South were less than the endowments of Harvard and Yale alone. The average schoolchild in the South had $25 a year spent on his or her education, compared to $141 for children in New York.

Generations of such deficiencies do not disappear overnight, and they affect the momentum of a culture. In 1974, a National Opinion Research Center (NORC) study of white ethnic groups showed that white Baptists nationwide averaged only 10.7 years of education, a level almost identical to blacks' average of 10.6 years, and well below that of most other white groups. A recent NORC Social Survey of white adults born after World War II showed that in the years 1980–2000, only 18.4% of white Baptists and 21.8% of Irish Protestants—the principal ethnic group that settled the South—had obtained college degrees, compared to a national average of 30.1%, a Jewish average of 73.3%, and an average among those of Chinese and Indian descent of 61.9%.

15 Policy makers ignored such disparities within America's white cultures when, in advancing minority diversity programs, they treated whites as a fungible monolith. Also lost on these policy makers were the differences in economic and educational attainment among nonwhite cultures. Thus nonwhite groups received special consideration in a wide variety of areas including business startups, academic admissions, job promotions and lucrative government contracts.

Where should we go from here? Beyond our continuing obligation to assist those African-Americans still in need, government-directed diversity programs should end.

Nondiscrimination laws should be applied equally among all citizens, including those who happen to be white. The need for inclusiveness in our society is undeniable and irreversible, both in our markets and in our communities. Our government should be in the business of enabling opportunity for all, not in picking winners. It can do so by ensuring that artificial distinctions such as race do not determine outcomes.

Memo to my fellow politicians: Drop the Procrustean policies and allow harmony to invade the public mindset. Fairness will happen, and bitterness will fade away.

Analyze

1. Webb argues that diversity programs have evolved such that they now favor anyone who is not what?
2. What does Webb say about President Lyndon Johnson's initial affirmative action program?
3. Webb says that government programs treat "whites as a fungible monolith." What does this mean?

Explore

1. Webb argues that changes in the law since 1965 have "moved affirmative action away from remediation and toward discrimination." What does he mean? Who is being discriminated against now? What factual evidence does Webb provide to support that claim? Why does Webb state that the government is now in the business of "picking winners"?
2. What call to action does Webb close with? Will his recommendations solve the problem he identifies? Why or why not?
3. Write a research brief that you could give to someone who wants to enter the debate on affirmative action. Research all sides of the issue and present them neutrally in a literature review. Note landmark moments in this issue—important legal rulings, key speeches, etc. Your brief should identify the key leaders within the major stakeholder groups. In your conclusion, identify common ground among the stakeholders. State a modest call to action that would fall within that common ground.

Adam Serwer
"Webb and 'White Privilege'"

A reporter for *MSNBC* who covers civil rights and social justice issues, Adam Serwer has written for *Mother Jones*, the *Washington Post*, the *New York Daily News*, and *The American Prospect*. This essay was originally published in *The American Prospect*. In it, Serwer challenges Webb's claims in the previous reading, arguing that white privilege is pervasive in the U.S.

Do you agree that the social advancement of minorities does not have to come at the expense of white Americans?

There are a number of things about Senator Jim Webb's op-ed "[Diversity and] The Myth of White Privilege" to dislike, starting with the fact that one of the awesome things about the existence of white privilege is that you can be part of a body like the U.S. Senate, which has a total number of zero elected black members, and write something titled "[Diversity and] The Myth of White Privilege" without anyone batting an eyelash. That said, Webb's op-ed is considerably more nuanced than the title, acknowledging that "The injustices endured by black Americans at the hands of their own government have no parallel in our history," although he makes the same mistake as Ross Douthat in repeating the conservative frame of zero-sum competition between whites and people of color.

For some reason, Webb sees the existence of poor whites as proof white privilege doesn't exist, when it's largely a non sequitur. The existence of Southie or Appalachia does not change the fact that a white man with a prison record has an easier time than a black person without one. But what I find really remarkable is this:

> The old South was a three-tiered society, with blacks and hard-put whites both dominated by white elites who manipulated racial tensions in order to retain power. At the height of slavery, in 1860, less than 5% of whites in the South owned slaves. The eminent black historian John Hope Franklin wrote that "fully three-fourths of the white people in the South had neither slaves nor an immediate economic interest in the maintenance of slavery."

Webb cites President Franklin Roosevelt's study of poverty and the region and notes, "Generations of such deficiencies do not disappear overnight, and they affect the momentum of a culture." How true. The gaping hole in Webb's argument, however, is that, as Ira Katznelson has written, the entire force of the American state spent decades helping the white people of the region to the exclusion of African Americans, at the behest of their representatives in the Democratic Party. The Social Security Act's three major provisions were constructed to deliberately exclude blacks, and previous programs with federal money aimed at the relief of poverty also gave discretion to the states for how to spend them precisely so Southern states could make sure they weren't being spent on black people. The National Labor Relations Act was constructed to exclude blacks, the GI Bill gave fewer benefits to black soldiers than to white soldiers, and the Federal Housing Authority's discrimination helped build the modern wealth gap between blacks and whites. These efforts "treated whites as a fungible monolith," to borrow Webb's own language, and in concert with other economic factors, helped speed the integration of white ethnics while maintaining a caste-system based on skin color. As if it isn't also obvious, the price for maintaining a system of apartheid in the South was diminishing the potential economic impact of these programs by excluding a large part of the region's residents.

I'm not uncomfortable with the government using its power to help poor people of any color, or people who are discriminated against. But to write about the poverty of the South without acknowledging the decades of massive government effort geared exclusively toward aiding white people is rather astonishing. More astonishing, perhaps, is that Webb, like all affirmative-action opponents, seems to forget the rather large number of white people helped by affirmative action. Webb notes that Johnson's "initial program for affirmative action" was grounded in the 13th Amendment. Sure. But arguing that Johnson meant for affirmative action simply to address the unique history of discrimination faced by African Americans is incorrect. It was Johnson, after all, who included "creed" and "national origin," along with "race" and "color," and in 1967 expanded his original executive order to include women. It's one thing for Republicans, who oppose government efforts to help the disadvantaged on ideological principle, to focus on race in arguments about affirmative action (or FinReg, or Health Care, etc.) because they think that this is the quickest way to get white people angry. But it's surprising to hear from a Democrat, especially one so clearly concerned with the stark racial injustices of the U.S. prison system.

5 Johnson's decision hints at affirmative action's real purpose, one that has been muddied by the legal arguments that have been necessary to keep it alive. The purpose is not merely the "compelling state interest in diversity," it is to help correct the societal biases, conscious and unconscious, that continue to curtail opportunity for certain groups of Americans. The fact that affirmative action, which is a relatively mild form of government action compared to the Democratic Party's deliberate creation of a modern whites-only welfare state, arouses so much anger is evidence of how powerful such biases continue to be.

In general, the argument over affirmative action is broad and nonspecific, and we don't discuss whether we mean college admissions, employment, or allocation of government contracts. I'm comfortable with moving to a more class-based system of affirmative action in college admissions, and I think a more aggressive class-based system might actually work better at creating diversity. But the fact remains that no one knows a white person is an Irish Protestant or a Baptist when they walk into a job interview. They do know when someone is black, and they know when someone is a woman, and we all know that still matters.

Finally, Pat Buchanan did not get into trouble merely for "pointing out that if Elena Kagan is confirmed to the Supreme Court, there will not be a single Protestant Justice." That remark was received in the context of Buchanan being someone whose definition of whiteness excludes white Jews and whose definition of Americanness excludes anyone who is not white. He believes any social advancement for people of color or non-Christians is necessarily to the detriment of white Americans, who are the people to whom America truly belongs. That perhaps explains why Buchanan didn't resign from the Reagan administration in protest when Justice Antonin Scalia was picked because Reagan thought, "We don't have an Italian American on the court, so we ought to have one." After all, if there's any lesson from history in all this, it's that certain forms of affirmative action aren't very controversial.

Analyze

1. Describe the tone of Serwer's opening paragraph. What does it suggest about Serwer's intended audience and purpose?
2. Serwer says that "Webb sees the existence of poor whites as proof white privilege doesn't exist." Serwer labels this argument as a logical fallacy

called a "non sequitur." Define this term. Did he label Webb's argument correctly? Explain.
3. What does Serwer say is the "gaping hole" in Webb's argument?

Explore

1. Research one or more of Serwer's claims about how the U.S. government continued to support white over black Americans even after slavery was abolished. Write a summary that either Webb or Serwer could use if they continued their discussion on this issue.
2. How does Serwer's account of the purpose of President Johnson's affirmative action policy contradict Webb's account? What is the significance of that different reading? How would you determine if one or the other reading is more accurate? Describe your process.
3. In the end, Serwer says that he is "comfortable with moving to a more class-based system of affirmative action" in such areas as college admissions, and he even thinks it might improve diversity. But, in his last line, he emphasizes what other key problem that affirmative action is intended to address aside from increasing diversity? Overall, does Serwer succeed in challenging Webb's argument? Base your assessment not on your own thinking on this issue but on the strength of Serwer's counterargument. Find at least one more response to Webb's op-ed (there were many) and determine which is most rhetorically successful.

Simon Kuper
"Poverty's Poor Show in the Media"

Born in Uganda and raised all over Western Europe and North America, Simon Kuper is a sports writer for *Financial Times*, a British newspaper covering international news with a focus on business and economics. Kuper authored the book *Football Against the Enemy*, and his work, which spans many subjects, has also appeared in *The Observer* and *The Guardian*. In this essay from *Financial Times*, Kuper explains the many reasons journalists often overlook the poor.

If you were asked to interview someone in your community who was poor, how would you go about finding and asking him/her to talk to you?

> "To become news, poor people have to cause disorder."

An actor recently left France after the government tried to raise rich people's taxes. Gérard Depardieu moved to Belgium (to be near friends, excellent meat and Paris's airport, he explained), acquired a Russian passport, and made friends with Vladimir Putin. Meanwhile earlier this month an unemployed father became the fourth Bulgarian to burn himself to death since February in despair at poverty. Guess which victim of the economic crisis got more publicity?

The media have probably always ignored the poor, but we continue to do so even as poverty becomes the most pressing problem in developed countries. One in seven Americans now lives below the official poverty line, ever more jobless people kill themselves, and my colleague Gillian Tett recently wrote of a child in Liverpool chewing the wallpaper as hunger rises in the city. Yet the media still look away. I'm as guilty as anyone. But we can change.

Poverty has never been sexy. In 2008, the Joseph Rowntree Foundation analysed 40 hours of British TV, and found that "the word 'poverty' appeared only twice, both in *Shameless*," a comedy drama. One reference was to the Live Aid concert; the other to Comic Relief. When poor people did get airtime, it was often as objects of derision on *Jerry Springer*-like shows.

You'd have thought the economic crisis would have made poverty newsy. "If it bleeds, it leads" is a journalistic maxim, and the Cambridge sociologist David Stuckler found sharp increases in suicides in recession-hit European countries after 2008. The crisis arguably caused 1,000 "excess" suicides in England alone.

5 But they weren't news. The global poor—2.5 billion people living on less than $2 a day—are considered even more boring, due to the triple whammy of being non-white, non-Anglophone and poor. To become news, poor people have to cause disorder. Middle-class people raise issues by writing;

poor people do it by rioting. I've read columns by prisoners and by people with terminal cancer, but I've never seen one by someone living on benefits.

The neglect isn't because journalists hate poor people. As the Tea Party likes to point out, most journalists are liberals. However, most are also upper-middle-class folk who never visit the poor areas of their city. We tend to interview people like us. There are rightwing media and leftwing media, but all are controlled by the well-fed. So are social media. On a map measuring global Twitter activity, the Netherlands dwarfs India, South Africa and Nigeria put together. And though journalists may be liberals, our proprietors and advertisers mostly aren't.

It's easier to meet a corporate PR for coffee in a nice hotel lobby near the office than to trek out to a chilly ghetto with poor transport links to find interviewees. Even when you get there, you don't always end up using their quotes. Something that's taboo to mention: poor Europeans (if asked) often express views on immigration that most journalists consider racist.

Poor people's analyses rarely fit neatly into the formats through which the ruling class interprets the world. A colleague told me how in Tunisia recently he'd interviewed a poor man who said he supported the ruling Islamist party. Then the man said he might vote for the secular far left. And then he expressed nostalgia for the departed dictator Zine el Abidine Ben Ali. These were probably valid responses to Tunisia's turmoil, but they didn't sound politically sophisticated, and my colleague was baffled.

I blame myself too. In the Palestinian West Bank this winter I interviewed a poor Bedouin family harassed by the Israeli authorities. I didn't write about them. Casting poor people as victims is boring. Anyway, nobody pressures you to quote them. Journalists get called up by corporate PRs, not by Bedouins.

Despite everything, there is a vigorous media debate about inequality. 10
However, it focuses on the 1 percent at the top. Most people profiled in the media—artists, athletes and many politicians—are millionaires. Depardieu probably received more coverage as an individual than the bottom 2.5 billion combined. That humanised him. Even when attacked, he gets a platform to complain about tax rises; people hurt by benefit cuts are rarely interviewed. It's as if you covered the Great Depression only by speaking to rentiers. In fact, we're exactly the media that an unequal world requires.

We don't have to be. We could take our lead from historians, who generations back dropped their exclusive focus on kings and queens to write "history from below." Fifty years ago E. P. Thompson, in *The Making of the English Working Class*, famously set out to rescue long-dead workers "from the enormous condescension of posterity."

Journalists still condescend, when we bother to notice the poor at all. Rather than presenting them only as victims, we could copy the narratives of triumph over adversity used in working-class women's magazines, suggests Amina Lone, social researcher in Manchester. It worked in *Educating Rita*, a film about a Liverpudlian hairdresser who goes to university. Morals aside: by ignoring the poor we are missing the economic story of the decade.

Analyze

1. "You'd have thought the economic crisis would have made poverty newsy," Kuper writes. What evidence does he provide that it did or did not?
2. What "triple whammy" makes poverty "boring"?
3. Kuper claims that the media neglect people who are poor not because they hate them but why?

Explore

1. Kuper writes: "To become news, poor people have to cause disorder. Middle-class people raise issues by writing; poor people do it by rioting." As support for this claim, Kuper says he's never seen something written by someone on benefits. Have you? How might he be right and/or wrong? Connect with a local social service agency to find someone who has experienced poverty who would like to be interviewed about that experience. Write a narrative or oral history that represents that story. Where could that story be shared?
2. Kuper claims: "[W]e're exactly the media that an unequal world requires." What does this mean? Do you agree or disagree? Explain.
3. Kuper gives both moral and practical reasons why the media's neglect of the poor is a problem. Explain those reasons. Write an essay in which you offer your own assessment of the media's attention to poverty. Cite examples from the media as support.

Dan Froomkin
"It Can't Happen Here: Why Is There Still So Little Coverage of Americans Who Are Struggling with Poverty?"

A senior Washington correspondent for the *Huffington Post*, Dan Froomkin is also a watchdog reporter who scrutinizes journalistic trends on *Nieman Reports*, a site dedicated to increasing accountability in journalism by highlighting questions that the press should ask. In the following article, Froomkin articulates the journalistic pressures that prevent poverty reporting and offers some solutions for restoring quality poverty reporting.

What makes a story about poverty engaging and compelling?

Poverty is hardly a new phenomenon in the hardscrabble highlands of Missouri's Ozarks. But to David Stoeffler, freshly arrived at the helm of the region's main paper, the *Springfield News-Leader*, the fact that two out of five families in the area with children under 18 lived below the poverty line seemed like a huge story. "We certainly had covered these issues," says Stoeffler, who became executive editor in May 2010, "but I would say it was more episodically, and not in any coordinated way."

> **16.1%** Percentage of Americans living in poverty (49.7 million total)[1]
> **0.2%** Coverage primarily about poverty in 50 major news outlets 2007–2012[2]

Stoeffler decided the paper needed to do more: "My sense was the community needed a little crusading."

After conversations with community groups and among staffers, the newsroom embarked on a major public service project called "Every Child" examining the range of challenges facing children in the region. There was still a problem, though, the one that plagues all poverty reporting: "What we were trying to do is figure out how could we paint this big broad picture and at the same time not bore everybody to death," Stoeffler says. "The goal was to try to raise awareness and get people to say, 'We need to do something about this.'"

So for five consecutive days last September, Stoeffler published stories across the entire front page of the print edition and the homepage of the paper's website. Each day focused on a specific problem: "No home," "No shoes," "No food," "No car," and "No peace." Many readers were shocked, saying they had no idea so many area families were living in such desperate circumstances. Some reached out to families that had been featured. Members of the community the *News-Leader* had initially brought together as an advisory group formed the Every Child Initiative to push for long-term policy changes. "There seems to be momentum toward wanting to do something sustainable and lasting," Stoeffler says. "We feel like we succeeded in getting the attention of the community."

5 Sadly, the *News-Leader*'s success is an anomaly in the news business. Nearly 50 million people—about one in six Americans—live in poverty, defined as income below $23,021 a year for a family of four. And yet most news organizations largely ignore the issue. The Pew Research Center's Project for Excellence in Journalism indexed stories in 52 major mainstream news outlets from 2007 through the first half of 2012 and, according to Mark Jurkowitz, the project's associate director, "in no year did poverty coverage even come close to accounting for as little as one percent of the news hole. It's fair to say that when you look at that particular topic, it's negligible."

Instead, as *Tampa Bay Times* media critic Eric Deggans notes, at most news organizations poverty comes up sporadically. "Poverty becomes a sort of 'very special episode' of journalism that we sort of roll out every so often," he says.

The reasons for the lack of coverage are familiar. Journalists are drawn more to people making things happen than those struggling to pay bills; poverty is not considered a beat; neither advertisers nor readers are likely to demand more coverage, so neither will editors; and poverty stories are almost always enterprise work, requiring extra time and commitment. Yet persistent poverty is in some ways the ultimate accountability story—because, often, poverty happens by design.

"Poverty exists in a wealthy country largely as a result of political choices, not as a result of pure economics," argues Sasha Abramsky, a journalist whose upcoming book is called *The American Way of Poverty*. "The U.S. poverty rate is higher than most other developed nations, and the only way you can square that is there are political choices being made—or not being made—that accept a level of poverty that most wealthy democracies have said is unacceptable. We make these policy choices that perpetuate poverty, and then because poverty is so extreme, it becomes impolite to talk about."

The media could try to force the issue but it doesn't—at least not anymore, according to Philip Bennett, managing editor of PBS's Frontline public affairs series: "There are basic questions about the way the country is today that aren't being addressed by the journalistic institutions that used to address them."

The rise (and fall) of the Occupy movement, along with data about the 10
increasingly skewed distribution of wealth and income in the United States, have led to greater interest in inequality. "There's been lots of really good stuff written about inequality, probably more in the last few years than in the previous 20," says Jason DeParle, who's covered poverty policy for the *New York Times* for 23 years. But much of the debate over inequality has focused on the excesses of the rich rather than the deprivations of the poor.

DeParle also notes that one frequent excuse for ignoring poverty is increasingly anachronistic. "We have tended to congratulate ourselves as a country that 'OK, there's more poverty, but that's because there's also more fluidity in our society,'" he says. But that's just not true anymore. Recent surveys show that Americans now have less economic mobility than Western Europeans. For instance, one study found that 42 percent of Americans raised in the bottom quintile of family income remain stuck there as adults, compared to 30 percent in the historically class-bound United Kingdom. For Bennett, the key unaddressed question is: Has America become a less fair society? "This is a major question of American life," he says. "It's part of our political divide in a really important way. [And yet it] is not receiving the kind of sustained, imaginative, aggressive coverage that it deserves. Shouldn't journalists—and not just one or two—be organizing themselves en masse to ask that question?"

One way to address the question is to confront pernicious myths about poverty. "The reason why people believe that '47 percent nonsense' [Republican presidential candidate Mitt Romney's leaked comment characterizing 47 percent of the population as "dependent upon the government"] that Romney was swinging is because they don't know the working poor," says Deggans, who is also author of "Race-Baiter: How the Media Wields Dangerous Words to Divide a Nation."

Despite stereotypes of "the lazy poor," for example, more than a third of adults in poverty have jobs; they just don't earn enough to support their families. According to the Economic Policy Institute, 28 percent of workers nationally earn less than $11 an hour. Even working full-time year-round, that still leaves a family of four below the poverty line.

> **10,489** number of presidential campaign stories carried by 8 major print, broadcast news outlets, Jan.–June 2012[1]
> **17** number of those campaign stories that were substantively about poverty

Modern low-wage workplaces can make for gripping stories. Noting Wal-Mart's promise to hire any recent honorably discharged veteran, Columbia University journalism professor Dale Maharidge suggests reporters follow one of those soldiers around for a few days. Half of Wal-Mart's more than one million U.S. workers make less than $10 an hour. "See how they cope on $8 or $9 an hour," says Maharidge, author of "Someplace Like America: Tales From the New Great Depression." Then consider the Walton family fortune, estimated to be more than $80 billion. "Look at how much money they're making versus how much their workers are making, through this soldier," Maharidge suggests.

There are also opportunities for business reporters to broaden questions beyond stock prices and acquisitions. Mimi Corcoran, director of the Special Fund for Poverty Alleviation at the liberal Open Society Foundations, urges journalists to grill CEOs about their companies' compensation plans and the ratio between what their employees make and their own income. "What are you doing to provide livable wages? What's the appropriate balance between return on income versus what you're doing to support your workforce?" Corcoran suggests as model questions.

Gary Rivlin, author of *Broke, USA: From Pawnshops to Poverty, Inc.—How the Working Poor Became Big Business*, points reporters to the businesses (payday lenders, pawnshops and check cashers) that profit from poverty. "Poor people don't just necessarily happen. The poor have a lot of help staying poor," he says. Rivlin and Barbara Ehrenreich, another writer with a long history of covering poverty, recently helped found a nonprofit group, the Economic Hardship Reporting Project, to encourage precisely that kind of coverage.

There's also a wealth of stories in anti-poverty programs. "You always hear, 'We waged a war on poverty and poverty won,'" says Greg Kaufmann, who covers poverty for *The Nation*. But the safety net has caught a lot of people who otherwise would have fallen much further, he points out: "It's like saying the Clean Water Act didn't work because there's still water pollution."

Indeed, one of the most overlooked stories of the decade may be the effects of anti-poverty measures that were part of the 2009 Recovery Act. "They had huge effects; they got virtually no attention," says Michael Grunwald, a *Time* reporter and author of *The New New Deal: The Hidden Story of Change in the Obama Era*. The provisions in the stimulus represent the biggest anti-poverty effort since President Johnson's Great Society in the 1960s.

In addition to expanding anti-poverty programs, the White House and Democrats in Congress made a concerted effort "to really do some innovative—and ultimately, in some areas, remarkably effective—things," Grunwald says. A $1.5 billion homelessness prevention fund allowed local governments to assist at-risk people with things like emergency rent payments, utility bills, and moving expenses. "During the worst economic crisis in 90 years, the homeless population actually decreased," Grunwald notes.

Mark Rank, a social welfare professor at Washington University in St. Louis, argues that poverty reporters also sometimes fall into a trap familiar to political reporters: giving both sides of the issue equal weight.

There's the conservative argument that poverty is largely a function of "people just screwing up, just not having the motivation," Rank says. The other argument, which Rank says is supported by the preponderance of research, is that poverty is the result of structural failings, most commonly, not enough jobs.

The most traditional kind of poverty coverage—the sob story—can actually backfire. A 1990 study by political scientist Shanto Iyengar found that "episodic" television news stories that focused on specific victims of poverty, especially black mothers, actually led white middle class viewers to blame the individuals more than social or government institutions. "In a capitalist society where success is judged in part by how much money you make, there's a strong impulse to want to attach personal choices and deliberate action to whether you are poor," says the *Tampa Bay Times*'s Deggans.

Context is key. Put individual stories in their wider context, look at the social factors at play, and examine possible solutions, says Calvin Sims, a former *New York Times* reporter who now manages the Ford Foundation's portfolio of news media and journalism grants: "Many readers walk away from stories about poverty thinking, 'Well, the poor, they'll always be with us. What can we do?' That's not something that we, as journalists, should leave people with."

News organizations need to "find ways for the work to have resonance in other spaces," according to Sims. That could mean convening follow-up conversations through panel discussions, on video, or through social media, with a particular focus on solutions. He also thinks there's great potential in traditional news organizations for sharing information with others, including the fast-growing ethnic media sector.

At the *Springfield News-Leader*, Stoeffler feels a sense of satisfaction. Like other newspapers, his has been retrenching; the newsroom is 20 percent smaller today than it was just three years ago. But Stoeffler argues that going after chronic community problems like poverty is more crucial now than ever. "From a journalistic standpoint, we become less and less relevant if we don't go after some of these bigger issues," he says. "It's the way we can distinguish ourselves from other media."

NOTES

1. Census Bureau Supplemental Poverty Measure.
2. Pew Research Center's Project for Excellence in Journalism.

Analyze

1. What is unusual about the poverty reporting in the *Springfield News-Leader* compared to the general media's poverty coverage?
2. Attention to growing inequality led the media to cover whom instead of the poor?
3. What question does Bennett, quoted in this article, say all journalists should ask?

Explore

1. Name at least two of the potential story areas Froomkin says the media are missing when it comes to covering poverty. Do these topics sound promising? Explain.
2. Why do some people argue that poverty reporters can "fall into a trap familiar to political reporters: giving both sides of the issue equal weight"? What's wrong with that?
3. Froomkin writes: "The most traditional kind of poverty coverage—the sob story—can actually backfire." Do you agree that the "sob story" genre exists in poverty reporting? Identify examples, if you think they exist. Why might this backfire?

Nazneen Mehta
"Opposing Images: 'Third World Women' and 'Welfare Queens'"

Nazneen Mehta wrote the following article as a third-year law student at Columbia University. Now serving as counsel for the U.S. Senate Committee on Judiciary, Mehta previously trained low-income women to become early childhood educators through the Connecticut-based nonprofit organization All Our Kin. In this article, Mehta argues that the images people construct of irresponsible "welfare queens" and oppressed "third world women" obscure their realities and negatively impact public policies.

What images of the poor do you see most often today?

Consider two familiar images of poor women: Both women are impoverished, raced, struggling to meet their children's basic needs, and living as marginalized members of their societies. But one woman lives in the

"Third World"—a victim of poverty in a developing country. The other woman lives in America—a "welfare queen" (Hancock 2004). While both images convey poverty and powerlessness, each one implies a different message about the woman's life and her ability to create a better future for herself and her family. These contrasting images and the assumptions they convey have a profound influence on U.S. public policy, creating a sharp contrast between international and domestic policies for assistance to poor women.

International development institutions and U.S. foreign policy makers have internalized the image of the Third World mother as a vulnerable woman who is trapped in a life of poverty because of "underdevelopment." The international and foreign policies created against the backdrop of this image seek to remedy the Third World woman's situation through empowerment; microcredit programs and cooperatives invest in women's economic and social empowerment as the key to increasing the well-being of the overall community and children. By contrast, underlying U.S. welfare policy for poor American women is the idea of the welfare queen—a mother who is seen not as an asset, but instead as a liability to herself, her children, and her community.

Both of these images are deeply problematic. They mask the historical and political processes that led to the poverty and structural inequality shaping these women's lives (Esteva 1992; Roberts 1999). But while the assumptions behind the image of the Third World woman—passivity and deprivation—have led to empowerment programs and policies (UNFPA 2005; U.S. Department of State n.d.), the image of the U.S. welfare queen—characterized as lazy, irresponsible, and uncontrollably fertile—has manifested in disempowering and dispiriting welfare reform laws that dismiss the poor woman's role as a source of strength and leadership to her family and community (Hancock 2004, 8).

Images and Policy: Power and Distortion

These two opposing images are so powerful both because they are literally images, which are flashed on television screens and circulated in print, and because they are fixed in our minds through our associations with labels and descriptions repeatedly cycled through public discourse. The interaction of the media, the public, and policy makers produces the constructed identities ("images") of social groups in public discourse; these images are then part of public debate and projected through social policy (Bickford 1999; Ingram and Schneider 1995).

Ange-Marie Hancock illustrates this point in her analysis of the congressional debate surrounding the welfare reform legislation of 1996. She describes the way a congressman read into the congressional record a *U.S. News* magazine report of an unemployed mother on welfare ("Bertha Bridges") as support for his vote to pass the Personal Responsibility and Work Opportunity Reconciliation Act of 1996 (PRWORA). The congressman's use of Bertha's story as representative of the experiences of millions of poor women meant that the journalist's description of Bertha and her "disruptive, severely depressed son" served not only to construct the popular image of a welfare queen, but also to indelibly etch the image into the legal documents of the policy-making process (Hancock 2004, 2).

Lawyers and policy makers may assume that legal policy and popular representations of it are separate, but law is rarely so hermetic. Policy efforts are often beholden to the popular images of law in action (Mégret and Pinto 2003, 468). For example, Frederic Mégret and Frederick Pinto (2003) argue that images in the "war" on global terrorism (photos and footage of detainees, soldiers, and prisons) have shifted legal and policy agendas by turning public attention away from the larger geopolitical issues underlying terrorism and focusing it instead on the few visible aspects of terrorism caught in the frame of a photograph. The images of the welfare queen and the Third World woman have a similar effect on policy agendas, blocking out other considerations and narrowing public attention to the issues we can "see" in the images. The result is policy prescriptions that address only poor women's most visible personal impediments: the welfare queen's failed work ethic and the Third World woman's oppression. What we do not see in these images is the complex web of history, power, and financial control that contributes at least as much as personal choice to the poverty these women experience.

For the Third World woman, the image of a passive victim, trapped and assailed by a poorly governed state, sets up a heroic narrative in which the international community acts as "savior"—the purveyor of financial assistance and protector of rights and economic security (Orford 1999, 696). This image of the Third World woman is set against the backdrop of a global economic hierarchy divided between the politically constructed "First" and "Third" worlds. Enshrining this division, the image of the victimized Third World woman is interwoven with a picture of heroic altruism on the part of the international First World community. This masks the history of the West as colonizers, complicit in causing the poverty and powerlessness of people in the developing world, and as perpetuators of colonial-style economic relations today (Schoepf et al. 2000, 96–101).

Similarly, the image of the welfare queen is the product of a denial of the legacy of slavery and segregation in the United States. These political institutions contributed to the historical denigration of African American motherhood and the economic disenfranchisement that underlies the persisting need for social aid programs (Roberts 1999, 22). By ignoring this history and its effects, the raced image of the welfare queen suggests poverty created by personal moral failing, without reference to social and historical context. Beyond simply ignoring the effects of macro political and economic forces on women's lives, the "welfare queen" image ascribes women agency in the apparent *decision* to live a life of poverty.

Implementing Images through Policy

This dichotomy of images has significant public policy consequences that are visible in the differences between U.S. federal welfare "reform" laws and the poverty alleviation programs promoted by U.S. policy makers and international development institutions.

The congressional and public debates on welfare reform leading up to the passage of the PRWORA were coded in gendered and raced language that targeted poor women's behavior as a root cause of family poverty. Analyzing shifts in the racial images of news coverage of the poor from the 1960s to the 1990s, Martin Gilens found that in the latter part of the period, images of African Americans were used at rates double their actual percentage of America's poor (Gilens 1999, 123). As noted above, the image of the welfare queen was actively invoked in congressional debate on the PRWORA, and the stereotypes underpinning the image seemed to justify the law's harsh restrictive conditions on aid to poor women and their children (Gilens 1999, 92).

The reforms targeted single mothers in poverty by enforcing term limits on their receipt of aid, instituting family caps barring additional aid to mothers who gave birth to children while on welfare, and strictly tying benefits to proof of work, while revoking benefits for mothers who were students (Pierson-Balik 2003). When the PRWORA was reauthorized in 2005, it included more than $100 million a year to implement programs encouraging women receiving welfare to marry (U.S. Department of

Health and Human Services n.d.). The federal law also allowed states to experiment with incentives and restrictions, which led some states to propose voluntary sterilization of poor women in return for more welfare benefits (Pierson-Balik 2003).

These reforms did nothing to cultivate poor women's education level, their autonomy, or their potential as leaders and advocates for their communities. The aim was to get women into work—any work—even if the work was dead-end, low-paying, far from their children, and without benefits (Schleiter and Statham 2002). The marriage initiative suggests one of poor women's problems is their lack of husbands, not opportunities. Thus, the message sent by the PRWORA is one of mistrust and degradation of poor women's life choices—a message made more tolerable to the public by the image of the welfare queen. U.S. foreign policy and international development policy, on the other hand, have sent a completely different message about the impoverished Third World woman. Development policy has been enthusiastic about supporting women's rights and increasing their educational, economic, and political opportunities (Coleman 2004, 82). For example, the World Bank's project to increase single mothers' employment in Tajikistan focused not on finding women any job placement available, but on the creation of microcredit institutions and local women's community centers where poor single mothers could receive the education and skills they need to start their own businesses (World Bank n.d., 8). This was in keeping with the dominant policy trend by international institutions; in 2000, when the United Nations instituted the Millennium Goals on global poverty, the promotion of gender equality and women's empowerment was included as one of the eight goals (United Nations n.d.).

Similarly, U.S. Secretaries of State Condoleezza Rice and Hillary Rodham Clinton have emphasized women's rights and empowerment in developing countries as a key component of U.S. foreign policy efforts to combat global poverty (Brand 2008; Landler 2009). The Obama administration recently created a new post of ambassador for Global Women's Issues to focus U.S. foreign policy efforts on the "political, economic, and social empowerment of women" (U.S. Department of State n.d.). In 2003, Congress specifically invested $10 million to empower Iraqi women by implementing leadership, political advocacy, and media training programs (Coleman 2004, 92). And in 2009, Senator Dick Durbin proposed the Global Resources and Opportunities for Women to Thrive Act (GROWTH Act) to increase funding for programs in developing countries that "ensure that the policies of the United States actively promote development and economic opportunities for women" (GROWTH Act 2009).

At the core of these foreign and international policies is a belief in what Nicholas Kristof and Sheryl WuDunn call the "girl effect," that is, the idea that *if only* women in developing countries had more opportunities, protections, and rights, they could better protect themselves and their children from poverty (Kristof and WuDunn 2009). This suggests optimism that, with the right support, poor women can be transformative actors, changing and improving their own lives as well as those of their children and communities. That message finds no counterpart in U.S. welfare laws; instead, U.S. policy evinces skepticism that U.S. women could be affected by the same kinds of oppressive economic and cultural forces that keep women in poverty in the developing world. This denies the potential of America's poor women to become the strong advocates and leaders of their communities that their sisters in developing countries are believed to be.

Exposing the dichotomy between foreign and domestic policy ap- 15
proaches suggests that U.S. welfare policy has been stunted by the confines of the harmful image of the welfare queen. By enacting welfare policies that seek to punish poor women's behavior, the United States loses out on the positive effects of women's empowerment that are already accepted and highlighted by the United States as sound policy abroad.

Analyze

1. Describe in your own words the contrasting images of poor women in the U.S. and poor women in the "third world."
2. What facts does Mehta say these images fail to acknowledge about the structural challenges and history behind these faces?
3. What is the "girl effect"? To whom is it applied?

Explore

1. Mehta argues that the images inspire compassion for the "third world woman" and disgust for the American "welfare queen." What evidence does she give that the images affect public policy? What analogy helps solidify her argument? Identify other cases in which media representations seem to drive public opinion/policy.

2. Locate images of these two types of representations. Do a rhetorical analysis of these images. How is meaning constructed through the way poor women are photographed (or drawn/painted)? How do they invite the type of audience response Mehta describes? Or, find images that challenge the frames Mehta describes. How do these images contradict the frames she defines?
3. Mehta writes: "U.S. policy evinces skepticism that U.S. women could be affected by the same kinds of oppressive economic and cultural forces that keep women in poverty in the developing world." What evidence does Mehta provide to support this claim? Write a researched letter to her in which you explain why you agree or disagree with her thesis.

Dean S. Karlan and Jacob Appel
"Introduction: The Monks and the Fish"

As a professor of economics at Yale University, Dean S. Karlan researches, writes, and works on implementing and evaluating micro-financing programs designed to help alleviate poverty in developing countries. Jacob Appel implements and evaluates programs through GOOD/Corps. In their book *More Than Good Intentions: How a New Economics Is Helping to Solve Global Poverty*, from which the following chapter is excerpted, Karlan and Appel explore how to invest money into more effective antipoverty efforts using such research as behavior economics to inform design and implementation of programs.

Should any attempt to address poverty that springs from a "genuinely altruistic impulse" be encouraged?

> "[W]e ought to find out where our money will make the biggest impact, and send it."

Morning in the harbor at Marina del Rey in Los Angeles is steely bright, and it smells of brine and of fish, and it is filled with the sound of pelicans. They congregate by the hundreds on the end of the jetty, strutting and chattering and throwing their heads back to slug down great bulging beakfuls of breakfast. Completely absorbed in the guzzling of their food, they seem not to notice the dinghies puttering by.

Jake was in one of those dinghies with his girlfriend Chelsea and her father, returning from a short ride out on the gentle rolling swell of the Pacific. They passed the gray-brown pelicans on the gray-brown rocks and continued into the marina. Coming down the causeway, they passed the gas pumps, the big prow of the Catalina ferry, and the Buddhist monks.

Yes, the Buddhist monks: those unassuming men and women, some dressed in saffron robes and others in street clothes, standing on the dock around a folding card table on which was erected a little altar with a statue of a sitting Buddha and an oil lamp. On the ground in front of the table was a plastic tub as big as a steamer trunk. From the boat, low in the water, Jake couldn't see what was inside. They were saying prayers over it.

Chelsea's father put the boat into idle and turned in a half-circle to stay even with the monks. They came to the end of their prayer and bowed deeply, and the two closest to the bin took it by the handles and dragged it forward to the edge of the dock. Then they tipped it.

5 Out came a great torrent of water and minnows, which landed in the causeway with a silvery clatter. The minnows disappeared instantly, darting away in every direction, and the ripples from the splash were drawn down the causeway to the ocean by the outgoing tide. The monks bowed again, deeply, and began to pack up their things.

What Jake had seen, Chelsea told him afterward, was a regular ritual. Those particular Buddhist monks set a tubful of fish free every couple of weeks. It was their small way of setting right something they believed was wrong. They didn't think those fish ought to be killed, so they bought their freedom. They would approach some fishermen, purchase their day's catch, say a prayer, and release the fish into the causeway to return to the ocean.

It was a moving gesture. Jake can attest to that. Whatever can be said against it—that it is merely symbolic, that those minnows might just be caught again later, that it does nothing to change the fact that fishing still goes on every day, that it is at best just a drop in a bucket (or a bucket in the sea)—it doesn't change the facts. The monks believed in something and they acted out of kindness and compassion.

When Jake and I talked about it together, though, there was one question we couldn't get around: The monks had clearly aimed to do a good thing—but could they have done better?

If their goal was to save a day's catch of fish from certain death, why not pay the fishermen ahead of time and just tell them to stay home? That would save the fish the trauma of being caught and dragged out of the water in the first place. It would save the fishermen the effort of waking up at dawn to complete the Sisyphean task of catching fish only to see them thrown back. It would save the gas they used to run the boat. And it would save the bait they used too.

10 The monks clearly had good intentions, but they may not have found the best way to act on them. Granted, some might argue that this is a relatively minor tragedy, that freeing baitfish is not a dire global concern. But the lesson still stands: We need more than good intentions in order to solve problems. Nowhere is this more relevant than in the fight against world poverty—a truly dire and global concern, in the service of which good intentions are usually the first (and all too often the only) resource to be mustered.

A Two-Pronged Attack for Fighting Poverty (and Saving Fish)

It is the best part of us that endeavors to be like the monks, to act out of compassion and do something positive for others. The vast majority of the work being done around the world to fight poverty fits this description, and anything that springs from such a genuinely altruistic impulse should be encouraged.

But there is a lesson in the monks and their tubful of minnows. Sometimes, even when we have all the good intentions in the world, we don't find the most effective or most efficient way to act on them. This is true whether we want to save fish, make microloans, distribute antimalarial bed-nets, or deliver deworming pills. What we really need to know is: How can we act with more than good intentions? How can we find the best solutions?

The only real consensus view on the issue is about the gravity of the problem. Three billion people, about half the world, live on $2.50 per day.

(To be clear, that's $2.50 *adjusted for the cost of living*—so think of it as living on the amount of *actual goods* that you could buy for $2.50 per day in the United States.) In the public dialogue about aid and development—that vast complex of people, organizations, and programs that seeks to alleviate poverty around the world—there are two main competing explanations for why poverty persists on such a massive scale. One camp maintains that we simply haven't spent enough on aid programs and need to massively ramp up our level of engagement. They point out that the world's wealthiest nations dedicate on average less than 1 percent of their money to poverty reduction. In their view, we haven't even given our existing programs a fair chance. The first thing we have to do is give more. A lot more.

The other camp tells a starkly different story: Aid as it exists today doesn't work, and simply throwing money at the problem is futile. They point out that $2.3 trillion *has* been spent by the world's wealthiest nations on poverty reduction over the past fifty years and ask: What have we accomplished with all that money? With poverty and privations still afflicting half the globe, can we really claim to be on the right track? No, they say; we need a fresh start. The aid and development community as it exists today is flabby, uncoordinated, and accountable to nobody in particular. It's bound to fail. They argue that we need to pull away resources from overgrown, cumbersome international organizations like the United Nations, wipe the slate clean, and focus instead on small, agile, homegrown programs.

Each camp claims prominent economists as adherents: Jeffrey Sachs of 15
Columbia University, an adviser to the United Nations, and Bill Easterly of New York University, a former senior official at the World Bank. Sachs and his supporters regale us with picture-perfect transformational stories. Easterly and the other side counter with an equally steady supply of ghastly the-world-is-corrupt-and-everything-fails anecdotes. The result? Disagreement and uncertainty, which leads to stagnation and inertia—in short, a train wreck. And no way forward.

Jake and I propose that there actually *is* a way forward. My hunch is that, at the end of the day, even Sachs and Easterly could agree on the following: Sometimes aid works, and sometimes it does not. That can't be all that controversial a stand!

The critical question, then, is *which* aid works. The debate has been in the sky, but the answers are on the ground. Instead of getting hung up on the extremes, let's zero in on the details. Let's look at a specific challenge or problem that poor people face, try to understand what they're up against, propose a potential solution, and then test to find out whether it works. If that solution works—and if we can demonstrate that it works consistently—then let's scale it up so it can work for more people. If it doesn't work, let's make changes or try something new. We won't eradicate poverty in one fell swoop with this approach (of course, no approach yet has managed to do that), but we can make—and are making—real, measurable, and meaningful progress toward eradicating it. That's the way forward.

To get there, we need a two-pronged attack.

The first prong is to understand the problems in the first place. Some problems are systemic, in the way entire populations interact and exchange information, and in the way they buy, sell, and trade. Increasingly we are recognizing that the problems are also with *us as individuals,* with the way we make decisions. Here we turn to behavioral economics for insight.

In the past, economists would have thought about the monks in a pretty wooden, mechanical way. They would have talked about the cost of the fish, the value the monks imputed to their survival, the opportunity cost of the fishermen's time, and the social impact of running the boat on diesel fuel. They would have put you to sleep. More important, at the end of the discussion the monks probably would still be dumping tubs of fish into the Marina del Rey causeway.

This is a narrow view of what makes us tick. Traditional economics gives us economic humans, the archetypes for rational decision-making. Borrowing a term from Richard Thaler and Cass Sunstein (from their book *Nudge*), I call these folks *Econs.* When they need to choose between two alternatives, Econs weigh all the potential costs and benefits, compute an "expected value" for each, and choose the one whose expected value is higher. In addition to keeping a cool head, they are very methodical and reliable calculators. Given accurate information about their options, they always choose the alternative most likely to give them the greatest overall satisfaction.

Behavioral economics expands on narrow definitions of traditional economics in two important ways. The first is simple: Not everything that matters is dollars and cents. In a sense, this is nothing new. For instance, Gary Becker—by many accounts a "traditional" economist—has been using economic analysis to think about marriage, crime, and fertility for years. The second expansion is a bit more radical. Behavioral economics recognizes that, unlike Econs, we do not always arrive at decisions by calculating a cost-benefit analysis (or even act as if we had done so). Sometimes we have different priorities. Other times we are distracted or impulsive. We sometimes slip up on the math. And, more often than we'd like to admit, we are shockingly inconsistent. To mark all of the ways we are different from Econs, Thaler and Sunstein use the powerfully simple term *Humans.* I will do the same.

Behavioral economics incorporates more nuanced behavior, and sometimes inconsistent behavior—like when we continue to sneak an occasional candy bar when we say we want to lose weight, or when we still eat dinners out while we try to pay down our credit card debt. It might suggest that the monks don't care what traditional economics has to say. Maybe they throw the fish back because paying for not-fishing wouldn't serve their purpose. Maybe it's important to them to hear that silvery splash, or to see the minnows dart away like a bursting firecracker. Maybe there is something psychological about the salience of seeing, with one's own eyes, fish jump free. And maybe the monks simply are willing to accept a less efficient solution in exchange for that moment of spiritual connection.

The breakthrough of behavioral economics has been to claim that if we want to understand the monks, then we must know how and why they make the decisions they do. Instead of deducing a way to think from a core set of principles, behavioral economics builds up a model of decision-making from observations of people's actions in the real world. As we will see throughout this book, this way of thinking can help us design better programs to attack poverty.

This does not imply that we should throw out the old models. Behav- 25
ioral economics is a powerful tool, but the proverb still applies: Just because you have a hammer, doesn't mean everything is a nail. The inspiration for some of the antipoverty programs we'll see comes straight from nuts-and-bolts economics. Combining the old and new approaches gives us the best chance to understand exactly what problems we're up against, and to design and implement the best solutions.

This first prong of the attack—understanding the problems we face—is a start, but it's not enough. Imagine you are stranded on a desert island with a rusted-out rowboat. Understanding the problem, even deeply, is like understanding why boats full of holes don't float. That alone will not get you home. You need to find a way to build a better boat.

Hence, the second prong of the attack: rigorous evaluation. Evaluation lets us compare competing solutions—like different boat designs or plugs for the holes—and see which one is most effective. Creative and well-designed evaluations can go even further, and help us understand *why* one works better than another.

Here's how it might work with the monks. I could propose setting up a new market, a market for hiring fishermen to not-fish, which would enable the monks to save fish more efficiently. It might sound good in theory, but then we'd go to the field and test.

Sometimes things that sound good fail. Suppose the monks actually don't care about seeing the splash of the minnows and would be happy to pay fishermen to not-fish; maybe they are simply up against a problem that makes it unfeasible. It could be a trust problem, where the monks fear the fishermen would accept payment for not-fishing and go out fishing anyway. Or maybe it is a monitoring problem, where there just aren't enough monks to tail around all the fishermen on not-fishing days to ensure they keep their word. A rigorous evaluation could point us to the specific problem that keeps the not-fishing market from saving more fish.

30 In the context of development, rigorous evaluation can help resolve the debate about how best to attack global poverty, by going to the field and finding out whether specific projects work. (It turns out that some projects work better—sometimes much, much better—than others.) You might think this goes without saying. You might assume that aid organizations have always routinely conducted careful and rigorous evaluations to see if they're doing the best they can. If so, you would be surprised.

Until recently, we knew astonishingly little about what works and what doesn't in the fight against poverty. We are now beginning to get the hard evidence we've lacked for so long, by measuring the effectiveness of specific development programs, many of which you'll read about in these pages. The next chapter will go into a bit more detail about how we do this.

Microcredit, the provision of small loans to the poor, is a perfect example of an idea that generated tremendous enthusiasm and support long before there was evidence on its impact. The excitement is largely understandable, for the very design of microcredit is appealing. It strikes a lot of chords: Microcredit often targets women, and many believe that the economic empowerment of women redounds to the benefit of the entire family; microcredit often focuses on entrepreneurs, and many believe that such individuals, given access to a modicum of working capital, are capable of dramatically improving their lives through their ingenuity and enterprising spirit; microcredit often involves communities, and many believe that by involving the community rather than just individuals, we are more likely to succeed.

But in some sense the enthusiasm is surprising: It seems to be predicated on a double standard about the useful role of high-interest debt. At the same time that we see millions of dollars pouring into microcredit programs to lend to poor microentrepreneurs at rates ranging from 10 to 120 percent APR (all in the hope of alleviating poverty), we also see millions of people outraged at payday-loans outfits at home, which lend at similar rates to the poor in America.

Without some basic facts about whether these loans actually make people better off, I would not know which side to believe, much less how to reconcile the two positions. But rigorous evaluation can—and does—help. Many were surprised by a study in South Africa, which we will see in chapter 4, that found that access to consumer credit, even at 200 percent APR, made people much better off on average. This does not imply that all credit is good for all people, but it should make us look critically at our strong opinions about what works and what doesn't, about what's good and what's bad. Do we have concrete facts to back them up?

The two-pronged attack we'll see throughout this book is a powerful economic tool. I use it (albeit in a slightly different form) whenever I teach development economics, both to undergraduates and doctoral students. Three questions organize our discussions. First: What is the root cause of the problem? Using both behavioral and traditional economics to answer this question is exactly the first prong of our attack in this book. Then two more questions: Does the "idea" at hand, whether a government policy, NGO intervention, or business, actually solve the problem? And how much better off is the world because of it? Using rigorous evaluations to answer these two questions together is the second prong of our attack.

Jump in Singer's Lake

Even in the absence of hard evidence about specific programs, people find compelling reasons to engage in and support the fight against poverty. One such reason comes from ethics, plain and simple: Suppose you are walking down a street by a lake on your way to a meeting, and if you miss the meeting you will lose two hundred dollars. You see a child drowning in the lake. Do you have an ethical obligation to stop and jump in and save the child, even though it will cost you two hundred dollars?

Most people say yes.

Don't you then also have an ethical obligation to send two hundred dollars right now to one of many organizations delivering aid to the poor, where it can save a child's life? Most people say no—or, at least, they don't cut that check.

The example comes from Peter Singer, a utilitarian philosopher at Princeton University and a hero of mine. I tend to think of it at some very specific moments, like when I am in a store and tempted to buy something that I don't really need. Couldn't that money go toward something better?

Singer's basic idea resonates, at least with me, but the logical conclusion of his argument is hard to swallow. The implication of his strict utilitarian reasoning is that we should all give away our money until we are so hard up that we honestly *couldn't* spare two hundred dollars to save a drowning child. Maybe an Econ would feel compelled by the cold force of logic to do so (assuming, of course, he'd had the heart to save the drowning child in the first place). But no Human I know of—not even Singer himself, a tireless advocate for doing more—goes that far.

Because the conclusion to the lake analogy makes us uncomfortable, we grope for holes in the logic. We raise objections. Often people's first response is to point out that when you dive in and pull the child to safety, there is no question that you've made a difference in the world. You can see with your own eyes that you've saved a life. But when you cut a check to an aid organization, the link is much less clear. How can you know your two hundred dollars is really doing good?

Most of this book is an attempt to respond to that objection. I hope that seeing some successes (and failures) up close convinces you that we *can* know we're doing good—if we commit to rigorously testing aid programs and supporting the ones that are proven to work.

The second objection people raise to Singer's lake analogy is about the "identifiable victim"—a vague sense that there's something morally significant about *seeing* the child flailing around in the lake, whereas we can't see the child our two-hundred-dollar check would be saving in, say, Madagascar. Logically, this objection is easy to refute. If someone runs to your house to tell you there is a boy drowning in the lake, you still have to go save him even though you haven't seen him with your own eyes. Wearing a blindfold does not solve ethical conundrums, and we cannot confine our responsibilities to a specific geographic area simply by narrowing our field of vision. A child is a child, wherever he is in the world, even if we cannot see him.

The trouble is that, while this refutation might be logically valid, it isn't viscerally compelling. We cannot simply reason our way into having a feeling of compassion, of responsibility for others. We need to be *moved* to act.

Behavioral Solutions Right Under Our Noses

Aid organizations, which depend for funding on our feelings of compassion, know from experience that appealing only to people's ethical obligations doesn't pay the bills. That's why tactics like the identifiable victim are longstanding staples of fund-raising. Think of Save the Children, which promises a photograph and a handwritten letter from *your* sponsored child in exchange for thirty dollars a month. Rather than approaching donors with facts, figures, and tables—which is what might sway an Econ—aid organizations take full advantage of the fact that we're Humans. They capitalize on our emotions.

This is exactly behavioral economics applied to the marketing of charities. Once you get inside the minds of those who give, you can come up with clever strategies to raise more money.

One such fund-raising strategy takes the financial sting out of giving by tacking donations onto other purchases. Recently I was in the checkout line at Whole Foods Market when the cashier asked me if I wanted to donate a dollar to the Whole Planet Foundation. She pointed to a small flyer on the counter. If I wanted to donate, she could scan a bar code on the flyer and add a dollar to my bill.

With a hundred dollars of groceries already rung up, an extra dollar is a tiny hit to take—so tiny you'd hardly notice it. And you get a lot of bang for that buck. Suddenly, you feel good walking out of Whole Foods Market with your bags of groceries. You've done something positive. It's not hard to see why the Whole Planet Foundation has been awash in donations.

Another behavioral approach to fund-raising involves separating the good parts of contributing (i.e., the satisfaction of doing a good deed) from the bad (i.e., the pain of parting with your money). Giving becomes much easier if you can enjoy the satisfaction up front, unencumbered by that irksome feeling that your wallet is thinner, and pay later.

That's exactly what happened in the phenomenally successful "Text to Haiti" campaign in January 2010. In the weeks following the devastating earthquake, people rose up in unprecedented numbers and acted to help those in need. Small individual contributions—the vast majority of them ten dollars or less—piled up at an unbelievable pace. Text donations from the first three days alone totaled more than ten million dollars.

Giving by text message takes a few seconds and is utterly gratifying. You type in "HAITI," press Send, and get an instant response thanking you for your generosity. You hardly have time to think of the phone bill coming at the end of the month. When it does arrive, your ten dollars is easier to part with because it's tacked onto the cost of phone service—a cost you're already prepared to bear.

Unless, that is, you are Cara. The following was pulled from a real Facebook page:

Cara's profile said: "I've texted Haiti to 90999 over 200 times . . . over $2000 dollars [sic] donated to Haiti relief efforts. Join me!"

Comments

Noah: Your parents might not like your cell phone bill this month.

Cara: It's not my money! Hah.

Cara: Wait a second . . . this doesn't get added to the phone bill does it? I thought it was just a free thing. . . .

Aaron: Cara shooot. No every text is $10!!!

Cara: Oh wow, are u sure? This could be very bad for me.

Aaron: Yeah I saw it on the football game they bill it to your cell phone bill.

Chloe: Yeah. Every text is 10 bucks. It said so when the Health and Human Services lady came on and told people about it on the Colbert Report. Uhh, Ask for people to help you pay your phone bill?

Cara: Thanks for letting me know! Haha Haiti must love me!

Kyle: A 2000 dollar phone bill? this is sitting in its own special zone of hilarious.

Aaron: Well . . . you may be screwed but, in this case there's a big upside at least.

Cara: Just counted my texts . . . grand total is 188 texts. $1,880 phone bill . . . this is not hilarious Kyle!!!!!!

Never mind, Cara—there are worse ways to make a mistake with $1,880. And this really doesn't happen very often—in the vast majority of cases, people know exactly what they are giving when they give it.

But behavioral marketing approaches can make it so donors may not always know exactly what, or whom, they are giving *to,* and this is more disquieting.

As an example let's look at Kiva.org, a tremendously popular Web site that raises money for microlenders around the world. Ask a user of the site how it works and this is what you're likely to hear: You log on and read through the stories of people who need loans. When you find one you like, you can fund her loan by clicking and sending money through Kiva. When the client repays her loan, you get your money back.

That's what most users would tell you, but most users would be wrong.

Suppose you click to fund a Peruvian client's hundred-dollar loan. Here's what happens behind the scenes: Some weeks before, bank staff went out to the field to take pictures and write up profiles of existing clients. Those profiles are what you see on the Web site. When you click to fund the woman's loan, you make a hundred-dollar no-interest loan to Kiva. Kiva then makes a hundred-dollar no-interest loan to the client's Peruvian microlender. The hundred dollars goes into the microlender's loan portfolio, and is lent out to clients (but not the one you clicked on, who already has her loan) at around 40 to 70 percent APR. If the client you clicked on actually defaults on her loan, you could lose your hundred dollars, but that's rare. Most of the time, either another client repays the loan for her, or the lender pays back the loan itself (in order to keep its "record" on Kiva.org clean, so that it can attract more money). That's how it really works.

In innumerable casual conversations, people have told me that they use Kiva exactly because they love the idea that *their* money goes to *that* particular person whose story they read, whose story moved them. They feel a connection, and that inspires them to give.

I have mixed feelings about this. Raising more money is a good thing, of course. Kiva is out there raising millions (over a hundred million as of November 2009) for microcredit. The problem is that pitching a development program on something other than its impacts puts some distance between the means and the ends. Tactics that work brilliantly to mobilize donations—focusing on the identifiable victim, for instance—don't necessarily work best to design programs that truly help poor people improve their lives.

The very best organizations pursue effectiveness in their fund-raising *and* in their programs with equal tenacity—and they usually end up with very different approaches to each. The point is that they have to recognize and respect that difference. We have to trust them to know that anecdotes are a far cry from real, systematic impact. And then we have to trust that, even as they use anecdotes to court donors, they will demand rigorous evidence to shape their programs.

For an organization to be worthy of that trust is no small feat.

We Can Demand Better

Fortunately, we don't have to rely on development organizations to come around entirely on their own. If we want aid programs to do the most good, we have to recognize that as donors—the ones who pay the bills—we are the people who ultimately have the power to steer the ship. Yes, us. You and me.

65 Large donors—governments, major philanthropic foundations, the World Bank—clearly matter. But small donors matter even more. Individual donors in America contribute over $200 billion to charity every year, three times as much as the sum of all corporations, foundations, and bequests. As we've just seen, aid organizations have spared no effort in developing an acute understanding of what works to raise funds from you and me. You can be sure they'll respond to the incentives we give them.

Jake and I will conclude this book with some practical suggestions for what you, as an individual, can do to help steer the ship. I hope I won't spoil the suspense, though, if I give you one bottom line up-front. Cutting checks is good, but it's not enough—especially when, thanks to behavioral marketing, we can do it with such little effort or deliberation.

Instead, we ought to find out where our money will make the biggest impact, and send it there. Some large donors, like the Bill & Melinda Gates Foundation and the Hewlett Foundation, try to do this as a matter of policy—and, sure enough, organizations respond by showing evidence that their programs work. Naturally, a small donor acting alone can't drive that kind of change. But if enough small donors start to reward aid organizations for providing credible demonstrations of their impacts, you can bet that better programs will ultimately result. And perhaps, if a critical mass of donors does this together, we can slowly but surely contribute to a shift in how we as a society view the act of giving money. This isn't just about making better use of the money raised, but also about helping to convince skeptics, who think aid isn't worth giving, that development can work if done right.

Remember Cara's Facebook page? There's a serious point lurking there. Cara's initial post showed not only that texting to Haiti was easy, but that it was cool—cool enough for her to think it was worth sharing on

Facebook. Whether we like it or not, for most of us there's an element of social display mixed up in our motivations for giving—and aid organizations know this, too, which is why visible signs of donation such as wristbands, stickers, and ribbons are also an effective fund-raising tool.

Anyone acting on good intentions deserves praise, no matter how far from optimal their actions may be. But how much more good could we do in the world if impact-informed giving came to be seen as the coolest kind of all?

Most of the research I'll talk about in this book is evaluation. It gives us concrete evidence, and concrete evidence truly should be the driving force in deciding which development approaches to support. But I don't believe it should be the only consideration. There is room for creativity, for trying new things, and for failure. We need new ideas to push us forward, and as donors we should reward those too.

Jake and I don't claim to have all the answers in this book. As we shall see repeatedly, behavioral economics reveals that, just like everyone else, poor people make mistakes that end up making them poorer, sicker, and less happy. (If they didn't, they could quickly escape poverty by selling self-help classes to the rest of us.) Identifying and correcting these mistakes is a prerequisite for solving global poverty, and we don't have a foolproof way of achieving that any more than we have a foolproof way to make every person in the developed world win all of his or her personal battles.

That said, we in the developed world are beginning to chip away at these insidious and persistent problems for ourselves, one by one. We *have* found specific ways to improve our decisions and make our lives profoundly better. We can and do use new tools—like the Save More Tomorrow program and stickK.com, which we'll see later—to spend smarter, save more, eat better, and lead lives more like the ones we imagine. The leap is in understanding that solutions like these, that have so enriched our own lives, can do the same for the people who need them most.

This book is about finding out which of them really work for the poor, and finding new solutions for the problems that remain.

Analyze

1. Define "Econs" and "Humans" as Karlan and Appel use these terms.
2. What are the two prongs in the two-pronged attack for fighting poverty that Karlan and Appel propose?

3. Karlan and Appel claim that there are two main camps with explanations for why poverty persists on such a massive scale. What are those two camps, and where do Karlan and Appel stand?

Explore

1. Describe Karlan and Appel's attitude toward the monks and their ritual of freeing fish. What do you think of that ritual and their response to it?
2. What key questions drive Karlan and Appel? Are these important? Explain.
3. First, explain how Singer's analogy about saving a drowning child relates to aid. Then, consider Karlan and Appel's response: "We cannot simply reason our way into having a feeling of compassion, of responsibility for others. We need to be *moved* to act." Write a reflection essay in which you recount a time when you were moved to act. *How* were you moved? What got you to donate money, time, or resources? Statistical data? A written narrative? Or was it meeting someone firsthand who was affected by the issue? Would the same approach move others? Explain.

David Bornstein et al.
"Solutions Journalism Network: Questions and Checklist"

David Bornstein is a journalist, author, and co-founder of Solutions Journalism Network, which aims to help journalists engage in "solutions journalism," reporting about responses to big social problems. He has authored books about developing social innovations and solving major social problems, including *How To Change the World*, *The Price of a Dream: The Story of the Grameen Bank*, and *Social Entrepreneurship: What Everyone Needs to Know*. He also co-authors the "Fixes" column in the "Opinionator" section of the *New York Times*, reporting on how people and organizations are working to solve major social problems. In the following list published on SolutionsJournalism.org, he offers 10 questions to guide journalists covering solutions-based stories.

In your own writing, do you tend to focus more on problems or solutions?

Here are 10 questions to ask yourself when writing a solutions-oriented story. Not every story will address all of these questions, and that's okay—but we hope this will inspire your thinking:

1. **Does the story explain the causes of a social problem?** A solution should be explained in the context of the problem it's trying to address. The causes of that problem should be documented in ways that make clear the opportunity for a solution to create leverage and impact.
2. **Does the story present an associated response to that problem?** The acid test; if the story doesn't describe a response, it's not solutions journalism.
3. **Does the story get into the problem solving and how-to details of implementation?** A great solutions story delves into the how-to's of problem solving, investigating questions like: What models are having success improving an educational outcome and how do they actually work?

4. **Is the problem solving process central to the narrative?** Solutions journalism, like all journalism, is about great story telling. It should include characters grappling with challenges, experimenting, succeeding, failing, learning. But the narrative is driven by the problem solving and the tension is located in the inherent difficulty in solving a problem.
5. **Does the story present evidence of results linked to the response?** Solutions journalism is about ideas—but like all good journalism, the determination of what works (or doesn't) and how is supported by solid data and evidence.
6. **Does the story explain the limitations of the response?** There is no such thing as a perfect solution to a social problem. Every response has caveats, limitations, and risks. Good solutions journalism does not shy away from imperfection.
7. **Does the story convey an insight or teachable lesson?** What makes solutions journalism compelling is the discovery—the journey that brings the reader or viewer to an insight about how the world works and, perhaps, how it could be made to work better.
8. **Does the story avoid reading like a puff piece?** Solutions journalism is expressly not about advocating for particular models, organizations or ideas. Journalists pursuing solutions stories are bringing their journalistic tools to bear on reporting, examining, and writing without a specific agenda.
9. **Does the story draw on sources who have a ground-level understanding, not just 30,000-foot expertise?** Beyond politicians and researchers from think tanks, solutions stories should consult and quote people who are working in the trenches and knowledgeable about the on-the ground realities of an issue.
10. **Does the story give greater attention to the response than to a leader/innovator/do-gooder?** We see a clear distinction between solutions journalism and what is often called "good news." "Good news" stories tend to celebrate individuals and inspirational acts. Solutions journalism is about ideas, how people are trying to make them work, and their observable effects.

Here's another way to think about solutions journalism—in a checklist format. Does your story do some of these?

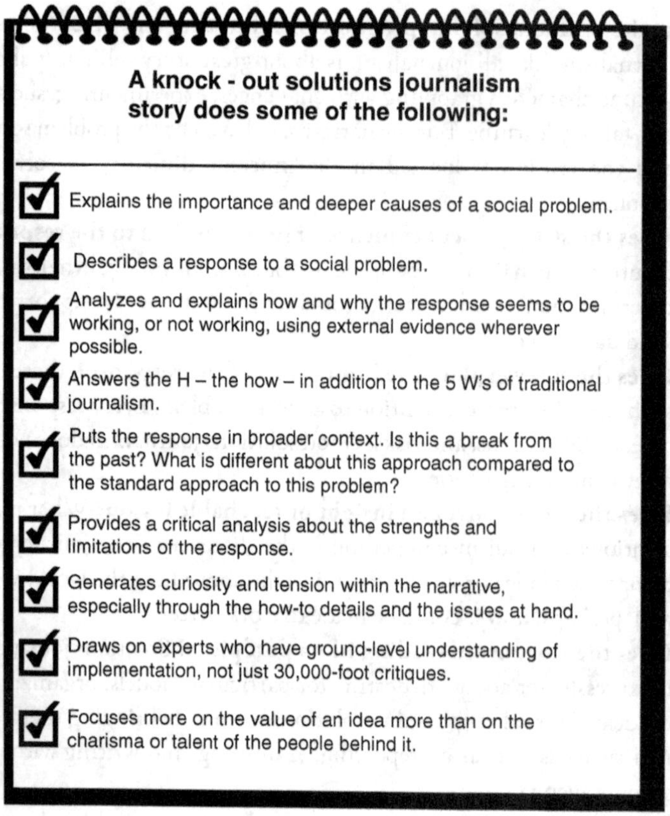
A knock - out solutions journalism story does some of the following:
Explains the importance and deeper causes of a social problem.
Describes a response to a social problem.
Analyzes and explains how and why the response seems to be working, or not working, using external evidence wherever possible.
Answers the H – the how – in addition to the 5 W's of traditional journalism.
Puts the response in broader context. Is this a break from the past? What is different about this approach compared to the standard approach to this problem?
Provides a critical analysis about the strengths and limitations of the response.
Generates curiosity and tension within the narrative, especially through the how-to details and the issues at hand.
Draws on experts who have ground-level understanding of implementation, not just 30,000-foot critiques.
Focuses more on the value of an idea more than on the charisma or talent of the people behind it.

Figure 6.1

Analyze

1. What is the "acid test" to see if a story about a social problem counts as solutions journalism?
2. Solutions journalism avoids the "puff piece" frame. What is that and why should it be avoided?
3. Solutions journalism also avoids the "good news" frame. What is that and why should it be avoided?

Explore

1. Visit SolutionsJournalism.org. Do a rhetorical analysis of one of their stories as a solutions journalism model. Does it meet the criteria outlined in the questions and checklist?

2. Apply the solutions journalism frame to a reading in this book. Do a rhetorical analysis in which you identify ways in which it meets or does not meet the criteria outlined here.
3. Identify a news story about poverty from the past week. In what ways does it meet or not meet the criteria for solutions journalism? If it diverges from those criteria, explain how and whether it seems successful in its purpose.

Forging Connections

1. Several of the readings in this chapter (e.g., Abramsky, Banerjee and Duflo, Buffett, Garrity, Karlan and Appel, Theroux, Yunus) stress the importance of creating solutions informed by people who live in poverty. That could mean people with many resources spending significant time with those in poverty, or it could mean inviting people in poverty to participate directly in solutions. Research one antipoverty program, either governmental or private, and analyze the extent to which people in poverty helped to design and implement that program. For example, Yunus included the poor in the administration of Grameen Bank (and in his acceptance lecture for the Nobel Prize). What are the practical and ethical advantages and disadvantages of designing programs for the poor *with* the poor?
2. Karlan and Appel write, "Whether we like it or not, for most of us there's an element of social display mixed up in our motivations for giving." What do they mean? Would we be as generous if people didn't know how generous we were? Does it matter if social display motivates giving if it results in gifts that help the poor? Consult readings in this chapter (e.g., Abramsky, Bornstein et al., Buffett, Karlan and Appel, Sanders and Lehrer, Theroux) and outside research to help you write a persuasive argument in which you analyze the role of social display (by individuals, politicians, even countries) in designing and implementing solutions to poverty.

Looking Further

1. Banerjee and Duflo quote their exchange with a poor man in Morocco whom they notice has bought a TV instead of the food he just told them he needs. He replies: "Oh, but television is more important than food!" Compare and contrast this idea to other readings

(e.g., McMillan Cottom, Rector and Sheffield) that address the role of material goods. Can a television, and other materials of high social value, benefit the poor more than food?

2. Compassion often drives people to act when confronted with suffering. But can compassion cloud judgment? If we want to reduce poverty and relieve suffering, shouldn't we be as efficient and effective as possible? Readings in this book (e.g., Banerjee and Duflo, Buffett, Cole, Karlan and Appel, O'Connor, Theroux, Wright) show ways that our good intentions can go wrong. Policies meant to encourage work sometimes discourage it. Programs meant to feed the poor can lead them to eat less. Write a researched proposal argument in which you recommend an antipoverty policy or program for a local, national, or international organization. Temper your compassion with informed argument. Explain why the stakeholders in this community should support this policy or program at this time.

Index

Not for Profit. *All* for Education.

Oxford University Press USA is a not-for-profit publisher dedicated to offering the highest quality textbooks at the best possible prices. We believe that it is important to provide everyone with access to superior textbooks at affordable prices. Oxford University Press textbooks are 30%–70% less expensive than comparable books from commercial publishers.

The press is a department of the University of Oxford, and our publishing proudly serves the university's mission: promoting excellence in research, scholarship, and education around the globe. We do not publish in order to generate revenue: we generate revenue in order to publish and also to fund scholarships, provide start-up grants to early-stage researchers, and refurbish libraries.

What does this mean to you? It means that Oxford University Press USA publishes books to best support your studies while also being mindful of your students' wallet.

OXFORD